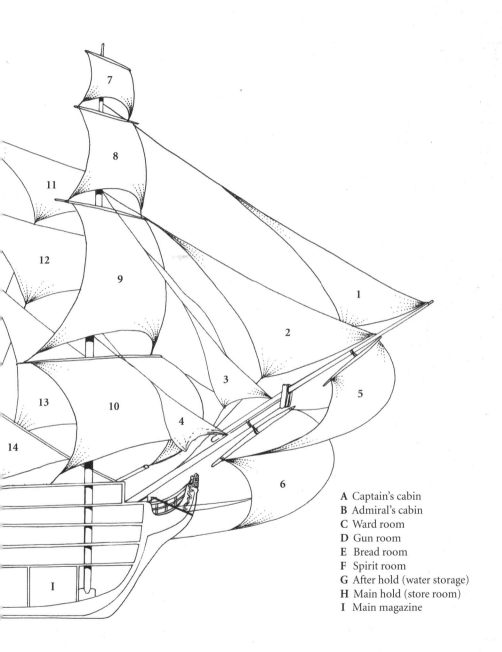

7

8

11

12

9

1

2

3

5

13

10

4

14

6

A Captain's cabin
B Admiral's cabin
C Ward room
D Gun room
E Bread room
F Spirit room
G After hold (water storage)
H Main hold (store room)
I Main magazine

I

# The War for All the Oceans

# The War for All the Oceans

From Nelson at the Nile to
Napoleon at Waterloo

ROY ADKINS

and

LESLEY ADKINS

Viking

VIKING
Published by the Penguin Group
Penguin Group (USA) Inc., 375 Hudson Street,
New York, New York 10014, U.S.A.
Penguin Group (Canada), 90 Eglinton Avenue East, Suite 700,
Toronto, Ontario, Canada M4P 2Y3
(a division of Pearson Penguin Canada Inc.)
Penguin Books Ltd, 80 Strand, London WC2R 0RL, England
Penguin Ireland, 25 St. Stephen's Green, Dublin 2, Ireland
(a division of Penguin Books Ltd)
Penguin Books Australia Ltd, 250 Camberwell Road,
Camberwell, Victoria 3124, Australia
(a division of Pearson Australia Group Pty Ltd)
Penguin Books India Pvt Ltd, 11 Community Centre, Panchsheel Park,
New Delhi – 110 017, India
Penguin Group (NZ), 67 Apollo Drive, Rosedale, North Shore 0745,
Auckland, New Zealand (a division of Pearson New Zealand Ltd.)
Penguin Books (South Africa) (Pty) Ltd, 24 Sturdee Avenue,
Rosebank, Johannesburg 2196, South Africa

Penguin Books Ltd, Registered Offices:
80 Strand, London WC2R 0RL, England

First American edition
Published in 2007 by Viking Penguin,
a member of Penguin Group (USA) Inc.

1 2 3 4 5 6 7 8 9 10

Maps on pages xvii, xviii, xix, 289 and 413 illustrated by John Gilkes

LIBRARY OF CONGRESS CATALOGING-IN-PUBLICATION DATA

Adkins, Roy (Roy A.)
   The war for all the oceans : from Nelson at the Nile to Napoleon at Waterloo / Roy Adkins and
Lesley Adkins.
      p. cm.
   Includes bibliographical references and index.
   ISBN 978-0-670-03864-0
   1. Second Coalition, War of the, 1798–1801—Naval operations. 2. Napoleonic Wars,
1800–1815—Naval operations. 3. Great Britain. Royal Navy—History—19th century. 4. France.
Marine—History—19th century.
I. Adkins, Lesley. II. Title.

   DC153.A245 2007
   940.2'745—dc22          2006101017

Printed in the United States of America

Set in Adobe Caslon

*To Mick Sharp and Jean Williamson,*
*photographers and friends*
*par excellence*

# CONTENTS

————— ◆ —————

# LIST OF MAPS AND PLANS

———— • ◆ • ————

# LIST OF ILLUSTRATIONS

———•◆•———

SECTION ONE

The Temple prison in Paris (*Naval Chronicle* 34, 1815)
Sir Sidney Smith (Author collection)
A plaque marking the burial of the many drowned in the wreck of the *Invincible* (Lesley and Roy Adkins)
A seaman being taken by the press-gang (*The Log Book; or, Nautical Miscellany*, 1830)
The north-west side of Diamond Rock (*United Service Journal*, 1833)
The north-east side of Diamond Rock (*United Service Journal*, 1833)
Action between a French squadron and *Vincejo* (*Naval Chronicle* 34, 1815)
The Dardanelles squadron under the command of Sir John Duckworth (Author collection)
A cannon from the frigate *Anson* (Lesley and Roy Adkins)
Bitche prison (Langton, 1836)
The 'Raie-de-Chat' near Blankenberge (Boys, 1864)
The memorial at Norman Cross (Lesley and Roy Adkins)
View from Batz up the River Scheldt towards Antwerp (Bourchier, 1873)
The *United States* defending the *Macedonian* ( J Frost, *The Book of the Navy; comprising a general history of the American Marine*, 1843)
The attack on Captain Philip Broke of the *Shannon* (Brighton, 1866)
Chesapeake Mill (Brighton, 1866)
The obelisk monument at Little Dunham (Lesley and Roy Adkins)
The White House (Lossing, 1868)
Plan of Dartmoor prison (Lossing, 1868)
Napoleon on board the *Bellerophon* (Las Cases, 1835)

SECTION TWO

John Wesley Wright (*Naval Chronicle* 34, 1815)
John Nicol (Nicol, 1822)
Captain Thomas Cochrane (Author collection)
Captain Charles Lydiard (*Naval Chronicle* 19, 1808)
Sir Samuel Hood (*Naval Chronicle* 17, 1807)
Donat Henchy O'Brien (O'Brien, 1839)
Captain Sir William Hoste (Hoste, 1887)
Sir Home Riggs Popham (*Naval Chronicle* 16, 1806)
Edward Codrington (Bourchier, 1873)
Stephen Decatur (Author collection)
James Lawrence (Lossing, 1868)
William Henry Allen (Lossing, 1868)

# ACKNOWLEDGEMENTS

———•◆•———

We are very pleased to acknowledge the help of many people and organisations during the writing of this book. The staff of numerous libraries and archives gave us invaluable assistance, most notably the Caird Library and the Manuscripts Department at the National Maritime Museum, Greenwich; the British Library; the National Archives at Kew; Colindale Newspaper Library; The London Library; University of Bristol Arts and Social Sciences Library; Exeter University Library; Exeter Cathedral Library; Devon Library and Information Services (particularly Exeter Central Library and St Thomas Library, most notably Jill Hughes, Lisa Podbury, Judith Prescott, Katie Forsey and Erica Stretton); the Admiralty Library of the Ministry of Defence; the Wellcome Library for the History and Understanding of Medicine; the Morrab Library in Penzance; the Centre for Oxfordshire Studies; the Naval Studies Section of Plymouth Central Library; the Service Historique de la Marine, Château de Vincennes, Paris; the Library of the Devon and Exeter Institution, especially Roger Brien and James Turner; and the Somerset Studies Library, particularly David Bromwich and Wilf Deckner. We are also indebted to the staff of the Royal Naval Museum Library, Portsmouth, particularly Kathryn Cooper, Allison Wareham and Iain MacKenzie; Matthew Sheldon, Head of Research Collections, Royal Naval Museum, Portsmouth; Ann Wheeler, Archivist, Charterhouse Archives; Laura Worth of Dartmoor Prison Museum; M. E. Hayes of the Nelson Society; and D. Johnson, Local History Librarian, South Tyneside Local Studies Library. Other individuals who have helped with specific aspects of the research include Elizabeth Sparrow, Alain Chappet, Dr Colin White, Professor David Crystal, Tom Pocock, Harry Watson and Howard Murphy of Cellardyke, Valerie and Richard Wheeler, Peter McRuvie and

Iain McRuvie. We are very grateful to Lord de Saumarez and to Mr W. R. Serjeant, Archivist to Lord de Saumarez, for information about Ann Hopping/Nancy Perriam. Further information about Nancy Perriam was provided by the staff of Exmouth Museum. Once again Sue and Tony Hall and Ray Hockin provided practical help.

We are very grateful to Anne Petrides and Parapress Ltd for permission to quote from *Sea Soldier, an Officer of Marines with Duncan, Nelson, Collingwood and Cockburn, the Letters and Journals of Major T. Marmaduke Wybourn RM, 1797–1813* (2000); and to the Trustees of the Royal Naval Museum for permission to use extracts from archive manuscripts 1995/48 and 1977/265. We are also grateful to the Hon. Editor and The Society for Nautical Research for permission to reproduce extracts from *The Mariner's Mirror*, and to the Military History Society of Ireland for permission to quote from *The Irish Sword*. The quote of Christiann White is used by courtesy of the Librarian, Wellcome Library for the History and Understanding of Medicine. We are also happy to acknowledge the help of Richard Dawes for copy-editing and proofreading, Jackie Brind for the index and John Gilkes for cartography.

Our greatest thanks must be to Bill Hamilton, Sara Fisher and everyone at A. M. Heath in London; to George Lucas of Inkwell Management; to Richard Beswick, Steve Guise, Roger Cazalet, Zoë Gullen, Viv Redman, Peter Cotton and the rest of the team at Little, Brown UK; and to Hilary Redmon at Viking Penguin US.

# PREFACE

———•◆•———

In 1789 the monarchs and aristocracies of Europe were shocked by the Revolution in France, and in subsequent years the execution of the French royal family and the bloodbath of the Terror lost the revolutionaries what little support they had among the ordinary people of other countries. As France embarked on what historians would label the French Revolutionary Wars in 1792, initially to defend its ideology from interference by neighbouring states, a young officer in the French army took his first steps to power. By 1798 Napoleon Bonaparte had risen to the rank of general, established a reputation as an invincible commander and was about to attempt to fulfil a personal dream – to retrace the footsteps of Alexander the Great and seize territory to form a French empire in the East. The war was to take on a global dimension, in a drawn-out conflict that would gain its name from the man who rose from a minor aristocratic Corsican family to become emperor, not of the East, but of western Europe: the Napoleonic Wars were about to begin.

This was the first worldwide war, and at its heart all the major powers of Europe were deeply involved in a kaleidoscope of constantly changing alliances and coalitions as the states surrounding France struggled to defend themselves or maintain a precarious neutrality. Further afield, the colonies and outposts of emerging European empires were captured or bartered like pawns in a giant game of chess, with little regard for the aspirations or welfare of the local populations. For a century, until World War I inherited the title, the Napoleonic conflict would be known as 'The Great War'.

It was a war won at sea. Although the Duke of Wellington led British and allied troops to a final victory over Napoleon at Waterloo, for many years French armies had reigned victorious on European soil, and only the natural moat of the English Channel, bristling with British Navy war-ships, precariously held the French at arm's length from mainland Britain. From the very beginning the British Navy blocked Napoleon's ambitions. At the Battle of the Nile, Nelson destroyed the French fleet, stranding Napoleon and his army in Egypt. His attempt to march overland to India was repulsed by Sir Sidney Smith's spirited defence of Acre, after which Napoleon postponed his plans for oriental conquest and returned to France to seize power, first as dictator and then as emperor.

While British naval intelligence officers gathered what information they could, wherever possible providing aid to the French Royalist oppo-sition, British warships struggled to keep the remaining French fleets confined to port by a constant blockade. This also hampered the assem-bly of a French invasion fleet for an attack on Britain, plans for which were shelved after the fleet of warships that was to escort them was destroyed by Nelson at Trafalgar. This was the turning point. For the next ten years the war at sea was one of attrition. France was bled of its resources to support Napoleon's armies, and the blockade of ports gradu-ally stifled French trade and prosperity, while the seizure of French territory in combined army and navy operations, or sometimes by a deter-mined assault by the crews from a couple of warships, diverted valuable commerce to Britain. Napoleon's dreams of global domination dissolved while Britain whittled away the French empire and found itself with a growing number of colonies almost by accident. Even a brief and unnec-essary war with America from 1812 to 1815, provoked by the war with France, did not distract the British Navy from its purpose, and by the time of Waterloo Britain controlled the world's sea-lanes and possessed the foundations of an empire on which the sun literally never set. The conflict that resulted from Napoleon's scramble to power out of the chaos of the French Revolution had developed into a war for naval supremacy and control of the world's seaborne trading routes – a war for all the oceans.

*Major place-names of the British Isles*

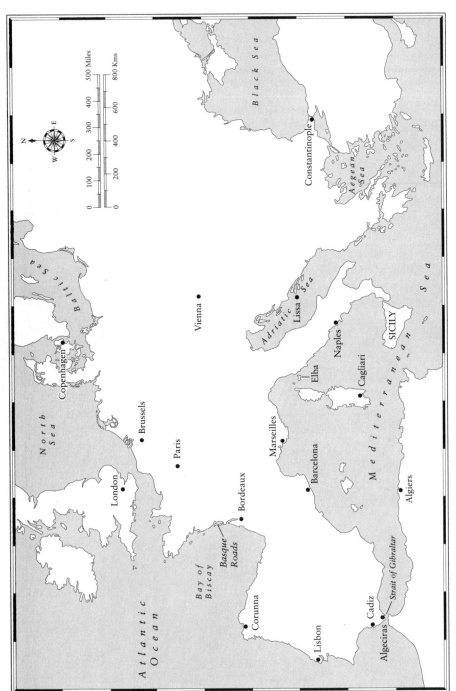

*Major place-names of Europe and the Mediterranean*

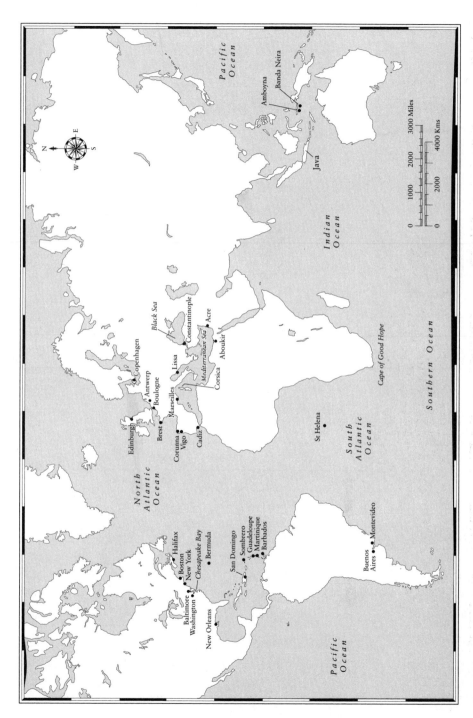

*Major place-names worldwide*

# PROLOGUE

—•◆•—

# WITH CANNON AND CUTLASS

Who would enter for small craft, when the *Leander*, the finest frigate in the world . . . still has room for a hundred active seamen . . . lots of leave on shore, dancing and fiddling aboard, and four pounds of tobacco served out every month.

From a recruiting poster for the *Leander*[1]

The *Speedy* certainly was a small craft. Optimistically described by the Admiralty as a sloop*, the British ship was considered by Thomas Cochrane as 'little more than a burlesque on a vessel of war . . . about the size of an average coasting brig, her burden being 158 tons . . . crowded rather than manned, with a crew of eighty-four men and six officers'.[2] Just promoted to commander, Cochrane nevertheless professed to be 'very proud of my little vessel'.[3] This did not mean he was blind to the ship's shortcomings, the main one being the armament, which 'consisted of fourteen 4-*pounders*! a species of gun little larger than a blunderbuss'.[4] A broadside from these guns was seven iron balls weighing in total 28 pounds, and Cochrane found that he could fit them all in his coat pockets and still comfortably pace the quarterdeck.

The ship was so cramped that Cochrane's cabin had 'not so much as room for a chair, the floor being entirely occupied by a small table surrounded with lockers, answering the double purpose of storechests and seats. The difficulty was to get seated, the ceiling being only five feet high,

---

* A small warship, usually carrying from fourteen to eighteen guns, commanded by a 'master and commander' with the courtesy title 'captain'.

so that the object could only be accomplished by rolling on the locker, a movement sometimes attended with unpleasant failure.'[5] The lack of space in the cabin was extremely uncomfortable for Cochrane, who was over six feet tall, and he found that the 'only practicable mode of shaving consisted in removing the skylight and putting my head through to make a toilet-table of the quarter-deck above'.[6]

Based in the Mediterranean, the *Speedy* was under the overall command of Admiral Lord Keith and in 1800 was being used as an escort for merchant convoys. This was essential but generally unrewarding work that maintained the flow of trade, particularly to and from the colonies, on which Britain's prosperity depended. On 10 May the *Speedy* sailed from Cagliari on Sardinia's southern coast to protect a convoy of fourteen merchantmen on their way to Leghorn (Livorno) on Italy's north-west coast, but within hours Cochrane was facing a crisis. The *Speedy*'s log for that day read, 'At 9 a.m. observed a strange sail take possession of a Danish brig under our escort.'[7] Faced with the choice of abandoning the Danish ship or leaving the rest of the convoy in a rescue attempt that might not succeed, Cochrane did not hesitate, as the log entry continued, 'At 11.30 a.m. rescued the brig, and captured the assailant.'[8]

The captured ship, Cochrane's first prize, was the French privateer *Intrépide*, and this was not the only threat because four days later the *Speedy* had to rescue two stragglers in the convoy which were seized by five armed boats that rowed out from the island of Monte Cristo. The voyage from Cagliari to Leghorn took eleven days, but after safely delivering the convoy, Cochrane was rewarded by being given a relatively free hand to harass enemy shipping, initially off the Italian coast and then off eastern Spain.

For nearly a year the *Speedy* cruised along the Spanish coast, capturing enemy ships as prizes and occasionally having to avoid warships that were too large and heavily armed, but on 5 May 1801 Cochrane and his crew came across some Spanish gunboats off Barcelona and immediately gave chase. The gunboats ran for the safety of the harbour, and from the way they behaved they were obviously acting as decoys, but this did not deter Cochrane. At dawn the next day he again took the *Speedy* in towards Barcelona, 'when the trap manifested itself in the form of a large ship'[9] – the Spanish frigate *Gamo*. This was a much larger vessel than the *Speedy*, with a crew of 319 men and armed with 8- and 12-pounder cannons and 24-pounder carronades. The weight of shot in the *Gamo*'s broadside was 190 pounds, nearly seven times that of the *Speedy*. Cochrane also had the disadvantage that his crew was reduced in number to fifty-four because some men were taking captured ships back to the *Speedy*'s base at Port Mahón on Minorca.

There was still time to escape from such an unequal contest, but Cochrane's officers had complained about not attacking a similar frigate and so 'orders were then given to pipe all hands, and prepare for action'.[10] Putting on a bold front, the *Speedy* 'made towards the frigate, which was now coming down under steering sails. At 9.30 a.m., she fired a gun and hoisted Spanish colours, which the *Speedy* acknowledged by hoisting American colours [America was a neutral country], our object being, as we were now exposed to her full broadside, to puzzle her, till we got on the other tack, when we ran up the English ensign, and immediately afterwards encountered her broadside without damage.'[11]

The only chance for the *Speedy* was to move in as close as possible to the *Gamo*, whose guns had a much longer range. The *Gamo* managed to fire another broadside, which again failed to damage the fast-approaching *Speedy*. Cochrane gave orders 'not to fire a gun till we were close to her; when running under her lee, we locked our yards amongst her rigging, and in this position returned our broadside, such as it was'.[12] The Spanish frigate towered above the *Speedy*, and, Cochrane recorded, 'to have fired our popgun 4-pounders at a distance would have been to throw away the ammunition, but the guns being doubly, and as I afterwards learned, trebly, shotted*, and being elevated, they told admirably upon her main deck; the first discharge ... killing the Spanish captain and the boatswain.'[13] The *Gamo* was now at a disadvantage, as Cochrane had calculated: 'My reason for locking our small craft in the enemy's rigging was the one upon which I mainly relied for victory, viz. that from the height of the frigate out of the water, the whole of her shot must necessarily go over our heads, whilst our guns, being elevated, would blow up her main-deck.'[14]

Although the *Speedy* had counteracted the superiority the *Gamo* had in fire-power, the crew was still outnumbered six to one by the Spanish, so to Cochrane the next move was obvious:

The Spaniards speedily found out the disadvantage under which they were fighting, and gave the order to board the *Speedy*, but as this order was as distinctly heard by us as by them, we avoided it at the moment of execution by

---

* Loaded with two or three cannonballs.

sheering off to prevent the movement, giving them a volley of musketry and a broadside before they could recover themselves. Twice was this manoeuvre repeated, and twice thus averted. The Spaniards finding that they were only punishing themselves, gave up further attempts to board, and stood to their guns, which were cutting up our rigging from stem to stern, but doing little farther damage, for after the lapse of an hour the loss to the *Speedy* was only two men killed and four wounded. This kind of combat, however, could not last. Our rigging being cut up and the *Speedy*'s sails riddled with shot, I told the men that they must either take the frigate or be themselves taken, in which case the Spaniards would give no quarter – whilst a few minutes energetically employed on their part would decide the matter in their own favour.[15]

The situation was desperate, and Cochrane did everything to improve their chances:

Calculating on the superstitious wonder which forms an element in the Spanish character, a portion of our crew were ordered to black their faces, and what with this and the excitement of combat, more ferocious looking objects could scarcely be imagined. The fellows thus disguised were directed to board by the head [at the bow], and the effect produced was precisely that calculated on. The greater portion of the Spaniard's crew was prepared to repel boarders in that direction, but stood for a few moments as it were transfixed to the deck by the apparition of so many diabolical looking figures emerging from the white smoke of the bow guns.[16]

While the Spanish were occupied by this diversion, Cochrane related, 'our other men, who boarded by the waist [amidships], rushed on them from behind, before they could recover from their surprise'.[17] He gambled everything on this attack, and his entire crew boarded the Spanish vessel except for 'the doctor, Mr. Guthrie, who . . . volunteered to take the helm. Leaving him therefore for the time being both commander and crew of the *Speedy* . . . in a few seconds every man was on the enemy's deck – a feat rendered the more easy as the doctor placed the *Speedy* close alongside with admirable skill.'[18] Initially the British had the upper hand because 'for a moment the Spaniards seemed taken by surprise, as though unwilling to believe that so small a crew would have the audacity to board them, but soon recovering themselves, they made a rush to the waist of the frigate, where the fight was for some minutes gallantly carried on'.[19]

At this point Cochrane shouted down to the doctor, the sole person aboard the *Speedy*, to send up another fifty men. He also sent a man to haul down the Spanish colours, and 'the Spanish crew, without pausing to consider by whose orders the colours had been struck\*, and naturally believing it the act of their own officers, gave in, and we were in possession of the *Gamo* frigate, of thirty-two heavy guns and 319 men, who an hour and a half before had looked upon us as a certain if not an easy prey'.[20]

Contrary to what might have been expected with the British so heavily outnumbered, the disparity between the sizes of the two crews was matched by a similar disparity in casualty figures, as Cochrane reported: 'Our loss in boarding was Lieutenant Parker, severely wounded in several places, one seaman killed and three wounded, which with those previously killed and wounded gave a total of three seamen killed and one officer and seventeen men wounded. The *Gamo*'s loss was Captain de Torres, the boatswain, and thirteen seamen killed, together with forty-one wounded, her casualties thus exceeding the whole number of officers and crew on board the *Speedy*.'[21]

When the Spanish had time for reflection, they were seemingly embarrassed to have been captured by so small a vessel, and Cochrane noted that 'some time after the surrender of the *Gamo*, and when we were in quiet possession, the officer who had succeeded the deceased captain . . . applied to me for a certificate that he had done his duty during the action'.[22] Cochrane duly gave him a certificate with the equivocal wording that he had 'conducted himself like a true Spaniard'[23], which pleased the officer, while to his amusement Cochrane 'had afterwards the satisfaction of learning that it procured him further promotion in the Spanish service!'[24]

Having won the battle, the British needed to escort the captured ship back to base before other Spanish warships intervened, and 'it became a puzzle what to do with 263 unhurt prisoners now we had taken them, the *Speedy* having only forty-two [fit] men left. Promptness was however necessary, so driving the prisoners into the hold, with guns pointing down the hatchway, and leaving thirty of our men on board the prize . . . we shaped our course to Port Mahon.'[25] The two ships reached Minorca safely, and in this they were lucky, with 'the Barcelona gun-boats, though spectators of the action, not venturing to rescue the frigate'.[26] As

---

\* Striking the colours (lowering the flag) was a recognised signal that a ship had surrendered.

Cochrane admitted, 'had they made the attempt, we should have had some difficulty in evading them and securing the prize, the prisoners manifesting every disposition to rescue themselves, and only being deterred by their own main deck guns loaded with canister, and pointing down the hatchways'.[27]

At the time the *Gamo* was captured in 1801, Cochrane was just twenty-five and the *Speedy* was his first independent command, but he would go on to terrorise the French by capturing over fifty vessels in the Mediterranean and harassing French troops in raids on the coasts of France and French-occupied Spain. He built a reputation as a captain who would not risk the safety of his crew unnecessarily, but was likely to make them rich with prize money. Yet Cochrane was only exceptional in the consistency of his success and his extreme independence of spirit. While frequently forced to endure the tedium of protecting merchant convoys or patrolling enemy ports, captains of small fast warships were also given a free hand to cruise particular areas, doing whatever damage they could to enemy forces and trade. The British Navy came to rely on these individual commanders who, with single ships or small squadrons rather than huge battle fleets, relentlessly reduced French naval power to a handful of warships confined to port by a continuous blockade.

The capture of the *Gamo* by the *Speedy* was only unusual because of the great difference in size and power between the two vessels – most battles were more evenly matched – but this incident is typical of the professionalism, ingenuity, daring and raw courage displayed by the seamen of the British Navy during the Napoleonic Wars. While Napoleon* went from one victory to another on land, all his plans for taking control of the seas were dogged by failure. The commerce of France was stifled, the French Empire shrank and the economy almost collapsed, while Britain expanded its trade, wealth and empire. Although Wellington dealt the final blow at Waterloo, ultimately the war against Napoleon was won by the officers and men of the British Navy.

---

* Napoleon adopted his first name as the title Napoleon I when he was crowned Emperor of the French in 1805. Before that he was generally known by his family name, Bonaparte, often with his military rank, as General Bonaparte. To avoid confusion, Napoleon is used throughout this book.

# ONE

———•◆•———

## GATEWAY TO INDIA

Had I been master of the sea, I should have been master of the East.

Napoleon, speaking about his expedition
to the eastern Mediterranean[1]

With hindsight, Tuesday 24 April 1798 was one of those pivotal days when history changes its course, but at the time it seemed no different from any of the days that came before or after. France had undergone a revolution and was now at war with Britain. The Directory, the present government of France, was engaged in a struggle with French Royalists who were trying to restore the Bourbon dynasty, which had ended with the execution of Louis XVI five years earlier. Having just arrested three leaders of the Parisian network of Royalists, the Directory's grip on power was more secure than it had been for some time and, on the surface at least, France seemed relatively stable. The rising star of the French administration, General Napoleon Bonaparte, was in Paris awaiting the Directory's decision on whether his planned expedition to invade Egypt would go ahead, or whether he would instead be sent on a diplomatic mission to Austria; Rear-Admiral Horatio Nelson, who was soon to become one of Napoleon's most effective adversaries, was at Lisbon on his way to join the British fleet in the Mediterranean; and Captain Sir William Sidney Smith, also of the British Navy, was a prisoner in Paris in a high-security prison called the Temple. This was a medieval tower, with a turret on each corner, that originally formed the heart of the fortified residence of the crusading Knights Templars in Paris. The forbidding stone structure was now mainly used for political prisoners: Louis XVI was held there before his execution, and Smith occupied the same apartments.

Smith had been in the Temple for much of the past two years, having been captured during a naval action at the mouth of the River Seine. The second son of a captain in the guards and gentleman-usher to Queen Charlotte, Smith had been born in Park Lane, London. He had joined the navy in 1777, at the age of thirteen, since when he had been in several notable actions. The French suspected that he was a spy and so refused to treat him as a prisoner-of-war. Although not able to prove it, they were right about his involvement in espionage, and from his prison cell in the French capital Smith acted as a spymaster, channelling funds from Britain to British agents and French Royalists in the Paris area. A fluent speaker of French, he was also a master of propaganda, and on the wooden panelling of his cell he had inscribed part of Jean-Jacques Rousseau's *Ode à la Fortune*. This inscription began: 'Fortune's wheel makes strange revolutions, it must be confessed; but for the term revolution to be applicable, the turn of the wheel should be complete. You are today as high as you can be. Very well. I envy not your good fortune, for mine is better still. I am as low in the career of ambition as a man can well descend; so that, let this capricious dame, fortune, turn her wheel ever so little – I must necessarily mount, for the same reason that you must descend.'[2]

The inscription was aimed at Napoleon and continued: 'I make not this remark to cause you any uneasiness, but rather to bring you that consolation which I shall feel when you are arrived at the same point where I now am – yes! at the same point where I now am. You will inhabit this same prison – why not [you] as well as I? I no more thought of such a thing, than you do at present, before I was actually shut up in it.'[3] Smith ensured that his message found its way into the French newspapers, ending with the proclamation: 'In short, I need not prove to you that you will come to this place, because you must come here to be able to read these lines. I presume also you will inhabit this apartment, because it is the best, and because the keeper of it is a civil man and will do for you the best he can, as he does for me.'[4] It came to be known as Smith's 'prophecy', and although Napoleon never saw the original inscription, the newspaper reports undoubtedly played on the superstitious streak in his character – he later ordered the Temple to be demolished, probably to prevent the prophecy from coming true.

On 24 April 1798 two officers arrived at the prison with an order to transfer Captain Smith and his fellow prisoner, Midshipman John Wesley

Wright, to another prison at Fontainebleau. This was unusual, as those held in the Temple were either released, executed or died there, and the head gaoler, Citizen Antoine Boniface, scrutinised the order carefully. There appeared to be nothing amiss, and so Boniface had his clerk copy the order into the register while the more senior of the waiting officers signed a receipt for the prisoners. Sir Sidney later recalled that the officer who came to collect him gave an assurance 'in the most serious manner, that the government were very far from intending to aggravate my misfortunes, and that I should be very comfortable at the place whither he was ordered to conduct me'.[5] When all the formalities had been completed, Boniface ordered six men from the guard to accompany Smith, which was agreed, but then the officer addressed Smith again, saying, 'Commodore, you are an officer, I am an officer also; your parole will be enough. Give me that, and I have no need of an escort'[6], to which Smith replied, 'if that is sufficient, I swear on the faith of an officer to accompany you wherever you choose to conduct me.'[7]

Once outside the prison, the small party of officers and their prisoners boarded a four-wheeled horse-drawn cab, apparently 'taken from the nearest stand'[8], but as Smith climbed inside he saw faces he recognised – faces of French Royalist agents – and his suspicions were confirmed that a rescue attempt was in progress. Once away from the prison, fearing immediate pursuit, they urged the cab driver to make haste, but their progress was immediately halted:

A trivial circumstance nearly defeated the bold enterprise. The driver had not gone a hundred yards, when he ran against a post, and not only damaged his wheel, but injured a foot-passenger [a child in the street]. An angry crowd collected; Sidney and his companions jumped out, took the valise, and were hurrying away, when the driver called them back, demanding his fare . . . [and one of the party] committed a rash act, which might well have compromised everything by arousing the suspicion of the by-standers; he threw the driver a double louis [an illegal Royalist gold coin], and hastily rejoined his companions.[9]

Hurrying away before the mistake was noticed, the fugitives set out on foot for a nearby Royalist safe house, where they spent the night. Smith left the next day in a carriage heading north-west, but he had no passport or papers and the most dangerous part of the journey was the checkpoint on the road leading out of Paris. Just as they approached this obstacle, the carriage collided with a wall and was damaged, but turning this accident to his advantage, Smith slipped through on foot while some of the checkpoint guards were occupied by the diversion. After being repaired, the carriage picked him up and continued towards the Normandy coast.

At the city of Rouen, Smith had to wait several days for a false passport, and here Midshipman Wright caught up with him. While they were at Rouen, their escape from Paris was finally noticed. On 2 May the Temple's doctor, who had come to know Smith well, was dining with a senior prison official and asked how Smith liked his new quarters. As he had not heard of the move, the official's suspicions were aroused, and when he checked with Fontainebleau prison the next day he realised Smith had escaped and raised the alarm. A reward was offered for the capture of Smith, who was described as 'middle-sized, very thin, brown hair, blue eyes, marked with the small pox, long nose, speaking French well, about 30 years of age'[10], but it was far too late. With false passports and dressed as fishermen, Smith and his companions rowed out from Le Havre in a small boat and were picked up by a British ship. As reported in *The Times*, 'They were taken on board the *Argo* frigate, which joyfully received these welcome strangers, who on Saturday morning [5 May] were landed at Portsmouth, amidst the acclamations and congratulations of all ranks of people, who lined the streets as they passed along. The same civilities were shewn Sir *SYDNEY SMITH* at every place where he was recognised . . . Sir *SYDNEY* is in a tolerable good state of health, though he looks very thin.'[11] In London Smith was received by the King and the Duke of Clarence and dined with Lord Spencer at the Admiralty.

The first time that Smith's path had crossed that of Napoleon was almost five years earlier at the siege of Toulon, in the summer of 1793. Toulon was the main French naval base in the Mediterranean, but that summer the largely Royalist population threw out the Revolutionary administration. As an army approached to take back control, the people of Toulon opened the port to the British and the Spanish, who were allies of Britain at that time. The resulting siege was a stalemate for some weeks while the British tried desperately to bring in reinforcements to counter the growing army of Revolutionary troops surrounding the town. At this point a twenty-four-year-old major of the French artillery, Napoleon Bonaparte, came to prominence by the skilful use of his guns. He persuaded his commanding officer to capture a key fort on high ground from where his artillery could threaten the British ships in the harbour, giving them the stark choice of retreat or destruction. The British fleet pulled out, leaving many of the local population to be massacred by the vengeful Revolutionaries. Smith volunteered to organise the burning of those ships that could not be sailed out of the harbour – fifty-eight warships, including thirty-two large battleships.

There was little time to lose. The Revolutionary army was pressing at the gates of the town, and many of the inhabitants had already thrown away their Royalist colours and were wearing the red, white and blue cockade of the Revolutionaries. In the end, the British sailed nineteen French ships out of the harbour, and Smith managed to destroy ten ships of the line* and four others, but this left eighteen ships of the line and seven others to be recaptured by the French. Even so, the loss of thirty-three ships was a greater blow to the French Navy than Nelson later inflicted at the battles of the Nile and Trafalgar, but in the subsequent search for scapegoats after the abandonment of Toulon, Smith was criticised for not destroying more ships, although in reality his achievement was remarkable.

Admiral Lord Hood, the commanding officer of the British fleet at Toulon, was himself well pleased with Smith's work and rewarded him with the honour of taking the dispatches back to London. Napoleon gave him the nickname 'Capitaine de Brûlot'[12] (fireship captain), and one far-reaching result of Smith's actions was that the French regarded him as an arsonist rather than a naval officer acting on orders, a charge frequently quoted when they refused him prisoner-of-war status during his captivity in the Temple. At the time of the Toulon siege Smith already had a reputation for gallantry, and a few years earlier, when working for the Swedish Navy, he had helped their trapped fleet escape from the Russians. For this, King Gustavus III had requested King George III to invest him with the Swedish honour of Knight Grand Cross of the Order of the Sword. From then on Sir Sidney was referred to by his enemies in Britain as 'the Swedish knight'.

By contrast, Napoleon earned great praise at Toulon and was promoted to brigadier-general, but he had yet to make his mark. His chance came in Paris two years later when the French government, then known as the Convention, was threatened by an armed mob of Royalists, anarchists and others opposed to the Revolution. Napoleon dispersed the crowd with

---

* The largest warships were known as 'ships of the line', because these were the battleships, carrying at least sixty-four guns (cannons) that traditionally formed the line of battle. The word 'battleship' is an abbreviation of 'line of battle ship'.

grapeshot fired from his artillery and earned the gratitude of General Paul Barras, the commander-in-chief. Barras hailed him as saviour of the French Republic, and suddenly Napoleon's name was known throughout France and his face recognised by Parisians. Barras had made him an overnight celebrity and basked in the reflected glory.

Within weeks Napoleon was promoted to full general, and a few months later, when the Convention was replaced by the Directory, he was given command of an army with orders to conquer northern Italy. Napoleon was still a protégé of Barras, who passed on to him Josephine Beauharnais. Her aristocrat husband had been guillotined during the Revolution and she was now the official mistress of Barras, who shared her with General Lazare Hoche. Napoleon soon also became her lover, in a bizarre and complicated relationship since she did not immediately give up the other two men, but Napoleon fell madly in love with her, and in March 1796 they were married – two days before Napoleon left Paris to invade Italy.

After winning twelve major battles in thirteen months, Napoleon not only achieved the objective of conquering northern Italy, but also occupied the Papal States. His charismatic and forceful character allowed him to impose a rigid discipline on his troops without their becoming rebellious. He marched them from place to place at a speed that amazed his enemies, who were equally outclassed by his tactics – he read the landscape and used it to his advantage during battles. This was not the dumpy, middle-aged Napoleon, with thinning hair and rather sullen expression, of portraits painted towards the end of his life, but a dashing, energetic young soldier.

To the Directory Napoleon was almost a miracle worker, who could be deployed against the enemies surrounding France, but they were aware of the dangers of someone who had risen from nowhere to a position of authority in an astonishingly short time. However, he was just one player in a constantly changing power struggle that had been raging ever since the start of the Revolution in the summer of 1789, and at this point there was little indication of his future destiny. He may have been an inspired general and one of France's greatest military assets, but the Directory did not trust his ambition. To keep him occupied, preferably away from Paris, and to hamper his flair for intrigue, the Directory put him in charge of the preparations for an invasion of Britain. His private secretary, Louis Antoine Fauvelet de Bourrienne, recalled Napoleon's irritation at being thwarted:

I do not wish to stay here [in France]; there is nothing to do. They are unwilling to listen to anything. I foresee that if I remain here, I am ruined in a short time. Everything here wears out; already I no longer have any glory. This little Europe does not supply enough. I must go to the East, all great glory comes from there. Nevertheless, I wish first to make a tour along the coasts, to assure myself about what can be undertaken . . . If the success of a raid into England appears doubtful to me, as I fear it will, the army of England will become the army of the East, and I will go to Egypt.[13]

This 'tour along the coast' took place in February 1798. It was a rapid two-week inspection of the Channel ports and of the preparations for an invasion of Britain, just a few weeks before Sir Sidney Smith escaped from Paris, and it resulted in a long letter from Napoleon to the Directory setting out in detail why an invasion attempt was premature. At a stormy meeting with the Directory in the last week of February, Napoleon was finally pushed to an outright refusal to continue with the invasion plans, and out of the confusion of the following days his suggestion of an alternative expedition to Egypt was accepted.

The prospect of acquiring Egypt as a colony was attractive not only for the fabled riches that the country possessed – fabled because there was relatively little accurate information about Egypt in western Europe – but also because it was a gateway to the overland route to the East. The Turkish Ottoman Empire that nominally controlled Egypt was fragile and starting to disintegrate. Its grip on the countries of the eastern Mediterranean was weakening and, in theory, a French army based in Egypt could push eastwards to India. Not yet the jewel in Britain's imperial crown, India was not even a British colony, but outposts there were vital for Britain's trade and prosperity. Any serious threat to trade with India would be a potential defeat for Britain, and at the very least might force the country to accept peace terms with France.

Added to these powerful incentives was the thought that an expedition to Egypt would keep Napoleon far from Paris and away from any conspiracies for quite some time, so the Directory did not take long to decide to sanction the expedition. For his part, Napoleon was aware that taking an invading army to Egypt ran counter to his immediate ambitions to seize power in France, but he had a grand vision of what might be achieved in the East. Egypt could provide a gateway to Africa as well as Asia, while a canal from the Mediterranean to the Red Sea at Suez would give a fast sea route to India and beyond. Napoleon believed it was his destiny to carve out an eastern empire to rival that of Alexander the Great, and he made his plans accordingly. 'A short time before leaving,' Bourrienne noted, 'I asked Bonaparte how long he intended staying in Egypt. "A few months, or six years; everything depends on circumstances. I will colonise that country; I will bring them artists, craftsmen of every description; women, actors, etc. We are only 29 years old, and we will then be 35. That is not old age. Those six years will enable me, if all goes well, to go to India."'[14]

The success of the expedition depended on misleading the British, and so preparations for the invasion of Britain continued in order to keep the British Navy tied up far from the Mediterranean. Meanwhile, the groundwork for the expedition to Egypt took place in the utmost secrecy. This was an incredible feat of military administration: Napoleon oversaw the project from Paris, delegating the work to subordinate generals in ports in southern France, Corsica and western Italy. In the end, an army of some thirty-eight thousand infantry and cavalry troops was assembled to be carried by a fleet of four hundred transport vessels, escorted by thirteen warships and seven frigates. Also embarked were sixty field guns and forty siege guns, but only twelve hundred horses for the three thousand cavalrymen because Napoleon expected to use camels. The ships were gradually gathered in the ports of Toulon and Marseilles in southern France, Genoa and Civitavecchia in Italy and Ajaccio in Corsica – and to the British warships patrolling off these ports, it was obvious that a huge campaign was in preparation.

The warships and frigates that were to escort the expedition could not possibly protect such a large convoy from a British attack: their best hope lay in deceiving the British about their destination. Napoleon was remarkably successful in this, and although British agents in France struggled to find out, they could not obtain any reliable information. Knowing that his movements were closely watched, Napoleon left it to the last moment before travelling to Toulon, but a week later Rear-Admiral Nelson, patrolling off that port, composed a dispatch to Admiral Earl St Vincent to report that 'Buonaparte arrived at Toulon last Friday, and has examined the troops which are daily embarking in the numerous Transports . . . it is not generally believed that Buonaparte is to embark, but . . . Reports say they are to sail in a few days, and others that they will not sail for a fortnight.'[15] A day later he was again writing to St Vincent, admitting, 'I have, in fact, no farther particulars to tell you . . . They order their matters so well in France, that all is secret.'[16] At this time

Nelson was commanding a small force of three warships (the *Vanguard*, *Alexander* and *Orion*), each carrying seventy-four guns, as well as three frigates, which were more lightly armed vessels, having about half the number of guns of a large warship, but were faster, more manoeuvrable and ideal for scouting purposes. This was a stronger squadron* than would normally be sent on a reconnaissance mission, and although it might hamper the sailing of the French fleet from Toulon, it could not stop it. For this reason Nelson was sending frequent reports to St Vincent, who was commanding a much larger fleet off the Spanish port of Cadiz, from which Nelson's ships had been detached.

In Toulon itself the French fleet had completed all its preparations, and according to Bourrienne, 'Bonaparte knew by the movements of the English that there was not a moment to lose; but adverse winds kept us for ten days.'[17] On the same day that Nelson was writing to St Vincent about the lack of information, the wind changed sufficiently for Napoleon's ships to start leaving Toulon. With a massive number of transports and warships to organise, it took over eight hours to assemble the fleet outside the harbour, and it was not until the next day, 20 May 1798, that they were ready to set sail. The very fact that Napoleon had planned this expedition, assembled its components and sailed in time to reach Egypt before the annual Nile flood made the Nile Valley impassable, was evidence not just of his ability as a commander, but of the strength of his power within France.

What was a good sailing wind for the French fleet at Toulon was actually the edge of a storm further out to sea – a storm that blew Nelson's ships south for two days before starting to moderate. Because the masts and rigging of Nelson's flagship, the *Vanguard*, were badly damaged, the ship was taken in tow by the *Alexander*. The warships, which had lost touch with the frigates, now looked for a sheltered spot to carry out repairs. They were off the Gulf of Oristano, on the west coast of Sardinia, roughly 250 miles south of Toulon, but the wind was keeping them off the coast, and as nobody had charts or personal knowledge of the area, they continued some 30 miles south to the island of San Pietro.

Parts of the world were still completely uncharted, and many places did not have adequate maps. Each seafaring nation had conducted surveys of

* At this time in Britain there was no real difference between the terms 'squadron' and 'fleet' except in reference to 'the Fleet' as a whole, which was divided into three squadrons (the red, white and blue). Generally, the terms were interchangeable, and have been used as such throughout this book.

some areas, but overall the coverage of sea charts was piecemeal and of variable quality. British naval captains were required to provide their own charts, but even if they could afford to buy everything available, it was often not practical to store so many charts on board ship, so they tended to be selective. When they found themselves in places not covered by their charts, they relied on anyone on board who had sailed in those waters before, so the situation that Nelson and his captains found themselves in was not unusual. Writing to his father-in-law afterwards, Captain Edward Berry of the *Vanguard* summed up the dangers of sailing into uncharted waters:

The storm did not abate till Tuesday afternoon [22 May], which enabled the *Alexander* to take us in tow. Our situation on Tuesday night was the most alarming I ever experienced: we stood in for the Island of Sardinia, and approached the S.W. side of the Island, intending to go into Oristan Bay, which we were not acquainted with, but it was absolutely necessary to go somewhere. Finding we could not fetch Oristan, the Admiral [Nelson] determined to try for St. Pierre's [San Pietro], which we could have fetched had the breeze continued, but unfortunately it fell light airs, and at times almost calm . . . All this time there was a heavy swell driving in towards the shore, so that at midnight we were completely embayed. You may easily figure to yourself our situation, and the feelings of those who *knew the danger*, when I tell you I could easily distinguish the surf breaking on the rocky shore; still there was hope anchorage might be found, though we knew of none.[18]

Berry described how they avoided shipwreck:

We therefore bent our cables [ready to anchor in an emergency] and prepared for the worst, anxiously wishing for daybreak, which at length arrived, and we found ourselves about five miles from the shore, the western swell still continuing to drive us in . . . Indeed, the *Vanguard* was a perfect wreck, but the *Alexander* still had us in tow. Fortunately, at about six o'clock on Wednesday, the 23rd of May, a breeze sprang up, the *Alexander's* sails filled, we weathered the rocks to windward of the Island of St. Pierre's, and before 12 we anchored in six fathoms*, and fine smooth water − a luxury to us scarcely to be equalled.[19]

---

* A fathom was 6 feet.

Despite the exhaustion of the crews after the storm, they were set to work to repair the three warships anchored off San Pietro, and remarkably the ships were ready to sail within four days, only to be delayed by variable winds. Before the repairs were complete, they were very vulnerable to capture, and Nelson commented that 'the meanest Frigate out of France would have been a very unwelcome guest'.[20] It was not until 3 June that they regained their station off Toulon, by which time they learned from passing ships that the French fleet had sailed, but nobody knew where. Two days later, while Nelson was still hoping to make contact with his missing frigates, Commander Thomas Masterman Hardy arrived in the British brig* *Mutine* with the welcome news that eleven warships were on their way to reinforce Nelson's fleet – he would now have a force capable of tackling the enemy fleet, but as yet had no knowledge of the destination of the French.

While Nelson's ships were blown southwards by the storm, Napoleon's fleet headed eastwards in order to round the northern tip of Corsica. After two days' sailing they met up with the French fleet from Genoa, and on 28 May this combined fleet reached the rendezvous point, west of Civitavecchia, to find the ships from Ajaccio already there. This huge convoy continued southwards, while the ships from Civitavecchia struggled to make contact, but they were not fast enough to keep up and sailed on a parallel course. For the rest of the journey to Malta, which was the first objective, the main French fleet had no idea where the ships from Civitavecchia were, but in fact they had the advantage of better winds and overtook the main convoy, arriving off Malta three days before the rest arrived on 9 June.

When the first French ships reached Malta, Nelson's fleet was still off Toulon, awaiting the last of the ships that were being sent as reinforcements and still ignorant about the route taken by the French. Impatient to start the search, Nelson left behind the *Leander* to meet the remaining ships that were expected. He himself took the rest of his fleet southeastwards towards Naples on 7 June, deducing that the various components of the French fleet were likely to rendezvous off the west coast of Italy. Three days later the *Leander* and the reinforcements caught up with Nelson, making his fleet complete except for his missing frigates: it was the same day that Napoleon began an assault on Malta.

For the French, the passage of nearly three weeks from Toulon to

---

* A brig was a small, two-masted vessel mainly used for running errands.

Malta had been relatively uneventful. At sea Napoleon 'passed the great-est part of his time in his cabin, lying on a bed, provided with four little castors, which alleviated the seasickness from which he almost constantly suffered'[21] – being liable to seasickness was one of the few things Napoleon and Nelson had in common. Many of the soldiers were seasick too, and conditions aboard the transports became more wretched day by day. Many were glad to reach Malta, a strictly neutral country ruled by the Knights of Malta, an organisation originating in the medieval crusades that had been in decline for some time and had come to rely heavily on recruitment from France. There was no legitimate reason for Napoleon to attack the island, but he needed the wealth accumulated by the Knights to help finance his expedition, and Malta would make a useful addition to Corsica and Corfu, two other islands invaded by the French, to increase their domination of the Mediterranean.

During the winter, in order to assess the likely level of resistance, Napoleon had sent a treasury official, Émile Poussielgue, on a spying mission to Malta. As well as gathering military intelligence, Poussielgue managed to bribe two key members of the Knights and returned to Napoleon with a completely favourable report: Malta could be taken with ease. According to Bourrienne, Napoleon was irritated that he had to put up even a token attack:

There was some misunderstanding, and consequently some cannon shots were exchanged . . . For those in the know, that was only for form's sake, and these hostile demonstrations were not followed up. We wished to preserve the honour of the knights, and that was all . . . The impregnable fortress of Malta is so sheltered from a raid that General Caffarelli, after examining the forti-fications with the greatest care, said to the General-in-Chief, in my presence, 'Well, General, we are very lucky there was someone in the town to open the gates for us.'[22]

On 13 June Napoleon issued a notification that Malta had surrendered and was under French control. He then organised systematic looting, carrying cartloads of treasure to his ships. His official report to the Directory would say that just over a million francs in gold and silver were taken from Malta, but the real figure was around seven million – the 'missing' five to six million was pocketed by Napoleon and his generals. Always conscious that a British fleet was hard on his heels, and anxious to prevent his invasion fleet being blockaded in harbour or caught at sea,

Napoleon was impatient to leave. Once the treasure had been loaded and a garrison of nearly four thousand French troops established in control, his fleet set sail again on 19 June, hoping to be in Egypt in under two weeks.

The same day that Napoleon declared Malta was taken, Nelson received his first piece of useful information from a passing ship: the French fleet had been seen off Sicily. With a chance to send letters home two days later, Nelson wrote to Earl Spencer, First Lord of the Admiralty: 'The last account I had of the French Fleet, was from a Tunisian Cruizer, who saw them on the 4th, off Trapani, in Sicily, steering to the eastward. If they pass Sicily, I shall believe they are going on their scheme of possessing Alexandria, and getting troops to India – a plan concerted with Tippoo Saib [the anti-British Sultan of Mysore], by no means so difficult as might at first view be imagined; but be they bound to the Antipodes, your Lordship may rely that I will not lose a moment in bringing them to Action.'[23] Clutching at this single straw of information, Nelson decided the likely destination of the French was Egypt: after so many setbacks, the chase was finally beginning.

Later Nelson was to write of this time that 'I had the happiness to command a Band of Brothers'[24], referring to the line 'We few, we happy few, we band of brothers'[25] in the king's famous speech before the battle in Shakespeare's *Henry V*. It was as they sailed in pursuit of the French that Nelson began to forge his captains into this band by inviting them to the *Vanguard* in small groups, often for dinner, in order to get to know them and discuss tactics. At a time when mobile phones have become essential possessions, it is difficult to appreciate the problems of communication at sea, even within a tightly packed fleet. Hailing could be used from ship to ship, but they had to be very close together, and even then the noise of the weather and the working of the ship could make shouted instructions incomprehensible. Generally, signal flags were used to pass messages from ship to ship, but these took time to hoist and be read, and the messages were limited in scope and open to misinterpretation, even when every flag was clearly visible. The only sure way of transmitting anything other than the most straightforward messages from one ship to another was to send someone with it in a boat, but frequently weather conditions intervened. There was simply no means of rapid and reliable communication, and so central control of a fleet from a flagship was often difficult – it was this obstacle that Nelson sought to overcome. By meeting with his captains and allowing them to become acquainted, he provided the conditions for them to understand and have confidence in one another. It was his genius for leadership, later known as the 'Nelson Touch'[26], that enabled him to rely on the simplest of strategies, instead of complicated battle plans and detailed instructions, confident that his subordinates had the ability to carry out his wishes, act independently, improvise where necessary and support one another as a team.

On the morning of 22 June Nelson's fleet had just passed the southern tip of Sicily when four ships were spotted to the south-east, and the *Leander* was sent to investigate. They were now moving into what were almost unknown waters, because the British Navy was used to operating in the western Mediterranean and seldom ventured east of Sicily. Between them, the British ships had very few charts of the area into which they were sailing. Lack of reliable charts was a minor inconvenience compared with the problem that Nelson was wrestling with − was he leading his ships in the right direction? In order to obtain their opinions, he summoned on board the *Vanguard* Sir James Saumarez of the *Orion*, Thomas Troubridge of the *Culloden*, Henry Darby of the *Bellerophon* and Alexander Ball of the *Alexander*. These captains discussed the information that had been collected and agreed that it was best to assume the French were heading for Egypt. Referring to this informal discussion, Nelson later wrote: 'I therefore determined, with the opinion of those Captains in whom I place great confidence, to go to Alexandria; and if that place, or any other part of Egypt is their destination, I hope to arrive [in] time enough to frustrate their plans. The only objection I can fancy to be started is, "you should not have gone such a long voyage without more certain information of the Enemy's destination": my answer is ready − who was I to get it from?'[27]

Just before the captains arrived on board the flagship, the *Leander* signalled that the four ships that had been spotted were frigates. Nelson recalled the *Leander* and let them go, not wanting to lose time chasing and capturing enemy frigates, even though he desperately needed such ships for reconnaissance. It was a mistake, as the frigates were outlying scout ships of the French fleet. While Nelson consulted his captains, the two fleets unknowingly passed within a few miles of each other − an opportunity to catch Napoleon at sea and change the course of history was lost.

On board Napoleon's flagship, the *Orient*, Bourrienne noted that 'while we were at sea he [Napoleon] seldom rose before ten o'clock in the morning. The *Orient* had almost the appearance of a town, from which women had been excluded, and this floating town had two thousand inhabitants, amongst whom were a great number of distinguished men.'[28] Napoleon was taking to Egypt an extraordinary party of civilian scholars. Despite his inviting them on a tropical voyage without revealing the destination, over 150 members of the French National Institute were willing to join the expedition. If Nelson had sunk the French fleet on its way to Egypt, the cream of France's intellectual and artistic talent would have been lost, including astronomers, civil engineers, draughtsmen, linguists, mathematicians, orientalists, artists, poets and musicians. For this very reason, the scholars were dispersed around at least seventeen ships.

It was an extraordinary idea of Napoleon's to take a large group of talented civilians on such a perilous military adventure – no other commander-in-chief would have even considered it, yet his exact motives are unknown. Their presence did allow Napoleon to claim that the expedition was a civilising mission, not one of imperial conquest. Perhaps more significantly, Alexander the Great had also taken a group of scholars and scientists on his Persian campaign, and Napoleon saw himself as following in the footsteps of Alexander.

With the wind in their favour, the British fleet was making a fast passage to Egypt, and on 24 June Sir James Saumarez on board the *Orion* wrote in his diary, 'The last two days we have not gone less than a hundred leagues*; and, as the wind continues favourable, we hope to arrive at Alexandria before the French, should their destination be for that place, which continues very doubtful. At the same time, if it should prove that our possessions in India is the object of their armament [military expedition], our having followed them so immediately appears the only means of saving that country from falling into their hands.'[29] Two days later Nelson sent Hardy ahead in the brig *Mutine* to forewarn the British consul at Alexandria and discover if there was any news of the French. By sunset on the 28th the British fleet was within sight of the port, but no French ships were to be seen. Nelson, with no hard evidence that the French were actually on course for Egypt, was suffering immense stress from apparently having made the wrong decision. Impatient to take action, he decided to search the eastern Mediterranean – again it was a mistake. The British fleet set sail north-eastwards on the morning of the 30th, and just twenty-five hours later the French fleet was anchored off Alexandria. Bourrienne recounted how they discovered their good fortune at being missed by Nelson:

* A league was 6116 yards – equivalent to 3 nautical miles. A nautical mile was equivalent to 6116 feet, but is now a distance of 6080 feet.

The expedition arrived off the coast of Africa on the morning of 1 July, and the [Roman] column of Septimus Severus indicated to us the city of Alexandria . . . Admiral Brueys [naval commander of the French fleet] had sent on beforehand the frigate *Juno* to fetch : . . . the French Consul. It was nearly four o'clock when he arrived, and the sea was very rough. He informed the general-in-chief that Nelson had been off Alexandria on 28 June and that he had straightaway sent a brig to obtain news from the English agent. On the return of the brig Nelson had immediately led his squadron towards the north-east. Without the delay that our convoy from Civita Vecchia has caused, we would have been in these waters at the same time as Nelson . . . It appeared that Nelson believed us to be already at Alexandria when he arrived there. He had reason for this, seeing that we had left Malta on 19 June, while he only left Messina on the 21st. Not finding us, and convinced that we should be there if that was our destination, he left these shores and sailed for Alexandretta in Syria, where he thought we might have landed in order to travel into Asia. This error saved the expedition a second time.[30]

Bourrienne next described Napoleon's actions – as impatient as those of Nelson:

Bonaparte, struck and convinced, as you might think, by the details which the French Consul gave him, resolved to disembark immediately. Admiral Brueys put to him the difficulties and dangers of disembarkation, the violence of the waves, the distance from the coast – a coast lined with reefs – the approaching night, and the complete ignorance of places suitable for landing. The Admiral urged him to wait for the following morning; that is nearly twelve hours, and that Nelson could not return from his move to Syria for several days. Bonaparte listened to these representations with impatience and ill-humour. He replied abruptly, 'Admiral, we don't have time to lose, fortune only gives me three days; if I do not make use of it, we are lost.' Fortune counted a lot with him. This chimerical idea constantly influenced his resolve. With General Bonaparte having command of the navy and army, the Admiral [Brueys] had to give in to his wishes.[31]

If Nelson's impatience had been unfortunate, leading him to miss the French fleet on two occasions, Napoleon's impatience was to prove equally unlucky. Preparations for landing began immediately. The fleet anchored as close inshore as they could, but Marabout beach was shallow and the nearest ships were 1½ miles offshore. With the rough weather it was several hours before all the boats were lowered and the first wave of troops had scrambled down into them. Fortunately for the French the landing was unopposed, because by the time they reached land the troops were seasick and exhausted, many were drenched, and some were injured where boats capsized or ran aground. In Napoleon's official report, he estimated that about twenty men lost their lives during the landing, but the real figure was probably higher.

Disembarkation of the army was not completed until 3 July, but only a couple of hours after the first soldiers landed, at dawn on the 2nd, Napoleon led a column of around five thousand troops in a march on Alexandria. No artillery, horses or even drinking water had been unloaded from the ships, and the tired and hungry soldiers carried nothing but their weapons and the clothes they marched in – many, suffering from seasickness, had left their food rations and water on board the ships. From the landing place at Marabout to Alexandria no road existed, and the few wells and water cisterns were sabotaged by nomadic Bedouin Arabs, who also continually harassed the French and captured and raped any stragglers.

The French reached the outskirts of Alexandria at eight in the morning, and although the troops were exhausted and suffering from extreme heat and thirst, Napoleon ordered an immediate attack. The inhabitants were poorly armed, terrified of the approaching army and had spent the night sending messages to Cairo begging for reinforcements. The French, desperate for water and facing only feeble resistance, had control of the city in under three hours. One French officer later wrote to his family, 'Confidentially, I can assure you that the thirst of our soldiers was the prime motive in capturing Alexandria. At the point the army had reached, it was a question of finding water or perishing.'[32]

If anything, there was less reason for an attack on Egypt than for taking Malta: it was unprovoked aggression against a neutral country that was part of the Turkish Ottoman Empire. Napoleon's excuse for the invasion was that the French were there to rescue the people of Egypt from the tyrannical rule of the Mamelukes, who were, in effect, the aristocrats of Egypt and ruled the country on behalf of the sultan of Turkey. Napoleon knew that it was only a matter of time before the Turks sent an army against him, and although such an army was unlikely to be as difficult to tackle as the Mamelukes, he could not defeat them both at once – he must press on and subdue the Mamelukes and take control of Egypt before the Turks arrived.

Five days after arriving in Alexandria, the troops were divided into three groups: Napoleon left on 7 July, leading a force to capture Cairo, the next day General Menou took his men to Rosetta by sea and the remainder stayed in Alexandria. From Napoleon's point of view, the invasion of Egypt was going well, but the soldiers saw the situation differently. One wrote to his parents:

We marched seventeen days without bread, wine, or brandy and five without water, over burning sands, with the enemy close at our heels! . . . We had to combat barbarians, wholly unacquainted with the rights of war, who exercised every species of cruelty upon the unhappy men who fell into their hands: cutting off the ears of one, the nose of another, the head of a third, and many other things . . . Which I tremble whenever I think of . . . Discontent was painted on every face, and the whole army was on the point of refusing to advance. A great number of soldiers blew out their brains, and many flung themselves into the Nile.[33]

Having been plunged from the cramped ships and unending seasickness into the fierce and waterless desert, without suitable clothing or equipment, the troops were rapidly becoming demoralised and were dying even before they fought any battles. Lieutenant Desvernois wrote that 'the soldiers accuse the generals for the unbelievable sufferings that they have endured since they left the ships; they cry, they ask what they have done wrong that the generals lead them in this way to die in a desert'.[34]

As Napoleon led his forces inland in search of the Mamelukes, Nelson continued to lead his fleet round the Mediterranean in search of the French. Having sailed northwards towards Turkey, the British fleet turned west on 2 July to head back towards Sicily and Naples, arriving at Syracuse in Sicily on the 20th. Here the ships loaded fresh supplies, and many took the opportunity to send letters home. Nelson wrote to his wife Frances, 'I have not been able to find the French Fleet, to my great mortification, or the event [British victory] I can scarcely doubt. We have been off Malta, to Alexandria in Egypt, Syria, into Asia, and are returned here without success: however, no person will say that it has been for want of activity. I yet live in hopes of meeting these fellows: but it would have been my delight to have tried Buonaparte on a wind [caught Napoleon at sea], for he commands the Fleet, as well as the Army.'[35] Nelson also wrote to Sir William Hamilton at Naples, giving him the latest news, or rather the lack of it: 'It is an old saying, "the Devil's children have the

Devil's luck." I cannot find, or to this moment learn, beyond vague con-
jecture where the French Fleet are gone to. All my ill fortune, hitherto,
has proceeded from want of Frigates.'[36] Without these fast scouting ships
to gather information and search for the enemy, Nelson was severely
handicapped, reliant on deducing the whereabouts of the French from
random snippets of information that came his way. Napoleon had
escaped him.

# TWO

---◆·---

# BATTLE OF THE NILE

I arrived there [*Aboukir Bay*] in the afternoon, and formed a line
of battle at two-thirds of a cable-length, the headmost vessel
being *as close as possible* to a shoal to the north-west of us, and the
rest of the fleet forming a kind of curve along the line of deep
water, so as not to be turned, by any means, in the south-west.
This position is the strongest we could possibly take.

Letter to the Minister of Marine in Paris from Admiral Brueys[1]

Nelson's fleet sailed eastwards from Sicily on 24 July 1798 and five days
later was off the southern coast of Greece, when at last reliable intelligence
about the French arrived. From the entries in his diary, Sir James
Saumarez gives some idea of how information percolated through the
British fleet, filling out the terse signal messages:

Sunday 29th July . . . A small vessel, captured yesterday by the *Culloden*, gave
some information of the enemy's fleet. The Admiral [Nelson] having made
the signal that he had gained intelligence of them, we are proceeding with a
brisk gale for Alexandria. If at the end of our voyage we find the enemy in a
situation where we can attack them, we shall think ourselves amply repaid for
our various disappointments. The *Alexander* also spoke [to] a vessel which
gave information; but, having had no communication with the Admiral, we
have not been able to learn the different accounts: we are however satisfied
with the purport of the signal he made yesterday. Monday. – I find from
Captain Ball [of the *Alexander*] that the enemy were seen steering towards
Alexandria *thirty* days ago, and we are once more making the best of our way

for that place. I also understand that two of our frigates were seen a few days since at Candia [Heraklion, Crete]; it seems decreed we shall never meet with them. I am rather surprised the Admiral did not endeavour to fall in with them, as they probably have certain information where the enemy's fleet are, from vessels they may have spoken with, and they otherwise would be a great acquisition to our squadron.[2]

In the four weeks since the British fleet had left Egypt, the French had gained control of the northern seaboard of the country. Once Alexandria was in French hands, the transport ships were brought into harbour, and the horses, artillery and stores were unloaded, but there was a problem with the warships. Some were carrying artillery and heavy equipment that was difficult to land in small boats, and so Napoleon ordered Admiral Brueys to take the warships into the two harbours as well. The forty-five-year-old Admiral, François-Paul de Brueys d'Aigalliers, was one of the few aristocratic naval officers to have survived the French Revolution, and Napoleon had specifically asked him to command the fleet. Brueys sent some officers to survey the harbours, and their report confirmed his suspicions. One harbour was too shallow and too open, and the only channel giving suitable access to the other one was so narrow that warships would have great difficulty sailing through. Once in this harbour they could easily be trapped by one or two enemy warships.

Brueys was in favour of taking his warships to a safe harbour in Corfu once the remaining artillery and stores were landed, but Napoleon wanted the ships close at hand. After a week of discussion Napoleon prevailed, and Brueys anchored the fleet in Aboukir Bay, 12 miles east of Alexandria. This anchorage was not ideal, with numerous sandbanks and little protection from the wind. Nevertheless, the bay offered the chance to unload the ships while they were anchored in a defensive formation. Within these treacherous waters, Brueys deployed his thirteen battleships in a line running approximately south-east to north-west, with their bows facing north-west and gaps of roughly 175 yards between the ships, so that the whole line was nearly 2 miles long. Four frigates formed a parallel line between the battleships and the shore, and there were two groups of gunboats nearer the beach, as well as artillery batteries set up on the coast and on a small island. It seemed a strong position, as the French assumed that the British would use traditional tactics of attacking in a line and so would sail down the outside of their formation.

One serious flaw was overlooked. The ships were anchored at the bow only, so that they were free to swing with the prevailing wind. This left the possibility of enemy ships anchoring between the ships, out of reach of the French guns. Their position could have been improved by springs on the anchor cables (ropes running from both sides of a ship to the cable so that the ship could be turned by hauling on one of these ropes), as this would have allowed guns to cover the blind spots. A stronger position would have been to close the gaps, with the ships immobilised by anchoring them at both bow and stern. Brueys, however, was satisfied with the arrangement, particularly as he had other distractions. The fleet was running desperately short of food, water and firewood – most of the supplies had been unloaded and taken by the army. On 12 July Brueys wrote to the Minister of Marine in Paris, 'We look forward with the greatest anxiety to the time when the conquest of Egypt shall furnish us with provisions. We are now obliged to supply the troops continually – every hour new drains are made upon us. We have now only fifteen days' biscuit on board, and we are in this anchorage just as if we were on the high seas – consuming everything, and replacing nothing.'[3] In addition, attacks by the Bedouin made it essential that foraging parties from the ships were large and well armed, so that considerable numbers of sailors were absent from their ships. In the same letter, Brueys complained: 'Our crews are weak both in number and quality. Our rigging, in general, out of repair, and I am sure that it requires no little courage to undertake the management of a fleet furnished with such tools! I do not think it necessary to enter into any further details on our present situation. You are a seaman, and will therefore conceive it better than I can describe it to you.'[4] In all, the impressive line of French warships anchored in Aboukir Bay was a good deal weaker than it looked.

After nearly three months of searching, the British fleet arrived back at Alexandria on 1 August to find the transports in the harbour, but no sign of warships. It was another bitter blow, as Saumarez admitted:

When on the morning of the 1st August the reconnoitring ship made the signal that the enemy was not there, despondency nearly took possession of my mind, and I do not recollect ever to have felt so utterly hopeless, or out of spirits, as when we sat down to dinner; judge then what a change took place when, as the cloth was being removed, the officer of the watch hastily came in, saying, 'Sir, a signal is just now made that the enemy is in Aboukir Bay, and moored in a line of battle.' All sprang from their seats, and only staying to drink a *bumper** to our success, we were in a moment on deck.[5]

At this point most of the British ships were about 9 miles from the French, although the *Alexander* and the *Swiftsure* were ahead, 2 or 3 miles away, and the *Culloden* was trailing about 7 miles behind because it was towing a French ship that had been captured off the Greek coast. With relatively light winds it would take about two hours to reach the enemy, yet it was now half past two in the afternoon, with sunset due around seven o'clock. If they were to fight straight away, the battle would be at night. Nelson did not hesitate and pressed on towards the French.

As soon as the British fleet was spotted, Rear-Admiral Blanquet du Chayla recalled that 'the signal was then made for all the boats, workmen, and guards to repair on board of their respective ships, which was only obeyed by a small number'.[6] Although the ships were short of men, the French were not unduly worried, as they expected the British to wait until the next day before attacking. Nevertheless, Blanquet du Chayla noted, 'At 3 o'clock, the Admiral [Brueys] not having any doubt but the ships in sight were the enemy, he ordered the hammocks to be stowed for action'[7], and two hours later, 'the enemy came to the wind [in order to turn] in succession. This manoeuvre convinced us that they intended attacking us that evening.'[8] This was very much to the advantage of the British, as it allowed the French only the minimum time to prepare, and although they would soon be fighting in the dark, Nelson was relying on his captains to use their initiative – essential when effective communication between ships would be impossible. In terms of the number of guns carried by the battleships, the French and British were evenly matched, but the guns of their frigates, gunboats and shore batteries gave the French the advantage.

On board Captain Thomas Foley's ship, the *Goliath*, a midshipman by the name of George Elliot celebrated his fourteenth birthday gazing at the French fleet as the British swept in to attack, being as he was in 'the leading ship of the fleet, in which no *order of sailing* was kept, but each ship got on as fast as she could, by way of gaining time'.[9] In fact, it was something of a race between the first two ships, and the *Goliath* was only 'first by half the length of a ship, but Captain Hood of the *Zealous* was very much senior to Foley, and was a likely man to make a push for the

* A glass or cup filled to the brim.

post of honour'.[10] Foley hoisted more sail and pushed on towards the French, with the added advantage of being the only British captain with an accurate chart of the area – a French one of 1764. Elliot assumed that 'Hood was annoyed but could not help it . . . Foley therefore stood on, and Hood followed him, but the third ship in the line, the *Audacious*, brought to [stopped], and of course forced the [following] two ships between her and *Vanguard* to do the same. A gap was thus made between the *Goliath* and the *Zealous* and the rest of the fleet of about seven miles, for we never shortened sail till we were coming to an anchor. The battle therefore began by only two ships against the whole of the enemy's van*.'[11]

The first French ship was the *Guerrier*, and Midshipman Elliot recorded how they decided to attack from the inshore side:

When we were nearly within gun-shot†, standing as aide-de-camp close to the Captain, I heard him say to the master that he wished he could get inside of the leading ship of the enemy's line. I immediately looked for the buoy on her anchor, and saw it apparently at the usual distance of a cable's length (*i.e.* 200 yards), which I reported; they both looked at it, and agreed there was room to pass between the ship and her anchor, (the danger was, the ship being close up to the edge of the shoal), and it was decided to do it . . . All this was exactly executed. I also heard Foley say, he should not be surprised to find the Frenchman *unprepared* for action *on the inner side* – and as we passed her bow I saw he was right, her lower-deck guns were not run out, and there was lumber, such as bags and boxes on the upper-deck ports, which I reported with no small pleasure.[12]

This was the advantage that would prove the key to success. Foley realised that because the French ships were only anchored at the bow, a strip of deep water must have been left between the ships and the shallows to allow them to swing inshore without grounding. If some British ships worked their way down the inside of the line, the French ships could be attacked from both sides. Brueys had not foreseen this tactic, and the guns on the inshore side were unmanned and obstructed. The British also had the wind behind them, while French ships further down the line could not sail directly into the wind and so were virtually powerless.

Foley took the *Goliath* along the inside of the *Guerrier* and fired a

---

* Van is short for vanguard – the leading ships of a line or fleet.
† Gun [cannon] shot was a distance of about 1000 yards.

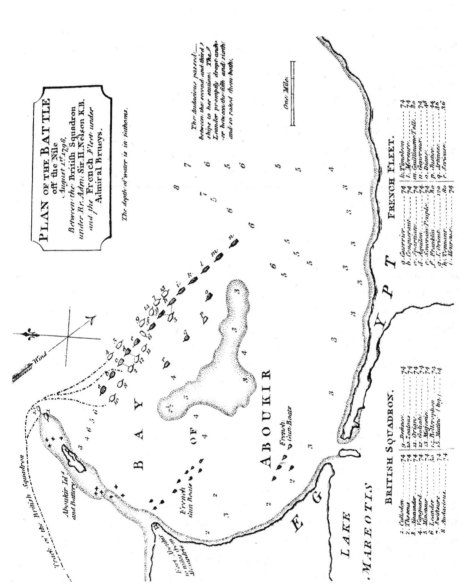

Plan of the Battle of the Nile

broadside at close range. This manoeuvre took Captain Samuel Hood by surprise, but he kept his ship, the *Zealous*, steadily within the wake of the *Goliath*, as he later recalled: 'The van ship of the enemy being in five fathoms water [we] expected the *Goliath* and *Zealous* to stick on the shoal every moment, and did not imagine we should attempt to pass within her . . . Captain Foley of course intended anchoring abreast of the van ship, but his sheet-anchor . . . not dropping the moment he wished it, [he] missed.'[13] By the time the sailors managed to drop the anchor, the *Goliath* had already passed the *Guerrier*. Captain Hood's *Zealous* had anchored just before the French line, but he now moved to fill the gap: 'I saw immediately he [Foley] had failed of his intention, [so I] cut away the *Zealous*'s sheet anchor and came to in the exact situation Captain Foley intended to have taken, the van ship of the enemy having his larboard bow toward the *Zealous*.'[14] This was a standard tactical move: because the majority of guns were positioned along both sides of a warship, the bow and stern were relatively unprotected blind spots – by anchoring just off the bow, the *Zealous* could fire all the guns of one side (a broadside) into the *Guerrier*, which could only return fire from a handful of guns at the bow.

Despite having known of the approach of the British fleet for at least three hours, the French had not believed the British would attack that night, and they were equally surprised by the speed of events, since the British ships did not even pause to regroup but sailed straight in with their guns blazing. In the *Goliath*, Midshipman Elliot observed the confusion and panic:

Foley's running on with only one ship to support him [the *Zealous*] . . . was also most fortunate. The French captains were all on board their admiral's ship [the *Orient*] and did not expect us to come in that night; they had sent for their boats to return from the shore, where they were procuring water. The senior officer of the *van division*, seeing us stand on under all sail, got anxious and sent his own boat to hasten off the boats of his division, without waiting to fill with water – she had not got back when we were getting very close, and as his own launch was passing the flagship, half laden with water, he got into her, but she pulled up slowly against the fresh sea breeze . . . I saw him waving his hat and evidently calling to his ship when still at a considerable distance. An officer was leaning against his ensign staff listening; at last this officer ran forward to the poop and down to the quarter deck. We knew what was coming, and off went their whole broadside but *just too late* to hit us.[15]

Having fired a broadside into the *Guerrier* in passing, the *Goliath* belatedly anchored between the *Conquérant* and the *Spartiate*, the second and third ships in the French line, while the *Zealous* took on the *Guerrier* as Captain Hood described: 'I commenced [such] a well-directed fire into her bow within pistol shot* a little after six [o'clock] that her fore mast went by the board in about seven minutes, just as the sun was closing the horizon, on which the whole squadron gave three cheers, it happening before the next ship astern of me had fired a shot and only the *Goliath* and *Zealous* [were] engaged. And in ten minutes more her main and mizzen masts [fell]. At this time also went the main mast of the second ship, engaged closely by the *Goliath* and *Audacious*.'[16]

By now the *Audacious,* third of the British ships, also managed to pass inshore of the French and anchored between the first and second of their ships. The next to arrive was the *Orion,* commanded by Sir James Saumarez, and he too decided to go on the inside of the French line. To do so the *Orion* passed on the inside of the *Zealous, Audacious* and *Goliath,* even closer to the shallow water, but without running aground. This course took the *Orion* within range of the French frigate *Sérieuse.* Frigates did not normally take part in full-scale battles, since their fire-power was much less than that of a battleship, and by convention battleships did not fire on a frigate unless the frigate fired first. This allowed frigates to sit on the sidelines of a battle, repeating signals, towing drifting vessels away and generally helping where they could. As the *Orion* passed by, Captain Jean Martin of the frigate *Sérieuse* decided he must act and fired a broadside into the *Orion* that did some damage and wounded two men. The total weight of the cannonballs fired by the *Sérieuse* was roughly 300 pounds. A broadside from the *Orion,* with the guns double-shotted, would be at least five times heavier, and officers on board proposed opening fire on the frigate immediately. Saumarez, though, wanted to be sure of his prey and replied, 'Let her alone, she will get courage and come nearer. Shorten sail†.'[17] Saumarez was right, and as the *Orion* slowed down, 'the frigate came up, and when judged to be sufficiently advanced [towards the *Orion*], orders were given to yaw the *Orion* [swinging off course to point the guns towards the *Sérieuse*], and stand by the starboard guns, which were double-shotted. The moment having arrived when every gun was

---

* Pistol shot was a distance of about 25 yards.
† Make some sails shorter, so reducing the overall area of sail exposed to the wind and thus slow down.

brought to bear, the fatal order to fire was given, when, by this single but well-directed broadside, the unfortunate *Sérieuse* was not only totally dismasted, but shortly afterwards sunk.'[18]

The *Orion* came to anchor off the bows of the *Peuple Souverain*, while Captain Ralph Miller, an American from New York serving in the British Navy, also took his ship, the *Theseus*, inside the French line. He manoeuvred between the *Zealous* and the *Guerrier*, to anchor in front of the *Goliath*. Midshipman Elliot in the *Goliath* was pleased that the *Theseus*, 'passing within ten yards gave us three most hearty cheers, which our men returned from their guns pretty well. The French were ordered by their officers to *cheer in return*, but they made such a lamentable mess of it that the laughter in our ships was distinctly heard ... It is a *disputed point*, whether cheering should be allowed. I say *decidedly yes*. No other nation *can cheer*. It encourages us and disheartens the enemy. I still distinctly recollect the stirring feelings of these men's cheers.'[19]

Five British ships were now inshore of the French, engaged with the first six ships of their line, and Nelson led his remaining ships down the outside of the line, anchoring his flagship, the *Vanguard*, opposite the *Spartiate*, which was already fighting the *Theseus*. For fear of hitting the *Vanguard*, the *Theseus* redirected fire from the *Spartiate* to the adjacent *Aquilon* as the *Vanguard* opened up with the starboard broadside. The *Minotaur* sailed in to anchor before the *Vanguard*, and the *Defence* anchored ahead of the *Minotaur*, while the *Bellerophon*, intending to pull up in front of the *Defence*, anchored too late, and instead of engaging the *Franklin*, took on the French flagship *Orient*. The battle was in full flow, with the first seven ships in the French line caught between five British ships on one side and four on the other.

By now it was seven o'clock and darkness had fallen. The British ship *Majestic* was next to arrive and tried to anchor off the stern of the *Orient* to help the *Bellerophon*, but instead drastically overshot, becoming entangled with the French ship *Heureux*. The *Culloden*, having left off towing the captured ship, made good speed to catch up with the rest of the fleet, but in his haste to join the action Captain Thomas Troubridge took the ship too close to Aboukir Island and hit a rock. The *Culloden* was stuck fast for the rest of the battle, and with the leaks increasing and the water rising, the entry in the log for the next day began: 'People employed throwing shot and provisions of all sorts overboard and sending some on board the *Mutine* [brig]. Found the ship make[s] more water. Sent all hands to the pumps.'[20] Seeing the *Culloden* aground, the *Alexander* and

*Swiftsure* steered well clear of the reef, and the *Alexander* joined the attack on the *Orient*, while the Canadian captain Benjamin Hallowell took the *Swiftsure* into a position between the *Franklin* and the *Orient*. The *Leander*, a 50-gun ship that was not really a frigate or a full-sized battle-ship, stopped to help the *Mutine* with the stranded *Culloden*, but then moved on to join the fight against the *Franklin*.

At nine o'clock the first part of the battle had run its course, as Captain Miller related in a letter to his wife :

Having now brought all our ships into battle, which you are to suppose raging in all magnificent, awful, and horrific grandeur, I proceed to relate the general events of it as I saw them. The *Guerrier* and *Conquérant* made a very inefficient resistance . . . and about 8 o'clock, I think, were totally silent. The *Spartiate* resisted much longer, and . . . her larboard* guns were fired on us in the beginning with great quickness, but after the Admiral [Nelson in the *Vanguard*] anchored on his starboard side, it was slow and irregular, and before or about 9 o'clock she was silenced, and had also lost her main and mizzen masts: the *Aquilon* was silenced a little earlier, with the loss of all her masts, having the whole fire of the *Minotaur* on her starboard side, and, for some time, nearly half ours on her larboard bow. *Le Peuple Souverain* was, about the same time, entirely dismasted and silenced.[21]

By this point, Nelson had been wounded. Around half past eight he was on the quarterdeck† of the *Vanguard* when the *Spartiate* fired a broad-side. He was 'struck in the forehead by a langridge shot, or a piece of iron, and the skin being cut by it at right angles, it hung down over his face, and as it covered his eye, he was perfectly blind'‡.[22] 'Langridge' was a general term for scrap iron, musket-balls or anything else likely to maim or kill, packed in a cylindrical tin case and fired from a cannon. As the case dis-integrated on firing, the effect was like a huge shot-gun, and was frequently used to cut a swath through groups of men on an exposed deck. Nelson fell, his face covered in blood, and Captain Berry caught him in his arms as he cried out, 'I am killed; remember me to my wife.'[23] Nelson was taken below to the surgeon, Mr Jefferson, exclaiming, 'I will take my turn with my brave followers!'[24] It was the general custom for the

* The left-hand side of a ship, later known as the port side.
† The quarterdeck was the aftermost deck and the place from where officers controlled the ship.
‡ He had lost the sight in his right eye at the siege of Calvi in Corsica on 12 July 1794, when the eye was grazed by gravel thrown up by a cannonball that struck the rampart in front of him.

wounded to be seen by the surgeon in the order in which they came to the cockpit, where he operated deep within the ship. Because of this, some men with minor wounds bled to death while waiting their turn. Nelson, who always took a pessimistic view when he was injured, 'felt convinced that his wound was mortal. Mr. Jefferson assured him, on probing the wound, that there was no immediate danger. He [Nelson] would not, however, indulge any hope.'[25]

This was an era when naval officers of most nations, and certainly those in the British, French and Spanish navies, had a paternalistic attitude to their men and a strong sense of honour and chivalry. They led from the front, winning the respect of their crews by an exaggerated disregard for their own safety. While the sailors used any available cover to avoid the worst of the enemy's broadsides, it was a point of honour among the officers that they paced the deck proudly in all their finery and did not flinch at the lethal showers of missiles. On board the *Tonnant* Captain Aristide Aubert Dupetit-Thouars certainly did not flinch. An experienced officer, he had rejoined the French Navy only a year before the battle. Under heavy fire, Dupetit-Thouars refused to surrender and had the French flag nailed to the mast*. In the hail of projectiles flying across the deck, he had one foot shot away and his leg was broken. After the lower leg was amputated, he continued to command the ship until he bled to death, and his last words were 'Never strike the flag!'[26] On his instructions his body was thrown overboard so that he would not fall into British hands.

By the time Nelson was wounded, Captain Westcott of the *Majestic* was dead, and several British officers were injured, including Sir James Saumarez on board the *Orion*, seriously wounded from a splinter in the thigh. The word 'splinter', given to any wooden fragments flying through the air, is misleading since it implies a very small piece of wood. Splinters were of any size, as the force of a cannonball at close range could smash pieces several feet long from any part of a wooden ship. The splinter that wounded Saumarez was the sheave (grooved wooden wheel) from a pulley block that had been smashed off a mast. Saumarez was lucky, since this splinter had already killed Mr Baird, his clerk, and severely wounded Midshipman Charles Miells, and so its momentum had been reduced, or Saumarez might have been killed outright. As it was, the blow knocked

---

* Lowering or 'striking' the flag ('colours') was an accepted signal of surrender: hence the expression 'nailing one's colours to the mast', indicating a refusal to surrender.

him over and he was stunned with pain and shock, 'but although he acknowledged it was painful, and might in the end be serious [requiring amputation to stop gangrene spreading], he could not be persuaded to leave the deck even to have the wound examined'.[27] Saumarez survived without needing amputation, but after the battle the wound was so bad that he was unable to leave his ship to join the other captains for a celebration.

In the *Vanguard* Nelson was eventually seen by the surgeon, who, 'having bound up and dressed the wound, requested the Admiral to remain quiet in the bread-room'.[28] Nelson found this impossible – it was observed that

nothing could repress his anxious and enthusiastic disposition. He immediately ordered his secretary, Mr. Campbell, to attend him in the breadroom, that no time might be lost in writing [his dispatch] to the Admiralty. This gentleman [Campbell] . . . had been himself wounded, and beholding the blind and suffering state of the Admiral, became so much affected, that he could not write. The Chaplain was then summoned, but the eagerness and impatience of Nelson increasing, he took the pen himself, and contrived to trace some words which marked at that awful moment his devout sense of the success he had then obtained.[29]

The battle was not yet over, but it was already clear to Nelson which side would win.

Of all the naval battles of the period, this one was unusual because few eyewitness accounts by ordinary seamen have survived. Officers were more likely to keep diaries and journals, and to write their memoirs in later life, but the letters to family and friends at home, which so often give a glimpse of the experiences of the sailors, were lost – thrown overboard with the code books when the *Leander*, carrying dispatches to England, was captured by the *Généreux*, one of the ships that escaped from the battle. John Nicol in the *Goliath* did write his memoirs, and he recorded helping the gunner in the powder magazine make up cartridges for the guns, away from the action, which was something he regretted: 'I would, if had I my choice, been on the deck; there I would have seen what was passing and the time would not have hung so heavy; but every man does his duty with spirit, whether his station be in the slaughterhouse or the magazine.'[30] The 'slaughterhouse' was what seamen called the middle section of the gun deck, where enemy fire tended to be concentrated and where the greatest damage and highest number of casualties usually occurred. By contrast, the vulnerable magazines where the gunpowder was stored were the most protected parts of the ship, usually below the waterline. Having been sealed off from the rest of the ship as much as possible, the magazines were always hot, stuffy and dark, but especially so on an August night off the Egyptian coast. No lantern could be allowed inside, and the magazines were illuminated by light cupboards or light rooms in which lanterns were placed so that they shone through thick glass windows into the magazine, so preventing the risk of explosion. The walls of the magazine were painted white to maximise the effect of the lanterns, but even so the light was dim.

Nicol complained that 'I saw as little of this action as I did of the one on the 14th February [1797] off Cape St Vincent . . . Any information we got was from the boys and women who carried the powder.'[31] The presence of women in navy ships at sea was against regulations, but many captains allowed the wives of petty officers to live on board, and during any fighting they either helped as 'powder monkeys', carrying gunpowder cartridges to the guns, or else assisted the surgeon as nurses. Nicol recalled that 'the women behaved as well as the men, and got a present for their bravery from the Grand Signior . . . I was much indebted to the gunner's wife, who gave her husband and me a drink of wine every now and then, which lessened our fatigue much. There were some of the women wounded, and one woman belonging to Leith [in Scotland] died of her wounds, and was buried on a small island in the bay. One woman bore a son in the heat of the action; she belonged to Edinburgh.'[32]

It was not unusual for women to give birth during a battle, as the noise and stress of the situation tended to induce labour. Nor was it unusual for the women to have their children with them on board ship. For the previous major battle off Cape St Vincent, where Nicol had also missed seeing the action, it has been calculated that at least twenty-three women and twenty children were in the British ships, but it is not known exactly how many women were on board the ships in Aboukir Bay. In the *Orion* there was at least one: Ann Hopping, wife of the second gunner, Edward Hopping, who is known to have earned money as a seamstress, working for Captain Sir James Saumarez. She had also been at Cape St Vincent, where she had helped her husband serve out cartridges from the magazine. She was now twenty-nine and had two young daughters, although it is uncertain if they were on board as well. Towards the end of her life (when better known as Nancy Perriam), Ann's memories of this battle at Aboukir were written down, and she recalled:

When the order to 'Clear for action' was given, she had just begun a flannel shirt for Sir James Saumarez. During the action she served out powder and also assisted the surgeons in the Cockpit. She was standing by when the surgeon took out from the socket [amputated] the arm of a midshipman . . . a protégé of Sir James Saumarez. During the operation the poor child never uttered a groan, and when it was finished he turned his head towards her and said, 'Have I not borne it like a man?' The words were scarcely uttered when a cold shiver seized him, and in an instant his young soul had entered the land of immortal life.[33]

On board the *Goliath*, as well as the gunner's wife mentioned by Nicol, at least four other women were present: Ann Taylor, Elizabeth Moore, Sarah Bates and Mary French. Three were wives of seamen, and Mary French was the wife a marine. All four men were killed in the battle. Afterwards Captain Foley took the unusual step of entering these women in the muster book, 'being the widows of men Slain in fight on the 1st Augt 1798 victualled at $\frac{2}{3}$ds allowance by Captains order, in consideration of their assistance in Dressing and attending on the Wounded'.[34] These women were provided with victuals from the ship's stores until 30 November, 'their further assistance not being required'[35]. This provision for widows was most unusual. Another widow, Christiann White, later wrote to Nelson asking for help:

Your petitioner Christiann White has taken the liberty to lay her case before your Lordship, that I lost my husband in your glorious action of the 1st of August 1798 at the Nile, and during the action I attended the surgeon in dressing the wounded men, and likewise attended the sick and wounded during the passage to Gibraltar which was 11 weeks on board his Majesty's ship *Majestic*, where we lost the Honourable Captain Westcott, and as for myself was left a widow and with 2 children to the mercy of God. Your petitioner humbly hopes that your Lordship will consider her worthy of your notice.[36]

In theory, widows of seamen who died on active service were entitled to the men's back pay and a small pension, but relatively few women received these as the bureaucratic process of claiming was so complicated. The way that the pension fund was financed was even more arcane. Every naval ship's muster book carried a number of 'widow's men', usually in the proportion of two for every hundred men in the crew, and the pay of these imaginary crew members was set aside as a contribution to the fund. In addition the personal belongings of a man who died at sea were usually auctioned off to other crew members, with the money going to the next of kin, and for famous battles that caught the public imagination subscriptions were raised to support widows and orphans, but for relatives of men killed in the many minor battles and skirmishes, or by accident or disease, support for dependants was haphazard. On top of this, the lack of regular and reliable communications meant that it could be months or even years before a widow found out that her husband was dead.

As the battle continued, the fighting around the *Goliath* was fierce, and in the magazine Nicol was kept informed of what was happening by the powder monkeys, who 'brought us every now and then the cheering news of another French ship having struck, and we answered the cheers on deck with heart-felt joy'.[37] Even the magazine was not a completely safe haven, though, as 'in the heat of the action, a shot came right into the magazine, but did no harm, as the carpenters plugged it up, and stopped the water that was rushing in'.[38] Then, at around ten o'clock, Nicol related that 'the *Goliath* got such a shake, we thought the after-part of her had blown up until the boys told us what it was'[39] – the French flagship *Orient* had exploded.

The *Orient* had been under attack by the *Bellerophon* from about seven o'clock – an unequal contest since the *Orient* had 120 guns on three decks, whereas the *Bellerophon* had only seventy-four on two decks. Within an hour the *Bellerophon*'s mizzenmast and mainmast were shot away, at least sixteen guns were out of action and the ship was badly battered. The anchor cable was cut and the *Bellerophon* began to drift away from the battle. The *Alexander* took up the fight by anchoring behind the *Orient* and firing into the vulnerable stern, while the *Swiftsure* attacked the *Orient*'s bow. The *Alexander*'s broadsides started a fire in the stern cabin of the *Orient* that quickly spread to the upper decks and was soon out of control.

On board the *Orient* was Brueys's chief-of-staff, Honoré-Joseph-Antoine Ganteaume, who later recalled 'an explosion took place on the aft of the quarter-deck. We had already had a boat on fire, but we had cut it away, and so avoided the danger. We had also thrown a hammock, and some other things, which were in flames, overboard, but this third time, the fire spread so rapidly and instantaneously amongst the fragments of every kind, with which the poop was incumbered, that all was soon in flames.'[40] Fire on board ship was something all seamen feared, because so little could be achieved with small pumps and buckets of water, but Ganteaume saw that 'the fire pumps had been dashed to pieces by the enemy's balls, and the tubs and buckets rendered useless. An order was given to cease firing, that all hands might be at liberty to bring water, but such was the ardour of the moment, that in the tumult, the guns of the main-deck still continued their fire. Although the officers had called all the people between decks, aloft, the flames had in a very short time, made a most alarming progress, and we had but few means in our power of checking them.'[41]

Once the flames were out of control, it was only a matter of time before the ship was destroyed. As the fire spread up the rigging and masts of the *Orient*, the effect was like a gigantic torch illuminating the battle area, and the ships nearest to the *Orient* began to move away to what was hoped would be a safe distance. Over a mile away, Midshipman Elliot was uncertain what ship was on fire: 'Long after it was quite dark, perhaps about ten o'clock, we saw a ship down the line on fire – it was long before we could judge which party she belonged to – *our* share of the action was all but over, and we looked on with great suspense – at last, as the fire increased, we saw her *three decks*, which decided the point, as we had but two-deck ships. We wished to send boats down, but, on examination, had not one that could be made to swim, so shattered were they all. It was an awful sight.'[42]

On board the *Swiftsure* the Reverend Cooper Willyams had a close-up view:

At three minutes past nine o'clock a fire was observed to have broken out in the cabin of *L'Orient* . . . The conflagration now began to rage with dreadful fury; still the French Admiral [Brueys] sustained the honour of his flag with heroic firmness; but at length a period was put to his exertions by a cannon ball, which cut him asunder: he had before received three desperate wounds, one on the head, two in his body, but could not be prevailed on to quit his station on the arm-chest. His Captain, Casa Bianca, fell by his side. Several of the officers and men seeing the impracticability of extinguishing the fire, which had now extended itself along the upper decks, and was flaming up the masts, jumped overboard; some supporting themselves on spars and pieces of wreck, others swimming with all their might to escape the dreaded catastrophe. Shot flying in all directions dashed many of them to pieces; others were picked up by the boats of the fleet, or dragged into the lower ports, of the nearest ships: the British sailors humanely stretched forth their hands to save a fallen enemy, though the battle at that moment raged with uncontrolled fury. The *Swiftsure*, that was anchored within half-pistol-shot of the larboard bow of *l'Orient*, saved the lives of the commissary, first lieutenant, and ten men, who were drawn out of the water into the lower deck ports during the hottest part of the action. The situation of the *Alexander* and *Swiftsure* was perilous in the extreme. The expected explosion of such a ship as *l'Orient*, was to be dreaded as involving all around in certain destruction . . . The van of our fleet having finished for the present their part in the glorious struggle, had now a fine view of the two lines illumined by the flames of the ill-fated foe; the colours of the contending powers being plainly distinguished. The moon, which had risen, opposing her cold light to the warm glow of the fire beneath, added to the grand and solemn picture. The flames had by this time made such progress that an explosion was instantly expected, yet the enemy on the lower deck, either insensible of the danger that surrounded them, or impelled by the last paroxysms of despair and vengeance, continued to fire upon us.[43]

The *Orient* then blew up, as Willyams graphically described:

At thirty-seven minutes past nine the fatal explosion happened. The fire communicated to the magazine, and *l'Orient* blew up with a crashing sound that deafened all around her. The tremulous motion, felt to the very bottom of each ship, was like that of an earthquake; the fragments were driven such a vast height into the air that some moments elapsed before they could descend, and then the greatest apprehension was formed from the volumes of burning matter which threatened to fall on the decks and rigging of the surrounding ships. Fortunately, however, no material damage occurred . . . An awful silence reigned for several minutes, as if the contending squadrons, struck with horror at the dreadful event, which in an instant had hurled so many brave men into the air, had forgotten their hostile rage in pity for the sufferers.[44]

The silence did not last. 'But short was the pause of death;' Willyams reflected, 'vengeance soon roused the drooping spirits of the enemy.'[45] After the explosion, the ships at the head of the French line were by now out of the battle, and so the British ships did running repairs and then moved down the line to take on fresh opponents. Here the fighting continued until about three in the morning, when there was another lull because both sides needed to pause to patch up their badly damaged ships. When the *Goliath* ceased firing, John Nicol 'went on deck to view the state of the fleets, and an awful sight it was. The whole bay was covered with dead bodies, mangled, wounded, and scorched, not a bit of clothes on them except their trowsers. There were a number of French, belonging to the French admiral's ship, the *L'Orient,* who had swam to the *Goliath* and were cowering under her forecastle. Poor fellows, they were brought on board, and Captain Foley ordered them down to the steward's room, to get provisions and clothing.'[46] An experienced seaman who had fought in the American War of Independence, Nicol was struck by the dejection of the prisoners: 'In the American war, when we took a French ship . . . the prisoners were as merry as if they had taken us, only saying, "Fortune de guerre" – you take me today, I take you tomorrow. Those we now had on board were thankful for our kindness, but were sullen, and as downcast as if each had lost a ship of his own.'[47]

The battle dragged on fitfully throughout the next day. Although it was obvious who were the victors, the French refused to surrender, and each ship had to be beaten into submission. Rear-Admiral Villeneuve in the *Guillaume Tell,* though, decided to escape with the remaining intact French ships, and took his ship out of the line, followed by the battleship *Généreux* and the two frigates *Diane* and *Justice.* Because the rigging and masts of the British ships were so badly mauled, there was no chance of catching these relatively undamaged French ships. After firing a few broadsides, they returned their attention instead to the remaining ships that had not surrendered. Willyams described how the last two French ships finally gave up:

In the morning of the 3rd of August there remained in the Bay only the *Timoleon* and *Tonnant* of the French line that were not captured or destroyed. The former being aground near the coast, the Captain (Trullet) with his crew escaped in their boats after setting fire to her, and in a short time she blew up. A flag of truce had been sent to the *Tonnant,* but she refused to submit; on which the *Theseus* and *Leander* going down to her, and the *Swiftsure* following, she struck without further resistance. This completed the conquest of the French fleet in the Bay of Aboukir.[48]

On the British side the initial estimate of casualties was 218 killed and 677 wounded, although men continued to die from their wounds. The number of women killed and wounded was not recorded. The French casualties were far worse, with an estimate of 5235 killed or missing and

3305 taken prisoner, of whom around a thousand were wounded. The *Orient* had a nominal crew of about one thousand men, but they were not all on board during the battle. Of those that were, the majority lost their lives – the exact casualty figures are unknown. Unable to feed and care for so many prisoners, Nelson returned all but about two hundred to the shore in the days following the battle.

At this time, Napoleon was pursuing a force of Mamelukes on the edge of the Sinai Desert, and news of the defeat did not reach him until 13 August. His private secretary, Bourrienne, recorded that 'on learning of the terrible catastrophe of Aboukir, the general-in-chief was overwhelmed . . . At a glance, he clearly measured its fatal consequences . . . He quickly recovered his presence of mind that controlled events; that moral courage, that strength of character, that loftiness of thought, which had wavered for a moment beneath the overwhelming weight of this news. He only repeated, in a tone difficult to describe, "*Unfortunate Brueys, what have you Done!*"'[49] Napoleon and his army were now trapped in Egypt.

The victory at Aboukir Bay was the greatest that had been achieved in the war against France and the first major setback for Napoleon, up to then claimed as invincible in French propaganda. The battle was to mark Nelson's life as deeply as it marked Napoleon's, for he became a British national hero. He was heralded as 'Lord Nelson' in *The Times* even before King George III decided to make him a peer. Rather than the Battle of Aboukir Bay, it became known in Britain as the Battle of the Nile, and Nelson became Baron Nelson of the Nile, with an annual pension of £2000. Other gifts and honours were showered on him, ranging from the sublime to the downright unbelievable. The East India Company considered that the immediate threat from Napoleon to its territories in India had been removed and voted Nelson a gift of £10,000, while the Ottoman Sultan Selim III awarded him the Chelengk (Plume of Triumph) – a gaudy, diamond-encrusted ornament, which Nelson sometimes wore on his hat. Probably the strangest gift came from Captain Hallowell of the *Swiftsure*, who presented Nelson with a coffin. The accompanying letter read: 'My Lord, Herewith I send you a coffin made of part of *L'Orient*'s main mast, that when you are tired of this life you may be buried in one of your own trophies – but may that period be far distant, is the sincere wish of your obedient and much obliged servant, Ben Hallowell.'[50] For Nelson, Napoleon and many other key players, the Battle of the Nile was the start of a new phase of the war, but for John Nicol, below decks in the *Goliath*, it was 'the glorious first of August, the busiest night in my life'.[51]

# THREE

———•◆•———

# SIEGE OF ACRE

Ten days before the departure of Bonaparte, who was heading towards Egypt and Syria, a prisoner escaped from the Temple who was to contribute so greatly to his reverses. An escape so simple in itself much later was to cause the failure of the most gigantic plans and bold ideas.

> Bourrienne, on the consequences of Sir Sidney Smith's
> escape from prison on 24 April 1798[1]

After the Battle of the Nile Nelson sent seven British ships and six French prizes to Gibraltar for repairs, and in the days that followed, the rest of the British ships were made seaworthy and the remaining captured French ships were either repaired or destroyed. At Aboukir, Midshipman Elliot was involved in the attempt to salvage anything useful from the submerged French frigate *Sérieuse* to refit his own ship, the *Goliath*:

The ship was laying on her side, the *upper part* of the lower deck hatches *under water*. Our greatest want was cannons, and I dived . . . in hopes of finding some, expecting to have air enough towards the upper side where it was above water; in this I was right, and I also found much more light than I expected . . . The first thing I met was a dead French marine, swelled up and floating like a cork; he was *by no means a pleasant companion* where fresh air was scarce, and it was with no little difficulty that I forced him under the beams into the open hatchway. Captain Hardy had come on board to see what was to be had, like myself, and just as he looked down the hatchway up bobbed the marine . . . I got most useful supplies from this ship, which

greatly assisted our refit. Hardy mentioned this . . . to Nelson who said no
wonder I smelt out a Frenchman in the dark. Poor Nelson had such a horror
of all Frenchmen, that I believe he thought them at all times nearly as corrupt
in body as in mind.[2]

At long last, five British frigates found their way to Egypt. Leaving two
battleships and three frigates to blockade Alexandria, Nelson took the
remaining ships to Naples. News of the battle had already been brought
there by the *Mutine,* and so boats were ready to welcome Nelson's ships.
An Englishwoman staying at Naples, Cornelia Knight, 'was with Sir
William and Lady Hamilton in their barge, which also was followed by
another with a band of musicians on board. The shore was lined with
spectators, who rent the air with joyous acclamations, while the bands
played "God save the King" and "Rule Britannia.".'[3] Following the barge
of the Hamiltons was the King of Naples, Ferdinand IV, but he 'did not
go on board either of the ships, but from his barge saluted the officers on
deck. His Majesty had expressed his desire to be incognito, so as not to
give the trouble of paying him the usual honours.'[4]

The British seamen, and especially Nelson, were given a rapturous
welcome, and afterwards Nelson wrote home to his wife: 'Sir William and
Lady Hamilton came out to sea, attended by numerous boats, with
emblems, &c. They, my most respectable friends, had nearly been laid up
seriously ill; first from anxiety, then from joy . . . Alongside came my
honoured friends; the scene in the boat was terribly affecting; up flew her
ladyship, and exclaiming, "Oh, God! is it possible?" she fell into my arm[*]
more dead than alive. Tears, however, soon set matters to rights, when
alongside came the king.'[5]

From a modern perspective, Lady Hamilton's reactions to the news and
meeting Nelson seem hysterical and perhaps insincere, but congratulations similar in tone came from various ladies, including Countess
Spencer in London:

Joy, joy, joy to you, brave, gallant, immortalized Nelson! May that great God,
whose cause you so valiantly support, protect and bless you to the end of your
brilliant career! Such a race surely never was run. My heart is absolutely
bursting with different sensations of joy, of gratitude, of pride, of every

---

[*] His left arm. His right arm was amputated in July the previous year after he was wounded by
a musket-ball.

emotion that ever warmed the bosom of a British woman, on hearing of her Country's glory – and all produced by you . . . All, all I *can* say must fall short of my wishes, of my sentiments about you. This moment the guns are firing, illuminations are preparing, your gallant name is echoed from street to street, and every Briton feels his obligations to you weighing him down.[6]

Nelson, the national hero, now found his fame was rapidly spreading across Europe – not for the strategic significance of the battle, which was important enough, but for the propaganda value. The French had enjoyed a long string of victories on land, and the rising young star, Napoleon, had been hailed as invincible. At sea, the defeat of a French fleet off Cape St Vincent in February 1797, and the defeat of the Dutch, allies of the French, at the Battle of Camperdown in October the same year, had been the only real causes for rejoicing. It did not matter that Napoleon was not on board ship at the time of the battle: his fleet had been decisively defeated, and Nelson was the commander who had led the attack.

When news of Nelson's victory reached London in October, the immediate reaction of the Foreign Office was to order Captain Sir Sidney Smith to Constantinople (now Istanbul). Both Nelson and Smith were lethal weapons that could be brilliantly effective against the enemy, but were not always controllable. Yet of all the differences between these two naval officers, one stood out: Nelson was very much a warlord, always anxious to go straight for the enemy and defeat them in open battle, whereas Smith was more subtle – a political animal deeply involved with the British Secret Service. Nelson was a fighter with limited diplomatic skills, Smith was a diplomat and spy who could fight.

Although Napoleon's fleet had been comprehensively defeated, and he himself was stranded in Egypt, a threat still existed to British interests in the eastern Mediterranean and even India, which the French could attack overland, beyond Nelson's reach. A British military expedition would take time and a great deal of finance to assemble, and if Napoleon moved quickly, as he often did, he could be in India long before the British Army caught up. The answer was to send Sir Sidney Smith to Constantinople, where his younger brother, John Spencer Smith, was the minister-plenipotentiary. When the latter was first appointed to the British Embassy there in 1792, his brother Sidney joined him and was involved in intelligence work. It was France declaring war on Britain early the following year that led to Sidney Smith rescuing and burning the

French warships at Toulon that summer. Sir Sidney was now instructed by the Admiralty 'to put to sea without a moment's loss of time in the ship you command, and proceed with all possible despatch off Cadiz, and putting yourself under the command of the Earl of St Vincent, admiral of the Blue and commander-in-chief of his majesty's ships and vessels in the Mediterranean and along the coast of Portugal, follow his lordship's order for your further proceedings'.[7] If St Vincent was not at Cadiz, Smith was to look for him at Gibraltar. The Foreign Office advised the two brothers to sign a treaty with the Turks and Russians to form an alliance to defend the Ottoman Empire, and Sir Sidney was given full powers with his brother. In a letter to Spencer Smith, his role was set out:

Your Brother Sir Sidney Smith shall proceed to Constantinople with the 80 Gun Ship the *Tigre*, to the Command of which he has lately been appointed. His Instructions will empower him to take the Command of such of His Majesty's Ships as He may find in those Seas, unless . . . it should happen that there should be among them any of His Majesty's officers of superior Rank, and he will be directed to act with such force in conjunction with the Russian and Ottoman squadrons for the defence of the Ottoman Empire, and for the Annoyance of the Enemy in that quarter.[8]

Such a dual mission was unusual, and the Admiralty knew that to invest a mere captain with such powers was likely to cause trouble when there were many senior officers available. Indeed, Nelson was to object most strongly. Sir Sidney met up with St Vincent at Gibraltar in December, and St Vincent subsequently responded to the First Lord of the Admiralty:

I certainly did conceive it to have been your lordship's intention, that Sir Sidney Smith should act independent of any other officer in the Mediterranean, except myself, and that he was only put under my orders *pro forma*; and I clearly understood from his conversation, that the great object of joining him in the commission with his brother, Mr. Spencer Smith, was to give him place [power] over the Turkish and Russian sea-officers serving in the Levant; and he expected, under the rank and precedence arising out of this commission, to command the combined fleets; and I so stated it to Lord Nelson, as the best apology I could make for permitting a captain of Sir Sidney's standing to pass through his lordship's district, without putting himself under his [Nelson's] command.[9]

While St Vincent knew that Smith was to be given a free hand and had only been put under his command for the sake of appearances, he did not like it any more than he liked Smith himself.

By the time Smith found St Vincent at Gibraltar, Nelson had been at Naples for some weeks, where he remained for the next few months, but it was not the quiet period of recuperation that he might have wanted. Ferdinand I, King of the Two Sicilies*, was not an intelligent man, and the real power was wielded by Queen Maria Carolina, sister of the guillotined Marie Antoinette. The King and Queen were inspired by Nelson's success to make a pre-emptive strike against the French, who were working their way south through Italy, and Ferdinand led his army in person, recapturing Rome with little difficulty. He was not prepared for the counterattack, however, and the battle turned into a rout, with the French hard on the heels of the Neapolitans. When the French reached Naples, the liberal Neapolitans, tired of misrule by a hereditary monarchy, rose in revolt and proclaimed a republic. In December 1798 the king and his family were forced to flee, being ferried to Sicily in Nelson's flagship through an extremely violent storm. Matters were further complicated for Nelson because he had fallen in love with Emma Hamilton, and at Palermo in Sicily they embarked on an affair.

Emma was originally the mistress of Sir William Hamilton's nephew, who had passed her on to Sir William, against her will, over a decade ago. By then Hamilton had been a widower for some years, after a happy marriage, and was at first uncomfortable with what his scheming nephew had done, but he realised that Emma was not just beautiful, but intelligent and gifted too. Hamilton set about educating her, noting her flair for languages, singing and drama, and eventually a strong bond formed between them, and they married. In the permissive, hedonistic atmosphere of the Royal Court at Naples, Emma was accepted as a British ambassador's wife and developed a deep relationship with the Queen that greatly benefited British diplomacy. Nelson believed she had intervened with the Queen to allow his fleet to replenish supplies at Syracuse before the Battle of the Nile, without which he would have been forced to sail even further afield and perhaps have missed the French altogether. For this he remained grateful to Emma until literally his dying day, when he mentioned it in a codicil to his will.

---

* Ferdinand IV of Naples. His kingdom consisted of Sicily and a wide area surrounding the city of Naples.

The relationship that developed between them was not a youthful infatuation, for Nelson was forty-three, blind in his right eye, missing his right arm and prey to other ailments, including malaria, while Emma was thirty-three, putting on weight and no longer possessing the fresh-faced beauty of her early portraits. There is no evidence that Emma was previously unfaithful to Sir William, and her involvement with Nelson did not replace her relationship with her husband, but Sir William was sixty-eight and his health was beginning to fail. The result was a three-sided relationship that lasted until Sir William's death – he was firm friends with Nelson and bequeathed him his favourite picture of Emma.

At this point, enjoying a blossoming love affair, still basking in public adulation and totally immersed in the work that he lived for, Nelson's pride suffered a severe blow with the arrival of Sidney Smith. On 26 December 1798 Smith entered Constantinople, just as Nelson reached Palermo in Sicily with the royal refugees from Naples. Smith was every bit as active as Nelson, immediately setting in motion his plans to oust the French from Egypt, and by the end of December Nelson learned that Smith had taken command of his own ships that were blockading Alexandria. He immediately wrote a furious letter to St Vincent: '*I do feel, for I am a man*, that it is impossible for me to serve in these seas, with the squadron under a junior officer . . . Never, never was I so astonished as your letter made me. The Swedish knight [Smith], writes Sir William Hamilton, says that he shall go to Egypt, and take Captain Hood and his squadron under his command. The knight forgets the respect due to his superior officer: he has no orders from you to take my ships away from my command . . . Is it to be borne? Pray grant me your permission to retire.'[10]

Nelson had not been fully informed of Smith's mission, nor had he yet received Smith's diplomatically worded letter written a few days earlier, in which he said: 'Your lordship will, I hope, likewise see that the selection of a captain [himself], of the year 1783 only, to fill this important post, has been dictated by a delicacy due to my brother . . . rather than to any undue preference of me to older and better officers, who have had the honourable advantage of distinguishing themselves under your orders, but who could not be so acceptable to my brother as his near relation.'[11] He added: 'I cannot conclude without offering my share of the tribute of admiration and gratitude, which is so readily and so liberally paid to your lordship, and to your gallant companions in arms at the Nile.'[12]

It was left to St Vincent to smooth over the situation, establishing that Smith in his role as naval officer was junior to Nelson, while Smith the diplomat was outside his jurisdiction. In truth both men were essential to stop the French. Nelson was rightly worried about Italy, and especially Naples, which was an important Mediterranean base for the British, while Smith was concerned to confine the French to Egypt. Nelson had missed his chance to catch Napoleon at sea, and his direct sea warrior's approach now had to give way to the subtle strategies of Smith. In the next few months, as Nelson came to appreciate Smith's mission, he became more amiable, ending one letter: 'Be assured, my dear Sir Sidney, of my perfect esteem and regard, and do not let any one persuade you to the contrary. But my character is, that I will not suffer the smallest tittle of my command to be taken from me, but with pleasure I give way to my friends whom I beg you will allow me to consider you.'[13]

Immediately after the Battle of the Nile, Nelson had clung to the idea of defeating the French in Egypt and wrote to one of his captains: 'I rely on the exertions of all my gallant friends in the squadron to complete the destruction of the French Army, &c. I shall not go home until this is effected.'[14] Yet Nelson had already done everything possible: the French war fleet had been destroyed, their transports were trapped at Alexandria, blockaded by the squadron of Captain Troubridge, while Napoleon and his army were inland. Once Sir Sidney Smith assessed the situation at Constantinople, a treaty was signed with the Turks, and he then set off for Alexandria.

By now Napoleon was preparing to march on Constantinople and possibly force a way down the Silk Road to India. From intercepted letters and from his spies among the French troops, Smith was well informed and took action to counter Napoleon. On 6 February 1799 the French advance guard was on the move, but urged into action by Smith, the governor of the city of Acre, Achmet Pasha, usually known as Djezzar the Cutter from his reputation for cutting throats, had sent a force of Turkish troops, Mamelukes and Albanian mercenaries to the small coastal fortress of El Arish, on the Egyptian border in the Sinai Peninsula. The French arrived there two days later and began to besiege the stronghold, but the siege guns had already been found too heavy and cumbersome to be moved through swamps and deserts. Instead they were loaded on to transport ships to take them to Acre once they could evade the British blockade, since Acre was the first place they were likely to be needed. The bombardment of El Arish was actually conducted with field guns, and it took a whole day of constant firing before there was the smallest breach in the walls. Djezzar's defenders put up a strong opposition, but finally surrendered on the 20th. The unexpected delay was a blow to the French, checking their momentum and allowing time for defences to be prepared against them in Syria. On top of that, when they finally took over El Arish they encountered people sick with the plague.

Napoleon continued northwards through Syria, leading around thirteen thousand French troops. The campaign went smoothly from then on until they reached Jaffa on 3 March. The city was taken by storm and the French slaughtered everyone they encountered, including all manner of civilians and some two thousand soldiers who were trying to surrender. At least two and a half thousand other soldiers took refuge in the citadel. After surrendering they were killed in cold blood because Napoleon felt he could not afford to leave such a large force in his rear any more than he had the means to keep them captive. It was a two-day massacre that appalled many French troops, and when the plague began to affect them immediately afterwards, some said it was divine retribution.

A serious problem for Napoleon was lack of information. He could send out scouts in advance of his army, but with the British Navy in command, he did not know what was happening along the coast. Communication between Egypt and France was all but impossible, and in one of many letters intercepted by the British a French soldier told his brother: 'I write you the present, hoping it will have the good fortune to reach you, in spite of the prodigious difficulties we find in sending or receiving a letter by sea, on account of the total destruction of our fleet. The English are at this moment complete masters of the Mediterranean. We are reduced, therefore, to the disagreeable necessity of trusting all our correspondence with France to neutral vessels. Even these can only hope to convey it by escaping the vigilance of the English, for if they are taken they are burnt.'[15] Ironically, his brother might just have seen the contents of this letter, as it was one of a selection that was published, in the original French and in English, as a British propaganda exercise. With naval intelligence denied him, Napoleon was forced to plan his campaign blindly, barely knowing the local situation, unaware of the wider picture and prey to any misinformation that Sidney Smith could fabricate.

Smith reached Alexandria in early March, taking over the blockade of that coast, and immediately wrote to the Admiralty that he was happy to allow the French to evacuate Egypt, as long as they left their weapons behind – contrary to Nelson's wishes, who wanted total surrender of the French. This difference in approach between Nelson and Smith reflected the contrary views in the Admiralty and Foreign Office that arose from opposing objectives – the Admiralty was seeking to win the war at sea, while the Foreign Office wanted to establish a peaceful and stable Europe, for which a change of regime in France was necessary. For years the British Secret Service had been working with French Royalists in an attempt to restore the monarchy in France, and the key to such a restoration was the French army. What Britain and its allies needed was a charismatic French general who could unite the army in a counter-revolution against the government and step aside in favour of the monarch. Several prominent generals had talked with the Royalists, but despite a few false starts, none had been galvanised into action. Napoleon himself had tentatively negotiated with French Royalists and British agents in France before being distracted by his Egypt expedition.

Even if the Turkish armies could be prodded into action, Smith believed they were unlikely to defeat the French. It was a better solution to allow the French to withdraw, and he ended his letter to the Admiralty: 'I mention this, thus early, to enable your Lordship to judge of probabilities in this quarter where everything is in embryo, dependent on Turkish armies which may never be what they are promised to be. *On n'attrape pas des mouches avec du vinaigre – ainsi je leur offre du miel* [one does not catch flies with vinegar – therefore I offer them honey]; and it is not to Buonaparte alone that I offer this *pont d'or* [golden bridge], but by other channels indirectly to all individuals of his army. I hope to come at those, by this means [subversion] that are out of the reach of our shells.'[16] To help him infiltrate the French, Smith had brought a group of French Royalists, including some who had assisted his escape from prison and who could no longer serve as agents in France because their identity was known. John Wright, who had escaped from the Temple with Smith and was afterwards promoted to lieutenant, was sent ashore on a spying mission, 'landed by Sir Sidney Smith, in his own barge, at a short distance from Alexandria in the night-time, not openly as a British naval officer, but bearded, moustachioed, and shawled *à la Turque*, and for the express purpose of gathering valuable information . . . he was constantly employed by Sir Sidney as a spy'.[17]

Smith remained off Alexandria for a few days only. Once he received intelligence that Jaffa had fallen, he set sail in the *Tigre* for Acre, deciding this was the best place to confront the French in their march northwards. He arrived there just before them. On 17 March Napoleon reached Haifa, from where he could look across the bay to the walled city of Acre. The sight did not please him, for in the bay were two British warships, as well as British and Turkish gunboats. The next day was foggy, and when the French ships arrived with the siege guns, with what appeared to be excellent timing, they did not see the British warships until it was too late. Six of the nine French ships were captured, and at a stroke Napoleon had lost his siege artillery. At first he was not worried by this setback. The fortifications of Acre were old, out of date and looked dilapidated, as Bourrienne reported:

Although surrounded by a wall flanked with good towers, with a broad and rather deep ditch, and defended by outworks, this little fortress did not appear capable of holding out for a long time against French bravery and the skill of our corps of engineers and artillery. But the ease and rapidity with which Jaffa had been taken blinded us a little over the apparent similarity of the two places and the difference of their respective locations. At Jaffa we had sufficient artillery; at St Jean d'Acre [St John of Acre, its French name] we didn't. At Jaffa we had to deal only with a garrison left to itself; at St Jean d'Acre we had to deal with a garrison propped up by reinforcements of men and supplies, supported by the English fleet, and assisted by European science.[18]

The fortifications at Acre had been built by the crusading Knights of St John. Acre was their final stronghold in Syria, and the walls were intended to last. The town was on a promontory, surrounded by sea for two-thirds of its circumference and protected on the landward side by a crenellated wall strengthened with several towers. The British Navy controlled the bay, and the French could attack only the landward side of Acre. Colonel Phélippeaux, a French Royalist who had helped Smith escape from prison in Paris and accompanied him to England, was landed at Acre a few days before Smith arrived. He was a skilled military engineer, and aided by Captain Miller of the *Theseus*, he immediately set about strengthening the defences, and Smith then supplied more cannons and a stock of gunpowder and ammunition. The unexpected delay in taking the fortress of El Arish allowed time for these defences of Acre to be refurbished – otherwise the French would probably have taken the town with ease, before so many of them fell sick with the plague, which was now taking hold.

A key factor in the struggle for Acre was the morale of the opposing sides. Before the arrival of Phélippeaux and Smith, Djezzar was seriously considering abandoning the town and retreating. The strengthened defences and the supplies that Smith brought in gave him new confidence. Turkish troops usually fought ferociously, but were ill-disciplined and at times their lines collapsed in panic, but the sailors and marines from the British ships stood fast and encouraged the Turks to keep fighting. Smith, a flamboyant figure, also used his personal charisma to the full to inspire the men he led, just like Napoleon. He was an easily recognisable figure, and one sailor described him as 'of middling stature, good-looking, with tremendous moustachioes, a pair of penetrating black eyes, an intelligent countenance, with a gentlemanly air, expressive of good nature and kindness of heart'.[19] Acre was so small that it could barely contain the defenders, yet their morale was rising – even though they were fewer than five thousand facing over ten thousand French troops. Morale among Napoleon's forces, digging in for a long siege and fearful about the spread of plague, was already flagging.

On 22 March, while the besieging French were preparing for an attack, Smith proposed an exchange of prisoners, pointing out that he had managed to keep one officer in particular out of the hands of Djezzar, who had a tendency to torture and kill such prisoners. Smith wanted back his own men who had been captured at Haifa the previous day while attempting to take some French sloops anchored there. Napoleon agreed to the exchange and sent Smith his thanks, continuing: 'Do not doubt . . . the wish that I have of being pleasant to you, nor of my eagerness to seize the occasion of being useful to the men of your nation who the hazards of war are making miserable.'[20] It was the last polite word that Napoleon ever said to Smith.

Having made camp out of range of the guns of Acre, the French set up their own batteries to concentrate fire on the largest of the landward towers, which they would soon name the Cursed Tower. The French, ignorant of the extent of the defences, sent an army officer, Captain Mailly, under a flag of truce to demand a surrender. His real purpose was to report back on the layout of the fortifications, but Djezzar, with customary ruthlessness, threw him in prison. French patrols attempting to reconnoitre were driven off by the defenders, and so Napoleon had only a partial knowledge of the fort when he ordered the first assault on 27 March.

The attackers aimed for a small breach that had been made the day

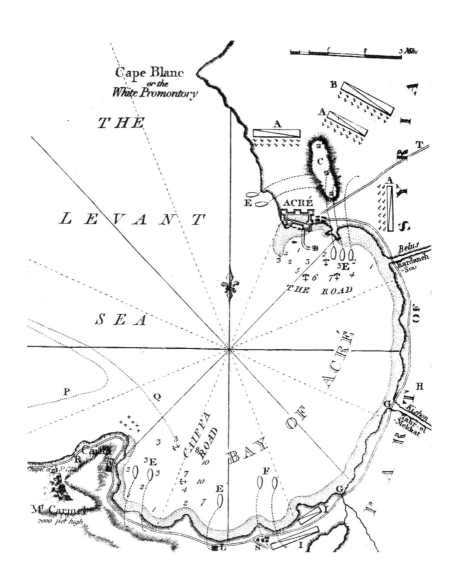

*Map of the French siege of Acre*

before when bombarding the walls. Smith, though, had already ensured the breach was blocked and the area covered by extra guns. The French charged the walls, but the attack faltered when they suddenly spotted the dry moat, which was 15 feet deep and 20 feet wide and could be fired on from the ships and boats in the bay. After climbing down the moat with ladders and up the other side, they found the ladders were too short to scale the wall and were forced to retreat under fire.

When he lost his siege guns, Napoleon had sent back to Egypt for more, but they would take some time to arrive. The cannons that the French were using to bombard the walls were running low on ammunition, and they were reusing cannonballs fired by the British, as General Montholon recalled: 'From time to time a few horsemen or waggons were made to appear, and then this commodore [Smith] approached the shore, and poured a rolling fire from all his batteries, and the soldiers, who got five sous for each ball which they brought to the director of artillery, ran and picked them up. They became so accustomed to this manoeuvre, that they pursued their search in the midst of the cannonade, while laughter resounded on every side.'[21] While the French were offering rewards for cannonballs, Djezzar was offering rewards for enemy heads. So far he had parted with little of his treasure, as none of the French had managed to get past the moat, which was now strewn with corpses, decomposing in the fierce sunlight and producing a noxious stench that was a constant torment to the defenders.

Among the dead in the moat was the mutilated body of a French general, who had worn an impressive uniform. The body had been stripped and beheaded by the Turks, and the sight particularly offended Daniel Bryan, a seaman of the *Tigre* described as an 'honest, though – the truth must be told – somewhat obtuse-minded tar'.[22] He asked why nobody had buried the corpse and was told, '*Go and do it yourself.*'[23] So he did. Other sailors tried to stop him and even offered to go in his place, but he replied, 'No! you are too young to be shot yet; as for me, I am old and deaf and *my* loss would be no great matter.'[24] They lowered him down the wall on a rope with a pick and shovel, and an eyewitness recalled how 'his first difficulty, not a very trivial one, was to drive away dogs'[25] that were feeding on the corpses. Then the French spotted him and 'levelled their pieces – they were on the instant of firing at the hero!'[26] Bryan called out, 'Mounseers, a-hoy! 'vast heaving there a bit, will 'e? and belay over all with your poppers for a spell.'[27] Fortunately a French officer who understood what he meant stopped the soldiers firing, and 'instantaneously the din of arms, the military thunder, ceased; a dead, a solemn silence prevailed'.[28]

With the French looking on, Bryan 'very leisurely then scrambled over the entrenchment into the ditch, the muzzle of the enemy's muskets still following his every motion. All this did not in the least disturb his *sang froid*; but going up to the French general, he took his measure in quite a business-like manner, and dug a very decent grave close alongside.'[29] Then Bryan, 'shaking what was so lately a French general very cordially and affectionately by the hand, he reverently placed him in his *impromptu* grave, then shovelled the earth upon and made all smooth above him'.[30] He next set up a stone at the head of the grave and 'with the peculiar air of a British sailor, took a piece of chalk from his pocket, and tried to write, "*Here you lie old* CROP [headless corpse]."'[31]

Back on board the *Tigre*, Smith sent for the sailor, and the following exchange took place: '"Well, Dan, I hear you buried the French general?" "Yes, your Honour." "Had you any body with you?" "Yes, your Honour." "Why Mr. — says you had not." "But I had, your honour." "Ah, who had you?" "*God Almighty*, Sir." "A very good assistant, indeed. Give old Dan a glass of grog."'[32]

While Napoleon was head to head with Smith at Acre, Nelson at Palermo in Sicily was occupied with keeping the Mediterranean free of the French and also with his new relationship with Emma. The British blockades of the French in Malta and Egypt had to be maintained, and in the short term Sicily had to be defended. Nelson's subordinate, Rear-Admiral Sir John Duckworth, was focusing on the western Mediterranean, but the biggest threat was the French fleet that had just escaped the British blockade of Brest, and which might head into the Mediterranean.

In Naples the republic was not a success and was not supported by the majority of the population. Being propped up by French troops, it would be vulnerable once they were withdrawn to fight elsewhere, and so in February 1799 King Ferdinand sent his agent, Cardinal Fabrice Ruffo, to rally Royalist support there. Ruffo was not just a cardinal, but a local magnate and a writer on military science. The King was pessimistic about Ruffo's chances and therefore gave him wide-ranging powers, but having recruited a band of peasants and assorted criminals, Ruffo was a runaway success. His undisciplined and uncontrollable 'army' rampaged through the countryside around Naples, butchering anyone even suspected of republican or French sympathies.

By the time of Napoleon's first assault on Acre at the end of March, Ruffo's ruffians were within 40 miles of Naples and closing in. Somewhat alarmed at his success, Ferdinand tried to reduce Ruffo's powers and instructed him that he was not, on any account, to offer terms of surrender to the rebels – in reality, Ruffo was not in sufficient control to guarantee anything. At this stage Nelson was not directly involved, but had to provide support for the Neapolitan monarchy because Naples was such an important strategic base for the British Navy. Nelson was still recovering from the wound over his eye, but he had the benefit of living ashore at Palermo, in surroundings more comfortable than aboard ship. Nelson's involvement with Emma was also deepening, but discreetly, and Cornelia Knight, who had been evacuated from Naples with the Hamiltons, recorded that 'there was certainly at that time no impropriety in living under Lady Hamilton's roof. Her house was the resort of the best company of all nations, and the attentions paid to Lord Nelson appeared perfectly natural. He himself always spoke of his wife with the greatest affection and respect, and I remember that, shortly after the battle of the Nile, when my mother said to him that no doubt he considered the day of that victory as the happiest in his life, he answered, "No; the happiest was that on which I married Lady Nelson."'[33]

While Nelson rested and applied all his intellectual energy to British naval strategy in the western Mediterranean, Smith at Acre was fully occupied with stopping Napoleon. The first failed French assault was followed by an attempt to set fire to the timbers blocking the breach in the wall by firing red-hot shot at it, but the engineer Phélippeaux had already anticipated that tactic and covered the wood with bales of cotton soaked in water. While Smith was away for a few days, his ships having been blown offshore by a storm, Djezzar took the opportunity to indulge his cruelty by murdering some of the French captives, including the unfortunate Captain Mailly, who had entered the city under a flag of truce. Their bodies were thrown into the sea, and as Bourrienne recalled, 'This cruel pasha undertook a great number of similar executions. The waves frequently washed dead bodies on the shore, and we came upon them while bathing.'[34] Djezzar was proving difficult to control, being more interested in butchering the French than organising effective resistance. Smith, however, had the measure of Djezzar, and wrote in a letter to St Vincent: 'What seems to have more effect on him, than anything else, is the idea I have thrown out, that if the enemy are suffered to come into the town I must, in my own defence, batter it down about their ears.'[35]

By the time Smith's ships were back on station in early April, the
French had launched another assault that failed, but more seriously they
had driven their trenches almost to the walls and were trying to dig a
mine under the Cursed Tower. The only way to counter this was by a
sortie outside the walls, an attack that was led by Lieutenant John Wright
and the Major of Marines, Thomas Oldfield, while the Turks provided a
diversion elsewhere. The sailors and marines charged through heavy fire
to the mouth of the mine, but when Wright entered with his men he
realised that the demolition teams had not been able to follow. They
pulled down the timber shoring so that the roof collapsed, but could not
destroy the mine completely. As they came out the French attacked, and
both Wright and Oldfield were wounded. Their bodies were visible to the
British from the walls, and so Smith called to one of his men,

a gigantic, red-haired, Irish marine . . . named James Close. Pointing to the
mass of carnage that lay sweltering in the ditch below, where the slightly
wounded and the actually dying were fast hastening into mutual corruption
under the burning sun . . . [Smith] said, 'Close, dare you go there, and bring
us the body of poor Wright?' 'What darn't I do, yer honour?' was the immediate reply, and, exposed to the musketry of the enemy, wading through
blood, and stumbling over dead bodies and scattered limbs, he, unhurt, at
length found Wright, not killed, but only wounded, and he brought him away
safely from these shambles of death.[36]

Other marines were searching for Major Oldfield and found him at the
same time as the French, who thought he was one of their officers. A fight
ensued over the body, which the French won and carried him off. He died
later from his wounds, but Wright survived. Reporting on the sortie,
Smith noted that at the end of the fighting 'the Turks brought in about
sixty heads, a greater number of muskets, and some entrenching tools,
much wanted in the garrison'.[37]

For the French, still without siege guns, mining remained the best
strategy, and by mid-April they had reopened the mine and driven it
under the Cursed Tower. On the morning of the 24th the mine was blown
up, but its position had been miscalculated, and instead of the whole tower
being brought down, only the front wall of the lower storey collapsed. The
French troops stormed into the breach, but could get no further, and were
driven back by the missiles showered from above.

Smith was expecting more Turkish troops by sea from Rhodes and overland from Damascus, as well as more guns and ammunition from Constantinople. To counter this, French forces were detached from the army at Acre, and in a series of skirmishes and battles they managed to rout the Turkish reinforcements that were travelling by land. Sometimes fighting against overwhelming odds, the discipline of the French infantry consistently defeated the flamboyant but erratic Turkish cavalry.

Despite these French successes, Acre remained a problem. Napoleon could not continue his march on Constantinople and the Silk Road, leaving such a stronghold to cut his lines of communication and supply. Nor did he have enough troops to leave behind to contain the fortress. Because of Smith, replacement siege guns could not be landed at Acre, but they began to be landed at Jaffa to the south and hauled overland. Napoleon, though, was not prepared to wait and ordered an assault on Acre for 24 April. Another mine had by now been dug under the Cursed Tower, and the blowing up of this mine launched the assault, but once again it only brought down part of the tower wall. As before, the charging French troops were blocked at the base of the tower and pelted with rocks and grenades from above, and finally powder kegs filled with a burning mixture of gunpowder and sulphur were dropped on to the attackers. These missiles, known as stink-pots, gave off clouds of choking smoke – those soldiers who were not suffocated by the blasts and fumes from the exploding kegs were forced to retreat.

Time was pressing, and Napoleon ordered another assault for the following day, but although the French managed to fight their way a little further into the tower this time, they were again beaten back. Smith seemed to be everywhere at once, constantly moving from his flagship, where he directed the naval operations and tried to maintain correspondence, into the city to lead the fighting on the walls during the assaults, and even outside the city on reconnaissance missions. The French recognised that he was a key figure of the resistance, and there were two failed attempts to assassinate him.

Ominously, the replacement siege guns began to arrive at the end of April. It would take another six days to set them up and bring them into action, but they would then dramatically increase the available fire-power. By 1 May Smith was so busy that his report to the Admiralty consisted of only two sentences: 'We have, since my letter of the 7th of April, been every hour employed in resisting the vigorous attacks of a most desperate enemy, and hitherto with success, which is all I have time to say at present, as the increased fire from his batteries gives us ample employment just at this moment. P.S. The enemy has made a fourth attempt to scale the walls, and is beaten back.'[38] The following day Colonel Phélippeaux, the French Royalist who had worked so hard to improve the defences and block any breaches, died of a fever.

On 7 May, the fifty-first day of the siege, the newly installed French guns began a continuous bombardment as preparation for another assault. Smith recorded that 'the constant fire of the besiegers was suddenly increased tenfold. Our flanking fire from afloat was, as usual, plied to the utmost, but with less effect than heretofore, as the enemy had thrown up epaulments and traverses [defences built of earth and sandbags] of sufficient thickness to protect them.'[39] According to Smith, their position as defenders was now desperate: 'We have been long anxiously looking for a reinforcement, without which we could not expect to be able to keep the place as long as we have.'[40]

Just when it looked as if Acre would fall to the French, the situation changed once again – that very evening, after only a few hours of bombardment, the first of the ships carrying reinforcements and supplies arrived. In reaction, Napoleon increased the effort to take Acre before the reinforcements were landed. This time the French troops at last occupied the second storey of the tower, having successfully demolished the upper part. They managed to hold this position overnight, but with reinforcements starting to land, Smith could see that this was a critical point. He therefore ordered ashore a party from the British ships and personally took charge of them in defence of the breach in the wall, holding it until the reinforcements arrived. These boosted the morale of the defenders, and despite fierce fighting the French assault was repulsed. Smith, though, was realistic in his assessment of the situation, writing to St Vincent on 9 May:

Buonaparte will, no doubt, renew the attack, the breach being . . . perfectly practicable for fifty men abreast; indeed the town is not, nor ever has been, defensible, according to the rules of [military] art, but according to every other rule, it must and shall be defended. Not that it is in itself worth defending, but we feel that it is by this breach Buonaparte means to march to further conquest. 'Tis on the issue of this conflict, that depends the opinion of the multitude of spectators on the surrounding hills, who wait only to see how it ends to join the victor . . . The magnitude of our obligation does but increase the energy of our efforts, in the attempt to discharge our duty, and though we may and probably shall be overpowered, I can venture to say, that the French army will be so much further weakened, before it prevails, as to be little able to profit by its dear bought victory.

The spectators on the surrounding hills were split into two broad factions, Christians and Muslims, and Napoleon had already tried to persuade both sides to join him. To the Christians he had distributed a leaflet claiming that he was a successor to the Crusaders and a defender of the Christian faith, while a proclamation in Arabic was circulated to the Muslims pointing out that he had already destroyed the power of the Pope in Rome and the Knights of St John in Malta and calling himself a defender of Islam. Smith distributed copies of these documents to the opposite faction to that for which they were intended. Napoleon was discredited, and some of the Christians went so far as to ally themselves with Smith. He also dropped bundles of leaflets into the French trenches, spelling out an offer from the Sultan at Constantinople for a free passage back to France for any soldier who surrendered. The initial effect was to raise indignation and harden the resolve of the French, but in the long term it helped undermine their morale. Napoleon was furious and accused Smith of various atrocities. Bourrienne noted Napoleon's reaction to Smith's propaganda campaigns, writing that 'he believed that by denigrating his adversary, he would mask his setbacks. He wrote on 2 June . . . "Smith is a crazy young man, who wishes to make his fortune and to make his presence felt. The best way of punishing him is never to respond to him . . . he is a man capable of doing anything."'[41]

Having survived the latest massive assault, and with the garrison bolstered by reinforcements, Smith was pleased with the effects that his propaganda was having on the Christians and Muslims, and declared that he had 'the satisfaction to find Buonaparte's career further northward effectually stopped by a warlike people inhabiting an impenetrable country'.[42] Napoleon realised that his position was almost untenable, but refused to give up as he told Bourrienne: 'I see that this wretched dump has cost me a good number of men, and wasted much time. But things are too far advanced not to attempt one last effort. If I succeed, as I believe I will, I shall find in the town the pasha's treasures, and weapons for 300,000 men. I will stir up and arm all of Syria . . . I will march on Damascus and Aleppo . . . I will reach Constantinople with a huge army. I will overthrow the Turkish Empire. I will found in the East a new and great Empire that will ensure my place in posterity.'[43] It was not to be.

The final French assault, the eleventh of the siege, was launched on 10 May. Napoleon was eventually persuaded not to lead the charge himself, but General Kléber took control instead, while the defenders at the breach were led by Smith. Despite starting well, the French were beaten to a standstill, and realising it was hopeless, Kléber ordered a retreat. In the aftermath of this battle, Smith wrote to Napoleon:

General, I am acquainted with the dispositions that for some days past you have been making to raise the siege; the preparations in hand to carry off your wounded, and to leave none behind you, do you great credit. This last word ought not to escape my mouth – I, who ought not to love you, to say nothing more: but circumstances remind me to wish that you would reflect on the instability of human affairs. In fact, could you have thought that a poor prisoner in a cell of the Temple prison – that an unfortunate for whom you refused, for a single moment, to give yourself any concern, being at the same time able to render him a signal service, since you were then all-powerful – could you have thought, I say, that this same man would have become your antagonist, and have compelled you, in the midst of the sands of Syria, to raise the siege of a miserable, almost defenceless town? Such events, you must admit, exceed all human calculations. Believe me, general, adopt sentiments more moderate, and that man will not be your enemy, who shall tell you that Asia is not a theatre made for your glory. This letter is a little revenge that I give myself.[44]

Napoleon decided to cut his losses and retreat to Egypt, and so on 20 May the French started to march back the way they had come just over two months before. The unexpectedly determined defence of Acre had stopped Napoleon's expedition in its tracks, sapping it of energy, and Smith's psychological warfare had turned the people of the country against it. Napoleon was so enraged by Smith's propaganda that he could not bring himself to open the customary negotiations about evacuation of the wounded. Instead, as Smith reported to Nelson, the French ships were 'being hurried to sea without seamen to navigate them, and the wounded being in want of every necessary, even water and provisions, they steered straight to his Majesty's ships, in full confidence of receiving the succours of humanity, in which they were not disappointed'.[45] Of the wounded Frenchmen who surrendered Smith wrote that 'their expressions of gratitude to us were mingled with execrations on the name of their general, who had, as they said, thus exposed them to perish, rather than fairly and honourably to renew the intercourse with the English'.[46]

Napoleon had selected the best of his troops for the campaign in Syria, and by the time he returned to Egypt over a third of them were dead or disabled.

It took four months for the news of the Anglo-Turkish victory at Acre to filter back to Britain, and it was greeted with quiet satisfaction rather than the rejoicing that had hailed Nelson's victory the year before. However, motions of thanks to Smith were passed by both Houses of Parliament and he was awarded an annuity of £1000. Nelson now had a clear picture of what Smith's mission had been, and generously wrote to him that 'the bravery shown by you and your brave companions is such as to merit every encomium which all the civilised world can bestow. As an individual, and as an admiral, will you accept of my feeble tribute of praise and admiration, and make them acceptable to all those under your command.'[47] The Turkish Sultan Selim III awarded Smith the Chelengk (Plume of Triumph), as had been awarded to Nelson for the Battle of the Nile, and for a time Smith joined Nelson as a British national hero.

In all probability, it was only Napoleon who fully appreciated the scale of Smith's achievement at this time. To the British, it seemed merely as if Smith had curbed French expansion, while Nelson had deprived them of a fleet. In fact, it was Smith who stopped Napoleon's advances on India, whereas Nelson had only hindered them, and Acre was the first defeat on land for the so-called invincible general. Without Smith and his men to strengthen the resolve of Djezzar, the Turks would have retreated, possibly as far as Constantinople, and it would have been much more difficult to stop the French army once it had gained momentum. Napoleon might not have made it as far as India, but it is quite likely he would have been left in control of Syria and the Silk Road trade route. Napoleon had now suffered two major defeats, both at the hands of officers and men of the British Navy. He himself would not be defeated on land by an Englishman again until the Battle of Waterloo. Napoleon admired Nelson, and even acquired a bust of the admiral, but Smith had shaken his nerve.

———·◆·———

# FOUR

# FROM NAPLES TO COPENHAGEN

Never mind manoeuvres, always go at them.

> Advice given by Nelson to the young lieutenant
> Thomas Cochrane at Palermo in 1799[1]

While Napoleon retreated from Acre to Egypt, Nelson prepared to return to Naples after his forced retreat. In early June 1799 Ruffo's army closed in on the city. The French troops and Neapolitan rebels took refuge in the forts, leaving the population to be terrorised by Ruffo's butchers, who took revenge on anyone they fancied, but were too disorderly to form a force capable of attacking the forts. Midshipman George Parsons of the *Foudroyant* described them as 'banditti under the [leadership of] primate Cardinal Ruffo, and who (I suppose in derision) were denominated the Christian army. These scoundrels, unchecked by law or justice, with no force to restrain them, freely indulged their licentious habits, and, with tiger-like ferocity, waded deep in blood.'[2]

Ruffo was powerless, and without consulting him Chevalier Micheroux, a Neapolitan envoy, granted the refugees in the forts an armistice. Ruffo rebuked him, as neither had the authority to negotiate, but they continued to engineer a treaty without consulting King Ferdinand. When rumours of what was happening reached Palermo, the King urged Nelson to return to Naples to sort out the mess, but he was reluctant to do so since he still had no definite news of the French fleet that had escaped from Brest. By late June the situation was worsening in Naples, so having heard that reinforcements had entered the Mediterranean to locate the missing fleet, Nelson agreed to risk a mission limited to eight days. He was authorised to restore order, secure the unconditional surrender of the forts and hand over the rebels to the King. Arriving on 24 June, Nelson issued the men in the forts an ultimatum: surrender unconditionally or they would be taken by force.

After several days' wrangling caused by the armistice and Ruffo's political manoeuvrings, the rebels bowed to the inevitable and surrendered. With detachments of seamen and marines Nelson moved quickly to restore some semblance of law and order in the city. The French troops were repatriated, while some eight thousand rebels were arrested and handed over to the Neapolitan authorities, who were more lenient than Ruffo's desperadoes would have been. Over seven thousand escaped punishment, 105 were condemned to death (but six were subsequently reprieved) and the rest were fined, imprisoned or deported. As representative of King Ferdinand, Nelson provided a British ship, the *Foudroyant*, which became nominally a Neapolitan ship for the court martial of Commodore Francesco Caracciolo of the Sicilian Navy. Having joined the rebels and commanded their gunboats, Caracciolo was tried by a board of Neapolitan naval officers for desertion and for firing on a Sicilian frigate. He was condemned to death. Nelson was later criticised for this, but his actions were entirely correct, as Cornelia Knight pointed out: 'It is only right to say that Caraccioli [Caracciolo] was taken in arms against the forces of his sovereign, that he was tried by a court-martial of Neapolitan officers, and executed on board of a Neapolitan ship.'[3]

Admiral Lord Keith, Nelson's superior, was still concerned about the French fleet from Brest and so ordered Nelson to take his ships to defend Minorca, but Nelson considered that Minorca was in no danger, whereas the Kingdom of the Two Sicilies was still not secure. Eventually Keith left the Mediterranean in pursuit of the French fleet, leaving Nelson the senior commander, but his decisions about Naples and his failure to obey Keith's orders led him into conflict with the Admiralty over the succeeding months. It only took a few weeks to secure Naples and the surrounding countryside, and as saviour of the kingdom, King Ferdinand awarded Nelson the Dukedom of Bronte and a diamond-hilted sword. The dukedom had an estate in Sicily and was valued by Nelson as a mark of his achievement that contrasted with the niggardly recognition he received from authorities in Britain. For the rest of 1799 he remained in command, using Palermo as his base and dealing mainly with the western

Mediterranean, where the main problem was the ongoing siege of the French garrison at Malta.

In the East, Sir Sidney Smith was still pursuing his war against Napoleon. The French retreat from Acre in late May 1799 was a miserable affair, as Napoleon's secretary, Bourrienne, acknowledged:

A raging thirst, the total lack of water, an excessive heat, and a fatiguing march over burning dunes demoralised the men, and made every generous thought give way to the most cruel selfishness and distressing indifference. I saw officers with limbs amputated thrown off stretchers, whose transport had been ordered and who had themselves paid money as a reward for the work. I saw abandoned . . . the amputated, the wounded, those with plague or only suspected of it. The march was lit by torches that were burning in order to set fire to the little towns, villages, hamlets and rich crops which covered the land. The whole country was on fire.[4]

The French were attacked and raided all the way back to Egypt by the Turks under the leadership of Major John Bromley – the alias of Jean de Tromelin, one of Smith's Royalist French agents. Bourrienne recorded that the surviving troops 'arrived in Cairo on 14 June, after the most awful march of twenty-five days, with the greatest hardships. The heat during the crossing of the desert between El Arish and Belbeis exceeded 33 degrees . . . Two days running my cloak was covered with salt that the evaporation of water that held it in solution left behind. The brackish waters of the deserts, which the horses greedily drank, made a great number of them die, falling a quarter of a league from the spring.'[5]

Napoleon needed all his charisma and skill to prevent the disaster at Acre sparking a mutiny among the troops in Egypt, and to that end Bourrienne recalled that 'Bonaparte had his entry into the capital of Egypt preceded by one of those lying bulletins that only took in fools. "I will bring with me," he said, "many prisoners and flags. I have razed the palace of Djezzar and the ramparts of Acre. Not a single stone remains. All the inhabitants have left the city by sea. Djezzar is severely wounded."'[6] Bourrienne claimed to disapprove of this: 'I confess that I experienced a painful feeling when writing these official words dictated by him, as each one was a deception. Aroused by everything I had just witnessed, it was difficult for me not to risk some observation; but his response was always, "My dear fellow, you are a simpleton; you don't understand anything." And he said this while signing his bulletin, which was going to satisfy the people and inspire historians and poets.'[7] Ultimately Napoleon was right, and there was no mutiny.

While Napoleon and his men straggled back to Egypt, Sir Sidney Smith was busy assembling a Turkish fleet of seven battleships, five frigates and fifty-eight smaller vessels to carry an army of twenty thousand troops of Turkish and various other nationalities in an attack on the French in Egypt. They landed at Aboukir Bay in early July before they could be opposed, but instead of marching inland, they dug in on the coast. As soon as he heard, Napoleon led a force of ten thousand men against them, arriving on the 24th. The battle the next day ended in a rout of the Turkish army, which left hundreds of Turks besieged in the fort at Aboukir while the rest retreated to the ships. In all about two thousand Turkish troops were killed in the battle, and the fort surrendered when it ran out of supplies.

Smith sent Major Bromley to negotiate an exchange of prisoners, but having learned his true identity, Napoleon refused to deal with him, and Smith's secretary, John Keith, had to take over. During the negotiations a French officer was allowed on board Smith's ship, the *Tigre*, and there Smith ensured that he obtained news of what was happening in Europe, as Bourrienne related:

After the battle ... Bonaparte sent a negotiator on board the English Admiral's ship. Our relations were full of politeness, such as might be expected between two civilised nations. The English Admiral gave the negotiator some presents, in exchange for what we sent, and also the French Gazette of Frankfurt of 10 June 1799. For ten months we had been without news from France. Bonaparte glanced through this newspaper with an eagerness easy to imagine. 'Good grief!' he said to me, 'my foreboding hasn't tricked me; Italy is lost!!! The scoundrels! All the fruits of our victories have disappeared! It's essential that I leave.'[8]

Napoleon made secret preparations to fit out two frigates and two smaller ships with a few weeks' provisions for about five hundred men. On 23 August he set sail for France. The British ships blockading Egypt had not been seen for several days, because the *Tigre* had gone to Cyprus for supplies and the *Theseus*, on a similar journey to Rhodes, had been delayed getting back. Only Turkish ships were left off the coast. With extraordinary luck Napoleon avoided not only the blockade, but all the British ships patrolling the Mediterranean. General Kléber was not told anything beforehand and was furious to find he had been left a letter giving him command of the troops in Egypt and a variety of instructions and promises. There was also a short proclamation to the soldiers from Napoleon, saying that 'In consequence of the news from Europe, I have determined to return immediately to France. I leave the command of the army to General Kléber: they shall hear from me speedily: this is all I can say to them at present. It grieves me to the heart to part from the brave men to whom I am so tenderly attached, but it will be only for an instant, and the General I leave at their head is in full possession of the confidence of the Government and of mine.'[9]

Napoleon deliberately left Kléber behind because he was a serious rival. He also ordered him not to negotiate with the enemy until the following May in an attempt to keep him out of the way. Both men respected each other's talents, but there was no love lost between them, and Bourrienne reported that several times Kléber made comments like: 'Your little bastard Bonaparte, who is as high as my boot, will enslave France. See what a damnable expedition he made us do.'[10] Kléber was left in an untenable position, yet the French soldiers were probably more loyal to him than to Napoleon. Sidney Smith realised that even the much larger Turkish army that was massing for another attempt to take back Egypt would find the task very difficult, so he approached Kléber with an offer to negotiate a French withdrawal. Kléber did not react immediately, but although another attack by the Turks was repulsed, the French soldiers mutinied, demanding their overdue pay and threatening to claim the Sultan's free passage home. Smith's propaganda was beginning to take effect, and at the end of October Kléber opened negotiations.

After forty-seven days at sea, on 9 October Napoleon landed at Fréjus, on the south-east coast of France. The news of his arrival reached the Directory in Paris three days later, and three weeks of political manoeuvring took place as different factions gained and lost power. On 9 November the fluid politics came to a crisis point when Napoleon was about to be outlawed for his illegal actions by the National Assembly – the body of delegates representing the third estate, those who were not aristocrats or clergy. Napoleon's brother Lucien saved the situation with a brilliant speech in his defence, and in the days that followed Napoleon and his supporters engineered a coup, replacing the Directory with a Consulate. This consisted of three consuls, but the main consul was

Napoleon, who eventually dispensed with the other two and ruled alone – he effectively established a military dictatorship.

Before seizing power, Napoleon and some of his supporters were negotiating with the Royalists, who needed a strong general to control the military and deliver power to the exiled King Louis XVIII. The British Secret Service knew about these negotiations through its involvement with the network of Royalist agents in France, and Smith also probably knew about them. It has even been suggested that he deliberately provoked Napoleon to escape, relaxing the blockade of Egypt. Certainly the Royalists in France and in exile initially welcomed Napoleon's rise to power, since the two other consuls favoured the restoration of the monarchy, but they waited in vain for power to be handed over to Louis.

By early 1800 Napoleon was showing no sign of co-operating with the Royalists, and Louis wrote him a letter reminding him of his supposed commitment to the monarchy: 'Whatever may be their apparent conduct, men like you, Sir, never inspire anxiety. You have accepted an eminent position, and I am grateful to you. You know better than anyone how much strength and power is needed to secure the good fortune of a great nation. Save France from her own violence, and you will have fulfilled the first wish of my heart. Restore her King, and future generations will bless your memory.'[11] According to Bourrienne, Napoleon was rattled by this letter and ignored it, but when Louis wrote again, Napoleon eventually answered: 'Sir, I have received your letter, and I thank you for the decent things you say to me. You must not desire for a return to France; it would be necessary to march over a hundred thousand corpses. Sacrifice your interest to the peace and well-being of France. History will take account of this . . . I am not insensible to the misfortunes of your family, and I will learn with pleasure that you are surrounded by everything that can contribute to the tranquillity of your retirement.'[12] Napoleon now felt himself in full control of France, with ambitious plans to dominate Europe, if not the world. There would be fifteen years of almost continuous bloodshed before he could be stopped.

In Egypt, negotiations continued between Smith and Kléber, until on 24 January 1800 an agreement for a French withdrawal was signed. The difficulties of long-distance communications now became apparent. Having taken charge of the British Embassy at Constantinople, Lord Elgin authorised Smith to conclude this treaty with the French, but by the time it reached London for ratification the government was influenced by intercepted letters betraying the desperate state of the French in Egypt.

The government therefore instructed Elgin and Smith to cancel the treaty, believing that the Turks could easily oust the French. Smith did not hear about this until late February, in a letter from Lord Keith, who took the same view as Nelson that the French must surrender. Keith had already written to Kléber with this demand, but Smith could see the wider picture and lamented the chance that was being lost. He pointed out to Keith that 'if the business is allowed to go on in the way it is now settled [ratifying the treaty with the French], the gigantic and favourite projects of Buonaparte are rendered abortive, and surely it is no bad general mode of reasoning, and particularly applicable in this case, to say that whatever the wishes of the *enemy* may be, we ought to cross *them*; *he* wishes this army to remain in this country, far from himself . . . And I have most positive ground for saying that Kléber is Buonaparte's most determined and most dreaded opponent.'[13]

As so often happened, while his superiors were concerned to win the battle, Smith was more concerned to win the overall war. The damage was already done, however, as Keith's letter infuriated Kléber, who immediately set about inspiring his men to a dogged defence of Egypt. On 20 March he successfully countered a Turkish attack and a week later had driven the Turks from Egypt. The process of removing the French from Egypt was set to drag on another year, even though Kléber was tragically assassinated by an Arab fanatic on 14 June.

While Napoleon in Paris was successfully manipulating French politics and Smith and Kléber were negotiating a withdrawal, Nelson at Palermo was struggling with his superiors. He was out of favour with some sections of the Admiralty and did not like or respect his immediate superior, Lord Keith, a frequent critic of Nelson. In early February 1800 both Keith and Nelson sailed from Palermo with a fleet that was taking reinforcements to Malta, where the French remained under siege. Nelson then sailed westwards in the hope of intercepting any French vessels sent to relieve the siege, and on 18 February captured the *Généreux*, one of the ships that had escaped from the Battle of the Nile. Soon afterwards Nelson met up with Keith, who tactlessly put in charge a lieutenant from his own ship, with orders to take the *Généreux* to Minorca, rather than leaving Nelson to delegate one of his own junior officers to command this prize.

The lieutenant Keith chose was a young fellow Scotsman, Lord Thomas Cochrane. He was heir to the Earldom of Dundonald, and just one year later would make his reputation by capturing the frigate *Gamo* with his tiny sloop *Speedy*. Cochrane took with him a few men from

Keith's flagship, including his brother Archibald, and later he reflected on this stroke of luck: 'Lord Keith permitted my brother to accompany me in the *Généreux*. By this unexpected incident both he and myself were, in all probability, saved from a fate which soon afterwards befell most of our gallant shipmates. On our quitting the *Queen Charlotte*, Lord Keith steered for Leghorn, where he landed, and ordered Captain Todd to reconnoitre the island of Cabrera, then in possession of the French. Whilst on his way, some hay, hastily embarked and placed under the half-deck, became ignited, and the flame communicating with the main-sail set the ship on fire.'[14]

One of the survivors from the *Queen Charlotte*, the carpenter John Baird, described what happened: 'I heard throughout the ship a general cry of *fire*! I immediately ran up the fore-ladder to get upon deck, and found the whole half-deck, the front bulk-head of the admiral's cabin, the coat of the mainmast, and the boats' covering on the booms, all in flames . . . The mainsail at this time was set, and almost instantly caught fire.'[15] All the crew were desperately trying to put out the flames, and Lieutenant Dundas was trying to soak the lower decks by pumping water through the gunports and close the hatches to prevent the fire spreading downwards. Baird recalled that 'the pumps [were] kept going by the people who came down, as long as they could stand at them. Owing to these exertions . . . the lower deck was kept free from fire, and the maga-zines preserved from danger for a long time: nor did Lieutenant Dundas or myself quit this station until several of the middledeck guns came through the deck.'[16]

With the deck above them burning so badly that cannons were begin-ning to fall through, there was no possibility of saving the ship. Baird and Dundas returned to the forecastle, where a group of men were still throw-ing buckets of water over the flames. 'I continued about an hour on the forecastle,' Baird reported, 'till finding all efforts to extinguish the flames unavailing, I jumped from the jib-boom, and swam to an American boat.'[17] Soon after, the *Queen Charlotte* blew up, and of a crew of 830 men, there were only 156 survivors. If Cochrane had been aboard, the acciden-tal loss of the *Queen Charlotte* would not just have been a terrible tragedy – it would probably have cut short the life and career of one of the British Navy's most remarkable officers.

By this time stress and exhaustion were making Rear-Admiral Nelson ill, and he returned to Palermo on leave while his flagship, the *Foudroyant*, underwent a refit. Because he was still unwell, the ship returned to the blockade of Malta without him, under orders to return to Palermo. Just as the *Foudroyant* reached Malta, the vessels of the British blockade there received news that the *Guillaume Tell* was about to break out from the harbour and head for Toulon for supplies. Along with the *Généreux*, the *Guillaume Tell* was the other battleship that had escaped from the Battle of the Nile, and the British were especially keen to take it. The Nile had been an unusual battle, marking a revolution in naval warfare. In previous battles hailed as British victories, relatively few enemy battleships had been taken – at the 'Glorious First of June' in 1794, six out of twenty-six were captured; at Cape St Vincent in February 1797, four out of twenty-seven; and at Camperdown the following October, eight out of fifteen. Nelson realised that the nature of warfare had changed and that it was 'annihilation that the country wants, and not merely a splendid victory . . . Numbers only can annihilate.'[18] It now only needed the capture of the *Guillaume Tell* to complete the annihilation of the French battleships of the Egyptian expedition.

The British intelligence was not wrong, and the French ship was spotted on the morning of 30 March. A chase ensued that lasted the rest of the day, and in the early hours of the next morning a fierce battle began as the British ships gradually caught up. The *Guillaume Tell* had on board Rear-Admiral Decrès, who was later to become Minister of Marine, and the crew put up a dogged resistance until the vessel had lost every mast and was almost a wreck. The British ships were also badly damaged, and there were many casualties on both sides, as revealed by Midshipman Parsons of the *Foudroyant*:

Down came the tri-coloured flag, and 'Cease firing!' resounded along our decks; but one of our lower deck guns gave tongue, and killed their first lieutenant, much praised and lamented by the prisoners, his brother officers. The slaughter on board the *Guillaume Tell* was about four hundred, and in our ship alone eighty, taking in the wounded [counting both dead and wounded]. Never was any ship better fought, or flag hoisted by a more gallant man than Rear-Admiral Decrès. Our captain [Sir Edward Berry] received his sword, and took it to the commodore* [Sir Manly Dixon], wearing half a cocked hat, the other half having been carried off by that impudent shot that dyed his cabin with the blood of two seamen . . . 'Good God! How did you save your head?' said the commodore. 'The hat was not on it,' replied our chief.[19]

---

* A captain appointed commander-in-chief of a squadron.

The capture of the *Guillaume Tell* completed the task begun at Aboukir Bay eight months before, and it also provided information about the siege at Malta. The ship had come from the capital, Valetta, and Parsons learned that 'famine prevailed in the town to such an extent, that the only thing found in *La Guillaume Tell* was the leg of a mule, hung for safety and his especial use over the admiral's stern-gallery'.[20] In British ships, too, it was sometimes the practice to hang food, particularly relatively fresh meat, from the stern to preserve it from the rats.

Nelson was still not fit, and in early April he applied to the Admiralty for leave in England to improve his health. On the 24th, with the damage to the *Foudroyant* repaired and while he awaited permission to return home, Nelson joined the blockading ships around Malta. This was something of a farewell cruise, as he took with him a party of guests including William and Emma Hamilton. On the way the ship was hit by bad weather. 'During the passage,' Midshipman Parsons recalled, 'we encountered a thunderstorm, and the electric fluid struck away our foretopmast, killing one man and wounding fourteen. The *Principo Real*, a Portuguese ship of the line, lost her mainmast that night from the same cause, with several men killed.'[21] Lightning strikes were a constant hazard for sailing ships, because electricity was not properly understood – and would not be for decades to come. A treatise on thunderstorms published in 1843 provided an analysis:

In one hundred and fifty cases [of lightning strikes], the majority of which occurred between the years 1799 and 1815, nearly one hundred lower masts of line-of-battle ships and frigates, with a corresponding number of topmasts and smaller spars, together with various stores were wholly or partially destroyed. One ship in eight was set on fire in some part of the rigging or sails; upwards of seventy seamen were killed, and one hundred and thirty-three wounded, exclusive of nineteen cases in which the number of wounded is returned as 'many' or 'several'. In one-tenth of these cases the ships were completely disabled.[22]

Some ships were fitted with lightning conductors, but these did not always work, and in many cases the lightning conductor was not a permanent fixture, but was hauled up the mast when it was thought to be needed. In the East Indies, the frigate *Resistance* blew up after being struck by lightning, and only two crew members survived, to be picked up by a Malayan ship. Without their rescue, the *Resistance* would have been added to the list of ships that mysteriously disappeared. This frigate was lost in July 1798, just a few days before the Battle of the Nile took place. Shortly after taking part in the battle, Midshipman Elliot of the *Goliath* was struck by lightning:

We were reefing for a squall, and I was on the mizen topsail yard-arm, the outer person, and about ten yards from the main top, when a flash passed between the top and me – a man in the top facing me was injured as nearly as possible to the same extent that I was – the next man to me was stupefied and blind for a short time, and the rest only blinded for the moment. I had no knowledge how I got in from the yard arm, or down on deck . . . I was placed in the dark cockpit, and though my sight returned in a few days I had my eyes bandaged, and was kept out of a stronger light on the lower deck for several days.[23]

Elliot remained very nervous of lightning, even though he recovered: 'There was no mark on my skin as if the lightning had struck me. My right eye was worst being next the flash, the left being perhaps sheltered by the nose. I do not remember suffering any pain. I never was a year in the Mediterranean without the ship being struck, but without serious injury to any of the crew.'[24]

At Malta, Nelson's flagship *Foudroyant* with the Hamiltons on board anchored at a point out of range of the French guns, but, as Midshipman Parsons recalled, 'a breeze unexpectedly came in from the sea, and the ship dragged her anchor'.[25] The mate reported it to the officer of the watch, and he woke Captain Berry, who, unconcerned, replied: 'Very well, Mr. Bolton, we will shift our berth at daylight.'[26] Parsons observed that at dawn the situation suddenly became serious:

Hunger, I suppose, kept the Frenchman waking, and at peep of day he made us a target for all his sea batteries to practise on. 'All hands up' – 'Anchor ahoy!' resounded fore and aft, and we hove short [the anchor cable] to the music of the shot, some of them going far over us. Lord Nelson was in a towering passion, and Lady Hamilton's refusal to quit the quarter-deck did not tend to tranquilise him. When short-a-peak [just before the anchor was raised], the breeze failed, leaving only a disagreeable concomitant – a swell.[27]

With the *Foudroyant* bobbing about on the choppy sea, an easy target for the French guns, it was only when a shot hit one of the masts that Lady

Hamilton finally consented to go below. Eventually the ship was towed out of range by boats. It would take another five months of blockade before the French garrison on Malta finally surrendered to the British.

Returning to Palermo, Nelson found his request to return to England was accepted, but Admiral Keith would not allow him to sail back in his flagship, and so he decided to travel overland through Europe. His last voyage in the *Foudroyant* was from Palermo to Leghorn, accompanied by the Hamiltons (because Sir William had been replaced as ambassador) and also by the Queen of the Two Sicilies, who was travelling to Vienna with some of her children to visit her family.

Nelson and his party arrived at Leghorn on 15 June 1800, the day after Napoleon won the Battle of Marengo against Austria. As Marengo was just north of Genoa in northern Italy, they realised that their direct overland route to England was blocked, and so were forced to travel to Ancona, then sail to Trieste and take a more roundabout route, swinging north through Austria. Wherever they stopped, Nelson was fêted as a celebrity, and the journey became a triumphal progress. Nelson and the Hamiltons eventually landed at Great Yarmouth on 6 November, and their travelling companion Cornelia Knight recorded that 'Lord Nelson was received with all due honours, which were rendered still more interesting to the good people of the town from his being a native of Norfolk. He was drawn in his carriage to the hotel (the Wrestlers' Arms) by the populace*, and the Mayor and Corporation came to present him with the freedom of the city. At his own request public service was performed in the church, to return thanks for his safe return to his native country, and for the many blessings which he had experienced. As he entered the church the organ struck up "See the Conquering Hero comes."'[28]

The lengthy overland journey had greatly improved Nelson's health, and he was already longing to go back to sea. Despite having to cope with the admiring crowds, he found time to write to the Secretary of the Admiralty: 'I beg you will acquaint their Lordships [of the Admiralty] of my arrival here this day, and that my health being perfectly re-established, it is my wish to serve immediately; and I trust that my necessary journey by land from the Mediterranean will not be considered as a wish to be [for] a moment out of active service.'[29] Three days after landing at Great Yarmouth, Nelson reached London, in the wake of a severe storm, and was celebrated here just as he had been across Europe. His expected

---

* Instead of horses, people dragged the carriage themselves as a mark of respect.

arrival had been heralded in the newspapers for days before, and comments were given on every last detail of the entourage, down to the presence of Emma's black servant. This was Fatima, a Nubian girl not yet twenty years old, bought by Nelson in Egypt. Slavery was then legal in Britain, but the vast majority of slaves owned by the British never set foot in the country: they were shipped straight from Africa to work on plantations in the West Indies. Although she had been bought and may technically have been a slave, Fatima was part of the Hamilton household, working as Emma's maid, and later was given the name Fatima Emma Charlotte Nelson Hamilton when she was baptised into the Anglican church.

In London, Nelson went directly to the Admiralty. 'The gallant Hero,' *The Times* reported, 'wore the Stars of the different Orders with which he has been invested for his achievements at Aboukir.'[30] Nelson's eagerness to return to sea seems inexplicable, especially with Emma being in an advanced state of pregnancy with their daughter Horatia. The problems that would inevitably stem from his continuing relationship with Emma, though, may have driven his decision. While the newspaper gossip columnists worked overtime, Nelson had to face the fact that his marriage to Frances was over. A difficult situation was not made any easier by Frances herself, who, entirely blameless and bewildered by Nelson's attitude, made strenuous efforts to reclaim her husband. Nelson left London on 13 January 1801 after two months of public acclaim and private chaos. A new threat to Britain's trade and security was looming, and the Admiralty was quick off the mark to take steps to counter it. Nelson was on his way to join his new flagship in Plymouth – and would never see Frances again.

With no censorship of the press in Britain, information was frequently published that was useful to the enemy. Even confidential material rapidly found its way into the newspapers, because politicians, senior civil servants, admirals and generals gossiped at social gatherings, and some deliberately passed information to journalists. Nelson's destination was supposed to be secret, but a week before he left London *The Times* carried a report about his mission: 'The Public will learn, with great satisfaction, that Lord NELSON is about to be employed on a SECRET EXPEDITION, and will hoist his flag in the course of a very few days. His instructions will not be opened till he arrives in a certain latitude. We shall only permit ourselves to observe, that there is reason to believe his destination is to a distant quarter, where his Lordship's personal appearance alone would preponderate over the influence or the intrigues of any Court in Europe.'[31] Although not obvious to a casual reader, to the diplomats and spies in Britain the mention of 'intrigues' indicated the Baltic, where negotiations were under way to form a League of Armed Neutrality.

Denmark was in dispute with Britain over the right to search neutral ships. As a neutral country, Denmark claimed the right to trade with any country and the colonies of any country, and to transport any goods except for a narrow range defined as specific war materials; neutral ships should not be stopped and searched by the British Navy, and they would ignore any blockade treaties unless warships stopped them entering a port. If neutral vessels were not to be searched, they could break the British blockade of enemy ports at will. Britain therefore wanted a wider definition of the goods forbidden to be carried by neutral ships, and crucially the power to search ships to enforce blockades. For Britain this policy was a matter of stopping French expansion and ultimately the very survival of the British Isles; for Denmark it meant money. Because of the war, neutral ships were in huge demand and the Danish merchant fleet was making massive profits. Many cargoes supposedly destined for Denmark were actually carried to France and French allies, and the situation was made worse by ships of other nations sailing under the Danish flag as a cover for similar trading ventures.

Before the Battle of the Nile, the British Navy had been on the defensive, with little spare capacity to deal with neutral ships, but Nelson's victory had changed all that. The Mediterranean was now under the control of the British Navy, which was trying to enforce a tight blockade of French and Spanish ports. What, for the Danes, had been merely profiteering now became a point of political principle. Britain maintained the right to search Danish ships, while Denmark denied that right. Danish convoys were escorted by warships, but these were often outnumbered by British warships, so from Denmark's point of view the answer was an alliance with other neutral nations to actively protect their merchant ships from being stopped. This was the League of Armed Neutrality – a change from passive, defensive neutrality to an aggressive assertion of the demand to carry on unrestricted trade.

The League was actually instigated by Russia, having been prompted to do so by Denmark. This was a dangerous political game for Denmark, though, as Tsar Paul was insane and his actions unpredictable. Tsars were autocrats, often tyrannical, who held total control over everything and everyone in Russia, in contrast to many other Continental monarchies where, at the very least, the king listened to advice from his ministers.

Denmark had a stark choice: bow to British pressure or join the Armed Neutrality. Gambling that Britain would not dare take action, Denmark joined Russia, Prussia and Sweden in the hope that with the backing of these allies, it could force favourable negotiations with Britain to provide free trade for Danish ships. The Danes were to be hoist with their own petard. Barely a month after the Tsar received the invitation from Denmark to head the League, he had made secret approaches to Napoleon.

The treaty that the Danes eventually signed with Russia was more militaristic than they would have wished, but as they were in a weak negotiating position they accepted the clauses requiring them to fit out extra warships. If war broke out between Russia and Britain, Denmark would be forced to take Russia's side. The treaty was ratified in Copenhagen on 4 November 1800, two days before Nelson's return to England. On the same day in St Petersburg, Tsar Paul placed an embargo on all British ships in Russian ports and arrested all British citizens. Tsar Paul's objective was an alliance to enable joint Russian and French domination of the Continent, using Denmark and Sweden as buffer states against Britain. While the Tsar was deluded with a vision of a European empire, Napoleon played him like a puppet and, Bourrienne observed, 'gained such a hold over the mind of Paul that he reached the point of doing without the cabinet of St Petersburg ... English ships were seized in all the ports, and, at the insistent urging of the Tsar, a Prussian army threatened Hanover [part of George III's territory]. Bonaparte lost no time, and, profiting from the friendship shown towards him ... endeavoured to make him carry out the far-reaching plan which he had devised: he wished to undertake an expedition by land against the English colonies in the East Indies.'[32] While the Tsar dreamed of Europe, Napoleon was still dreaming of the East.

With the League members now effectively enemies of Britain, it was no longer just a question of preventing neutral ships from being searched. Access to trade with the Baltic states, which provided the British Navy with essential supplies such as hemp for ropes and fir wood for spars, would now be blocked, because Russia, Sweden and above all Denmark were in a position to control the trade route and capture merchants ships that passed through their waters. As the situation slipped towards war, the Danes refused all diplomatic overtures from Britain, despite knowing that their country was likely to be the first target of British hostility. They had left themselves without a choice: defiance of Britain might mean heavy casualties, bombardment of coastal settlements and even the loss of their fleet, but defiance of Russia could prompt a Russian invasion and the loss of everything.

On the day that Nelson had started out from London for Plymouth, the British government decided on its response to the crisis. Those Danish, Swedish and Russian ships already in British ports would be detained, while any encountered at sea would be captured. Danish and Swedish colonies in India and the West Indies would be occupied, and a British fleet was to be sent to the Baltic to ensure that British trade continued. Although Russia was seen as the main aggressor, its ports were further north and were still icebound when the thaw freed Danish ports − its geographical position determined that Copenhagen would be the first target.

This was warship diplomacy on a grand scale, and to head the mission the Admiralty chose Admiral Sir Hyde Parker. Sixty-one years old, Parker was from an old naval family, and had spent the latter part of his career in the West Indies, becoming rich from his share of the prize money that his subordinate captains brought in. Parker was considered politically sound and was chosen to conduct the diplomacy. As his second-in-command, Nelson provided the threat to back up the diplomacy. His reputation was well known to the Danes, and in theory this was the ideal combination of commanders − the embodiment of the carrot-and-stick approach. Inevitably, the partnership was doomed to failure. The two men were utterly different in approach and temperament. From the outset, Nelson was pressing the need for urgency, because strategically the Danish and Swedish fleets had to be neutralised before the Russian ships could join them, yet Parker's instinct for correctness and caution caused constant delays.

In the wider picture there was a further complication. Through the British Secret Service it was known in London that plots existed to assassinate both Napoleon and Tsar Paul. Since government involvement with assassination of foreign heads of state would meet with international outrage, little evidence has survived as to the extent the British government was implicated and which members of the administration knew about it. A change of regime in Russia was likely to solve the problem posed by the Armed Neutrality without the need for bloodshed, and if an assassination attempt was imminent, Parker might have been instructed to stall as long as possible.

Even before he met up with Parker, Nelson at Plymouth was fretting at the delays. His own flagship was not yet ready to sail, and there was little he could do to speed up the repairs and loading of supplies. He spent much of his time on administration and writing letters, but this took its toll on his health, which was perhaps not as good as he had assured the Admiralty. On 28 January he wrote to Emma:

My eye [left eye – he was blind in his right] is very bad. I have had the Physician of the Fleet to examine it. He has directed me not to write, (and yet I am forced this day to write [to] Lord Spencer, St. Vincent, Davison . . . &c., but you are the only female I write to;) not to eat anything but the most simple food; not to touch wine or porter; to sit in a dark room; to have green eyeshades for my eyes – (will you, my dear friend, make one or two? – nobody else shall) – and to bathe them in cold water every hour. I fear, it is the writing has brought on this complaint. My eye is like blood; and the film so extended that I only see from the corner farthest my nose.[33]

Emma did make some green eyeshades, and one was sewn, like a short peak, on to the front of his hat. Three days after writing this letter, he learned that Emma had given birth to his daughter, Horatia.

It took until 7 March for Nelson to make sure his ships were all in good order and then sail to Great Yarmouth to rendezvous with Parker. There was immediate friction between the commanders as Nelson took issue with Parker's indecision, and this set the pattern for the whole campaign. Parker's final instructions from the government were to attack the Russian fleet in the Baltic once Copenhagen had been dealt with, and under constant pressure from Nelson, they at last set sail. On 19 March, while rounding the northern tip of Denmark, the British diplomats who had been trying to negotiate a last-minute settlement joined the fleet. They reported that they had failed, and the only option was war with Denmark. To Nelson the situation was clear and he wanted to attack immediately.

At this stage very few people on board the ships knew what was going on, and bad weather was preventing the usual method of detailed communication – officers visiting each other's ships. Just two days earlier Thomas Fremantle, captain of the *Ganges*, wrote to his wife: 'We have since we sailed experienced a second winter; it has snowed every day since, and the ship's company are hacking from morning to night with coughs; in other respects we are perfectly well but I have had no communication with the flag ship since we left Yarmouth . . . I am more at a loss to guess exactly our destination; we are certainly not in sufficient force to attack Copenhagen, and war is not declared against the Danes. A very little time will unravel this business as we are not at this time above forty leagues from Elsinore [just north of Copenhagen].'[34] George Elliot, now a lieutenant on board the *St George*, mentioned that 'we usually anchored at night on account of the snowstorms, and it took us nearly an hour at daybreak to shovel down the snow from our tops and yards before we could weigh. It was very trying to my Mediterranean skin and feelings. Towards the end of March it all at once cleared up and became fine weather.'[35]

Captain Fremantle next wrote to his wife about the delays:

You find us almost in the same situation as we were in when last I wrote to you, except that we are a few miles nearer the [Cronborg] Castle, which the Danes are making as formidable as they can. Sir Hyde in his present disposition means to pass the Castle, and Lord Nelson with the Van Division of the fleet is to attack the floating batteries. I confess myself I think if we had had the good fortune to have undertaken this business a week ago we should have more probability of succeeding . . . if I were to give an opinion on this business, I should say the Danes are exceedingly alarmed, but delay gives them courage, and they will by degrees make Copenhagen so strong, that it may resist the attack of our fleet. The whole Coast is lined with Guns and Mortars, but yet I think if we pass the Castle in a day or two, we may succeed. Lord Nelson is quite sanguine, but as you may well imagine there is a great diversity of opinion . . . You will take into consideration that we are now not contending with Frenchmen, or Russians, but with people who have not been at war for 70 or 80 years, and consequently can never have seen a shot fired.[36]

The holdup in striking at Copenhagen was partly due to contrary winds but mainly to disagreement between Parker, Nelson and the senior captains as to the plan of battle or even whether to attack at all. As Fremantle mentioned, the Danes were using every last minute to strengthen their defences, but at least the interlude allowed the straggling British ships to catch up with the fleet. One ship that did not arrive was the warship *Invincible*. Sailing from Great Yarmouth, carrying troops and stores, this vessel struck a sandbank off Happisburgh on the Norfolk coast and gradually sank. Even though another ship took off some of the survivors, it was not possible to rescue more than a fraction of those on board. In all, over four hundred lives were lost in this shipwreck – more than the total number of British who would be killed in the forthcoming battle. For days afterwards bodies were washed up on the nearby beaches and cartloads were taken to a mass grave by Happisburgh church, although others were buried at various points along the coast.

The Danes may not have had much recent experience of war, but it was their capital city and in many cases their homes that were threatened by bombardment, so they were particularly determined to put up a strong resistance. Copenhagen was a small city straddling a deep-water channel that separated the large island of Zealand from the very much smaller island of Amager, the channel itself within the city walls providing a sheltered harbour. The walled city was barely 20 feet above water at its highest point, so the fortifications were too low to be secure against bombardment from the sea. To counter this, a line of warships, hulks and barges was anchored to the north-east of the city, on the edge of the channel, to keep the British ships away from the land. At the northern end of this line was the Trekroner fort, positioned at the tip of a shoal, while another line of ships and hulks protected the entrance to the harbour. All these vessels, fitted out as floating gun batteries, formed a rough V shape or arrow pointing northwards, with the Trekroner fort at the apex.

To the east of the channel was the large but invisible Middle Ground Shoal, but all the marker buoys had been lifted. The hurried Danish defences were backed up by gunboats that could move through the shallows, as well as boats to ferry powder and ammunition to the floating batteries. These defences looked very strong, but as the British well knew, the crews of the floating batteries had very little experience, and in fact many of them were recent conscripts from the streets of Copenhagen and the surrounding countryside. The British assessment was that the floating batteries were strong, but the men inside were the weak point. In both cases they were wrong: the ships and hulks were in poor repair, but the Danes made up for their inexperience with raw courage and a tenacious determination to fight to the last.

Almost due east from Amager was the Swedish coastal town of Malmö, separated from Copenhagen by the Sound, a stretch of sea strewn with treacherous shoals and the island of Saltholm. British ships approaching Copenhagen would have to steer a course out of range of both enemy shorelines, while keeping in deep water to avoid running aground. Despite concerted efforts in Britain to obtain detailed charts of the waters off Copenhagen, the fleet was desperately short of information.

On 30 March, the day after Fremantle had written to his wife, the fleet

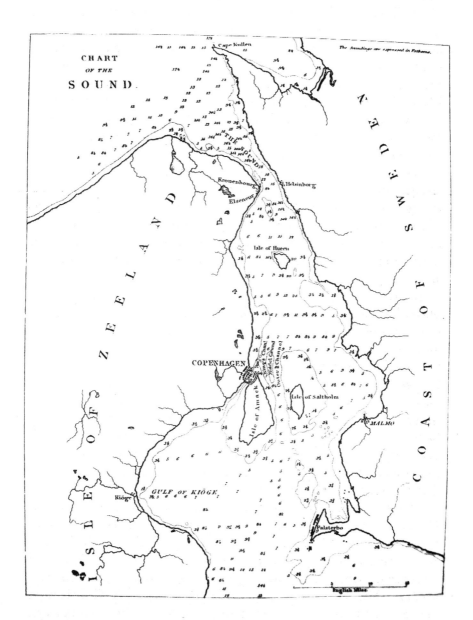

*Chart of the Copenhagen area in 1801*

sailed south past Cronborg Castle at Elsinore. Here the ships had to pass through a channel between Elsinore in Denmark and Helsingborg in Sweden and could expect to come under fire from both sides. As the Swedes did not open fire, the British ships moved to that side of the channel. Traditionally regarded as a gateway to the Baltic, the channel was nowhere near as formidable as its reputation, and unless fierce fire was co-ordinated from both Danish and Swedish sides, ships could sail out of range of the guns. The British fleet had several bomb vessels with them – ships specially designed and rigged to carry one or two large mortars that could fire explosive shells, called bombs, over a greater distance than ordinary naval cannons. As they passed Cronborg Castle, out of all the British ships that opened fire it was the bomb vessels that did the damage. An anonymous officer aboard Fremantle's ship, the *Ganges*, wrote a letter home:

In my last, of the 30th March, I informed you of the intention of the Fleet to pass Elsineur [Cronborg] Castle the first fair wind: it came that very day. We weighed Anchor, formed the Line, and stood past it with all sail set: during the time we were passing, a very great fire was kept up by the Enemy, but not one of our Ships received a shot. The Swedes, very fortunately, did not engage us at all: we were not above a mile from their guns, as we kept their shore on board, to be out of the Danes' gun-shot; in the mean time we had several Bombships firing on their Town; the shells which they fired killed 160 people ashore at Elsineur.[37]

The British anchored some 7 miles north of Copenhagen, within sight of the city but well out of range. Immediately they started to reconnoitre and take depth soundings close to the defences, although the Danes were vigilant and opened fire whenever possible. Midshipman John Finlayson on board the *St George* noted that 'the night also of the 30th was employed by some of our most intelligent masters and pilots, several of whom we had brought from England with us, in sounding and laying down fresh buoys'.[38] One thing was obvious – the bombardment of Copenhagen was only feasible if the offshore defences were neutralised first. A plan of attack was finally decided upon. The fleet would divide in two, with Nelson (now in the *Elephant*) taking his ships south, keeping to the east of the Middle Ground Shoal. Once the wind was favourable, he would sail northwards on the west of that shoal to attack Copenhagen. Parker would stay to the north of the city to provide support and guard against enemy ships approaching from that direction. Another factor that had to be considered was the necessity for the British fleet to remain relatively unscathed, so that the Russian fleet could be attacked afterwards.

On the afternoon of 1 April Nelson took his ships south and anchored off the southern tip of the Middle Ground Shoal. After nearly seven weeks of constant frustration and delays, while the ice imprisoning the Russian fleet continued to melt, Nelson was finally poised to attack.

# FIVE

——·◆·——

# WAR AND PEACE

A fleet of British ships of war are the best negotiators in Europe, they always speak to be understood, and generally gain their point.

Nelson, writing to Emma Hamilton before the Battle of Copenhagen[1]

The next morning, 2 April 1801, there was a favourable wind to take the British ships north past the floating batteries, but first the ships would have to sail between the Refshale Shoal and the Middle Ground Shoal. Neither shoal was visible or marked properly, and the pilots disagreed about the best course to steer. As Nelson struggled to make sense of conflicting advice from the pilots, the crews of the ships were getting ready for battle, and in the Monarch Midshipman William Millard noticed the surgeon's station:

As soon as reports had been delivered from all parts of the ship that every thing was prepared for action, the men were ordered to breakfast . . . Our repast, it may fairly be supposed, under these circumstances, was a slight one. When we left the berth [on the starboard side of the cockpit], we had to pass all the dreadful preparations of the surgeons. One table was covered with instruments of all shapes and sizes; another, of more than usual strength, was placed in the middle of the cockpit: as I had never seen this produced before, I could not help asking the use of it, and received for answer 'that it was to cut off legs and wings [arms] upon'.[2]

As the midshipmen returned to their posts, Millard heard the banter between them and the surgeon's assistants: "'Damn you, Doctor," said one, "if you don't handle me tenderly, I will never forgive you;" to which the mate answered, "By George, sir, you had better keep out of my clutches, or depend on it I will pay you off all old scores." Some such compliments as these were passed with almost every one.'[3]

It was nearly ten o'clock by the time a pilot volunteered to guide the lead ship, the *Edgar*, up the channel to Copenhagen. The *Edgar* was followed by the *Ardent*, *Glatton* and *Isis*, but as the remaining ships also weighed anchor and prepared to follow, the *Agamemnon*, which should have been fifth in the line, ran aground on the Middle Ground Shoal. The navigable channel was not wide, and the shoals made it impossible to position the ships close to the Danish batteries. Because of these difficulties, Nelson had worked out a precise sailing order in advance, matching the fire-power of specific ships against what was known about the individual floating batteries. This was ruined at the outset, but he quickly improvised, ordering the *Polyphemus* to take the *Agamemnon*'s place. From the *Monarch*, which would be almost the last ship, Millard was impressed by the sight of the *Edgar* sailing into action: 'A more beautiful and solemn spectacle I never witnessed. The *Edgar* led the van, and on her approach the battery on the Isle of Amak [Amager] and three or four of the southernmost vessels opened their fire upon her. A man-of-war under sail is at all times a beautiful object, but at such a time the scene is heightened beyond the powers of description. We saw her pressing on through the enemy's fire, and manoeuvring in the midst of it to gain her station; our minds were deeply impressed with awe, and not a word was spoken throughout the ship but by the pilot and helmsmen.'[4]

The sailing order was further wrecked when the *Bellona* and then the *Russell* ran aground. Although the stranded ships did at least mark the edge of the shoal, they became added obstacles to be avoided. The whole process of deploying the British ships was already very slow, and some of the smaller ships took nearly all day to reach their proper positions, while others never made it at all. The wind was with Nelson's ships, but once those commanded by Admiral Sir Hyde Parker to the north began to get under way to support the attack, they found the wind directly against them, and it was obvious that they would take a long time to reach the area of the battle. Nelson was kept busy organising the line to maximise his fire-power by hailing and signalling to the ships as they prepared to enter the channel. On board Nelson's flagship, the *Elephant*, an army officer, Lieutenant-Colonel William Stewart, watched what was happening: 'The Action began at five minutes past ten. In about half an hour afterwards,

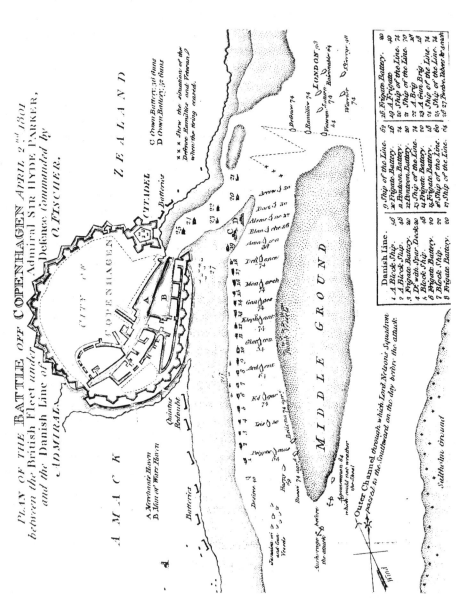

Plan of the Battle of Copenhagen in 1801

the first half of our fleet was engaged, and before half past eleven, the Battle became general. The *Elephant*'s station was in the centre . . . our distance [from the batteries] was nearly a cable's length [200 yards], and this was the average distance at which the Action was fought; its being so great, caused the long duration of it. Lord Nelson was most anxious to get nearer; but the same error which had led the two Ships on [to] the shoal, induced our Master and Pilots to dread shoaling.'[5]

Edward Riou, captain of the frigate *Amazon*, was in charge of five frigates that were stationed towards the northern end of the battle line. Normally frigates were considered too small and lightly armed to take part in battle, but Riou saw that where Nelson had reorganised the battleships to close the gaps left by the grounded vessels, the battle line did not extend as far north as was planned. Riou moved his frigates to lengthen the line northwards, which took some pressure off the northernmost battleships, but at great cost to the frigates.

On board the *Monarch*, stationed to the north of the *Elephant* with the *Ganges* anchored between them, Millard recorded the start of the battle: 'We anchored about ten [o'clock], but not precisely in the station originally intended, for this reason, that two of the ships stationed by Lord Nelson ahead of us never made their appearance [because they ran aground] . . . When the ship came to, I was on the quarter-deck, and saw Captain Mosse on the poop; his card of instructions was in his left hand, and his right was raised to his mouth with the speaking trumpet.'[6] This picture remained in the young midshipman's memory because it was the last time he saw his captain alive: 'I returned to my station at the aftermost guns; and in a few minutes the Captain was brought aft perfectly dead. Colonel Hutchinson was with me, and was asked if he thought it right that the Captain should be carried below; he answered that he saw no sign of life, and it might only damp the spirits of the men. He was then laid in the stern walk, and a flag thrown over him. Colonel Hutchinson turned round and exclaimed with tears in his eyes, "Poor man! he has left a wife and family to lament him."'[7]

This was not an auspicious start to the battle for the crew of the *Monarch*, and Millard commented: 'I was conscious that employment was the surest mode to escape those unpleasant sensations which must arise in every one's breast that has time for reflection in such a situation. I therefore pulled off my coat, helped to run out the gun, handed the powder, and literally worked as hard as a dray-horse.'[8] Like many of the ships, the *Monarch* had an extra complement of soldiers on board in case they were needed for a ground assault on the harbour, but being at extreme musket range (about 200 yards) from the enemy, there was little they could do. Millard saw that they 'were dressed in full uniform and stationed upon the poop and on the gangway where they kept up a fire of musketry, till they were mowed down so fast that they were ordered below to wait further orders. The remainder, in their working-jackets without accoutrements, were attached to [help with] the great guns.'[9] Lieutenant-Colonel Hutchinson was their commanding officer, and to set an example he continued to pace the quarterdeck, resplendent in his full uniform, but, as Millard related, 'This brave officer had, strictly speaking, no particular duty to do . . . he begged I would employ him if I thought he could do any good. I was at this time seated on the deck, cutting the wads asunder for the guns; and the Colonel, notwithstanding the danger attending his uniform breeches, sat himself down and went to work.'[10]

On board the *Elephant* Lieutenant-Colonel Stewart, who also had no specific duties, paced the deck with Nelson watching the progress of the battle: 'Nelson was . . . walking the starboard side of the quarter-deck; sometimes much animated, and at others heroically fine in his observations. A shot through the mainmast knocked a few splinters about us. He observed to me, with a smile, "It is warm work, and this day may be the last to any of us at a moment;" and then stopping short at the gangway, he used an expression r ever to be erased from my memory, and said with emotion, "but mark you, ˙ would not be elsewhere for thousands."'[11] Splinters were a major hazard, as Millard in the *Monarch* recounted:

Our signal-midshipman (the Honourable William Bowes) was bruised from head to foot with splinters in such a manner as compelled him to leave the deck . . . When the wheel was shot away, I was in a cloud [of splinters]; but being some little distance before the wheel I did not receive any of the larger pieces. When I passed backwards and forwards between my quarters and the mainmast, I went on the opposite side to that which was engaged, and by that means probably escaped a severe wound; for as I was returning with two shot in one hand and a cheese (or packet) of wads in the other, I received a pretty smart blow on my right cheek. I dropped my shot, just as a monkey does a hot potato, and clapped my hand to the place, which I found rather bloody, and immediately ran aft to get my handkerchief out of the coat-pocket.[12]

Millard's wound was slight and so he continued his work on the quarterdeck, but soon after he had to go to the magazine and was shocked to find that conditions below were much worse: 'When I arrived on the maindeck, along which I had to pass, there was not a single man standing the whole way from the mainmast forward, a district containing eight guns on a side, some of which were run out ready for firing; others lay dismounted; and others remained as they were after recoiling. In this dreary scene I shall be excused for shuddering as I walked across the body of a dead soldier.'[13]

As the morning of the battle wore on, some Danish batteries ceased firing and some surrendered, but others continued to put up a strong resistance. Several British ships were being badly mauled, and in the *Monarch* Millard was horrified that 'after my return from the magazine Mr. Ponsonby (midshipman), who had been quartered on the forecastle, came on to the quarter-deck, his face and the collar of his coat partly covered with a coagulated compost of human blood and brains. He presented himself and three of his men . . . as all that were left [of those stationed on the forecastle].'[14] A little later Millard was sent to the poop deck, but found this too was devoid of anyone left alive, although he noticed 'a musket, the barrel of which was bent in a semicircle; this I apprehended must have been struck on the muzzle at the very instant the man was presenting it; it could not otherwise have been driven into that form'.[15]

Parker's ships were playing no part in the battle as they had made virtually no progress against the headwind, and around noon Parker sent the captain of his flagship, Robert Otway, in a boat to Nelson. Otway was one of the most senior officers in the fleet and a personal friend of Parker's. Nearly 700 miles to the north-east, at St Petersburg, Tsar Paul of Russia had been assassinated nine days earlier, on 24 March. In summer, news of such a momentous event, travelling by sea, would have reached Copenhagen long before the battle, but the Russian ports were still icebound, and for much of their journey couriers had to take a longer, overland route. There is a mystery about exactly when the news arrived at Copenhagen, and it has been suggested* that it came while the battle was still raging and influenced subsequent events. This theory may explain some aspects of the battle that otherwise appear irrational, particularly Parker sending Otway, in the heat of the battle, on an errand to Nelson's flagship. It is tempting to suppose that news of the Tsar's death had reached Parker, who, realising the political significance, entrusted the

---

* By the historian Elizabeth Sparrow (1999, pp.223–40; 2001).

information to one of his closest companions. Neither at the time, nor in subsequent years, did Parker, Nelson or Otway record or comment on this incident.

Otway was in a hurry and hailed a passing launch, which proved to be heavily laden and made slow progress. It was a long distance to row and after more than an hour Parker could see that Otway had still not reached Nelson's ship. He seems to have panicked, and at a quarter past one the admiral hoisted signal number 39 commanding all ships to leave off the action. On board the *Elephant* it was observed by the signal lieutenant, who made his report. Nelson, according to Stewart,

continued his walk, and did not appear to take notice of it. The Lieutenant meeting his Lordship at the next turn asked, 'whether he should repeat it?' Lord Nelson answered, 'No, acknowledge it.' On the Officer returning to the poop, his Lordship called after him, 'Is No. 16 still hoisted?'* the Lieutenant answering in the affirmative, Lord Nelson said, 'Mind you keep it so.' . . . After a turn or two, he said to me, in a quick manner, 'Do you know what's shown on board of the Commander-in-Chief, No.39?' On asking him what that meant, he answered, 'Why, to leave off Action.' 'Leave off Action!' he repeated, and then added, with a shrug, 'Now, damn me if I do.' He also observed, I believe, to Captain Foley, 'You know, Foley, I have only one eye – I have a right to be blind sometimes;' and then with an archness peculiar to his character, putting the glass to his blind eye, he exclaimed, 'I really do not see the signal.'[16]

Nelson's action was the origin of the saying 'to turn a blind eye'.†

The signal caused confusion among Nelson's ships – some obeyed and started to pull out of the battle, while others, observing that the *Elephant* had not repeated the signal, carried on fighting. The frigates under Riou's command, which by this time had suffered dreadful damage and casualties, were at the head of the British line nearest to Parker. Riou decided he must obey and reluctantly ordered the frigates to move out towards Parker's ships. Moments later Riou was killed by a cannonball.

---

* Signal number 16 was 'engage the enemy more closely'.
† Some people believe that the blind eye incident never happened, but was a later embellishment by Stewart. In another report he merely says that Nelson ignored the signal, but 'at the very time observed, that he was determined to "give it to them till they should be sick of it; and that if three hours would not do, he would be responsible that four hours' such fire as we were then keeping up would do for them"' (Stewart 1801, p.24).

Nelson was right to disobey Parker's direct order even though, after the battle, he commented to Stewart: 'I have fought contrary to orders, and I shall perhaps be hanged: never mind, let them.'[17] For the frigates to sail out of the line of fire was relatively easy, because they were at the head of the line, and as they had taken such a battering it was only sensible to retreat. The largest warships further down the channel were in a different situation. Any attempt to sail up through the channel under fire from the Danish batteries would have led to a chaotic situation, perhaps more ships being grounded and certainly the abandonment of those ships already aground. To have obeyed Parker's signal would have snatched defeat at the point of victory, and just as Nelson did not mention the signal in his official reports, Parker never commented on why he sent it. It was inexplicable to Nelson and his officers at the time, and remains so today.

It became obvious that the Danish defence was crumbling, and yet the Danes fought on doggedly. Midshipman Finlayson was helping out in one of the boats, and when the Danes slackened their fire he was ordered 'to pick up as many as possible of the poor Danes, who were jumping overboard from the blazing Hulks. We saved a great many, some without arms or legs, and others in some way or other dreadfully wounded, and put them on board . . . the first ship we could get near.'[18] Half an hour after the signal was hoisted, and with Otway having reached the *Elephant*, Nelson decided to call for a truce. The purser of the *Elephant*, Thomas Wallis, said that 'Lord Nelson wrote the Note [suggesting a cease-fire] at the casing of the rudder-head, and as he wrote, I took a copy, both of us standing. The original was put into an envelope, and sealed with his Arms; at first I was going to seal it with a wafer [gummed paper in the form of a seal that would take some time to fully dry], but he would not allow this to be done, observing that it must be sealed, or the Enemy would think it was written and sent in a hurry. The man I sent below for a light [to melt the sealing wax] never returned, having been killed in his way.'[19]

A second messenger was more successful, and the letter was sealed and dispatched under a flag of truce with Captain Frederick Thesiger, a Danish speaker who volunteered to act as courier. The letter read: 'To the Brothers of Englishmen, the Danes. Lord Nelson has directions to spare Denmark, when no longer resisting; but if firing is continued on the part of Denmark, Lord Nelson will be obliged to set on fire all the Floating-batteries he has taken, without having the power of saving the brave

Danes who have defended them. Dated on board his Britannic Majesty's Ship Elephant, Copenhagen Roads, April 2nd, 1801.'[20]

If Parker knew that the Tsar was dead and the whole political and diplomatic landscape had been turned upside down, every minute more of fighting produced unnecessary bloodshed and made a diplomatic settlement harder. It was only after Otway reached the *Elephant* that Nelson wrote this letter to the Danes proposing a cease-fire. Although this was possibly a clever ploy to allow his ships to pull out of a difficult situation, Nelson always maintained that he sent the letter on humanitarian grounds. He knew he had the upper hand and would ultimately win the battle, and his normal policy, once committed, was annihilation of the enemy, so perhaps learning of the Tsar's death forced the cease-fire offer.

Because Thesiger's boat had to take a circuitous route to avoid the worst of the gunfire, it was around three o'clock when he finally landed at the Citadel of Copenhagen. Nelson's timing was perfect: when the letter was delivered, it was apparent that further resistance from the Danes would only cause more bloodshed without achieving anything. The Danes agreed to a cease-fire. The letter was not just a humanitarian gesture, but a useful political move, limiting the damage already done to Anglo-Danish relations. The cease-fire also allowed time for the British ships to work their way out of the channel, as they had been ordered to do by Parker several hours earlier. Even without being under fire, ships ran aground, but eventually the warships cleared the channel to be replaced by the bomb vessels that were ready to bombard the city and dockyard if fighting broke out again.

The day after the battle, Nelson went on shore and was astonishingly well received, as one Danish observer recorded:

In the course of the forenoon, Admiral Nelson came in his barge in the inner roads, and went on board the *Denmark*, where he partook of some refreshment, and then proceeded ashore. On his landing he was received by the people, neither with acclamations nor with murmurs; they did not degrade themselves with the former, nor disgrace themselves with the latter. The admiral was received as one brave enemy ever ought to receive another – he was received with respect. A carriage was provided for his lordship, which he, however, declined, and walked amid an immense crowd of persons anxious to catch a glimpse of the British hero, to the palace of the Prince Royal. After dinner the Admiral was introduced to the Prince, and the negotiations commenced.[21]

Once the firing had stopped, both sides could pay full attention to the casualties. Midshipman Edward Daubeny in the *Bellona* wrote to his father that there had been 'great slaughter, I am very sorry to say, on both sides, particularly on the enemy's. Some of their ships were manned three times [with reinforcements from the shore]; eight hundred were killed and wounded in one of their ships, and almost as many in their others. Our ships have suffered very much from the enemy's shot.'[22] Daubeny himself was wounded, but made light of it so as not to alarm his relatives: 'We have besides about 80 killed and wounded by the bursting of our guns. I am, thank God, only slightly burnt by the bursting of one; don't be at all alarmed when you see my name amongst the wounded in the papers; to be sure I am weak, but that is occasioned by the length of the engagement, and I was not very well before.'[23] The actual casualty figures on the British side were around two hundred and fifty killed and seven hundred wounded, some of whom later died of their injuries. Estimates of casualties on the Danish side vary widely because the floating batteries were continually supplied with fresh crews during the battle, but around four hundred were killed and perhaps a thousand wounded.

It is usually accepted that reliable news of the Tsar's death did not reach the Danes at Copenhagen until 8 April, while they were still negotiating terms for an armistice with the British, but Peter Cullen, a surgeon in the *Agamemnon*, recorded in his journal that 'it was in consequence of the intelligence received of the death of the Emperor Paul of Russia, that the Truce was extended from 24 hours to 14 weeks. This intelligence was received at Copenhagen the day after the battle [the 3rd], and which if received previously would in all probability have prevented this melancholy affair.'[24] The news changed the negotiating position of the Danes. After six days of diplomatic wrangling, agreement was suddenly reached and an armistice was signed the next day.

Official news of the Tsar's death and a change of Russian policy reached London on the 13th, and the British fleet, which had moved on from Copenhagen to threaten the Russian ports in the Baltic, was recalled. Parker was also recalled, leaving Nelson in charge. Despite much public and private criticism of Parker's actions, there was no formal investigation or censure, and the whole episode was quietly covered up. Whatever the truth of the Battle of Copenhagen and the death of the Tsar, Britain was ultimately triumphant – the Armed Neutrality fell apart within a matter of weeks. With the emergency over, Nelson had time to consider his health, which was still not good, and he applied for leave to return home to recuperate. On 1 July he was back in Great Yarmouth.

A year had passed since Nelson was in the Mediterranean, but the French and Spanish continued to be harassed by the British, while blockades were maintained at various ports, including Alexandria and Toulon. Lieutenant Thomas Cochrane was appointed commander of the 14-gun sloop *Speedy*, and in May 1801, a month after the Battle of Copenhagen, he captured the Spanish frigate *Gamo*, an act of bravado that passed into legend. Shortly after, he was back on convoy duty – Cochrane's little sloop *Speedy* was now an escort for the packet ship carrying mail between Minorca and Gibraltar. It was tedious work with little chance of capturing prizes, but on 3 July three ships were unexpectedly spotted in the distance.

Cochrane recounted that 'at daybreak, on the morning of July 3rd, these large ships were observed in the distance, calling up to our imaginations visions of Spanish galleons from South America, and accordingly the *Speedy* prepared for the chase'.[25] Such galleons carried so much bullion that the prize money from the capture of just one, divided among the small crew of the *Speedy*, would have made each man the equivalent of a modern millionaire, so doubtless Cochrane's enthusiasm was mirrored by his men. The dream was short-lived, although Cochrane admitted that 'it was not till day dawned that we found out our mistake, the vessels between us and the offing being clearly line-of-battle ships, forbidding all reasonable hope of escape'.[26] They were French battleships, under Rear-Admiral Charles Linois, that had evaded the blockade of Toulon and were heading for Cadiz. The *Speedy* was trapped between them and the coast, with limited room to manoeuvre, but Cochrane was determined to try:

Being to windward, we endeavoured to escape by making all sail, and, as the wind fell light, by using our sweeps [large oars]. This proving unavailing, we threw the guns overboard, and put the brig before the wind; but notwithstanding every effort, the enemy gained fast upon us, and, in order to prevent our slipping past, separated on different tacks, so as to keep us constantly within reach of one or the other; the *Desaix*, being nearest, firing broadsides at us as she passed when tacking, at other times firing from her bow chasers, and cutting up our rigging. For upwards of three hours we were thus within gunshot of the *Desaix*, when finding it impossible to escape by the wind, I ordered all the stores to be thrown overboard, in the hope of being able, when thus further lightened, to run the gauntlet between the ships, which continued to gain upon us.[27]

Having failed to outrun the French ships, the last resort was to try to outmanoeuvre them, a dangerous gamble that would initially take the *Speedy* closer to the French ships, when a broadside from any one of them could have blown the sloop out of the water. Cochrane described what happened next:

Watching an opportunity . . . we bore up, set the studding sails [to maximise speed], and attempted to run between them, the French honouring us with a broadside for this unexpected movement. The *Desaix*, however, immediately tacked in pursuit, and in less than an hour got within musket-shot. At this short distance, she let fly at us a complete broadside of round and grape [shot], the object evidently being to sink us at a blow . . . Fortunately for us . . . her round shot plunged in the water under our bows, or the discharge must have sunk us; the scattered grape, however, took effect in the rigging, cutting up a great part of it, riddling the sails, and doing material damage to the masts and yards, though not a man was hurt. To have delayed for another broadside would have been to expose all on board to certain destruction, and as further effort to escape was impotent, the *Speedy*'s colours were hauled down.[28]

Cochrane was taken prisoner, but because the French captain had been impressed by his courage and seamanship, he happily found that 'on going aboard the *Desaix*, and presenting my sword to the captain, Christie Pallière, he politely declined taking it, with the complimentary remark that "he would not accept the sword of an officer who had for so many hours struggled against impossibility," at the same time paying me the further compliment of requesting that "I would continue to wear my sword though a prisoner."'[29] This was an unusual honour, as surrendered swords were regarded as trophies. Cochrane was treated well by his captors, and the French battleships sailed on into the Spanish port of Algeciras, across the bay from Gibraltar, with the *Speedy* and the packet ship as their prizes. The Rock of Gibraltar commands a good view of Algeciras, and although no British ships there were large enough to make an attack, little time was lost in sending a message to Sir James Saumarez, now a rear-admiral, who was blockading Cadiz.

The French began taking on stores and refitting with the intention of sailing west into the Atlantic with the first available wind, but on 6 July Saumarez arrived in the Bay of Gibraltar with nine battleships. Captain Pallière asked Cochrane if he thought an attack was imminent, to which Cochrane replied 'that before night both British and French ships would be at Gibraltar', adding that, 'it would give me great pleasure to make him and his officers a return for the kindness I had experienced on board the *Desaix*!'[30] Despite this warning, Pallière resumed his normal routine, inviting Cochrane to breakfast: 'Before the meal was ended, a round shot crashed through the stern of the *Desaix*, driving before it a shower of broken glass, the *débris* of a wine bin under the sofa. We forthwith jumped up from table, and went on the quarter-deck, but a raking shot from Sir James Saumarez's ship sweeping a file of marines from the poop, not far from me, I considered further exposure on my part unnecessary, and went below.'[31]

Although outnumbered, the French were in a strong position, being protected by Spanish gunboats and by batteries of guns on the shore. To prevent the British ships sailing between them and the coast, the French ships had begun moving inshore, but they were too slow and so Linois ordered them to cut their cables and run ashore. Being under fire from British ships and prudently taking cover, Cochrane could gain only glimpses of the action. The British ships tried to get in closer, but the 74-gun *Hannibal* ran aground and sustained heavy fire, which, as Captain Jahleel Brenton of the *Caesar* noted, resulted in 'seventy-three killed and sixty-four wounded, – a very unusual proportion, as, in general, the wounded trebles the number of the killed; but this may be accounted for by the *Hannibal* being so near that the enemy's shot passed through her sides without making any splinters, to which the greater number of wounds are attributable'.[32]

With adverse winds, Saumarez decided it was fruitless to continue the attack, and the remaining British ships withdrew to Gibraltar, leaving the shattered *Hannibal* along with the crew in French hands. The day after this Battle of Algeciras, the British negotiated an exchange of prisoners, including Cochrane and the crew of the *Speedy* and those on board the *Hannibal*.

Both the French and British ships were badly damaged, and it was a race to repair them – if the French won, they could escape before the British were ready to attack again, but for added protection they called for reinforcements from the Spanish fleet at Cadiz. Several days later six

Spanish battleships under Vice-Admiral Moreno arrived at Algeciras from Cadiz, having evaded the now much-reduced blockade of that port. On the afternoon of 12 July the French and Spanish all sailed together. Though the repairs of the British ships were incomplete, they gave chase, and from Gibraltar Cochrane watched the fighting begin in the Strait:

Of the action which subsequently took place I have no personal knowledge, other than that of a scene witnessed by myself from the garden of the commissioner's house [at Gibraltar], in which I was staying. The enemy were overtaken at dusk, soon after leaving the bay, and when it had become dark, Captain Keats, in the *Superb*, gallantly dashed in between the two sternmost ships, firing right and left, and passed on . . . The movement was so rapidly executed, that the *Superb* shot ahead before the smoke cleared away, and the Spanish ships, the *Real Carlos*, 112 [guns], and the *San Hermenegildo*, 112 [guns], mistaking each other for the aggressor, began a mutual attack, resulting in the *Real Carlos* losing her foretop-mast, the sails of which – falling over her own guns – caught fire. While in this condition the *Hermenegildo* – still engaging the *Real Carlos* as an enemy – in the confusion fell on board her and caught fire also. Both ships burned till they blew up.[33]

With expert seamanship, at a cost of two broadsides, Captain Richard Keats had caused the destruction of two of the largest Spanish battleships, and Cochrane recorded that 'nearly all on board [the Spanish ships] perished; a few survivors only escaping on board the *Superb* as Captain Keats was taking possession of a third Spanish line-of-battle ship, the *San Antonio* . . . the remainder of the combined squadron got safely back to Cadiz'.[34] As the sight and sound of the fighting disappeared in the distance, Cochrane was left to reflect that his association with the *Speedy* was at an end. He was subsequently court-martialled on board the *Pompee* at Gibraltar. This was an automatic proceeding for any officer who had lost his ship, but as Cochrane had done everything possible to save the *Speedy*, it was no surprise that he was acquitted. In the few months under his command, he claimed the little sloop had captured fifty vessels and 122 guns, as well as taking 534 prisoners. The *Speedy* was renamed *Saint Pierre* by the French and was presented by Napoleon to the Pope. Cochrane himself was promoted to captain, but was furious that his first lieutenant was turned down for promotion following the capture of the *Gamo*. He refused to let the matter rest on his return to England, and Earl St

Vincent eventually replied to him that 'the small number of men killed on board the *Speedy* did not warrant the application'.[35] Cochrane's bravery and seamanship tended to avoid such casualties, and never afraid to speak out, he retorted that 'in the battle from which his lordship derived his title there was only *one man* killed on board his own flagship'.[36] This made him a bitter enemy of St Vincent and those around him, but, Cochrane commented, 'it was a common remark in the Navy that the battle of St. Vincent was gained by the inshore squadron, under Nelson, the commander-in-chief being merely a spectator, at a distance which involved the loss of one man in his own ship'.[37] It would be a long time before Cochrane was given another ship to command.

At the other end of the Mediterranean in August 1801, a few weeks after these two battles off Algeciras, the French signed a treaty to leave Egypt: after the assassination of General Kléber the previous year, overall command had passed to General Menou – Jacques Abdallah Menou as he now called himself, for he had married an Egyptian woman and converted to Islam. Unlike Kléber, Menou was not in any hurry to quit Egypt, and he was also eccentric, which made negotiations difficult. To break the deadlock an expeditionary force of British troops was sent to take Egypt by force, and in the autumn of 1800 Admiral Lord Keith was given the task of organising the transportation of this army. The British government had underestimated the strength of the French troops in Egypt and overestimated the efficiency of the Turks, with the result that the force sent out under the command of Lieutenant-General Sir Ralph Abercromby was inadequate. Keith took personal charge of British ships in the eastern Mediterranean, relieving Sir Sidney Smith of his command, so that on the face of it Smith was just another captain of a ship. However, Keith did recognise that Smith had extensive knowledge of the area and found his advice invaluable.

The British expedition assembled in the bay of Marmaris on the southern coast of Turkey, where Abercromby, awaiting supplies, prudently allowed his soldiers to acclimatise while he trained them in the tactics of beach landings. This also gave Abercromby time to gain intelligence about Egypt and to realise that his Turkish allies were likely to prove useless. The French were aware of the preparations for a British invasion well in advance, but Menou failed to reinforce their positions along the coast, so that when the attack came in March 1801, the French were repulsed, despite putting up a stiff resistance. Had Menou counterattacked immediately with a large force, he would have thrown the

British back into the sea, but he delayed, and when he did oppose the British landing at Aboukir, his force was too small. Even so it was a closely fought battle with many casualties on both sides, including Abercromby, who died of his wounds a week later. Menou retreated to Alexandria, and the British, now reinforced by Turks, Mamelukes and Bedouins, gradually pushed inland from the coast. At the end of August 1801 Menou finally signed a treaty allowing him to repatriate his men, which was ratified by Keith on 2 September, at last bringing an end to Napoleon's expedition to the East.

Sidney Smith was given the honour of taking dispatches back to Britain, announcing the final removal of the French from Egypt, and he sailed in the frigate *Carmen*, which was commanded by Captain Selby. It was to be an eventful journey. As they were sailing along the coast of Libya strong winds almost blew the frigate ashore. Midshipman George Parsons, awakened from his sleep by the noise, heard the master shouting, 'hold on, lads . . . for here comes a topper'.[38] Parsons recounted that 'the frigate, from having little way [no speed], had fallen off in the trough of the sea, and a mountainous wave rolling on the beam seemed determined to swamp us; onward it came in its resistless might, breaking over the frigate, and sweeping away the boats and spare spars. "Hold on, good sticks [addressing the masts]", said Sir Sidney, who, with the captain, being aroused by the concussion, came running on deck . . . "It is Cape Dern [modern Derna]," said Sir Sidney, "and I fear we are embayed. All hands wear ship."'[39] As the men struggled to turn the ship Parsons saw that 'the mainsail blew to ribbons as she came to the wind on the other tack; and, fortunately for the old frigate, it so happened, for we were taken flat aback in a heavy squall, and, had the mainsail still remained set, we most certainly should have gathered stern way, and foundered'.[40]

Having survived this emergency the frigate continued to battle against unusually rough weather, but it was not seasickness that blunted Parsons's hunger: 'Sir Sidney, among many peculiar eccentricities, asserted that rats fed cleaner, and were better eating, than pigs or ducks; and, agreeably to his wish, a dish of these beautiful vermin were caught daily with fish-hooks, well baited, in the provision hold, for the ship was infested with them, and served up at the captain's table; the sight of them alone, took off the keen edge of my appetite.'[41] Smith was right that the rats lived off the best provisions and thus could provide a good meal, and it was not uncommon for seamen to cook and eat rats to supplement their rations: what was unusual was serving them at the captain's table.

The bad weather of the Mediterranean worsened as soon as they passed the Strait of Gibraltar. In the Bay of Biscay they met a merchant ship flying the American flag upside down as a distress signal. Parsons, with no great regard for Americans and less for their skill at navigation, dubbed the commander of the vessel 'Captain Corncob'. He hailed the *Carmen* with the news that they had a leak and were sinking. When he requested a boat, Captain Selby offered to accompany the ship into port, as he thought the sea too rough for a boat. It became clear that the crew were panicking, so Smith volunteered to take a carpenter across in a boat to see what could be done. On boarding the American ship Smith was greeted by the captain, as Parsons sardonically recorded:

'I guess you are the captain of that there Britisher,' said Jonathan Corncob . . . 'and I take your conduct as most particularly civil.' 'I am only a passenger in yon frigate, and am called Sir Sidney Smith; but let your carpenter show mine where he thinks the leak is, and I shall be glad to look at your chart.' 'You shall see it, Sidney Smith (we do not acknowledge titles in our free country);' – and Jonathan [a name for an American] unrolled a very greasy chart before Sir Sidney. 'I do not see any track pricked off. What was your longitude at noon yesterday? and what do you think your drift has been since that time?' 'Why, to tell you the truth, Sidney Smith, I 'av'n't begun to reckon yet; but mate and I was about it when the gale came on. I think we are about here.' And Jonathan Corncob covered many degrees with the broad palm of his hand. 'Mate thinks we are more to the eastward.' This convinced Sir Sidney, that he rightly guessed, that the man was lost. . . . The carpenter, by this time, had diminished the leak; and Sir Sidney, giving Captain Corncob the bearings and distance of Brest, only a day's sail dead to leeward, offered to take him and his crew on board the *El Carmen*, leaving the boat's crew to run the tarnation leaky hooker into Brest, and claiming half her value as salvage. But Jonathan gravely demurred, and calling to mate, 'Reverse our stripes, and place our stars uppermost again, where they should be,' while he kindly slapped Sir Sidney on the shoulder, calling him an honest fellow from the old country; and in the fulness of his gratitude offered him a quid of tobacco and a glass of brandy.[42]

The *Carmen* finally reached Portsmouth on 9 November, but the ship carrying duplicate dispatches from Egypt had overtaken them, as *The Times* reported: 'Yesterday morning at eight o'clock Sir SIDNEY

SMITH arrived at the Admiralty from Portsmouth. The vessel in which he came home having been charged with duplicates of the despatches which have already been published, Sir SIDNEY brings no news: he has, however, brought with him a great number of letters from our country-men in Egypt, which will no doubt prove highly acceptable to their relatives. Sir SIDNEY was attired in the Turkish dress, turban, robe, shawl, and girdle round his waist, with a brace of pistols, and appeared in good health and spirits.'[43] The flamboyant Sir Sidney found that he was also eclipsed by Nelson, who was still being fêted in London after his victory six months earlier at Copenhagen, and that people were now more concerned about the prospect of peace. The heroes were home, Napoleon had gained control of France, though he had lost Egypt, the Armed Neutrality had collapsed and the British controlled the Mediterranean. It was a stalemate, with both Britain and France exhausted by the war effort and desperately needing to recuperate. Because of continual warfare, Britain's national debt stood at £537 million, causing much suffering as taxes and the cost of living rose steadily. Food prices had nearly doubled, and bad harvests and a reduction in imports brought many of the poor to the edge of starvation. Food riots began to break out across the country in almost every major city, including London. This led to the suspension of the Habeas Corpus Act, allowing imprisonment of anyone indefinitely, without charge or trial.

Even while the fleet had been gathering off Copenhagen in March, the British government had indicated to Napoleon a willingness to negotiate a peace settlement, but as one historian commented a century ago, 'It fairly took the Ministry by surprise when, on Wednesday, the 30th of September [1801], an answer was received from Napoleon, accepting the English proposals. Previously, the situation had been very graphically, if not very politely, described in a caricature [political cartoon] by Roberts, called "Negotiation See-saw," where Napoleon and John Bull were repre-sented as playing at that game on a plank labelled, "Peace or War".'[44] For the moment, the see-saw favoured peace.

In October 1801 a provisional peace treaty between Britain and France was signed. There was rejoicing on both sides of the Channel, but it was agreed that Britain would relinquish virtually all overseas territories that had been recently annexed, including Egypt and Malta, and not just those captured from France but also ones taken from Spain and Holland. Even strategically important bases such as the Cape of Good Hope, on the main sea route to the East, were given up. In the Caribbean only Trinidad (previously Spanish) was held, while in the East Indies the former Dutch colony of Ceylon was retained. In return France agreed to recognise the neutrality of states such as Holland and Switzerland in a set of conditions designed both to appease Napoleon and curb French expansion.

In truth it was no more than a respite allowing the two opponents to draw breath before renewing the conflict, and many politicians and military men saw it as such, yet the majority of people genuinely wanted peace, and there was almost every possible shade of opinion about the treaty. For many British naval officers the peace was not welcome, since it meant being cast ashore on half-pay with little prospect of further employment, promotion or prize money, but for many ordinary seamen it was a chance to return home. For John Nicol, who had served at the Battle of the Nile, it was a time of mixed feelings:

I was once more my own master, and felt so happy, I was like one bewildered. Did those on shore only experience half the sensations of a sailor at perfect liberty, after being seven years on board ship without a will of his own, they would not blame his eccentricities, but wonder he was not more foolish. After a few days my cooler reason began to resume its power, and I began to think what should be my after pursuits . . . the thoughts of Sarah [a woman he had loved and been forced to leave ten years earlier] had faded into a distant pleasing dream. The violent desire I at one time felt to repossess her was now softened into a curiosity to know what had become of her. As I was now possessed of a good deal of pay, and prize-money due, when I received it, I went down to Lincoln to make inquiry, but no one had heard of her since I was there myself, nine years before.[45]

Finding the quest hopeless because he 'knew not in what quarter of the globe she was, or whether she was dead or alive',[46] Nicol returned to his native Edinburgh, but he already knew that his father was dead and his brothers had gone, and he found the city changed: 'I scarce knew a face in Edinburgh. It had doubled itself in my absence. I now wandered in elegant streets where I had left corn growing; everything was new to me . . . I felt myself, for a few weeks after my arrival, not so very happy. As I had anticipated, there was scarcely a friend I had left that I knew again; the old were dead, the young had grown up to manhood and many were in foreign climes . . . I could not settle to work, but wandered up and down.'[47] Yet Nicol was one of the lucky ones, because in the following months he gradually overcame his sense of alienation, found a job and married. Many other seamen spent their money all at once and were reduced to begging, since there was now no call for sailors and few could turn to another trade.

In March 1802 the treaty between France and Britain was formally ratified in what became known as the Peace of Amiens, but even before this the effects of peace were being felt. The price of food in Britain fell, and increased trade with the Continent provided greater variety. Many people, unable to visit France for so many years, flocked there as soon as they had the chance. One of these was the Francophile Henry Redhead Yorke. Like many British people, Yorke had initially supported the French Revolution in the days before it became a bloodbath. Now visiting France for the first time since 1792, he found many things had altered in a very short time. Soon after he landed he talked to a fisherman who stated that 'in no part of France had the peace of England caused more joy than at Calais, which had suffered extremely by the war, where the inhabitants were in a most deplorable condition; the young and middle-aged, to avoid being famished, had no other resource than to join the armies, which chiefly subsisted upon the plunder of foreign countries, for they had no alternative between famine and conquest'.[48] Other people had different views, and some who spoke to Yorke said that 'in their opinion the Peace was in favour of England, and when I enumerated the names of the different colonies we had restored to France they laughed at me and said, "You have taken away our commerce, and what have we taken from you?"'[49]

In Paris Yorke noted many changes, both in the appearance of the city, where many buildings had been demolished during the Revolution, and in the life of the people. He visited the Temple prison:

The place is now greatly altered . . . all the surrounding buildings have been pulled down and a large opening formed which absolutely secludes it from all immediate communication with the city. It is impossible to obtain admission into this State prison – it is rigidly guarded within and without the walls. Persons are daily conveyed there by a lettre de cachet from the Grand Inquisitor Fouché, without any preliminary examination and often without the knowledge of their friends. This is the real history of those sudden disappearances of a number of persons, which the French journalists ascribe to robbers and assassins.[50]

It was most apparent in the capital that France had become a police state, and Yorke observed that 'spies of the police prowl in every coffee house . . . no one dares now talk politics in them'.[51]

Poverty was much in evidence, and Yorke thought that conditions were much worse than in Britain: 'In France at this time there are neither parochial rates nor workhouses such as we have in England . . . no kind of provision exists which affords employment to persons who, from sickness, misfortune, or lack of employment, have been thrown out of work. Hence the poverty of a French pauper is the consummation of wretchedness; rags, filth and disease waste his constitution and destroy his body, while despair for ever settles on his soul.'[52] In contrast to the poverty, gambling dens and brothels, Yorke also found luxury goods on sale in shops.

With France in such a situation many people favoured a strong leader like Napoleon, and he was as skilful a politician as he was a general. The novelist Fanny Burney, married to a Frenchman who had escaped to Britain during the Revolution, returned to France in the spring of 1802. She stopped at a rural hamlet on the road from Calais to Paris, where she met 'two good old women [who] told us that this was the happiest day ('twas Sunday) of their lives; that they had lost *le bon Dieu* [the Good Lord] for these last ten years, but that Bonaparte had now found him! In another cottage we were told the villagers had kept their own Curé all this time concealed, and though privately and with fright, they had thereby saved their souls through the whole of the bad times!'[53] Napoleon had no respect for religion, but restoring it after its being banned by the revolutionaries was a cost-effective way of winning support. Because he was still securing his power base within France, peace with Britain would give him more time to deal with domestic concerns.

This was only the beginning, because Napoleon had ambitions to transform just about every aspect of French life in addition to extending his power well beyond the borders of France. After the horrors of the Revolution he appeared to offer a better future, and Bourrienne recorded the optimism: 'The period of the peace of Amiens must be considered as the most glorious in France's history. I exclude neither the time of the conquests of Louis XIV nor the more brilliant era of the Empire. The Consular glory was at that time pure, with only rosy expectations in prospect.'[54]

———— •◆• ————

# SIX

# HOT PRESS

We made use of the Peace, not to recruit our Navy, but to be the cause of its ruin. Nothing but a speedy battle, a complete annihilation of the Enemy's Fleets, and a seven years' Peace, can get our Fleet in the order it ought to be.

Nelson, writing to Hugh Elliot, a British
diplomat at Naples, in July 1804[1]

By the spring of 1803 it was clear that peace with France was not going to last – it was nothing more than an armed truce. France was preparing to renew the war, and yet again Britain was faced with the threat of invasion. When the Peace of Amiens was signed the year before, the First Lord of the Admiralty, Earl St Vincent, had drastically cut the navy, but now it needed to expand rapidly to meet the threat. On 8 March 1803 a message from King George III was delivered to Parliament: 'His Majesty thinks it necessary to acquaint the House of Commons, that, as very considerable military preparations are carrying on in the ports of France and Holland, he has judged it expedient to adopt additional measures of precaution for the security of his dominions.'[2] The French were claiming that they were building up military strength merely to protect their own colonies. The British did not believe them.

The very next day there began frenzied activity to prepare the laid-up naval ships for possible war and to enlist thousands of seamen. Warrants authorising press-gangs were issued in the greatest secrecy so that nobody could hide beforehand, and orders were given to ships' captains to start a hot press – a vigorous and ruthless mobilisation. To obtain extra crew, a ship's captain could send on shore a gang of trusted seamen commanded by a lieutenant or even board merchant ships, but many press-gangs were part of the Impress Service. At the Peace of Amiens, the Impress Service had been virtually dismantled, and so it was now hurriedly reinstated around the coast of Britain, with each press-gang headed by a lieutenant under a regulating captain.

Once the decision was taken to conduct a hot press, an Admiralty messenger raced to Plymouth in just thirty-two hours, arriving there early in the morning of 10 March. The news he brought led to the gates of the barracks being immediately shut, and

about 7 P. M. the town was alarmed with the marching of several bodies of Royal Marines, in parties of 12 and 14 each, with their officers, and a naval officer, armed, towards the Quays. So secret were the orders kept, that they did not know the nature of the service on which they were going until they boarded the tier of colliers [coal boats] at the New Quay, and other gangs the ships in Catwater, the Pool, and the gin-shops. A great number of prime seamen were taken out, and sent on board the Admiral's ship. They also pressed landmen of all descriptions; and the town looked as if in a state of siege . . . one press gang entered the Dock Theatre, and cleared the whole gallery, except the women.[3]

The same sort of activity occurred simultaneously at Portsmouth, where 'not a single vessel of any description, lying in the harbour, but what has been completely searched, and the men, and even boys, taken out. It is with the utmost difficulty that people living on the Point can get a boat to take them to Gosport, the terror of a press-gang having made such an impression on the minds of the watermen that ply the passage.'[4] The first few days of the hot press caused consternation and mayhem in places such as Portsmouth and Plymouth, and quickly moved further afield.

At the start of the hot press, twenty-two-year-old Lieutenant William Henry Dillon was struck with horror at being asked to work for the Impress Service in Hull. He had been in the navy for twelve years, and to him 'the news was so astounding that I was completely taken aback, as I thought it a degrading appointment. None, generally speaking, but worn-out lieutenants were employed in that Service.'[5] William Marsden, Second Secretary at the Admiralty in London, persuaded him to take up the post because 'he told me that Lord St. Vincent had changed the whole system relating to the Impress Service by nominating young and active officers to it instead of old ones'.[6] Dillon left for Hull the following day and 'had not been out of the stage[coach] one minute when I met one of my shipmates of the *Crescent*, the sailmaker [they had served together in the West Indies]. He hailed me with a cheerful countenance, but when he heard the reason for my presence in that town, he took to his heels and was out of sight in no time.'[7]

Although the Royal Navy had no problem recruiting officers, seamen were always needed, especially in times of war, and the key method of recruitment was forcing them to enlist through impressment. Other methods of recruiting, such as calling for volunteers, were much less effective. The word 'prest' came from the French word *prêter*, to lend or pay in advance. It was originally a small sum of money paid to a seaman upon recruitment, who was then said to be 'prest'. It took on a more menacing meaning when conflated with 'press', implying coercion. A group of seamen given a particular task was called a 'gang', but the press-gang – responsible for impressment – became hated and feared, and so the word 'gang' acquired sinister and criminal associations.

Impressment had its origins in a feudal society, but by the time of the Napoleonic Wars it was regarded by many people as nothing short of 'legalized slavery'[8], although others felt that impressment was an evil necessity in time of war and that the king had every right 'to compel the services of the seamen, when their element (the ocean) is invaded'.[9] Inevitably, those most opposed to it were the ones at greatest risk from being pressed. Torn from their families, men were forced into the navy with no idea how long they would serve – often until the end of a war unless they deserted, died or became unfit for service. No seaman had any guarantee of shore leave, as captains feared they would desert, which often made them more determined to run away as soon as they had an opportunity.

By law a press-gang was allowed to take only seafaring men and those associated with river craft, but they interpreted this ruling loosely and at times operated far inland. Only men between eighteen and fifty-five were supposed to be pressed, but age was difficult to prove since there were no birth certificates at this time and no system of recording births: parish registers, kept in churches, only recorded baptisms, marriages and burials. With all the difficulties of keeping impressment within the legal guidelines, any rumours of the approach of a press-gang tended to cause mass panic.

Although thousands of recruits to the navy were needed, experienced men were most valued, in particular merchant seamen. Crews of outward-bound merchant ships were exempt, as were several other categories of people, such as apprentices, some fishermen, custom-house employees and captains and mates of merchant ships, but they all had to carry a certificate of protection. Foreigners were also exempt, although Americans often found it difficult to prove their nationality. It was up to men taken by the press-gang to show they were exempt. Merchant ships returning home, even after a prolonged voyage, were targeted and their crews often cruelly depleted when boarded by the press-gangs within sight of Britain's shores.

The process of impressment was often brutal. The press-gangs snatched men from the streets, taverns and even their own homes to be taken to the Impress Service's headquarters, known as the 'rendezvous' or 'rondy' – usually a local inn. Here they were locked up until they could be transferred to a pressing tender, a small ship moored nearby. This was because until they were aboard their allotted ship, where they were asked whether they wanted to volunteer, the men were subject to civil law, not the law of the navy. Once they were asked, many did volunteer, since the only practical difference between a volunteer and a pressed man was that the volunteer was given a cash bounty for joining. Accommodation in the rendezvous and tenders tended to be cramped and filthy, conducive to the spread of diseases such as typhus. William Robinson described the conditions in which newly pressed men were held:

We were ordered down in the hold, and the gratings put over us; as well as a guard of marines placed round the hatch-way, with their muskets loaded and fixed bayonets, as though we had been culprits of the first degree, or capital convicts. In this place we spent the day and following night huddled together, for there was not room to sit or stand separate: indeed, we were in a pitiable plight, for numbers of them were sea-sick, some retching, others were smoking, whilst many were so overcome by the stench, that they fainted for want of air. As soon as the officer on deck understood that the men below were overcome with foul air, he ordered the hatches to be taken off, when day-light broke in upon us; and a wretched appearance we cut, for scarcely any of us were free from filth and vermin.[10]

Scenes of violence occurred throughout the country in the desperate attempts to escape the press-gangs. In early May, two press-gangs were attacked less than 400 yards from the Admiralty in London, the very headquarters of the Impress Service – 'two gallies, each having an Officer and press-gang in it, in endeavouring to impress some persons at Hungerford Stairs, were resisted by a party of coal-heavers belonging to a wharf adjoining, who assailed them with coals and glass bottles: Several of the gang were cut in a most shocking manner on their heads and legs, and a woman who happened to be in a [nearby] wherry was wounded in so dreadful a manner, that it is feared she will not survive.'[11] Hungerford Stairs were wooden steps leading down to the River Thames, since destroyed by the building of the Victoria Embankment.

One of the ships in the Thames that was looking to impress seamen was the frigate *Immortalité*, with Midshipman Abraham Crawford on board. He recorded that his ship was there 'to enter or impress a new ship's company as quickly as possible; the old one, which had served in the late war, being promised their discharge from the service as soon as the new crew should be completed'.[12] With the prospect of the old crew being released, 'all now was eagerness and anxiety to raise men . . . no vessel inward or outward bound escaped a search'.[13] Even with such enthusiasm it took a while to raise the new crew, and Crawford recalled that 'some time before we were complete, the ship still wanting perhaps some forty or fifty good hands, the captain learned that two Indiamen, which had just dropped down to Gravesend, had received their crews that morning'.[14] Ships of the East India Company were known for the high quality of their officers and men, in comparison with other merchant seamen, and they were well armed and capable of fending off pirates and privateers. They would have just the type of seamen that were needed. The captain of the *Immortalité* decided to send several boats full of armed men to search two East Indiamen, the *Ganges* and the *Woodford*. By the time the boats reached the sides of the ships they 'found the whole crew at quarters, armed with pikes and cutlasses, and every description of missile that the ship could supply'.[15] It was obvious that the Indiamen would not submit without a fight, and Crawford recorded what happened after the lieutenant in charge of their boats ordered his men to board the ships:

This order was more easily given than accomplished. The sides of the Indiamen were high, and everything which might aid a man in mounting had been carefully hauled in board; besides, she was terribly wall-sided [sides nearly vertical], which rendered the ascent still more difficult. The boats' crews, as they attempted to board, were thrust back by those long pikes with which the Indiamen are supplied, one of which was hurled with great force into the boat I was in, and nailed a poor fellow's foot to the bottom of the boat. Once more the lieutenant cautioned our stout opponents as to the consequences of conduct so refractory and illegal, ordering the marines in the boats at the same time to load. At length, finding every remonstrance unavailing, and every species of missile, including cold shot hurled into the boats, his patience became exhausted, and he ordered half a dozen muskets to be fired. This fire, though fatal, wounding two men mortally, had only the effect of exasperating the Indiaman's crew more and more, and rousing them, if possible, to a fiercer and still more determined resistance.[16]

The boats were ordered to move away from the ships a short distance, and a message was sent back to the *Immortalité*. There was now a stand-off, as Crawford related: 'The boats continued to row guard round the two Indiamen, but I fear not very watchfully; for towards midnight, when they were hailed, and told that they were then at liberty to search the ships, we found only a few men on board the *Woodford*, and those of a sorry description. Thus terminated this most untoward affair, fatally and unsuccessfully, and at the same time reflecting but little credit upon the men-of-war.'[17] The coroner at Gravesend gave a verdict of wilful murder against the lieutenant who had ordered the marines to fire. He was later tried but acquitted, and Crawford commented: 'In the present state of uncertainty regarding the authority under which warrants for impressment are issued, many consider they have a right to resist them; – and they do so even to the death, and, as far as I know, without ever having been punished, or even prosecuted for such resistance. It is not fair, it is not just, to impose a painful, a hateful duty upon officers – in the execution of which, should wounds or death ensue, they alone, it appears, are liable to be criminally prosecuted and punished.'[18]

Other controversial deaths had occurred during impressment a month earlier in Dorset. On 1 April the frigate *Aigle*, under the command of Captain George Wolfe, anchored off Portland, having sailed over 55 miles from his station at Portsmouth. Before it was light the following day a small boat rowed Wolfe, three of his officers, a lieutenant of marines, twenty-seven marines and a similar number of seamen to land close to the dilapidated castle on the north side of Portland. Thomas Hardy was right to call the forbidding, virtually treeless Portland the 'Gibraltar of Wessex'.[19] Rising abruptly from the sea and just 4 miles long, the rocky island was an impregnable fortress, linked only to the Dorset mainland by the immense shingle beach of Chesil Bank. Many of its men worked in the quarries that produced fine Portland building stone, as well as holy-stones* for scrubbing down decks of naval ships. These men had a fierce reputation, and in order to hide from the press-gangs, the fishermen of nearby Poole used Portland as a refuge.

Wolfe and his men marched half a mile from the castle to the village of Chiswell, where they successfully 'impressed Henry Wiggot and Richard Way, without any interruption whatsoever'[20], and these two men were placed under guard in the castle. The other inhabitants of Chiswell ran up the hill to escape and raised the alarm, pursued by the press-gang, and at the village of Easton the chief constable of the island's court leet asked the press-gang by whose authority they were on the island. They replied that they had a warrant signed by the Mayor of Weymouth, but, as they were told, Portland was a Royal Manor, whose inhabitants owed allegiance directly to the king. The mayor's jurisdiction did not extend to Portland, and so Wolfe's press-gang had no legal right to be there. This did not deter them, and they rushed down Reforne Street to confront 'the mob . . . [who were] soon reinforced by nearly three hundred men, armed with muskets, pistols, and cutlasses, which had been plundered from the transports wrecked on that coast in 1795'.[21]

The press-gang then tried to seize several men, but a scuffle broke out, and Wolfe fired his pistol into the ground, 'at which signal the Lieutenant of Marines ordered his men to fire, which being done, three men fell dead, being all shot through the head'.[22] These men, all married, were killed instantly: Alexander Andrews, a quarryman aged forty-seven, Richard Flann, also a quarryman, aged forty-two and William Lano, a twenty-six-year-old blacksmith, who had been 'in the act of cocking a musket'.[23] Two others were dangerously wounded: Richard Bennett and Mary Way, sister of the impressed man Richard Way. She was shot in the back, and on 13 April *The Times* reported that 'the ball is still in her body, and but little hopes are entertained of her recovery'.[24] Sixteen men of the press-gang were also wounded in this skirmish, nine so severely that they were discharged from the navy.

No effort was made to stop the inhabitants fleeing in all directions,

---

* Holystones were rectangular stones for scrubbing the maindeck and came in three sizes. The largest had rings fitted at each end to which ropes were attached. These were pulled to and fro across open areas. Smaller stones, called 'bibles' because of their size, were used in more confined areas by sailors kneeling down to push the stones backwards and forwards by hand. In tight corners, hand-sized stones called 'prayer books' were used. Before holystoning, the deck was wetted and sprinkled with sand, and afterwards rinsed off with sea-water.

while Wolfe's press-gang made their way dejectedly back to the castle and took on board the two men they had seized earlier. An inquest was held at Weymouth in mid-April, at which contradictory accounts of the incident were given, resulting in a verdict of wilful murder. Following this, Captain Wolfe, Lieutenant Hastings, Midshipman Morgan and Marine Lieutenant Jeffries were charged with the crime.

Mary Way died seven weeks after she was shot, and along with the other victims she was buried in the graveyard of St George's Church, a magnificent Georgian building that had been consecrated some thirty-seven years earlier. The inscriptions in the graveyard set in stone the anger felt by the Portlanders at what became known as the Easton Massacre, with that on William Lano's headstone stating that he was 'wantonly Shot by some of a Pressgang'.[25] Mary's inscription reads: 'To the Memory of MARY Daughter of JOHN and MARY WAY who was Shot by some of a Press gang on the 2nd of April 1803 And died of the Wound the 21st of May the same Year. Aged 21 Years.'[26] When Captain Wolfe and his colleagues were tried at Dorchester Assizes in the summer, a surgeon of Weymouth 'stated that a young girl [Mary Way] who had received a wound in the late tumult, declared to him before her death that Captain Wolfe was the person who had shot her'[27], but despite his evidence all the men involved 'were fully acquitted, the jury agreeing that they had merely acted in self defence'.[28]

At the other end of the country, the press-gangs during this hot press ranged as far north as the Shetland Isles in search of men, as sixteen-year-old Midshipman George Vernon Jackson described:

We were at Shields [at the mouth of the River Tyne] with other men-of-war, engaged in the impressment of men for the service. Our instructions were to spare no effort in procuring fresh hands, and we succeeded beyond our hopes. From Shields we went to Shetland, and . . . we carried off every able-bodied male we could lay our hands upon. I think the number we captured in Shetland alone amounted to seventy fine young fellows. When the ship was on the point of leaving, it was a melancholy sight; for boat-loads of women – wives, mothers, and sisters – came alongside to take leave of their kidnapped relatives. Being young at the business I was not always proof against some of the trials I encountered ashore, and often repented having made a capture when I witnessed the misery it occasioned in homes hitherto happy and undisturbed . . . These were strange times when a youngster of my age could lay violent hands upon almost any man he came across and lead him into bondage, but such was the law, and to resist it was dangerous and sometimes productive of even greater evils. There is a fine touching old song which was composed about this period illustrating the cruelties of impressment. It became a universal favourite with the poorer classes. Such an influence did this song exercise upon the people that it was forbidden to be sung in public.[29]

The song that Jackson mentioned was 'The Voyage Was Past', which told the story of a sailor taken by the press-gang just as he reaches his home after a long time at sea.

Further south, John Nicol was beginning to earn a living as a cooper in Edinburgh. He was now forty-eight, a very experienced seaman who had sailed around the world twice and seen many battles. He had also given his new wife a promise that he would not return to sea and yet, as he recorded, 'the press-gang came in quest of me. I could no longer remain in Edinburgh and avoid them. My wife was like a distracted woman, and gave me no rest until I sold off my stock in trade and the greater part of my furniture, and retired to the country. Even until I got this accomplished I dared not to sleep in my own house, as I had more than one call from the gang.'[30] Nicol moved into the countryside to Cousland, 9 miles from Edinburgh, and eventually took a job he disliked in a quarry just to survive. Even here he was not safe: 'I was becoming a little more reconciled to my lot, when the press-gang came out even to Cousland, and took away a neighbour of the name of Murray. He had a large family, and, through the interest [influence] of the minister and neighbouring gentlemen, he got off. His impressment was a great blow to my tranquillity for many months. For a long time I slept every night either in Dalkeith or Musselburgh, and, during the day, a stranger could not appear near the quarry without causing the most disagreeable sensations to me.'[31]

The whole of the north-east coast of England and Scotland was frequently raided by press-gangs, and Tyneside was a favourite target. At North Shields one gang was under the command of Lieutenant John Mitchell. On 19 April he took his men across the River Tyne to South Shields, where he was 'attacked by a Multitude of Pilots and Women, who threw a quantity of Stones and Brickbatts at him, they likewise threatened to hew him down with their Spades, which are very dangerous Weapons, they being round and quite Sharp, with Shanks of about Six feet in length, and likewise threatened to Murder him if he ever came back.'[32]

Despite the threats, his gang did in fact return on several occasions to South Shields, but never with great success. Only a week later Mitchell and his men went to South Shields early in the morning, and 'after going a short way along the [river] bank he saw two Seamen run down into the street, when he immediately pursued them and was again attacked by a Mob of Women'.[33] One of those who frequently attempted to stop the press-gang's activities was Dolly Peel, a notorious fishwife and smuggler, and a woman of great wit and humour. She was so tall that she could hide fugitives beneath her voluminous skirts. On one occasion her husband, Ralph (or Cuthbert) Peel, rushed into their home at the top of a house in Shadwell Street (now Wapping Street), right by the river, pursued by the press-gang, who forced open the door. She stopped them pushing past 'for she possessed phenomenal strength and had the muscles of a man. Thus Dolly held them at bay until her husband had contrived to make his exit through a window in the roof of the house.'[34]

The following day, 'when the party landed for a final round-up, they were accompanied by cutlass-armed reinforcements from the receiving ship, lying at Pegg's Hole, South Shields. They rushed from the boats like an invading army into Pilot Street, brandishing their weapons and impressing all remaining men young and of mature years . . . This time Ralph (Peel) was not allowed to go scot-free.'[35] Dolly managed to follow Ralph to sea and is recorded as having helped the surgeon in the warship's cockpit during battle. She died at South Shields in 1857 at the age of seventy-five, and a statue of her, unveiled in 1987, overlooks the River Tyne from close to where she lived.

Also in South Shields, the twenty-three-year-old merchant seaman John Wetherell was saying goodbye to his family before he headed back to London to join a merchantman to the West Indies. Hearing rumours of the coming of the press-gang, he hurriedly left by sea for London only to be pressed at the mouth of the River Thames by a gang from the frigate *Hussar* commanded by Captain Philip Wilkinson. The *Hussar* was part of a small squadron under the overall command of Sir Sidney Smith that was then actively boarding merchant ships to seize their crews. Wetherell had been travelling with a carpenter's certificate of protection, but to no avail. With the navy desperate for new recruits, permission had been given by government for the suspension of protections, and since there was a great need for carpenters, Wetherell was taken.

Not all the sailors were pressed men, and even at this time there were still volunteers, like the thirteen-year-old Robert Hay, who ran away from the life of a weaver in the cotton mills of Paisley in Scotland to seek his fame and fortune. He made his way to Greenock with the idea of joining a merchant ship, but he met two other boys who persuaded him that the navy offered better prospects. 'After rambling about the greater part of the day,' he recalled, 'we towards evening repaired to the naval rendezvous. Here we found a lieutenant of the navy, to whom we offered our services . . . We then underwent a surgical [medical] examination, found to be sound in body, and in less than an hour after found ourselves on board of the war vessel a mile or two from shore.'[36] It took several days for Hay's father to track down his runaway son, and as the warship had not sailed, he came on board. Hay recorded that 'at our meeting where both joy and grief were mingled I could observe in his paternal countenance a mixture of anger and pity . . . he could not refrain from shedding tears on my account. He applied with urgency to the Captain for my discharge, but it would not be obtained without advancing a sum of which alas! he was not master. "Furthermore," the Captain said, "Hands are too scarce just now . . . and hot as the press is, we cannot get a sufficient supply of seamen. Your son, it is true, will not be of much use to us for some time, but if I can judge from the cut of his jib (eyeing me as he spoke, from head to foot) we have here the makings of a smart fellow." To all further solicitations he remained inflexible.'[37]

Robert Hay would have been rated as a Boy, being under the age of eighteen. Those under the age of fifteen were Boys Third Class and those over fifteen were Second Class. Those rated Boys First Class were training to be officers. Adults who had no sea-going experience (of whom many had been pressed) were rated as Landmen, while expert sailors were rated as Able Seamen. Between these two levels of competence were the Ordinary Seamen, who had been to sea before but were not recognised as skilful sailors. This rating system was based on the level of competence of the crew member, although men could be disrated as a punishment, since it meant a drop in pay and privileges, so it was possible to have a skilled seaman rated as a Landman.

Even a few women tried to enlist, and in mid-April 1803 *The Times* reported that on 'Thursday morning a young woman, dressed as a seaman, came to one of the rendezvous in Falmouth, for the purpose of entering herself for the navy; but her sex being soon discovered, she was of course rejected. It appears that she belongs to a parish at a small distance from Falmouth, and that her attachment to a young man, who is gone into the navy (and by whom she is by child), actuated her in this extraordinary proceeding, for the sake of following him.'[38] The idea of a woman disguising herself as a sailor to find a missing lover was something that captured the popular imagination, and songs such as *William Taylor* and *The Handsome Cabin Boy*, now surviving as traditional folk songs, were composed on the theme. In fact a few women did serve in both navy and merchant vessels by passing themselves off as men, but such cases were comparatively rare.

As at the Battle of the Nile, the women on board warships were largely the wives of petty officers, but they were accompanying their husbands, not working as sailors. Just as they took no part in the working of the ship and were there contrary to Admiralty rules, so they were generally free to leave at any time. In May the frigate *Hussar*, still involved in the hot press, was off Harwich, and John Wetherell recorded in his diary that 'our Corporal of Marines . . . had his wife on board, a fine young woman. She took sick and died on board. The Boat was order'd to be mann'd next morning, her body put in a shell made by the ship's joiner, taken out to sea and sunk, at the same time the ship lay within three miles of Harwich.'[39] Not burying her on land was regarded by the crew as a grossly inhumane action on the part of Captain Wilkinson, and on 12 May Wetherell noted: 'This morning several of our Married men's wives left the ship and went on board the tender and landed in the evening at Harwich. They would not remain on board where such an unfeeling Monster commanded.'[40]

While mobilisation of the British Navy was in full swing before war was declared, in France unease increased among the British visitors. Fanny Burney wrote to her father on 6 May of her 'suspense and terror . . . from the daily menace of war'.[41] With her husband now employed in France, Fanny had the agonising decision of whether to stay with him or return to Britain before hostilities broke out. On 13 May she added a final paragraph to a letter: 'Ah, my dearest friends – what a melancholy end to my hopes and my letter. I have just heard that Lord Whitworth set off for Chantilly last night; war therefore seems inevitable; and my grief, I, who feel myself now of two countries, is far greater than I can wish to express.'[42]

That Lord Whitworth, the British Ambassador, was on his way out of France was a sign that diplomacy had failed, and it was only a matter of time before war was expected to break out. Some British visitors were preparing to leave, and one of these was John Wesley Wright, now a captain, who was still involved with the British Secret Service. He left Paris clandestinely, accompanied by an official from the British Embassy and a locked trunk. The embassy official ensured it passed customs at Dover without being searched, and it reached London unopened, with over two hundredweight of secret maps, plans and manuscripts.

During the peace, travel to France had been relatively cheap, and hundreds of people had made the journey – not just upper-class travellers with their servants, but ladies and gentlemen to see the latest fashions, many young people for whom it was the first opportunity to see France, and businessmen and merchants. With war looking more likely, wary travellers in Britain postponed their plans, but others continued to arrive in France, and the French newspapers encouraged them to stay. On 18 May 1803, only a few days after Wright had reached London, Britain declared war on France.

Many of those still in France rushed to get back home, but on the 23rd a furious Napoleon issued a decree to General Junot, one of his top aides, ordering the arrest of all British men then in France, both civilians who might be liable to military service and those already holding a commission: 'All Englishmen from the ages of eighteen to sixty, or holding any commission from His Britannic Majesty, who are at present in France, shall immediately be constituted Prisoners of War.'[43] Napoleon further insisted that 'this measure must be executed by seven this evening. I am resolved that to-night not an Englishman shall be visible in the obscurest theatre or restaurant of Paris.'[44]

The British were outraged, believing this action to be a breach of international law. Lieutenant William Dillon, who had recently moved from the Impress Service at Hull to blockade duty in the frigate *Africaine*, recorded:

On the 18th the war was declared. I believe I am correct as to the date. In the newspapers received by the Packet we were informed of Prizes being taken daily. Bonaparte was terribly annoyed at not being able to humbug us any longer, and the capture of two vessels in Hodierne Bay [Audierne Bay, south of Brest] became the subject of severe controversy, as he insisted that we had taken these vessels previous to the declaration of war. Therefore in retaliation (as he said) he laid hands upon all the English travellers and residents in France, who thought themselves safe while in possession of their passports. He did not care what he said, if it answered his purpose; the press and the *Moniteur* being solely under his control.[45]

Dillon was right – the French vessels were only seized after the declaration of war. He went on to describe the rapid sequence of events: 'Scarcely had Lord Whitworth quitted Paris before the telegraph spread the order for the detention of his countrymen, and in one night, from

Brussels to Montpel[l]ier, from Bordeaux to Geneva, all the British subjects were arrested. Travellers on the road to Spain, Germany or England, even those who were waiting at Calais for a favourable wind, shared the same fate. Some were called out of theatres, others were waked in their beds to sign a paper declaring themselves prisoners of war.'[46] The Dover to Calais packet boat, the *Prince of Wales*, was stopped from sailing back to England with its full load of passengers, and not another packet would sail between the two countries for eleven years.

By his decree, Napoleon was expecting thousands of civilians to be taken, but only about seven or eight hundred were detained. Even boys and elderly men were held, on the grounds that the British could force them into military service, but women were not included in the decree, although some were arrested. Generally, women were at liberty to go free if they wished, along with very young children, but Fanny Burney made her decision to stay in France with her husband and son.

Once war broke out, John Nicol in Scotland resented his own situation, constantly hiding from the press-gangs: 'I hoped that every month would put a period to the war, and I would be allowed to return to Edinburgh . . . When the weather was good, night after night have I sat, after my day's labour by the old windmill in Bartholomew's field, first gazing upon Edinburgh, that I dare not reside in, then upon the vessels that glided along the Forth. A sigh would escape me at my present lot . . . I was like a bird in a cage, with objects that I desired on every side, but could not obtain.'[47] He longed for peace, and the man in charge of the quarry kept him informed about the progress of the war: 'As Mr Dickson knew I was anxious for the news, he was so kind as [to] give me a reading of the newspapers when he was done. The other workmen assembled in my cottage on the evenings I got them, and I read aloud; then we would discuss the important parts together.'[48] Often heated arguments followed because Nicol, despite his situation, was a staunch supporter of the government, but the majority of the quarry men were not. Nicol and his wife would be fugitives for many years to come.

The decision to send out as many British naval ships as possible after the short-lived peace was essential for the strategy of keeping control of the seas, particularly around the coast of mainland Europe. The first task was to ensure a tight blockade of enemy ports to prevent French warships massing into large fleets capable of posing a serious threat, and to destroy those warships whenever possible. Napoleon realised that in the long term he could not succeed in his ambitions if he was still opposed by

Britain – the only solution was to neutralise the British Navy and to invade the country. With superiority at sea, France would have much greater access to trade and the chance to build a global empire, while the profits would fund his attempts to conquer Europe and the East. Even before war was declared, Napoleon was preparing plans for the invasion of Britain, and the British Navy was preparing a blockade to prevent it.

In the weeks before war broke out many British naval officers, knowing what was coming, applied to the Admiralty for posts. Sir Sidney Smith was made commodore of a small squadron to patrol and blockade ports off northern France and the Dutch coast. He was probably glad to leave behind the scandal of his involvement with Princess Caroline – the Princess of Wales, the estranged wife of the future King George IV. Caroline took a series of lovers, of whom Smith was one, and she was rumoured to be pregnant with his child, but she cast him aside for another naval lover, Captain Manby, and the relationship ended acrimoniously. In 1820 the Prince was to lose the affection of the public when he put Caroline on trial for adultery in an attempt to divorce her and then forbade her to attend his coronation, but in 1803 the public only knew that the couple were formally separated. Nelson, too, had scandalised high society by his association with Emma, but at least that relationship was enduring and happy, and now he had one of his long-term ambitions fulfilled by being given command of the Mediterranean fleet, while Admiral Lord Keith took the North Sea fleet and Admiral Sir William Cornwallis headed the Channel fleet. One officer under orders from Cornwallis was the Cornishman Sir Edward Pellew, a very experienced seaman with over thirty years' service in the navy. During the peace he had become Member of Parliament for Barnstaple in north Devon, but with the threat of war he too applied for a post and in March 1803 was appointed captain to the *Tonnant*, an 80-gun warship captured from the French at the Battle of the Nile.

After delays at Plymouth recruiting sufficient crew and fitting out the ship, Pellew set sail in early June to join the blockade of Brest. Here he received orders from Cornwallis to sail with the *Spartiate* and *Mars* to the port of Ferrol on Spain's north-western coast, where a Dutch squadron was believed to have called in on the way to the East Indies. Pellew's orders were to detain the Dutch ships and to seize or destroy any French vessels, but 'to give no interruption to any Spanish ships or vessels whilst they continue to act as a neutral Power'.[49] Although Spain was supporting Napoleon financially, the country had not yet resumed war with Britain, and so technically ports such as Ferrol were neutral and open to all shipping. At Ferrol Pellew's ships joined the *Aigle* under Captain Wolfe (sent there to gather intelligence, before facing trial at Weymouth for the murders at Portland), only to discover that the Dutch ships had slipped away the evening before. After three weeks engaged in a fruitless chase as far as Madeira, Pellew's ships returned to begin a blockade of the adjacent ports of Corunna (La Coruña) and Ferrol, where a French squadron had just arrived after leaving the West Indies on the resumption of the war.

In November the frigate *Hussar* sailed from Cornwallis's squadron off Brest to take dispatches to Pellew and join the blockade at Ferrol. Six months earlier the *Hussar* under Captain Philip Wilkinson was ordered to cease impressment on the North Sea coast and join the blockade of Brest. The seaman John Wetherell loathed the brutal Wilkinson, a 'great brave tyrannical cross unfeeling coward . . . Sodom and Gomorrah were destroyed for their wickedness and Wilkinson ought to have been in the midst of them'.[50] Typical of the class structure and snobbery of British society at this time Wetherell, the son of a whaling captain, also despised Wilkinson for being of low birth, since he was the son of a Harwich barber. British society was highly stratified, in contrast to that in France, where the Revolution had swept away the aristocracy and suppressed the middle classes. Wetherell recorded that the *Hussar* was 'stationed off the harbour mouth to break off all communications between Ferrol and Corunna. The French lay in Ferrol harbour 9 sail and in Corunna one 74 and two frigates. We used to go on shore to market frequently and have fresh beef for all the squadron.'[51] Several of the crew were also in the habit of exchanging tobacco and even their own clothing for alcohol and fruit.

At the end of the year, after the British ships had spent months on blockade duty, fierce storms inflicted serious damage, and so when the gales abated in early January 1804, Pellew risked taking shelter in Betancos Bay, between Ferrol and Corunna, which he correctly suspected was not a dangerous anchorage as the Spanish firmly believed. The French expected his ships to be driven on to shore, but instead Pellew rode out the storms and kept the enemy ships securely blockaded, while maintaining good relations with the Spanish. The British and French squadrons were 3 miles apart, and Pellew would send his men on shore to a windmill from where they could look down on Ferrol. Here they met up with their French counterparts, and such was the respect between officers that an amicable understanding was easily reached, which Pellew mentioned in a letter to Cornwallis: 'We are not permitted [by the Spanish] to go near their ships, but our look-out Lieuts meet at the Wind-Mill on a hill between the two ports – out of one window my Lieut. spies them, and out of the opposite one their [French] officer upon us. Buller proposes a Pic-Nic there with Mons. Gourdon*, as we find they dine there frequently.'[52] Sir Edward Buller was captain of the *Malta*, and it was cruelly said that he was 'even in his sober moments about as much a seaman as his grandmother'.[53]

The westerly winds that kept the French in port allowed Pellew to shelter in Betancos Bay, but when the winds turned easterly he quickly anchored his ships across the entrance to the harbour mouth to keep the French cooped up. Not only was Pellew worried about these French ships escaping, but he was also constantly afraid that a French squadron would slip out of Brest to overwhelm his small number of ships or that Nelson in the Mediterranean would be unable to contain the French in Toulon harbour, who could be an even greater threat. Apart from the anxiety of an unexpected attack, blockade duties were always tedious, and often physically demanding and dangerous. Added to this was the difficulty of obtaining adequate supplies. Ships from England were supposed to bring provisions to the blockading fleets, but frequently in winter the weather prevented this or delayed the transfer of supplies once they did arrive. Fresh water could be obtained from places on the nearby coast, but food was not plentiful there, and British seamen ended up travelling as much as 40 miles inland. In general the Spaniards were happy to allow this, although the French tried to stir up opposition.

As well as food, the blockading ships were running short of other essentials, and Pellew complained to Cornwallis that they were suffering in the wretched weather:

As we were not caulked† when commissioned, we have not a dry hammock in the ship, and what is worse the magazine becomes more damp every day, so that [gun]powder filled three days cannot be lifted by the cartridge; 1600 and odd [cartridges] have been condemned by survey – and the regular loss of above 100 weekly. Every pound of pitch in the ship has been long since expended, so that our caulkers are at stand: nor are they able to do any more than stop partial leaks. I shall hope therefore whenever relieved that we may go to a port, when the defects can be made good, otherwise this fine ship will be ruined.[54]

* Captain Adrien-Louis Gourdon.
† Caulking was the process of making a ship watertight by filling the gaps between the planks of the hull. Into these gaps, called seams, was hammered a tangled mass of tarred hemp fibres, made from shredded rope, called oakum. Over this a waterproof layer of melted pitch or resin was applied.

In early February Pellew received important dispatches from John Frere, the British minister at Madrid, warning him of a Spanish military expedition of several thousand soldiers that was to set sail from Ferrol in the next few weeks, and explaining that it was essential to prevent it because of the probable hostile intent. Pellew therefore decided to send the *Hussar* with dispatches to England, though they were to communicate first with Cornwallis off Brest and inform him of this threat. Wetherell noted that 'Sir Edward gave us orders to prepare for England with all speed. He had orders from the Admiralty to dispatch the *Hussar* home to England with all haste.'[55] Not knowing the reason for their mission, Wetherell was quite convinced that the Admiralty had issued the order because of complaints about Captain Wilkinson's brutality. The *Hussar* prepared to sail, but they were delayed by a terrific thunderstorm. Eventually the weather abated, and they set sail for England.

Donat Henchy O'Brien, an eighteen-year-old master's mate from County Clare in Ireland, expressed their excitement: 'Every heart was elated with the joyful expectation of being safely moored in a few hours in the land of liberty. Some were employed in writing to their friends and relatives; but, alas! how frail and delusive are the hopes of man!'[56] After leaving Ferrol, the *Hussar's* journey through the Bay of Biscay was marred by faulty navigation. The ship took a course too far to the east, so that just before midnight on the night of 8 February the *Hussar* struck rocks on the Île de Sein (known to the British sailors as the Saints), as Wetherell described:

The night was very dark and a little squally. Took in the royals, and were in the act of furling them when something sounded like the distant roll of a drum. All hands stood in a state of surprise for a moment and anxiously listened to hear from whence the noise proceeded, when a most dreadful crash ensued which nearly sent the masts over her bows. That was followed by another when she stuck fast . . . All hands in a state of confusion; some let go halyards, others let go sheets and braces, in fact all was terror and confusion. By this time the ship was half full of water, the pumps were rattling, boatswain's mates roaring, ship striking, sails flapping, and officers bawling, which formed a most dismal uproar. At last some person on the forecastle saw a large rock under the bows quite above the water.[57]

In order to try to attract assistance, Wetherell recorded that they 'fired minute guns and rockets until daylight made its welcome appearance and then Oh,—horrid! All round as far as we could see from the deck was sharp ragged black rocks.'[58] Wetherell thought that their course had been disputed by the officers on board, and that Captain Wilkinson had insisted this course should be followed in a death wish to destroy the ship and crew. The fact they were saved, Wetherell believed, was because 'kind heavens protected us from his horrid design and safely landed us in the midst of our open enemies, as a place of refuge and deliverance from the hands of oppression'.[59]

They were lucky to be wrecked on the edge of an inhabited island, but a story instantly spread that the island was full of French troops, and so some of the crew and marines managed to get on shore and marched to the fishing settlement, terrifying the few inhabitants by this invasion. Wetherell described that they found the house of the governor and asked a young boy where he was:

The boy burst out crying and said, 'You will kill my Father and my Mother and then take me away to England.' 'No, my good boy,' says Smithson [a seaman who spoke French]; 'Your Father nor yet any soul in the town shall suffer the least harm from any of our shipwrecked officers or men. All we want is to see your Father, so that he may instruct us how to act in regard to lodging our men on shore.' At last the boy took Smithson as interpreter . . . into the next apartment where sat an elderly lady weeping. 'Where is the governor?' says Smithson. 'Under the bed,' says the woman, 'but pray spare his life.'[60]

The governor emerged from his hiding place and said that no lodgings were available but they could take refuge in the church. As he had orders to report any enemy ships, he advised them to take possession of the boats in the harbour, about thirty in all, and to save as much food as possible from the wrecked *Hussar*. Wetherell reported that with difficulty they managed to salvage 'bags of bread beef pork cheese butter candles grog tea sugar, in short everything that was not damaged'[61], carrying it all to the safety of the church. The next day it was decided to prepare the fishing boats for their escape before French troops made an appearance. According to Wetherell, 'we ransacked the town, took all the sails we could find, which they mostly used for their beds, and tubs bottles pitchers, or any vessel we thought any use to carry water'.[62] Next they set fire to the *Hussar* and 'destroyed everything we thought of any use to the enemy. As for her magazines they were full of water. All the guns were loaded and double shotted on our first leaving Ferrol. We hove all the arms over the side, and finding the fires burning furiously . . . we all started on shore and went up to the town.'[63]

In the evening they left the island in boats belonging to both the *Hussar* and the fishermen, to whom 'bills of exchange were given to the full amount of their value upon the English government'.[64] They intended reaching one of the British warships cruising off Brest, but by six in the morning 'the wind shifted round to the N.W. followed by a heavy squall of hail and constant lightning followed by dreadful crashes of thunder. The gale kept still increasing, the sea rose in entire confusion thro' the sudden change of wind, and our sails all blew away . . . We were one minute in total gloomy fog so thick we could not see one of our dispersed fleet, and the next minute wrapt in flames, as it were, by the continual lightning.'[65] Captain Wilkinson in his boat was picked up by the battleship *Magnificent*, but the weather was so bad that the remaining boats were forced to make for Brest harbour. The men, 'almost perishing and starved from the fatigues and sufferings of the night'[66], were taken prisoner on board the French warship *Alexandre*. In six weeks' time and 18 miles to the north, the *Magnificent* would also be wrecked on rocks.

As a prisoner on board the *Alexandre* in Brest harbour, O'Brien was impressed by his initial treatment, noting that the French 'gave each of my men a glass of liquor, and ordered breakfast for them, with every thing else that was necessary to recruit exhausted nature, and to console them under their sufferings and misfortunes. The poor fellows were in a most deplorable state, shivering and shaking like aspen leaves: some of them were so worn out with fatigue, hunger, and the extreme severity of the weather, that they could scarcely articulate when spoken to.'[67] The French admiral addressed them: 'Be of good courage, my men. Your confinement in France will not be long, and as it is the laws of our two nations to hold fast all prisoners at this present time, my duty to my nation compels me to transfer you to some place of confinement as prisoners of war.'[68] They could hardly imagine that most of them would remain prisoners in France for the next ten years.

In late February the crew of the *Hussar* set off from Brest on a long and arduous march of 500 miles across France to their prison depot at Givet.* This was a fortified town on the left bank of the River Meuse overlooked by the substantial fortress of Charlemont high on the cliffs above. Many prisoners-of-war came to be held in fortresses and walled towns on this

---

* Also known as Little Givet. Great Givet was on the other side of the river.

eastern side of France, at places such as Valenciennes, Givet, Verdun, Bitche and Besançon. These fortified strongholds were no longer needed to protect France, because Napoleon had pushed his frontier much further east by invading neighbouring countries. At the time of Napoleon's first abdication in 1814 there were over sixteen thousand foreign prisoners in France, about three-quarters of whom were sailors, most from the actions of French privateers capturing merchant vessels and also from naval vessels being shipwrecked, especially during constant close blockade duties on the dangerous Atlantic coast.

Conditions for prisoners depended very much on local circumstances, such as the gaoler in charge and the wealth of individual prisoners. For poorer prisoners, some money was handed out by relief funds administered by charities, such as the Lloyd's Patriotic Fund in London. From the outbreak of war in May 1803, the gentlemen civilian prisoners, known as *détenus* ('detained people'), were held on parole wherever they wished to live, giving their word of honour, *parole d'honneur*, not to escape. As they were illegally held, many civilians did not regard this parole as a moral obligation and so attempted to escape. Consequently, in November there was an order that the upper-class *détenus* should be held at Verdun, on parole, and the rest elsewhere. Verdun, the prison where military and naval officers were held, was on the left bank of the Meuse, like Givet, which was further to the north.

As well as the illegal detention of civilians, some seamen were kept prisoner contrary to accepted wartime rules, and one such was Lieutenant William Dillon. Having joined the frigate *Africaine* after his press-gang work in Hull, he became involved in the blockade of the Dutch port of Hellevoetsluis near the Hook of Holland. In July he was sent with dispatches from Admiral Keith to the Dutch commodore under a flag of truce, a convention recognised by all nations. He was asked to wait for a reply from the Dutch government, and after eight days was given an answer to the dispatch and told he was at liberty to leave, at which point the crew from a nearby French frigate, the *Furieuse*, boarded his unarmed boat and took him and his crew captive.

Towards the end of 1803 Dillon was taken to Verdun, where he would remain for nearly four years. He was the first naval officer to arrive at this prison, but was soon joined by others from captured or wrecked vessels, such as the officers of the frigate *Hussar*. Another early arrival was Captain Jahleel Brenton, originally from Rhode Island in America, but serving in the British Navy. His frigate, the *Minerve*, had grounded off

Cherbourg harbour in thick fog, and the entire crew was taken prisoner, most of whom were sent to Givet.

With both officers and the civilian *détenus* present at Verdun, many with their wives and children and often lodging in the town, the place was unlike any of the other prisons and developed into a microcosm of English society, with schools, theatricals, clubs, hunting, gambling and horse-racing much in evidence. One Verdun prisoner commented that 'not only a hare hunt, and consequently a tally ho club, but racing was among the English amusements . . . A jockey club was formed. Every midshipman was becoming a horseman, every sailor a groom.'[69] The fortunes of the French citizens of Verdun rose greatly with the arrival of these prisoners with money. James Choyce, born in Finchley, had been a seaman on merchant ships for many years, but in March 1804 he was captured in the Atlantic by a French privateer. On his long march of over 1000 miles to Sarrelibre prison, he and his fellow-prisoners were held for several days at Verdun, where he observed the character of the place:

At last we drew near to Verdun, and when still some miles away we met many Englishmen, some on foot, some on horseback, and some in carriages with livery servants behind them; but never a word had they for us – not even so much as to say, 'Countrymen, we pity your condition.' There were such a number of them I thought half London had come to Verdun. When we got within sight of the town we met another Englishman . . . We enquired of him the meaning of meeting so many Englishmen on the road, and he told us they were some of those who had come to France before the war, some to spend their own money and some, no doubt, that of their creditors*, and that when war broke out Buonaparte had laid an embargo on them all and sent them to Verdun as prisoners of war. They were only allowed to leave the town when given a passport by the general; and that all those we had seen were going to some races about five or six miles away which were much patronized by Lord Yarmouth and many of his friends. On entering Verdun we saw many of our countrymen about, some as complete dandies as one would see in Bond Street or the piazzas of Covent Garden.[70]

Even among prisoners-of-war held in Republican France, the British class structure remained unbroken.

---

* France was a favourite destination for those fleeing the threat of the debtors' prison.

# SEVEN

———•◆•———

# INVASION FLEET

Does haughty Gaul invasion threat?
    Then let the louns beware, Sir.
    There's wooden walls upon our seas,
    And volunteers on shore, Sir.

Poem by Robert Burns[1]

Some prisoners had travelled great distances by sea before even reaching France, having been captured in the Far East or the West Indies, because as well as the close blockade of Europe to keep the ships of the French and their allies in port, another strand of British strategy was the recovery of colonies that had been relinquished as part of the Peace of Amiens. This was intended to increase the British trading empire at the expense of the French, and out of all the colonies the most lucrative were those in the West Indies – the sugar islands. The problem was that few ships could be spared, and when war was declared in May 1803 the task of recapturing the islands fell to Samuel Hood. At this time Hood was a commissioner in Trinidad, which had remained a British colony, and dispatches arrived appointing him commodore and commander-in-chief in the West Indies. He was responsible for a vast swathe of islands stretching over 800 miles from Trinidad in the south, off Venezuela, to as far north as the Virgin Islands. The small force at his disposal consisted of two battleships, the *Centaur* and *Blenheim*, six frigates and a handful of smaller vessels and troop transports. With this he was supposed to patrol the islands, protect British shipping and retake the lost colonies, starting with St Lucia.

In the event, the recapture of many islands was accomplished fairly rapidly. St Lucia was attacked on 21 June and taken in two days, and Tobago was secured shortly afterwards. These two islands had been occupied by the French, but now Hood turned his attention to those colonies in Guyana that had been restored to the Dutch, and by September Demerara, Essequibo and Berbice became British possessions. Further to the north-west, Commodore Loring's ships were blockading the ports of Cape François and St Nicholas Mole, the last footholds the French had on the island of Hispaniola. Just before the Peace of Amiens, Napoleon had revoked the emancipation of slaves and reintroduced slavery in the French colonies. His expedition against the former slaves in Hispaniola had been a dismal failure, though, and it was now cornered in the two blockaded ports. Squeezed between the British at sea and the black armies on land, some French escaped but most eventually surrendered to the British. By the end of 1803 nearly all the French had left the island, and on 1 January 1804 it became the Free Black Republic of Haiti.

Now the French had only two major naval bases left in the Caribbean: Guadeloupe and Martinique. Napoleon realised that the French colonies in the West Indies were expensive, and it was becoming almost impossible to keep control of them, particularly with Britain dominating the sea lanes. This also applied to the Louisiana territories on mainland America, which he had bought from Spain in 1800. These territories covered a vast area of over 800,000 square miles, land that Napoleon sold to President Jefferson for around $15 million in April 1803 – an acquisition that doubled the area of the United States. With interest costs on the payments, the price finally rose to just over $27 million, but even this only amounted to around five cents an acre. Since Napoleon knew it would be extremely costly to defend if the Americans were determined to take the territories by force, it is debatable who made the most out of the deal, but it gave Napoleon a substantial boost to his war chest in Europe.

The French islands of Guadeloupe and Martinique acted as shelters for numerous privateers that preyed on British merchant ships, capturing valuable cargoes and forcing British Navy ships to be diverted to escorting convoys. It was now the responsibility of the ships in Hood's squadron to patrol the area, capture or destroy privateers, and protect the merchant fleets, and his small force was badly stretched. Realising that if he could set up an efficient blockade of Martinique it would curtail the actions of the privateers and prevent supplies reaching the French garrison, Hood decided on an unusual course of action – to capture Diamond Rock.

Patrolling the southern side of Martinique, where the two main ports of St Pierre and Fort Royal (known to the French as Fort de France) were located, he realised that the rock on the south-east of the island was in an ideal position to control the main shipping route. This was because the prevailing currents and winds determined that the easiest way to approach both ports, but particularly Fort Royal, was to sail within sight of Diamond Rock.

This rock, about a mile off Martinique, rises to a height of 574 feet and is roughly square, with sides about 400 yards long. As Hood soon discovered, the only landing spot was on the western side, and even here access was very difficult. It was a natural fortress, surrounded by sea, and he considered that 'thirty riflemen will keep the hill against ten thousand . . . it is a perfect naval post'.[2] Men were landed on 7 January 1804 to establish the first base and begin the task of fortifying the island. James Maurice, first lieutenant of Hood's flagship, the *Centaur*, volunteered to command the landing party, which Midshipman John Donaldson described:

A working party of fifty seamen and twenty-five marines . . . with fourteen days' provisions, were landed on the Diamond Rock. As the party was to keep the launch completely armed with her 24-pounder carronade, she was secured at the only landing-place, and the gun mounted on a projecting point, commanding this little cove. Immediately opposite the landing-place a very large cave was discovered, in which the forges were erected, and the carpenters and other artificers established their workshops; indeed it was so capacious, that it contained the whole party and material for the first night. The interior of this cave, generally with the whole rock, being grey limestone, was very dry. From the roof were suspended numerous stalactites, which made a most brilliant appearance when the forge and other lights were burning; added to which, the mirth and fun of the party at getting on shore after long confinement on board, and our very novel employment of fitting out such a nondescript vessel as his Majesty's sloop the Diamond Rock, made this evening pass off very cheerfully; and at the next dawn our party entered most zealously into the various duties they had to do, so very different from what they had lately been accustomed to.[3]

With no easy paths to the summit, they also began the essential task of fixing safety ropes and rope ladders at the most difficult points. Apart from the danger of falling off, there was an additional hazard from a deadly poisonous snake, the fer-de-lance, with which the rock was infested. Many of the men who lost their lives on the rock died from snakebite. Other caves were also found, but they needed work to make them habitable. Bales of hay were burnt to drive away the bats before the accumulated guano could be shovelled out and then the caves offered shade from the fierce Caribbean sun and shelter from storms and hurricanes. Midshipman Donaldson noted that 'a number of small dry caves and openings at the base of the rock were selected by the seamen for suspending their hammocks, and forming themselves into messes, while the officers were in tents, pitched on the flattish part of the ground, containing about three quarters of an acre'.[4] Food, gunpowder and ammunition were supplied to the rock by boats in fair weather, and it was found that water also had to be brought in as the few springs were totally inadequate for the needs of the garrison. In time, tanks were constructed for water storage.

Gradually the defences of Diamond Rock were organised, with two 18-pounder guns on the top, a 24-pounder halfway up, and two more 24-pounders just above sea-level, as well as boats, one of which had a 24-pounder carronade, that were used to intercept passing ships. Getting the guns into position on the rock required superb engineering skills, particularly for the ones on the summit. Here a platform was cleared by blasting and holes were bored in the rock to secure the two guns. The operation to transport these guns to the top of the rock began in early February. A cable was rigged from the mainmast of the *Centaur* to the top of the cliff, which itself was some way below the summit. A cannon was hung in a sling from a pulley block riding on that cable to take the majority of the weight, and another rope attached to the cannon was used to haul it to the top of the cliff. When everything was in place, Donaldson said that

the word was given at the capstan *to heave round*; and to all the inspiring tunes the band could play, away marched the first gun up its tremendous and perilous journey of seven hundred feet from the level of the sea, and four hundred feet horizontally from the ship. The men at the capstan were relieved every hour; and commencing at half-past ten A.M., the gun was landed at the upper end of the stream-cable at five o'clock P.M., having been seven hours in heaving him up to the first landing-place, when the party on shore parbuckled him up to his berth on the top of the rock with three cheers . . . The next day they began on board the ship earlier, and the second gun was got up about three P.M., by the same means as the first: but the men were nearly nine hours at the capstans, in consequence of the wind blowing very fresh this day, causing the recoil of the waves from the base of the rock to be so powerful, that the ship became unsteady, swinging the gun at such a fearful rate, that three times the end of the stream-cable was cast off from the ship, and the gun remained suspended from the rock. Indeed, they almost despaired on board of getting it up, but fortunately they did succeed, as the gun was scarcely landed, when one of the cables which held the ship was discovered severely cut by the rocks.[5]

During this operation the *Centaur* and the rock itself were very vulnerable to attack by the French, because the shallow waters left the British ship little room to manoeuvre against gunboats, and being anchored so close to the rock would have made escape difficult. The French missed their chance, though, and were generally slow to react to Hood's invasion of the rock, probably because they did not believe what was happening. When the British interest in Diamond Rock was first noticed by the French, the governor of Martinique, Vice-Admiral Louis-Thomas Villaret de Joyeuse, had ordered the repair of the road from Fort Royal to the coast opposite the rock, in preparation for establishing a gun battery. The black population of Martinique favoured the British and were already secretly selling fresh food to the garrison of Diamond Rock, as well as providing information. At the end of January the British were informed that an engineer and his men had arrived to set up the battery, and so a raiding party was sent on shore and captured him and three of his men without a shot being fired. After further raids on the area the French abandoned attempts to threaten the rock from the coast of Martinique.

The defences on Diamond Rock proved very successful, as Midshipman Donaldson related:

About four days after, Sir Samuel Hood made a signal to the rock to try the range of the 18-pounders, which was done, and found to command the passage between the rock and the main island so effectually, that no vessel could attempt it without great risk; and from the great height of the guns above the horizon, the shot were carried to such a distance, that vessels passing the rock on the outside, or great channel between Martinique and St. Pierre, were obliged to keep so far off the land, that the winds and strong westerly currents would not let them fetch into Port Royal Bay. Thus the object of taking possession of the Diamond Rock fully answered the purpose intended.[6]

The administration of Diamond Rock had to be put on a proper footing, with a permanent commander. Impressed by the exertions of Lieutenant Maurice, Hood promoted him to that post, and on 7 February reported to the Admiralty:

In the singular situation of the Diamond, so close to the enemy's shore . . . I thought it right a superior command to a Lieutenant should be held, and have, in consequence of the very zealous conduct of Lieutenant Maurice, first [lieutenant] of the *Centaur*, in arranging its works since the commencement of hostilities, given him an acting order as Commander and one hundred men for the present establishment of the *Fort Diamond* as a sloop of war, including the Rock, by which warrant officers will be useful for the security of the stores, etc., with a Lieutenant to command the vessel when she might leave the Rock on any service. A Purser will also very much facilitate the arrangement, and the Surgeon will superintend a small hospital for thirty men or, if necessary, a few more, in any casualties or bad fevers from the ships, and which will allow me to do away totally [with] the hospital at Barbados which is not half so healthy. I hope their Lordships will approve this measure which will be executed with little expense and may save thousands to the country, independent of its utility in consequence to the enemy and protection of the trade passing this channel.[7]

In order to circumvent the administrative problems of manning an offshore rock as a captured enemy ship, Diamond Rock was treated as if it was an appendage of one of the ship's boats stationed there. This boat was commissioned as the sloop *Diamond Rock* by the Admiralty (changing the name from Hood's *Fort Diamond*), but this was a technicality – the boat was later captured by the French, and was merely replaced by another without any effect on the rock's status. In time, the technicalities were forgotten and the rock itself came to be known as the 'Sloop Diamond Rock'.

The hospital was very successful, and Donaldson described how it was set up: 'The . . . cave, on the east side of the rock, was built up in front to the height of three stories, and converted into a most excellent and well-aired hospital, (where the sick and wounded were sent, instead of conveying them to Barbadoes or Antigua) amply supplied, after we left it, with a good medical staff, and every comfort for such an establishment.'[8] Garrison duties on the rock were popular with sailors. It was regarded as a healthy place, the men enjoyed fresh food, and there appears to have been some fraternisation with the black female population on the nearby coast of Martinique. Visitors from passing British ships were a welcome distraction, and one of these was Midshipman George Vernon Jackson. After his spell of impressing men in the Shetland Isles, the frigate in which he served escorted a convoy of merchant ships to Barbados and then cruised through the islands looking for privateers. This visit to the rock left a lasting impression on Jackson: not from admiration of the skill of the sailors who had managed to occupy it, nor of the insight of Hood, who had first seen its strategic potential, but because it was on the rock that he first tried smoking a pipe and did not like it, as he recalled:

One of the Lieutenants at the Rock insisted on trying to make me a disciple of the 'fragrant weed', and failed most disastrously in his kind intentions. I became so horribly ill, and took such a dislike to him, and tobacco, and the place in consequence, that I never think of them without a qualm. Perhaps I lacked energy to persevere and conquer, but I have never touched tobacco since, and perhaps am all the better for it. From being considered a filthy indulgence, it has reached the character of a gentlemanly habit, so I must not abuse 'what all the world approves.' A long way off, and in the open air, I do not mind it much, and even this is a great admission to make. There are some young fellows I know who, when they come to see me, are sure to have a stale pipe in their pockets, and I can scent them afar off; but they assure me the more beastly a pipe looks and smells, the nicer it is to smoke. So much for taste.[9]

On board navy ships smoking was allowed below decks only in the galley, and opportunities to smoke on deck were infrequent, especially in bad weather, so most sailors chewed tobacco rather than smoked it in clay pipes. The increased freedom to smoke on the rock would have been an added attraction to some sailors.

Once the garrison was self-supporting, bringing in supplies and water in its own boats, Hood was eager to reap the benefit of this permanent blockade post and took the *Centaur* to prey on French shipping among the other islands. Seeing the ship leave, the French put together a hasty plan to attack the rock before the *Centaur* should return, and four boats full of soldiers were launched. The sailors rowing these boats knew that the currents would make the attack all but impossible, and everyone involved viewed the whole plan as ill-conceived and suicidal. Exhausted by rowing out from the coast and into position for landing at the one accessible spot, the men found that they could not resist the strong current, which swept them past the rock and out to sea, though they did eventually get back to Martinique safely. Fortunately for them the attack was at night, and the garrison only heard about it several days later: in daylight they could easily have sunk the boats. After this ignominious failure the French on Martinique abandoned all thoughts of dislodging the British and appealed for assistance from France. With visibility of up to 40 miles from the summit, the garrison could intercept any shipping in the vicinity and fire on those passing close by – over the next few months this blockading rock would continue to be an irritation to the French on Martinique and a constant humiliation to the naval administration in France.

While Samuel Hood in the West Indies was making the best of limited resources, a great deal of effort was expended by the British Navy in blockading the enemy ports of Europe to prevent the terrifying prospect of Napoleon invading Britain. Most closely watched were those ports across the Channel, in easy reach of England's shores. Before the peace Napoleon's soldiers could not be spared for such an enterprise, but just as Britain welcomed the respite from financing allies on the Continent, so France was relieved of the burden of actively defending its borders. Gradually over one hundred thousand troops were moved to camps concentrated on the French coast around Calais and Boulogne, as little as 25 miles from the beaches of Kent. Although packed into a small area to minimise the time and effort of embarking the troops on transport ships, the military encampments nevertheless spread along 75 miles of coastline and were soon visible from the shores of Kent. While the French soldiers were kept occupied with training and drilling to defuse the general air of suspense, a huge flotilla of landing craft was also accumulating that seemed especially threatening. Midshipman Abraham Crawford of the British frigate *Immortalité* was patrolling the English Channel in the summer of 1803 and observed the situation:

The flotilla meant for the invasion of England began to assemble at Boulogne – Bonaparte was loud and boastful in his threats of what he should perform – and the whole French nation seemed confident that at length the conquest and humiliation of their hated rival was about to be achieved; all seemed awakened and inspired by the energy and ever-active mind of their chief. From Brest to Boulogne he inspected all that was in progress, and

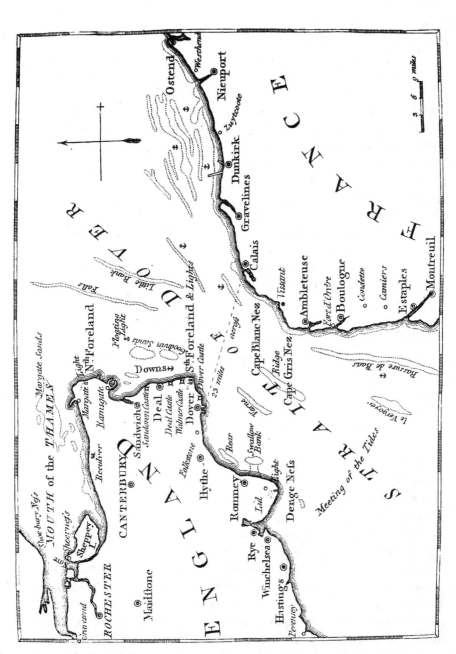

Map of the English Channel and the Downs anchorage

wherever he appeared, his presence inspired new life and animation. Boulogne was the grand rendezvous for the flotilla and army of invasion, and he stopped there a few days to trace the sites of the camps, and to give directions about enlarging and improving the contiguous harbours of Vimereux and Ambleteuse.[10]

Napoleon was hoping to amass two thousand boats to carry his invading army across to England, but the British Navy stood in the way, and only temporary dominance of the Channel by French warships could ensure that the invasion stood a chance. What was needed was French control of the sea between Britain and France for a few days – Napoleon boasted that all he needed was a few hours: 'I know not, in truth, what kind of precaution will protect her [England] from the terrible chance she runs. A nation is very foolish when it has no fortifications and no army to lay itself open to seeing an army of 100,000 veteran troops land on its shores. This is the masterpiece of the [French invasion] flotilla! It costs a great deal of money, but it is necessary for us to be masters of the sea for six hours only, and England will have ceased to exist.'[11] Now that the possibility of invasion was concrete, something close to hysteria gripped the British people and government.

The French troops were trained, experienced and inspired by their generals: they were of the same high standard as the men of the British Navy. The British Army at this time, though, was badly organised and inexperienced compared with Napoleon's troops. Even with the impetus of fighting to save their homeland and backed by the volunteer militias drawn from the civilian population, the British troops were not likely to prove a match for the French. The British government still relied on the navy as the foremost protection against invasion, and serious plans for fortifying the coast against invasion were not put into effect until the autumn of 1804, most of which would take years to complete. In the short term, when the danger of invasion was greatest because Napoleon had no distractions elsewhere on the Continent, Britain was totally dependent on the 'wooden walls' of its navy.

Volunteers were needed for the local militias, but it was feared that many working-class men were sympathetic to Napoleon's invasion plans. An address to 'English Day Labourers' tried to alarm them by claiming that Napoleon 'gives his soldiers leave to ravish every woman or girl who comes in their way, and then – to cut her throat. The *little children* perish (of course) by hunger and cold, unless some *compassionate* soldier shortens their misery by his bayonet . . . If you will not hazard your lives to preserve your wives, daughters, boys, and sweethearts, from such a dreadful fate, then refuse to take up arms; grumble at the laws about Militia, Supplementary Militia, Army of Reserve, and Army in Mass; look out for the French gun-boats, and hail them to the shores of Britain.'[12]

The Admiralty was closely monitoring the effects of the measures it had already taken. The rapid blockade of European ports had won a breathing space that had been used to prepare more ships for sea and increase the effectiveness of the navy. Everything possible was being done to prevent the French gaining control of the Channel, and ships were deployed to continually harass the accumulation of the invasion fleet at Boulogne, with various plans put forward to achieve its destruction. On the French side, though, measures were being taken to protect their invasion vessels, as Midshipman Crawford detailed:

The whole line of coast from Calais to Havre being strengthened, all the old defences were augmented, and new ones sprang up wherever they were found to be useful or necessary. On our part we gave them all the interruption that we could, and, besides bombarding the towns of Tréport, Dieppe, St. Vallery en Caux, Fecamp, and Havre, in company with the *Sulphur* bomb [vessel], we were constantly engaged in harassing and annoying the men employed on the new works. These new batteries, or towers, they appeared particularly anxious to complete. They were intended for the further defence of the bay of Boulogne, and were situated, one at the eastern extremity of the bay, one in the centre immediately at the entrance to the harbour, and the third off Point D'Alpreck. On these a number of workmen were actively employed day and night, whilst we lost no opportunity of retarding their operations.[13]

The whole coastline around Boulogne was the scene of a constant war of attrition, as the British Navy did what they could to prevent the build-up of the French invasion flotilla. One incident that occurred around the same time as Hood's capture of Diamond Rock was typical of hundreds of small actions in this area, and was described by Crawford:

Some night in January, 1804, when the *Immortalité* was again off Boulogne, and at anchor, her barge, under the command of the first lieutenant, was sent in-shore, towed by the *Archer*, gunbrig. I am not sure that they had any definite object when they left the ship – most likely it was to observe whether anything was moving alongshore, and to *pick* up whatever they could. They had not been gone an hour when a brisk fire of musketry and the report of a few guns was heard inshore. The firing did not last many minutes, and we remained in darkness and uncertainty as to its cause for some time. In an hour, however, the brig and boat returned, bringing with them a French lugger, a small schuyt [Dutch flat-bottomed boat] laden with gin, and a dogger [two-masted fishing boat] in ballast. All three had sailed together from Calais early in the day, bound for Boulogne, and were met with farther off-shore than they calculated upon. After an exchange of musketry and a few shot, it being nearly calm, the barge shoved off from the brig, and, boarding the lugger, carried her after a slight resistance, two of her crew only having been wounded; the barge had not a man touched. The lugger was to have formed one of the flotilla, and was commanded by an *enseigne de vaisseau*\*; she mounted two guns – a twenty-four pounder forward, and one of twelve pounds aft. Besides her crew, she had twenty-five soldiers on board; and there were also a few embarked in the schuyt and dogger; making the number of prisoners amount altogether to fifty.[14]

The conflict off Boulogne was not as one-sided as would appear from this incident, because gradually the French found more effective – though very costly – ways of protecting ships and boats on their way to the rendezvous of the invasion fleet. Usually these vessels sailed close to the coast, which slowed their progress but allowed artillery batteries on the shore to protect them. This made attacks increasingly hazardous for the British, as Crawford recorded:

In the month of February we were again off Boulogne, when we had several sharp bouts with the batteries and flotilla. On the 8th, I think it was, we were hotly engaged, with short intervals, from noon until half-past five. During the day's work we had a marine killed, two midshipmen, the captain's clerk, and three or four men wounded. A good many shot hulled the ship, the mainyard was shot through, and the sails and rigging a good deal cut. Several of the enemy's vessels were on shore; but as they were all flat-bottomed, drawing very little water, and never ventured to move from port to port, except with a leading wind inclining off the land, they were in this, as in almost all

* This was the lowest rank of commissioned officer in the French Navy, roughly equivalent to a midshipman. The next rank was *lieutenant*. Above this was the *capitaine de frégate*, who had less than three years' seniority and was subordinate to a *capitaine de vaisseau*, the equivalent of a senior captain in the British Navy. From *capitaine*, French officers were promoted to *contre-amiral* (rear-admiral), *vice-amiral* (vice-admiral) and then *amiral* (admiral).

other cases, enabled to stop the shot-holes when the tide ebbed sufficiently, and float them again at high water. In moving alongshore, the Flotilla was invariably accompanied by a brigade of horse-artillery specially organized for that purpose; and as they were all covered and protected by numerous batteries and musketry from the beach, any attempt by the [British] boats to destroy them, or bring them off, must have been attended with a wasteful sacrifice of life.[15]

The Admiralty began to consider more unusual methods of attack and turned to the inventor Robert Fulton, an American from Pennsylvania who had spent much of his youth in England. In 1798 he had been employed in France to build an experimental submarine, and this vessel, the *Nautilus*, was launched in May 1800. It underwent a number of trials, which were relatively successful, but the vessel was slow and difficult to manage when fully submerged. In 1802 Monsieur St Aubin, an official in Paris, published a letter giving an account of this *bateau plongeur**, as the French called it:

In making his experiments at Havre, Mr. Fulton not only remained a whole hour under water with three of his companions, but held his boat parallel to the horizon at any given depth. He proved the compass-points as correctly under water as on the surface; and that while under water, the boat made way at the rate of half a league [1½ miles] an hour, by means contrived for that purpose . . . It is not twenty years since all Europe was astonished at the first ascension of men in balloons: perhaps in a few years they will not be less surprised to see a flotilla of Diving-boats, which, on a given signal, shall, to avoid the pursuit of an enemy, plunge under water, and rise again several leagues from the place where they descended! . . . What will become of maritime wars, and where will sailors be found to man ships of war, when it is a physical certainty, that they may every moment be blown into the air by means of a Diving-boat, against which no human foresight can guard them?[16]

St Aubin's letter was as much propaganda as it was accurate reporting, because there were still serious problems with Fulton's submarine that were mainly to do with its method of propulsion. This was by means of a propeller attached to a gearing mechanism turned by hand by the men

* The English name for a submarine at this time was 'plunger' or 'diving boat'.

inside, so speed and distance depended on their strength. Inevitably the speed of the *Nautilus* was slow and its underwater range was small, although on the surface it could hoist a sail and perform like a boat. These problems were a factor in the French rejection of the submarine in early 1804, but there was also a feeling that it was not a reputable invention. Like the British, French naval officers were used to standing on the deck and facing enemy fire – to lurk unseen beneath the waves was rather dishonourable. A general reluctance to embrace new technology also existed, which was found in Britain as well as France.

At the time Fulton's ideas were finally rejected by the French, an old friend of his, Tom Johnson*, was in prison at Flushing in Holland. Often referred to as 'Johnson the Smuggler', he was already notorious, and many myths and legends were subsequently attached to his name, making it difficult to sift fact from fiction. Like many other smugglers, Johnson had been employed by the British Navy and Secret Service as a spy and as a pilot in the Channel, responsible for gathering information as well as guiding naval vessels and landing agents on the coast of France. While in France he was approached with an offer to work as a spy for the French, but was thrown into Flushing prison when he refused. In mid-1804 he escaped to America, where he called himself an unemployed Channel pilot and obtained work as a clerk with the British Consulate in New Orleans, but when Fulton arrived in England, after his rejection by the French, Johnson was invited back to Britain to assist him. Fulton, who began work in Britain under the cover name of Mr Francis, had also invented several types of 'torpedo' – bombs that could be attached to warships by a submarine and later exploded – and these were the Admiralty's main interest. Fulton had been the first to adopt the term 'torpedo', taken from *Torpedo nobiliana*, a species of North Atlantic ray that was capable of producing a strong electric shock to stun its prey, but torpedoes were more often known by the term 'carcasses'. These floating bombs could be weighted with ballast to lie just beneath the surface, so as to be almost invisible, and they could be attached to an enemy warship by stealth, even using a boat during darkness, manned by sailors dressed in black with blackened faces – there was no absolute need for a submarine.

The most obvious application of these carcasses was against the French invasion flotilla at Boulogne, so it was not long before they were put to use, as Midshipman Crawford witnessed:

* Also spelled Johnston.

When the ship was at anchor off Boulogne, on dark nights and during calm weather, the first lieutenant and [Midshipman Thomas] Clarke frequently went in the *gig* to endeavour to blow to pieces, or, at least, to keep on the *qui vive*, the Flotilla, which lay in the Roads*. This was to be effected by means of coffers, or carcasses – a newly-invented engine of murderous contrivance and most destructive force. These engines were made of copper, and . . . spherical in form; hollow to receive their charge of powder, which by means of machinery, that worked interiorly, and so secured as to be perfectly water-tight, exploded at the precise moment that you chose to set it to.[17]

The fuses for these submerged bombs were run by a clockwork mechanism that provided a time delay. Despite the technical aspects, the carcasses provided a relatively cheap means of attacking anchored ships and also risked fewer British casualties as they could be released offshore and allowed to drift to their targets on the incoming tide. Crawford noted how they were used against the French vessels at Boulogne:

Two [carcasses], attached together by means of a line coiled carefully clear, were placed in the boat ready to be dropped over-board. The line was buoyed by corks, like the roping of a seine [fishing net], so as to allow the carcasses to sink to a certain depth, and no further. When you had approached near enough to the vessel or vessels against which you meant to direct the carcasses, and saw clearly that you were in such a position that the line could not fail to strike her cable, one carcass was first dropped overboard, and when that had extended the full length of the line from the boat, then the other, both having been carefully primed and set to the time, which would allow of their floating to their destined object before they exploded. Of course it is presumed that wind and tide set in the direction, so as to ensure their not deviating from their course. These preliminaries being attended to, the carcasses drifted until the line which attached them together struck the cable of the vessel, when it was presumed that the carcasses, one on either side, would swing under her bilge, and, at the fated moment, explode and shatter her to pieces.[18]

As the darkest nights were used in order to give the best cover for the boats releasing the carcasses, it was generally only the explosions that could be seen, so it was difficult to assess the damage, as Crawford admitted:

---

* Roads, short for roadstead, is a safe anchorage near the shore.

Often as this attempt was made we never could ascertain that it was completely successful, although the first lieutenant, with a determination to effect his object, approached so near the flotilla, and remained so long, in order to see everything in proper train, as to draw upon his boat a heavy fire of musketry from the nearest vessel, which not unfrequently killed or wounded some of his men. Sometimes, after an expedition of the kind, we saw a vessel in the morning with her jib-boom gone, but without any confusion appearing in their line; and if any one sustained greater damage, they took care that we should be none the wiser, by removing her whilst it was dark, and supplying her place with another, so that they always appeared in precisely the same order at daylight, and the same number was counted as had been at sunset on the previous evening.[19]

While the French did their best to conceal the effectiveness of the carcasses, their concern at the potential damage and their counter-measures were more difficult to disguise: 'As a proof, however, that the enemy was kept on the alert, and had a just apprehension of the dangerous powers of those engines, whenever a division of the flotilla was at anchor outside the harbour, they always latterly moored a boat at the buoy right a-head of each vessel, so that she would be sure to bring up [intercept] anything that might be set adrift for the annoyance of the flotilla.'[20]

Despite all the efforts of the British Navy, the French flotilla had now grown so large that it could no longer be accommodated within the harbour area at Boulogne and was spreading out into the adjacent area of sea, where the vessels were potentially more vulnerable to attack. Such was the determination to stop the invasion fleet in its tracks that almost any scheme was considered, including what came to be known as 'stone ships'. As Crawford explained, 'the harbour of Boulogne is dry at low-water, the entrance to it being shoal and narrow, and liable to be choked or obstructed by the accumulation of sand, which the north-west winds are constantly throwing in. To prevent this obstruction, the little river Liane, which flows through the harbour, was carefully kept free, and also, as at Dieppe, dammed up, having a sluice, which, when opened at low-water, suffered the whole river to rush with such force, that it swept everything before it, and kept the harbour and the channel leading to it perfectly clear.'[21] It seemed a simple matter to sink some ships laden with stone at the entrance to the harbour and so render the port of Boulogne totally useless. Captain Edward Owen of the *Immortalité* was given charge of the operation, and Crawford noted that three vessels were prepared which

were 'old three-masted merchant-ships, in each of whose holds was built
a piece of masonry, well cemented, and having the stones cramped
together with iron, so as to render the whole mass more solid and
durable'.[22] There was an obvious flaw – even if the ships could be sunk in
exactly the right position, they would be uncovered at low tide and the
French could walk out to them from the shore.

Crawford was scathing in his assessment of the plan, which he felt was
ill-conceived and naive:

I am not prepared to say what might have been the opinion of Captain
Owen with regard to the scheme; but this I know full well, that he spared no
pains to put it into execution . . . But although our captain could effect much,
he could not render the elements propitious, and after several abortive
attempts to place the ships in a fitting situation for scuttling, which lasted a
full month, and was constantly baffled by calms and contrary winds, the
whole plan was abandoned. It is difficult to comprehend how any men, much
less men supposed to be capable of managing the affairs of this great nation,
unless stunned and bewildered by the projects of the arch-enemy, and his
threats of invasion, could incur an expense so considerable, and adopt a
scheme which, if practicable in the execution, might be useless and inopera-
tive in a few tides. For what more easy than to place a few barrels of
gunpowder under those masses of stone at low-water, and blow them to
pieces, when, at the next tide, the little 'Liane' would flow as uninterruptedly
as heretofore into the ocean.[23]

As well as blockading and harassing the French, the British ships off
the Channel coast near Boulogne were also engaged in intelligence-
gathering and espionage, and Crawford recorded one episode that involved
his own vessel:

We again proceeded off Boulogne, taking with us a gentleman, whom, as his
name never transpired, I must still designate by the appellation of 'Mr
Nobody', the cognomen by which alone he was known to the midshipmen.
During the fortnight that this gentleman passed on board the *Immortalité* she
was kept constantly close in shore, whenever the state of the tide and weather
would permit, in order to give him an opportunity of pursuing certain
researches upon which he seemed intent, and which, to give him his due
praise, he did with the greatest earnestness and coolness, unruffled and undisturbed by the showers of shot and shells that fell around the ship, splashing

the water about her at every instant. The object of this scrutiny seemed to be to ascertain, as correctly as he could, the fortifications around Boulogne, and the position and bearings of the different batteries which faced the sea, and also the exact distance at which the flotilla in the roads was anchored from the shore.[24]

Naval officers did not generally welcome being at the disposal of members of the Secret Service, and on this occasion, although the mission appeared successful, Crawford recalled that 'when these purposes were accomplished, I conclude to his satisfaction, we ran back to the Downs*, where he was landed, I confess to my no small satisfaction, and, I suspect, without regret by any one on board, for his presence imposed a load of additional trouble on the ship, besides making her serve every day, whilst he was on board, as a target for our friends to amuse themselves by practising at'.[25]

The man Crawford only knew as 'Mr Nobody' was not the only secret agent at work along the French coast, and Sir Sidney Smith's friend, Captain John Wesley Wright, was particularly active. Having left Paris without being recognised just before the renewal of war with France in May 1803, Wright continued his espionage work, gaining intelligence about Napoleon's proposed invasion and assisting Royalist agents in their conspiracy to assassinate Napoleon and restore the Bourbon monarchy. Not everybody in the Admiralty supported Wright's hazardous work, especially when he by-passed official channels and failed to show sufficient respect for his superior officers. As early as September 1803 Sir Thomas Troubridge, an Admiralty commissioner who had been at the Battle of the Nile, grumbled to Admiral Lord Keith that 'Captain Wright is talking large about being sacrificed, that he was nearly taken by our not giving him a sufficient force. Now it so happened that we knew nothing of Captain Wright being in the [gun-brig] *Basilisk*.'[26]

Despite his own antagonism towards Wright, Lord Keith had only the day before informed the captain of the *Speculator* that 'Captain John Wright of H.M. Navy is employed on a secret and delicate service, and I have thought fit that he should embark in H.M. armed lugger under your command; you are hereby required and directed to receive Captain Wright on board and to proceed with him from place to place as he may require, furnishing him with boats and chosen men for the accomplishment of his

* The anchorage off Deal in Kent.

object, vigilantly attending to his safety and protection, and that of any persons who may be with him; and keeping your vessel in constant state of preparation for resisting any attack that the enemy may make upon you.'[27] Doubtless to many men in the *Speculator*, they were carrying several 'Mr Nobodies'.

Over the following months Wright's operations took him along much of the northern coastline of France, which led him to complain about the lack of British vessels keeping a close watch. In December John Markham, also of the Admiralty, wrote to Lord Keith that 'Captain Wright writes to say that he has been some days on the enemy's coast and met their boats coasting almost every night, and never saw one of our cruisers'[28], and in March 1804 Markham again wrote to Keith that 'As to Capt. W[right] he has long since given out that he is continually among the enemy flotilla and on their coast and that you have nothing there to stop them.'[29] This did not endear Wright to the officers responsible, who were struggling to bring the blockade up to maximum efficiency with limited resources after the navy establishment had been run down during the peace.

On several occasions Wright secretly landed Royalist agents. These included the Breton General Georges Cadoudal, who had been implicated in the first attempt to assassinate Napoleon nearly three years earlier, and General Jean-Charles Pichegru, who met General Victor Moreau in Paris to finalise the new plans to overthrow Napoleon. It emerged that Moreau was willing to depose Napoleon but not install a monarchy, which threw the conspiracy into confusion. The plot began to leak out, and over 350 arrests were made, including Moreau and Pichegru in February 1804 and Cadoudal in March – they were all imprisoned in the Temple. Napoleon was convinced that the Duke d'Enghien, a contender for the royal throne, was involved. On his orders, d'Enghien was kidnapped from his home just beyond the French border at Ettenheim in the state of Baden and was brought to the castle of Vincennes outside Paris. After a peremptory trial he was shot dead on 21 March and buried in a shallow grave in the dry moat. The murder of d'Enghien caused horror throughout France and the rest of Europe. The bloodshed did not cease, because a fortnight later Pichegru was murdered in the Temple prison, though it was reported as suicide by strangulation.

In mid-March 1804, just before these murders, Captain Wright headed for the Quiberon Bay area of Brittany in the *Vincejo*, a brig armed with sixteen 18-pounder carronades. Here he spent some weeks 'without a pilot, within the enemy's islands, in the mouths of their rivers, in the presence of an extremely superior force, continually in motion'.[30] He was constantly harrassing the enemy and obtaining information, but disaster struck in May when the *Vincejo* was blown by an Atlantic gale into the Gulf of Morbihan, only for the wind to die down, leaving the brig defenceless just off Port Navalo. Several French gunboats began a bombardment, forcing Wright to surrender after two hours of fierce fighting.

Initially he and his crew were rowed upstream to the town of Auray, with the seamen taken to the prison and the officers to houses guarded by gendarmes. Having been recognised by a former officer in Egypt, now the Prefect of the Department of Morbihan, Wright was sent after a few days to Paris in case he could provide useful information on 'the frightful Conspiracy which has struck all France with alarm'.[31] Just before leaving he was unexpectedly presented with a letter by the mayor of the town, in front of several other dignitaries, in which they thanked him for his immense kindness for past actions towards French citizens: 'Yes, sir, we will never forget that it was thanks to your kind concern that Citizen Thevenard, son of the Maritime Prefect of the port of Lorient, and the crews of two French boats condemned at Rhodes to hard labour, obtained their release; even more recently in cruising our area, we have learned with feeling that you released fathers of families, old men and children that fate of war had made fall into your hands.'[32]

Wright related that 'conducted by two soldiers, one by my side in the carriage, and the other upon the coach-box, I arrived in ten days' painful journey, accompanied by my little nephew [John Rogerson Wright] and my servant . . . the agitation of the journey had extended the inflammation of my wound to the bladder'.[33] He was taken to the Temple, from which he had escaped six years previously, and was subjected to repeated interrogations about landing the Royalist agents. Moreau and Cadoudal were also still in the prison, and towards the end of May they and many others were put on trial. On the sixth day Wright was summoned to the court as a witness, but refused to answer any questions:

The president, calling me by name, enjoined in a certain formula, to answer all the questions that would be asked me, without partiality, hatred, or fear. I replied, in French, that I had to observe, in the first place, that military men knew no fear; that I was a British prisoner of war; that I had surrendered by capitulation, after an action with a very superior force; and knowing my duty to my King, and to my Country, whom I loved, and to whose service I had devoted myself from my youth; and owing no account of my public services to any authority but my own government, I would not answer any one of the questions that might be put to me.[34]

There was much popular support for Moreau, who was sentenced to two years in prison, but was instead banished to America. Cadoudal was guillotined, along with several other conspirators, on 25 June.

As a spy, Wright knew he was also in danger, and William Dillon, imprisoned at Verdun, commented that 'the very circumstance of keeping him in prison whilst his officers were allowed their parole had a most suspicious appearance'.[35] He added that Wright 'was locked up in the same apartments he had formerly occupied [with Sidney Smith], and in examining the locality he found some files which had been hidden by him, and with which he intended to sever the bars of his window'.[36] Several other crew members of the *Vincejo* were initially taken to the Temple, but were later marched to prisons in eastern France – the officers went to Verdun. Before they left him Wright warned that nothing would induce him to take his own life and 'therefore, if you hear of my death, depend upon it I shall have been murdered. I make this statement to you that you may repeat it should you hear of my having quitted this life.'[37]

Sir Sidney Smith himself was still patrolling off northern France and the Dutch coast, gathering very detailed intelligence about the military build-up in the area. In March 1804 he reported:

An account from Ostend . . . [is] as follows: One hundred luggers, all new, adapted for rowing, with two guns, one fore and the other aft; one hundred and forty large gaff schuyts, from about 100 to 120 tons; two hundred and sixty of smaller sort, different sizes, which makes five hundred; but exceed that number. At the west part a large camp, and another at the east side of the tower, which consists of twenty-one thousand men: they have a large quantity of artillery in the camp . . . The new harbour is full of schuyts, taken in requisition, adapted for carrying horses. The troops are much thinned on the island, there being very few in the barracks: on the island of Schowen at present there are about one thousand Dutch troops, burghers excepted, and hardly any batteries round it.[38]

Detailed reports concerning the preparations for the invasion of Britain continued to flow from the ships under Smith's command, but he was frustrated at not being able to effectively attack and harass the vessels about which he reported, because they were protected by the shallow coastal waters. Warships could not sail close enough to destroy many of them, and the only craft that were effective were gunboats, but Smith had very few of these at his disposal. Worn down by the constant coastal vigil, Smith's health deteriorated and he was advised to take shore leave, so in May 1804 he returned to England. During his leave he brooded about the problems of warfare in the shallow waters off the North Sea coast of the Low Countries, and designed a shallow-draught landing craft based on descriptions of catamarans that were brought back by South Seas explorers such as Captain Cook. The main difficulty was transporting field guns ashore to support soldiers attacking the ports, and prototypes of Smith's designs were tested and found to solve this problem. As a result the Admiralty ordered two versions to be built: one capable of carrying a field gun and fifty soldiers that was 48 feet long, and another twice that length, both of which could float in 18 inches of water.

It would take time to build a sufficient number of landing craft to be effective, and so short-term solutions were continually considered, particularly when in August information from a secret agent in France confirmed that the invasion of Britain and Ireland was imminent. By now British newspapers were giving a running commentary on events in the Channel whenever reports of naval actions off the French coast were brought by ships returning for repairs and supplies. The proximity of the fighting greatly reduced the usual time-lag caused by the slowness of communications, so that even newspapers that appeared only once a week could keep pace. Accounts from the blockade vessels augmented the comments from actual observers on the Kent coast who often had a good view of what was happening.

The French had now perfected their defences of Boulogne, but ironically their invasion plans were in disarray. Admiral Latouche-Tréville at Toulon, who was in overall command, died suddenly on 19 August, and it proved difficult to find a replacement. After several candidates were considered, the officer eventually chosen was Vice-Admiral Pierre-Charles de Villeneuve, who had escaped from the Battle of the Nile. The British ships patrolling off the port of Boulogne continued their vigil, and Midshipman Crawford of the *Immortalité* reported:

Whenever the state of the weather permitted, a strong division of the [French] flotilla was constantly anchored outside the harbour . . . to give regular exercise to their crews, as [well as] to brave [confront] and set the

English squadron at defiance. When the tide suited they sometimes got under way, and manoeuvred, but always under the protection of their formidable batteries. A grand attack [by the British], which had been maturing for some weeks, against this part of the flotilla was ready to be put into execution in the beginning of October, the general management and conduct of which was intrusted to Sir Home Popham.[39]

This was originally planned as a surprise attack in September, but for some reason Lord Keith postponed it until October, much to Crawford's amazement: 'For several days prior to the attack there was a great display of our force before Boulogne, amounting to between fifty and sixty vessels of all kinds, for no object that I can conceive, except to put the enemy on his guard, and give him timely notice of our intentions.'[40]

The purpose of the attack was to destroy as much of the invasion flotilla as possible, and Crawford commented that the British force included 'sloop-rigged vessels, prepared as fire, or rather explosion vessels, the number of which I forget, but not exceeding, I think, four or five. These vessels were filled with combustibles and powder, and supplied with explosive machinery similar to that which was fitted to the carcasses.'[41] The attack went ahead on the evening of 3 October, but Keith's inept approach had given the enemy all the warning they needed, as Crawford complained:

The French (how could they be otherwise?) were perfectly awake to all that was going forward. The [invasion] flotilla had been moved as near to the beach as it could anchor with safety; and in addition to the precaution of mooring a boat a-head of each vessel to arrest anything floating in its progress towards the flotilla, they had alarm boats, and pinnaces rowing guard round the whole; our leading boats were, therefore, soon descried. The enemy's sentinels hailed and discharged their muskets nearly at the same moment; and long before the carcasses could be set adrift, the whole bay was lit up by vivid flashes of musketry that was soon increased to almost noonday brightness by a blaze of artillery from the flotilla and batteries, which continued to pour heavy, though happily with few exceptions, harmless showers of grape [shot] in the direction of our boats.[42]

One after another the explosion vessels blew up, but the French, with plenty of warning, had prepared their defences well, and Crawford described how the explosions were spectacular but ineffective: 'As they entered the [French] line, and at the time for which their machinery had been set, they exploded, and shot in columns of flame into the air, adding by the splendour of their meteor-flight to the brilliancy of a scene, which . . . proved nothing but a grand and expensive, though harmless *feu de joie*. In the morning we observed no change or alteration in the French line, and we counted precisely the same number but one, which composed it on the evening before.'[43] Only one French gunboat was sunk, and Crawford was dismissive of the whole enterprise, 'which had been concocted with much thought and ingenuity, and was preparing, with great labour and expense, during several weeks. If it ended in smoke, and served no other purpose, at least its previous show and parade kept our friends in the flotilla on the *qui vive* for several nights; and when at length it did come off treated many thousand spectators, both ashore and afloat, to one of the most splendid fire-works I ever beheld.'[44]

In the days that followed the attack on Boulogne, much more momentous events were taking place off the coast of Spain. Intelligence had warned that a substantial quantity of treasure would soon reach Cadiz from South America, intended for the French. Spain was still theoretically neutral, but it was known that this neutrality was being bought by providing finance to Napoleon in return for immunity from invasion by the French. From Britain's point of view, the Spanish ships could not be considered as strictly neutral. Captain Graham Moore was ordered to Cadiz with a squadron of four frigates, and on 5 October four Spanish frigates were spotted. They ignored his warning shots and advice that he had instructions to detain them. A battle ensued, and in less than ten minutes one ship, the *Mercedes*, blew up with the loss of most of the crew. The other ships surrendered, one of which was found to be carrying a huge quantity of silver dollars. The diplomatic repercussions were inevitable – neutral Spanish ships had been attacked, 240 Spaniards had been killed, including friends of the Spanish royal family who were civilian passengers, and an extremely valuable cargo had been seized. Midshipman Lovell commented on the battle many years later:

I always did think, and my opinion has never changed, that it was a cruel thing to send only four frigates to detain four others, when by increasing the force by two or three line-of-battle ships, this might have been effected without loss of blood, or honour to the Spaniards. If it was necessary to detain these vessels and treasure from political motives, in order to make the king of Spain declare his equivocal conduct, it would have been humane to have sent such a force as would have put resistance out of the question; for what man, who was not a traitor, could yield without fighting (and with such a valuable cargo on board), to a force, in all appearance, not greater than his own.[45]

In the next few months Napoleon was distracted from his invasion plans, although they were not abandoned but continued at a slower pace while he prepared to be crowned Emperor of the French. This event took place amid great pomp and ceremony on 2 December. As a direct result of Captain Moore intercepting the Spanish treasure ships two months before, Spain declared war on Britain on 12 December. With 1804 drawing to a close, the situation was at last clear. Napoleon was bent on invading Britain, and with Spain now openly an ally he was in a powerful position – the next few months would be critical.

# EIGHT

## TURNING POINT

England expects that every man will do his duty.

Nelson's signal to the British fleet at the Battle of Trafalgar[1]

The first days of 1805 saw a major breach in Britain's defences – a snow-storm on 10 January forced the 'wooden walls' away from the French coast around Rochefort, and Rear-Admiral Édouard-Thomas de Burgues Missiessy led his fleet out through the disrupted blockade. Napoleon's grand strategy was for Missiessy to take various islands in the West Indies, while a fleet led by Vice-Admiral Villeneuve would capture several others. They were then to harass the merchant shipping of the area, causing as much commercial damage as possible, before returning to support the invasion of Britain. At the very least, British interests in the West Indies would be severely disrupted, and if this diversion drew off enough British battleships from the Channel, it would be possible to mount the invasion. Like all Napoleon's grand naval schemes it was too complicated and did not allow for any necessary deviations from the plan, so right from the start the strategy began to unravel.

The storm that forced the blockading British ships to seek shelter hit Missiessy's fleet with full force, causing serious damage to some of the ships. Several days later in southern France high winds swept the British blockade, which was under Nelson's overall command, away from Toulon. This allowed Villeneuve to take his fleet out of port, but his ships were in turn battered by the storm, and so he decided to head back. Missiessy did not yet know it, but he was on his own. The French admiral managed to move unseen into the Atlantic, and the first the British in the West

Indies knew of the danger was when the French were spotted off Barbados. Missiessy had five battleships, three frigates and two brigs and was also carrying a force of 3500 troops, and so was a much stronger fleet than the British one there, which was in any case dispersed over a wide area.

The sight of the French caused a certain amount of panic and the news spread through the islands, so that the garrison of Diamond Rock knew what to expect even before they gained their first view of the enemy fleet on 20 February. Commander James Maurice prepared his guns, hoping that he might catch the French unawares, but they had been well briefed and kept out of range, sailing on to the port of Fort Royal on Martinique, where several hundred men were landed as they had already succumbed to illness, and Missiessy himself was unwell.

Disease was the invisible scourge of sailors, killing far more seamen than were killed in battles, accidents or even shipwrecks, because virtually nothing was known about the real causes of sickness. Particular places were regarded as especially dangerous, though, and the West Indies were notoriously unhealthy. The most feared ailment there was yellow fever, often called 'yellow jack' because of the yellow quarantine flag flown on ships where men had contracted the disease. The yellow fever virus was spread by mosquitoes, and the disease was marked by fever, vomiting of dark blood and the skin turning yellow through jaundice caused by the breakdown of the liver. Midshipman George Jackson, who had visited Diamond Rock, caught the disease shortly afterwards at English Harbour in Antigua, where there was an epidemic. His ship was in port for repairs after running aground, and before these were complete he was taken ill and treated in the hospital. He left a detailed account of his progress:

Next to confluent smallpox, I should imagine yellow fever to be the most malignant and incurable of the epidemic diseases. Its real nature can be conceived only by those who have witnessed its horrors. The Spaniards call it 'vomits' from the black vomit that nearly always ensues, after which there is little or no hope of the patient's recovery. When attacked by this accursed retching, the sufferer frequently springs up in his bed and expels the dark thick fluid from his mouth several feet beyond him in a moment of intense agony; and at times the patient is suddenly seized with such violent convulsions that the force of several powerful men is hardly sufficient to hold him down. This singular malady is so deceptive that the patient will sink at intervals into a calm and apparently refreshing sleep, as still as a child's slumber, and start suddenly thence without the slightest warning into one of those terrible fits.[2]

Some precautions against the spread of disease, such as quarantine, were used on a basis of trial-and-error, because it was not understood how diseases were spread. Jackson thought that visiting the hospital and just seeing other patients had caused him to catch yellow fever:

Before my attack I had been constantly to the hospital in charge of the sick, and the sights I there witnessed no doubt made an injurious impression upon me and accelerated my illness. On the last occasion I was greatly affected and depressed by a scene in the wards. One unfortunate creature lay in the throes of death. From every orifice in his body a thin bloody serum was oozing, and the natural colour of his skin was changed to a ghastly muddy yellow. To add to the hideousness of the spectacle, his person was literally swarming with minute white ants, called by the natives, I believe, 'walky-walky ants'; and where the secretion exuded these detestable insects were collected thickest, gathered round the margin of the fluid, and feasting upon their odious banquet. Wherever a dead body is they are certain to congregate, but in this instance they were too eager to wait until death had finished his work. I called the Doctor's attention to the case, and he declared it impossible to remedy the evil. The legs of the bed were standing in pans of water, but no other resources were equal to the emergency, and the wretched victim lingered on under the additional affliction to his appointed hour.[3]

Feeling unwell, Jackson consulted the doctor, who recommended that he should remain in the hospital, but he contrived to stay out for another day until he became so ill he was ordered back. He was still sufficiently alert to insist on better treatment, which may have saved him:

On entering the hospital I flatly refused to take the room allotted to me, and asked to be put into the one at the other end of the building. The Doctor kindly humoured me. Then I objected to the bed; there was an ugly stain upon the pillow. 'I will not go there,' I cried, 'a man has died in that bed!' 'Give him another bed,' said the Doctor, and after a few more objections had been satisfied, I gave myself up entirely to the faculty and prepared to meet the enemy. What occurred during the next fortnight I do not recollect, but as soon as the virulence of the malady had subsided, I began to realise the mistake I had made in the choice of a room. The window next to my bed, and from which I could easily look, commanded an uninterrupted view of the dead-house outside, so that I could plainly see the bodies being carried there from the hospital.[4]

Jackson was one of the lucky few who survived and was forever grateful to those who had nursed him: 'The kindness and care bestowed upon us during the illness left an indelible impression on my mind and heart, and had I possessed the means I should certainly have requited, as far as it lay in my power, the services of the nurses who were in constant attendance upon myself and the other patients. But I was entirely without resources save those only of which a Midshipman could boast.'[5]

At Martinique, Missiessy stayed only long enough to land his sick men and take on supplies before sailing north to carry out a successful raid on the British-held port of Roseau, the capital of the island of Dominica. Raids were also carried out on St Kitts, Nevis and Montserrat. The British had far too few resources to oppose Missiessy, but in the absence of Villeneuve's fleet he himself did not have a large enough force to hold on to any of the places he captured – he could harass the islands, but not occupy them. On 14 March 1805 Missiessy received dispatches informing him that Villeneuve was still at Toulon and that there might now be a British fleet on its way to the West Indies. Subsequent dispatches ordering him to wait in the Caribbean until reinforcements arrived never reached Missiessy, and he set sail for Europe without capturing any British-held islands, nor achieving his specific objective, the recovery of Diamond Rock. When Napoleon heard what had happened he was furious: 'I choked with indignation on reading that he had not taken the Diamond Rock . . . I would have preferred to lose a warship.'[6]

While Missiessy was making his way back to France, Villeneuve finally managed to leave Toulon on 30 March, with yet another set of orders that were supposed to culminate in the invasion of Britain. Sailing south-west along the coast of Spain and through the Strait of Gibraltar, his fleet reached Cadiz on 9 April, and he sent a message to his Spanish ally, Admiral Federico Carlos Gravina, to warn that he thought a British fleet was already in pursuit. Gravina replied that he would set sail with his fleet immediately, but Villeneuve did not wait and pressed on to the West Indies. He arrived at Martinique six days before Missiessy reached France on 20 May, the two fleets having unknowingly passed each other in the

Atlantic. Gravina's ships rapidly caught up with Villeneuve, whose greatest fear was Nelson's Mediterranean fleet. Nelson, though, had been misled by reports that the French ships were carrying troops and had initially assumed their destination was Egypt.

It was only on 11 May, when Villeneuve was already in West Indian waters, that Nelson set sail across the Atlantic in pursuit – for the moment, Villeneuve had a free hand, and he took the opportunity to study Diamond Rock on his way into Fort Royal. Two days later, on 16 May, the *San Rafael*, a straggler from Gravina's fleet, sailed too close, and Commander James Maurice reported:

I saw a large ship rounding Point Saline, and from her appearance I plainly saw she was a ship of the line, and from the cut of her sails an enemy. At eight, she hoisted a Spanish ensign and pendant; I immediately directed French colours to be hoisted as a decoy, which fully answered my wishes, for at twenty minutes before nine she had got under the lee of the Rock, at the distance of three-quarters of a mile, when I shifted the colours, and opened a well-directed fire of round and grape from Fort Diamond*; the first shot striking her under the fore channels, she directly put her helm up, and in the act of wearing returned one feeble shot. From the little winds she did not get out of range of shot until nine, but continued running before the wind until twelve. At two, an enemy's brig of war stood out of Fort Royal and beat to windward of the Rock, where she continued to cruise. I was now fully satisfied in my own mind of the intention of the enemy to attack the Rock.[7]

Although Maurice's guns had done no serious damage, they did cause the Spanish ship to run for cover. Maurice was satisfied with his defensive position, yet almost immediately everything changed. It was found that all the water had leaked out of the main storage tank, a month's supply, leaving Diamond Rock short of water. A crack beneath the specially constructed concrete tank had been widened by earth tremors that had been common during the past eighteen months, and now the vibration from the guns had turned the trickle into a flood. Even with strict rationing, there was barely two weeks' water left. If the British were to hold on to the Rock, fresh supplies were essential, but that was now impossible, as Maurice recorded: 'From the 16th to the 29th the Rock was

---

* Fort Diamond or Diamond Battery was the name given to the gun battery on the summit of Diamond Rock.

completely blockaded by frigates, brigs, schooners and small boats, sloop-rigged, which prevented any supplies being thrown in to me; for on the 25th a sloop from St. Lucia, with my second Lieutenant, who had carried dispatches to Barbadoes, and the Purser, who had gone over to complete the provisions to four months, were taken under my guns, endeavouring to throw in some barrels of powder, although we covered her with a spirited fire from Fort Diamond.'[8]

The French did not know it, but they only had to maintain the blockade a little longer and Diamond Rock would be forced to surrender. Instead they continued their preparations for an all-out assault. On 31 May a force of French warships was visible near the Rock, and Maurice saw that the attack was imminent:

From the number of their signals, and having cast off their boats, I was convinced the attack would be made soon. At seven the enemy bore up in a line for the Rock, the gun-boats &c. keeping within them, crowded with troops. Seeing the impossibility of defending the lower works against such a force, and the certainty of our being prevented from gaining the heights [later] without considerable loss, and which could not be defended for any time without us, with the greatest reluctance I ordered the whole [garrison] above the first lodgement, having a man at each gun to give the enemy their discharge, which they did, and joined me over the North Garden Pass, excepting the cook, who was made a prisoner. What powder was left below we drowned, and cut away the launch, that she might not be serviceable to the enemy.[9]

Having retreated to the summit, it was not long before the wisdom of his decision was made very clear to Maurice:

At ten minutes before eight we had every person up, and the ladders secured, when the [French ship] *Berwick* opened her fire within pistol shot, and at eight the whole of the enemy's squadron of ships and gun-boats were in action, which was returned by Hood's Battery* and Fort Diamond; the whole of the troops in the boats keeping up a heavy fire of musketry. It was a fortunate circumstance we quitted the lower works when we did, as our own stones hove down [from the cliff face] by the enemy's shot would have killed and wounded the whole of us.[10]

---

* This 'battery', named after Samuel Hood, was a single 24-pounder cannon sited in a cave.

Such falls of rock were a hindrance to the French troops and added to the dangers of attacking up a cliff face through a hail of missiles from above. Major Boyer, who commanded part of the French assault force, later wrote an account for the *Martinique Gazette*, where he detailed the problems:

The fortifications of the Rock, and the positions of the enemy, were exactly as I had conceived them to be . . . the scaling of it appeared to me to be perfectly easy, and I had made my dispositions accordingly; but the moment we had landed, this illusion ceased – I saw nothing but immense precipices, perpendicular rocks, a threatening enemy, whom it was impossible to reach, and insurmountable difficulties on all sides. We naturally enough concluded, that from the facility with which the enemy had suffered us to occupy the bottom of the Rock, they had reserved all their force, to destroy us more securely from the heights of their inaccessible retreat. Our troops suffered severely from a most galling volley of musketry, large fragments of the rock, cannon balls, and casks filled with stones, which they poured upon us.[11]

The time the garrison had spent in musketry practice now bore fruit, and the French were forced to retreat or take shelter, as Boyer described:

From the tremendous fire of the enemy, the boats had been obliged to retreat, without having landed any of the articles with which I had furnished myself for the attack; the ships also had drifted into the offing, and we remained without support or provisions: I saw we had no resource, but to retreat into two cavities in the Rock . . . where we should at least be under cover: I had all our wounded carried into them . . . In order to prevent as much as possible the effects of the enemy's destructive fire, I made all the out-posts fall back into the two caverns, to wait for the approach of night.[12]

At this point the British had the upper hand, despite the continuing bombardment of the Rock from the French ships, and Boyer recounted how the spearhead of the French attack was trapped in two caves not far above sea-level:

Our situation was truly dreadful; we were exhausted with fatigue, and the want of nourishment was more severely felt by the troops, who had been prevented by the sea sickness from taking any for the two preceding days that they were on board the ships. The boats had not had time to land any provisions, nor could we expect they would run the risk of bringing us any. The enemy too had by now, by the quantity of shot and stones which they continued to direct at us, cut off the communication between the two caverns, notwithstanding their vicinity to each other: in short, to add to the horrors of this calamitous scene, we had nothing to offer our wounded, of whom some were in a most deplorable state, but barren consolations.[13]

Commander Maurice related that they could do little to stop the French bringing in more supplies under cover of darkness:

At night the whole of the men [of the garrison] were posted on different lodgements, to harass the enemy as they threw in supplies and reinforcements: on the 1st [June] the enemy's squadron employed constantly bombarding the Rock, the fire from the troops much more spirited: on the 2nd the enemy's squadron bombarding as before, who had been reinforced with another brig, but the fire from the troops this day very severe, as they had during the night got under the rocks in the surf, and were covered by the overhanging rocks, and as our men appeared they fired up.[14]

The British still had plenty of food, but after suffering nearly two and a half days of bombardment, they were running out of ammunition, and the shortage of water was becoming serious, so while his men still had enough strength to climb down from the summit, Maurice realised that the only option was to negotiate a surrender:

At four in the afternoon [of 2 June], on examining into our ammunition, I found we had but little powder left, and not a sufficient quantity of ball cartridges to last until dark, and being firmly of the opinion the enemy meant to endeavour to carry the heights by assault that night, I thought it a duty I owed to those brave fellows who had so gallantly supported me during three days and two nights constant battle, to offer terms of capitulation; and having consulted my first Lieutenant, who was of the same opinion, at half-past four, the unhappiest moment of my life, I threw out a flag of truce, which returned at five, with honourable terms for the garrison, and the next morning we embarked [as prisoners-of-war] on board the *Pluton* and *Berwick*.[15]

With direct orders from Napoleon that Diamond Rock, which had proved such an irritation and insult to the French on Martinique, should be captured, Boyer was at pains to exaggerate the achievements of the French and play down the difficulties that the British garrison faced:

The number of effective men [in the British garrison] amounted to 107, one half of whom were sent on board the *Pluton*, and the other on board the *Berwick*. I inspected the whole of the Rock, and had the two 18-pounders at the top of it thrown into the sea, as well as the platform, and all the powder and shot; I also cut down one of the flag-staffs, leaving only that on which the French colours were flying. To judge from the great quantity of powder, shot, water and provisions of all kinds, which we found in the different cavities near the summit of the Rock, it would be supposed that the enemy could have held out much longer. The prodigious buildings which they had constructed, evidently prove that they considered themselves as well established here. I cannot even yet conceive how they should be so soon dislodged – it required, no doubt, Frenchmen to do it . . . From a hasty calculation, I am afraid we have to regret the loss of 50 men, both killed and wounded, which is certainly great, when we reflect that it is so many brave men who have fallen; but from the difficulty of the enterprise, we might have calculated upon a much greater one.[16]

On the British side two men were killed and one wounded, but all had suffered from the effects of the heat and lack of water, as Maurice recorded:

Their fatigue and hardships are beyond description, having only a pint of water during 24 hours, under a vertical sun, and not a moment's rest day or night; and several of them fainted for want of water, and obliged to drink their own. A schooner had brought out sixty scaling ladders, to attempt us that night under cover of the ships, and four more ships of the line were to have come against us the next day. Indeed the whole of the combined squadron's launches were employed on the service, and not less than three thousand men . . . My only consolation is, that although I unfortunately lost the Rock, I trust its defence was honourable.[17]

Taking Diamond Rock was Vice-Admiral Villeneuve's greatest victory, and he hoped it would restore him to Napoleon's favour, since the emperor had been enraged by his taking so long to break through the blockade at Toulon. The assault on the Rock had depleted the stores on board the French ships, but Villeneuve decided his next objective would be the capture of Antigua and Barbuda. On 8 June, however, before he reached these islands, he came across a British convoy carrying sugar, which he promptly captured. Although this was a rich prize, it also carried the bad news for Villeneuve that Nelson was in the Caribbean with eleven warships and seven frigates. Short of supplies, with his ships in need of repair and now with many crewmen sick, the last thing Villeneuve wanted was a pitched battle with Nelson: two days later the French sailed for Europe.

The captured ships from the convoy were sent to Martinique escorted by a French frigate, but soon after parting company from Villeneuve they ran into two British sloops. These were not a danger in themselves, but the jittery French took them to be scouts for Nelson's fleet and burned all fifteen of the merchant ships to prevent their being returned to the enemy. Even before he had finally left the vicinity of the West Indies, a large part of Villeneuve's success had turned to ashes on the water.

Once Nelson heard of the return of the French to Europe, he set off in hot pursuit, and just as in the chase to Egypt before the Battle of the Nile, Nelson's fleet unknowingly overtook the French. Nelson had taken a southerly route that eventually brought him to Gibraltar, but Villeneuve had steered north and on 22 July was intercepted by a British fleet commanded by Vice-Admiral Sir Robert Calder. The encounter was blanketed in fog, and the resulting battle inconclusive, although both sides claimed victory. Villeneuve lost two Spanish ships to the British, but managed to reach the safety of Vigo in north-west Spain, and Calder was later censured for not doing more to stop the French. Napoleon was furious, ranting: 'What a chance Villeneuve has missed! He could, on arriving at Brest from the open sea, have played prisoners' base [a popular game] with Calder's squadron . . . defeat the English and gain a decided supremacy.'[18] His achievements in the Caribbean were ignored, and again Villeneuve remained out of favour with his emperor.

Since Vigo had no resources to refit his ships or cope with the large number of men needing hospital treatment, he took his fleet south along the Spanish coast, arriving at Cadiz on 21 August. The weak British blockade of that port was soon strengthened, and the scene was now set for the Battle of Trafalgar, which would take place two months later when Villeneuve sailed from Cadiz.

While Nelson had been fruitlessly pursuing Villeneuve across the Atlantic and back, Thomas Cochrane had captured a string of prizes. The previous year the government fell and his enemy St Vincent was replaced as First Lord of the Admiralty by Lord Melville, who appointed Cochrane to the new frigate *Pallas*, with orders to cruise off the Azores. In early March *Pallas* caused a sensation by sailing into Plymouth with huge golden candlesticks lashed to the masts. The prize money from his spoil amounted to around £300,000, most of which was generated by capturing a single ship, the *Fortuna*, as reported by the *Naval Chronicle*:

The *Pallas*, Captain Lord Cochrane, on his late Cruise off the Coast of Spain and Portugal, fell in with and took *la Fortuna*, a Spanish Ship, from Rio de la Plata, to Corunna, richly laden with Specie, (Gold and Silver) to the amount of £150,000, and about the same sum in valuable Goods and Merchandise, in all near 300,000 dollars value. When the Spanish Captain came on board with the Supercargo, who was a Merchant and Passenger from New Spain, they appeared much dejected, as their private property on board was lost, which amounted to 30,000 dollars each person, in Specie and Goods. The Papers and Manifest of the Cargo of *la Fortuna* being examined, the Spaniards told Lord Cochrane that they had Families in Old Spain, and had now lost all their property, the hard earnings by commerce in the burning clime of South America, the savings of nearly 20 years . . . Both the Spaniards appeared to feel their forlorn situation so much, that Lord Cochrane felt for them; and with that generosity ever attendant on true bravery, consulted his Officers as to the propriety of returning each of these two Gentlemen to the value of 5000 dollars of their property, in specie, which was immediately agreed to be done . . . On this his Lordship ordered the Boatswain to pipe all hands on deck, and addressed the Seamen and Royal Marines with much feeling, and in a plain seamanlike way stated the above facts. On this the gallant Fellows, with one voice, sung out, 'Aye, aye, my Lord, with all our hearts!' and gave three cheers. The Spaniards were overcome with this noble instance of the generosity of British Seamen, and actually shed tears of joy, at the prospect of once more being placed in a state of independence.[19]

Cochrane himself had sorted through some of the spoils of his victories, recording some material that was rejected: 'In one of the captured vessels was a number of bales, marked "invendebles". Making sure of some rich prize, we opened the bales, which to our chagrin consisted of pope's bulls, dispensations for eating meat on Fridays, and indulgences for peccadilloes of all kinds, with the price affixed. They had evidently formed a venture from Spain to the Mexican sin market, but the supply exceeding the demand, had been reconsigned to the manufacturers. We consigned them to the waves.'[20]

For the rest of 1805 Cochrane was involved in escorting a convoy to Canada, but in Britain the people became increasingly worried about an invasion happening soon. It was not until 9 August that some of the terror was dissipated, when newspapers reported that Nelson was back from the West Indies. There was a general feeling that a significant battle was imminent and that Nelson would triumph. The only doubt was when the battle would take place; the only worry, that the French would yet again give Nelson the slip.

The confidence that Nelson would eventually meet and beat the French did not altogether allay concern about the invasion fleet at Boulogne, especially as Napoleon was known to be there himself. Newspapers, while still giving detailed accounts of the minimal successes of British attacks on Boulogne, also tried to defuse the tension with humour, and *The Times* published a satirical version of a speech from Shakespeare's *Hamlet*:

> BUONAPARTE's SOLILOQUY
> ON THE CLIFF AT BOULOGNE
> T'invade, or not t'invade – that is the question –
> Whether 'tis nobler in my soul, to suffer
> Those haughty Islanders to check my power,
> Or to send forth my troops upon their coast,
> And by attacking, crush them. – T'invade – to fight –
> No more; – and by a fight, to say I end
> The glory, and the thousand natural blessings
> That England's heir to; – 'tis a consummation
> Devoutly to be wish'd. – To invade – to fight –
> To fight – perchance to fail: – Ay, there's the rub;
> For in that failure, what dire fate may come,
> When they have shuffled off from Gallia's shore,
> Must give me pause. – There's the respect,
> That makes me thus procrastinate the deed:
> For would I bear the scoff and scorn of foes,
> The oppressive thought of English liberty,
> The pangs of despis'd threats, th'attempts delay,

The insolence of Britain, and the spurns,
That I impatient and unwilling take,
When I myself might head the plund'ring horde,
And grasp at conquest? Would I tamely bear
To groan and sweat under a long suspence,
But that the dread of something after battle,
That undecided trial, from whose hazard
I never may return, – puzzles my will,
And makes me rather bear unsated vengeance,
Than fly from Boulogne at the risk of all.
And thus my native passion of ambition
Is clouded o'er with sad presaging thought:
And this momentous, tow'ring enterprise,
With this regard, is yearly turn'd aside,
And waits the name of action.[21]

The Admiralty was taking the threat from Boulogne more seriously, and through the summer of 1805 Sir Sidney Smith pressed for an attack on the port using the new technology of Fulton's torpedoes and Congreve's rockets, but he met with some resistance. The rockets were the invention of William Congreve, but while they could terrify the enemy, they were unpredictable and often regarded as no more than expensive fireworks. Louis Simond, a Frenchman brought up in America who lived for a time in England, described them as

made like common rockets [fireworks], only of an enormous size. The cylinder, or case of iron, contains 20 or 30 pounds of powder, rammed hard, and the fore-part loaded with balls. The rocket is impelled by its own recoil. It is held, in the first instance, by a pole 20 or 25 feet long, sloping to the proper angle like a mortar. The pole is carried away by the rocket, and keeps in its proper direction like the feather of an arrow. But when the wind blows strong with it, or sidewise, the pole or tail is apt to steer the wrong course; and the rockets go right only against the wind, or with no wind.[22]

Fulton's torpedoes were also regarded with suspicion, because they had already failed to live up to their promise when used at Boulogne earlier in the year. Many doubted that they were even capable of sinking a ship, so a practical demonstration was arranged off Walmer in Kent for the middle of October, which the *Annual Register* reported:

An experiment of a newly-invented machine for destroying ships at anchor was tried in the Downs, and succeeded in the most complete manner. A large brig was anchored abreast of Walmer-castle, about three quarters of a mile from the shore. Two or three gallies then rowed off, and placed the machine across the cable of the brig, which, by the running of the tide, was soon forced under her bottom, about the centre of the keel, where it attaches itself. In a few minutes, the clockwork of the machinery having performed its operation, a small cloud of smoke was seen to rise from the vessel, which in a moment after was blown to atoms, without any noise or appearance of fire. In about 27 or 28 seconds, not a vestige of the brig was to be seen, as the fragments were then level with the water's edge . . . a number of military and naval officers, went with Sir Sidney Smith to Mr. Pitt's*, at Walmer-castle, to witness the experiment, and expressed the utmost astonishment at the destructive power of the invention.[23]

Despite continuing opposition from some senior admirals, the demonstration was successful, and Smith was given permission to make an attack on Boulogne, even though by now Napoleon had removed much of his invasion army to counter threats to his eastern borders. Midshipman Crawford of the *Immortalité* was still part of the blockade and saw the build-up to the attack: 'In November, Commodore Sir Sidney Smith arrived off Boulogne with his squadron, and assumed the command. The force, when united, consisted of twenty-five sail, which did not include three explosion-boats and a mortar-ketch. Of this number five were bombs; the remainder were vessels of all descriptions. Several fire-vessels joined afterwards, which swelled our force to more than thirty sail, enough to alarm the whole flotilla; and, in truth, our new commander seemed bent on desperate deeds.'[24]

The plan was to burn the invasion flotilla, and it was obvious even to the anxious French in Boulogne that the vessels in Smith's fleet were of types used to set fire to or blow up closely grouped ships and boats. Crawford noted that 'after the vessels had all assembled, few preparations were necessary . . . all now depended on the weather'.[25] This was the crucial factor, for the fireships and explosion vessels needed a good following wind from the right direction because they travelled the last part of their voyage without men on board to steer. Over the next few days several attempted attacks were made, but the weather was against them – either

* William Pitt, the Prime Minister.

the wind failed at a crucial point, leaving the attack becalmed, or the weather was too stormy for it to have any chance of success.

The *Immortalité* continued patrol duties with specific orders to intercept two French frigates, since there was information from spies that these ships were about to set out from Flushing. The situation then changed dramatically, as Crawford related:

It was during this cruise that we first heard of the mighty victory of Trafalgar: a victory of such vital importance at the time to England, neutralizing in some degree the consequences of the vast successes of the French upon the continent; and I can well remember how much the pride and exultation, which we should otherwise have felt at our country's success, were saddened and subdued by the irreparable loss of her favourite hero. Instead of shouts and songs of triumph and [con]gratulation, the subject was mentioned in broken whispers, and all seemed to feel, not only that some great national calamity had befallen the land, but as if each individual had lost a friend and leader, with whom it would have been the happiness of his life to serve and follow.[26]

Like Crawford, almost everybody in Britain was to remember where they were and what they were doing when they first heard of the victory at Trafalgar and the death of Nelson. The battle had been fought off Cape Trafalgar, on the Spanish coast between Cadiz and Gibraltar, on 21 October 1805, but the news did not reach London until 6 November and took much longer to spread through Europe and reach outlying ships and colonies. A combined fleet of eighteen French and fifteen Spanish battleships led by Vice-Admiral Villeneuve had broken out from Cadiz and was confronted by Nelson's fleet of twenty-seven battleships. Although the British were outnumbered in ships, guns and men, Nelson adopted a daring strategy of dividing his fleet into two columns that sailed at right-angles to the battle line of French and Spanish ships, rather than forming the traditional parallel line of battle. The danger of this strategy was that during their approach, the British ships were under heavy fire without being able to retaliate with anything other than a few guns mounted in the bows. Once the British ships reached the enemy line, however, the effect was devastating as the whole formation deteriorated into a confused mass. Nelson's captains had been briefed to act on their own initiative, whereas the French and Spanish were forced to do so in the absence of instructions from their commander, because they could no longer read his signals amid the clouds of smoke. Also, the leading ships of the French and Spanish line had been cut off from the main group by Nelson's column of ships, and it was with great difficulty that they managed to turn round and join the battle. By this time the British had won.*

Nelson's aim had been to destroy the heart of the French and Spanish navies, and the task that he began was completed by a fierce storm that raged for a week immediately after the battle. By the time the weather subsided, a total of nineteen ships had sunk or been destroyed, and four more that escaped were captured soon afterwards. Around two and a half thousand French and Spanish seamen were killed and over seven thousand taken prisoner. The British did not lose a single ship and fewer than five hundred men were killed. It was a crushing blow that demoralised the French and Spanish navies. It was also a turning point in the war against Napoleon.

Now that his navy had suffered a serious defeat, there was no possibility of attempting an invasion of Britain in the immediate future. After Trafalgar, the French dominated Europe but did not manage to mount a serious challenge to Britain's domination of the sea. Despite some successes against Britain in subsequent years, the threat from the French Navy was contained and diminished, helped by the disillusionment of Napoleon, who concentrated on his armies. Crawford remarked that shortly after hearing the news of Trafalgar, 'it being ascertained that the frigates, which we were on the look-out for, had made their escape, and gone north-about, the *Immortalité* returned to the Downs. We had now done for a time with Boulogne. Work enough had been cut out for Bonaparte's Grand Army in Germany: his threat of invasion was suspended *sine die*, and the *Immortalité* could be spared for other service.'[27]

For the people of Britain the long-term effects of Trafalgar were as yet unproven, and only two simple facts were recognised: there would be no invasion by the French, and Nelson was dead. Feelings of relief were mingled with sadness and gratitude towards the sailors who had obtained the victory. The newspapers were full of notices of fund-raising events for financial support of the dependants of those men killed or wounded in the battle, and for a time it seemed that everyone was involved. A newspaper for 16 November reported:

---

* For a gripping narrative of the battle illustrated by vivid accounts from eyewitnesses, see *Trafalgar: The Biography of a Battle* by Roy Adkins.

On Friday morning Sir Sidney Smith went on board the *Diligence* sloop of war in Dover Harbour, and ordered the crew to be mustered. As soon as they were assembled, after a few prefatory observations, he read the Extraordinary Gazette to them with much firmness, until he came to that part of it which mentions the manner of Lord Nelson's death, when his voice faltered, and tears were perceived to trickle down his cheeks. When he had concluded, he resumed his observations and informed the crew of the *Diligence*, 'that in consequence of an address from him, the ships company of the *Antelope* had come to a determination to give ten days' pay towards the relief of the sufferers in the glorious action off Trafalgar, and the families of those who fell in it.' The whole crew of the *Diligence* immediately exclaimed, 'ten, twenty, thirty days' pay – any thing Sir Sidney pleases.'[28]

Even John Nicol, still hiding from the press-gang near Edinburgh, was affected by the news of Trafalgar. Despite his situation he remained patriotic and a staunch supporter of the government, constantly taunted by the men he worked with:

One would ask what I thought of British freedom; another, if I could defend a government which did such things [as force men into the navy]? I was at no loss for my answer. I told them, 'Necessity had no law'. Could the government make perfect seamen as easily as they could soldiers, there would be no such thing as pressing of seamen, and that I was happy to be of more value than them all put together, for they would not impress any of them, they were of so little value compared with me. When the news of Trafalgar arrived, I had my triumph over them in return. None but an old tar can feel the joy I felt. I wrought none [did not work] the next day, but walked about enjoying the feeling of triumph. Every now and then I felt the greatest desire to hurra aloud, and many an hurra my heart gave that my mouth uttered not.[29]

Nicol continued to be a fugitive, but at least he was not a prisoner, unlike Lieutenant William Dillon, who was still at Verdun. In December he was called upon to comment on the news of Trafalgar that had just arrived:

I happened to enter the Caron Club about 11 o'clock one day when one of the committee came in with the English newspapers containing the account of Nelson's victory over the combined fleets of France and Spain. Lord Yarmouth, Col. Abercromby and several others of my friends seized hold of me as if by one accord, and, lifting me on the table, desired me to read in a loud voice the official report of that splendid victory. The most perfect silence having been secured, I communicated the details of Collingwood's letter to the Admiralty. When I had finished it, three hearty spontaneous cheers were given by at least one hundred members present, and those who were not near the table closed up and requested me to read the account a second time, to which I readily agreed to do.[30]

Afterwards Dillon found that the French just could not believe the news:

Going out to the street, we met a crowd of French gentlemen who were anxious to know the reason of all that cheering. I told them of our splendid victory, and they were sadly cast down on the occasion. My French friends overloaded me with questions. They allowed they could not contend with us upon the ocean. 'We do not doubt,' they said, 'that you have triumphed. But that you should have taken and destroyed so many ships without losing any is a case we cannot admit. Our seamen can fight as well as yours, and surely you do not mean to maintain that our shot has not sunk *some* of your ships?' My only reply was that they might see Lord Collingwood's official report for themselves, by which it was perfectly clear that they had lost twenty sail of the line: but not one on our side, either lost or taken, a British admiral not daring to send home a false report.[31]

A little later, Captain Mathieu-Anne-Louis Prigny de Quérieux, Villeneuve's chief-of-staff, passed through Verdun, and Dillon learned from him more details of the battle:

He had been wounded at the battle of Trafalgar, and had been sent to take the waters of that place (Barège), which had been beneficial in curing him. This gentleman's name was Prigny. He was Adm. Villeneuve's flag captain, and I do not recollect at any period of my life having enjoyed a more interesting conversation than I did in that officer's company. I found in Capt. Prigny an amiable and well-informed officer who did not, at the meeting which took place between us, conceal any of the facts or principal incidents which occurred between the hostile fleets on that important occasion. His ship, the *Bucentaure*, was taken possession by the *Mars*, 74, commanded by my former captain, George Duff of the *Glenmore* (who was killed on that glorious day). After a conversation that lasted until 2 o'clock in the morning, wherein the gallant Frenchman made the most satisfactory replies to all my questions, I at length, fearing that I had made too many, said in conclusion, 'I am truly sensible of your polite attention in conveying to me the interesting details which you have so frankly given.' 'Not in the least,' he replied. 'We did not gain the victory, and the truth will out [to the French people] in due time. Therefore it would be absurd to conceal the events as they really happened.'[32]

On 6 November, the same day that news of Trafalgar reached London, the death of Captain John Wesley Wright was announced in *The Times*. Wright had been in solitary confinement in the Temple prison for many months, but no doubt hoped that through the intervention of Sir Sidney Smith and Royalist agents he would be helped to escape. He kept in touch by letter with his first lieutenant, James Wallis, who was at Verdun, and six weeks before the Battle of Trafalgar he wrote: 'I rejoice also to hear at length that you are near those dear boys [three young protégés on board the *Vincejo*] in whose progress my whole solicitude at present centres . . . I have taken the liberty to make you a sort of foster father to my little admirals in embryo'[33] – he knew that he was unlikely to be sent to join them at Verdun, but was anxious they should be looked after. The three boys from his crew about whom he was so concerned were William Mansell, John Rogerson Wright (either his nephew or illegitimate son) and George Sidney Smith (Sir Sidney Smith's nephew).

Six days after Trafalgar, on the night of 27 October 1805, the thirty-six-year old Wright was reported by the official French newspaper as having committed suicide. Dillon at Verdun recorded that 'the article in the Moniteur stated that he was found dead in his bed, having cut his throat whilst reading the bulletins announcing the victories of the French Army over the Austrians. What, in God's name, had the victories of the French in Austria to do with Capt. Wright, an English officer?'[34] General Mack and his fifty thousand Austrian troops surrendered at Ulm on 20 October, but it is also possible that Wright had just heard the news of the British naval victory at Trafalgar on the 21st. Nobody believed the suicide theory, and *The Times* commented: 'We fear, there is no doubt of the fact of Captain WRIGHT's decease, but we cannot believe that a gallant officer, who has so often looked death in the face, and was proverbial for courting danger, fell in the manner mentioned. They who ordered, and perpetrated the midnight murders of PICHEGRU, and the Duke D'ENGHIEN, can, no doubt, explain the nature of Captain WRIGHT's death.'[35]

Years later, after the war was over, Sidney Smith made extensive enquiries of former prisoners and gaolers about what happened to Wright, and he discovered a damning story from the porter of the Temple prison:

They found him extended in his bed, his eyes open, his body covered up to the chin with the sheets and counterpane, as if in a state of repose; that one of them ... remarked an opening in the neck, which extended across the same from side to side ... the edges as it were, stuck together. This opening appeared to him at first no more than a scratch, from whence death could not ensue ... The captain was found as has been described, dead, in his bed-gown, (which he however never wore at night), holding in his right hand a razor with a white handle, the arm extended along the right thigh ... the bed was narrow. Captain Wright's head was between two pillows, and not bloody ... By order of the steward, the deponent, with Savar, carried the body down stairs, to a room where it was customary to depose the dead, the one holding it by the head, the other (Savar) by the feet; in doing which the head became all at once so reversed, that he thought it was coming off. It was the deponent who (together with his wife) was charged with the burial, and to cleanse the chamber, that is to say, to remove the marks of blood from the ground *near the bed*, although there was *none on* or under the bed, unless it were a little on the edge of the sheet on the side where the ground was bloody. He ended by saying, that the captain, whose disposition was generous, and his heart endowed with sensibility, always treated him in a manner full of amenity ... on the eve of Captain Wright's death, the deponent heard him playing on the flute till an hour after midnight; which recreation did not indicate the despair of a person who had the intention to destroy himself.[36]

It was obvious that Wright had been murdered, unless a death by natural causes had been made to look like suicide. The same fate seems to have befallen Vice-Admiral Villeneuve. Following the Battle of Trafalgar, he was taken to England as a prisoner-of-war and was one of the few officers to be exchanged, but soon after arriving in France he was found stabbed to death.

During his journey to St Helena on board the *Northumberland*, Napoleon talked for many hours with the surgeon, William Warden, and insisted that he had no part in Wright's death. On one occasion, Warden recalled, Napoleon 'asked me, to my great surprise, if I remembered the history of Captain Wright. I answered, "Perfectly well; and it is a prevailing opinion in England, that you ordered him to be murdered in the

Temple." With the utmost rapidity of speech, he replied, "For what object? Of all men he was the person whom I should have most desired to live. Whence could I have procured so valuable an evidence as he would have proved on the trial of the conspirators in and about Paris? The Heads of it he himself landed on the French coast"[37]

On St Helena, Napoleon repeated his assertions to Barry O'Meara, his physician there:

If Wright was put to death, it must have been by my authority . . . If he was put to death in prison, I ordered it. Fouché, even if so inclined, never would have dared to do it. He knew me too well. But the fact is, that Wright killed himself, and I do not believe that he was even personally ill treated in prison . . . Sidney Smith, above all men, knew, from having been so long in the Temple, that it was impossible to have assassinated a prisoner, without the knowledge of such a number of persons as would have rendered concealment impossible.[38]

The memory of Wright preyed on Napoleon, and he was especially agitated when O'Meara showed him a copy of the *Naval Chronicle* with an engraving of an elaborate monument that had been set up by Sir Sidney Smith over the grave of Wright in the Père Lachaise cemetery (which Napoleon had established outside the walls of Paris). The Latin inscription included the uncompromising words: 'Awhile successful in his career, at length, assailed by adverse winds, and on a hostile shore, he was captured, and being soon after brought to Paris, was confined in the prison, called the Temple, infamous for midnight-murders, and placed under the most rigid custody. But in bonds, and suffering severities still more oppressive, his fortitude of mind, and fidelity to his country remained unshaken. A short time after, he was found in the morning with his throat cut, and dead in his bed . . . To be lamented by his country – avenged by his God.'[39] Napoleon retorted, 'If I had acted properly, I should have ordered Wright to be tried by a military commission as a spy, and shot within twenty-four hours, which by the laws of war I was enti-tled to do.'[40] Less than a century later one visitor to Paris remarked: 'Strange to say this monument is now undiscoverable, and the cemetery keepers deny that Wright is on their registers.'[41]

By the last days of 1805 it was obvious that the struggle between France and Britain had entered a new phase. Nelson was dead, but the defeat of the French and Spanish at Trafalgar had given Britain the upper hand at sea. There would be no more major fleet actions between France and Britain, and increasingly the French Navy would become second in importance to the many privateers that preyed on British trade. But while Britain could now manage to keep control of the sea, France was tightening its grip on the land. John Wesley Wright was dead, and much of the network of British spies and French Royalists had been disrupted or destroyed. Napoleon's position in France was becoming more secure, and he would shortly have control of Europe, so the immediate future presented an uneasy stalemate that would not be resolved until Napoleon's final defeat in 1815. In December 1805 the words of Britain's Prime Minister, William Pitt, were to prove eerily prophetic – when he heard that the Austro-Russian armies had just been decisively crushed by Napoleon at Austerlitz, he said of a map of Europe, 'Roll up that map; it will not be wanted these ten years.'[42]

# NINE

———◆———

# IN EVERY SEA

I used to say that there were four privations in my situation on board the *Devonshire* – fire, water, earth, and air. No fire to warm oneself on the coldest day, no water to drink but what was tainted, no earth to set foot on, and scarcely any air to breathe.

Mary Sherwood's summary of her experience
as a passenger from England to India[1]

After Trafalgar there was a sense of relief and a tendency to relax. The continuous close blockade put a terrible strain on the ships and men involved, and the Admiralty now thought it safe enough to allow the Channel Fleet to take refuge from the winter weather in the shelter of Torbay rather than suffer constant battering by storms. This was a mistake. On 13 December 1805, less than two months after Trafalgar, the blockading British fleet withdrew from its station outside Brest because of foul weather, and the French seized their chance. A formidable battle fleet escaped, but the French were not looking for a pitched battle – they soon divided their forces, with one squadron heading for the West Indies, where it ran into a squadron commanded by Vice-Admiral Duckworth.

Less than four months after Trafalgar, Duckworth at the Battle of San Domingo engineered another resounding victory:

The French admiral, who was greatly inferior in strength, endeavoured to make his escape on the appearance of the English squadron, but being speedily overtaken, an action commenced, which lasted with great fury for near two hours, at the conclusion of which three of the French line of battle ships remained prizes to the English, and two were driven on shore and burned. The two French frigates and corvette put to sea and made their escape. The loss of the English in this engagement was 64 killed and 294 wounded. No officer above the rank of midshipman was killed, but several were severely wounded. The French had 760 killed and wounded on board of the three ships that were taken, and they no doubt lost a proportional number in the two others that were destroyed.[2]

In fact, Duckworth's success was founded more on luck than judgement. He had been blockading what was left of the defeated combined fleet of French and Spanish ships at Cadiz when news arrived that a French fleet was at sea. His decision to raise the blockade and go in pursuit did not make him popular with Vice-Admiral Cuthbert Collingwood, who, on the death of Nelson, had become commander-in-chief of the Mediterranean fleet. Duckworth was also out of favour because earlier he had actually sighted the other part of the fleet from Brest, led by Rear-Admiral Jean-Baptiste-Philibert Willaumez, but had mistakenly let it go. The breakout of one part of the fleet from Brest may have been neutralised relatively quickly, but not before reinforcements had been delivered to the French at San Domingo, and Willaumez was still at large. This was a practical demonstration of how much harder it was to find and destroy French fleets once they were at sea than to keep them cooped up in their ports. It was a salutary lesson to the British that a great battle had been won at Trafalgar but they had yet to win the war.

The blockade of French and Spanish ports was tightened as much as possible, and Collingwood, mollified by Duckworth's achievement, felt that the situation in and around the Mediterranean was under control. The blockade might be the most effective weapon against Napoleon, but it was hard and monotonous work, offering little of interest and no financial rewards. Social etiquette prevented admirals from mixing too much with subordinate officers, and so the boredom of blockade duties affected them deeply. Napoleon, when on board a British warship heading for exile, commented that 'I used to go amongst them [the seamen], speak to them kindly, and ask different questions. My freedom in this respect quite astonished them, as it was so different from that which they had been accustomed to receive from their own officers. You English are *aristocrats*. You keep a great distance between yourselves and the people.'[3] When one of his officers in whom he could confide left the blockade, Collingwood felt quite alone and wrote to his wife and daughters:

I shall miss Admiral Grindal [Richard Grindall, captain of the *Prince* at Trafalgar, and afterwards promoted to rear-admiral] very much, for he has been a companion for my evenings: and when he is gone I shall have only Bounce [Collingwood's pet dog] to talk to . . . The only subject that gives a gleam of cheerfulness is the hope that the fleet in Cadiz may venture out again: they will soon be strong enough. I have only been ten days in port since I left England. It would weary any thing. Would that we had peace, that I might laugh again, and see you all merry around me.[4]

The men in the ships were not happy either, and many of those who had fought at Trafalgar felt aggrieved that their efforts had not been better rewarded. The crew of the *Royal Sovereign* went so far as to present a formal petition to the Admiralty when the ship reached Plymouth, in which they listed their grievances, including only a few men being granted shore leave when in harbour for repairs, and not being allowed to send dirty clothes to be washed on shore. They concluded that 'your Lordships' petitioners further sheweth that contrary to the rest of the Ships that were in the said Action of 21st of Oct[obe]r they have not received the smallest encouragement since the action, not even a single drop of extra liquor'.[5]

Privileges such as shore leave and receiving letters from home were granted at the discretion of captains of individual ships – and some were more generous than others. Many captains feared that allowing seamen ashore encouraged them to desert, especially as a large percentage had been pressed into the navy, but keeping them on board ship in a British port after long tours of duty also made many of them determined to escape at the first opportunity. It was because the men were rarely given shore leave that women were frequently permitted on board the anchored ships, and this was also felt to reduce the likelihood of homosexuality among the men. Homosexual acts were crimes brought before a court martial, such as one that took place 'on board the Salvador, in Plymouth Dock, for the trial of William Taylor and Thomas Hobbs, two seamen, charged with committing an unnatural crime, which being proved against them, they were sentenced to receive 500 lashes each, to forfeit all their pay, and be imprisoned two years in solitary cells. They underwent a part of their punishment on Monday last, alongside the ships in Hamoaze and Cawsand Bay; one of them received 300, and the other 370 lashes.'[6] Such harsh punishment was not unusual, and the men could even be hanged.

Ostensibly, only the wives and children of seamen were granted the privilege of joining them on board, but they were actually far outnumbered by prostitutes. Wives seldom knew which port their husbands had arrived at, or even which ships they were in, and so on top of the problems of travelling it was very difficult for them to join their husbands. In most cases ships were anchored offshore rather than moored in the docks, and boatloads of prostitutes were rowed out to the ships. Usually all a seaman had to do was claim that one of them was his wife, which gave rise to the saying that sailors have a wife in every port. The French army officer René-Martin Pillet, a prisoner-of-war in England for several years, observed that 'the vessel is opened to all the girls of a dissolute life, who offer themselves. Sometimes moreover, for form's sake, a hypocritical captain requires the female visitors to take the title of the sister, niece, cousin or relation of the sailor they designate.'[7]

The seaman William Robinson gave a graphic account of the women who greeted the arrival of his warship at Spithead*:

After having moored our ship, swarms of boats came round us; some were what are generally termed bomb-boats [bumboats], but are really nothing but floating chandler's shops; and a great many of them were freighted with cargoes of ladies . . . So soon as these boats were allowed to come alongside, the seamen flocked down pretty quick, one after the other, and brought their choice up, so that in the course of the afternoon, we had about four hundred and fifty on board. Of all the human race, these poor young creatures are the most pitiable; the ill-usage and the degradation they are driven to submit to, are indescribable; but from habit they become callous, indifferent as to delicacy of speech and behaviour, and so totally lost to all sense of shame, that they seem to retain no quality which properly belongs to [a] woman.[8]

The process by which the women were brought on board was next described in detail by Robinson, who made a pointed comparison to slavery:

On the arrival of any man of war in port, these girls flock down to the shore, where boats are always ready; and here may be witnessed a scene, somewhat similar to the trafficking for slaves in the West Indies. As they approached a boat, old Charon [the boatman], with painter in hand, before they step on board, surveys them from stem to stern, with the eyes of a bargaining jew;

* The sheltered anchorage between Portsmouth and the Isle of Wight.

and carefully culls out the best looking, and the most dashingly dressed; and, in making up his complement for a load, it often happens that he refuses to take some of them, observing, (very politely) and usually with some vulgar oath; to one, that she is *too old*; to another, that she is *too ugly*; and that he shall not be able *to sell them*; and he'll be d———d if he has any notion of having his trouble for nothing.[9]

Robinson also pointed out just how much the officers were involved in controlling the traffic in prostitutes, contrasting their behaviour with their pretensions to being gentlemen:

The only apology that can be made for the savage conduct of these unfeeling brutes is, that they run a chance of not being permitted to carry a cargo alongside, unless it makes a good shew-off; for it has been often known, that, on approaching a ship, the officer in command has so far forgot himself as to order the waterman to push off — that he should not bring such a cargo of d———d ugly devils on board, and that he would not allow any of his men to have them. At this ungentlemanly rebuff, the waterman lays upon his oars a-while, hangs his lip, musing on his mishap; and in his heart, no doubt cursing and doubly cursing the quarter-deck fool, and gradually pulls round to shore again, and the girls are not sparing of their epithets on the occasion. Here the waterman is a loser, for he takes them conditionally: that is, if they are made choice of, or what he calls *sold*, he receives three shillings each; and, if not, then no pay, – he has his labour for his pains . . . these were the terms at Portsmouth and Plymouth in war-time, at these great naval depôts. A boat usually carries about ten of these poor creatures at a time, and will often bring off three cargoes of these ladies in a day; so that, if he is fortunate in his *sales*, as he calls them, he will make nearly five pounds by his three trips. Thus these poor unfortunates are taken to market like cattle.[10]

As a parting shot, Robinson explained the sole reason for the system: 'It may seem strange to many persons, that seamen before the mast* should be allowed to have those ladies on board; whilst the officers must not, on pain of being tried by a court-martial, for disobedience of orders, the Admiralty having made a regulation to that effect. The reason of this is, that the seamen are not allowed to go on shore, but the officers are, and may partake of what pleasure they choose.'[11]

---

* Common sailors, whose berth was the forecastle, in front of (before) the foremast.

Accommodation below deck was crowded enough under normal circumstances, but the influx of so many women filled it to overflowing, and Admiral Edward Hawker provided a vivid picture of life on board a warship in port in a pamphlet he published anonymously in 1821:

The whole of the shocking, disgraceful transactions of the lower deck is impossible to describe – the dirt, filth, and stench . . . and where, in bed (each man being allowed only sixteen inches breadth for his hammock) they [each pair] are squeezed between the next hammocks and must be witnesses of each other's actions. It is frequently the case that men take two prostitutes on board at a time, so that sometimes there are more women than men on board . . . Men and women are turned by hundreds into one compartment, and in sight and hearing of each other, shamelessly and unblushingly couple like dogs. Let those who have never seen a ship of war picture to themselves a very large low room (hardly capable of holding the men) with five hundred men and probably three hundred or four hundred women of the vilest description shut up in it, and giving way to every excess of debauchery that the grossest passions of human nature can lead them to, and they see the deck of a seventy-four-gun ship the night of her arrival in port.[12]

To upper-class observers such as Hawker, the women were hard-bitten, drunken and debauched. At Portsmouth they were known as 'Spithead Nymphs' and 'Portsmouth Polls', and the surgeon George Pinckard described what he regarded as a typical specimen in his account of a visit to Portsmouth:

In respect to streets, houses, markets, and traffic, Portsmouth is not unlike other country towns, but Portsmouth Point [by the docks], Portsea Common, and some other parts of the town have peculiarities which seem to sanction the celebrity it has acquired. In some quarters, Portsmouth is not only filthy and crowded, but crowded with a class of low and abandoned beings, who seem to have declared war against every habit of common decency and deco-rum . . . To form to yourself an idea of these tender languishing nymphs – these lovely sighing *ornaments* of the fair-sex, imagine something of more than Amazonian stature, having a crimson countenance, emblazoned with all the effrontery of Cyprian confidence, and broad Bacchanalian folly: give to her bold countenance the warlike features of two wounded cheeks, a tumid nose, scarred and battered brows, and a pair of blackened eyes, with balls of red; then add to her sides a pair of brawny arms, fit to encounter a Colossus, and set her upon two ankles like the fixed supports of a gate. Afterwards, by way of apparel, put upon her a loose flying cap, a man's black hat, a torn neckerchief, stone rings on her fingers, and a dirty white, or tawdry flowered gown, with short apron and a pink petticoat; and thus, will you have something very like the figure of a '*Portsmouth Poll*'.[13]

The women depicted by Pinckard were prostitutes who plied their trade on shore, as he mercilessly described:

Callous to every sense of shame, these daring objects reel about the streets, lie in wait at the corners, or, like the devouring kite, hover over every landing-place, eager to pounce upon their prey; and each unhappy tar, who has the misfortune to fall under their talons, has no hope of escape till plucked of every feather. The instant he sets foot on dry land he is embraced by the neck, hugged round the waist, or hooked in the arm by one or more of these tender Dulcineas; and, thus, poor Jack with pockets full of prize-money, or rich with the wages of a long and dangerous cruize, is, instantly, dragged (though, it must be confessed, not always against his consent) to a bagnio, or some filthy pot-house, where he is kept drinking, smoking, singing, dancing, swearing, and rioting, amidst a continued scene of debauchery, all day and all night, and all day and all night, until his every farthing is gone. He is, then, left to sleep till he is sober, and awakes to return, pennyless, to his ship – with much cause to think himself fortunate, if an empty purse be the worse consequence of his, long wished for, ramble ashore.[14]

While many of the women who survived for any length of time as seaport prostitutes may well have come to resemble the caricature figure that Pinckard represents, most were despairing young women who had turned to prostitution merely to survive in a brutal society that offered little other employment for an unattached woman not protected by her family. The seaman Robert Mercer Wilson recorded an incident at Spithead in his journal for September 1805 that demonstrates just how desperate some of the prostitutes were:

While we lay taking on board our stores, the ship's company [of the frigate *Unité*] were allowed to have women on board, and really I could almost fill a volume with the different scenes I saw, and the frequent discourses I heard; but as it would be no agreeable thing to those who never heard of the like, and no new thing to those who have, I shall only mention one circumstance which came immediately under my eye. A good-looking woman was taken in one day by a messmate of mine. When he brought her below, I observed that in spite of her trying to be cheerful, she was sad and many a sigh escaped her – also [this escaped] the notice of my thoughtless messmates, who were more mindful of pleasure than noticing whether their girls were glad or sad. Even if they had observed the latter the consolatory reflexion would have been replete with a few hearty dry curses – though in justice to those who uttered them, they meant no harm, so much are seamen in general addicted to swearing. For my part I observed her sighs, and from her discourse I found her to be a woman of some learning . . . I was surprised and amazed when I perceived her to be big with child. 'Good God!' said I to myself, 'well might she sigh and look sad.' What had hindered myself and my messmates from observing it before was [that] she had so artfully concealed it with her cloak in such a manner that it was impossible to perceive it till she took off her cloak.[15]

Wilson asked her how she had come to be a prostitute and was given a familiar story:

It was briefly thus; that 'she had seen happier days, and might have done so to this time but for a young man who, although he was the occasion of all her woes and [of] her present situation, she could not hate'. She told her story so pathetically that I was sensibly touched with the narration; I only grieved I was not in a situation to relieve her . . . In spite of my remonstrances with my messmate (her partner) not to have any connections with her, my offering to take her off his hands, which made him think I was anxious to possess her charms, made him the more determined . . . Poor girl! It was a dear bought pleasure for her, for next morning she was seized with convulsions severe, which indicated the quick birth of the infant in her womb. When her situation was made known, our First and Second Lieutenants (to their honour be it said) gave her a guinea each; I contributed a small matter, but not half so much as I could wish, and she went on shore. The next day a letter came from her (though not written by her) to this effect; 'that she [had] scarcely arrived on shore before she was delivered of a fine boy, in a promising state.'[16]

There was not always a clear distinction between a sailor's wife and a prostitute – sometimes sailors married prostitutes, but more often sailors' wives were forced to turn to prostitution to survive. Despite all that the Admiralty did to help seamen send money to their wives, many received only irregular payments and were often living in poverty. This was not necessarily because sailors did not want to send money, but because the system for doing so was erratic and unreliable. A seamen's wife was not told where or when her husband's ship would return to Britain and often had to travel across country to see him. The only method of social support was the workhouse, but these were organised on a local basis and paid for, grudgingly, out of local taxes. For this reason a destitute woman was taken back to her parish of origin rather than being given help where she was then living. In places overcrowded with seamen's wives from all over the country, such as Portsmouth and Plymouth, the burden on local people would have been crippling if such a strict regime had not been in place. As it was, the cost of returning the impoverished families of seamen to their home parish was very high in the major ports and naval bases. In any case, the workhouse was an absolute last resort, as they were badly run, miserable places with a high mortality rate, largely because the sick and the destitute were housed together with hardly any medical help. In the ports, little work was available for women, and begging was not a realistic option. Beggars who were caught were also taken back to their home parish, but there were so many of them that the competition rather than fear of arrest made begging uneconomic for a sailor's wife. Faced with such a harsh existence, accompanying their husbands on board a warship may have been the least daunting alternative for those wives who had the opportunity.

The navy might turn a blind eye to the custom of taking prostitutes aboard ships anchored at British ports, but did not openly acknowledge it. When Princess Caroline, who earlier had a brief relationship with Sir Sidney Smith, made an official visit to the *Caesar* in Cawsand Bay at Plymouth, Gunner William Richardson recorded the event:

On May 11, 1806, Her Royal Highness Caroline, consort to His Royal Highness George, Prince of Wales, being on a visit to Edgecumbe House, paid our Admiral [Rear-Admiral Sir Richard Strachan] a visit on board the *Caesar*, accompanied by Lady Hood and some others of distinction, and were received with a royal salute of twenty-one guns. The ship had been cleaned and prepared for the purpose, and all the girls (some hundreds) were ordered to keep below on the orlop deck and out of sight until the visit was over. As Her Royal Highness was going round the decks and viewing the interior, she cast her eyes down the main hatchway, and there saw a number of the girls peeping up at her. 'Sir Richard,' she said, 'you told me there were no women on board the ship, but I am convinced there are, as I have seen them peeping up from that place, and am inclined to think they are put down there on my account. I therefore request that it may no longer be permitted.' So when Her Royal Highness had got on the quarterdeck again the girls were set at liberty, and up they came like a flock of sheep, and the booms and gangways were soon covered with them, staring at the princess as if she had been a being dropped from the clouds.[17]

For the seamen a return from port to blockade duties was often considered the worst, keeping them at sea for months on end in all weathers, but many officers hated protecting convoys of merchant ships even more. Because of the risk of attack from enemy warships and privateers, it had been necessary right from the start of the war to organise civilian ships into convoys, and under an Act of Parliament they were only permitted to set sail under the orders of their naval escort. Few of the people involved liked sailing in convoys. Merchant ship captains felt that they restricted trade and made their crews much more vulnerable to press-gangs, who would often meet homecoming convoys and strip the merchant ships of the best seamen. They also resented being told what to do by the officers of naval escorts, who invariably regarded them as inferior seamen. On the other side, the naval officers considered convoy duty hard and frustrating work with no compensations. They had little prospect of capturing enemy ships, so no expectation of prize money, and they were responsible for the safe passage of slow and unwieldy merchant vessels, crewed by civilians who would not obey orders. The only trading ships the navy respected were the East Indiamen. There was frequent friction between merchant crews and naval escorts, and on occasion this became open hostility.

Every kind of cargo was carried by British convoys, including slaves from Africa bound to plantations in the West Indies, a trade that would become illegal in British ships in 1807. There were mixed feelings in Britain over slavery, and even Nelson opposed those such as William Wilberforce who were in favour of abolition, writing to one Jamaican plantation owner just a few months before Trafalgar:

*Victory, June* 10, 1805.– I ever have been and shall be a firm friend to our present colonial system. I was bred in the good old school, and taught to appreciate the value of our West Indian possessions, and neither in the field nor the Senate shall their just rights be infringed whilst I have an arm to fight in their defence or a tongue to launch my voice against the damnable, cruel doctrine of Wilberforce and his hypocritical allies, and I hope my berth in heaven will be as exalted as his who would certainly cause the murder of all our dear friends and fellow-subjects in the Colonies.[18]

Lieutenant Frederick Hoffman, who escorted one of the last slave convoys in his sloop the *Favourite*, was one of those struck by the plight of the slaves in West Africa before they had even set foot on board ship:

During the time I was at Bence Island, which was the great mart for slave dealing, forty of those unfortunate beings arrived, most of them half famished. The principal merchant, who was a mulatto, told me that the greater part of them had been pledged for rice, which is the principal food in Africa, that they had not been redeemed at the time appointed, and in consequence had become the property of those who supplied the food. The remainder were those taken prisoners in the skirmishes occasioned by their trespassing on each other's ground, particularly on the rice patches when the grain was nearly ripe. A black woman offered me her son, a boy about eleven years of age, for a cob – about four-and-sixpence. I gave her the money, and advised her to keep her son. Poor thing! she stared with astonishment, and instantly gave me one of her earrings, which was made of small shells. It was like the widow's mite, all she had to bestow.[19]

The convoy eventually sailed to Barbados, taking seven weeks for the journey, during which Hoffman, with 'some of the officers, visited the Guinea men, and found them orderly and clean, and the slaves healthy'.[20] Doubtless the slaves were crowded together below deck, but in itself this may not have seemed unduly inhumane to an officer accustomed to the hammock decks of warships where the seamen were allowed a space only 14 inches wide in which to sling their hammocks – the hammock plan of a warship was very similar to the 'stowage' plan for people on a slave ship. Sailors were of course free to move about the ship, whereas the slaves were frequently chained up within their cramped space, often lying on bare boards or the deck itself.

Perhaps the only people who were grateful to be sailing in convoys, because of the protection they provided, were the civilian passengers, especially on the long journeys to and from India. It would be over half a century before the opening of the Suez Canal allowed merchant ships from Britain and Europe to dispense with the journey of several months' duration round the Cape of Good Hope to India and the East. The Cape was originally Dutch, but had been seized by the British in 1795 and then returned to the Dutch as part of the Peace of Amiens. As soon as war was declared in 1803, the British government had ordered an expedition to recover it, but this was delayed until autumn 1805, when five thousand soldiers under Major-General Sir David Baird set out in sixty transports escorted by a squadron of warships commanded by Commodore Sir Home Riggs Popham.

It was essential to reclaim the naval base at the tip of South Africa, because merchant ships on the vital east–west trade route were so vulnerable, even when travelling in a convoy. In April 1805, a few months before Popham's expedition set sail, one such convoy of East Indiamen left Portsmouth. Mrs Mary Sherwood and her husband Henry, an army officer, were late embarking in H.C.S.* *Devonshire* and could only hire one of the least desirable cabins, which she graphically described:

No woman who has not made a voyage in such a cabin as this can possibly know what real inconveniences are. The cabin was in the centre of the ship, which is so far good, as there is less motion there than at either end. In our cabin was a porthole, but it was hardly ever open; a great gun ran through it, the mouth of which faced the porthole. Our hammock was slung over this gun, and was so near the top of the cabin that one could hardly sit up in bed. When the pumps were at work the bilge water ran through this miserable place, this worse than a dog-kennel, and, to finish the horrors of it, it was only separated by a canvas partition from the place in which the soldiers sat and, I believe, slept and dressed . . . [the cabin] was just the width of one gun, with room for a small table and single chair. Our cot, slung cross-ways over the gun, as I have said, could not swing, there not being height sufficient. In entering the cabin . . . we were forced to stoop under the cot, there not being one foot from the head or the foot of the cot from the partition. The ship was so light on the water that she heeled over with the wind so much we could not open our port, and we had no scuttle [air vent]. We were therefore also in constant darkness. The water from the pump ran through this delectable cabin, and I as a young sailor, and otherwise not in the very best situation for encountering all these disagreeables, was violently sick for days and days.[21]

* H.C.S. stood for 'Honourable Company's Ship', the East India Company being 'The Honourable East India Company'.

Mary Sherwood was eventually able to cope with the motion of the ship and the hardships of life on board, but after three months the convoy was spotted in the Indian Ocean by French warships:

In a very short time after the enemy had been seen, one of the strangers lay to, whilst the other two came down, and, passing close to our rear, hoisted French colours almost before we had time to form our conjectures of what they were. The colours were no sooner up than they began to fire, and at the same crisis all hands were engaged on board our ship to clear for action. Every cabin which had been erected between the last gun and the forepart of the ship was torn down, ours of course amongst the rest, and everything we possessed thrown in heaps into the hold or trampled under foot. All the women without respect of person were tumbled after the furniture of the cabins into the same dismal hole at the very bottom of the ship, and the guns prepared in the shortest possible time to return the compliment which the enemy had already paid us. One of the enemy's ships was a seventy-four, or eighty gun, the other a large frigate. They were commanded by Admiral Linois.[22]

Nearly three years earlier the French Rear-Admiral Charles Alexandre Linois had sailed from Brest to India and had become notorious in menacing merchant shipping belonging to the British. Accompanied by the frigate *Belle Poule*, Linois in the warship *Marengo* had recently captured the East Indiaman *Brunswick* off Ceylon. He next sailed southwards to escape from a superior British force that he learned was out looking for him. This was part of the squadron of Rear-Admiral Sir Edward Pellew, who was now in command of the East Indies. For political reasons, though, Rear-Admiral Thomas Troubridge was on his way to take over the eastern half of this command, much to the anger of Pellew. What Linois did not realise was that Troubridge was sailing in the *Blenheim*, an old battleship that was accompanying the convoy of East Indiamen in which Mary Sherwood was sailing. Troubridge described how the French, on 6 August 1805, suddenly appeared out of the fog: 'I fell in with Mon'r Linois . . . in very thick squally weather, and just at the close of day exchanged a few shots with him, I fancy he thought we were all Indiamen, for the moment he made the *Blenheim* out through the haze, he bore away . . . I trust I shall yet have the good fortune to fall in with him when unencumber'd with convoy . . . This convoy has given me much trouble to drag them on.'[23] Unlike Troubridge, Mary Sherwood found the whole encounter extremely frightening:

At the commencement of the contest the *Devonshire* was one of those near-est to the enemy, and their shot passed through our rigging, but, as we advanced, the seventy-four fell back and the battle became unequal. One of the Indiamen singled out the frigate, and would have fought her, but after some broadsides the French showed a disposition to withdraw, and it seemed to us that they had been quite as much surprised at meeting us as we had been at seeing them. Linois did not show his usual spirit at this time. It was quite dark when the contest ceased and we poor women were set at liberty.[24]

The convoy was not safe yet, however, and at daylight the French reap-peared:

It was suspected that the frigate had met with some damage, and that she was changing her masts; the third ship, which was a merchantman [the captured *Brunswick*], was not in their company. Several times they bore down as if to attack, but always stopped out of reach of our guns. Our admiral followed by some Indiamen, made a show of pursuing them, but did not go far . . . at day-light [the following day] they were no longer to be seen, and we sent on board different ships of the fleet to ascertain what damage had been done. The rig-ging of the *Hope* and of the *Cumberland* had been much cut, a Mr. Cook on board the *Blenheim* was killed, a man of the 67th had lost his life on board the *Ganges*, and a sergeant of our regiment had lost both his legs on board the *Dorsetshire*. From that time we saw no more of the French, but we afterwards ascertained that we had made Linois suffer so severely that he was glad to get away. The man-of-war was the *Marengo*, eighty guns, and the frigate the *Belle Poule*, of forty.[25]

After this skirmish the convoy had a relatively easy passage to Madras, and Linois headed towards the Cape of Good Hope, where he waited for the *Brunswick* and the frigate *Atalante* to join him. The *Brunswick* came into the bay in a storm in mid-September and was totally wrecked after running aground. A few days later the *Atalante* arrived, and then ran aground in another fierce storm six weeks later. Repairs were impossible, and the crew of the *Atalante* was distributed between the *Marengo* and the *Belle Poule*, with 160 seamen left behind at the Dutch colony. On 9 November Linois headed into the Atlantic in order to cruise along the western African coast. Among the men transferred from the *Atalante* to the *Belle Poule* was the French naval officer Louis Garneray, and he noted the reasoning behind Linois's decision: 'As the slave trade was then flourishing, we put to sea, in the hope that the English slave ships would provide us with fine catches. We sailed along the entire west coast of Africa. Our crews, exhausted and badly rewarded by the insignificant and infrequent prizes that we had taken, complained bitterly, all the more so because they knew that the corsairs of India had resumed their privateering with astonishing success.'[26]

Popham's expedition to recapture the Cape of Good Hope arrived at the beginning of 1806 and just missed Linois. Thomas Howell, a soldier with the 71st Highlanders, said that 'it was early in the morning [of 4 January], when we first beheld the land about the Cape of Good Hope. We soon after could distinguish a hill, called the Sugar Loaf; and next reached a low island, called Robben [Robin] Island. We anchored in Table Bay, and were disembarked next day.'[27] Marine Lieutenant Robert Fernyhough described the difficulties in landing:

We now made preparations for our debarkation, fired guns, and hoisted English colours; a broad hint to the enemy of our errand, which was quickly taken, for the town appeared in great confusion. We saw a party of cavalry, riding in various directions. As soon as we were close enough in, the General and Commodore went in a boat to reconnoitre the place, where they intended to disembark the troops. Accordingly at daylight, the first, or Highland brigade, consisting of the 71st, 72nd, and 93rd regiments, were ready in the boats, but unfortunately it came on to blow fresh, causing a tremendous surf, which rendered it utterly impossible for the troops to land . . . In the morning of the 6th of January, a very heavy surf still running, created a good deal of anxiety on the part of the commanders, but abating a little towards evening, the General was determined at all events to attempt another landing, further down the bay, at a place called Lospord's Bay, which was effected, but not without some difficulty.[28]

Even at this new landing place, there were many casualties, as Fernyhough related:

Forty-one privates of the 93rd regiment were lost in the surf. The 72nd regiment was first put on shore, and it behaved nobly. Whilst our brave comrades were landing, we observed a party of the enemy's cavalry and riflemen advance from behind one of the hills, near the beach, and commenced a smart fire upon them; but as soon as the Highlanders got sight of the enemy, they rapidly advanced, opened a fire upon them, which did much execution,

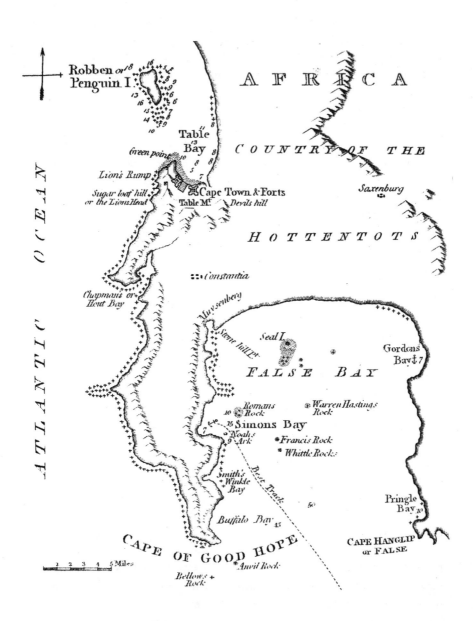

*Map of the Cape of Good Hope*

and they speedily retreated . . . Their main body, consisting of about five thousand men, including Hottentots, was encamped behind the mountains, six or seven miles off, and intended to give us battle next evening. We were disembarking all that evening, until the middle of the next day, January the 7th; an order then came from the General for the marine battalion, with some artillery, to re-embark, and land higher up the bay, to cut off the enemy's retreat.[29]

This next phase was even more difficult, according to Fernyhough:

It is astonishing to me, how we did land through such a tremendous surf, for this was the very place where the first brigade attempted to do so on the 5th, and were obliged to return on board . . . The nearest point we could get to the shore, was forty or fifty yards, so that we were obliged to wade that distance, up to the middle, before we could reach it. I was completely ducked, for in getting out of the boat, a sea came, and dashed me over head, and I thought I should have been obliged to swim for it, but another wave set me on my legs again; I then took to my heels, and ran till I got safely beyond the reach of the sea . . . The *Diadem*, *Leda* frigate, and gun-brig, covered our landing; and just as we were leaving the boats, some of the enemy advanced down the hill, towards us, but the gun-brig opened a fire of grape shot among them, killed two, and the rest retreated. Another part of the enemy, during our debarkation, attempted to get a piece of cannon upon an eminence, but a well-directed fire from our ships completely baffled the attempts; so effectually had the squadron covered our landing.[30]

The Dutch took up a position between the coast and Cape Town, and the British troops followed and prepared to attack, but they had to wait until the artillery arrived, which was dragged up by seamen from the warships, as Lieutenant Samuel Walters of the *Raisonable* described:

We did not reach the Army till noon with the Artillery cannon owing to the extreme difficulty of the country to the drawing [of] Artillery. Seamen on this service drop'd down from their drag ropes almost lifeless – our water all expended – and gain'd a little strength, and came running to join their shipmates. Most of the enemy's cavalry kept on the Heights during the action. The flank companies of the respective Regiments were sent after them, and a smart action took place . . . Our kill'd and wounded about two hundred, that of the enemy double the number.[31]

While the British seamen were helping to haul artillery in place, the Dutch artillery was assisted by the crew of the *Atalante*, who had been left behind by Linois. To no avail. The Dutch were forced to retreat to a natural stronghold, leaving the road to Cape Town clear. The next day, 9 January, the British set out for their main objective, as Walters recounted: 'At daylight the Army set forward for Cape Town, and at 3 p.m. halted near the lines. A Flag of Truce was sent out from the town to offer terms and treat for a capitulation, and was acceded to the following day, by which the Dutch were to give up to us Cape Town, Citadel, Forts, and lines, all the ships in Table Bay, all public buildings and stores, &c. &c., all Naval and Military men to be sent to Holland at the expense of the British Government, all French in the Colony to quit it.'[32]

The Dutch finally surrendered on the 10th, and Walters was one of the naval officers who occupied the town: 'The evening of this day, march'd on to Cape Town, took possession of it, halted in the parade square, a Royal salute was fired by our Artillery, and returned Commodore Popham's Ship, the *Diadem*, the Squadron having all anchor'd in the Bay . . . The Dutch Colours was haul'd down and the English Union hoisted in their stead. The Cape of Good Hope once more an English Colony.'[33] The recapture of the Cape did not just help to protect Britain's trade with India and China, important though that was, but it also provided another check on Napoleon's ambition to expand his empire eastwards. As a result of safeguarding British trade and denying trade opportunities to the enemy, Britain's wealth was bound to grow while that of France dwindled.

It took some time for news of Cape Town being in British hands to reach all the French naval forces, and on 4 March the French frigate *Volontaire* was spotted sailing into the bay, as Lieutenant Fernyhough related:

We took a French frigate, of forty-eight guns, under the following circumstances. She ran into Table Bay, being deceived by the Dutch ensign flying on the flag-staff of the forts and ships, which was on our parts a ruse de guerre. When she came alongside of us, we hauled down the Dutch colours and hoisted the English ensign, opened our ports, showed our broadside, and ordered her to strike. She lowered her colours, and I was directed by Sir Home Popham to take possession of her, with a party of marines. As soon as I got on board, I saw a number of English officers and soldiers, belonging to the 2nd or Queen's, and the 54th regiments of foot. The joy they expressed on our appearance I am unable to describe. One of the officers came and shook me by the hand, and burst into tears, he was so overjoyed: the poor soldiers were in such a state of feeling, that they appeared ready to jump overboard. Poor fellows! they had been prisoners between seven and eight weeks, and during the greatest part of that time had been confined below. A number of them had died for want of air. We now began to bring upon deck the poor sufferers who were confined below. Some of them were so ill, from their long restraint from liberty, that they expired as soon as they were exposed to the air.[34]

The soldiers told Fernyhough that they had been taken prisoner on their way home to England from the garrison of Gibraltar – after capturing troop transports in the Bay of Biscay, the *Volontaire* had been detached from Willaumez's squadron, which was still at liberty after escaping from Brest the previous December, and had sailed to the Cape.

In late January Rear-Admiral Linois learned from an American vessel that the Cape was in British hands, though the news was embellished with warnings that they were waiting for him there, and at St Helena and Mauritius (Île de France to the French). Short of supplies, he decided to risk heading back to France without orders. News of his capture in March reached Plymouth just a few days before Princess Caroline's visit to the *Caesar* with all the prostitutes on board, and *The Times* triumphantly declared:

The *John-Bull* cutter arrived at Plymouth on Friday night, with dispatches from Admiral Sir J. BORLASE WARREN. She had brought the important intelligence of the capture of the *Marengo*, commanded by Admiral LINOIS, and the *Belle Poule* frigate . . . It must be highly gratifying to every English mind that victory is a never-failing attendant on the British flag, in every sea, and on every coast. We see on this occasion, as we have observed on all others of a similar nature, that intrepid conduct, active spirit, and steady resolution, which do so much honour to the naval character, and produce such continual addition to the glory of our country.[35]

The overblown language of the newspaper report obscured the fact that it was bad luck on the part of Linois to have been caught. The squadron led by Vice-Admiral John Borlase Warren was actually searching for Willaumez. On 12 March, in the area of sea between St Helena and the Canary Islands, Linois thought he had spotted a convoy, and Louis Garneray on board the *Belle Poule* witnessed what happened: 'We noticed three vessels sailing towards us before the wind on the opposite tack. The biggest of these vessels made signals, which the others repeated, and two of them soon disappeared from sight thanks to the darkness. Our captain, Mr Bruillac, warned Admiral Linois that the biggest we had just seen and which was now pursuing us, probably belonged to an English squadron . . . Admiral Linois took this advice badly and maintained that this ship was, on the contrary, only protecting a merchant convoy.'[36]

Linois soon realised his mistake, but before he could veer away, Warren's squadron turned to attack. The British maintained their pursuit overnight and the next day caught up with the French ships. Midshipman William Bowyer from the *Ramillies* wrote to his parents, describing the action once the two French ships had been spotted:

It was the middle watch, I was on duty. At 4 o'clock all hands were called: we waited with impatience until daylight appeared, then we saw from the mast-head the *London* engaging a French line-of-battle ship and a frigate; the signal was instantly made for a general chase; our little ship being a prime sailer, came up first to the combatants, when the French frigate made sail, and endeavoured to get away from her companion, but the *Amazon* frigate, of 36 guns, who had all the time stuck close to her, followed her, and as she passed the enemies' line-of-battle ship, poured a broadside into her, as an *English salute* on such occasions: in a short time she came up with the French frigate, which after a sharp engagement at last struck to the *Amazon*; she proves to be the *Belle Poule*, of 40 guns . . . By this time we were coming very near to the *London* and her opponent; we beat to quarters, and double shotted our guns, and as we were about passing the *London*, who had most nobly sustained a severe conflict, she bore up a little and fired another broadside into the enemy; then cheered us as we passed; we returned the compliment, and immediately got between the French ship and them.[37]

Before the *Ramillies* fired, the *Marengo* surrendered because, Midshipman Bowyer reported, of the terrible damage sustained, 'the last broadside from the *London* having made such havock amongst her men, as having killed or wounded above twenty by that fire alone . . . The ship taken was the *Marengo*, Admiral Linois, from the East Indies, who was then on board, and severely wounded in the leg, and his first Captain having lost his right arm. The total number of the killed and wounded on board the enemy I believe to be about 150: I am sorry to say a number are dangerously so, and dying fast.'[38]

Both French ships were captured, and Bowyer told his parents that he was one of the crew ordered to take the prize ship *Marengo* back to England, but in his next letter to them, written at Spithead in mid-May, he recounted how they nearly came to grief on the journey home:

Nothing particular happened until the 23d [of April], when it began to blow one of the heaviest gales of wind (for the time it lasted) that seamen ever experienced, which, with the crippled state of our ship, rendered our situation still more dangerous . . . About nine o'clock in the morning the atmosphere appeared thick and black, and clouds hanging very heavy over our heads; we saw the threatening storm approaching by degrees . . . at seven our mizen-top-mast was blown away close to the mizen-cap . . . we soon cut the rigging away, and overboard it went; then all hands were called, as the ship was making three feet water per hour: we kept constantly pumping, until the moment arrived, when, with a tremendous crash, the once high, lofty, and towering main-mast, with the mizen, fell . . . nothing now appeared before our eyes but the tottering foremast; which in a few minutes fell down also.[39]

Over three hundred men were aboard the captured vessel, but only five men lost their lives, and by rigging a jury mast*, the *Marengo* eventually reached Spithead, along with the *Belle Poule*. The survivors of both crews, including Louis Garneray, were imprisoned in England and would not be released for another eight years.

In early June 1806 Vice-Admiral Warren's squadron left Spithead to return to the hunt for Willaumez's elusive ships. Two weeks earlier Rear-Admiral Sir Richard Strachan's squadron had left Plymouth, also in pursuit of the French admiral – they had been on the point of departure when Princess Caroline had paid a visit to Strachan's flagship, the *Caesar*. Willaumez had for several months been raiding the convoys of merchant vessels in the South Atlantic and West Indies. He was now heading for the coast of Newfoundland, but on 18 August encountered a vicious hurricane that dispersed and damaged his entire squadron.

A fortnight later two of Willaumez's crippled battleships, the *Éole* and *Patriote*, made their way into the safety of Chesapeake Bay, on America's eastern seaboard, while a frigate, the *Valeureuse*, made it to the Delaware river estuary further north. Strachan's squadron was also scattered by a storm, but in mid-September his battleships *Belleisle* and *Bellona* and the

* A temporary mast to replace a damaged or broken one.

frigate *Melampus* caught up with another damaged French battleship, the *Impétueux*, which was also limping towards Chesapeake Bay. Spotting the British ships, the *Impétueux* deliberately ran ashore, and the *Melampus* rescued the French prisoners and set fire to the ship – technically a breach of neutrality as this was carried out in American waters. The British ships now began the tedious process of laying in wait for the French ships, which would trigger a series of events culminating in the attack on the American frigate *Chesapeake* the following year and nearly lead to war between Britain and America.

While the captured ships of Linois were being taken to England, Sir Home Popham was preparing to leave the Cape of Good Hope. He had received information that the Spanish colonies on the Río de la Plata (River Plate) in South America were ripe for liberation, with the additional prospect of rich pickings since Buenos Aires was a repository for treasure that was periodically shipped to Spain. Although an expedition to these colonies had been discussed on previous occasions, and Popham had been involved in the discussions, he had no specific orders from the Admiralty. Nevertheless, he managed to persuade General Baird to loan him some troops under the command of General Beresford, and on 20 April 1806 he set out for South America, sending a message to the Admiralty once he was at sea, informing them of his intentions. The fleet sailed to St Helena to pick up water and supplies, and Popham persuaded the governor there to provide him with reinforcements. From St Helena the fleet moved on to the mouth of the River Plate in early June, and Marine Lieutenant Fernyhough recorded their subsequent progress:

We made sail up the river, but were frequently obliged to anchor, on account of foul winds, and the strong tides, which were continually running against us. The mouth of the river is upwards of 150 miles wide; and in approaching Buenos Ayres, the navigation became extremely difficult, and dangerous to strangers . . . We arrived off Buenos Ayres on the 25th, near Quilmes, about fifteen miles from the city. Here General Beresford deemed it prudent to land. We now observed that the Spaniards were collecting in great numbers at a small village, called Reduction, situated upon an eminence, a short distance from the beach, and upon our appearance, commenced firing alarm guns. About four o'clock p.m. we began to disembark the troops, which we accomplished by midnight, without any material accident, though we had a heavy surf to wade through.[40]

The massive estuary of the River Plate was flanked by Montevideo on the northern shore and Buenos Aires on the south, so the *Raisonable* and another battleship were stationed off Montevideo to cut communication while Buenos Aires was attacked. With his ship separated from the main force, it was nearly a month before Walters had any news of the assault:

On the 9th [July] came down from Buenos Ayres the *Willington*, transport with a supply of water, vegetables, &c., with the following account of the progress of our friends. They did not effect their landing til the 26th June, from having continual fogs with heavy rains, together with the *Narcissus* having got aground on the upper part of Oyster Bank, greatly retarded their progress. On the 29th they had an Action with the Spaniards. Tho' four times the number of ours they soon gave way in all directions, and the English advanced towards the City of Buenos Ayres. When General Beresford arrived before that City with his little force, a Flag of Truce was sent into the Citadel to summons it to surrender at discretion. When the Spanish troops march'd out and those of the English march'd in and took possession of the City, Citadel, Forts, &c., treasure to a great amount was found.[41]

Although most private property was respected, the Spanish treasury was ransacked and warehouses were stripped of valuable merchandise. The viceroy of the colony had escaped with a large amount of treasure, but the British soon found out, as Walters related: 'The General [Beresford] from good information was made acquainted that, the same day that he landed the English Force . . . the Viceroy went off with immense treasure, ten or twelve waggon loads . . . immediately he had got things a little arranged, detach'd a force in quest of them, and was fortunate enough to come up with and take a part of it. It was determined that the dollars should be immediately embarked on board His Majesty's Ship *Narcissus*, and for her to proceed for England.'[42]

The expedition began to run into serious resistance. In August an attack was mounted on Montevideo, but after initial success Beresford's forces were overwhelmed, and on the 12th he was forced to surrender to the Spanish. Popham then tried to blockade Montevideo, but numerous shoals prevented him moving in sufficiently close to be effective, so he shifted his ships along the coast and landed Brigadier-General Backhouse, who, at the end of October, took the town of Maldonada with a small force of troops bolstered by seamen and marines. According to Walters,

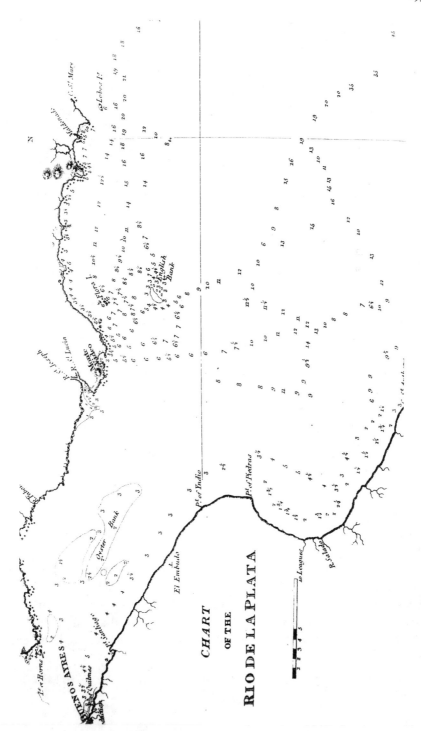

*Chart of the mouth of the River Plate showing Buenos Aires, Montevideo and Maldonado*

the intention in taking Maldonado was that our Force being too small to land against Monte Video, and the Commodore and the Colonels being of opinion that reinforcement shortly would arrive, induced them to take this place for the purpose of getting fresh beef, &c., for the troops and crews, of which we stood greatly in want of. This country being so well stock'd with oxen (upwards of five hundred in herds) and this place being situated about a half mile from the place where the boats land, from the town, we had only to send on shore a few men arm'd with muskets and drive as many as was wanted for present use down towards the place where we used to kill them and take off the beef.[43]

It was probably the arrival of the *Narcissus* in Britain that saved Popham's career. The Admiralty had unsuccessfully tried to stop his expedition as soon as they realised his precise intentions, but the amount of treasure and merchandise seized was valued at several million Spanish silver dollars, and when a large part of this was landed at Portsmouth the expedition was hailed as a triumph. Having been committed to action by Popham, the British government decided that it was better to carry it through than give up, so they sent out Rear-Admiral Stirling to take control. He arrived off Montevideo on 3 December, and Walters wrote in his journal, 'Arrived the *Sampson*, Rear Admiral Stirling, two India ships and some victuallers, who took command of the Squadron, &c., in the River Plate. The Commodore [Popham] haul'd down the broad pendant, and resigned the command. The Admiral would not allow him even a transport to take him home. Sir Home, Captain Wm. King, the First Lieut. and Secretary and other followers* obliged to take a passage in the *Rolla* [an American ship not part of Popham's expedition].'[44]

By now the British had lost control of Buenos Aires, and so with the newly arrived troop reinforcements it was decided to abandon Maldonado and make an assault on Montevideo. This city fell on 3 February 1807, but it took nearly five months to mount a further campaign against Buenos Aires. This proved to be a catastrophe, and after the loss of over 2500 British troops, prisoners were exchanged under a flag of truce, including General Beresford and his men. The British ships evacuated all their remaining forces to England and the Cape of Good Hope, leaving the Spanish in control once more. Popham was

---

* Protégés of Popham who followed him from ship to ship; most senior officers had such a group who relied on their favour for promotion.

court-martialled at Portsmouth, and the verdict was that 'the conduct of the Captain Sir Home Popham, in the withdrawing the whole of the naval force under his command from the Cape of Good Hope, and the proceeding with it to the Rio de la Plata, was highly censurable; but in consideration of circumstances did adjudge him to be ONLY SEVERELY REPRIMANDED'.[45] This was a very lenient verdict, but Popham had influential friends, and the tragic disaster barely made a dent in his career.

To the Admiralty and the Government the fiasco of Popham's unauthorised adventure was an unfortunate distraction from a more immediate problem. Part of the reason that the attempt on the Spanish colonies was not abandoned earlier was that Britain needed fresh markets for its exports, which South America could provide. Because the British Navy now dominated the seas around western Europe, it could blockade the ports and control the flow of imports and exports. Napoleon could not challenge this with a physical blockade so he devised what became known as the Continental System in order to destroy Britain's economy. From November 1806 the ports of western Europe were closed to British ships in an attempt to prevent the export of supplies to Britain and the import of British goods. Even neutral vessels were not allowed to enter ports if they had previously been at a British one, and if strictly enforced it could have brought Britain to the point of negotiating with Napoleon before the country became bankrupt.

In reality, the Continental System was not strictly enforced because it was soon realised that it hurt France and its allies as well as Britain, and also affected neutral countries. Even Napoleon and members of his entourage circumvented the system when it suited them, and numerous methods were devised to evade the blockades and embargoes. Barely a year after the system was put in place, the *Calcutta Gazette* was reporting that indigo dye from India was selling at a high price, since it had 'found its way into the very countries occupied by the armies of our most inveterate enemy. France herself is our best customer, since all the French soldiers are clothed in blue, and all the French are soldiers . . . we cannot but be highly gratified by the consideration that, whilst Bonaparte is straining all his nerves and exerting all his arts to destroy the proud independence of England, he is effectually a dependent upon her maritime sovereignty.'[46]

# TEN

————◆————

# CONFLICT AND COMMERCE

At the dinner at Tilsit, at which the Emperor of Russia &
Buonaparte were present, the following Toast was given '*The
Freedom of the Seas*'.

Diary entry by Joseph Farington for 27 July 1807[1]

The start of 1807 not only saw the beginning of the disastrous loss of a
foothold in South America, but a similar fiasco much closer to home.
During the autumn of 1806 Turkey had become an ally of France, giving
Napoleon a good land route to the East. This could only be cut by the
British Navy at the Dardanelles – the narrow stretch of water separating
Europe from Asia at Constantinople. Britain was reluctant to regard
Turkey as an enemy and so sent a fleet to cruise the Dardanelles in the
hope that a show of force would persuade the Turks to change their
policy. As a last resort, the Turkish fleet at Constantinople could be
destroyed to prevent them helping Napoleon's armies to cross into Asia.
It was a task requiring the kind of subtle diplomacy at which Sir Sidney
Smith excelled. He also had extensive knowledge of Turkish waters and
links with the Turks from the time of the siege of Acre, but he was out of
favour with both the government and the Admiralty, and so Vice-Admiral
Sir John Duckworth was to lead the mission instead. Duckworth was
instructed to be guided in diplomatic matters by the British Ambassador
at Constantinople, Charles Arbuthnot, who had little experience of diplomacy in the Middle East. Because Smith accompanied the force in a
subordinate role as the admiral in charge of the rear division of the fleet,
this led the *Naval Chronicle* to comment that Smith had been placed 'not

The Temple prison in Paris, viewed from the interior courtyard

Sir Sidney Smith defending the breach in the walls at Acre in April 1799

A plaque recording the burial in the churchyard at Happisburgh, Norfolk, of many who drowned in the wreck of the *Invincible* in March 1801

A seaman being taken by the press-gang

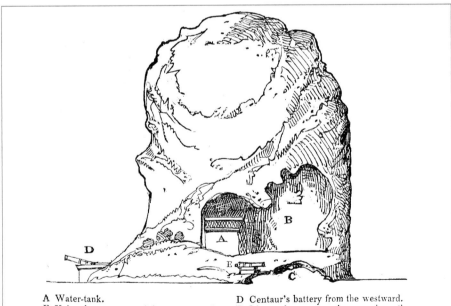

A Water-tank.
B Vulcan's cave, containing coppers for cooking, smith's forge, with purser's, gunner's, boatswain's, and carpenter's store-places.
C The only landing-place on the rock.

D Centaur's battery from the westward.
E 24-pounder carronade covering the landing-place. Here there was a pair of boat's davits for hoisting a barge up.

The north-west side of Diamond Rock in January 1804

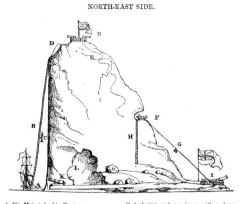

NORTH-EAST SIDE.

A His Majesty's ship Centaur.
B Jack-stay and purchase, with the long 24-pounder slung.
C Gun, vial-block, and slings.
D Projecting piece of rock at top, where upper end of the jack-stay was secured.
E Foot-path to upper battery.
F Hood's battery, 24-pounder carronade, grand magazine. Provisions were also kept here for a month or six weeks.
G Jack-stay and purchase, with a large tub, called the Royal Mail, as a communication between Hood's battery and low ground, for provisions, &c.
H Jacob's ladder, also communicating to Hood's battery, and hauled up every night.
I Centaur battery.
K Diamond, or Queen's battery.
L Hospital Cave.
h̄ h̄ h̄ Caves where the people slept and trussed.
N Upper, or Chicel's battery, two long 24-pounders.

The north-east side of Diamond Rock, hauling guns into position on the summit in January 1804

Action between a French squadron and John Wright's *Vincejo* in the Gulf of Morbihan, in May 1804

The squadron under the command of Vice-Admiral Sir John Duckworth in the Dardanelles, February 1807

A cannon from the frigate *Anson*, wrecked in December 1807, on display at Helston in Cornwall

Bitche prison in eastern France

The 'Raie-de-Chat' near Blankenberge where Edward Boys and other prisoners-of-war hid

The memorial at Norman Cross to the prisoners-of-war who died there

Bird's-eye-view looking from Batz up the River Scheldt towards Antwerp during the 1809 Walcheren expedition

The *United States* defeating the *Macedonian* in October 1812

The attack on Captain Philip Bowes Vere Broke of the *Shannon* after boarding the *Chesapeake*, June 1813

Chesapeake Mill in Wickham, Hampshire, in 1864, made from timbers of the *Chesapeake*, captured in June 1813

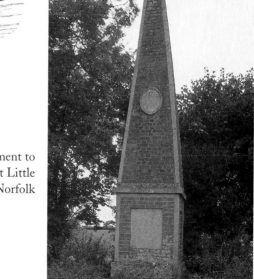

The obelisk monument to peace in 1814 erected at Little Dunham in Norfolk

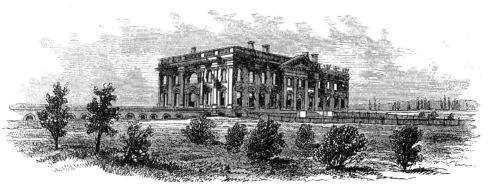

The White House, Washington, after being burned in August 1814

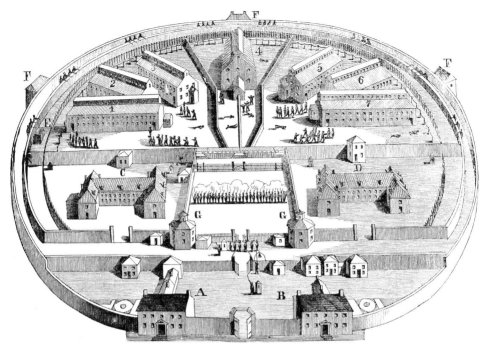

Plan of Dartmoor Prison at the time of the massacre on 6 April 1815

Napoleon on board the *Bellerophon* in 1815

*first*, nor SECOND, but THIRD, in command of an expedition, of which he alone was competent to be the commander-in-chief'.[2]

The victory at Trafalgar had been an inspiration to the navy, but a tendency towards overconfidence now prevailed. Midshipman Crawford on board the *Royal George* commented that 'if Mr. Arbuthnot and the Admiral [Duckworth] had any misgivings as to the issue of the coming enterprise, certain I am, that they were not shared by the inferior officers and men; not a doubt of the sufficiency of the force, or of its complete success, ever crossed their minds'.[3] The fleet reached Turkish waters in early February 1807, and those officers familiar with the story of the siege of Troy in Homer's *Iliad* were keenly aware of their surroundings, as Crawford noted:

Off this classic coast, how many recollections of early years floated through my brain! – freshly and vividly recalling my schoolboy days, and renewing all those feelings of enthusiasm and delight with which the soul-stirring story of those countries is wont to inspire the youthful mind! Scarcely could I bring myself to believe that I beheld, indeed, the battle-field of the contending hosts of Ilion [Troy] and Greece! – the arena where fought the heroes, fabulous or real, of the master-bard! – that I was in the very waters that bathed the shores of immortal Troy![4]

Almost immediately, however, disaster struck. While anchored at the mouth of the Dardanelles on the night of 14 February, one of the battleships caught fire. Crawford's sleep was broken by the subsequent commotion: 'Soon after I had turned in, I was suddenly roused by an alarm of fire. Jumping out of my hammock, I learned from the sentry in the cockpit that it was not the *Royal George*, but one of the squadron. I was dressed and on deck in a moment, when I saw volumes of dense smoke, illumined by occasional flashes of lurid flame, issuing from the stern-ports of the *Ajax*.'[5] The fire rapidly took hold of the entire ship, as a lieutenant on board the *Ajax* recorded in an anonymous letter to the *Naval Chronicle*:

At half past nine on the evening of that day, the *Ajax* took fire in the bread-room, and in ten minutes she was in a general blaze from stem to stern . . . when the first Lieutenant, and many others, broke open the door of the Surgeon's cabin, the after bulk-head was burst down by the accumulated flames and smoke abaft it, and so rapidly made its progress through the cockpit, that it was with difficulty he could regain the ladder, and most of those who accompanied him were suffocated in the attempt. On reaching the quarter-deck he found the fire had out-run him, and Captain Blackwood agreeing with him that she was past all remedy, they both ran forward where the majority of people were assembled, calling most piteously on their God for that help they despaired of getting, although many boats were approaching them, so rapidly did the fire work its way forward, and [so they] leapt from the sprit-sail-yard.[6]

Boats from the surrounding ships were sent to pick up survivors as fast as possible, but the fire was so fierce that most were forced to jump overboard before they arrived. The lieutenant of the *Ajax* gave some details: 'The Gunner, unhappy father! had thrown one child overboard, which was saved; but going down [below deck] for another, perished in the flames. Of forty-five Midshipmen of every description, about twenty are saved . . . Three Merchants of Constantinople were on board, two perished; also a Greek Pilot. One woman, out of three [on board], saved herself by following her husband with a child in his arms down a rope from the jib-boom-end . . . several people died after they were got on board the different ships, the rest are distributed among the squadron.'[7]

In all, about four hundred people were saved, but over two hundred and fifty lost their lives. The ship burned for a long time, watched by those aboard the nearby ships. Crawford observed that 'after the fall of the masts, the smouldering hull long remained unmoved, nor did it drift until two o'clock in the morning, when, the light wind having veered a little more to the eastward, it was slowly borne towards the island of Tenedos, upon which it struck; and at five o'clock, a partial explosion of the magazine shattered to pieces what the fire had not consumed. Thus miserably perished the noble but ill-starred *Ajax*! – a most inauspicious omen for the success of our enterprise.'[8] The ship being named after a Greek hero from Homer's *Iliad*, some inevitably saw its loss so close to Troy as a bad omen, but it was much more serious that Duckworth's fleet had lost one of its larger battleships before the first shot had been fired.

Five days afterwards the fleet sailed into the Dardanelles. Confined within a narrow stretch of water 38 miles long and at times less than a mile wide, the fleet was at the mercy of the currents flowing between the Black Sea and the Aegean, and sometimes had little room to manoeuvre. As the ships sailed up the Dardanelles they soon came under fire from Turkish shore batteries and warships, which Captain of Marines Thomas Marmaduke Wybourn on board the *Repulse* recorded the next day:

This day [20 February] we arrived at Constantinople through a *vortex of fire*. I could never conceive much more experience. I often thought ... I had seen service, but every shot I have seen for twelve years past, would not amount to half fired yesterday. We got under way by daylight on Thursday Morning, passed the two great Castles at the entrance, with but little loss and fought our way up till we came to the grand Key to the Capital 15 miles up – here we saw what even Mars [Roman god of war] himself might have trembled to behold, a narrow passage in the form of 'S' dividing Europe from Asia, and so narrow one might fancy in approaching there was no inlet, – two immense Castles, situate on each point with Batteries on all sides, that threw shot from 40 to 60 pounds weight. After looking on this, I must not be thought a *Coward* if I declare I felt an unusual tremour at my heart, for I sincerely thought no power could *save* us.[9]

In this first stretch of the Dardanelles, the British ships ran the gauntlet of the shore batteries equipped with mortars that fired huge balls of granite and marble weighing up to 800 pounds. With such projectiles it did not require many direct hits to do a great deal of damage, as Wybourn witnessed: 'To return was *impossible* ... 700 pieces of Cannon opened upon us, the Ships were cut to pieces in their Ropes, Masts, and rigging. The smoke so thick they could not see to fire with precision – their large stone shot fell short, and passed over us, as second Ship – the first Ship was mawled dreadfully, and also the *Royal George* the 3rd Ship, the one received a shot which killed and wounded six men, and weighed 554 pounds, the other one of 640 pounds, I never heard of such a thing, and no doubt it would appear incredible at home.'[10]

Despite the damage, the fleet sailed by these forts without losing a ship and then passed relatively unprotected settlements along the shore. Duckworth's instructions were to bombard the Turks until they surrendered their fleet if diplomatic negotiations failed, and so firing was directed at these towns. Wybourn recorded the result: 'The strong wind [that] we had soon cleared the first three ships of the danger, then *what a sight* presented itself. Round the Castle were towns two miles long: as the other ships and the two bombs [bomb vessels] came through we had nothing to do for half an hour but look on; the slaughter on shore was beyond all calculation, the houses flew in thousands of pieces, never was anything so dreadfully awful.'[11]

The fleet next encountered more serious opposition from Turkish ships backed up by shore batteries, and Sir Sidney Smith at the rear was ordered to use his three battleships and a frigate to deal with this, while the rest of the fleet sailed on to Constantinople. Smith's ships were remarkably successful, as he informed Duckworth:

In reporting to you the entire completion of the service you were pleased to order should be executed by the rear division under my immediate directions, I need not inform you that the ships were anchored in the thick of the Turkish squadron, and in close action with them, as you must have observed it; but as the intervention of the land, after you passed the point, prevented your seeing the subsequent operations, it is my duty to acquaint you therewith. The Turks fought desperately, like men determined to defend themselves and their ships as long as they could; but the superiority of our fire, within musket-shot, obliged them in half an hour to run on shore.[12]

Having put the Turkish ships temporarily out of action, Smith followed up the advantage by attacking the shore batteries. With control of the beach, he landed seamen and marines to destroy the ships and shore batteries, in the process of which they took many prisoners. Smith had orders not to keep prisoners, who were released once the Turkish opposition was neutralised, as he told Duckworth: 'The whole of the Turks were landed, in pursuance of your orders, including the wounded, with due attention to the sufferings of our misguided opponents, as I must call them; for the term enemy does not seem applicable, considering their evident good disposition towards us nationally.'[13] In all, Smith's small force destroyed nine Turkish ships, two gunboats and a large shore battery of thirty-one cannons, but it was not as easy a victory as the measured prose of Smith's report to Duckworth suggested. On board the *Repulse,* Marine Captain Wybourn set down his own version of events:

We now approached a point of *three fronts* and which had kept up a triangular fire with the Castles some time, the Channel led us inevitably to pass this enormous Battery also, when lo! as we turned a corner, we discovered ten men of War, with all broad sides turned to us & which we passed within a few yards of. What did the noble Sir Sidney [Smith] do, but run with two ships in between them *all*, and so astonished them, that our 3 first Ships passed with little damage from them. Our signal was now made to assist Sir Sidney, when we engaged a 64 and one point of the villainous Battery for one hour: now was the sport of the day at issue, thank God we were out of the reach of those frightful Castles and granite shot. The Turks took *panic* – they never think of quarter as they do not give it, they began to jump overboard. Cables were cut by our shot, the ships ran on shore, we now boarded & saved the people, and the day was our own. The Admiral had run with his squadron of about 6 Ships into a Bay out of danger – and we four ships took, and destroyed a squadron of 10. We made signals of victory, and the Admiral ordered all the prizes to be burnt. Alas! Money out of my pocket, but he had other objects.[14]

Wybourn, and doubtless many others on board Smith's ships, lamented the loss of prize money when the captured Turkish ships were destroyed rather than being sailed back to a British port to be sold. As a captain of marines, Wybourn was entitled to a share of one-eighth of the value of all prizes taken by his ship, divided up among captains of marines, captains of soldiers and ship's lieutenants and masters. A fixed scale distributed the prize money between all the officers and men who took part in the action, so in this case any prize money would be divided between the four ships involved. If the ships were acting under orders from an admiral, he would also receive a share, and if they were particularly successful, admirals could become very rich men without lifting a finger. Until 1808 admirals stood to receive an eighth of the value of all prize ships captured under their orders, but then the scales were changed and an admiral's share was reduced from one-eighth to one-twelfth. The seamen were known to grumble that the musket shot and cannonballs ought to be distributed in the same proportion as the prize money, with the largest share going to the officers, but in many battles the officers were at greater risk because their sense of honour did not allow them to take cover, whereas the men thought it sensible to duck behind a cannon to avoid incoming shot. The only officer about whom such grumbles were frequently valid was the commanding admiral, who received his share even if he was miles away from the action and did not know about it until afterwards.

Smith was forced to burn his prize ships because he could not spare any men to form the skeleton crews that would normally be detached to sail the prizes back to British territory. He needed every man he had, as Wybourn was well aware: 'The Turks covered the hills & country for miles around – we destroyed the Battery of above 50 Guns, took above 3,000 prisoners, and liberated them, to their *wonder* and *amazement* – and they perhaps, or even ourselves, never beheld a sight as grand as all their ships on fire, and blowing up one after another. We now joined the Admiral, and fought our way without much difficulty past Gallipoli, into the sea of Marmora, and were safe at eight o'clock for the present. Took something to eat, cracked our jokes and laid down for a Nap, but who could sleep?'[15]

The entire fleet anchored together late in the evening of 20 February, but without the advice of Smith, who knew the locality very well, Duckworth had made a fatal mistake. In his report written the next day he glossed over the problem: 'The squadron . . . came to anchor at ten o'clock, near Prince's Island, about eight miles from Constantinople, when I dispatched Captain Capel, in the *Endymion*, to anchor near the town, if the wind, which was light, would permit the ship to stem the current, to convey the ambassador's despatches to the Sublime Porte in the morning, by a flag of truce; but he found it impracticable to get within four miles, and consequently, anchored at half-past eleven P.M.'[16] In sailing towards Constantinople Duckworth's ships should have kept to the western side of the channel, but they had anchored on the east and found that without a strong following wind they were prevented by the fierce current from approaching the opposite shore. The whole point of the mission was for a strong naval force to threaten the Turkish fleet at Constantinople, as well as the city itself, in order to provide leverage for diplomatic negotiations in Britain's favour. It was exactly the same bullying strategy that had been successful for Parker and Nelson at Copenhagen nearly six years earlier, but now and in subsequent days there were at best only light breezes, and no chance of Duckworth's ships moving within range of the Turkish fleet.

At first the Turks refused to negotiate at all, and then prevaricated as much as possible, aware that all the available time could be used to strengthen their fortifications and take other defensive measures. On 3 March, when it had become obvious that the city had become too well defended for an attack to succeed, Duckworth abandoned negotiations. He led his ships back through the Dardanelles to the open sea, and although the fleet was sailing with the current and had a following wind to speed the ships along, the Turkish batteries were waiting for them, as Crawford in the *Royal George* related:

We now found that the enemy fired with much more precision than upon our ascent; for, though we were borne along with great velocity, the squadron was struck more frequently, and suffered more than it did upon its upward passage. By noon it had cleared the Dardanelles, and soon after anchored between Tenedos and the main. The *Royal George* had three men killed, her first lieutenant and twenty-seven men wounded, in the descent of the passage. These casualties were chiefly caused by a huge stone-shot, that struck the upper sill of the third quarter deck port from forward, and with the surmounting hammocks, swept every man from the gun, and tearing away in its course the whole of the bulwark between the two opposite guns, expended its remaining force in the water. I watched this monster-shot almost from the cannon's mouth till it struck the ship; and, so little swift was its flight that, had it come in the direction in which I stood, I should have had time to avoid it. Indeed, the whole scene on shore more resembled the bursting of some mountain's side, which, vexed and torn by the throes of a laboring volcano, vomits forth, in fire and smoke, fragments of rock and iron, than the sharp, quick fire of a well-served battery.[17]

In the end, the British gained nothing from this expensive venture, and it was left to the Russian allies of Britain, with a fleet under Admiral Dmitri Seniavin, to blockade the Dardanelles. On 1 July the Russians finally removed the threat by defeating the Turkish fleet, in a battle known to them as the 'Russian Trafalgar'.

While the Admiralty reacted on an ad hoc basis to specific threats, such as the changing loyalties of the Turks, the blockade of French ports remained relentless, disrupting French merchant shipping and trade. In response to Napoleon's Continental System, Britain placed restrictions on neutral vessels, and in turn Napoleon declared it illegal for a neutral vessel to comply with these British regulations: America was caught in the middle. Neutral American merchant ships were circumventing the blockade of French ports by re-exporting goods from the French West Indies to Europe, resulting in a dramatic surge in business for America. The Royal Navy caused deep resentment in America by seizing the ships that were involved in this re-export business, but attempts to resolve the various problems between America and Britain failed, and Anglo-American relations rapidly deteriorated.

While trade was a major source of aggravation between Britain and America, the impressment of seamen raised equal concerns. Thousands of

British seamen – including deserters from the British Navy – volunteered for service in American merchant ships, because pay and conditions were much better, with less likelihood of encountering a British press-gang. The Royal Navy believed that it had the right to board American and other neutral merchant ships, even on the high seas, in order to impress British citizens and take off deserters. To the Americans this was a violation of their sovereignty, a controversy that 'constituted a part of the historic struggle for the establishment of the principle of the freedom of the seas'.[18]

If British seamen had been the only ones taken from American vessels, there might have been much less rancour, but many Americans were also taken. One problem was deciding who was an American, because at that time there was no especially distinctive American accent and anyone born before the declaration of independence in 1776 had once been a British subject. Certificates of citizenship were issued to many American seamen to prevent their being seized by press-gangs, but bogus protection documents were freely purchased, both in America and in major British seaports, so the Royal Navy tended to treat them all with suspicion.

Only a year before, in the spring of 1806, Lieutenant William Stanhope Lovell of the frigate *Melpomene* observed one case of bogus documents when they took 'a very fine young seaman'[19] from an American ship while they were moored off Messina in Sicily: 'On being brought on board he produced his United States' protection, and requested to be sent back to his ship . . . Having strong suspicion that he was an English subject, – notwithstanding the clamour raised by the Yankee master and consul, and the production of his protection; yet, from his not having any nasal twang when he spoke, and not using the general slang words of that country, such as "I guess," "I calculate," etc., – we kept him on board that night.'[20] The following day the seaman admitted that he was a native of Swansea in Wales and described how he had bought a false protection when last in New York:

I was told that by paying two dollars I could get a protection of citizenship, which would prevent my being pressed on board an English man-of-war. The way it was managed was this:– I was put into a large cradle made on purpose to hold men; I was then rocked by them for a minute or two, and afterwards taken before the proper authorities by the old couple, who made oath they had known me ever since I was in my cradle – no further questions were asked, the matter being quite understood between the parties, – I paid the fees, the protection was granted, and, having given the old folks two dollars for their trouble, I became a 'registered American citizen,' . . . in short, it is a regular trade, and hundreds of seamen that have protections got them in the same manner.[21]

Louis Simond, who had emigrated to America just before the French Revolution, travelled in Britain for many months during the Napoleonic Wars. He himself was a shipowner in America and was of the opinion that 'it is notorious that nearly one half the crews of American ships sailing from southern ports, beginning at New York, were composed of British seamen. Every individual of them, however, most probably had protections; one-half of which were consequently false: how could it be expected that such documents as these should be respected?'[22]

Another problem was that America was happy to grant citizenship to immigrants, while Britain held the view that nationality could not be renounced unless by permission of that nation, so anyone born in the British Isles could not escape the obligation of serving in the navy simply by becoming a naturalised American citizen. Most Americans were not issued with protection certificates, and Britain thought it had the right to impress anyone without a protection who spoke English, resulting in thousands of Americans being mistakenly or deliberately impressed into the Royal Navy. It has been estimated that from the start of the war with France in 1793 to the outbreak of war with America, between eight and ten thousand American seamen were pressed into the Royal Navy, while others served as volunteers.

Although war with America did not start until 1812, a major incident occurred almost exactly five years earlier. In June 1807 British warships were lying in wait off Chesapeake Bay in the expectation of intercepting the two French warships, the *Patriote* and *Éole*, that had taken refuge there nearly a year before. The British ships had set up a blockade, and they regularly anchored in Hampton Roads while obtaining provisions and fresh water in the town of Norfolk. During one such revictualling, men had deserted from the frigate *Melampus* and the sloop *Halifax* and enlisted with the American frigate *Chesapeake*, so complaints were made to Vice-Admiral Sir George Berkeley, the commander of the British squadron, who was based at Halifax in Nova Scotia. In early June he issued an order to his captains to search the *Chesapeake* for deserters if the American frigate was met 'at sea, and without the limits of the United States'.[23] In turn Berkeley ordered that if the Americans made a similar demand, they should be allowed to search for any deserters, 'according to the usages of civilized nations on terms of peace and amity with each other'.[24]

On 22 June, after months of delays, the *Chesapeake* sailed into the Atlantic at the start of an intended voyage to the Mediterranean to relieve the frigate *Constitution*, which had been away nearly four years. The *Chesapeake* had around four hundred crew and several passengers. In mid-afternoon the British frigate *Leopard*, under Captain Salusbury Pryce Humphreys, approached the *Chesapeake* and signalled that they had dispatches. Lieutenant Meade boarded the *Chesapeake* with Vice-Admiral Berkeley's orders, which complained that while British ships were at anchor in Chesapeake Bay, 'many seamen, subjects of his Britannic Majesty . . . deserted and entered on board the United States frigate called the *Chesapeake*, and openly paraded the streets of Norfolk, in the sight of their officers, under the American flag, protected by the magistrates of the town'.[25]

Captain James Barron of the *Chesapeake* refused to allow a boarding party, and after Meade left he ordered his officers to prepare for action. Before they could do so, the *Leopard* fired two shots across the American frigate's bow and stern, followed by three broadsides from a distance of only 200 feet. The *Chesapeake* managed to fire just one gun in fifteen minutes and sustained much damage, with eighteen men wounded and three killed. When Barron surrendered, the *Leopard* ceased firing and sent a boat to the frigate. Although the *Chesapeake* had many British seamen, only four deserters could be identified, and they were taken off. Three were in fact Americans: John Strachan, Daniel Martin and William Ware. These men had volunteered for service in the Royal Navy, though before that they had been illegally pressed but returned to their merchant ships – only to desert to the Royal Navy.

The only man who was English was a thirty-four-year-old by the name of Jenkin Ratford, and he had deserted from the sloop *Halifax* and enlisted with the *Chesapeake* as John Wilson. He was now dragged from his hiding place and put on board the *Leopard*. Because the British declined to take the *Chesapeake* as a prize, the American frigate limped back to Norfolk, and on 1 July Stephen Decatur took over the command. The following day President Jefferson ordered all British warships to leave American waters.

Barron was later court-martialled and suspended without pay from the American Navy for five years. The court martial of the *Melampus* men and the deserter Ratford took place at Halifax on 26 August 1807. Vice-Admiral Berkeley ordered the three Americans to receive five hundred lashes each, but this punishment was never carried out, and instead they were held in prison, where one of them died, though the other two were eventually returned to the *Chesapeake*. Ratford 'was found guilty of mutiny, desertion, and contempt, and hanged at the fore yard-arm of the *Halifax*, the ship from which he had deserted'.[26]

In America there was outrage at what had happened, the citizens of Norfolk rioted and war with Britain was demanded. Attempts were made to resolve the issue, but Britain refused to budge from the right to search American merchant vessels for deserters. Later in the year, on 16 October, the British government issued a proclamation that ordered all British seamen engaged in the service of foreign vessels and states to return home and for all British naval officers to seize any such seamen, as well as reinforcing the right of impressment from foreign merchant vessels, but disclaiming the right to search naval ships of other nations, all of which increased the anger felt in America. The actions of Berkeley, though, were disowned, and he was recalled by the Admiralty. Fellow naval officers were horrified at what he had done, and Collingwood wrote from his ship, the *Ocean*, based off Syracuse in Sicily, that 'the affair in America I consider as exceedingly improvident and unfortunate, as in the issue it may involve us in a contest which it would be wisdom to avoid. When English seamen can be recovered in a quiet way, it is well; but when demanded as a national right, which must be enforced, we should be prepared to do reciprocal justice. In the return I have, from only part of the ships, there are 217 Americans. Would it be judicious to expose ourselves to a call for them?'[27] He added: 'What should we say if the Russians were to man themselves out of English ships?'[28]

In Europe, the political landscape had changed again. On 14 June a Russian army had been defeated by Napoleon at the Battle of Friedland, and on 7 July Napoleon met the Russian Tsar Alexander I at Tilsit, a small town on the Polish-Lithuanian border. Here a peace treaty was signed between France and Russia, and it was obvious that with Russia under the sway of Napoleon the Continental System would soon begin to have a serious effect on Britain. Russia also agreed to give up its naval bases in the Adriatic to the French and vacate the Mediterranean. Of more immediate concern was one part of the treaty that was meant to remain secret – how France and Russia would divide up Europe between them with an aggressive application of the Continental System and the amalgamation of the French and Russian fleets. These were to be increased by more shipbuilding and by seizing the fleets of Portugal and Denmark, both neutral states.

The secret treaty was known almost instantly in Britain, and the government realised that it must act quickly to pre-empt Napoleon's plan. The more dangerous threat lay with the Danish fleet, and within weeks seventeen battleships and twenty-one frigates commanded by Admiral Lord Gambier sailed for Copenhagen as the first wave of an expeditionary force, while other battleships, frigates and transports for twenty-five thousand troops under Lieutenant-General Lord Cathcart were assembled. Once again Britain was threatening force against a nominally neutral country for much the same reasons that Copenhagen had been attacked by Parker and Nelson in 1801. If Napoleon gained control of Denmark, Britain would be excluded from essential trade with the Baltic states, and the Danish fleet could be used to renew the possibility of invading Britain.

Barely one step ahead of the military, with a ring of British ships already in place around the Island of Zealand, the British diplomats met the Danish Crown Prince to demand 'whether Denmark intended to declare for or against England, as its neutrality, owing to the violent measures adopted by France, could no longer be acknowledged'.[29] The Prince is said to have declared 'that he would consider every power as his enemy that should attempt to violate his neutrality'.[30] The lessons of 1801 had been taken to heart, and not only had the expedition been dispatched more quickly this time, but it did not rely on naval fire-power alone. Troops were landed and quickly laid siege to the city of Copenhagen to back up British demands that the Danes surrender their fleet and naval stores. Charles Chambers, a surgeon on board the fireship *Prometheus*, noted the disembarkation of the troops in his diary entry for 16 August:

At 2 this morning, the Troops began to land, which occupied all the forenoon. They made a very grand appearance on the beach, and an appropriate spot being selected, of course met with no opposition from batteries, &c. This portion of the Country is one of the finest I ever beheld, and considerably surpasses in rusticity that . . . in the neighbourhood of Elsineur; the woods have a great similitude to those of Radway in Warwickshire, but are more extensive, and there are some celestial cottages situated in various parts of them. I felt for the disconsolate inhabitants on the disembarkation of the Troops, many of whom I afterwards saw marching over the hills, and in the heat of the day sitting down under the shade of the trees in a state of tranquillity that could scarcely be expected, when reflecting on the serious and awful purport of their errand.[31]

The reserve troops were commanded by Major-General Sir Arthur Wellesley, who had travelled with an entourage of servants and his own supplies, which by now were running low, and Chambers related that 'it having been intimated to Captain Parker [of the *Prometheus*] that Sir Arthur Wellesley was getting short of provisions, he very liberally sent him some wine, hams, &c., on shore for his use'.[32] He added:

An order has been given by Admiral Gambier to fit out a small captured Danish sloop as a fire-ship, to send in to destroy their floating battery should an opportunity avail, the entire superintendence of which is entrusted to Captain Parker, who is to have the management of her when she is burnt. As she is rigged out with part of the *Prometheus*'s combustibles, we have denominated her the *Young Prometheus*. A poor dog was found in her, which unhappily fell overboard, and with much difficulty I saved its life by employing a man who had much trouble to haul it in; the sensible animal evinced its gratitude by a peculiar attachment [to Chambers].[33]

While Chambers acquired a pet dog, the bombardment of Copenhagen was intensifying, and the next day he had a grandstand view of the conflict. His diary entry for 23 August recorded the awesome sight:

Sunday morning at 10 o'clock a firing commenced and proved far more tremendous than any yet experienced; the enemy began, and in less than 10 minutes it became general with the navies and armies. More grandeur and magnificence could not possibly be displayed: the elements appeared at war with each other, and the incessant roaring of guns, mortars, &c., resembled . . . an unremitted peal of thunder, the repeated echo of which baffles all description. I wish it to be understood the *Prometheus* this day was only a spectator . . . I therefore from our quarter-deck beheld, in cool blood, the desperate proceedings of each party. From the windmill battery, lately erected by our soldiers, they fired red-hot shot, the distinct hissing of which through the air was awful indeed. Our mortar-boats sallied forth to lend their assistance, but were shortly obliged to return, being unable to cope with the enemy's heavy metal, especially of Copenhagen Crown Battery, the most formidable one of all. I saw several of our shells burst over the city and blockships, and

two fell apparently very near one of the large spires. We could plainly perceive
where shot and shells dropped on both sides; those which fell in the water
produced an extraordinary splashing, and those on shore raised immense
clouds of dust; the chief of them appeared very well directed . . . Some of Mr.
Congreve's pyrotechnic rockets were let off at the town, though it was generally supposed the distance too great for them to do execution. I saw two
stick in the beach which burnt a considerable time. Including the standard of
wood to which they are attached the same as common rockets, the weight of
each is 32 lb.; they make a most curious noise as they traverse the atmosphere,
by far more audible than the hissing of shells or red-hot shot. The action continued till 4 in the afternoon, when the firing of each party ceased, as if
reciprocally; however, wishing to act as an impartial umpire, I must confess
our ships appeared unable to maintain the contest longer, and I fear sustained
no inconsiderable injury. The cutter from which the rockets were discharged,
was repulsed in a very short time. Congreve was not in her himself, which
some attributed to *sagacity* on *his* part. In the afternoon, a stag was conveyed
past the *Prometheus* in a boat, which I presume was taken from some park on
shore, and sent as a present by the military officers to Admiral Gambier.[34]

Day after day bombardment and counter-bombardment continued, as
the British grip tightened around the city, and the Danes held out in hope
of the siege being broken by a relieving army. On board ships such as the
*Prometheus*, which were not directly involved in the fighting, life went on
as normal. On the 29th Chambers recorded: 'A general order has been
issued stating that a Danish vessel laden with oranges and lemons being
detained by the Fleet, any Officers desiring to procure some for their
refreshment may obtain them at the rate of £1 12 0 per chest, the price of
which in England I fancy would be nearly double that sum. Our lower
deck was whitewashed this morning, which gave it a much neater and
lighter appearance than before.'[35]

It was on this day that the only real battle between two large forces of
troops took place – Danish troops were moving in to break the siege, and
the British reserve under Wellesley decisively defeated them at Kioge,
which left Copenhagen completely at the mercy of the besiegers. The next
day Chambers wrote: 'At 3 P.M. the following Telegraph communication
was conveyed to us from the Admiral's ship . . . "General Wellesley has
gained a complete victory and taken 1 General, 64 officers, 1,200 prisoners and 12 cannon and was pursuing the enemy flying." I understand Sir
A. Wellesley's Brigade were sent after a detachment of Danes to the

number of 7,000 in the direction of Elsineur, the chief of whom consisted of armed peasantry, and I presume were not partial to the smell of gunpowder, as Sir A.W.'s force consisted of only 2,000 but the flower of the Army.'[36] Without a break Chamber's diary entry continued with more mundane news: 'Had a most excellent turkey for dinner which came from Sweden and cost no more than 4 shillings. Congreve the rocket maker is become the jest of the whole Fleet, insomuch that every person is sporting wit upon him, some have conferred on him the appellation of Commodore Squib, &c. ; he appears determined to make himself conspicuous, as he wears a white hat and coat; consequence [desire for celebrity] seems his leading characteristic, which cannot be wondered at with a salary of £2,000 per annum for an invention which hitherto has proved futile.'[37]

On shore, Captain Harry Ross-Lewin of the 32nd Regiment was critical of the soldiers' behaviour after their victory:

On the 29th he [Wellesley] defeated the Danes near Kioge, and took about eleven hundred prisoners. This duty was performed effectually, but the men were guilty of many excesses. The Danes pay the greatest respect to the remains of their deceased relations, keeping the churchyards uncommonly neat, and adorning them with well-executed monuments, chiefly of white marble. Some of these were wantonly injured by the soldiers, and several of the tombs were broken open by them in the expectation of finding money, rings, and other trinkets. Not content with these insults to the dead, they stripped many living females of their necklaces and ear-rings, sometimes tearing the latter through the flesh; but immediate steps were taken to put a stop to such outrages.[38]

Wellesley's defeat of the Danish force proved to be the turning point, after which the British gradually gained control of the city. By 2 September Chambers was able to report that 'our Army have cut off the source of water from the City of Copenhagen',[39] but the Danes refused to surrender and the bombardment continued. Three days later Chambers was called from his bed in the early hours:

At 5 this morning was informed the largest church* in Copenhagen was on fire . . . I instantly jumped out of bed and ran on deck with only a great coat

* Vor Frue Kirke (Church of Our Lady), rebuilt after the great fire of 1728.

on. I then cast my eyes to the accustomed quarter and derived a melancholy gratification on beholding the sacred edifice so roughly handled by that all-devouring element. The Spire – a very lofty one – *was* an octagonal building, beautifully ornamented with gilded decorations, but alas! had fallen to the ground from near its base . . . the remaining steeple, which is also considerably high, exhibited a woeful spectacle, being encompassed to its now uncouth summit by the sacrilegious flames which were vomited out in torrents from the different windows and outlets . . . Having gazed till novelty was overbalanced by sorrow for such an event, I proceeded below.[40]

The terrifying bombardment continued through the day, but Chambers then remarked: 'This evening to our astonishment there was no repetition of the bombardment, which made us suspect that a negotiation might possibly be carrying on, for scarcely a gun was fired on either side.'[41] His suspicion was correct and the next day, 6 September, the Danes agreed to give up their fleet and naval stores in return for a British withdrawal and an exchange of all prisoners. It had been a costly episode for the Danes. The authorities had ignored British offers for civilians to be evacuated before the bombardment began, and around two thousand people lost their lives, including many women and children, as well as about two hundred and fifty of the defending troops and seamen. Many more lost their homes. Some of the officers went into the city, including Robert Blakeney, an eighteen-year-old ensign in the 28th Regiment:

The spectacle was lamentable and well calculated to rouse every feeling of sympathy. Many houses were still smouldering, and in part crumbled to the ground; mothers were bewailing the melancholy fate of their slaughtered children, and there was not one but deplored the loss of some fondly beloved relative or dearly valued friend. Yet they received us with dignified, though cool courtesy, in part suppressing that horror and antipathy which they must have felt at our presence, though some indeed exclaimed that their sufferings were the more aggravated as being inflicted contrary to the laws of all civilised nations. The unfortunate sufferers seemed not to reflect that war was will, not law.[42]

In the days that followed the cease-fire Chambers, who had already bought some Danish items and rescued the dog, continued to add to his souvenirs, and on 10 September he noted:

Was this day presented with a Danish tourniquet, and pair of pistols, found in one of the enemy's gun vessels; the latter are evidently more constructed for utility than ornament. Lieut. Setford likewise having a brace, thoughtlessly pointed one at me and snapped the trigger, luckily it didn't go off, for on examination immediately afterwards to our astonishment it was found primed and loaded. The ball I now have in my possession. A large concourse of Danes have been looking on from the beach at *our* Sailors employed with *their* shipping, at whose manoeuvres they do not seem well satisfied. Heard that four Lieutenants are ordered under arrest by Sir Samuel Hood [of Diamond Rock fame] for marooning as the nautical phrase is, i.e., embezzling a few small articles for their own use, during the time they were employed in Copenhagen Dockyard.[43]

The siege and bombardment also furnished the name for the horse that Wellesley (as the Duke of Wellington) would ride at the Battle of Waterloo. Major-General Thomas Grosvenor took his favourite mare with him on the expedition to Copenhagen, but on arrival the horse was found to be in foal and was sent home. The chestnut foal, named Copenhagen, was later bought by Wellesley and became his favourite horse, which carried him all day at Waterloo. The horse retired to the Duke's house at Stratfield Saye in Hampshire, and was buried with full military honours in 1836.

The Danish warships were taken out of the dockyard, and all the naval supplies removed or destroyed, as Blakeney described: 'In less than six weeks after the fall of Copenhagen (which time was occupied in rendering the Danish ships seaworthy, and spoiling its well-stored arsenal to the last nail and minutest rope-yard) we departed, carrying away with us, as prizes, eighteen sail of the line, fifteen frigates, five brigs, and twenty gunboats.'[44] Ross-Lewin was aggrieved at the lack of prize money awarded: 'The ships and stores brought off from Copenhagen were valued in England at four millions and a half sterling, and it was supposed cost the Danes about ten millions; but as no formal declaration of war had been made, it was decided that the captors were not entitled to prize-money, and a sum of only eight hundred thousand pounds was granted by way of compensation to that portion of the army and navy which had been engaged in the siege of Copenhagen.'[45]

The success of the Copenhagen expedition did nothing to diminish the outcry against what was seen by many as an unprovoked attack on a neutral state. Others had no such doubts. When news of the action reached him in early November. Marine Captain Wybourn in the *Repulse*, now part of Admiral Collingwood's Mediterranean fleet, happily wrote:

The Captain sent us various papers up to the 8th of October, which was a great treat indeed. The full particulars of the Danish affairs were in them, stating that Copenhagen Capitulated on the 7th of September with all their Fleet, Stores & Ammunition etc., etc. fell into our hands – 114 Ships & Vessels of War & more naval stores than will fill all our fleet & their own. This must be a death blow to Boneparte, as it is certain he meant to seize that Country & employ all its force against us, as there was five times the quantity of stores more than was necessary for all the Danish fleet. It will also again check a Northern Confederacy &, by all the papers, Russia appears dissatisfied with the Peace of *Tilset* [Tilsit].[46]

Despite the optimism of the newspapers that inspired Wybourn's enthusiasm, Napoleon was anything but finished, and many years of conflict lay ahead before there would be a lasting peace in Europe. The Mediterranean was still a key battle ground, but ever since Trafalgar the main danger was from privateers and pirates* rather than enemy fleets, which were kept in port by the blockade. Three days after Wybourn had received his 'great treat' Captain Thomas Cochrane was taking his ship, the *Imperieuse*, to join Collingwood's fleet when he was becalmed within sight of another ship that he believed was a privateer. The only way to investigate was by boat, and three boatloads of marines were sent. Cochrane reported what happened in a letter to Collingwood:

I am sorry to inform your Lordship of a circumstance which has already been fatal to two of our best men, and I fear of thirteen others wounded two will not survive. These wounds they received in an engagement with a set of desperate savages collected in a privateer, said to be the *King George*, of Malta, wherein the only subjects of his Britannic Majesty were three Maltese boys, one Gibraltar man, and a naturalised captain; the others being renegadoes from all countries, and great part of them belonging to nations at war with Great Britain. This vessel, my Lord, was close to the Corsican shore. On the near approach of our boats a union-jack was hung over her gunwale. One

---

* A privateer was a privately owned vessel of war that had an official commission from a state authorising the capture and destruction of enemy ships on its behalf, in the same way as a naval ship. A pirate had no legal sanction and preyed upon ships of all countries.

boat of the three, which had no gun, went within hail, and told them that we were English. The boats then approached, but when close alongside, the colours of the stranger were taken in, and a barbarous volley of grape and musketry discharged in the most barbarous and savage manner, their muskets and blunderbusses being pointed from beneath the netting close to the people's breasts.[47]

It was this first volley that caused most of the casualties, and knowing that if the boats pulled away they would have to retreat under fire, the marines swarmed aboard. A fierce fight followed and the crew of the privateer was cut to pieces by Cochrane's men. The few who were not wounded eventually surrendered, but it was then found that the ship was a British privateer. Both ships had mistaken the other for the enemy. Cochrane was dismayed, but since the papers of the *King George* were not in order and the crew seemed anything but British, he sent the vessel to the authorities at Malta. In a typical instance of duplicity the prize court ruled that since the papers were not in order, the *King George* would be seized as a prize, but being a friendly vessel, all prize money would go to the crown. Everyone involved in the incident was a loser by this decision, and Cochrane keenly felt the loss of his men by such a mistake, which is why his letter to Collingwood read more like an admission of failure than a report of success. He ended it with the words, 'The bravery shown and exertion used on this occasion were worthy of a better cause.'[48] Collingwood saw things differently and was impressed by the initiative of the latest addition to his command. It would not be many months before Cochrane was released from the tedium of blockade and convoy duties to carry the war to the enemy in his own individual way.

Also in late 1807, the American government was still considering what response to make after the attack by the *Leopard* on the *Chesapeake*. In Britain it was felt that America was not truly neutral, and in his diary entry for 7 December the artist Joseph Farington echoed that view:

This day appeared in the papers the message of Mr Jefferson, President of the United States, to Congress delivered the 27th of Oct. It evinces more partiality to France than any document which the American government has for a long time published. While Mr. Jefferson declaims with great warmth against what He calls the depredations of this country on American commerce, the numerous aggressions of France are passed over without

observation . . . The affair of the *Chesapeake* is mentioned with much irritation. The finances of the United States are stated to be very flourishing.[49]

While Farington was reading this in newspapers in England, the
Americans were pushing through the Embargo Act, in which all
American commerce with foreign countries was prohibited. It became
law on 22 December, and its aim was to withhold raw materials and
manufactured goods from the warring European nations, forcing the
war to a close. Instead its immediate effect was to cripple the American
economy.

In reality the embargo made very little immediate difference to Britain's
economy, and the British Navy was more concerned about the disruption
of trade by privateers. This threat was still most serious in the West
Indies, and in December the 18-gun brig *Recruit* was sailing out to join the
squadron that Britain was forced to maintain to protect the merchant
ships. The *Recruit* was commanded by the twenty-six-year-old lieutenant
the Honourable Warwick Lake, who had already served more than ten
years in the navy. At Falmouth in Cornwall, to bring the crew up to
strength, ten men had been pressed from the privateer *Lord Nelson*,
including a local man called Robert Jeffery. Born at Fowey, he had moved
to Polperro with his family as a young boy, and after being reasonably well
educated he went to work in his stepfather's smithy. He found the lure of
the sea irresistible and signed on as a seaman with the *Lord Nelson*, only to
be forced into the navy. When he was taken on board the *Recruit,* he was
only seventeen and legally below the age of impressment.

The *Recruit* was not a happy ship and during the voyage to the West
Indies several crew members were flogged for being ill-disciplined and
drunk, and Jeffery was held in irons for two days for stealing rum, before
receiving a flogging of twenty-four lashes. About two weeks later he was
caught stealing beer from a cask, which he admitted, claiming that he was
dying of thirst in the heat – it was later reported that the men were kept
short of water, although the officers had plenty. Captain Lake ordered
Jeffery's name to be added to a list of those to be allocated unpleasant jobs,
but late in the afternoon on the same day he was again summoned before
the captain, who was by now in a fury, declaring that 'he would not keep
such a man in his ship'.[50] Lake told Jeffrey that he was going to be left on
the island they were approaching, and he was forbidden to take food,
water and spare clothing.

The island of Sombrero is in the very north of the Leeward Islands, some 40 miles from the nearest inhabited land. Just three-quarters of a mile long and up to 400 yards wide, the island had seabirds and lizards, but no water or trees. It had been given its name by the Spanish, because its profile resembled that of a sombrero hat. The second lieutenant, Richard Mould, remonstrated with Lake, but was ordered to take Jeffery in the jolly-boat to the island. On looking round the tiny sliver of land, the boat's crew 'found nothing on it; it was a barren spot, covered in the middle with a rough grass weed'.[51] Some of them gave Jeffery their own possessions – a knife, handkerchiefs and even a pair of shoes as his bare feet were by now cut and bleeding after climbing up the side of the cliff. They returned to the *Recruit*, leaving a greatly distressed Jeffery, who 'expected every moment that a boat would be put off to take him on board'.[52] This was an unprecedented type of punishment, as Robert Jeffery had in effect been left to die. It was 13 December 1807, two days after his eighteenth birthday.

The log books recorded that Jeffery had been left on the island, but in the muster book, in which all members of the crew were listed, the purser added 'R' for 'run', incorrectly signifying that he had deserted. This was later erased and replaced with 'Sombrero Island 14th December'.[53] The *Recruit* continued patrolling to the south until reaching Barbados at the end of January 1808, where the flagship of the fleet commander, Rear-Admiral Sir Alexander Cochrane, was anchored. On learning about Jeffery, he immediately sent Captain Lake back to Sombrero to rescue him, but by the time the *Recruit* reached the tiny island, two months had elapsed since Jeffery's abandonment. The search party found only the remains of a pair of trousers and the handle from a tomahawk or hatchet: of Jeffery there was no trace. In years to come, his treatment of Jeffery was to return to haunt Captain Lake, but for now that was the end of the matter.

# ELEVEN

———•◆•———

# THE SEA WOLF

Five thousand men, at the disposal of Lord Cochrane or Sir Sidney Smith . . . would have rendered more service to the common cause *than five times that number on shore*, because they could at all times choose their points of attack, and the enemy, never knowing where to expect them, would everywhere be in fear.

Opinion of Sir Walter Scott[1]

In November 1807 news began to filter back to Britain about another incident that had taken place on the other side of the Atlantic – the capture in the West Indies of a French privateer, the *Génie*, that operated out of Guadeloupe. A letter describing the action, from a passenger on board the British ship *Windsor Castle*, was published in the *Naval Chronicle*:

In the morning of the 1st of October, the man at the masthead called out 'a sail': we were soon convinced that all hopes of escape, by swiftness, were vain. We therefore had the netting stuffed with hammocks and sails, the arms all prepared, and the hands at quarters, when the enemy began to fire at about 40 minutes past eleven, A.M., but as his shot did not reach us, we did not return his fire till about half past twelve, and so continued till he closed, and grappled us on the starboard quarter, at about quarter past one. In this situation it became quite calm, and the vessels could not have separated even had they been inclined. As soon as they grappled us, our boarders were prepared with their pikes, but our nettings were so lofty, and so well secured, that they did not attempt to board; our pikemen, therefore, again flew to their muskets, pistols, and blunderbusses; our captain all the while giving his orders with the most admirable coolness, and encouraging his men by his speeches, and example, in such a way, that there was no thought of yielding, although many of our heroes now lay stretched upon deck in their blood; but then we saw the enemy's deck completely covered with their dead and wounded, and the fire from our great guns doing dreadful execution at every discharge. We now began to hear them scream, which so inspired our gallant little crew, that many of the wounded returned again to their quarters. At length, about a quarter past three, the rascals ran from their quarters, when our captain, with five or six of his brave comrades, rushed on board, killed their captain, tore down their colours, and drove the few remaining on deck below, and the privateer surrendered.[2]

The *Windsor Castle* passenger described how the odds had been against them:

Our force consisted of a small ship of 180 tons, mounted with six 4-pounders and two sixes, manned with 28 people, officers and boys included, of which there were four of the latter under 17 years old. The privateer was called the *Genii*, . . . mounting six long sixes, and one long 18-pounder fixed upon a swivel in the centre of her main-deck, and traversing upon a circle, so that this enormous piece of ordnance was worked just as easily as a common sized swivel; and having on board, at the commencement of the fight, 86 men, of which number 26 were killed, or died in a few hours after the action, and 30 more are wounded, many of whom will also die: not one of their officers escaped being killed or wounded. Both vessels were greatly damaged in the action . . . On our side we lost three brave fellows, two of whom were killed on the spot, and the third died the same evening; another, I fear, is mortally wounded through the breast and shoulder. We had, besides, nine men wounded, and three or four of them badly.[3]

The fact that the crew of a small British ship, outnumbered by over three to one, had captured a more heavily armed privateer, was remarkable enough, but the *Windsor Castle* was a Falmouth packet – a civilian ship, not a warship. These packet ships were only lightly armed, for self-defence, usually relying on speed to outrun any attackers, so the capture of a more powerful privateer was a significant achievement. Packet ships were run by the Post Office to carry mail, freight and passengers overseas, and although not part of the Royal Navy until 1823, the Packet Service had

close connections with it. Much of the ordinary mail and less urgent dispatches were carried to and from naval vessels by packet ships, which were
sometimes given a navy escort in particularly hostile waters, and they
regularly operated over vast distances. Their main base was at Falmouth
in Cornwall, from where they sailed to many transatlantic destinations as
far off as Halifax in Canada and Buenos Aires in South America, as well
as the important Mediterranean route to Corfu via Gibraltar and Malta.
Other packet ships were stationed at Harwich and Dover for Continental
destinations, Weymouth for the Channel Islands and Holyhead and
Milford for Ireland. Falmouth was chosen as the main base because it was
a good, sheltered anchorage giving easy access to the transatlantic routes,
and was far enough west to be out of the way of most privateers from the
Continent. The disadvantage of Falmouth was its distance from London,
over 270 miles, but this was regularly covered by mail coaches in three to
four days.

In their role as transport for passengers, packet ships were the fore-
runners of the great ocean liners that were such a popular method of
travel at the end of the nineteenth century. Soon after the Napoleonic
Wars were over, several companies established rival packet services using
steamships, and in 1839 the partnership of Samuel Cunard, George Burns
and Davis MacIver established the British and North American Royal
Mail Steam Packet Company, which soon became widely known as the
Cunard Line.

In the weeks following the news of the capture of the *Génie*, a crisis
emerged in Europe resulting from the Treaty of Tilsit, which had been
signed between France and Russia in July. Admiral Seniavin's Russian
fleet, so recently successful against the Turks in the Dardanelles, now
found itself virtually an enemy of the British and without a Mediterranean
base. Unable to reach the Black Sea, it was attempting to reach the far-off,
friendly waters of the Baltic when bad weather in mid-November forced
it to take shelter in the mouth of the River Tagus at Lisbon. The timing
was unfortunate as Napoleon was planning to invade Portugal, and
Lisbon was soon to become the next brief focus of the struggle between
the British and the French.

Aware of the shadow of Napoleon looming over his country, the Prince
Regent of Portugal had already expelled the British business community
and later detained those British subjects still in the country, confiscating
all remaining British property. This was not enough to appease his French
ally, and while the Russians were sailing into the Tagus, General Jean

*Map of Lisbon and the mouth of the River Tagus*

Junot was marching through Spain at the head of a French army to capture Lisbon, marking the start of the Peninsular War in Spain and Portugal. Rear-Admiral Sir Sidney Smith, meanwhile, had been dispatched from England with orders to ensure that the Portuguese fleet and Portuguese government should not fall into the hands of the French. Smith also had orders to prevent the Russian fleet from sailing into an enemy port, but he was too late to stop them slipping into the Tagus on 16 November, just as his own ships were approaching. Smith had a powerful fleet of eight battleships and two frigates, and he immediately set up a blockade of the Tagus where the bulk of the Portuguese fleet, and now a Russian fleet of nine battleships and a frigate, lay at anchor.

The Prince Regent was reluctant to leave, despite intense diplomatic pressure from the British, but at a Council of State on 24 November the decision to flee to Brazil was taken – the deciding factor seems to have been news that the French had crossed the border into Portugal and were less than 75 miles from Lisbon. It was now a race to prepare the ships for the long voyage to South America and move out of the anchorage before General Junot and his army arrived. Five days later the Portuguese fleet set sail, but they were forced to leave behind four battleships and several smaller warships, most in poor condition. As the Portuguese ships crossed the bar of the Tagus into the open sea, the French took control of Lisbon.

Smith had been working closely with Viscount Strangford, the British Ambassador, and in persuading the royal family of Portugal to leave for Brazil and remove the Portuguese fleet from the grasp of Napoleon, they had achieved a strategic blow against the French at least equal to Nelson's rescue of the Neapolitan royal family in 1798. The Admiralty's appreciation was shown in a letter to Smith dated 28 December, signed by the Admiralty Secretary, William Wellesley Pole: 'I am commanded by their lordships to express their high approbation of your judicious and able conduct in the management of the service entrusted to your charge . . . [and] the respectful attention which you appear to have shown to the illustrious house of Braganza . . . their lordships are satisfied of the necessity of your resuming, in person, the strict blockade of the Tagus, and they approve of your having detached from your squadron four sail of the line, under the command of Captain Moore, to escort the royal family of Portugal to Rio [de] Janeiro.'[4]

Once clear of the coast, Smith ordered Captain Graham Moore, whose interception of Spanish treasure ships in October 1804 had led Spain to declare war on Britain, to escort the Portuguese to Brazil, while Smith

himself returned to command the continuing blockade of Lisbon and
the Portuguese coast. A few weeks later, in February 1808, Smith was
relieved by Vice-Admiral Sir Charles Cotton and sailed to take up command of the squadron in Brazilian waters. The Russians had made no
move to stop the Portuguese leaving, and continued to favour the British
rather than the French, hoping that national alliances would soon shift
back again. During the following months, while trapped in the Tagus,
they maintained a discreet and friendly contact with the British ships on
blockade duty, while at the same time resisting pressure from Junot for
closer co-operation with the French.

Blockade remained the most effective naval strategy against Napoleon
and his allies, confining their warships to port and severely restricting
their trade, and just as battles and other engagements took their toll in
ships and men, blockade duty also continued to be hazardous. Often
ships had to be at sea in the worst of the weather to maintain a blockade,
and inevitably some were lost. On Christmas Eve 1807, the frigate *Anson*
sailed from Falmouth to rejoin the blockade of Brest, but after being hit
by a severe storm, generally described at the time as a hurricane, Captain
Charles Lydiard decided to return to port. For several days the frigate
fought against the weather, but visibility became so bad that they were
uncertain of their exact position along the Cornish coast. When they
found out, on the morning of 29 December, it was too late as the *Anson*
was already trapped in Mount's Bay, near Penzance. The wind was blowing the ship relentlessly towards the shore, and there was not enough
room to sail out to open sea without striking the headlands at either end
of the bay. One survivor described how the anchors failed:

Captain Lydiard's mind [was] made up to come to an anchor; for had we kept
under weigh, the ship must have struck upon the rocks in a few hours. The
top-gallant-masts were got upon deck, and she rode very well until four
o'clock on Tuesday morning, when the cable parted. The other anchor immediately let go, and the lower yards and topmasts [were] struck. At daylight the
other cable parted, and we were then so close to the land, that we had no
alternative but to go on shore, when Captain L. desired the master to run the
ship into the best situation for saving the lives of the people, and fortunately
a fine beach presented, upon which the ship was run.[5]

The 'beach' was actually a sand bar that divides Loe Pool from the open
sea. Although deceptively soft and sandy in appearance, it is actually hard

and stony, with a shelf just offshore where the depth drops abruptly by some 15 feet. On impact the wind and waves rolled the ship over towards the shore and the mainmast snapped. What happened next was reported in *The Times* several days later: 'The sheet anchor was then let go, which also brought up the ship; but after riding end-on for a short time, this cable parted from the same cause, about eight in the morning, and the ship went plump on shore, upon the ridge of sand which separates the Loe-pool from the bay. Never did the sea run more tremendously high. It broke over the ships masts, which soon went by the board; the main-mast forming a floating raft from the ship to the shore, and the greater part of those who escaped, passed by this medium.'[6]

With the ship starting to break up and huge waves washing over the hull, many tried scrambling to shore by means of the mainmast, but most were washed off and drowned. Ironically, many more of those who waited several hours, when the weather improved slightly, were saved. It was a gamble of life or death: stay on a ship that might break up at any moment, or risk being swept away and drowned while trying to cover the 60 yards that separated the ship from the shore. By the time the *Anson* ran aground, people had begun to gather along the shore from neighbouring settlements, but they were largely powerless to help. An account of the rescue attempts, by an anonymous eyewitness, was published in the *Naval Chronicle*:

Now commenced a most heart-rending scene to some hundreds of spectators, who had been in anxious suspense, and who exerted themselves to the utmost, at the imminent risk of their lives, to save those of their drowning fellow men; many of those who were most forward in quitting the ship lost their lives, being swept away by the tremendous sea, which entirely went over the wreck . . .. One of the men [who was] saved reports that Capt. Lydiard was near him on the main mast; but he seemed to have lost the use of his faculties with the horror of the scene, and soon disappeared. At a time when no one appeared on the ship's side, and it was supposed the work of death had ceased, a methodist preacher, venturing his life through the surf, got on board the wreck of the main mast, to see if any more remained; some honest hearts followed him. They found several persons still below, who could not get up; amongst whom were two women and two children. The worthy preacher and his party saved the two women, and some of the men, but the children were lost. About two P.M. the ship went to pieces; when a few more men emerged from the wreck. One of these was saved. By three o'clock no appearance of the vessel remained. The men who survived were conveyed to Helston, about two miles distant, where they were taken care of by the magistrates, and afterwards sent to Falmouth, in charge of the regulating captain at that port. Of the missing, we understand many are deserters, who scampered off as soon as they reached the shore.[7]

It is not surprising that many of the surviving crew, presumably pressed men, took the opportunity to regain their freedom, but it made it impossible to calculate casualty figures with any accuracy. Over three hundred people had been on board. They came from all across the United Kingdom, including Tavistock, Weymouth, Portsmouth, Bristol, Dublin, Tipperary, Belfast, Cork, Liverpool, Manchester, Lancaster, Aberdeen, Newcastle, Norwich, Colchester and many from London. Quite a few were from much further afield such as Holland, Sweden, France and America. Estimates of those killed and missing varied from fifty to well over one hundred, with one witness claiming to have seen at least seventy bodies on shore, but later reports indicated that fewer than fifty people lost their lives. The fact that anyone was saved was due largely to Captain Lydiard's decision to deliberately beach the ship.

Accounts appeared in the press, very similar to that in the *Naval Chronicle*, implying that Lydiard had become unhinged and relinquished command, which provoked a furious reaction from Thomas Gill, a lieutenant on board the *Anson* who survived the wreck. In a letter to the *Sun* newspaper, Gill was at pains to clear the name of Captain Lydiard, who, he said, 'never lost his faculties to the last, but was heard singing out, "don't be in a hurry, my lads, watch a favourable opportunity, and get a rope to the shore." Weakened (by want of rest, and the dreadful sea that was pouring over him) he certainly was – the Methodist Preacher who kindly lent him assistance was a Mr. Roberts, of Helston, a worthy industrious tradesman, but certainly no Methodist Preacher . . . a Seaman of the name of Robert Henly, who went on board, after he had saved himself . . . was the means of preserving a Midshipman, two women, and a young child.'[8] Gill's letter, reprinted in various newspapers, sparked a controversy over the disputed bravery of the captain that obscured the facts even more, but this was soon overtaken by another controversy – the burial of the dead – with far-reaching consequences.

Only a few weeks earlier, on 6 November, the transport ship *James and Rebecca*, which was returning with troops from Buenos Aires, had also been wrecked in Mount's Bay, less than 2 miles from where the *Anson* was beached. Many troops on board had their wives and children with them, and those sailors, soldiers, women and children who lost their lives were buried in a mass grave in unconsecrated ground, with little in the way of a burial service. The dead from the *Anson* were similarly buried in anonymous makeshift graves overlooking the bay, and yet great efforts were made to salvage as much as possible of the ship and its cargo. In law bodies cast ashore from wrecks were not required to be given a proper funeral or to be properly buried. No one was officially responsible for such bodies, and it was not uncommon for them to be moved from one part of the coast to another, so that they became someone else's responsibility, but not before being stripped of clothing and possessions. This tradition of casual salvage and robbing of the dead was carried on all round the coast of Britain, giving rise to legends of gangs of wreckers deliberately luring ships on to rocks in order to plunder them. In fact, virtually no hard evidence exists that deliberate wrecking ever took place, and shipwrecks were so frequent that there would have been little incentive to risk the harsh retribution of English law to add to their numbers.

In response to what was seen as the inhumane treatment of the bodies of the dead from these shipwrecks, efforts were made to try to change the situation, and the local Member of Parliament took up the cause as his maiden speech on 27 April 1808. The *Naval Chronicle* reported:

Mr. Tremaine obtained leave to bring in a bill to enforce the burial of dead bodies cast ashore from wrecks, &c. He had been induced to make this motion by strong representations from the county for which he was member (Cornwall), of the nuisance occasioned by a neglect on this head upon its coast. It often happened that bodies were cast ashore among poor people, who were prevented by the expence from burying them. He mentioned two cases in which this had happened; one on the loss of the *Anson* frigate, the other on the loss of a transport with troops from Buenos Ayres. The bodies were either left unburied, or buried in heaps. The provisions of the bill would be to encourage the giving notice of such cases to the nearest parish officers to bury the bodies in the parish church-yards, and to reimburse them, in certain instances, from the treasurer of the county.[9]

John Hearle Tremayne's Dead Bodies Interment Bill became 'The Burial of Drowned Persons Act, 1808', and proved a turning point in the way that bodies washed up by the sea were treated. Once the law stipulated proper burial, much greater efforts were made to identify bodies, and accurate records began to be compiled. For the first time it became clear just how many people lost their lives each year in the numerous shipwrecks around the coasts of Britain. From 1902, much of the remains of the *Anson* itself was salvaged, and one of the cannons from the ship, restored and mounted on a new gun carriage, stands outside the museum at Helston in Cornwall.

In the spring of 1808, while Parliament debated how to deal with dead bodies from shipwrecks on the coast of Britain, Captain Thomas Cochrane was harassing the French and Spanish along the Mediterranean coast of Spain. Despite the disastrous attack on the Maltese privateer the previous October, Collingwood gave Cochrane the chance to do what he did best – use his own initiative against the enemy. In late February his ship the *Imperieuse* captured some Spanish gunboats near Cartagena, and learning of a French vessel nearby, Cochrane was determined to capture it. He later recorded the attempt in his autobiography: 'Having received information from the prisoners taken in the gunboats that a large French ship, laden with lead and other munitions of war, was at anchor in the Bay of Almeria, I determined on cutting her out\*, and the night being dark, it became necessary to bring to [stop]. At daylight on 21st [February], we found ourselves within a few miles of the town, and having hoisted American [neutral] colours, had the satisfaction to perceive that no alarm was excited on shore.'[10]

In an audacious move the *Imperieuse* sailed down on the prey, and as soon as the ship anchored, the boats were deployed immediately to make the most of the element of surprise, as Cochrane recalled: 'The boats having been previously got in readiness, were forthwith hoisted out, and the large pinnace, under the command of Lieutenant Caulfield, dashed at the French ship, which, as the pinnace approached, commenced a heavy fire, in the midst of which the ship was gallantly boarded, but with the loss of poor Caulfield, who was shot on entering the vessel. The other pinnace coming up almost at the same moment completed the capture, and the cable being cut, sail was made on the prize.'[11] So far the operation had gone relatively smoothly, some smaller vessels had also been captured and all that was needed to seal Cochrane's success was to sail out of the bay with his prizes before the shore batteries could do serious damage.

---

\* To 'cut out' means to capture one or more ships from an enemy port in a surprise attack, usually at night, often by boarding from boats.

Then the wind dropped, leaving the *Imperieuse* at the mercy of the guns on shore.

Cochrane had the anchors dropped and springs put on them so that he could at least turn the ship in order to bring the guns to bear. Midshipman Marryat, later better known as the novelist Frederick Marryat, witnessed the gunnery duel from the quarterdeck: 'The *Imperieuse* returned the fire, warping round and round with her springs, to silence the most galling [fire from the shore]. This continued for nearly an hour, by which time the captured vessels were under all sail, and then the *Imperieuse* hove up her anchor, and, with the English colours waving at her gaff, and still keeping up an undiminished fire, sailed slowly out the victor.'[12] It had been a daring gamble to pluck the French ship out of the bay from under the protection of the shore batteries, and one that only just paid off, as Cochrane acknowledged:

It was fortunate for us that a breeze sprang up, for had it continued calm, we could not have brought a vessel out in the face of such batteries, not more than half a mile distant. Neither, perhaps, should we ourselves have so easily escaped, on another account,– for about four o'clock in the afternoon a Spanish ship of the line suddenly appeared in the offing, no doubt with the intention of ascertaining the cause of the firing. We, however, kept close to the wind, and got clear off with the French ship, mounting 10 guns, and two brigs laden with cordage [ropes]. The scene must have been an interesting one to the people of Almeria, great numbers of the inhabitants lining the shore, though at some risk, as from our position many shots from the *Imperieuse* must have passed over them.[13]

Cochrane continued preying on enemy shipping around the southern coast of Spain, periodically taking his prizes to Gibraltar, and while there in June he received news that completely changed the focus of his operations: 'On the 1st of June, the *Trident* arrived from England with convoy, and the intelligence of a revolution in Spain, which, being shortly afterwards confirmed by proclamation, a friendly communication was opened between the garrison and the Spaniards, and on the 8th Lord Collingwood arrived at Gibraltar in the *Ocean*, to be in readiness to act as circumstances might require.'[14] Napoleon's response to the Spanish uprising was swift, forcing King Ferdinand VII to abdicate, while Napoleon's brother Joseph was proclaimed king of Spain, which was now reduced to a satellite of France controlled by an army of occupation, as Cochrane explained:

On the 6th of June 1808, Napoleon issued a decree, notifying that, as it had been represented to him by the Spanish authorities that the well-being of Spain required a speedy stop to be put to the provisional government, he had proclaimed his brother Joseph, King of Spain and the Indies! To this extraordinary proclamation the Supreme Junta, *on the same day*, replied by another, accusing Napoleon of violating the most sacred compacts, forcing the Spanish monarch to abdication, occupying the country with troops, everywhere committing the most horrible excesses, exhibiting the most enormous ingratitude for services rendered by the Spanish nation to France, and generally treating the Spanish people with perfidy and treachery, such as was never before committed by any nation or monarch . . . On these and other accounts the Junta declared war against France by land and sea, at the same time proclaiming durable and lasting peace with England.[15]

After refitting at Gibraltar, the *Imperieuse* set sail on Midsummer's Day and met up with Collingwood off Cadiz, where Cochrane was ordered to return to the Mediterranean and give assistance to the Spaniards against the French. The *Imperieuse* cruised along the Spanish coast while Cochrane took stock of the situation, and in several places where the French had not yet taken control the British landed and were welcomed by the Spanish. General Philibert-Guillaume Duhesme and his French troops, based at Barcelona, had been trying to reopen the main route to France, as communications had been already cut. Cochrane goaded the enemy at Barcelona by flying the English and Spanish flags with the French flag below, in the position indicating defeat. He then fired a 21-gun salute in mockery:

The French, who were in possession of the place, to our great amusement resented the affront by firing at us from all their batteries, but their shot fell short. We could distinctly see the inhabitants crowding the house-tops and public places of the city by thousands, and the French cavalry and infantry meanwhile patrolling the streets. Knowing that the French held their own with difficulty, especially in the adjacent towns, we again hove-to and displayed English colours over French, and then Spanish over French, firing an additional salute, which increased the cannonade from the batteries, but to no purpose.[16]

While the French were willing to waste precious gunpowder and shot firing at a frigate that was out of range, Cochrane continued to annoy them. He then 'bore up along the coast, and when clear of the enemy's lines, a number of [Spanish] boats came off complaining bitterly of the French troops who were burning their towns on the least resistance, or even pretended resistance, and were permitted by their officers to plunder and kill the inhabitants with impunity. Perhaps it would be more in accordance with military justice to say, that with the ideas of equality and fraternity then prevalent amongst the soldiers, their officers had no control over them.'[17] The brutal way Duhesme's troops were treating the local people while trying to secure the route to France caused much anger, and Cochrane received similar complaints about the French further along the coast. With only a frigate he could not confront the French forces head on, but began to liaise with the Spanish to cause maximum disruption using amphibious assaults. The town of Mataró, to the north of Barcelona, had already been taken by the French, but in July Cochrane set about attacking the coastal road, since, as he described, the landscape gave the *Imperieuse* the chance of controlling one of the main routes from France into Spain:

The *Imperieuse* could effect nothing against the French in Mataro, from its unassailable position, but having received intelligence that a considerable force under General Duhesme was advancing towards Barcelona [actually from Barcelona to Mataró], it occurred to me that their progress might be checked. Landing accordingly with a party of seamen, we blew down the overhanging rocks and destroyed the bridges so effectually as to prevent the passage either of cavalry or artillery, at the same time pointing out to the Spaniards how they might impede the enemy's movements elsewhere along the coast by cutting up the roads,– an operation on which they entered with great alacrity, after being shown how to set about their work. The nature of these operations will be readily comprehended by the statement that a considerable portion of the main road ran along the face of the precipitous rocks nearest the sea.[18]

Unfortunately for the Spanish, the *Imperieuse* was running short of supplies and had to sail to Port Mahón in Minorca for provisions and water. The ship was only absent for a few days, but the French seized the opportunity of forcing their way from Mataró to the fortified town of Gerona, which they began to besiege. On his return Cochrane 'learned the mode in which the French had surmounted the obstacles interposed by the Spaniards in cutting up the roads, viz. by compelling the inhabitants to fill up the gaps with everything movable, even to their agricultural implements, furniture, and clothes. After this, the French, by way of deterring the Spaniards from again interfering with the highways, sacked and burned all the dwelling-houses in the neighbourhood.'[19] The response of Cochrane was to attack the road yet again: 'Taking a party of marines on shore, we again blew up additional portions of the road to the eastward, and as the gaps made on our last visit had been chiefly filled up with wood, and other inflammable articles . . . we set fire to them, and thus not only renewed the obstacles, but created fresh ones, in the assurance that as everything movable was now destroyed, the obstruction must become permanent. Whilst this was going on the seamen and marines of the *Imperieuse* destroyed a battery completed by the French, and threw over the cliff the four brass 24-pounders.'[20]

These cannons were recovered from the beach the next day, and then the *Imperieuse* sailed down the coast to Canet de Mar, where the French garrison was greatly depleted because troops were dealing with the sabotage of the road. This enabled the British to capture more guns from another shore battery and create utter confusion, as Cochrane related:

After these [the guns] had been secured, I again took a party of seamen and marines on shore, and broke down or blew up the road in six different places. On paying a visit to the town, there was scarcely a house which the French had not sacked, carrying off everything that was valuable, and wantonly destroying the remainder. The inhabitants were in a miserable condition. The two next days were employed in blowing down rocks, and otherwise destroying roads in every direction which the French were likely to take, the people aiding heart and soul, anxiously listening to every suggestion for retarding the enemy's movements, and evincing the greatest alacrity to put them into practice.[21]

With much of Duhesme's army occupied with besieging Gerona, Barcelona was left poorly defended, itself under siege. One outpost was the castle of Mongat, 10 miles north-east of Barcelona, and on 29 July the local Spanish resistance fighters approached Cochrane with a promise of eight hundred men to help him take the fortress. Overnight Cochrane landed men who simultaneously blew up and blocked with rockfalls the road on either side of the fort, cutting off the garrison from reinforcements sent from Barcelona. On the 31st, when the *Imperieuse* again anchored off the fort, the Spanish stormed, captured and held a French outpost on the hillside, despite heavy fire from the castle. Cochrane described the difficult process of surrender that followed:

By this time I had got the *Imperieuse* well in, and had given the castle [Mongat] a couple of well-directed broadsides when the enemy hung out flags of truce. On this I landed with a party of marines, but the exasperated Spaniards, elated by their recent victory, paid no attention to the flags of truce, and were advancing up the hill to storm the place, the French still firing to keep them in check. I was immediately conducted to the castle, where the French troops were drawn up on each side of the gate. On entering, the commandant requested me not to allow the peasantry to follow, as they would only surrender to me, and not to the Spaniards, of whose vengeance they were evidently afraid. After giving the commandant a lecture on the barbarities that had been committed on the coast, and pointing out the folly of such a course, inasmuch as, had his troops fallen into the hands of the Spanish peasantry, not a man would have escaped with life, I acceded to the request to surrender to us alone, and promised the escort of our marines to the frigate. The commandant then gave me his sword, and his troops forthwith laid down their arms.[22]

The British were now faced with another battle, to protect their prisoners from the Spanish while they boarded the *Imperieuse*. As Cochrane commented, 'what became of the men forming the captured outpost I never knew, and was not anxious to enquire'[23] – he already had enough trouble dealing with the Spanish around the main fort:

It was not without a few blows, and forcing some of the assailants over the parapet, that we succeeded in keeping them off. The Spaniards were with some difficulty made to understand that, however exasperated they might be at the conduct of the French, the latter were British prisoners, and not a hair of their heads should be hurt. When we were somewhat assured of their safety, the prisoners were marched down to the boats; and glad enough they were to get there, for the Spaniards accompanied them with volleys of abuse, declaring that they might thank the English for their lives, which, had the Spanish party succeeded in storming the fort, should have been sacrificed.[24]

Mongat castle was then blown up, and the Spanish flag hoisted over the ruins. When General Duhesme's army retreated from Gerona two weeks later, they were forced to reach Barcelona by a long detour inland, abandoning their ammunition and field guns. The disruption caused to the French was out of all proportion to the cost of deploying a single frigate off the Spanish coast for a few days, and the French in Barcelona were now in a difficult position as the Spanish increasingly disrupted inland routes, while British ships ensured that supplies and reinforcements could not reach the French by sea.

After the destruction of Mongat, Cochrane decided to take the war directly to France, thinking that 'as the French troops kept out of our reach, there was no beneficial object to be gained by remaining on the Spanish coast; and it occurred to me, that by giving the French, in the neighbourhood of Marseilles, a taste of the evils they were inflicting on their Spanish neighbours, it would be possible to create an amount of alarm, which would have the effect of diverting troops intended for Catalonia, by the necessity of remaining to guard their own seaboard'.[25] In mid-August 1808 the *Imperieuse* arrived in the Bay of Marseilles and for over a week Cochrane conducted an intense campaign of burning any boats he could find and destroying shore batteries and semaphore stations, which completely disrupted French coastal communications and tied up troops destined for Spain. The campaign, he said, had another benefit, as they obtained secret codes:

In this cruise against the French signal stations, the precaution of obtaining their signal books before destroying the semaphores was adopted; and in order to make the enemy believe that the books also were destroyed, all the papers found were scattered about in a half-burnt condition. The trick was successful, and the French authorities, considering that the signal books had been destroyed also, did not deem it necessary to alter their signals, which were forwarded by me to Lord Collingwood, who was thus informed by the French semaphores, when re-established, of all the movements of their own ships, as well as of the British ships from the promontory of Italy northward.[26]

At the beginning of September Cochrane moved eastwards and boldly attacked the port of La Ciotat, midway between Marseilles and Toulon, but was eventually driven off by French ships from the latter port. Sailing back to Marseilles the *Imperieuse* was joined on the 7th by the *Spartan*, commanded by Captain Jahleel Brenton, and together they carried out further raids along the French coast. Near Port Vendres, close to the

Spanish border, they encountered a large force of French troops protecting the shore batteries. The French were too strong to attack directly, and
so Cochrane devised a plan to divide their forces:

We now passed close to a small fishing town, where other guns were observed
in position, both on the right and on the left, these being manned by regular
troops and backed by hundreds of armed peasantry . . . By way of feint, to
draw off the attention of the cavalry, both *Spartan* and *Imperieuse* manned
their small boats and the rocket boats with the ships' boys, dressed in marines'
scarlet jackets, despatching these at some distance towards the right, as
though an attack were there intended. The device was successful, and a body
of cavalry, as we anticipated, promptly set off to receive them.[27]

While the French cavalry raced to cut off what appeared to be a major
attack by marines, the *Imperieuse* and *Spartan* incessantly pounded the
town, and after an hour Cochrane's real marines landed, took the battery
and spiked the guns. The French cavalry had by now realised the deception and were galloping back. They looked likely to cut off the British
force, and from the direction in which the British ships were sailing, their
guns could not easily be brought to bear on the French, particularly since
for much of their route they were not visible from the ships. It seemed
certain that the landing party would be captured, but Captain Brenton
described what happened next:

The *Spartan* was following the *Imperieuse*, at less than a cable's length distance, the ships going about three knots, when the *Imperieuse* was observed
suddenly to swing round, with much more rapidity than any action of the
helm could have produced. The fact was, that Lord Cochrane from the mast
head saw a squadron of the enemy's cavalry galloping towards a gorge on the
coast, which had they passed, they would have cut off the retreat of our
people, who were employed in spiking the guns. His Lordship immediately
ordered the ship's anchor to be let go, and the swinging round brought her
starboard broadside to enfilade this gorge, by which the cavalry were instantly
turned [forced to retreat].[28]

By this manoeuvre Cochrane could train his guns on the one point on the
route where the cavalry were exposed, firing at the precise moment they
reached it. The broadside of grapeshot from the *Imperieuse* was so effective, Cochrane commented, that 'all who were not knocked out of their

saddles rode off as fast as they could'.[29] Brenton described the manoeuvre as 'a beautiful instance of ready seamanship'.[30]

Cochrane often led the attacks himself and inspired his men at least as well as Nelson had done. A large part of his success was his concern for the crew's safety, and Captain Brenton testified that 'he admired nothing more in Lord Cochrane than the care he took of the preservation of his people. Bold and adventurous as he was, no unnecessary exposure of life was ever permitted under his command. Every circumstance was anticipated, every precaution against surprise was taken, every provision for success was made, and in this way he was enabled to accomplish the most daring enterprises, with comparatively little danger, and still less of actual loss.'[31] Napoleon called Cochrane '*Le loup des mers*'[32] – the sea wolf – and such was his reputation that when he ran short of water he sailed up the River Rhône to beyond the point where it changed from salt water to fresh and took on water without any opposition.

With very limited resources, Cochrane demonstrated just how effective naval raids could be against troops and communications in coastal areas. The raids along the Mediterranean shores of France meant that French troops were diverted from Spain to meet the threat, but most important of all French morale was profoundly affected. Back in Britain, Sir Walter Scott was to comment:

Lord Cochrane, during the month of September 1808, with his single ship the *Imperieuse,* kept the whole coast of Languedoc in alarm, – destroyed the numerous semaphoric telegraphs, which were of the utmost consequence to the numerous coasting convoys of the French, and not only prevented any troops from being sent from that province into Spain, but even excited such dismay that 2000 men were withdrawn from Figueras [the fortress just over the border in Spain] to oppose him, when they would otherwise have been marching farther into the peninsula. The coasting trade was entirely suspended during this alarm; yet with such consummate prudence were all Lord Cochrane's enterprises planned and executed, that *not one of his men were either killed or hurt*, except one, who was singed in blowing up a battery.[33]

In early November the French General Laurent Gouvion St Cyr crossed into Spain on his way to Barcelona to relieve the beleaguered Duhesme, who was cut off. Rather than besiege the fortress of Gerona, St Cyr decided to march past with his thousands of troops, but before that the town of Rosas, a key point of Spanish resistance, needed to be destroyed. This small coastal town lay 10 miles to the east of his route, just south of the border, and it had an excellent harbour that was used by British warships and was a potential landing point for Spanish guerillas. The surrounding land was marshy, but the town was guarded by a dilapidated citadel, while a mile away the harbour was protected by the formidable Fort Trinidad – Fort Trinity – built high on the cliffs.

When Cochrane arrived on 21 November, Rosas and Fort Trinidad were under siege and had already been heavily bombarded. Despite help from other British warships, the citadel was on the point of collapse and the Spanish were preparing to evacuate the area. Cochrane went on shore to assess the situation and decided that Rosas could be held for some time yet if assisted by the *Imperieuse*. Possibly the appearance of his ship persuaded the enemy forces to act, for Cochrane had not long been back on board before they tried an assault on Fort Trinidad, as he recorded: 'After pounding away at the fort for several days, the French made up their minds to storm, but on coming within range of musket-shot, they got such a reception from the garrison as to render a hasty retreat imperative. As their discomfiture was visible from the ship, we fired a salute of twenty-one guns by way of sarcastic compliment, but the enemy had not the politeness to return the courtesy.'[34] Cochrane followed up his salute by moving against the French: 'The *Imperieuse* now got under weigh, and cleared for action, taking up a position to the left of the citadel, and within musket-shot of the French lines, into which we poured such a storm of shot as to drive out the enemy.'[35] After this a French gun battery on top of the cliffs began to shower the *Imperieuse* with shells, forcing Cochrane to move away from the shore.

From his reconnaissance Cochrane knew that although the French had a gun battery on the cliff above Fort Trinidad, they could only fire on one small area of the fort. The fort itself backed right on to the cliff edge – making it easy to defend, but almost impossible to evacuate in an emergency, except by ropes down the cliff to the sea, as he described:

The Castle of Trinidad stood on the side of a hill, having by no means a difficult descent to the sea, but this hill was again commanded by a higher and more precipitous cliff, which would have enabled an enemy to drive out the occupants with ease, but for the peculiar construction of the fortress. Next to the sea was a fort constructed with strong walls some 50 feet high. Behind this and joined to it, rose another fort to the height of 30 or 40 feet more, and behind this again was a tower rising some 20 or 30 feet still higher, the whole presenting the appearance of a large church with a tower 110 feet high, a nave 90 feet high, and a chancel 50 feet. The tower, having its back to the cliff, as a matter of course sheltered the middle and lower portions of the fortress from a fire of the battery above it. Nothing, in short, for a fortress commanded by adjacent heights could have been better adapted for holding out against offensive operations, or worse adapted for replying to them.[36]

Being the key to Rosas, Cochrane decided to hold Fort Trinidad for as long as possible, in the hope of Spanish reinforcements arriving from Gerona – if they did not arrive, he would demolish it. After an attempt to destroy the French gun battery failed, Cochrane landed on the 24th with over a hundred men to repair the fort and strengthen the garrison, leaving the *Imperieuse* to bombard the French positions. He continued his comparisons with church architecture in describing how the French created a hole high up in the tower:

In consequence of the elevated position of the enemy's battery on the cliff, they could however only breach the central portion of the tower, the lowest part of the breach being nearly sixty feet above its base, so that when practicable, it could only be reached by long scaling ladders. A pretty correct idea of our relative positions may be formed if the unnautical reader will imagine our small force to be placed in the nave of Westminster Abbey, with the enemy attacking the great western tower from the summit of a cliff 100 feet higher than the tower, so that the breach in course of formation nearly corresponded to the great west window of the abbey. It will hence be clear that, in the face of a determined opposition, it would be no easy matter to scale the external wall of the tower up to the great west window, and more difficult still to overcome impediments . . . so as to get down into the body of the church. These were the points I had to provide against, for we could neither prevent the French from breaching nor storming.[37]

The fort was under constant heavy bombardment, especially the tower, from which Cochrane evacuated all his men, but he also set up explosives to destroy the fort: 'The next object was to prepare trains for the explosion of the magazines, in case evacuation of the fort became compulsory. This was done in two places; the first deposit of powder being placed underneath the breach, with the portfire [fuse] so arranged, as to go off in about ten minutes; the other beneath the remaining part of the fortress, with a portfire calculated to burn until we ourselves were safe on board the frigate.'[38]

With everything in place to cover their retreat and destroy Fort Trinidad, it was now a case of holding on as long as possible, but the French bombardment had caused another breach in the defences, as Cochrane recorded:

Our men were now engaged in blocking it up as fast as it was made, and working as they did under cover, no loss was sustained, though every shot brought down large masses of stone within the fortress; the French thus supplying us with materials for repair, though rendering a sharp look-out against [stone] splinters necessary. On this day I received a wound, which caused me intolerable agony. Being anxious, during an ominous pause, to see what the enemy were about, I incautiously looked round an angle of the tower towards the battery overhead, and was struck by a stone splinter in the face; the splinter flattened my nose and then penetrated my mouth. By the skill of our excellent doctor, Mr. Guthrie, my nose was after a time rendered serviceable.[39]

Two days later, after a midnight assault, the French managed to overrun the town of Rosas. All the pressure of the French forces was now directed towards Fort Trinidad, but despite bombardments and assaults the fort continued to hold out and refused a French offer of honourable surrender. On the morning of the 30th Cochrane awoke with a premonition:

Long before daylight I was awoke[n] with an impression that the enemy were in possession of the castle, though the stillness which prevailed showed this to be a delusion. Still I could not recompose myself to sleep, and after lying for some time tossing about, I left my couch, and hastily went on the esplanade of the fortress. All was perfectly still, and I felt half ashamed of having given way to such fancies. A loaded mortar, however, stood before me, pointed, during the day, in such a direction that the shell should fall on the path over the hill which the French must necessarily take whenever they might make an attempt to storm. Without other object than that of diverting my mind from the unpleasant feeling which had taken possession of it, I fired the mortar. Before the echo had died away, a volley of musketry from the advancing column of the enemy showed that the shell had fallen amongst them, just as they were on the point of storming.[40]

The sound of the mortar roused the defenders, and, as Cochrane put it, 'to the purposeless discharge of that piece of ordnance we owed our safety, for otherwise they would have been upon us before we even suspected their presence'.[41] Several waves of infantry were thrown against the fort in this assault, and Cochrane was particularly impressed by the Italians:

They were gallantly led, two of the officers attracting my especial attention. The first was dropped by a shot, which precipitated him from the walls, but whether he was killed or only wounded, I do not know – probably wounded only, as his body was not seen by us amongst the dead. The other was the last man to quit the walls, and before he could do so, I had covered him with my musket. Finding escape impossible, he stood like a hero to receive the bullet, without condescending to lower his sword in token of surrender. I never saw a braver or prouder man. Lowering my musket, I paid him the compliment of remarking that so fine a fellow was not born to be shot down like a dog, and that, so far as I was concerned, he was at liberty to make the best of his way down the ladder; upon which intimation he bowed politely, as though on parade, and retired just as leisurely.[42]

Having repulsed this attack the garrison experienced a relative lull for a few days, during which time the *Imperieuse* was joined by the *Fame* and *Magnificent* warships. On 5 December it became clear that the French had been waiting for reinforcements and were now massing for a final assault – it was time to evacuate Fort Trinidad using rope ladders. Boats from the ships came in to the shore below the fort to take off the garrison, and when they realised what was happening, the French ceased firing: it was more important to them to remove the obstacle of the fort than kill a few more of the enemy. With all the garrison on board the ships and the fuses burning, Cochrane waited for the fort to blow up: 'The French having become practically acquainted with some of our devices were on their guard, and did not take possession of the castle immediately on our quitting it, and it was lucky for them that they did not, for shortly after we got on board the first explosion took place, blowing up the portion of the fortress which they had been breaching; but the second train failed, owing, no doubt, to the first shock disarranging the portfire. Had not this been the case, scarcely one stone of the castle would have remained on another.'[43]

Nevertheless, Cochrane was pleased with the outcome, having delayed the French for a number of days, giving the Spanish more time to organise their defences and demonstrating once again the vulnerability of the coast road to attacks from the sea. He pointed out that 'in the defence of this fortress, we lost only three [British] killed and seven wounded; the loss of the Spaniards amounting to two killed and five wounded . . . The destruction of the French must have been very great. We who were cooped up in the fortress had only one collision with them, but in that they suffered fearfully, whilst we escaped scot free. But the fire of the ships must have told upon them to a great extent.'[44] The nearby citadel of Rosas was not so lucky, because over two thousand Spanish troops were taken prisoner.

Through the summer and autumn of 1808 Cochrane had created chaos along the main French invasion route from the Rhône Valley in France to southern Spain at the many points north of Alicante where the road ran along the coast. As he commented, 'actions between line-of-battle ships are, no doubt, very imposing; but for real effect, I would prefer a score or two of small vessels, well handled, to any fleet of line-of-battle ships'.[45] Collingwood was delighted with Cochrane's success, praising him in successive letters to the Admiralty. In one he commented: 'Nothing can exceed the activity and zeal with which his Lordship pursues the enemy. The success which attends his enterprizes clearly indicates with what skill and ability they are conducted; besides keeping the coast [of France] in constant alarm, causing a total suspension of the trade, and harassing a body of troops employed in opposing him.'[46] The Admiralty, however, did not share Collingwood's enthusiasm and even went so far as to reprimand Cochrane for using more 'gunpowder and shot than had been used by any other captain in the service'.[47] By looking merely at cost rather than cost-effectiveness, the penny-pinching Admiralty took a blinkered view of the war in the Mediterranean and threw away the opportunity to encourage other captains to emulate the exploits of Cochrane, who was destined to remain the only one with the title of 'sea wolf'.

# TWELVE

———•◆•———

# BY LAND AND SEA

It appeared to me a physical impossibility to escape from it, and I was filled with despair. Nothing but madness could entertain a thought of attempting to escape.

Judgement of Midshipman O'Brien when
he first saw the fortress of Bitche[1]

While Cochrane was doing his best to disrupt the French occupation of Spain, some of the British prisoners in France, most of whom had been captured at sea, were becoming tired of waiting to be exchanged for French prisoners in Britain and began planning their escape. In September 1808 Midshipman Donat Henchy O'Brien successfully broke out of the high-security prison fortress of Bitche in north-east France after over four and a half years in captivity. The escape was to become a legendary episode of the war.

Having been shipwrecked in the *Hussar*, O'Brien was initially held at Givet, mistaken for an ordinary seaman, but he was transferred, in July 1804, to the officers' prison at Verdun. Another prisoner there, Midshipman Edward Boys, described the parole conditions: 'Prisoners on their arrival at Verdun were invariably conducted to the citadel, when their names, age, birth place, profession, and description were entered in a book. They were then obliged to sign a paper, promising upon honour to conform to the regulations of the depôt, and not to escape, if permitted to reside in the town. A direct violation of this engagement was so unreservedly condemned by all classes, that during the five first years of the war, I recollect but three who so disgraced their country.'[2] Even midshipmen were honour-bound not break their parole, but they were still obliged to turn up for roll-call twice a day, as Boys explained: 'Captains in the navy, and field officers, once a month; lieutenants, every five days; midshipmen and others twice a day (thus calculating the word of a midshipman as equal only to one-sixtieth part of that of a field officer).'[3]

It was generally assumed that prisoner exchanges between the two countries would be rapidly agreed, as had occurred earlier in the war. After Boys was captured off Toulon in August 1803 and was being marched to Verdun, he met some English *détenus* at Nîmes, who 'considerably allayed the ennui and mortification of captivity, by confidently assuring us, that an exchange of prisoners had been arranged between the two governments, and that in six weeks we might rest satisfied of a happy return to the service of our country'.[4] Six weeks turned to six years – and more. Negotiations between the British and French for exchanging prisoners made no progress, and Napoleon invariably failed to honour his side of the bargain whenever French prisoners were returned. One officer lucky enough to be exchanged was Lieutenant William Dillon. Although technically not a prisoner-of-war (having been captured under a flag of truce) Dillon had not given his parole, yet he never made an attempt to escape from Verdun. He was eventually exchanged for a French officer, Captain Éléonore-Jean-Nicolas Soleil, who had been captured in September 1806. Dillon reached England in September 1807, only the fourteenth naval officer to be exchanged since the resumption of war over four years earlier. Most prisoners were destined to be held in French prisons, well away from the sea, until the peace in 1814, and inevitably a number of them died in captivity.

By 1807, after three years at Verdun, Midshipman O'Brien had no hopes of release, and he was in a state of despair: 'I was losing the prime of my youth in captivity. I saw no prospect of peace, or an exchange of prisoners; no hope or possibility of being promoted.'[5] Around the time that Dillon was exchanged, O'Brien decided to escape with three trustworthy friends, Midshipman Christopher Tuthill, Midshipman Henry Ashworth and Lieutenant John Essel, but they first honourably settled their affairs and deliberately set out to have their parole withdrawn by various misdemeanours.

O'Brien and his party were terrified of being found out, because of paid informers among the prisoners: 'These spies were so numerous,' O'Brien complained, '. . . that it was morally impossible to know them all;

consequently [even] the most watchful and cautious amongst us were liable to be entrapped.'[6] Throughout the course of the war only a few hundred prisoners from a total of some twelve thousand managed to escape, and informers were an especial threat – at least fifty at Verdun alone. On 28 August 1807 O'Brien and his friends escaped and made their way towards the Channel, but three weeks later they were recaptured near Boulogne. During their interrogation before a local court, O'Brien was asked how they had managed to find their way from Verdun without guides, so he replied provocatively 'that English sailors could always steer with sufficient correctness by the stars; and that, when those celestial objects were visible, they were never at a loss'.[7] Next the court wanted to know how well he knew the French coast. 'It struck me,' O'Brien remembered, 'that the shipwreck of the *Hussar* was a pretty clear proof that there was one part of the coast, at least, of which it would appear we had but an imperfect knowledge.'[8] Instead, he smiled and answered 'that every naval officer of England was by far better acquainted with the French coast than even with his own . . . That we could hardly go up and down Channel without acquiring a knowledge of the northern coast of France.'[9]

As punishment, the four were ordered to the terrible penal depot of Bitche, a mountain fortress that was dubbed 'the place of tears'.[10] Along with other prisoners, they were marched to their destination and had no opportunity to escape until the final day of their journey, when they were left unfettered. Three of them, including O'Brien, managed to run for the cover of a nearby wood, where they split up, but towards the end of November O'Brien was recaptured at Lindau in Germany and escorted back to Bitche:

At about noon, on the 21st of December, 1807, the high turrets and massive towers of the gloomy fortress in which I was going to be incarcerated, presented themselves to my sight. Their very appearance was sufficient to strike the mind with horror . . . The prospect of being shut up in that detestable fortress, perhaps for the remainder of my days, could only be relieved by the probability that my length of life would be shortened by the nature of my imprisonment. Death itself was preferable to protracted persecution, and I sometimes devoutly wished to be at rest.[11]

It was with mixed emotions that he met up with his companions Ashworth and Tuthill, having imagined them safely in England by now, and to hear of the death of Lieutenant Essel, who 'had been dashed to pieces in endeavouring to get over the walls [at Bitche], in a fresh attempt to escape'.[12] The fortress, O'Brien noted, 'is reckoned one of the strongest fortifications of France, and is built on the summit of an immensely high rock, out of which all its subterranean caves are hollowed'.[13]

Many of the prisoners were kept in dungeons deep underground, and for months O'Brien plotted ways of escaping. In August 1808 there was a failed attempt in which he avoided being implicated, but, as he related,

I had the mortification to see my poor companions heavily ironed and bound in chains. After being closely confined in their filthy and pestiferous den for many days, they were to be marched twenty-five leagues, in order to be put upon their fictitious trials ... In a few days I received a letter from my friend Mr. Ashworth, giving me a melancholy narration of the trial; and he concluded by stating that himself, and several of our friends, were sentenced *'as slaves to the galleys for fifteen years.' Mr. Tuthill was sentenced to only nine.*[14]

O'Brien was so shocked that he dropped the letter and rushed to inform his fellow-prisoners what had happened: 'The feelings of indignation it excited were extreme, and though under the absolute power of the enemy, we loudly exclaimed against the barbarity.'[15] When one of his friends retrieved the letter, they discovered that the sentence had in fact been rescinded, but that two other seamen they knew had been sentenced to six years in the galleys for forging passports. This form of punishment – slave labour rowing French galleys in the Mediterranean or working in their dockyards – was abhorrent to O'Brien, who thought it 'to the eternal disgrace of a nation that styled itself civilized'.[16]

A month later he devised another escape plan with Midshipman Maurice Hewson, who a few months earlier had also escaped from Verdun and had been arrested far away in southern France. They were joined by Archibald Barklimore, a surgeon who had originally been captured by a French privateer off Ireland when returning from the West Indies and was sent to Bitche after an unsuccessful escape from Verdun. The final member of the group was Mr Batley, a dragoon officer who had been captured on the way to India and sent straight to Bitche, so that this was his first escape attempt. O'Brien had made a piece of linen cloth into a rope, which he had been wearing round his waist for many weeks and he had also manufactured a key. They set 13 September as their escape day, but on the evening before O'Brien's anxiety increased when the prison governor stopped to chat about escape attempts:

'Well, Monsieur O'Brien . . . you must not think of escaping, for there is no chance whatever for an Englishman to get off from the Continent.' I replied, 'That is very true, Monsieur le Commandant, but if that had not been the case, Monsieur le Commandant, where is the possibility of getting out of this strong fortress, and so well guarded too?' 'True,' said he, smiling; 'but the attempt has been made more than once, and which certainly, I must say, invariably proved unsuccessful, and frequently fatal to some of the party.' He continued by saying, 'My opinion is, that if prisoners-of-war, I mean English, could manage to get out of confinement, their only course would be that towards Flushing or Rotterdam, where they are always pretty certain of finding English smugglers ready to embark them.' I assured Monsieur le Commandant that his remarks were quite correct, and that if I thought there was the slightest chance of escaping from the fort, I would not hesitate to try and do so to-morrow, or as soon as possible.[17]

O'Brien wondered if their plans were suspected: 'I could not help thinking this conversation at so critical a moment very extraordinary. However, this opinion of his did not make us alter our intended course for Austria.'[18] The weather was stormy the next night, and worst of all was the incessant lightning, which seemed set to reveal them. The guards remained vigilant all night, and so they postponed their plans, despite having cut up all their sheets to make additional ropes. Unlocking their cell door with the key before dusk the following evening, they crept past the guards and climbed down the first stage of the ramparts. Terrifyingly, the rope snapped, but a long enough piece survived for tackling the two lower ramparts – in all, a descent of around 200 feet. They climbed out of the deep ditch and 'shook each other cordially by the hand, overwhelmed with exultation at our almost miraculous success. When we looked at the stupendous heights of the rock and fortress, it seemed as if a miracle alone could have enabled us to descend them, suspended by so slight and ill-made a cord as that which we had been able to construct out of our shirt-linen, and a little cobbler's twine.'[19] The soldier, Batley, was especially overjoyed, having considered himself a dead man from the moment he agreed to join the escape party, but fearing an accusation of cowardice if he withdrew. Keeping his own counsel, he merely commented: 'You sailors are Devils.'[20]

With no time to lose, they moved rapidly from Bitche to the border, and travelled across south Germany, but by the time they reached the neighbourhood of Radstadt Batley's legs and feet were too swollen to continue. They pretended to be Frenchmen travelling on leave from their regiment which was then in Prussia, to give Batley a cover story so that he could be safely left to recover. The people he was lodged with looked after him until he was well, and despite not knowing the language, Batley eventually followed the same escape route.

The others continued and in mid-October 1808, once inside the Austrian border, the three men pretended that they were Americans who had escaped from the Danes at Altona (Hamburg), but on discovering that the authorities were going to verify their story with the American consul, they took a risk and admitted being escaped English prisoners-of-war, because it was obvious that many Austrians were well disposed towards the British. They were advised that it would take about a fortnight to sort out matters, but they should make themselves as comfortable as possible at a local inn and maintain their American story. With nothing else to do, they made great efforts to learn German, and at the inn, 'the landlady and waiters declared, that, until they had seen us, they had imagined that all Americans were negroes'.[21] Hewson commented that 'we endeavoured to chat to every one who had patience to bear with us. The great victories of Sir Arthur Wellesley [including Vimiero, in Portugal] were in every one's mouth – his letters detailing the battles were in every paper, and caused general exultation . . . we grieved much that we were denied the privilege of acknowledging ourselves [as Englishmen].'[22]

Still very nervous, they searched out places from which they could escape in an emergency, but on their eleventh day Hewson was summoned before the police director, who told them they were free to go. On 4 November they arrived at the port of Trieste: 'I need not dwell on the pleasure we felt this morning at beholding the gulf of Trieste, and the ships and vessels lying in the harbour; amongst which was a Russian squadron, consisting of four sail of the line, one frigate, and a store-ship. We also discovered a ship at anchor some leagues out, which, to our very great satisfaction, we were informed was his Britannic Majesty's frigate, *L'Unité*, Captain Campbell, who, they said, blockaded that port. This was the most welcome news imaginable.'[23] The Russian ships were stuck in port, blockaded by the British, while the rest of their fleet at Lisbon had only just been escorted to Spithead by the British. For three days the escaped prisoners were also stuck in Trieste, because of strong winds, but they took the time to write to their friends Ashworth and Tuthill in Bitche – their use of the German language deceived the guards there, who did not bother checking the letters. They gave details of their route to Trieste, enabling the pair to escape in December.

Hewson recorded that on their second night O'Brien 'accompanied me to the heights outside the town to refresh ourselves in looking at the broad ocean, and feasting our eyes on the sight of a small British Frigate proudly standing in, daily reconnoitering a large Russian Squadron moored in the Mole, and capturing vessels hourly, in their view, even under their guns – 'twas truly flattering that we belonged to a country and service that swayed so triumphantly – feared and admired by all Europe.'[24] As soon as the weather moderated, O'Brien related, they hired a boat and under cover of darkness 'rowed towards the point where I had calculated we should find the English frigate; but, to our mortification, we were disappointed'.[25] Once the moon had risen, O'Brien, Hewson and Barklimore rowed in all directions until at daybreak another boat was spotted:

The boat ran alongside us, and asked in English what we were. I sprang up at hearing the English language, and, with inexpressible joy, saw that it was a British ship-of-war's boat. I answered that we were three British subjects who had escaped from a French prison. Having been informed it was the *Amphion*'s boat, I assured the officer we should be very happy to quit our present conveyance, and take a passage with him to the frigate. He replied, 'The ship is at present at a considerable distance off; I shall not return until eight o'clock.' I answered, that this was of little consequence; two of us belonged to the navy, and we would willingly take a cruise along the coast with him, if he had no objection.[26]

The frigate *Amphion*, commanded by Captain William Hoste, had only replaced the *Unité* the night before in blockade duties outside Trieste, and to O'Brien's great joy an old friend, Lieutenant Jones, was in the boat. He began to amuse the crew with anecdotes of their escape when two strange vessels were spotted heading towards the coast. The chase was on, and a cutlass and musket were immediately thrust into O'Brien's hands:

We fired several muskets to bring the enemy to . . . We could not perceive many men on her deck, but those that were there kept up a smart fire. At length we got alongside, in the right English style, when upwards of twenty men suddenly shewed themselves, with an officer at their head, decorated with the Legion of Honour, and at whom I discharged my musket, which I believe took fatal effect, but at the moment I received a musketoon ball in my right arm, that disabled it. They poured into us a volley from muskets, musketoons, blunderbusses, &c. Our bowman and another sailor fell dead; three other seamen dropt from their wounds, and Green Dick, the pilot, one of them, died the next day. Jones was also severely wounded. Our little party was thus sadly thinned; the conflict was severe.[27]

The larger French vessel backed off, and the *Amphion*'s boat had no choice but to give up, with O'Brien thankful that he had not been taken prisoner again:

The frigate was not then in sight, and the confused state of our little crew, two killed and five wounded, including our brave and gallant officer, would have rendered us no difficult conquest to so superior a force, had they but persevered in the attack, for our retreat was covered by the musket of only one marine, whose name was Hunt, and whom I supplied with cartridges as fast as he could load and fire, biting them off and giving them with my left hand to him. My friend, Barklimore, was of essential service to us, in binding up our wounds with handkerchiefs, &c., for there were not a sufficient number of tourniquets . . . My wound, through the right arm . . . disabled it so that I never recovered the strength of it.[28]

They finally reached the safety of the frigate, where Captain Hoste addressed Hewson angrily in French, thinking him the captain of the enemy vessel, but once the officers on board realised the true story, Hewson considered that their reception 'was at once the most generous and liberal, each officer vying with each other in supplying me and my companions with whatever we wanted in clothing and linen, and one of the officers was kind enough to give up his cabin to O'Brien'.[29] His arm was saved, despite the surgeon's initial worries, though O'Brien bitterly noted: 'For this very serious wound, I have never received any pension, as it was not considered equivalent to the loss of a limb . . . and yet, what is the difference to a sufferer, between the loss of a limb, and the loss of all use of a limb?'[30]

On 16 November 1808, just when O'Brien, Hewson and Barklimore were safely on board the *Amphion*, four midshipmen – Edward Boys, Robert Hunter, William Mansell and Frederick Whitehurst – were escaping from Valenciennes prison in north-east France. Mansell, 'a delicate and high spirited youth of about eighteen years of age',[31] was one of the young protégés of Captain John Wright who had been taken prisoner when the *Vincejo* brig was captured in 1804. Boys and Whitehurst had been captured off Toulon the year before and were forced to march all the way to Verdun prison, where midshipmen were initially held. They arrived at Verdun early in 1804 and remained there until the summer of 1808, when, as Boys explained, 'three midshipmen (I blush to state it) were taken in the very act of violating parole . . . the result was an order for the whole class [of midshipmen] to be removed. Accordingly, on the 7th of August, on going to the afternoon "appel," [roll-call] we were arrested, to the number of 142, and sent to the citadel.'[32] Although the midshipmen were somewhat concerned, Boys reckoned that the townspeople were more worried, because they were owed so much money. Early the next morning, 'the drum summoned us to muster. All those who were to depart were drawn up in two ranks; one of seventy-three, destined for Valenciennes and Givet, the other of sixty-nine (most of whom were masters of merchant vessels), destined for Sarre Louis and other depôts, to the eastward. The northern expedition being ready, we were placed two by two, upon bundles of straw, in five waggons, and set out, escorted by the greater part of the horse gendarmerie of the district, aided by infantry.'[33]

Boys was desperate to escape: 'Parole had, hitherto, tended, in some measure, to reconcile me to captivity, but being now deprived of that honourable confidence, and feeling my pride wounded, at the oppressive act of punishing the innocent for the guilty, no obstacle could avert my intention of finally executing, what I now felt a duty.'[34] Every opportunity to escape was thwarted by the vigilance of the guards, and once the Givet contingent had departed, a further obstacle of honour was placed in their path, as Boys explained:

This day the guard being relieved, we were entrusted to the care of a 'Marechal de logis,' who, entertaining the most liberal opinions of the character of British officers, immediately placed us on parole, and took us to an inn, where we slept. In the morning he selected eight, of whom I was one, and gave us permission to take the diligence [coach] to Valenciennes; adding—'Gentlemen, I rely upon your honour.' Now, severity would have been more acceptable than this act of politic kindness; but to have declined the offer, would have exposed my intentions.[35]

During the journey in the diligence to Valenciennes, Boys related that they

met four English seamen without scarcely a rag to cover them, strongly guarded, chained to each other by the neck, and handcuffed. They told us, that having escaped from Arras, they had gained the coast, seized a vessel, and put to sea. After beating about for several days in a gale of wind, and splitting all the sails, they were blown back, wrecked on the coast, and, on being retaken, were shamefully treated by the gendarmes. We made a subscription for them, and the poor fellows, with hearts of oak, not to be subdued, gave us three cheers, adding—'Never mind, gentlemen, we'll catch 'em again off Trafalgar, some of these days.'[36]

Arriving at Valenciennes, Boys immediately began to plot his escape, though 'from the citadel, escape appeared impossible, it being surrounded with ditches containing about six feet of mud, on the surface of which was not more than a foot of water; so that swimming was deemed impracticable'.[37] The many men held at Valenciennes experienced desperate boredom, as Boys described:

The ingenuity of fourteen hundred men were put to the test, to furnish amusement for the most wearisome hours that can be imagined, and in utter ignorance of their termination, or what was passing in the busy world of strife. The greater part, by lifeless ennui, were reduced to such a state of apathy, that they were worn down into mere brute existence; whilst those who had still any energy left, magnified the most trifling occurrence into an important event. On the 21st of October, being the [third] anniversary of the Battle of Trafalgar, almost every window in the citadel was illuminated, and several transparencies were exhibited in honour of that glorious victory. The repeated and almost incessant cheering of the prisoners continued for nearly two hours; many of the inhabitants of the town obtained leave to visit the citadel, and appeared to join in the sport with all their characteristic frivolity.[38]

Soon after, a guard mistook the sparring of two seamen as a quarrel and brutally attacked them, leading to the intervention of the gendarmes. Midshipmen Whitehurst and Boys pushed in, trying to stop the bloodshed, but were arrested. During their confinement they agreed an escape plan and next persuaded Robert Hunter and William Mansell to join them. The preparations were hurried, their plan being 'to scale a wall, to ascend the parapet unseen, to escape the observation of three or four sentinels and the patroles, to descend two ramparts, of about forty-five feet each, to force two large locks; and to get over two drawbridges'.[39]

The night of 16 November they made their escape, but at dawn an escape was suspected when their rope was spotted, and Boys was later told that 'the roll to muster was instantly beaten, and the alarm given to the neighbouring peasantry by the firing of guns. The midshipmen, on whom suspicion first fell, were hurried into ranks, half-dressed, and when the names of the absentees were called over, some one tauntingly replied, "Parti pour l'Angleterre" [left for England]—This tone of triumph considerably exasperated the gendarmes, and inflamed the zeal of the pursuers.'[40] An order was immediately given to take the prisoners dead or alive.

Over the following days Boys, Whitehurst, Hunter and Mansell trudged across fields and along lonely roads, travelling largely by night and sleeping in woods in the daytime. Thoroughly soaked with the constant rain, they 'were overtaken by two horse gendarmes; but it being exceedingly dark, they took us for conscripts, part of their own escort, for one of them, in a muffled tone, as if fearful of exposing his nose, said, "Make haste, you will be too late for your lodging tickets;" reply was made that we were fatigued; soon afterwards, the rain increasing, they trotted on, repeating, "Make haste, make haste."'[41] A large party of conscripts was on the move to Ghent, and so the four escaped prisoners were able to deceive the landlord of a public house and obtain lodgings for their first night in the dry. Two more days were spent outside in the cold and wet, until they reached the outskirts of Bruges in Flanders. Boys described what happened next:

At this time we were all in a most deplorable condition—wet to the skin, our feet bleeding, and so swollen, that we could scarcely walk at the rate of three miles an hour. Near the gates we observed a public-house, and, having hitherto found such places to afford relief and safety at this hour of the night, we entered, and saw nobody but an old woman and a servant. At first they appeared somewhat surprised, but asked no questions except such as regarded our wants, frequently exclaiming, 'pauvres conscripts.' We dried our clothes, when the sudden transition from cold to heat split Hunter's feet; several of his nails also were loose, and Whitehurst had actually walked off two . . . Having, however, enjoyed a comfortable supper, we laid ourselves down as before, keeping watch in turn, until four A.M., when we paid the old woman, and departed.[42]

They hid in a nearby wood and at sunset took the main road to Blankenberge, a village on the Belgian coast to the east of Ostend, where they expected to get hold of a boat to cross the Channel. Late at night they passed a solitary public house, as Boys related:

We observed through the window, an old man, two women, and a boy, sitting round a comfortable fire at supper. Hunter and I entered for the purpose of purchasing provisions to take on board any vessel we might be enabled to seize, being then about four miles from the sea. We asked for gin – the woman of the house rose and stared at us, apparently alarmed at our appearance; we repeated the demand without obtaining a reply; still gazing for a few seconds, regardless of our request, she rapturously exclaimed, 'Mon Dieu, ces sont des anglais!' [My God! They are English!][43]

The woman who ran the public house, the Raie de Chat (Mark of the Cat), was Madame Derikre, and despite their insistence that they were conscripts on their way to Blankenberge, she refused to believe them, having once worked for an English gentleman. She insisted they sit down and eat supper, all the while talking 'of nothing but her dear English'.[44] They left Madame Derikre, still declaring that they were conscripts, and made their way to the village, where 'finding a footpath leading over the sandbank, we ran down to the sea, forgetting our wounds, and exulting as though the summit of our wishes were attained, and we were on the point of embarkation. Indeed, so exquisite was the delight, that, regardless of consequences, we dashed into the water, drank of it, and splashed about like playful schoolboys, without being in the least disconcerted that the few vessels which could be seen were high and dry, close under the battery.'[45]

After their initial euphoria they realised that there were virtually no boats to take and that the tides were wrong. Then they heard footsteps running behind them and the clash of muskets, but managed to give their pursuers the slip. At dawn the following day they decided to seek the help of Madame Derikre, and while they tried to explain the truth, she exclaimed, 'Hold your tongues, I knew that you were English gentlemen the moment I saw you.'[46] Congratulating themselves on their good fortune, Boys confessed that they 'were so overpowered, so choked with joy, that we could scarcely articulate; the tear of gratitude trickled down the cheek, whilst the hand of friendship simultaneously met that of its neighbour; even the old woman (notwithstanding her vivacity) could not refrain from participating in our feelings'.[47]

In true Resistance style, Madame Derikre sheltered them secretly in the loft of the 'Cat' for the next few months, while a family friend by the name of Winderkins tried to find a fisherman to take them to England, but the patrols along the Channel coast were now very rigorous. One evening in mid-December, Boys related, 'Winderkins sent word that the vessels were all preparing for sea; but the next morning our expectations were again disappointed, by the information that the Government had laid an embargo on all the Blankenberg craft, until they furnished five seamen for the navy. The vessels were again hauled up above high-water mark, and the fishermen fled in all directions.'[48]

The four men remained in their loft but were constantly fearful of being discovered, as gendarmes and custom-house officers frequently used the public house, as well as soldiers looking for fugitive seamen. Hunter and Boys therefore decided to venture into the woods to see where they could hide, but they had only gone a mile along the road when two gendarmes on horseback noticed them. They rushed into a ploughed field and reached a thicket on the other side just as the gendarmes entered the wood, then plunged into a wide ditch which was flooding that part of the wood. They remained hidden in a dense part of the wood until dark, and on their return Boys was surprised to learn from Madame Derikre 'that she had heard of our adventure from the gendarmes, who, halting to bait [for refreshment], told her, they were very nearly catching two of the Blankenberg sailors, "but the rogues swam like ducks"'.[49]

After numerous setbacks and being forced to live in the woods because Madame Derikre was now under suspicion, Mansell went into Bruges disguised as a girl. At the very end of the year, with the help of a lawyer acquaintance of Madame Derikre by the name of Moitier, Mansell finally returned to England from Flushing in a small open boat belonging to a man known as Peter the Smuggler. The boat never returned for the rest of them, and in the end Moitier was persuaded to go to Verdun to obtain more money from a friend of Boys, Thomas George Wills, who had been a prisoner-of-war since 1804. Boys knew that Wills 'would risk his all to serve me'.[50] Before he left, Moitier introduced Boys to a businessman, Auguste Crens Neirinks, who secretly lodged the three escaped prisoners in an uninhabited house in Bruges.

Once Moitier knew for certain he would be paid well, he was spurred into action and next left for Flushing to make arrangements with Peter the Smuggler. On 28 April Neirinks gave word that a guide would be ready the following evening to lead them to Flushing, but on Moitier's return Boys related that 'he declared that Peter, from the imminent risk he had run in his late trip, would not undertake to carry us across the Channel under 80*l*. [£80]; that he, Moitier, had calculated on paying him only 40*l*.; Peter was to receive one-half on landing in England, and a note of hand was to be left with Moitier for the other. The 80*l*. were paid; but, I have since learned from Neirinks, that this story was a fabrication of Moitier's, who pocketed the additional 40*l*.'[51]

Having expressed their gratitude to Madame Derikre and the family of Neirinks for their immense kindness, Boys, Whitehurst and Hunter disguised themselves as Flemings and left Bruges by mingling with the crowd, accompanied by Neirinks and the guide. Boys described what happened next:

On arriving near the coast, we met Peter's wife, who ordered us to lie down on the ground, whilst this Amazonian chief reconnoitred the strand. She had scarcely proceeded a hundred yards, when she was hailed, and saluted with a shot; like a skilful general, she instantly made good her retreat, and bivouac'd with the main body. In this position we remained for about two hours, whilst Peter and his chief were occasionally watching the motions of the enemy, and looking out for the private signal from the boat. Our anxiety was now at its utmost stretch, and every passing moment appeared an age. The look-out, every now and then, was obliged to retreat, to avoid the patroles . . . The boat not coming, when day dawned we retreated to Peter's hut, for concealment.[52]

Finally, on 8 May 1809, Boys learned that all would be ready at ten o'clock that night:

Accordingly, at that hour, the weather fine, and the night dark, we marched down to the beach, and as soon as the patrole had passed, the private signal was made and answered. The boat gliding silently in shore with muffled oars, we rushed in with the rapidity of thought, and in an instant were all safe afloat; each seized an oar, and vigorously applying his utmost strength, we soon reached beyond the range of shot . . . It were in vain to attempt a faithful description of our feelings at this momentous crisis . . . nor, indeed, could we relinquish the oar, but continued at this laborious, though now delightful, occupation, almost without intermission the whole night. When day dawned the breeze freshened from the eastward, and as the sun began to diffuse his cheering rays, the wide expanse of liberty opened around us, and in the distant rear, the afflicted land of misery and bondage was beheld.[53]

With Neirinks and Peter the Smuggler, they continued rowing from Flushing until the white cliffs of Dover were spotted at three in the afternoon, and the harbour was reached five hours later. They landed at daylight on 10 May. The family of Boys lived only a few miles away, at Betteshanger, and he now found out that when Mansell had returned to England over four months earlier, he had gone to his family and tactlessly 'assured a younger sister, whom he happened to find alone, that "we should be either dead or in England in three weeks, as we had vowed not to be taken alive." Many months having elapsed since any letters from France had reached home, my parents received this information with mingled feelings of joy and fear, and immediately set on foot every method ingenuity and affection could devise, to render assistance through the smugglers'[54] – nearby Deal was a notorious haunt of smugglers, who themselves had strong connections with Flushing, but it had become increasingly difficult to operate because Napoleon was using that port and Antwerp, further up the River Scheldt from Flushing, as a naval base. By now, Boys's parents were in complete despair.

At Dover he hired a carriage, later remarking that 'at a moment when my attention was directed towards a neighbouring village, in search of the roof under which I had received the first impressions of discipline, Neirinks, whom I had taken with me, and who was admiring everything he saw, as "magnifique," suddenly exclaimed— "Regardez ce vénérable dans cette belle voiture."'[55] This 'venerable gentleman in the fine carriage' was Boys's father, and Boys simply related that they 'speedily drove to Betshanger, where a scene awaited me that I had little anticipated'.[56]

After a week Neirinks and Peter the Smuggler returned to Flushing with the aid of a naval vessel, and Boys was well pleased that 'with the money they received, and which they considered amply sufficient to recompense them for their services, they had previously purchased a quantity of indigo and coffee, which yielded them a profit of about 600 per cent. We had, therefore, not only the satisfaction of knowing that they were content with the result of their present trip, but that it would be an inducement for them to afford every assistance in their power to any of our countrymen, who might at a future period, escape from confinement, and reach that part of the coast.'[57]

Of the others who had escaped, Boys recounted that 'Hunter was soon afterwards employed, and promoted in 1811. Whitehurst was sent to the Halifax Station [Canada], where he had not been long before he was again made prisoner in the *Junon*, and detained in France during the remainder of the war. Mansell, a short time after, died at sea.'[58] Many more British seamen were to be taken prisoner during the remainder of the war, but to be taken prisoner twice like Frederick Whitehurst was very unlucky. He was serving in the frigate *Junon* off Guadeloupe and was captured by the French in mid-December 1809, only seven months after returning to England. One of those captured with him was Lieutenant George Vernon Jackson, who had taken such a dislike to tobacco on Diamond Rock. Boys himself was given special dispensation to take his lieutenant's examination almost immediately, and only a month after returning to England he was appointed as lieutenant of the recently launched brig-sloop *Arachne*. A few weeks later, in July 1809, Britain would launch a massive expedition against Flushing and the surrounding area, from where the prisoners had just escaped, in order to destroy what had become the second-largest French naval arsenal after Toulon.

With Cochrane's raids against the French on the southern coast of Spain and Sir John Moore (brother of Graham Moore) leading a British army into northern Spain after Sir Arthur Wellesley had defeated General Junot at Vimiero in August, the autumn of 1808 gave a false promise that the tide of war was turning against the French in Europe. Napoleon was impelled to take charge himself, marching into Spain at the head of his troops, and Moore boldly struck at his rear, but was forced to retreat in the depths of winter. An evacuation of the British troops looked inevitable, and warships and transport ships began to arrive at Spain's Atlantic port of Vigo for that purpose, many of them sailing from Corunna. In the south, Gerona was lost: the Spanish surrendered on 11 December, freeing the besieging French troops to be deployed elsewhere and opening up the possibility of supplying Barcelona overland by road from France. As the year 1808 drew to a close, Napoleon's grip on Spain tightened to a stranglehold.

On the last day of the year the British rearguard reached Astorga, and by now Moore's sole object was to save as many of his men as possible, destroying stores and ammunition and abandoning the sick in order to maintain the speed of the main body of troops. At Astorga the two light brigades were sent almost due west to the port of Vigo, while the remaining troops continued north-west towards Corunna. Thomas Howell, a soldier with the 71st Highlanders, vividly recalled the start of the journey:

From Villa Franca we set out on the 2 January, 1809. What a New-year's day had we passed! Drenched with rain, famished with cold and hunger, ignorant when our misery was to cease. This was the most dreadful period of my life. How differently did we pass our hogmonay, from the manner our friends were passing theirs, at home? Not a voice said, 'I wish you a happy new year;' each seemed to look upon his neighbour as an abridgement to his own comforts. His looks seemed to say, 'One or other of the articles you wear would be of great use to me; your shoes are better than those I possess: if you were dead, they would be mine!' . . . Dreadful as our former march had been, it was from Villa Franca that the march of death may be said to have begun.[59]

Without supplies and having worn out their boots with marching, they now had the French hard on their heels, and another Scottish soldier of the 71st, who no longer had boots, recalled:

Many of the officers were in the same state; some of them attempted to defend their feet by wrapping pieces of blanket round them. MY sufferings were now dreadful; every thing in the shape of stockings being long since gone, the constant friction of the wet trowsers rubbed the skin completely off my legs, and the raw flesh, feeling as if cauterised, increased my torments to an indescribable degree. But many were in a far worse condition, and lay down completely exhausted with excess of fatigue and misery, waiting impatiently for death to relieve their pangs . . . About this time I saw a dragoon sprawling in the mud, quite drunk, and seemingly unconscious of his miserable situation, laughing and yelling out his bacchanalian ribaldry. This poor wretch undoubtedly became food for the crows in a few short hours. Our cavalry and artillery horses died in such numbers, that nearly the whole road between Lugo and Corunna was strewed with their bloated carcasses.[60]

While one section of the remains of the British army struggled towards Corunna, the situation of those headed for Vigo was no less desperate, as John Harris of the 95th Rifles (and once a shepherd in Dorset) recorded:

The shoes and boots of our party were now mostly either destroyed or useless to us, from foul roads and long miles, and many of the men were entirely barefooted, with knapsacks and accoutrements altogether in a dilapidated state. The officers were also, for the most part, in as miserable a plight. They were pallid, way-worn, their feet bleeding, and their faces overgrown with beards of many days' growth . . . Many of the poor fellows, now near sinking with fatigue, reeled as if in a state of drunkenness, and altogether I thought we looked the ghosts of our former selves.[61]

If anything, the suffering of the camp-followers was even worse than that of the soldiers, and many of the incidents of the retreat were seared into the memories of those who survived, including Rifleman Harris:

One of the men's wives (who was struggling forward in the ranks with us, presenting a ghastly picture of illness, misery, and fatigue,) being very large in the family-way, towards evening stepped from amongst the crowd, and lay herself down amidst the snow, a little out of the main road. Her husband remained with her; and I heard one or two hasty observations amongst our men, that they had taken possession of their last resting-place. The enemy were, indeed, not far behind at this time, the night was coming down, and their chance seemed in truth but a bad one. To remain behind the column of march in such weather was to perish, and we accordingly soon forgot all about them. To my surprise, however, I, some little time afterwards (being myself then in the rear of our party), again saw the woman. She was hurrying, with her husband, after us, and in her arms she carried the babe she had just given birth to. Her husband and herself, between them, managed to carry that infant to the end of the retreat, where we embarked. God tempers the wind, it is said, to the shorn lamb; and many years afterwards I saw that boy, a strong and healthy lad. The woman's name was M'Guire, a sturdy and hardy Irishwoman; and lucky it was for herself and babe that she was so, as that night of cold and sleet was in itself sufficient to try the constitution of most females.[62]

Stories with a happy ending were the exception, and Harris could hardly bear to recall another sight:

Soon after our halt beside the turnip-field the screams of a child near me caught my ear, and drew my attention to one of our women, who was endeavouring to drag along a little boy of about seven or eight years of age. The poor child was apparently completely exhausted, and his legs failing under him. The mother had occasionally, up to this time, been assisted by some of the men, taking it in turn to help the little fellow on; but now all further appeal was in vain. No man had more strength than was necessary for the support of his own carcass, and the mother could no longer raise the child in her arms, as her reeling pace too plainly shewed. Still, however, she continued to drag the child along with her. It was a pitiable sight, and wonderful to behold the efforts the poor woman made to keep the boy amongst us. At last the little fellow had not even strength to cry, but, with mouth wide open, stumbled onwards, until both sank down to rise no more. The poor woman herself had, for some time, looked a moving corpse; and when the shades of evening came down, they were far behind amongst the dead or dying in the road. This was not the only scene of the sort I witnessed amongst the women and children during that retreat. Poor creatures![63]

When the exhausted troops finally reached Vigo on 12 January, they were completely at the end of their strength, as Harris graphically recorded:

As we proceeded down the hill [to Vigo] we now met with the first symptoms of good feeling from the inhabitants, it was our fortune to experience during our retreat. A number of old women stood on either side of the road, and occasionally handed us fragments of bread as we passed them. It was on this day, and whilst I looked anxiously upon the English shipping in the distance, that I first began to find my eyesight failing, and it appeared to me that I was fast growing blind . . . As it was, when I did manage to gain the seashore, it was only by the aid of my rifle that I could stand, and my eyes were now so dim and heavy that with difficulty I made out a boat which seemed the last that had put off. Fearful of being left half blind in the lurch, I took off my cap, and placed it on the muzzle of my rifle as a signal, for I was totally unable to call out . . . making one more effort, I walked into the water, and a sailor stretching his body over the gunwale, seized me as if I had been an infant, and hauled me on board. His words were characteristic of the English sailor, I thought. 'Hollo there, you lazy lubber!' he said, as he grasped hold of me, 'who the hell do you think is to stay humbugging all day for such a fellow as you?'[64]

The sailors then rowed Harris to the waiting transport ship*:

The boat, I found, was crowded with our exhausted men, who lay helplessly at the bottom, the heavy sea every moment drenching them to the skin. As

---

* Transport vessels carried soldiers and stores, mainly to places overseas. Merchant ships were usually hired for this role.

soon as we reached the vessel's side, the sailors immediately aided us to get on board, which in our exhausted state was not a very easy matter, as they were obliged to place ropes in our hands, and heave us up by setting their shoulders under us, and hoisting away as if they had been pushing bales of goods on board ... It was not very many minutes after I was on board, for I lay where the sailors had first placed me after dragging me through the porthole, ere I was sound asleep.[65]

The tattered remnants of the other section of the British army staggered into Corunna on 11 January, only to find that there were no transports waiting. The man in charge of the navy ships and transports off the west coast of Spain was Sir Samuel Hood, now a rear-admiral, but a message only reached him two days before with the news that Moore had changed his mind and was heading for Corunna rather than Vigo. In Corunna at that time was Henry Crabb Robinson, a thirty-three-year-old journalist who had been sent by the editor of *The Times* to write about the British campaign in Spain, making him the very first war correspondent. His report for 11 January, published some days later, accurately summed up the situation:

In the course of this day, the whole English army has either entered within, or planted itself before the walls of this town. The French army will not fail to be quick in the pursuit; and as the transports which were so anxiously expected from Vigo, are still out of sight, and, according to the state of the wind, not likely soon to make their appearance, this spot will most probably become the scene of a furious and bloody contest. At the same time, it is not probable that the conflict will instantly begin. Hitherto, the enemy has but a small quantity of infantry in the field; his cavalry, which does not exceed 5000, may be at no great distance from this place; and on this side [of] Lugo, there may be 8000 infantry ... It is, therefore, unlikely that any serious attack will be made upon the town for some time, perhaps not till our troops manifest an intention to embark: because, incapable as we are of receiving supplies, except those which the transports from Vigo may bring with them, our worst foe may ultimately be hunger.[66]

In the following days the army began to destroy supplies and equipment that were to be abandoned, including a large quantity of gunpowder, as Robert Blakeney, a young officer with the 28th Regiment, recalled:

On this morning [the 14th] a large quantity of powder sent for the use of the Spaniards was destroyed, to prevent its falling into the hands of the enemy. The casks were piled up in a large and lesser magazine, built together upon a hill about three miles from the town. The smaller one blew up with a terrible noise, which startled us all; but scarcely had we attempted to account for the occurrence, when, the train igniting the larger one, the crash was dreadful. A panic seized all; the earth was agitated for miles, and almost every window in Corunna was shattered. This was the largest explosion of powder which had ever taken place in Europe – four thousand barrels. On this evening the long-expected transports hove in sight, and soon entered the harbour of Corunna. Preparations for embarkation immediately commenced.[67]

The transports, over two hundred in number, had been delayed by gale-force winds blowing against them, and they reached Corunna on the same day that the French came within sight of the town. Lieutenant Basil Hall of the frigate *Endymion* accompanied the vessels from Vigo: 'The wind blew dead in from the south, and so hard, that not one of the transports could be moved . . . On the 11th of January, the wind lulled a little, and, by dint of whip and spur, we got our immense fleet fairly under weigh . . . we arrived [at Corunna] on the morning of the 15th of January, surrounded by upwards of two hundred and fifty sail of ships.'[68] Lieutenant Hall many years later wrote that 'I have often since heard officers who were then with the army, in position along the ridge . . . describe the feelings with which they turned round to look at the ships crowding into the harbour, under all sail, right before the wind.'[69] Napoleon had returned to Paris after the British had given him the slip at Astorga, and the French were now led by Marshal Nicolas Jean de Dieu Soult, who decided to pause, allowing his men to rest while the stragglers caught up with the main French army. This gave Moore a breathing space, and embarkation of the British continued unopposed over the next two days.

Unexpectedly delayed in his departure, Robinson wrote his last report to *The Times* from Corunna on the night of the 15th:

Yesterday evening, the fleet of transports which had been dispersed in their passage from Vigo, began to enter the harbour, and the hearts of thousands were relieved by the prospect of deliverance. I beheld this evening the beautiful Bay covered with our vessels, both armed and mercantile, and I should have thought the noble three-deckers, which stood on the outside of the harbour, a proud spectacle, if I could have forgotten the inglorious service they were called to perform. In the meantime the stairs which led to the water were thronged with boats, in which were embarking the British cavalry. The English soldiery appeared to have taken possession of all public places, while the inhabitants looked on with mortification and sorrow . . . I proceeded to the quay; and the scattered lights from the numerous shipping would have been a gay scene, but for the long waving line of light which we saw and knew the enemy had kindled above. During the whole of the day there have been skirmishes between French and English, at less than a league's distance, in small bodies: much firing, but little execution. To-morrow there is no doubt that our embarkation will proceed, and the enemy will probably be prudent enough to witness this without interfering, until a large proportion of our force is thus rendered useless.[70]

Among the troops still on shore at Corunna was Thomas Howell of the 71st Highlanders, who recorded the final hours before the French took over the town, including the destruction of equipment and thousands of horses and draught animals:

I witnessed a most moving scene. The beach was covered with dead horses, and resounded with the reports of the pistols that were carrying this havoc amongst them. The animals, as if warned by the dead bodies of their fellows, appeared frantic, neighed and screamed in the most frightful manner. Many broke loose, and galloped alongst the beach, with their manes erect, and their mouths wide open. Our preparations continued until the 16th, when every thing was completed, and we were to begin our embarkation at four o'clock. About mid-day we were all under arms, when intelligence arrived that the French were advancing . . . They commenced a heavy fire, from eleven great guns placed in a most favourable manner on the hill. Two strong columns advanced on the right wing; the one along the road, the other skirting its edges: a third advanced on the centre; a fourth approached slowly, on the left; while a fifth remained half way down the hill, in the same direction.[71]

As the French advanced, the rearguard action, known later as the Battle of Corunna, was commanded personally by Moore, as Howell recalled: 'Sir John was at the head of every charge . . . and the 42d drove all before them . . . The Guards were ordered to their support. Their ammunition being all spent, through some mistake, they were falling back: "Ammunition is coming, you have your bayonets," said Sir John. This was enough; onwards they rushed, overturning every thing. The enemy kept up their hottest fire upon the spot where they were. It was at this moment Sir John received his death-wound. He was borne off the field by six soldiers of the 42d, and the Guards.'[72] Lieutenant Hall and the purser of the *Endymion* had been allowed ashore and witnessed the entire battle. An army colonel standing close to them commented, 'Well, gentlemen, I don't know how you get on at sea, but I certainly never saw on land a hotter fire than this.'[73]

The British held the French off until darkness put a stop to the fighting – though the embarkation continued. Howell, one of the last to leave, recorded the final phase of retreat:

At dawn there was little to embark, save the rear-guard and the reserve, commanded by Major-General Hill, who had occupied a promontory behind Corunna. We were scarcely arrived on the beach, ere the French began to fire upon the transports in the harbour, from the heights of St Lucia. Then all became a scene of confusion. . . . There was no regularity in our taking the boats. The transport that I got to, had part of seven regiments on board. The Spaniards are a courageous people: the women waved their handkerchiefs to us from the rocks, whilst the men manned the batteries against the French, to cover our embarkation. Unmindful of themselves, they braved a superior enemy to assist a friend who was unable to afford them further relief, [and] whom they had no prospect of ever seeing again.[74]

Another soldier from Howell's regiment was in a transport that nearly ran aground, as he later recounted:

Daylight coming on, the French opened a heavy fire of shot and shells upon the transports, from some batteries on the heights and this unexpected salute terrified the transport captains so much, that several of them gave orders to cut their cables, without first taking the necessary precaution to brace their yards. Five vessels, in consequence of this, ran ashore in the greatest disorder. The foolish master of our vessel, seized with the same consternation, (a shell having burst at the stern, filling the whole ship with smoke), was hastening to follow the rash example the others had set, in cutting the cable, when we thought proper to prevent him. An officer of the 38th regiment, who seemed to have some nautical skill, then took the command, ordering the sails to be all set first, and afterwards that the cable should be cut. Although the balls were whizzing through the rigging now and then, the officer's orders were obeyed with great promptitude and coolness, and we were soon running out to sea in fine style; not, however, without having the satisfaction of seeing a British seventy-four come in, and silence with a single broadside the battery which had annoyed us so much.[75]

Despite the last-minute confusion, the evacuation was a resounding success for the British Navy. Around twenty-six thousand experienced troops, the core of the British army in the field, along with wives and children, were snatched from the Iberian Peninsula. Their loss would have been a catastrophe for Britain, and in that context the evacuation was as important as the later evacuation of a British army from the beaches of Dunkirk in 1940. Rear-Admiral Hood was the hero of the hour, receiving official thanks from Parliament. For the soldiers, though, there was still a gruelling and stormy journey by sea to be endured, through the Bay of Biscay. This was described by Rifleman Harris, who had fallen asleep as soon as he was safe on board at Vigo:

It was only the terrible noise and bustle on board consequent upon a gale having sprung up, that at length awoke me. The wind increased as the night came on, and soon we had to experience all the horrors of a storm at sea. The pumps were set to work; the sails were torn to shreds; the coppers were overset; and we appeared in a fair way, I thought, of going to the bottom. Meanwhile, the pumps were kept at work night and day incessantly till they were choked; and the gale growing worse and worse, all the soldiery were ordered below, and the hatches closed; soon after which the vessel turned over on one side, and lay a helpless log upon the water. In this situation an officer was placed over us, with his sword drawn in one hand, and a lantern in the other, in order to keep us on the side which was uppermost, so as to give the vessel a chance of righting herself in the roaring tide. The officer's task was not an easy one, as the heaving waves frequently sent us sprawling from the part we clung to, over to the lowermost part of the hold, where he stood, and he was obliged every minute to drive us back. We remained in this painful situation for, I should think, five or six hours, expecting every instant to be our last, when, to our great joy, the sea suddenly grew calm, the wind abated, the vessel righted herself, and we were once more released from our prison, having tasted nothing in the shape of food for at least forty-eight hours.[76]

The storm had scattered some of the transports, which made their way to many different ports as best they could. Only two transport vessels were wrecked, off the Cornish coast, with the loss of nearly three hundred

men. Sailing from Corunna, rather than Vigo, Howell had a better journey, but still far from comfortable:

For two days after we came on board, I felt the most severe pains through my
whole body: the change was so great, from the extreme cold of the winter
nights, which we had passed almost without covering, to the suffocating
heat of a crowded transport. This was not the most disagreeable part: vermin
began to abound. We had not been without them in our march: but now we
had dozens for [each] one we had then. In vain we killed them; they appeared
to increase from the ragged and dirty clothes, of which we had no means of
freeing ourselves. Complaint was vain. Many were worse than myself: I had
escaped without a wound; and, thank God! though I had not a shirt upon my
back, I had my health, after the two first days, as well as I ever had it. On the
morning of the tenth day after our embarkation . . . 'Land ahead! Old
England once again!' was called from mouth to mouth . . . We anchored
that same day at Plymouth, but were not allowed to land: Our Colonel kept
us on board until we got new clothing. Upon our landing, the people came
round us, showing all manner of kindness, carrying the lame and leading the
blind. We were received into every house as if we had been their own relations. How proud did I feel to belong to such a people![77]

The appearance throughout southern England of troops in such a state
was shocking to the inhabitants. A few days after Howell's ship arrived,
*The Times* published an eyewitness report from Plymouth:

A telegraphic order was received this day for the transports, with the troops
on board, to proceed round to Spithead, where I understand near 200 sail
have already arrived, and which is to be the general rendezvous of the whole.
The weather having moderated, early this morning, the landing of the sick
and wounded of our brave army proceeded with great alacrity; and considerable numbers were brought on shore, and conveyed to the hospitals. Their
situation and wretched appearance were truly pitiable. Several were brought
on shore dead; and some have died in the streets within the last three days, on
their way to the hospitals. It is impossible for me to portray the confusion and
distress which has prevailed here the whole week – women searching through
the fleet for their husbands and relatives – officers and men looking after their
wives, children and comrades. Nor can our loss be in any degree ascertained
till a general muster takes place, and correct returns of the respective corpses
are given in. I have, however, learnt, from several intelligent officers who were

present in the last engagement, that our loss in killed, wounded, prisoners, and those who expired by fatigue, and the want of proper food, does not fall short of 9 or 10,000 men.[78]

Those who survived made the most of it, as Robert Blakeney of the 28th Regiment wryly recorded:

Our appearance on landing was very unseemly, owing principally to the hurry attending our embarkation at Corunna, which took place in the dark and in the presence of an enemy. Scarcely a regiment got on board the vessel which contained their baggage; and the consequence was, that on quitting our ships we presented an appearance of much dirt and misery. The men were ragged, displaying torn garments of all colours; and the people of England, accustomed to witness the high order and unparalleled cleanliness of their national troops, for which they are renowned throughout Europe, and never having seen an army after the termination of a hard campaign, were horror-struck, and persuaded themselves that some dreadful calamity must have occurred. Their consternation was artfully wrought up to the highest pitch by the wily old soldiers, who, fully aware of the advantage to be gained by this state of general excitement and further to work on the feelings, recited in pathetic strain the most frightful accounts of their sufferings and hardships.[79]

Another soldier, from the 71st, reported that one of the wives similarly obtained money:

Among the women who were put ashore on our arrival at Portsmouth, there was one belonging to our regiment who had rather the appearance of a bundle of rags than of a human being. Upon some of the men calling out to her not to expose the regiment, by telling the good English people that such a scarecrow belonged to it, she answered, that she would soon have more prize-money than any of us. This eventually turned out truth; not long afterwards she joined us again, finely dressed, and having £30 in her pocket: – her lamentable story had taken well; but, I dare say, she got the money more readily on account of having a beautiful child in her arms.[80]

After all the hardships of the campaigns in Spain, even this was small compensation.

# THIRTEEN

———•◆•———

# THE GRAND EXPEDITION

This is to certify that Mr. Frederick Marryat, midshipman of
H.M.S. *Imperieuse*, was in the explosion brig under my command
in the attack of the enemy's fleet in Basque Roads, on the night of
the 11th of April, 1809, and conducted himself very much to his
own credit and my entire satisfaction.

Certificate of service given to the naval officer
and later novelist Frederick Marryat[1]

The British Navy's success in evacuating Corunna was almost instantly
counterbalanced by the failure of the blockade off Brest. When the
squadron of Rear-Admiral Willaumez was disastrously hit by a hurricane,
some of his ships had taken refuge in American waters. In early 1807
he managed to return to Brest, where he had been blockaded ever since.
Admiral James Gambier – now elevated to Lord Gambier after his attack
on Copenhagen – was in charge of the Channel Fleet, but severe weather
forced his blockading ships from Brest, and on 21 February 1809 Willaumez
seized the opportunity and escaped with eight battleships and seven
frigates.

The failure of the blockade was blamed on Gambier, who had a reputation, regarded by many sailors as a *bad* reputation, for being a Christian
evangelist. The poet and humourist Thomas Hood mocked his extreme
views in an ode :

> Oh! Admiral Gam—— I dare not mention *bier*
> In such a temperate ear,—

Oh! Admiral Gam—— an Admiral of the Blue,
Of course, to read the Navy List aright,
For strictly shunning wine of either hue,
You can't be Admiral of the Red or White.[2]

Many thought that Gambier was more concerned with saving the souls of his crew than saving Britain from the French, an attitude frowned on by several of his fellow officers and most of the men, who christened him 'Dismal Jimmy' and 'Preaching Jemmy'.

The squadron of Willaumez was spotted by Commodore John Beresford, whose four battleships were blockading the nearby port of Lorient, and he attempted to attack them, but they gave him the slip. On the 23rd Willaumez reached as far south as Rochefort, which was blockaded by Rear-Admiral Robert Stopford. There was no chance of stopping the French force, and Stopford sent a ship to Gambier to raise the alarm while harassing the stragglers and forcing two frigates to be wrecked on the French coast. Stopford, though, could only watch as Willaumez led his remaining fleet into the safe anchorage known as Basque Roads, from where Napoleon intended him to go to Toulon.

The place where Willaumez had taken shelter was just off the Atlantic coast of France between La Rochelle to the north and Rochefort to the south. This anchorage was protected by several islands, with the Île de Ré west of La Rochelle, the Île d'Oléron off Rochefort and the Île d'Aix, much closer to the shore, lying between the two. Basque Roads was the area of sea to the north of the Île d'Aix, and Aix Roads was to the south. Not only were these anchorages protected from the weather, but enemy attack was made more difficult by shore batteries on the islands and the fact that the smaller islands and shoals made navigation of the area difficult and slow. The natural protection of the shoals was not always beneficial, because as Willaumez led his fleet into the greater safety of Aix Roads, the battleship *Jean Bart* ran aground on a shoal due south of the Île d'Aix and had to be abandoned as a wreck. The nature of the area, with its shoals and fortified islands, made it extremely difficult to blockade, particularly with the small force at Stopford's disposal, but Willaumez made no move to escape, and merely strengthened his defensive position by fixing a heavy boom across the passage into his anchorage. This passageway, a shallow channel less than 2 miles wide, led between the shoals and the Île d'Aix to the estuary of the River Charente, and it was here that the French were anchored.

Gambier arrived with his fleet on 7 March, which at least provided extra ships for a more effective blockade, but neither the Admiralty in London nor the Ministry of Marine in Paris was happy with events. When it was known that Willaumez had failed to tackle Beresford's inferior force and was now bottled up in Aix Roads, he was replaced by Vice-Admiral Zacharie-Jacques-Théodore Allemand. In London, the general opinion was that if the French could give Gambier the slip at Brest, they could easily do so here. The Admiralty was no longer content merely to blockade the French fleet but wanted action, proposing an attack on the French ships at anchor. Gambier reluctantly replied that 'an attack by means of fire-ships was hazardous, if not desperate . . . [but] if the Board of Admiralty wished to order such an attack, it should be done secretly and quickly'.[3] When the idea became known in Gambier's fleet, a number of officers volunteered to take part, including the Trafalgar veteran Rear-Admiral Eliab Harvey. The decision was not in Gambier's hands, though, and the Admiralty had already formed a plan.

Captain Thomas Cochrane had barely set foot on land at Plymouth after his successes against the French in Spain, when he received a message from William Johnstone Hope, Second Lord of the Admiralty: 'There is an undertaking of great moment in agitation against Rochefort, and the Board [of Admiralty] thinks that your local knowledge and services on the occasion might be of the utmost consequence, and, I believe, it is intended to send you there with all expedition; I have ventured to say, that if you are in health, you will readily give your aid on this business.'[4] On reaching London, Cochrane learned that it was proposed to put him in charge of the fireship attack. He instantly objected – being only a junior captain, he knew his plans would be met with ill-feeling by those higher in rank. Cochrane was curtly told that 'the present was no time for professional etiquette'[5] and was sent off immediately to Rochefort, arriving there on 3 April.

His appearance produced just the effect he had feared: Admiral Harvey, initially assuming it was all Gambier's doing, flew into a rage and publicly accused him of being unfit to command. Cochrane commented that the 'the abuse of Lord Gambier to his face was such as I had never before witnessed from a subordinate'.[6] Harvey returned to England to face the inevitable court martial, which found him guilty of using 'vehement and insulting language to the Right Hon. Lord Gambier, and of having otherwise shewn great disrespect to him as commander-in-chief'.[7]

He was dismissed from the navy, and although he was reinstated to his rank the following year in recognition of his previous years of service, he was never employed at sea again.

Cochrane immediately set in motion his plan for attack, with explosion vessels full of shells and Congreve rockets, and fireships to burn the French fleet. There had been continuing skirmishes between both sides, and one incident on the day of his arrival was recorded by William Richardson, gunner of the *Caesar*: 'In the forenoon of this day we observed many large boats, some with guns [cannons] and full of men, rowing along shore on the Oleron side [near the Île d'Oléron], and we supposed with intent to capture some of our victuallers, who were lying becalmed outside of the roads; we therefore sent the launches of our fleet armed with carronades and other boats manned and armed to stop them; a smart fight soon ensued, and the enemy retreated. Our loss in the boats was one lieutenant and one seaman killed and another seaman wounded.'[8] The 'victuallers' were merchant ships bringing supplies to the blockading fleet, but Cochrane had another purpose in mind for them, as Richardson related:

Having got the victuallers cleared of the provisions and water, twelve of them were selected for fire-ships, and the *Mediator*, 36-gun frigate, was to be fitted for another, in order to go in ahead of the others and clear away all obstacles; eight others were expected from England, making in all twenty-one, and besides we fitted up three explosion vessels, to lead in the fire-ships and blow up first, to throw the enemy in consternation: all these ('twas thought) were sufficient to destroy the enemy's fleet. We got along-side one of the victuallers, a brig of 350 tons named the *Thomas*, and belonging to a Mr. Cowey of North Shields, and immediately began to fit her up for a fire-ship; we made narrow troughs and laid them fore and aft on the 'tween decks and then others to cross them, and on these were laid trains of quickmatch [fuses]; in the square openings of these troughs we put barrels full of combustible matter, tarred canvas hung over them fastened to the beams, and tarred shavings made out of brooms, and we cut four port-holes on each side for fire to blaze out and a rope of twisted oakum well tarred led up from each of these ports to the standing rigging and up to the mast-heads; nothing could be more complete for the purpose.[9]

Gunner Richardson was then employed on an explosion vessel:

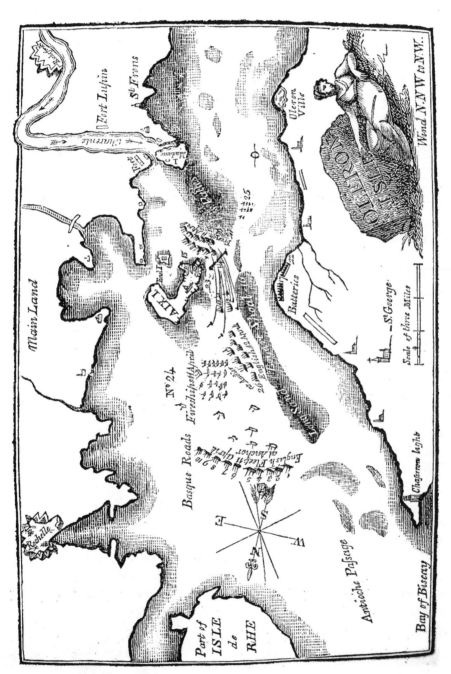

Chart representing the French and British fleets in Basque Roads

My next job was to fit up a chasse-marée* (lately taken) for an explosion vessel; but she rolled so much alongside as to endanger her masts being carried away against our rigging, so she was dropped astern, and hung on by a rope [was towed], and then continued to roll as much as ever; so that I had to change first one and then another of the carpenter's crew who were on board cutting the fuses, they being seasick. We stowed thirty-six barrels of gunpowder (90 lb. each) in her hold upright and heads out, on each was placed a 10 inch bomb-shell, with a short fuse in order to burst quickly. A canvas hose well filled with prime powder was laid for a train from the barrels to a small hole cut in her quarter for the purpose, and the train was led through it to her outside, which was well fastened – a port fire which would burn twelve or fifteen minutes so as to give the people alongside in the boat who set it on fire sufficient time to escape before she exploded.[10]

James Choyce had until recently been a prisoner-of-war at Sarrelibre, but had joined the French Navy as a means of escaping and a few days later rowed out to a British warship. He was now involved in fitting out transport ships as fireships, with all sorts of combustible material. 'In all this what stuck most in our gizzards,' he lamented, 'was that two or three of these vessels were loaded with hay, and a number of puncheons of rum, of which we were not allowed to taste a drop, the puncheons being all stove [in] and the contents poured over the hay to make it burn the better. This . . . grieved us very much.'[11]

Once the fireships and explosion vessels were ready, it was only necessary to have favourable winds and tides, and the attack was launched on the evening of 11 April, just over a week after Cochrane had taken charge. The plan was that an explosion vessel towed into position by Cochrane's *Imperieuse* would drift against the boom and blow up, clearing the way for the other ships. These would be steered in by a handful of men who were to light the fuses and escape in boats, to be picked up by frigates waiting nearby. William Robinson on board the *Revenge* commented that 'however dangerous the service, yet there are never wanting British seamen to embark in it, and on this occasion a boat's-crew, from each ship of the line, volunteered their services to take those fire-ships in . . . it is a mode of warfare dreadful to resort to, and should not be practised by any civilised nation'.[12]

---

* A chasse-marée, French for 'chase-tide', was a three-masted coasting ship particularly favoured by privateers and smugglers.

The conditions seemed ideal, and Richardson described it as 'being very dark, and a strong tide setting with blowing weather right towards the enemy's ships'.[13] Characteristically, Cochrane not only led the way with his ship, but joined the crew of the boat that was to set fire to the explosion vessel. What happened next was described by an anonymous correspondent of *The Times*:

When Lord Cochrane had conducted his explosion-ship as near as was possible; the enemy having taken the alarm, he ordered his brave little crew into the boat, and followed them, after putting fire to the fuse, which was calculated to give them 15 minutes to get out of the reach of the explosion. However, in consequence of the wind getting very high, the fuse burnt too quickly; so that, with the most violent exertion against wind and tide; this intrepid little party was six minutes nearer than they calculated to be, at the time when the most tremendous explosion that human art ever contrived took place, followed by the bursting at once in the air, of near 400 shells, and 300 hand-grenades, pouring down a shower of cast-metal in every direction! But fortunately our second NELSON was spared; the boat having reached, by unparalleled exertion, only just beyond the extent of destruction. Unhappily this effort to escape cost the life of the brave Lieutenant, whom this noble Captain saw die in the boat, partly under fatigue, and partly drowned with waves, that continually broke over them. Two of the four sailors were also so nearly exhausted that their recovery has been despaired of.[14]

In fact, the boat was not yet beyond the falling debris, according to Cochrane:

To our consternation, the fuses which had been constructed to burn fifteen minutes, lasted little more than half that time, when the vessel blew up, filling the air with shells, grenades, and rockets; whilst the downward and lateral force of the explosion raised a solitary mountain of water, from the breaking of which in all directions our little boat narrowly escaped being swamped. In one respect it was, perhaps, fortunate for us that the fuses did not burn the time calculated, as, from the little way we had made against the strong head wind and tide, the rockets and shells from the exploded vessel went over us. Had we been in the line of their descent, at the moment of explosion, our destruction, from the shower of broken shells and other missiles, would have been inevitable.[15]

The blast dislodged the boom, and the fireship *Mediator* broke through this massive obstacle of cables and anchors, leaving the channel free for the other, smaller fireships. With the high winds, they sped down towards the French, and the attack looked to be a success, but already Cochrane was disappointed. Only four of the twenty-one fireships managed to reach the enemy, and Cochrane blamed the crews for setting light to their fuses and abandoning them too soon. However, at least part of the problem was the unexpected ferocity of the wind, which made the fuses burn faster than normal. Nevertheless, faced with the wall of fire racing towards them out of the darkness, the French panicked and cut their anchor cables, allowing the wind to blow them away from the danger. By daylight only two French battleships were still afloat, and the other eight were heeled over at awkward angles, having run aground. Not a single French ship had been burned.

The victory was only half won, and it was obvious to Cochrane that it could easily be completed by the British battleships sailing in and bombarding the stranded French ships before they had a chance of refloating. Cochrane sent anxious signals from the *Imperieuse*, asking for support from Gambier, who was anchored some 10 miles away. A few hours later Gambier at last brought his ships in closer, only to anchor 6 miles from the enemy ships. He was unwilling to risk his battleships in an attack, underestimating the width of the channel and overestimating the strength of the French shore batteries. As James Choyce commented, 'this would have been the time to have destroyed them; but this favourable opportunity was neglected, which caused not a little murmuring among us, and was considered most unseamanlike by many experienced men in our fleet.'[16]

After midday, some of the French ships began to refloat and Cochrane, furious at what he saw as a lost opportunity, could wait no more. He went in to attack the *Calcutta*, an East India ship that had been captured in 1805, sending urgent signals that he needed assistance. Gambier initially ordered some of the smaller vessels to go in and assist, followed up by battleships and frigates. Faced with a possible assault, two French ships cut their cables but soon afterwards grounded, and in the late afternoon three ships (the *Aquilon*, *Ville de Varsovie* and *Calcutta*) surrendered after being attacked. Captain Jean Lafon of the 50-gun *Calcutta* was later court-martialled and shot dead for having surrendered to Cochrane's inferior *Imperieuse* (of only 38 guns). The French set fire to the *Tonnerre* to prevent the vessel being taken, and the British set fire to the *Calcutta* in the belief that the ship was stuck fast. Gunner Richardson on board the *Caesar*, though, commented that 'it was thought she might have been got off by lightening her'.[17]

Some British ships grounded for a while, including the *Caesar*, but Richardson explained that they got clear late at night and moved away from the *Calcutta*, 'which had been all in a blaze only a short distance from us; the latter when she blew up made a most dreadful explosion, having a great quantity of gunpowder on board and other stores which were intended for Martinique, had we not prevented her. It was said she was worth half a million sterling. Fortunately none of her fiery timbers fell on board our ship: everything went upwards, with such a field of red fire as illuminated the whole elements.'[18]

The *Revenge* with William Robinson on board also grounded: 'Our ship having touched the ground, we were obliged to lay under their batteries all night . . . their shots were whistling over us, some a-head, some a-stern, and a great many fell short: there was not one in fifty that hit us, but those that did, effected great execution. Amongst them was a very distressing and mischievous one, which knocked a man's head completely from his shoulders, and struck a lieutenant on the breast: the lieutenant was knocked down by the force of the head striking him.'[19] During the night, Choyce recorded, 'a constant fire was kept up from our bomb and rocket vessels, for no decision had been come to as to how we should act, it not being considered prudent to risk many of our heavy ships among the sands and shoals'.[20] Fireships were preparing to attack the remaining ships, but the winds changed. Instead the *Aquilon* and *Ville de Varsovie* were set on fire in the early hours of the 13th, as Gunner Richardson recalled:

Captain [John] Bligh of the *Valiant* was sent in with the boats manned and armed to reconnoitre the enemy more closely, and on his return informed us that they had got three lines of boats manned and armed to keep off any more fire-ships, and, it beginning to blow strong at the time, the attempt was given up. So we set fire to the *Varsovie*, a new 90-gun ship (for she carried that number), and to the *Aquilon* (74 guns), as they were waterlogged. They burnt to the water's edge, and then blew up. As for the *Tonnère* (74 guns), the enemy set fire to her themselves, and then escaped in their boats. In the place where we now had anchored we found our ships to ground at low water. And early in the morning, the wind having become favourable, we got under way with the other line-of-battle ships, and left this place, which may be compared to Portsmouth Harbour, and soon after anchored among our other ships in Basque Roads, which may be compared to Spithead.[21]

By now Cochrane had been ordered by Gambier to withdraw and hand over to Captain Wolfe of the *Aigle*, so that he could transport back to England Flag Captain Sir Harry Neale with dispatches. Overall the attack had been a success, as well as a psychological blow to the French, demonstrating that their ships were not even safe within their most protected anchorages. In Britain it was hailed as a victory, and *The Times* produced a gushing report extolling Cochrane's virtues in the same vein that had so often been used for Nelson. Many French were taken prisoner, and the removal of some of the crew from one ship that had surrendered was transformed into a 'rescue': 'Our Hero soon turned his attention to rescue the vanquished from the devouring elements; and in bringing away the people of the *Ville de Varsovie*, he would not even allow a *dog* to be abandoned, but took a crying, and now neglected little favourite up into his arms, and brought it away. It may be supposed that he has conveyed this fortunate little trophy into the bosom of his family, where it ought to be ever cherished as an instance of his generous care.'[22]

Cochrane was rewarded by being made a Knight of the Bath, but still annoyed by Gambier's caution he made it clear that in his position as Member of Parliament for Westminster he would oppose the customary vote of thanks to Gambier. This, along with a whispering campaign against Gambier that the victory was not as complete as it might have been, led Gambier to demand a court martial to clear his name. This was held in July and he was exonerated, but Cochrane refused to accept its findings. When the vote of thanks to Gambier was eventually proposed Cochrane spoke in opposition, but it was still passed, not least because it would have been a blow to the government had it failed. Opinion among naval officers was divided, but many thought Cochrane was right. The physician O'Meara later published a conversation that he had with Napoleon on St Helena about this episode:

I [O'Meara] said that it was the opinion of a very distinguished naval officer whom I named, and who was well known to him, that if Cochrane had been properly supported, he would have destroyed the whole of the French ships. 'He could not only have destroyed them,' replied Napoleon, 'but he might and would have taken them out [captured them], had your admiral supported him as he ought to have done . . . The terror of the *brûlots* (fire-ships) was so great that they actually threw their powder overboard, so that they could have offered very little resistance. The French admiral was an *imbecille*, but yours was just as bad. I assure you, that if Cochrane had been supported, he would have taken every one of the ships.[23]

Cochrane was still a hero in the eyes of the British public, although in some quarters a tarnished one. While the Admiralty still saw him as an asset, it was not willing to employ him on his own terms, turning down his suggestions as to where he might best be used. He was soon distracted by his political interests and did not see active service again during the rest of the war.

One of Cochrane's suggestions rejected by the Admiralty was that he should be an observer with the expedition against Napoleon's naval base in the Scheldt estuary. Captain George Wolfe of the frigate *Aigle* was also affected by the Basque Roads dispute as he was obliged to resign his command in order to attend the court martial of Lord Gambier. In his place Lieutenant William Dillon, who had been released from imprisonment at Verdun nearly two years earlier, was appointed acting captain. Dillon reached Plymouth to take over the *Aigle* on 13 June 1809 and was not impressed: 'I found her in a most dirty, slovenly state, the cabin full of rolled-up sails, without any circulation of air . . . I saw at a glance that extraordinary exertions would be required to get the ship ready for sea.'[24] He considered the discipline far too lax and complained that 'Capt. W. had the mania of placing himself upon a very familiar footing with the seamen, giving them the preference to his officers. On the first day that I went on board [before Wolfe left] I had noticed one or two seamen entering the cabin with as much freedom as if in their own homes, and speak to their Captain in the most familiar tones. He seemed to encourage that, as he styled them Tom, Jack, Bill, etc. My plan of proceeding was diametrically opposed to this, my opinion being that familiarity breeds contempt.'[25]

After only eight days the frigate was almost prepared for sea, when at four in the morning the crew mutinied by refusing to scrub the deck. Dillon ordered his first lieutenant to seize the first man who refused the order and have him flogged, commenting that 'that punishment, and the decision with which it was performed, made a strong impression upon all hands. The officers were not prepared for it, declaring that Capt. Wolfe would not have acted so.'[26] Later the same morning, Dillon recorded, he met Admiral Young, commander-in-chief of Plymouth, who advised him that the crew were about to be paid, after which they should proceed to Spithead:

'As the Aigle is going to Portsmouth,' said he, 'they can lay out their cash there. You will explain that to them before you weigh anchor.' When I returned to the ship, the pay officers were on board. Plenty of Jews occupied the Main Deck: there were many women on board: nothing to be seen but confusion. I had considerable difficulty getting rid of Moses and his party, but perseverance drove them all out. The hands were ordered to unmoor, and when they were ready I had them aft, and told them that, by the ship's being ordered to Portsmouth, they would not be deprived of their usual indulgence. I hoped they would show their good will, and I would, in return, make up to them what might be required. They then gave three vociferous cheers, and unmoored ship in double quick time. These fellows were fractious at 4 o'clock in the morning, and 12 hours afterwards they were ready to do anything they were ordered. Such is the material of a frigate crew.[27]

At Spithead, Dillon learned, 'reports were in circulation that an expedition amounting to 40,000 men would soon be fitted out . . . Its destination was all a matter of speculation, excepting those who were in the secret.'[28] Despite the supposed secrecy, newspapers daily carried details of the preparations for what they called the 'grand expedition', with great optimism about what it might achieve. In mid-July *The Times* reported: 'While the destination of the expedition, which is now on the point of setting out, remains, in some degree, a secret at home, the enemy, it appears, fancies he knows exactly whither it is to go. The most recent papers from Flushing state, that in Holland it is universally believed that the first object of the expedition is to take possession of the island of Walcheren, and after having seized the naval treasures at Flushing, then to proceed up the Scheldt and attack Antwerp.'[29]

This account was entirely correct, but the expedition was also a diversion. Because Napoleon's army in central Europe was much weakened owing to the campaigns in Spain and Portugal, Austria in early 1809 decided to attack the French, initially with some success. In April Britain had signed a treaty of alliance with Austria and was persuaded not only to assist financially, but also to keep the French occupied elsewhere so that his troops on the Danube could not be reinforced. Being severely short of specie – gold and silver coins – the British government decided on a second front close to home: an attack on the French shipping, arsenals and dockyards along the long, winding River Scheldt, which flowed into the North Sea.

The River Scheldt was formerly the boundary between the Austrian Netherlands (Belgium) and the United Provinces (Kingdom of Holland). While nominally independent, Holland was ruled by Napoleon's brother, Louis Bonaparte. The river, though notorious for its shifting sandbanks and fierce tidal currents, could be navigated by large ships all the way to Antwerp (Anvers in French) in Belgium, and it was here that Napoleon was rebuilding his navy, with heavy supplies such as timber transported along the numerous tributaries and canals. The Scheldt had become Napoleon's second-largest naval base, after Toulon. As the River Thames was less than twenty-four hours away, it had long been feared that Napoleon would launch an invasion of England from here. The Admiralty kept a permanent close watch on the area, and spies and naval vessels constantly reported on the situation. Intelligence had been received that the troops on the northern coast of France and Holland had been ordered to join Napoleon's Grand Army in Austria, leaving only a small force to guard Antwerp and Walcheren, and so this was a good time to attack. Towards the end of April Captain John Martin Hanchett of the sloop *Raven*, who had been gathering information in the Scheldt estuary, advised that Flushing should be a prime target:

Having served with Sir Sidney Smith in the *Antelope*, during the time he commanded the squadron off Flushing, in the early part of the present war, and from that circumstance being well acquainted with the anchorage, fortifications, &c. of that port, I have no doubt that the enemy's fleet, if they are laying in the outer Roads, may be easily destroyed by fire-ships, or, should they lay in the Basin, from the depth of water and the navigation, with which I am well acquainted, a line-of-battle ship may be run alongside the walls of the town so close, that men may land from the yard-arms; and I volunteer to be the first man that lands from them.[30]

Flushing (Vlissingen in Dutch) was a town on the southern side of the island of Walcheren, and although the island was Dutch, Flushing had been ceded to France. The so-called secret plan was for a combined army and navy expedition that would destroy the French fleet and arsenals along the River Scheldt, as well as Napoleon's shipbuilding capability. It was a formidable expedition, the largest that had ever been assembled in Britain. Some of the troops were to be landed on the islands of Walcheren and South Beveland in the Scheldt estuary (part of the Dutch province of

Zeeland or Zealand*) and on the island of Cadsand to the south. Most of the islands were below sea level and were protected from flooding by sand dunes and massive dykes. At the estuary, the Scheldt split into two channels, but as the East Scheldt on the north side of Walcheren was especially difficult to navigate, the navy was to force its way past Flushing along the West Scheldt. Most of the troops would disembark at the village of Sandvliet and then march 20 miles to attack the port of Antwerp. What was required was speed, surprise and efficient co-operation, but when the plan was first devised, the army could not supply enough men, as so many had been lost in the recent campaign in Spain and Portugal, and those who had returned safely from Corunna and Vigo after their retreat were in a poor physical state. Delay followed delay, and the element of surprise was lost.

Once the expedition had been decided upon, an overall commander was needed, but to widespread consternation, John Pitt, the second Earl of Chatham, was chosen, 'a man reputed to possess excellent understanding, but whose very name was almost proverbial for enervation and indolence'.[31] Lord Chatham was an army officer, the elder brother of the former prime minister, William Pitt, and a favourite of George III. Captain James Seton of the 92nd Highlanders remarked: 'He may be a very able statesman, but I am afraid he is a d——d bad general.'[32] Rear-Admiral Sir Richard Strachan, known to his men as 'Mad Dick' because of his fierce temper, was appointed naval commander. These two contrasting characters proved incapable of working together, but the captain of the *Marlborough*, Graham Moore, was very confident: 'The Naval part of it is well commanded. Strachan is one of those in our service whom I estimate the highest. I do not believe he has his fellow among the Admirals, unless it be Pellew, for ability, and it is not possible to have more zeal and gallantry.'[33] For the past few months Strachan had been in charge of a squadron watching the Dutch coast, but now he was placed in charge of a huge fleet of nearly four hundred transports and around 265 warships, including thirty-five ships of the line. Serving under Strachan were Sir Home Popham and Sir Richard Keats.

Preparations for the expedition continued slowly, over many weeks, as it was an immense undertaking to gather together all the ships, over six thousand horses, artillery, ammunition and other stores, as well as over seventy thousand men belonging to the army and navy. The biggest prob-

---

* Not to be confused with the Danish island of Zealand.

lem was the lack of transport ships, particularly those for horses. Sir Home Popham, who knew the Scheldt waters well, was giving much thought to the combined operation, and in mid-June he wrote anxiously to Lord Castlereagh, the minister for war: 'I see the season advancing fast; and, if we are imperceptibly led on till the midsummer fine weather is past, we shall have the most dreadful of difficulties, the elements, to encounter.'[34] By the end of the month preparations were gathering pace, and thousands of troops, cavalry and infantry began to march from all over the country towards the embarkation ports of Deal, Dover, Chatham, Harwich, Ramsgate and, primarily, Portsmouth, so as to give the impression that they were preparing for renewed action in Portugal.

In the last week of June 1809 the artists Benjamin Robert Haydon and David Wilkie travelled from London to Portsmouth, where, with a letter of introduction, they were shown over the dockyard by Sir Roger Curtis, the port admiral. The two tourists were taken out to look round one of the largest ships of the line, and Haydon recorded his impressions as an artist: 'In the afternoon we went out to see the *Caledonia* [Gambier's flagship at Basque Roads], 120 guns, at Spithead. What a sublime and terrible simplicity there is in our navy! Nothing is admitted but what is absolutely useful. The cannon, the decks, the sailors, all wore the appearance of stern vigour, as if constituted only to resist the elements. No beautiful forms in the gun-carriages, no taste or elegance in the cannon; the ports square and hard; the guns iron; the sailors muscular. Everything inspired one with awe.'[35] Haydon was also struck by the presence of so many vessels: 'What grandeur in the sight of three hundred and fifty sail of men-of-war and transports destined for a great enterprise! We rowed or sailed among them for the rest of the day and did not return until the evening to Portsmouth.'[36]

The artists Haydon and Wilkie were not the only sightseers, because all along the coast of south-east England thousands of people were watching the preparations, as the *Annual Register* described:

The present age had not witnessed so numerous a body of British soldiers, marines, and sailors assembled for the purpose of invading the continent. The number of the whole amounted to about 100,000 men. The expectations of the nation were raised to the highest pitch. The fleet while it lay, or was leaving the Downs, was a spectacle grateful to the pride, and flattering to the hopes of Britain. Dover, Deal, Ramsgate, and Margate were full of visitors, of persons of the most respectable classes of both sexes, come to see the sailing of this great armament. Among these was lord Castlereagh, accompanied by his lady and a number of his particular friends, contemplating with delight a work of his own creation, from which farther glory was anticipated, from its success confidently expected. Among the visitors of the fleet, was one who attracted much notice by the pomp of his appearance, or what may be called his equipage. This was sir William Curtis*, who was wafted to the Downs in a yacht, either of his own, or hired for the purpose, or borrowed, beautifully painted, adorned with a streamer bearing devices prognosticating victory and glory, and carrying delicate refreshments of all kinds to the military and naval commanders, and the principal officers.[37]

Most of the warships and transports were not docked alongside wharfs, but remained offshore in deeper anchorages, so huge numbers of smaller craft were needed to convey supplies and men to the vessels. To Private William Wheeler of the 51st Regiment, 'Spithead is all bustle, crammed with vessels, from the huge three decker to the smallest craft, thousands of lighters and boats are on the move continually.'[38] Gunner William Richardson arrived at Spithead on board the *Caesar*. He related that 'a report came on board that we were going on some grand expedition and will have to take troops on board',[39] adding that in order to make room for these troops 'soon after a lighter came from the gun wharf to take on shore our lower deck guns and carriages'.[40] The troops began to embark in mid-July, and John Harris of the 95th Regiment, a survivor of the retreat from Spain, recorded a distressing picture as thousands of families were parted:

At Deal, the Rifles embarked in the *Superb*, a seventy-four, and a terrible outcry there was amongst the women upon the beach on the embarkation; for the ill consequences of having too many women amongst us had been so apparent in our former campaign and retreat that the allowance of wives was considerably curtailed on this occasion, and the distraction of the poor creatures at parting with their husbands was quite heart-rending; some of them clinging to the men so resolutely, that the officers were obliged to give orders to have them separated by force. In fact, even after we were in the boats and fairly pushed off, the screaming and howling of their farewells rang in our ears far out to sea.[41]

* Member of Parliament for the City of London and formerly the mayor.

Private Wheeler described how his regiment boarded a ship at Spithead: 'We embarked on board several cutters . . . It being the first time I was ever on salt water nothing could be more pleasant; our little cutter skimmed over the waves like a seagull . . . The whole Regt. was put on board [the warship *Impetueux*], she had her lower deck guns taken out and the larboard side of the lower deck was all the room allotted to us, the remainder was occupied by the ships company . . . When the gun fired all the soldiers were ordered down except the watch.'[42] As *The Times* reported, the soldiers 'take very little baggage, and only one blanket for each man – no beds'.[43] They slept squashed together on the planking of the lower deck, and the next day there was an awful scene: 'The decks had been newly caulked, the heat of so many bodies had drawn the pitch and tar, so that we were stuck fast in the morning. It was the most ludicrous sight imaginable, some were fast by the head, others had got an arm secured, those who had laid on their backs were completely fast, some who were wrapped in their blankets came off best, but their blankets were completely spoiled. It was a fine treat for the blue jackets to see all the lobsters [redcoats] stuck fast to the decks.'[44]

On 19 July news arrived of the French victory against the Austrians at the Battle of Wagram two weeks earlier. It was now too late for the diversion to save Austria. The weeks of delay also meant that Napoleon was long forewarned of unusual activity along the English coast and of a possible attack on the Scheldt, and he had already ordered increased fortifications and additional troops to be brought in. A few days before the expedition sailed, Rear-Admiral Strachan received word from Captain William Bolton of the frigate *Fisgard* that 'the enemy's fleet, amounting to eleven sail of the line, have this instant dropped down the Scheldt, and are anchored close off the town of Flushing'.[45] In order to cope with this unexpected news, the expedition plans began to be altered, most notably in deciding to land the troops on the north side of Walcheren rather than close to Flushing.

Although they did not yet know their destination, the soldiers learned that 'a certain number of seamen from the different line of battle ships are to serve on shore with us, they will be employed in dragging guns, ammunition stores etc. These men are to be equipped with a cutlass and pistols, a broad canvass belt to fasten to the gun . . . This will prove a treat to the seamen, some of whom has not been on shore many years.'[46] Gunner Richardson in the *Caesar* likewise recorded that while waiting for the order to sail, they were employed 'in training up eighty seamen for a brigade to land with the army, and emptying all the 32-pr. cartridges and filling more 24-pdr. cartridges, intending, if necessary, to put half the main-deck guns (24-prs.) on the lower deck, so that we might fight both tiers, one side or the other, or all on one side, as our lower-deck guns were left on shore to make room for the troops'.[47]

The expedition began to set sail from the Downs at dawn on Friday 28 July, with Strachan and Chatham on board the flagship *Venerable*. One Scottish soldier, just back from Corunna, later commented: 'Never will I forget the glorious sight of the most powerful and numerous fleet which ever left the British shores, – the sea looked as if it groaned under the weight of so many vessels, and as far as the eye could reach a wilderness of masts was seen.'[48] There was huge excitement at Deal, as portrayed by Robert Blakeney of the 28th Regiment: 'Thousands of superbly dressed women crowded the beach; splendid equipages were numerous; all the musical bands in the fleet, as well military as naval, joined in one general concert, playing the National Anthem, which, with the loud and long-continued cheering on shore, enlivened the neighbourhood for miles around, and caused the most enthusiastic excitement through-out the whole . . . The show was august, the pageant splendid, the music enchanting.'[49]

That evening scores of ships anchored a few miles off the north-west coast of Walcheren at the entrance to the East Scheldt, and the remain-ing ships set sail from the Downs over the next few days. The role of pilots was crucial in ensuring that the vessels did not ground on the sandbanks in the shallow waters, but there were never enough good pilots, and years later Captain Edward Brenton commented that 'the North Sea pilots, during the late war, were shamefully and alarmingly ignorant of their business . . . The fault is with our own Government, which never gave encouragement to young officers to become pilots . . . Two were generally put on board a ship of war at a time, and both sup-posed to possess equal knowledge; but this was far from being the fact.'[50] Brenton thought it a ridiculous policy to rely so heavily on pilots from the enemy, who were in effect traitors to their own country. Many of those employed for this expedition, though, were previously engaged in the thriving smuggling trade to and from Flushing and therefore knew the waters well. In a memorandum written by Lord Castlereagh, the employment of the smuggler Tom Johnson was specifically authorised:

Lord Chatham being of opinion that Mr. Johnson's assistance may be materially useful in carrying into execution the service with which he is entrusted,
Lord Castlereagh authorizes him to employ him on the following terms: he
is to receive [blank] shillings a day, while employed, and travelling charges at
the rate of [blank] per mile. Mr. Johnson having represented that he has a
plan, which he has undertaken to carry into execution in person, by which he
conceives Flushing can be taken by a coup de main, upon Lord Chatham and
Sir R. Strachan certifying that this object has been accomplished by Mr.
Johnson's means, he will receive full pay at the above rate, or the value of it,
for life. For any other extraordinary service Mr. Johnson may render of less
importance, he will receive such reward as his services may appear to Lord
Chatham and Sir R. Strachan to merit.[51]

Once news of their arrival reached the French commander at Flushing,
General Louis-Claude Monnet, he sent his second-in-command, the
Dutch general Pierre-Jacques Osten, with troops to defend the north
side of the island. Osten was astonished at the sheer number of ships and
knew he was unable to prevent a landing, but would do his utmost to
harass the British troops as they made their way to Flushing. The weather
now intervened, because the next morning it became cloudy and windy,
followed later in the day by rain and gales, and an attempt to land troops
on the exposed beaches of northern Walcheren was abandoned owing to
the high seas.

A squadron of ships that had anchored off Blankenberge (where
Madame Derikre was helping escaped prisoners-of-war) was supposed to
land troops on the beaches of Cadsand, aided by boats from Lord
Gardner's squadron, which was blockading the West Scheldt. The
instructions and arrangements were confused and the winds were initially
too strong. Gardner also refused to help, not having received precise
orders, and so insufficient small boats were made available to land the
troops in one go. French reinforcements were by now pouring into
Cadsand, and the plan to take the island was abandoned. Captain
Hanchett of the sloop *Raven*, who had volunteered to be the first to
take Flushing, was involved in trying to stop the French reaching
Cadsand:

The batteries soon opened on the gun-boats, when Capt. Hanchett most
spiritedly ran his vessel up between the gun-boats and the fire of the enemy,
which was instantly transferred to his ship. He was fired at from five

batteries on Cadsand, from the whole sea-front of Flushing, and from thirty-nine gun-boats. For four hours he bravely maintained the unequal contest, and . . . silenced the battery of Breskens, in Cadsand, though not before he had three of his own guns dismounted*, his vessel dismasted, and several times set on fire, and above a thousand shot discharged against him from all sides . . . it has been achieved without much comparative loss, only the gallant Captain and 18 of his brave crew having been wounded, none of them badly, and not a single man having been killed.[52]

In calmer weather another attempt was made to land troops on the north side of Walcheren. Private Wheeler of the 51st Regiment recorded the action:

The Gunboats had taken up their position along the shore, the flats [shallow-draught landing craft] full of soldiers and towed by the ship's boats, formed in rear of the Gunboats. On a signal the flats advanced. All now was solemn silence, saving the gunboats, who were thundering showers of iron on the enemy [Osten's troops]. Their well-directed fire soon drove them to shelter, behind the sandbank. The flats had now gained the Gunboats, shot through the intervals and gained the shallow water, when the troops leaped out and waded ashore, drove the enemy from behind the hills where they had taken shelter from the destructive fire of the Gunboats. Some batteries and forts were soon taken, the enemy fled and we lost sight of the contending parties.[53]

William Richardson was watching the events from the *Caesar* and commented that 'it was a grand sight to see so many heroes in boats extending for miles dashing along to meet their enemies on a foreign shore',[54] adding: 'A firing of musketry was soon heard between the sandhills, and in the evening we had fifty-two prisoners brought on board (two of them female). Our naval brigade of eighty seamen under the command of Captain Richardson [no relation] were landed at this time.'[55]

Throughout the day the British troops advanced across Walcheren, capturing fortifications. Many villages and the main town of Middelburg surrendered, and on the morning of 31 July the fortified town of Veere, on the north-east coast of Walcheren, was surrounded by troops. The bomb vessels pounded the area and gunboats began a sustained attack.

---

* The gun knocked off the wooden carriage.

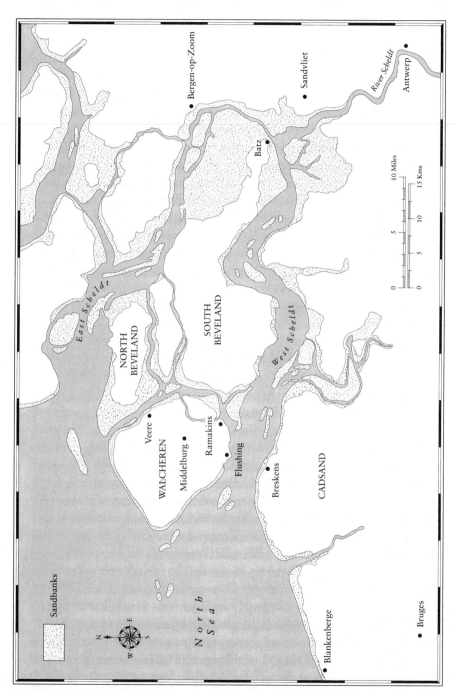

*Map of Walcheren, South Beveland and the River Scheldt*

This was described in his journal by Surgeon W. Cullen Brown, who commented on the power of the large mortars on board his ship, the bomb vessel *Aetna*:

Eleven o'clock. The ice is now broken! We have fired off our ten and thir-teen-inch mortars, from the explosion of which I had been taught to apprehend so much. By stuffing my ears with cotton, and pressing them with my fingers on the word for making ready being given, I find no manner of inconvenience from the concussion. I have had the hardihood, standing close by the great brass mortar, to try the effect of its sound on my ears open, and never experienced a more disagreeable sensation. My ears have continued ever since ringing. At the very first firing of the mortar, the lock of my cabin has been forced off, and the boards of the bulkhead have drawn their nails. This, however, is but the prelude to what is to follow . . . The tide is now turning; and such a force of bomb-vessels, gun-brigs, gun-boats, and flat-bottomed boats, will shortly assail the place, almost in close contact with it, as there will be no resisting. The multiplicity of ships to be seen almost as far as the eye can carry, forms a beautiful sight, and highly gratifying to the feelings of an Englishman.[56]

In the evening incendiary rockets were fired into the town, and Gunner Richardson of the *Caesar* was in the thick of the action:

Next morning [31st] an order came for me to land and bring the Congreve's rockets I had on board along with me for the investment of the place [Veere] . . . I was soon landed with the assistance of the seamen's brigade, who were my shipmates; we cut off the upper part of a small tree and put the rocket ladder for elevation against it, placed and primed the rockets, and began to blaze away at a fine rate, and I was soon covered with volumes of smoke. In a short time one part of the town was set on fire by the rockets, and soon after two other parts; some of our gunboats were also firing shot at the town at the time, and two of them got sunk; a shell burst over our heads without hurting a man. However, the rockets terrified them so much (having never seen such things before) that in the evening they sent out a flag of truce to capitulate.[57]

Once Veere had surrendered, the garrison troops became prisoners-of-war. Afterwards Richardson was one of the first to enter the place: 'I next took a ramble round this neat and clean town, which put me in mind of Portsea (only it has a harbour in the middle of the town) . . . Great havoc had been made among the houses by the shot from our gunboats; one had begun at the corner of a house, and ripped its way along the front of eight more before it stopped; at the outside of the gate lay three of the 71st and two horses dead and unburied, and a painter's shop burnt down by one of the rockets. I was told that a rocket entered into one of the embrasures, killed seven men at the gun, and wounded another.'[58]

The rout of Osten's troops (comprising French, Dutch, Prussians and Irish) continued as far as Flushing, and many islanders also fled in that direction. Once the troops and civilians were safely inside, the city's guns were turned on the pursuing British, forcing them to halt. Another British army division headed towards Ramakins, a small fortress east of Flushing that controlled a strategic waterway. Although under fire from the fortress, the British engineers began to construct a gun battery, finishing it by evening. Some of the warships also sailed from Veere towards Ramakins, where they came under fire. Surgeon Cullen Brown on board the *Aetna* noted some of the injuries:

August 2d . . . At half-past eleven, in consequence of being sent for, I went on board the *Harpy* brig. A poor man, belonging to one of the gun-boats, manned from the *Bellona*, had been shot through both arms from Rammekens, and was brought, in consequence, for assistance to the *Harpy*. Before my arrival, Mr. Parsons, surgeon of the *Harpy*, with Mr. Mortimer, assistant-surgeon of the *Charger* gun-brig, had amputated the right arm; and the tourniquet was already fixed on the other. Both arms had been shockingly fractured and lacerated. The man expired in five or six minutes after my arrival. He had been shot an hour and a half before getting on board of the *Harpy*: his death, as it appeared to myself, Mr. Mortimer, Mr. Parsons, and the assistant-surgeon of the *Safeguard*, was imputable to the loss of blood he had sustained, and the shock the nervous system had received. I dressed another man, who had been shot in the integuments of the head by a grape-shot, or musket-ball, and one who had received a severe bruise on the nose, without any of the bones being shattered, in the same gun-boat.[59]

Ramakins surrendered on the 3rd before the British fired a shot in return. Now only nearby Flushing needed to be captured on the island of Walcheren, and Johnson the smuggler was involved in these plans. At the instigation of General Sir William Congreve, the sloop *Galgo* had been fitted out as a rocket ship from which to fire his missiles, but the *Galgo* was too late reaching Ramakins. At Ramakins Seaman Joseph Wrangle on board the *Galgo* observed that 'A great deal of small craft lay about the place, and a complete fleet of Deal men were employed on this service. Johnson the smuggler was a conspicuous character: this man was much esteemed in the fleet and was of great service, having been employed by the government to buoy the channel and point out the difficulties attendant on the coast. I saw his brig pass through the fleet with his yards manned giving three cheers.'[60]

Another army division had been transported further up the East Scheldt so that the troops could land on the island of South Beveland, to the east of Walcheren, but bad weather delayed disembarkation. Six thousand troops were eventually landed, only to find that the key positions had already been abandoned by the Dutch troops, including Fort Batz in the south-east corner of the island, which commanded the confluence of the East and West Scheldt. The British now controlled all of South Beveland and were ever closer to Antwerp.

What was remarkable was that a few tourists sailed across the North Sea from England to view first-hand what was happening, including Sir William Curtis in his yacht. After Ramakins was taken Surgeon Cullen Brown met two such tourists when he and other officers from the *Aetna* went ashore on South Beveland, 'where a torrent of rain forced us to scamper in different directions. Mr. Steele, the marine artillery officer, and myself, took refuge in a barn, where we entered into conversation with two very agreeable men in uniform, who had betaken themselves to the same retreat. They afterwards proved to be Lord Yarmouth and Major Dormer, who are here at present, in a small vessel they have hired from Dover, for the purpose of observing the operations of the Expedition.'[61]

The British now needed to push on towards Antwerp, but according to Rear-Admiral Strachan, it was impossible to reach Antwerp by sailing further up the East Scheldt, 'on account of the shallowness of the water, and the intricacy of the narrow channel'.[62] It was also impossible to sail up the West Scheldt while Cadsand and Flushing remained in enemy hands – but Gunner Richardson of the *Caesar* strongly disagreed, bemoaning that 'our commanders were misled by the Dutch pilots, who told them that the batteries in Flushing and Cadsand would soon destroy any ships that passed between them'.[63] With the surrender of Ramakins, though, ships could pass from the East Scheldt to the West Scheldt via the Slough – the waterway between the islands of Walcheren and South Beveland – which bypassed Flushing and Cadsand. The way was open to Antwerp – if only the commanders could agree a plan of action.

# FOURTEEN

———————◆———————

# DISASTER

Such a fleet and army never left the shores of Great Britain together before.

Gunner William Richardson, who took part in the expedition[1]

Less than a week after landing on South Beveland, some of the troops unaccountably began to fall ill, and Rifleman Harris related that many men were struck down with fever:

The first I observed of it was one day as I sat in my billet, when I beheld whole parties of our Riflemen in the street shaking with a sort of ague, to such a degree that they could hardly walk; strong and fine young men who had been but a short time in the service seemed suddenly reduced in strength to infants, unable to stand upright – so great a shaking had seized upon their whole bodies from head to heel . . . Under these circumstances, which considerably confounded the doctors, orders were issued (since all hopes of getting the men upon their legs seemed gone) to embark them as fast as possible, which was accordingly done with some little difficulty. The poor fellows made every effort to get on board; those who were a trifle better than others crawled to the boats; many supported each other; and many were carried helpless as infants.[2]

The assault continued, despite the increasing numbers of sick troops, but Lord Chatham decided that Flushing should be taken before the expedition could tackle Antwerp. Surgeon Cullen Brown commented that 'the wise ones afloat begin to accuse the Earl of Chatham of dilatoriness'.[3]

A severe gale prevented ships being anchored above and below Flushing, as was planned, and the unseasonal weather was described by Cullen Brown as 'a continued gale of wind, accompanied by heavy rains, and as much cold as we might expect to find in the month of December'.[4] By 7 August improved weather meant that an effective blockade of Flushing was at last in force by land and sea. Lieutenant Dillon's *Aigle* was one of the blockading ships, and two days later he wrote with irritation: 'I was surprised at the appearance of Capt. Wolfe, who had returned from the Court Martial on Lord Gambier to resume the command of his ship. This placed me in rather an awkward situation, as we were blockading Flushing, and I had no means of quitting the ship, but was obliged to remain on board. Capt. Wolfe did not fail in his attentions, but I could not help noticing the familiarity of the seamen who came into his cabin as suited them, to compliment him upon his return . . . He brought the report of Lord Gambier's trial, who had been exonerated.'[5]

In the end it was agreed that Dillon should leave the ship, and so he packed two trunks and was taken to a point along the beach that he calculated was the British advance post: 'When I ascended the sand hills, I found I had exactly hit upon the right spot. An officer of our Army, who was here on the watch, seeing me, called out in extreme anxiety, "For God's sake, drop down, Sir, or you are a dead man. Slide down, roll yourself down. You have not the slightest idea of the danger you are in." Perceiving by his countenance, as well as the agitated tone of his address, that I had unknowingly exposed myself, being in uniform, cocked hat, etc., I slid down instantly as the officer advised.'[6] After his narrow escape Dillon moved on to Middelburg, and on his way he noticed that 'the enemy had cut one of the dykes, and the water was nearly level with the bottom of the tents. In fact, the appearances were anything but agreeable, the worst of all being that the coming in of the sea would spoil the drinkable water.'[7] General Monnet had ordered some of the sluices around Flushing to be opened so as to flood the land held by the besiegers, though the British managed to drain some of the sea-water away, following the advice of the peasants. All supplies for the siege were being landed at Veere, in the north-east of Walcheren, and were then transported along the narrow roads to Flushing, but the constant rain and thunderstorms, and now Monnet's deliberate opening of the sluices, made this work extremely difficult.

Private Wheeler described the efforts that were being made to reduce Flushing:

We are going on with the necessary work for the destruction of the town. There is not an idle hand to be found, some are building batteries, digging trenches, filling sand bags, making large wicker baskets, carpenters making platforms, Sailors bringing up guns, Mortars, Howitzers, ammunition, Shot, shell etc. All this work is going on under the beautiful music of all the guns and mortars the garrison can bring to bear on any of our works ... Two nights ago we were visited by a dreadful Thunder storm, such were the torrents of rain we were washed out of our camp, the barns and houses of two farms gave us shelter for the night. This has slightly hindered our work, but the progress made under so many difficulties is astonishing, every thing is nearly complete, and begins to assume a very formidable appearance.[8]

On 11 August ten frigates forced their way up the West Scheldt, firing on Flushing and damaging several enemy guns. Marine Lieutenant Robert Fernyhough, in the frigate *Statira*, took part in the action:

If you had seen me ... you would have taken me for any thing but an officer, for I was as black as a sweep. In the middle of the conflict it became so hot, that I threw off my uniform and neck-cloth, and unbuttoned my shirt collar, consequently, the powder had so completely blackened my shirt and face, that had a soot bag been shaken over me, I could not have been worse. I have scarcely been able to use my right hand since, the skin having been taken off four of my fingers, by the friction of the ropes, in working the guns; for I pulled and hauled as well as my men, not choosing to remain inactive, when the shot were flying about.[9]

In his official dispatch Strachan reported: 'The gallant and seaman-like manner in which this squadron was conducted, and their steady and well-directed fire, excited in my breast the warmest sensations of admiration. The army witnessed their exertions with applause ... No very material accident happened, except by a shell striking *L'Aigle*, and which fell through her decks into the bread room, where it exploded; one man was killed, and four others wounded; her stern frame is much shattered.'[10] From the roof of a building at Middelburg, Lieutenant Dillon witnessed the frigates forcing their way up the Scheldt and the shell hitting his former ship, the *Aigle,* after which he encountered some of the tourists:

I now became a perfect idler, my time being taken up with sightseeing at

Middelburg and its environs. English travellers were arriving daily to witness the exploits of our Army: among the number Alderman Curtis, whom I shall never forget. He paid great attention to gastronomy, and came in a pleasure boat, bringing with him a fine turtle which I believe was presented to Lord Chatham. Among the strangers I was agreeably surprised to meet my friend Lord Yarmouth. These gentlemen were longing to have a view of a siege of a fortified town, and Flushing was considered one of the first order: it was therefore expected that it would not easily surrender. A col. Congreve, with whom I became acquainted, had invented a rocket of destruction, which bore his name. They were in high request on this occasion.[11]

Chatham's turtle was duly cooked and eaten, and news of this, as well as Chatham's reputation, reached Paris, where it was mockingly said that 'his countrymen reproached him with being occupied almost exclusively about his health and his turtle-soup, instead of troubling himself with details of the expedition placed under his command'.[12]

On the day that the frigates attacked Flushing, Monnet ordered more of the surrounding area to be flooded by sea-water, and a worried Strachan wrote in his dispatch that 'the enemy has cut the dyke to the right of the town, and the island is likely to be inundated. I have ordered Rear-admiral Otway to send the *Monmouth* and *Agincourt* to England for water . . . and earnestly entreat that other means may be adopted for supplying the army and navy from England, as I apprehend all the water in this island will be spoiled by the inundation, and that there is not more in the other islands than is necessary for the subsistence of the inhabitants.'[13]

Now that the gun batteries were ready, Seaman William Robinson related that 'a summons was sent in for the town of Flushing to surrender; to this the commandant [Monnet] sent in a negative, unless compelled by the force of arms: a second message was then sent, requesting that the women and children might be sent away, as the intention was to bombard the town, and it would be desirable that their lives should not become the sacrifice; and the commandant's reply was, that he would not allow any person to leave the town'.[14] As the flooding was getting worse, threatening some of the gun batteries, the decision was taken to begin the bombardment of Flushing from the newly constructed batteries and from a flotilla of gunboats and brigs under Captain George Cockburn situated above Flushing and another flotilla under Captain Edward Owen situated below. Gunner Richardson of the *Caesar* reported what happened in his journal: 'Sunday, August 13.—While the good people in Old England were this day offering up their prayers to the Almighty God of peace, we here were serving the devil by destroying each other as fast as we could; for at half-past one in the afternoon, our batteries being all ready, began to fire on the town of Flushing, and a tremendous roar (such as has seldom been in battle) was kept up with shot, shells, rockets, and musketry, enough to tear the place in pieces.'[15]

Thomas Howell of the 71st Highlanders and a veteran of the Corunna retreat, was shocked by the result:

I was stunned and bewildered by the noise; the bursting of bombs and falling of chimneys, all adding to the incessant roar of the artillery. The smoke of the burning houses and guns, formed altogether, a scene not to be remembered but with horror, which was increased, at every cessation from firing (which was very short), by the piercing shrieks of the inhabitants, the wailings of distress, and howling of dogs. The impression was such as can never be effaced. After night fell, the firing ceased, save from the mortar batteries. The noise was not so dreadful: the eye was now the sense that conveyed horror to the mind. The enemy had set fire to Old Flushing, whilst the New Town was kept burning by the shells and rockets. The dark flare of the burning, the reflection on the water and sky, made all the space, as far as the eye could reach, appear an abyss of fire. The faint tracks of the bombs, and luminous train of the rockets, darting towards, and falling into the flames, conveyed an idea to my mind so appalling, that I turned away and shuddered.[16]

The French advance posts were attacked during the night, forcing them to be abandoned. In their retreat, the French set fire to the old town, but the intense smoke the next day hid from view the British gun batteries, especially those manned by the seamen, and allowed them to bombard Flushing even more vigorously. According to Captain Harry Ross-Lewin of the 32nd Regiment, the seamen proved formidable artillerymen: 'A strong division of sailors was landed, when we appeared before Flushing, to assist in the erection of batteries. Their station was on the extreme right [west]; they threw up a considerable work, armed with twenty-four pounders, and their fire from it soon became so incessant as to excite general astonishment.'[17] At times, the sailors were rather too enthusiastic and impeded the assault, as Seaman Robinson observed: 'I will here remark, that on one of the sallies made by the enemy out of the gates of the town, the soldiers and small-arms-men from the ships, were employed in engaging them, and the small-arms-men being seamen, with an impetuosity not to be controlled, they rushed on the enemy with such rapidity, while the military were waiting the word of command, that they actually drove the enemy within the gates of the town, with the loss of very few lives . . . Several times during the conflict, the soldiers would have fired on the enemy, but could not, for fear of killing our seamen.'[18]

By early morning seven battleships under the command of Rear-Admiral Strachan moved towards Flushing, but his flagship, the *St Domingo*, came too close and grounded, as did the *Blake*, which was following. Marine Captain Thomas Marmaduke Wybourn was on board the *Blake*, under Captain Edward Codrington, and he described the dangerous situation in a letter to his sisters:

Sir R. Strachan formed the desperate resolution of attacking by Sea (he is the bravest fellow in the world). We had lain just out of reach of Shot since the 11th & yesterday the signal was given to prepare for battle, at Sea; we & the other Flagship* got within Pistol shot of the Walls – the havoc we made was *shocking*, when to our consternation we both struck the Ground, all the other Ships passed by further off, seeing the danger; for three hours & a half we were thus left to ourselves, the batteries cutting us to pieces and no alternative but to wait the Tide rising. *We* all thought there could be no possibility of escaping. We on the poop, which is the roof of the Capt's Cabin, were in such a line with the Guns, that it is amazing *any* of us escaped; almost the first shot killed my best Sergeant, a fine fellow, it took off both *thighs*, left *Arm* & right *hand*, the poor fellow called out to me, but I could not bear to look at him. Fortunately he died in half an hour, under amputation . . . The Troops & all our Fleet were spectators of the danger the *two Admirals only* were in . . . By the blessing of God, we lost but 13 men killed & wounded. The Shot actually flew about us at all angles, & it is a miracle how so many could pass among us with so little effect; 150 shot struck the Ship in the main Mast and the other masts & rigging cut to pieces – one shot carried 30 of my Muskets with it & shivered them to atoms. We have learnt since, that so destructive was our fire before we got aground that the French could not stand at their Guns – the '*Blake*' killed 87 at the first Volley. But when they saw our situation, & that we could not fire, they rattled and peppered us finely. About an hour before we floated, we got about 7 Guns (out of 46) to

---

* The *Blake* was the flagship of Rear-Admiral Lord Gardner, and the other flagship was the *St Domingo* with Strachan on board.

bear, & these, with the '*San Domingo's' few* guns who had swung towards the Shore, kept them in check – & by half past one, we made sail from this Perilous position, *happy enough*.[19]

The bombardment from land and sea continued until four in the afternoon, when Chatham ordered a cease-fire. After being in so much danger, Captain Codrington confessed to his wife that 'to us it was a worse battle than that of Trafalgar, because we were in so very perilous a situation and the particular object [target] of the enemy . . . There are but two killed and nine wounded, although there are six wounds in the mainmast and several *warm* shot sticking in parts of the hull.'[20] Writing from Walmer in Kent, where she was passing the summer, Mrs Jane Codrington hopefully asked: 'Will your wounds in the masts require your coming here or your going to Portsmouth?'[21], adding: 'I hope the two sailors' wives on board *Blake behaved properly* in *action*.'[22]

By now fires were raging out of control in the town, but the French rejected the cease-fire, and so the firing resumed, lasting all evening and through the night. Private Wheeler was awestruck:

The Bombardment continued all day, and increased at night. This night [14th] I was on picquet, it was beautiful and fine, one half of Flushing was in flames, the Fleet and the whole of the Batterys were at it pel mel. At midnight, when on sentry, I often counted fifteen shells and twelve rockets at one time hovering over and descending in to the devoted town. The roaring of guns and mortars, the hissing of Rockets, shot and shells, the chiming of the church bells, the French sentries calling at intervals 'Alls well,' [they were actually calling out 'sentinelles'] the noise of the people trying to extinguish the fires, but above all, the heart rending cries of the poor women and children, beggars decription.[23]

Seaman Robert Stafford Clover on board the bomb vessel *Thunder* had trouble finding words to convey the scene: 'At 8 o'clock a sight presented itself to the spectator, not often to be seen in modern times. Fifteen or sixteen shells flying like so many flaming meteors through the air, all up at once, and this repeated as often as the Mortars could be loaded, the shells also that we, and the other Bombs were throwing, the terrible carronading of the Gun Boats and the Congreve Rockets streaming liquid fire through the sky all combined to form a scene better to be imagined than described.'[24]

Early on 15 August the French surrendered. In his journal Gunner Richardson wrote: 'The bombardment continued more than thirty-four hours (except an interval of three), when on the 15th, at three in the morning, it surrendered, although the commander-in-chief, General Monnet, had declared that he would be buried in its ruins first. However, it was said that he surrendered only at the intercession of the inhabitants, to save the town from destruction.'[25] Richardson remarked that the townspeople 'represent General Monnet as a tyrant, and that when the women solicited him to surrender in order to save the town from destruction, he ordered the soldiers to fire on them; but of the second in command [Osten] they spoke in high terms'.[26] Napoleon thought that Monnet surrendered to the British to avoid justice at home: 'The general who commanded Flushing did not defend it as long as he ought to have done. He had made a large fortune by the smugglers (as there was another depot of them there) and had been guilty of some malpractices, for which he was afraid of being brought to a court-martial, and I believe he was glad to get away.'[27]

The destruction of buildings at Flushing was terrible, as were the civilian casualties, and everyone who visited the wrecked town was shocked by what they saw, including Gunner Richardson:

It has suffered much, many of its noble buildings being in ruins, and nearly four thousand troops and inhabitants slain. A church, said to be built in memory of Bonaparte when he visited this place, was in such a blaze that the very bells were melted, on the day and very near the hour of his nativity. Our loss was nearly as follows: The Navy, 9 killed and 55 wounded; the Army, 103 killed and 443 wounded ... The town was in a miserable state from the effects of the bombardment, hardly a house escaped injury, and many totally destroyed; their fine Stadthouse is burnt down, and so was a fine elegant church. In looking at the ruins of it I got close to the mouth of a pit, nearly full of both sexes who lost their lives in the siege; the uppermost was a female of bulky size, and I was told that a number of people of both sexes were in the church when it fell, and were buried under its ruins, and this is very probable, as the bombardment began on a Sunday.[28]

Seaman Robinson also touched on the fate of women and children: 'The sight was melancholy and distressing to behold. There was scarcely a street but in which the greater part of the houses were knocked down, with women and children buried under their ruins. Some were dug out scarcely alive and much mutilated, whilst others found a ready grave amidst the devastation. One third of the town was completely destroyed, and other parts much damaged; even the church did not escape, it received much injury by catching fire.'[29] Lieutenant William Dillon hurried from Middelburg to see Flushing and was likewise appalled by the devastation. When it suddenly began to rain, he took shelter in a wooden shed: 'Here I was accosted by a French artillery blacksmith, who had been at work in his department. I obtained more information from him than from any of the better-classed individuals. He was extremely intelligent, and stated that the authorities had been expecting our attack six weeks earlier. Preparations for defence had been made in all directions, but as our ships did not appear it was conceived to have been a false alarm.'[30] A few days later Dillon secured a passage home.

Three days after the surrender of Flushing the French-Dutch garrison of just over 5800 men was marched across Walcheren to embark on ships that were to take them as prisoners-of-war to England. Shortly afterwards large numbers of soldiers on the island of Walcheren fell severely ill, and among them was Thomas Howell of the 71st Highlanders, who like most others attributed his sudden illness to the bad atmosphere:

The wet and fatigue of the last few days had made me ill. I was scarce able to stand, yet I did not report myself sick. I thought it would wear off. Next night I was upon guard. The night was clear and chill; a thin white vapour seemed to extend around as far as I could see; the only parts free from it were the sand heights. It covered the low place where we lay, and was such as you see early in the morning, before the sun is risen, but more dense. I felt very uncomfortable in it; my two hours I thought never would expire; I could not breathe with freedom. Next morning I was in a burning fever, at times; at other times, trembling and chilled with cold: I was unfit to rise, or walk upon my feet. The surgeon told me, I had taken the country disorder. I was sent to the hospital; my disease was the same as that of which hundreds were dying. My spirits never left me; a ray of hope would break in upon me, the moment I got ease, between the attacks of this most severe malady.[31]

The British expedition was totally unprepared for such illness, as the medical authorities had not been consulted beforehand, even though it was known that this sickness was prevalent in this low-lying land, because the army had suffered during campaigns in 1747. John Pringle, physician to the army at that time, had observed that only those on land were affected, though he did not understand why: 'Commodore Mitchell's squadron, which lay at anchor in the channel between South Beveland and the island of Walcheren, in both which places the distempers raged, was neither afflicted with fever nor flux; but amidst all that sickness enjoyed perfect health. A proof that the moist and putrid air of the marshes was dissipated, or corrected, before it could reach them; and that such a situation open to the wind, is one of the best preservatives against the maladies of a neighbouring low and marshy country.'[32]

During the current Walcheren expedition Captain Codrington also noted that those who remained on board were healthy, but of the many who fell ill, 'in the navy we have, I believe, only those who have formed the sea brigade on shore, and I have only heard of these in the *Dryad* and *Imperieuse*'.[33] Although dysentery and typhus were a problem, what was mainly affecting the troops was malaria, a disease that is characterised by periodic attacks of shivering, sweating and weakness, and can be fatal. It was only in the late nineteenth century that it was discovered to be caused by parasites passed to humans by the bites of mosquitoes that thrived in the (now drained) marshlands of Zealand. The first attack of malaria appears some eight to twenty-five days after a person has been bitten. Lacking this knowledge, Robert Renny, the army's assistant-surgeon, tried to explain why this fever was prevalent here: 'The two islands of Walcheren and Beveland are, like all the Dutch European territories, flat and watery . . . it is not surprising that strangers, who have hitherto breathed a comparatively pure and healthful atmosphere, should be subject to febrile diseases, and more especially in autumn, when, from the heat of the sun, and the putrefaction of vegetable bodies, the effluvia from marshes are more active, more plentiful, and more obnoxious than at any other season of the year.'[34] Although the disease and its causes were not understood, it was known that the bark of the cinchona tree (containing quinine) was an effective treatment. The French knew that the marshes were unhealthy, with the population prone to fever, and one French officer wrote that 'it was rarely fatal for men acclimatised to the area, but it caused great harm amongst foreigners. The French only sent the minimum number of their own troops to Walcheren island; the permanent garrison of Flushing was for the most part composed of Prussian, Spanish and Irish prisoners.'[35] The British army medical authorities declared that they could have made provision for this illness if the destination had not been kept secret. As it was, a disaster began to unfold.

After the fall of Flushing some soldiers were left as a garrison on

Walcheren, while those who were not ill crossed into South Beveland by ferry and marched to Batz or else were transported by ship from Ramakins, in readiness for the onslaught on Antwerp. In one of the warships that sailed from Flushing were several marine artillerymen who had been responsible for firing Congreve rockets during the bombardment, and Seaman Joseph Wrangle was amused at the sight of them:

They exhibited a strange appearance. The most part of them had been engaged in discharging the Rock[ets] from machines on a ladder. It was truly laughable to witness the appearance they made. The practice of discharging the Rocket by the ladder machine was a new invention and proved a great injury to the men, burning their hands and faces. Some had no hair on their heads and their hands and shoulders severely scorched. It appears that upon discharging the Rocket it will rebound and envelop the person discharging them in what appears in the day to be but smoke but at night is a flame of fire. The Rocket rebounds and then springs forward with great rapidity and it is according to the altitude that you give it that it will fall with great force upon the intended object.[36]

During the past fortnight the troops already on South Beveland had fortified the fortress of Batz, but were otherwise awaiting orders. The French therefore had plenty of time to send thousands of additional troops to the Scheldt and to the coast between Cadsand and Boulogne, because they were uncertain where the British planned to strike next. The neglected defences of Antwerp were also being improved, and, in order to prevent British warships reaching the city, a boom of chains and logs secured with anchors was constructed across the river just above the village of Sandvliet, with a gap wide enough to allow only one vessel at a time to pass through. In charge of the defences was Vice-Admiral Missiessy, who was disgraced after failing to take Diamond Rock and meet up with Villeneuve before Trafalgar. He was now commander of the French fleet in the Scheldt, and he withdrew to safety behind the boom.

As a further defensive method sluices were opened on both banks of the Scheldt between Antwerp and Bergen-op-Zoom, flooding some areas. Even so, the alarmed people of Antwerp fully expected their city to face bombardment. French soldiers heading to the city 'met scared citizens who had just abandoned Antwerp, fearing to be exposed to the horrors of a bombardment that they regarded as inevitable . . . A crowd of worried sailors and inhabitants had gathered on the banks of the Scheldt; they gazed ceaselessly towards the north, as if some terrifying apparition had recently appeared on the horizon.'[37] To the French it looked as if they were doomed: 'This thick forest of masts, this immense gathering of floating fortresses that had come and placed itself so boldly within cannon reach of us, presented the most imposing sight.'[38]

On 15 August 1809, the day that Flushing surrendered, Marshal Jean-Baptiste Bernadotte arrived at Antwerp to take overall command of the army there. He set in motion other measures, including flooding more areas and strengthening the forts on the right and left banks. A boom between Lillo and Liefkenshoek forts was also constructed, this time completely blocking the river. On board the rocket ship *Galgo*, Seaman Wrangle observed the frantic activity:

The whole of the French fleet was getting up towards Antwerp as fast as they could, and there appeared no opportunity of following them as the fortifications up the river was too strong. The French had well secured the passage to Antwerp with a boom thrown across the river, and the channel was well fortified with batteries erected all along the banks. But had our ships been allowed to proceed in the chase, some of the larger ones keeping the batteries in bay, our small craft might have turned the point on them and by dint of British seamanship have given a good account of some of them, but this was not permitted . . . From the place where we now lay we could plainly discover the fortification of Antwerp, and the cathedral was very plain as we could see the dial with the naked eye and could count the number of large ships laying in the basin at Antwerp, likewise the great fort of Lillo was plainly perceived.[39]

Although in sight of Antwerp, the British soldiers and sailors were left idle, either camped on South Beveland or on board vessels near Batz. In the *Blake*, Codrington wrote to his wife: 'Our coming here yesterday produced us an introduction to Sir Home Popham . . . He lays blame on pretty thick, I assure you, and attributes to the great indolence of Lord C. [Chatham] the want of success which is likely to attend an attack on Antwerp . . . I just hear that the Commander-in-Chief is now expected *to-day*; having been expected yesterday; and to be further probably expected to-morrow!'[40] Wrangle thought that it was hard for the troops to be confined to the transport ships and that 'it was a curious sight to see them of a morning running round the deck by companies and this was done several times a day to keep them in motion. We often amused

ourselves in looking at them for hours.'[41] Surgeon Cullen Brown on board
the *Aetna* also had little to do – no battle wounds to treat in this period of
inactivity, while the men had not been on land and so remained healthy,
well away from the ravages of the mosquitoes. He spent some of his time
climbing up and down the mainmast to gain a better view: 'I have just
come down from the main-top-gallant-mast, from whence I have been
contemplating the city and environs of Antwerp, than which nothing
can cut a more splendid appearance. We are able to make out nine apparently line-of-battle ships, and between forty and fifty gun-boats, and
other small vessels.'[42]

Marine Captain Wybourn on board the *Blake* with Codrington was
disgusted by the delays:

It is certainly provoking to see Antwerp, all their Fleet & immense Flotilla
just above us, & not be able to get at them, when it is beyond a doubt, that
had *we dashed* up here at *first* & left Flushing invested (as it was) there were
not 5,000 Men to oppose us . . . Thus will fifty thousand Men, at an
Enormous Expense to the Country, have been *trifling* at *Flushing* to capture
a handful of *Men* & a place little better than a fishing town, when such fine
desperate fellows, instead of laying 16 days in the Trenches & *wet ditches*
might absolutely have eaten their way (both man and beast) to Antwerp in
the *first week*. Now General Hope says it will cost us 10,000 to attempt anything more. Besides, the Troops are falling off by sickness – many thousands
have been laying 3 weeks in Beveland, in a Marsh, waiting for the *Gallant
Chief* [Chatham] who was investing little Flushing with 21,000 troops, &
living himself in beautiful Middleburg eating *Turtle*.[43]

Private Wheeler, anchored near Batz in a transport ship, recorded the
antics of the French that succeeded in enraging the British sailors:

Some of the dirty rascals on board the French fleet had been amusing themselves by —— on the Union Jack, on board one of their ships in the mouth
of the harbour. In sight of the whole of our fleet, they have placed the British
Jack under their bows for the ship's company to evacuate on. I could not help
laughing at one of our honest Jacks, who feeling a personal insult at such an
unwarrantable dirty trick, could not help exclaiming 'D—n their s—n cow-
ardly eyes and limbs, if it was not for the cursed chain across the harbour, we
would soon make the frog eating sons of B—s lick the filth off with their
tongues.'[44]

Lord Chatham only reached Batz on 24 August, followed by the transport vessels with the cavalry and ordnance. A flotilla under Sir Home Popham went up the Scheldt to attack the forts and select a landing site, but by now over three thousand men were sick. Three days later the seven army lieutenant-generals advised Chatham that a siege of Antwerp was not feasible, and he decided to suspend operations and retreat from South Beveland. Before the army retreated, Rear-Admiral Strachan wanted at the very least to break the booms across the river, destroy the flotilla behind and sink the ships in the Scheldt to create an obstruction. Chatham refused.

On South Beveland the guns began to be dismantled and the next day an evacuation of the island began. The number of sick was increasing at an alarming rate, reaching nearly five thousand by 1 September and over eight thousand two days later. On 4 September the last soldiers were withdrawn from South Beveland, and the last of the British ships descended the Scheldt. The French flotilla quickly made their way to Batz, and Dutch troops reoccupied the fortress. The sick troops started to be moved to England, because conditions for them on Walcheren were terrible, but the number of returning sick became so great that the coastal towns had difficulty housing them.

Writing to her husband, Jane Codrington said that 'I was told that there had been a most dreadful scene on the beach [at Deal] the whole morning . . . landing the sick, actually some dying as they landed. And even here so inefficient are the arrangements that there was not room enough for the numbers that did arrive, and the poor fellows were lying about in the barrack yard for hours without refreshment and exposed the whole time.'[45] Three days later she wrote: '1,039 sick arrived here to-day; out of 100 in a transport eight were thrown overboard between Flushing and this place, and they generally die six or eight every day! It is really too dreadful to think of.'[46]

John Harris of the 95th Rifles remarked that 'there were three brothers in the Rifles named Hart – John, Mike, and Peter – and three more perfectly reckless fellows, perhaps, never existed'.[47] They had survived the Corunna retreat, but Harris was appalled how Walcheren destroyed them: 'Nothing, indeed, but that grave of battalions, that unwholesome fen, Flushing, could have broken the spirits of three such soldiers as John, Mike, and Peter Hart. A few weeks, however, of that country sufficed to quiet them for evermore. One, I remember, died; and the other two, although they lived to return, were never worth a rush afterwards, but, like myself, remained living examples of what climate can bring even a constitution and body framed as if of iron to.'[48]

On 10 September Lord Chatham received an official command from Lord Castlereagh to return to England once arrangements had been made for those left behind to garrison Walcheren. Major-General William Dyott noted that 'on the 14th Lord Chatham at last embarked for England. He had been detained by contrary winds for several days. I should imagine his lordship's feelings must be uncomfortable, as the newspapers had been most liberal in their abuse of him.'[49] Robert Blakeney of the 28th commented acerbically that 'finding too late that late Court hours and measured movements were ineffectual against rapid and early rising revolutionists, Lord Chatham . . . returned to England',[50] while on 18 September Captain Codrington wrote to his wife:

I shall commence with an epigram, which Sir Richard [Strachan] received in a letter yesterday, which tells the story of the expedition at once:—
    Says Strachan to Chatham, 'Come let us be at 'em!'
    Says Chatham to Strachan, 'No, we'll let 'em alone.'
Another epigram going about at this time:—
    Lord Chatham with his sword undrawn,
      Was waiting for Sir Richard Strachan.
    Sir Richard, longing to be at 'em,
      Was waiting too–for whom?–Lord Chatham.[51]

George Canning, the foreign secretary, had for several months been plotting to have Castlereagh removed from his post as minister for war, blaming him for events in Portugal and now Walcheren as well. When Castlereagh found this out, rather than retaliate politically, he challenged Canning to a duel, which took place on 21 September:

The parties met on Wimbledon Common, Lord Castlereagh attended by Lord Yarmouth, Mr. Canning by Mr. Ellis . . . Having taken their ground precisely at seven o'clock, they fired by signal, and Mr. Canning received the ball of his protagonist in the fleshy part of the thigh. He was preparing for another fire, but Mr. Ellis perceiving a great effusion of blood from the wound, interposed, and, after a conference with Lord Yarmouth, the parties retired . . . It was found on examination that the ball had passed quite through Mr. Canning's thigh on the outside of the bone, but fortunately none of the large blood vessels were injured, and the wound is not considered dangerous.[52]

While the politicians in London fought among themselves, on Walcheren Lieutenant-General Sir Eyre Coote was left as commander-in-chief, with Dyott his second-in-command. Shortly afterwards Dyott spent two days visiting all the hospitals, commenting that 'a more wretched melancholy duty no man ever performed; indeed I don't suppose it ever fell to the lot of a British officer to visit in the course of three days the sick chambers of nearly 8000 unfortunate men in fevers; and the miserable, dirty, stinking holes some of the troops were from necessity crammed into, was more shocking than it is possible to express'.'53 Now that Chatham had gone, much more began to be done for the plight of the sick and dying, causing Codrington to write home that 'the extent of this disease does not surprise those who have seen our men packed together in hovels such as would be thought unfit for dogs, exposed to the noxious night-airs, and in some cases with only damp straw to lie on . . . Indeed, till Lord C. went, and Sir E. Coote, with Dyott and Acland visited the whole of the hospitals and barracks, even the sick were no better provided, and death has consequently followed the convalescence.'54 Not understanding the reasons for the disease, Codrington believed himself safe and urged his wife to join him.

By the end of September about 9300 out of seventeen thousand men on Walcheren were sick. Because of the emergency, Dr James McGrigor, Inspector of Army Hospitals, was requested to go there immediately. In just a few hours he reached Deal, where there were four transports and the 74-gun *Venerable* warship of Sir Home Popham, then commanded by Acting Captain Andrew King. The port admiral gave Captain King orders to convey Dr McGrigor and any other medical officers without delay to Walcheren, but the captain was furious at being used as a transport ship. Despite the urgency, he was in no hurry to leave, as McGrigor reported: 'After the vessel was under weigh, and had stood out to sea, and after repeated signals from the admiral on shore, she made no way on her passage, and intended, as it appeared, to make little, till a lady came on board. That lady was the wife of an officer at Walcheren, Captain Codrington . . . She was at Canterbury [actually Walmer], whither I was informed an express had been sent for her.'55

McGrigor's sudden arrival had obviously upset a prior arrangement to convey Codrington's wife to Walcheren, and 'although we got under weigh, and so far as to get beyond the reach of the admiral's glasses; I soon found out that we were not making our passage. In reality, Captain King was waiting for Mrs. Codrington, and it was not till late at night, or perhaps the following morning, that she, with a lady her companion, came on board.'[56] The companion of Jane Codrington, who was six months pregnant, was Miss Mary Treacher. At seven in the evening they reached the Stone Deep anchorage to the north-west of Walcheren, and Mary Treacher related that 'Captain King wished to remain, for the tide had begun to ebb – we were still ten miles from the fleet, and there were symptoms of a coming storm – but he was overruled by the pilot, who affirmed that he could take the ship in safety. She had not, however left the anchorage five minutes when she struck upon the sandbank. The second shock she received carried away the rudder, and her ultimate fate then became very precarious.'[57] McGrigor gave a graphic account of the ship in distress:

On my reaching the deck, I found Captain King questioning the two Deal pilots, whose faces were of the colour of ashes. We had struck on a sand bank; and the vessel, on swinging round from this, struck upon another. An anchor was let go, which we lost. Another was thrown out, and with consternation it was found we had got into a quarter where we ought not to have been. We were in fact surrounded by sand banks. As night advanced, the scene became terrific. The ship was constantly thumping at a terrible rate, and I could hear the sailors say—'Her bottom will not bear this long.' The night was very dark; and about ten o'clock, after a violent thump, her rudder was carried away, and we heard a gush of water rush in. She was found to admit water very fast, although all hands were to the pumps. At this time, Captain King, taking me aside, begged I would take the ladies below into the ward room, for he was about to cut away the mainmast, and in its fall it might injure the cabin and the persons in it.[58]

McGrigor duly led the women below, where, he said:

we could distinctly hear the heavy blows of the carpenters at the main mast, which at length fell with a tremendous crash; and getting entangled with the foremast, carried it overboard with it in its fall. The water was still continuing to gain in the leaks. A great deal of stowage was thrown overboard, and all the guns, six only excepted, which were retained for signals. The water increasing much, and the men and officers being exhausted, a last expedient was had recourse to; that of thrumming a tarred sail under her bottom, at the place where the leaks were. But, after a long trial, the men were found to be so much exhausted, as not to be able to accomplish this; and we gained little upon the leaks . . . A great many bags of biscuit were stored in the ward room for exigencies. Over these, in deep sleep, were the midshipmen, who, poor little fellows, had been quite exhausted. In their sleep I observed the fine countenances of young gentlemen or noblemen; some brought up in the lap of luxury, and whose parents no doubt never dreamed of their dear boys being in such a situation as I then saw them.[59]

Jane Codrington later told her daughter 'that at first she counted the shocks which the ship received by striking upon the bank, but when they *passed one hundred* she left off her counting'.[60] McGrigor observed their increasingly dangerous state:

At this time our situation became truly awful; the vessel appeared at every thump to take in more water . . . As day broke upon us, the spectacle of the wreck was frightful. The whole deck was a mass of ruin, and the sides were all out, torn away in part by the guns in throwing them overboard; one mast, the mizen, only, was standing. We were at this time firing signal guns of distress, every five minutes. We had about eighty women on board, mostly Irish, the wives of soldiers going to their husbands at Walcheren. After every signal from the guns, a general screech and yell followed from the women, who were most troublesome, running about below and above.[61]

As daylight increased, everyone was looking out for help:

A vessel was descried. We made her out to be an American. But to our utter dismay it was observed, that although she must have seen us in our distressed condition, and heard our guns, she bore away from us, and made for Flushing. It was then that an officer of the ship unfortunately was heard to say. 'We are doomed to destruction. The *Venerable* will not hold out till other vessels can near us.' I had never been actually depressed till I heard this . . . We were constantly firing guns of distress, and every volley from them was followed by a general screech from the soldier's wives. The two ladies however behaved well; Mrs. Codrington, who showed an extraordinary degree of fortitude, was always collected, and prepared to meet the worst. At length another sail was descried from the top of our remaining mast. Every eye was applied to the nearest accessible glass. It was discovered that she was a small vessel, a brig. The utmost anxiety prevailed. To our infinite joy it was discovered that she had observed our signal of distress, and heard our guns, and finally that she made for us. She came not very close, but kept rather at a respectful distance, fearing, I believe, that we might go down and carry her with us in our vortex.[62]

The ladies were transferred to the brig, along with the papers and plate of Sir Home Popham, as Mary Treacher explained: 'At about ten o'clock, a brig was seen in the distance . . . but it was one o'clock before we left the *Venerable*, which we had great difficulty in doing, for she was then high out of the water, and was rolling heavily in a very rough sea. We got down her side, however, without accident, as well as up the less formidable one of the brig, which lay to for us at the distance of a quarter of a mile; she was laden with wine for the fleet, and was going into Flushing.'[63] The next day the badly damaged *Venerable* was brought into Flushing under jury masts and later towed back to England for repair.

McGrigor's first task was to inspect all the hospitals, following which he urged that veteran soldiers be sent from England as orderlies and that local Dutch people should be employed to help. He also stressed that the sick should be evacuated to England in 'six or seven ships of the line, with no greater complement of men than would be sufficient to navigate them; the guns of the lower deck being taken out, with a sufficiency of hammocks for 500 men'.[64] McGrigor also managed to obtain more quinine (bark), which was in such short supply: 'I learned that an American vessel, which came with a large supply of champagne and claret for the sutlers, had brought some chests of bark on a venture; having most probably heard of the deficient state of the stores of all the belligerents, in that article. I immediately ordered the purveyor to make a purchase of whatever stock of bark the Americans might have; and the supply we obtained [1460 pounds] lasted till the quantities forwarded by the mail coaches at Deal, and thence by packets to Walcheren, arrived.'[65]

The commander-in-chief, Sir Eyre Coote, wrote constantly to Lord Castlereagh about the dire situation, and on 6 October he informed him: 'This day I have ordered 1000 sick and convalescents, selected from the whole army, to be put on board ship, and I hope that, if the wind continues fair, they will sail this evening. In the course of a day or two a second embarkation of nearly double that extent will take place, which will tend greatly to clear out our crowded hospitals, and relieve our medical officers of some part of their laborious duty. An experiment is likewise to be tried by sending a portion of the convalescents to board the *Asia* and *Britannia* hospital ships, to try the effect of a change of air.'[66] He added: 'Your lordship will also pardon my anxiety to be informed of the intention of his

Majesty's government as to the future fate of Walcheren, as that knowledge will very essentially affect the measures which I shall then deem it necessary to pursue.'[67]

Only a week later Sir Eyre Coote found out that a treaty had been signed between France and Austria.* The Grand Expedition had been a disastrous failure. Too late to provide the diversion needed to relieve the pressure on Austria, the attack on Antwerp was not pressed home, and most of the French ships based in the Scheldt had escaped. Part of Napoleon's naval base was still usable, and many of the troops saved by the naval evacuation of Corunna and Vigo were now lost to malaria. Lack of planning and lack of leadership had reduced the expedition to a shambles.

In late October Sir Eyre Coote was replaced by Lieutenant-General George Don, who also asked the government to send more ships to evacuate the sick, but by the end of the month he was informed that Walcheren should be abandoned and Flushing destroyed. Private Wheeler, who returned to Walcheren towards the end of October in a transport vessel to take off the sick soldiers, outlined what was planned:

We . . . dropped anchor between the Islands of Walcherine and South Beveland. Since we left these islands our people have evacuated South Beveland and the enemy has taken possession of it, the troops are so sickly in Walcherine. It is intended to destroy the works and dock yards together with every place belonging to the French Government, then leave the place; we are to remain on board as circumstance shall require; the enemy is throwing up works on the Island they occupy, and it is said they are meditating an attack on Walcherine. The river is full of our Gunboats, which are constantly annoying them, and they in return keep up a constant fire on our boats, so nothing is heard all day and night but the clang of war, and seemingly without effecting any purpose whatever. Our situation here is not very pleasant, the weather is cold and we have not much room to exercise ourselves on deck; one comfort attending us is gin, and tobacco is cheap, so we can enjoy ourselves over a pipe and glass; the cause of our remaining on board is for the preservation of our health.[68]

All through November and early December, great efforts were made to dismantle everything of use in Flushing, and Gunner Richardson in the *Caesar* described some of the scenes: 'A hundred men from each

* Treaty of Schönbrunn, on 14 October 1809.

line-of-battle ship are employed on shore daily in dismantling the batteries and putting the guns and mortars on board the transports: we received nineteen on board of different calibres, some brass and copper. Some are employed in breaking up the piers of the new harbour, and filling it up with rubbish, to prevent the enemy's ships from entering in and lying up in winter (to be clear of the ice coming down the Scheldt).'[69] On 9 December most of the troops came on board the ships, and Codrington declared that 'I only wish to get home with the rest of this *no longer* GRAND EXPEDITION.'[70]

William Robinson also documented the destruction: 'Previous to our coming away, we did all the mischief we could; we set fire to every thing in the dock-yard, and filled up the entrance of the different canals with stones and rubbish; this obtained for us no good name, for on leaving, we were much ridiculed and jeered by the Dutchmen, who exclaimed that we had brought a large force there, and had done nothing worthy of war, but to knock down their houses, and distress the poor inhabitants.'[71] For several days storms prevented the final evacuation from Walcheren, but on the 22nd they got under way, sailed for a mile and a half and anchored again. The following day the entire British force finally set sail and were in sight of Beachy Head on Christmas Day. Richardson felt sorry for those they left behind:

The inhabitants of Walcheren, poor creatures, are at this time to be pitied, and they may well call themselves unfortunate: about two years ago the sea broke over the dykes, destroyed much property, and many lives were lost; in the late bombardment their ancient town has been nearly destroyed, and two thousand of the inhabitants slain; and the dread of Bonaparte coming (who they expect will lay heavy taxes on them to make good the works we have destroyed) fills them with despondency. Such is the ruin of warfare! As for our part, we are tired enough of the place; when we left England it was thought three weeks would finish the business.[72]

Over four thousand troops died in combat or of disease, and another twelve thousand fell sick, mainly of malaria, some of them suffering for years afterwards. The *Annual Register* was severe in its criticism: 'The failure of this expedition, in its main object, is beyond all doubt, to be attributed not in any degree to the army or navy, whose alacrity in the cause could not have been exceeded, but by the shameful ignorance of those who planned it . . . The French crowed over the expedition into the Scheldt . . .

The British nation acknowledged that the exultation and ridicule of the French was not for once misplaced.'[73] Robert Blakeney reckoned that 'the unwieldy expedition, although it furnished cause of merriment all over the Continent, deluged the British empire with tears. There was scarcely a family in Great Britain which did not mourn the fate of a gallant soldier.'[74]

Napoleon believed that the expedition should have succeeded. Talking years later with his physician, Barry O'Meara, on the island of St Helena, he expressed his thoughts:

I am of opinion, that if you had landed a few thousand men at first at Williamstadt, and marched directly for Antwerp, that between consternation, want of preparation, and the uncertainty of the number of assailants, you might have taken it . . . It was a very bad expedition for you. Your ministers were very badly informed about the country. You afterwards had the stupidity to remain in that pestilential place, until you lost some thousands of men. It was the height of stupidity and of inhumanity. I was very glad of it, as I knew that disease would carry you off by thousands, and oblige you to evacuate it without any exertion being made on my part.[75]

A Parliamentary Inquiry was held the following year, against the wishes of the ministers, to investigate the causes of the failure, and the American Louis Simond wrote in his diary: '*April 2.*—The Walcheren question was finally decided the day after I was at the house, or rather the next day after that, the debates having been protracted till long after daylight. A small majority of 21 – that is 253 for, and 232 against the ministers – approves all! This is certainly quite contrary to public opinion, which is altogether against ministers . . . The members of Parliament seem to feel singularly relieved by the final termination of this Walcheren question.'[76] Three weeks later he wrote:

A new panorama is now exhibiting in London; it is of Flushing. The spectator is placed in the middle of the town, on the top of some high building: bombs and rockets pierce the roofs of the houses, which are instantly in flames, or burst in the middle of the streets, full of the dismayed inhabitants, flying from their burning dwellings with their effects, and carrying away the sick and wounded. It is a most terrifying picture. At the sight of so much misery, all the commonplaces about war become again original, and the sentimental lamentations on suffering humanity oppress and sicken the soul, as if they were uttered for the first time.[77]

# FIFTEEN

———— ·◆· ————

# PRISONERS AND PRIVATEERS

There was something horrid in the treatment of the prisoners in England. The very idea of being put on board a ship, and kept there for several years, has something dreadful in it.

Napoleon in exile on St Helena, talking to his physician, Barry O'Meara[1]

Although the Walcheren expedition was a disaster, many prisoners were captured and taken to England. Most would not be released for years. From the resumption of the war in 1803 until its end eleven years later, over one hundred thousand French prisoners were brought back to Britain, as well as thousands of prisoners of other nationalities, such as Spanish, Dutch and Danish – in 1807 more than eighteen hundred Danish prisoners were taken during the bombardment of Copenhagen alone. Soon captured Americans would be added to their numbers. They included seamen and officers from naval, merchant and privateer vessels, some of whom were only boys. While the Walcheren expedition significantly increased the number of captured troops, there was still a greater proportion of sailors than soldiers. This ratio altered as the Peninsular War in Spain and Portugal progressed and large numbers of soldiers were imprisoned.

The Transport Board (a department of the Admiralty) had responsibility for all prisoners. Lower-rank prisoners and those officers who refused to give their parole or broke their parole were interned on board prison hulks – known to the French as *les pontons* – and in land prisons, called depots. Initially these depots were close to southern ports, such as

Millbay in Plymouth, Stapleton near Bristol, Forton near Gosport and Portchester Castle near Portsmouth, and there was also a prison at Norman Cross near Peterborough. As prisoner numbers increased, more land prisons were constructed across the country, including Dartmoor in Devon and Valleyfield near Penicuik, south of Edinburgh.

It was the hulls of obsolete naval vessels, both British and captured foreign ships, that were used as prison hulks – usually two- or three-deckers, with their masts removed. Hulks were used by many countries as prisons, for both civilian convicts and foreign prisoners-of-war, but in Britain exceptional numbers of prisoners-of-war (up to one-third) were held in hulks. Most of these were moored at Plymouth, Portsmouth Harbour, nearby Langstone Harbour and along the River Medway at Chatham. Conditions for prisoners varied, and some were cruelly treated and the victims of corrupt contractors supplying poor-quality food and clothing, but the worst conditions for prisoners were in the hulks, which were very cramped and with poor ventilation. After his release Captain Pierre-Charles-François Dupin of the French naval engineers complained to his government:

The Medway is covered with men-of-war, dismantled and lying in ordinary [with no masts and the upper deck roofed over]. Their fresh and brilliant painting contrasts with the hideous aspect of the old and smoky hulks, which seem the remains of vessels blackened by a recent fire. It is in these floating tombs that prisoners of war are buried alive – Danes, Swedes, Frenchmen, Americans, no matter. They are lodged on the lower deck, on the upper deck, and even on the orlop-deck . . . Four hundred malefactors are the maximum of a ship appropriated to convicts. From eight hundred to twelve hundred is the ordinary number of prisoners of war, heaped together in a prison-ship of the same rate.[2]

Some of the prisoners wrote accounts of their experiences, and one of the most detailed was by the Frenchman Louis Garneray, who had been on board the frigate *Belle Poule*, which was captured with the *Marengo* in March 1806 when Rear-Admiral Linois was trying to return to France. Arriving at Spithead, Garneray was handed over to the *Prothee* hulk (a warship captured from the French in 1780), and in a vivid narrative of his many years as a prisoner, he claims to have been transferred to the *Crown* hulk about three years later and then to the *Vengeance*. It is often difficult to isolate the factual comments from his somewhat fictionalised account, but it is certain that he was not reduced to the squalor experienced by many prisoners. He learned English and became an interpreter, and also developed his skill as an artist. After his eventual release, Garneray followed a career as a marine artist for four decades. He gave a description of his living quarters:

You know that on the upper deck of a vessel there exist the forecastle and quarterdeck, which are linked by the gunwale and by a large opening which leaves uncovered part of the gun deck . . . This open area and the forecastle were the only places where the prisoners were allowed a little air and to walk – and that not always. With the ironic gaiety that never fails the French in adversity, the inmates referred to this open area by the pompous name of the Park. It was about 44 feet long and 38 feet wide. The forecastle, the second place to walk on board the hulks, was not so big and was therefore not so well regarded as the Park; moreover, the chimneys, which were right up close, enveloped it almost always with a thick cloud of coal smoke, which was a horrible nuisance . . . The lower gun deck and the orlop deck were the parts of the hulk given over to the living quarters of the prisoners; this gun deck as well as the orlop measured about 130 feet by 40 feet. It was in this narrow space that we were accommodated, to the number of almost 700![3]

General René-Martin Pillet, taken prisoner in 1808 at the battle of Vimiero, also condemned the hulks, having first-hand experience of them at Chatham after breaking his parole:

The hulks are moored in the midst of fetid and stagnant mud, which at every tide is left bare. The air which is breathed being putrid, damp, and salt, would be sufficient without ill treatment, or unwholesome food, to impair and destroy in a very short time the health of the most robust . . . The height of the deck of the *Brunswick,* on board of which I was confined, is exactly four feet ten inches, so that a man of the shortest stature can never stand erect. This is a mode of perpetual punishment which none of those tyrants who have dishonoured the human species, have ever devised against the greatest criminals.[4]

The low ceilings were not such a problem for seamen serving on board ships, because they had much more freedom to move around the vessel.

Apart from the restricted height, the space allotted to the hundreds of prisoners on board each hulk was also minimal, as Pillet explained: 'The space allowed to a prisoner to suspend his hammock, is six English feet long, and fourteen inches wide; but these six feet are reduced to four and a half, because it is so contrived that the cords of the hammocks run into each other, and consequently the head of every man in the second rank when lying down, is placed between the legs of two men who are in the first rank of the deck, and his feet are placed between the two heads of those of the third rank, and so on from one extremity of the deck to the other.'[5] Many of the foreign prisoners also found the climate in Britain hard to bear, as winters were harsher than today. Pillet complained that 'the prisons on land or water where Frenchmen are confined in England, never have any glass, although the temperature of that climate is generally wet and cold, and the winters very long. The heat occasioned by the crowding together of the prisoners is so great that the airports [gunports] of one side only, that exposed to the wind, can be shut; and this is done with old rags.'[6]

Midshipman Bonnefoux likewise commented that 'in the winter, the cold was excessive during the day, and never was our quarters heated'.[7] Pierre-Marie-Joseph de Bonnefoux, like Louis Garneray, had been on board the frigate *Belle Poule* when it was captured. Many officers were sent on parole to Thame, but Bonnefoux broke his parole in several escape attempts. Of the hulks, he commented, 'it is, indeed, difficult to imagine a more harsh form of torture. It is cruel to incarcerate and subject to it, for an indefinite time, prisoners-of-war who deserve much consideration and who are arguably *the innocent victims of the fortunes of war!*'[8] Because of family influence, Bonnefoux was released from the hulks at Chatham and allowed to go to Lichfield on parole, but in 1811 he successfully escaped with the help of a smuggler.

For some unfortunate prisoners, these hulks were their home for over a decade, and escape was difficult, because few prisoners could swim, and they were mostly too poor to pay bribes or buy outside assistance. Desperate escape attempts were made, though, often by cutting through the wooden hull. In the spring of 1808 such a daring breakout succeeded at Portsmouth:

Early on Thursday morning, the 7th April, eleven French prisoners made their escape out of the *Vigilant* prison-ship, at Portsmouth, by cutting a hole through one of the ports of the ship, and swimming to the *Amphitrite*, a ship in ordinary which is fitted up for the abode of one of the superintendant-masters. There they clothed themselves with the great coats of his boat's crew, lowered down the boat, and went and took possession of one of the finest unarmed vessels in the harbour, called the master-attendant's buoy-boat.—They immediately got her under weigh, and sailed out of the harbour at about five o'clock that morning, and, it is supposed, reached either Cherburgh or Havre in the evening . . . There were three [British] men on board her, whom they have taken to France.[9]

In France, the escaped prisoners sold the vessel for £700, which was fitted out as a privateer known as *Le Buoy Boat de Portsmouth*, but this was captured a few months later, as *The Times* reported:

Arrived this afternoon the cutter called the *Buoy Boat of Portsmouth*, captured from the French by his Majesty's brigs *Coquette* and *Daring*. This cutter, it will be remembered, was, about nine months ago taken possession of in this harbour by several Frenchmen, who made their escape from the *Vigilant* prison-ship, and who arrived in her in safety at a French port. From the circumstance of her having been employed as a buoy boat in his Majesty's service at this port, her name was not changed by those who became proprietors of her in France; and, from her excellent sailing, she was fitted out as a privateer, since which, until the present time, she has bid defiance to our ships, and had great success in capturing British coasting vessels. She took an English vessel on her present cruise, which gave rise to the vigilance of our cruisers at the time of re-capturing and the taking of the above annoying privateer.[10]

As days of tedium became years of relentless boredom, with little hope of release or escape, a number of prisoners on board the hulks and in the land prisons became addicted to gambling and alcohol. This most desperate group of prisoners even sold their bedding, clothing and rations for gambling, and were reduced to scavenging. Some of these men in the land prisons were taken to the hulks in order to isolate them, and during the winter of 1807 a newspaper reported on one such group:

There is such a spirit of gambling existing among the French prisoners lately arrived at Chatham [hulks] from Norman Cross, that many of them have been almost entirely naked during the late severe weather, having lost their clothes, not excepting even their shirts and small-clothes, to some of their fellow prisoners; many of them are also reduced to the chance of starving by the same means, having lost seven or eight days' provisions to their more fortunate comrades, who never fail to exact their winnings. The effervescence of mind that this diabolical pursuit gives rise to, is often exemplified in the conduct of these infatuated captives, rendering them remarkably turbulent and unruly. Saturday a quarrel arose between two of them in the course of play, when one of them who had lost his clothes and food, received a severe stab in the back.[11]

Even in this wretched state, the prisoners were a tourist attraction, with visitors being rowed out from shore to the hulks. Colonel Lebertre, who was a prisoner at Chatham after breaking his parole, complained that 'even the women showed a really shocking indifference. You could see them remain for whole hours with their eyes fixed on the Park where the prisoners were kept, without this spectacle of misery, which would so terribly affect a French woman, making them shed a single tear. On the contrary, an insulting smile was on their lips. The prisoners only knew of a single example of a woman who fainted at the sight of the Park.'[12] Some women did live on board these hulks, either as wives of the British officers, or as prisoners, usually the wives of soldiers or sailors.

Not all prisoners allowed themselves to despair. Many turned their hand to making things – often exquisite artefacts that were sold to the public in markets held in the prisons. These included intricate objects carved out of meat bones, such as models of warships, and many are today on display in museums. On one Sunday, Betsey Wynne (wife of Captain Fremantle) wrote in her diary: 'Took a ride in the carriage as far as Portchester Castle where we saw the French prisoners, there are 3000 of them; they are industrious and make all kinds of little works. We bought a Guillotine neatly done in bone.'[13] Most of the names of the men who made these models are lost, but Corporal Jean de la Porte, who was captured at the Battle of Trafalgar and held at Norman Cross for almost nine years, is known as the artist of a view of Peterborough Cathedral done in straw marquetry.

Other occupations, such as straw-plaiting, where wheat and barley straw were used to make decorative baskets, boxes and bonnets, were less welcome. Making straw hats and bonnets was illegal, and later all straw work was prohibited, in order to protect local industries that were taxed. Even so, a thriving black-market trade existed in many prisons, and the Transport Board issued a plea for 'the magistrates to help in stopping the traffic with prisoners of war in prohibited articles, straw hats and straw plaits especially'.[14] They were also concerned that 'it has been the means of selling obscene toys, pictures, &c, to the great injury of the morals of the rising generation'.[15] At Portchester Castle many prisoners were employed in the lace industry, but complaints from local lace makers led to this being stopped, and the popular theatre run by the prisoners was closed down to prevent competition.

Forgery was another persistent problem, and Dartmoor Prison was renowned for its forgers. In April 1810 it was reported that 'a great number of Bank of England forged notes and counterfeit seven shilling-pieces, are now in circulation in Plymouth and its neighbourhood: several persons detected in uttering them were taken into custody on Saturday night. They are supposed to be the manufacture of French prisoners, whose ingenuity this way is very astonishing.'[16] For murder and forgery, prisoners were subject to civil law and could be sentenced to death.

Dartmoor Prison had been constructed in response to the overcrowding in the hulks at nearby Plymouth and also because of fears that the prisoners were too close to the naval base. It had the worst reputation of all prisons, because it was on top of the moor, very bleak, often bitterly cold and suffered high rainfall. The foundation stone was laid in March 1806 and three years later two and a half thousand French prisoners were transferred there from the hulks at Plymouth, with numbers rising to twelve thousand. That first winter an epidemic led to nearly five hundred deaths, and these men were buried in an adjacent cemetery.

While British officers were held on parole at Verdun, up to four thousand French officers were also on parole in Britain, but they were not concentrated in a single place; instead, they were dispersed among fifty to sixty small parole towns where they could live in the community. Wincanton and Chesterfield had the most Frenchmen on parole. They had to give their word of honour – *parole d'honneur* – not to travel beyond the boundaries of the town, which were marked by stones. Very few British officers in France broke their parole, as they knew they would be reprimanded, demoted and even ostracised by their family for doing something so dishonourable, but hundreds of French officers broke their parole and escaped. The French authorities did not reprimand these 'broke-paroles' but allowed them to continue their employment. Because the officers had money, they were frequently helped to escape, especially by young women bedazzled by the French and by professional smugglers. Advertisements constantly appeared in newspapers offering a reward, such as this one at the beginning of 1810:

His Majesty's Transport Service, &c. do hereby offer a REWARD of FIVE GUINEAS for the recapture of each of the said prisoners, to any person who shall apprehend them, or either of them, and deliver them at this Office, or otherwise cause them to be securely lodged in any of the public gaols. JOSEPH GOUET, Captain, La Josephine, merchant vessel, 30 years of age, 5 feet 5¾ inches high, middle-sized person, oval visage, brown complexion, brown hair and hazel eyes. JACQUES CLEMENDOL, Lieutenant de Vaisseau, La Ville de Varsovie, man of war, 30 years of age, 5 feet 4¼ inches, middle-sized person, oval visage, sallow complexion, black hair, and black eyes.[17]

Clemendol had been captured in April 1809. His ship, the *Ville de Varsovie*, was a new warship that had run aground during Cochrane's fireship attack at Basque Roads and was burned after surrendering.

General Osten, the second-in-command at Flushing captured during the Walcheren expedition, also made his escape. He was living on parole at Lichfield, along with his daughter. As was her right, she returned to Holland in December 1809, taking with her all their heavy baggage. The following February Osten met a Folkestone smuggler by the name of James Moore, who operated as a highly successful escape agent over an extensive area of England and Scotland. Less than two days later the general was back in Holland. Moore used several aliases, but he was known to the French as Captain Harman. Two months later he was helping General Pillet to escape, along with the Italian marine captain Paolucci, both at that time on parole at Alresford. They 'left their quarters at Alresford, and were met half a mile out by Harman with a post-chaise, into which they got and drove to Winchester, alighting in a back street while Harman went to get another chaise. Thence they drove circuitously to Hastings via Croydon, Sevenoaks, Tunbridge, Robertsbridge, and Battle, Harman saying that this route was necessary for safety, and that he would get them over, as he had General Osten, in thirty-four hours.'[18] The pair were captured and sent to Norman Cross, with Pillet subsequently transferred to the hulks at Chatham for bad behaviour. Harman was arrested but escaped lightly, promising to supply information about these escape routes – but he was back in business before too long.

Jack Rattenbury, from Beer in Devon, was another smuggler involved in assisting French officers to escape. In early 1808 he purchased an oared galley, but during a smuggling run to the Channel Islands he was caught by two revenue cutters, handed over to the press-gang and taken to the coast of Ireland to serve in the Royal Navy. He managed to escape, and back home in Beer he immediately returned to his smuggling ways: 'I made an agreement with four French officers, who had made their escape from the prison [parole town] at Tiverton, to take them to Cape La Hogue, for which I was to receive one hundred pounds. They came to Beer, and I concealed them in the best manner I was able, in a house near the beach, where I supplied them with such provisions as they wanted. But a vigilant inquiry was commenced; their steps were traced, and the place of their retreat discovered.'[19]

Rattenbury led a charmed life and managed to extricate himself from this predicament, though the French prisoners undoubtedly forfeited their parole:

The next morning, there was a special warrant out against myself and five others, who were connected with the affair, and the constables came to my house, while I was up-stairs considering how I had best act. Finding that my companions had absconded, and being captain of the boat, I immediately surrendered myself to them. I was then taken before the magistrates, where I found the French gentlemen in custody. They were examined through the medium of an interpreter, but their replies were cautious, and they said very little that could tend to implicate me in the transaction. My turn then came; and, in reply to the questions from the bench, I briefly stated that I was engaged to take the gentlemen to Jersey, of which island I understood they were natives. A lieutenant of the sea-fencibles* being in the room, asked me if I did not know a native of Jersey from a Frenchman; to which I was going to have replied, but my attorney, who was present, said that this was a question which he had no right to prefer, and which I was not bound to answer. The magistrates then conversed together; and, after a little consultation, dismissed me, with a gentle admonition to go home, and not engage in any similar transaction for the future.[20]

Until 1811 helping a prisoner-of-war to escape was only a minor crime, but then it became punishable by imprisonment or transportation, as in one case the following year:

At the late Lewes Assizes, *James Robinson*, who holds a mill in the neighbourhood of Oswestry; *John Hughes*, landlord of the Red Lion, and

---

* A sea-going equivalent of the militia, drawn from fishermen and boatmen, for defending the coast against invasion.

Post-Master at Rye; and *William Hatter*, fisherman of that town, were convicted before the Right Hon. Lord ELLENBOROUGH, of a conspiracy to effect the escape of General PHILLIPON, and Lieutenant GARNIER, two French Officers, who, in breach of their parole of honour, absconded from Oswestry, on the 30th of June last. The evidence adduced in support of this charge satisfied the Jury, not only that these men were guilty of this conspiracy, but that Robinson and Hatter had actually conveyed the two Frenchmen to the enemy's coast; and the Jury, without hesitation, found them *Guilty*. His Lordship, in a most impressive manner, after expatiating on the enormity of this offence, which he declared was scarcely to be distinguished from high-treason, adjudged Robinson and Hughes to be confined in the common gaol of the county of Sussex, for the space of two years, and within the first month to be placed in and upon the pillory on the sea shore, near the town of Rye, and as near as could be within sight of the French coast, that they might be viewed, as his Lordship observed, by those enemies of their country, whom they had by their conduct so much befriended.[21]

The majority of foreign officers respected the conditions of parole and added a cosmopolitan air to many towns that had up to now been very inward-looking. Lieutenant Pierre-Guillaume Gicquel des Touches was one of over four thousand prisoners brought to England after Trafalgar. He was placed on parole at Tiverton in Devon but considered it dishonourable to try to escape: 'The population of Tiverton, moreover, made us very welcome; some of the inhabitants were even kind enough to suggest they should help me to escape . . . I did not have much trouble in resisting these temptations, but it grieved me more to tear myself away from the obsessions of some of my friends, who, not having the same ideas as me about the sacredness of one's oath, simply wanted me to escape with them.'[22]

Officers on parole mixed with the local population, at times marrying local women, and earned additional money by teaching a range of activities such as French, fencing and dancing, while others established theatrical groups and became part of local society. Lieutenant Gicquel des Touches thought that the parole town of Tiverton 'was quite a pleasant town, but which seemed to me remarkably monotonous after the restless life to which I was accustomed . . . I made the most of my leisure time to refresh and complete my education. Some of my more well-read friends gave me lessons in literature and history; I repaid them by teaching them fencing, in which I always remained well practised.'[23] Relations were not always harmonious, however, as violence could break out between prisoners and the local people.

As the war dragged on a few prisoners were released, usually as a reward for acts of bravery and kindness, and over seventeen thousand prisoners were sent back to France because they were sick and injured, although this was not reciprocated. Even so, over ten thousand prisoners died during their confinement in Britain. Some of their gravestones survive, but most were buried in unmarked mass graves. Decades later an elderly man recalled that as a young boy he often watched the burial of those who died at Millbay Prison in Plymouth and that 'they were taken from the prison gates to the grave in a cart made for the purpose, drawn by a donkey belonging to old Samuel Fuge, who had the contract for the work'.[24] He related one particular incident:

A boy was in the burial ground one morning for the purpose of catching birds with bird lime on a thorn-bush. Seeing a grave not filled in, he got down on the coffin to hide himself from the birds; hearing a noise in the coffin he was soon out again, and ran away, quite alarmed and frightened, down to the entrance gate that stood near, where the Athenaeum now stands. Some persons who were passing, seeing the poor boy, asked him what was the matter, when he kept crying out, 'A man buried alive.' Several persons went up to the grave, when they found the boy's story was true. The lid of the coffin being raised, the poor French prisoner was soon taken up, and immediately conveyed to the prison infirmary. After a few months he got quite convalescent, and was sent home to France – one of the exchanged prisoners. After his arrival home, he wrote to the Rev. Herbert Mends, minister of Batter-street Chapel, Plymouth, asking if he would be kind enough to find the boy who was the means of saving his life. Mr. Mends, after making inquiries, was fortunate enough to discover who the boy was, and replied to the letter by giving particulars respecting him. In the course of a few days he received another letter from France, with an enclosure for five pounds, asking him if he would kindly hand it over to the boy, also stating that he (the Frenchman) would forward him the same amount yearly so long as he lived. The money was duly received for four or five years, when Mr. Mends received an account of the Frenchman's death.[25]

As the burials were frequently not marked with gravestones, they were soon forgotten after the end of the war. In 1882 several bodies from Millbay Prison were rediscovered at Plymouth: 'In excavating on the site of the

Athenaeum extension building, the workmen have disturbed the supposed remains of several of the French prisoners of war, who . . . were interred in what is known at present as the *Crescent*. Great numbers of these unfortunate exiles appear to have been buried in this spot, as scarcely a yard of the ground in and around the Crescent can be disturbed but some human remains are turned up by the workman's shovel.'[26] They were reburied 'with befitting marks of respect'[27] in Plymouth's Ford Park Cemetery. A television centre building at nearby Derry's Cross, constructed over part of the burial ground, was reputedly haunted by ghostly appearances.

Those who died on board the River Medway hulks were buried on St Mary's Island, between Chatham and Gillingham, but a major extension to Chatham Dockyard from 1864 led to many of the bones being dug up. Due respect was paid to these men:

The remains were . . . collected and reinterred, in the presence of the French naval attaché in England, within a railed-in enclosure two hundred feet square, laid out with flower-beds, shrubs, and gravel paths. In the centre the Admiralty had a memorial stone erected; comprising, on a raised pedestal, a finely carved female figure in armour, cloaked and holding in her hand an inverted torch, the figure being surmounted by a canopy of stone, also fittingly carved and decorated. A granite panel was placed on one face of the pedestal with this inscription in gilt letters:—

> Here are gathered together
> The remains of many brave soldiers and sailors
> Who having once been the foes and afterwards
> The captives of England,
> Now find rest in her soil,
> Remembering no more the animosities of war, or
> The sorrows of imprisonment.
> They were deprived of the consolation of closing
> Their eyes
> Among the countrymen they loved,
> But they have been laid in an honoured grave
> By a nation which knows how to respect valour
> And to sympathise with misfortune.[28]

Only a few years later, in 1904, owing to a further extension of the dockyard, the remains of the 521 bodies and the memorial were moved to the grounds of the naval barracks in Gillingham, in front of the chapel. This is now St George's Centre, itself a major naval memorial to those Chatham-based ships lost in the world wars.

The expedition to Walcheren may have yielded the prize of numerous prisoners-of-war, but the disastrous British withdrawal at the end of 1809 was in contrast to the French successes in Spain just beforehand that had given them control of much of the southern part of the country. Europe was now within Napoleon's grasp, but at the extreme edges his empire was slipping away. In South America Sir Sidney Smith, who was commanding the British naval presence there, had sent Captain Yeo to lead a combined force of British, Portuguese and Brazilians to attack the colony of French Guiana in December 1808. By 14 January 1809 the whole territory had been captured and was given over to Brazilian rule. That same month Rear-Admiral Sir Alexander Cochrane and Lieutenant-General George Beckwith had led almost the whole of the British forces deployed in the West Indies in an attack on Martinique. The island (and Diamond Rock) fell within a matter of weeks, although desperate attempts by the French to regain control continued for several months. Willaumez was supposed to sail to Martinique, but instead his squadron had become stuck in Basque Roads and suffered the fireship attack of Thomas Cochrane (nephew of Alexander Cochrane). The Spanish uprising against France isolated the remaining French colonies, leaving them no local allies, and the Spaniards, with support from some of Alexander Cochrane's ships, managed to take the remaining French area on Haiti by early June. Many of the French troops from here were evacuated to New Orleans and were still there to join in the defence of that city against the British nearly five years later. This left Guadeloupe as the only surviving French colony in the West Indies.

For years Guadeloupe had been a safe haven for the French privateers that preyed on the trade between the West Indies and Britain, but now that it was isolated Rear-Admiral Cochrane, again with Beckwith, was determined to leave them no hiding place. At the start of 1810 he led his fleet in a major assault on the island. On board Cochrane's flagship, the *Pompee*, Midshipman William Bowers kept a record of the attack:

On the 22nd of January, the men-of-war and transports, having completed the embarkation of the troops destined for the reduction of the enemy's remaining possessions in this quarter, sailed from Fort Royal Bay, Martinico [Martinique], and proceeded to Prince Rupert's in the island of Dominica, where the final dispositions were made. The military force consisted of six thousand seven hundred men. These were divided into five brigades, forming two divisions, and a reserve; the whole under the chief command of Lieutenant Sir George Beckwith. All being prepared, on the morning of the 26th the fleet weighed, and quitted Prince Rupert's; the second division proceeding to the Saintes, where it anchored the same day, while the first, with the commander-in-chief under charge of our ship, steered for Gosier Bay, or Roadstead, on the southern coast of that part of Guadeloupe called Grand Terre, and between three and four leagues east of the large and handsome town of Point à Petre, the emporium of the island, where we anchored on the following day.[29]

The British lost no time in landing troops, as they were unopposed, but with such a strong force no attempt was made to surprise the French. Instead a message was sent to the nearest French position demanding their surrender, as Bowers described:

We had no sooner anchored than a summons was despatched to Fort Fleur d'Epée, a strong post, about a league distant from the anchorage, which was not however complied with. During the night, and early the following morning, the whole of the first division and reserve were disembarked without accident or opposition, at the Village of Marie, Capes Terre, a few leagues distant, covered by the squadron; the whole instantly pushed forward to the southward, keeping the coast, and on the 30th, at noon, advancing by the pass of Somme Chien, reached Trois Rivières, sending forward some advanced posts in the direction of the enemy, who had concentrated his principal force, consisting of between three and four thousand troops in the neighbourhood of Basse Terre. These were strongly entrenched on a range of heights to the north-east of that city, their right flanked by the sea to the west, and their line extending thence to the strong post of Matabau, the outposts of which, forming their extreme left, were flanked again by the sea to the eastward.[30]

At the same time, the second division that had initially sailed to the Saintes now landed to the rear of the French. Caught in this pincer movement, the French were forced to give ground, as Bowers observed from his ship:

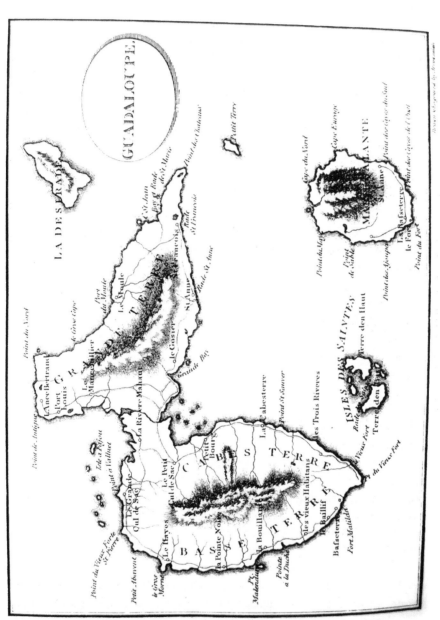

*Map of the Island of Guadaloupe*

The following morning [30 January], anchoring a little to the northward of Basse Terre, [the second division] disembarked . . . a little in the rear of the enemy's right; a movement which caused him to abandon the posts of Palmiste and Morne Hauel on his left in order to extend his line to the westward. Meanwhile the first division and reserve advanced rapidly, the enemy abandoning in succession the heights of D'Olot and others. On taking possession of Palmiste on the 2nd February, we lost sight of them, among the mountains, and our co-operation being no longer necessary on this side of the island, we bore up to join the left wing to leeward. This we found strongly posted on some heights on the enemy's right, an incessant cannonade being kept up between the hostile batteries.[31]

As so often occurred in amphibious attacks, seamen were landed from various ships to man the guns, as Bowers described: 'On our side [of the island], these [batteries] were principally served by the seamen of the squadron*, now further reinforced from our ship, and nothing could exceed the alacrity and good-will with which each and all performed their arduous duties, for service by night and day was one of unremitted fatigue. Seamen indeed are in general as unrivalled in serving in, as in storming, a battery, and in all operations, particularly along shore, have ever been found effective auxiliaries to the army.'[32]

One of the seamen landed was the Irishman Henry Walsh, from the *Alfred*, who left a record of his involvement:

Our fleet anchored before the town of Bastar and landed one hundred sailors that night, and brought up to our army two mortars and plenty of ammunition before morning, I being one of those sailors that was chose to go on shore on said duty to assist our army. This was the time I thought of making my fortune. But believe me I was greatly deceived in this for we were employed in conveying cannon and ammunition to the army both night and day, which I am very sure was the most toilsome and wearisome time I ever passed in my lifetime. There is no roads or highways in this island excepting pathways which nature has formed itself, and these indeed is most beautifully interwoven in the form of arches in many places which is most elegant to behold, as the orange and lemon trees chiefly composes these delightful shades so that you might reach your hand on either side and pull fruit of almost any kind that is delightful. We had no horses to assist us in dragging these mortars and field pieces through

---

* The cannon being dragged into position and fired by gun crews from the fleet.

those lonely pathways which in many places is almost impassable and particularly when we ascended the mountains. We upset these mortars several times down into ditches which was very difficult to get them out again.[33]

Some of the seamen were wounded, including an impressed American, James Durand, who related that 'I was one of a party which, on the fifth morning, was making a breast works and platform on which we were to plant some more mortars. While working there, an 18 pound shot from them struck the planking next me and a splinter of it broke my leg just below the calf.'[34] On the next day came the pitched battle that both sides were preparing for, and from his position as part of a gun crew Walsh witnessed the ebb and flow of the fighting:

Morning coming on being the 3rd day of February, by break of day the house which we remained in all night was entirely knocked down over our heads almost before we could get out of it. As the enemy's shots and shells reached from their batteries on us, the British army then immediately beat to arms and drew their troops in battle array on the plains of Matabar, which was about ten miles in circumference. The French army immediately gathered together and marched out of this garrison down to this plain in order to engage our army. Our artillery being entirely few in number the sailors being stationed to the field pieces to assist them in working the cannons as we understood that exercise. So I being stationed to a gun also and so we advanced against our enemy. We engaged and fought for some time but was obliged to retreat. But we rallied again and regained our ground but was obliged to retreat a second time. But we rallied again and forced them to retreat again, and when the French seen that we were pursuing them eagerly they seemed to decoy us on to a place where they had undermined [and planted explosives] and a train [fuse] laid to blow us all up. But our general being a skilful man in war, he deemed that some danger was nearby by the manoeuvres of our enemies, and accordingly sounded retreat and by this means saved the lives of his army. For there was close to us a snare laid for us which surely would prove our destruction, had our army advanced a little further.[35]

Walsh described how the French, having failed in their plan, surrendered:

The French seeing they were deceived in their scheme or stratagem immediately entered their garrison and hoisted a flag of truce, in order to bury the dead which indeed was very numerous for the plain for some miles was over-spread with killed and wounded. There must have been great slaughter on both sides, when this engagement lasted from daylight in the morning until 4 o'clock in the afternoon. As the weather being so excessively warm it became very necessary for both sides to bury their dead immediately, lest it should cause a plague. But our army had slaves continually burying the dead during the time of the engagement. However next day a French ambassador came to sue for peace, and in some days entirely surrendered the island up to our general.[36]

It had taken just eight days to capture the island of Guadeloupe, but while it lasted Midshipman Bowers considered that the battle was hard fought:

The contest, though short, was severe; the enemy defended himself on some points with much obstinacy, and made some determined charges; in one of which a certain regiment, composed principally of foreigners, was only saved from a total rout by the brave Forty-sixth. Our loss in killed and wounded was between three and four hundred. With Guadeloupe fell its two dependencies – St. Martin's and St. Eustatius, the last of the enemy's transatlantic possessions. The field of enterprize for the navy was but limited, and the promotion, to our great disappointment, corresponded. Our casualty only occurred among the officers of this arm; this was with a lieutenant of the *Sceptre*, who had his head knocked off by imprudently exposing himself on the rampart of the battery, in which he commanded a detachment of seamen.[37]

The injured American James Durand, on board the *Narcissus*, reckoned that 'the British lost, in killed and wounded, more than 300 men. The islanders' loss was said to be more than 700. The wounded were all taken on board and, after a common attendance with our own people, were received as prisoners of war.'[38] He added ruefully: 'I had been in the service of the British for more than a year and if I continued seven more, I decided I would see my limbs scattered all over the globe . . . "If I kill or am killed," said I to myself, "who is there to benefit except King George?"'[39]

With the fall of Guadeloupe France had lost all its bases in the Caribbean, which greatly benefited the security of British trade as well as being a severe blow to French trade, as was noted in *The British Neptune* newspaper:

The capture of Guadeloupe, the last of the enemy's colonies in the West Indies, cuts the knot of contest which has so long existed between this country and America, as France has no longer any colonial produce to carry in neutral bottoms [mostly American ships]. Guadeloupe annually exports about 190,000 quintals of sugar, 70,000 of coffee, 15,000 of indigo, 1000 of cocoa, 6000 of cotton, besides cinnamon, balsam capivi, honey, hides, sulphur &c. . . . The quantity of sugar now in the island is very considerable, although this article is now selling at 8s. a pound in France. The supply must affect the English market, and reduce sugar to a more moderate price than it has lately sold for.[40]

The loss of the French colonies would also have an effect on the continuing decline of slavery. After a long campaign the British slave trade had been stopped in 1807. The following year the United States made it illegal to import slaves into America, but it was left to individual states to enforce the law. Slavery itself was still legal in America, as in the British colonies, but in Britain there was growing public opinion against it. Within a very few years slavery would become an issue of righteous indignation on the part of the British, and a subject for outcry in the newspapers, as in one comment in early 1811:

To the disgrace of America, we copy the following advertisement from a recent New York paper: – 'Wanted to purchase, a smart Black Boy, of good temper and character: one accustomed to house-work will be preferred. Also, a steady, middle-aged Black Woman, who is a good cook, washer, and ironer, and can be well recommended for both or either. A good price will be given – Apply at Warne's Register and Commission Office, No. 2, Robinson-street. – Nov. 15'

How dare any country pretend to either honour, delicacy, or a spark of the real spirit of freedom where such a system is the law of the land, and the trade and pursuit of its people!!![41]

Since the British slave trade had carried nearly three and a half million Africans to slavery in America and the West Indies between 1662 and 1807, this was a very rapid change of attitude, but in the West Indies at least, slavery was withering. In the twenty-six years between the stopping of the British slave trade and the final abolition of slavery, the slave population of the West Indies fell by nearly 19 per cent. With British naval supremacy now undisputed in the Caribbean after the fall of Guadeloupe, there would be increasing pressure on the slave trade carried on in non-British ships.

# SIXTEEN

## THE HAND OF PROVIDENCE

A spirit of Commerce, and strength at Sea to protect it, are the
most certain marks of the Greatness of Empire . . . whoever
Commands the Ocean, Commands the Trade of the World, and
whoever Commands the Trade of the World, commands the
Riches of the World, and whoever is Master of That, Commands
the World itself.

Comment on navigation and commerce by John Evelyn in 1674[1]

Vice-Admiral Alexander Cochrane's success in expelling the French from
the West Indies was rewarded with the governorship of Guadeloupe. It
also probably helped to protect him from the repercussions over the
marooning of the seaman Robert Jeffery, who, three years before, had
been left to die on the uninhabited island of Sombrero by the captain of
a ship in Cochrane's fleet, the Honourable Warwick Lake. When Captain
Lake was ordered by Cochrane to rescue Jeffery, there had been no sign of
the man. Very few ships passed by the remote island, yet the most likely
explanation was that Jeffery had been rescued, and so Cochrane had
decided to take no further action, as he explained: 'I was well aware of the
irregularity of the proceedings at the time it occurred, and when it was
reported to me, I immediately sent Captain Lake back to the island, to
take the man off, but he was already gone; and having heard soon after of
the circumstances being reported in an American paper, and of the man's
arrival there, which assured me of his safety, I consented, after seriously
admonishing Captain Lake, to let the business rest.'[2]

No effort was made to verify this rumour of Jeffery's rescue, and a few months later Lake had been allowed to return to England on sick leave. Shortly after, he was ordered back to the West Indies as captain of the *Ulysses*. In September 1809 Lake was court-martialled for an incident in July, when the *Ulysses* was waiting to set sail as part of the Walcheren expedition. He was accused of drunkenness and of having neglected discipline by allowing the officers to be treated with disrespect. Lake was acquitted, but at the time of this court martial nobody knew about Jeffery, and the incident probably would never have come to light, but for the actions of Charles Morgan Thomas, a former acting purser in Cochrane's fleet who had a grudge against the admiral. In order to stir up trouble, Thomas wrote from Martinique to his Member of Parliament about his grievances in March 1809, adding: 'I deem it a duty I owe to humanity, to inform you that Captain Lake, when Commander of the *Recruit*, set a man belonging to that vessel on shore at Sombrero, an uninhabited Island in the Atlantic Archipelago, where he died through hunger, or otherwise, for more was never heard of him. This was likewise known to Sir Alexander Cochrane, who suffered this *titled murderer* to escape, and he now has command of the *Ulysses*.'[3]

The Admiralty in London was informed of this letter, and enquiries were made, leading to Lake facing a court martial on 5 February 1810 on board the *Gladiator* in Portsmouth harbour. He was accused of 'having, when Commander of his Majesty's ship *Recruit*, on the 13th of December, 1807, at six o'clock in the afternoon, caused a seaman, of the name of Robert Jeffery, to be put on shore on the desert island of Sombrero, in the West Indies'.[4] In his defence Lake 'admitted that he put the man on shore, but denied that he ever intended to put his life in jeopardy, as he thought the island was inhabited: that in landing him, he thought he would be more sensible of his want of conduct, and would reform in future'.[5] While punishments for seamen could be very harsh and their lives made intolerable by some brutal officers, captains did not have the power to invent their own system of justice. Nobody questioned the flogging that Jeffery had received for stealing rum, as that was an accepted punishment, but the court martial decided that Lake was guilty of abandoning the seaman, for which he was dismissed from the Royal Navy.

After Lake's court martial there immediately followed a frenzy of speculation in newspapers across the country about whether or not Jeffery was alive, and what action should be taken. At that time the artist Joseph Farington was touring Cornwall, and at Polperro he happened to ask about Jeffery, but he wrote in his diary that 'All of those I spoke to believed Jefferies [Jeffery] to be dead, and that all the reports to the contrary were published by the friends of Capn. Lake hoping thereby to prevent any further discussion of this subject which so greatly agitated the public mind.'[6] Later Farington received a visit from Jeffery's mother, Mrs Coade, who explained that she too was doubtful that Jeffery was alive. Farington tried to comfort her 'by saying that there has appeared in the newspapers accounts of her son being well and settled in America, and that they did seem to be authentic'.[7]

Farington's words of comfort turned out to be true, because Jeffery had actually been rescued from Sombrero on his tenth day there. When first abandoned on the island, he admitted that he was very frightened and in utter despair. His attempts to find food were unsuccessful: '*Second day.*–At the dawn of this day, I went out in search of food; but could not find any, not even a blade of grass, a weed, or a limpet . . . *Third day.*–I again traversed the rock, in search of food, and found an egg; but could not eat it, as it was in a very putrid state, it being out of season for birds to lay. It rained on this day, which enabled me to get a little fresh water. Hunger became more violent.'[8] In the following days his desperation increased:

*Fifth night.*–Night drawing on, I again laid me down to sleep; but was continually alarmed by what had troubled me before, *black lizards crawling over my face*, and being ignorant of the harmlessness of those creatures, I remained restless *the whole* of that night! . . . *Sixth day.*–I was refreshed by more showers of rain, and supplied with a little more fresh water. I saw two vessels pass at a great distance! *Seventh night.*–On this night, the heavens were as light as noon-day, arising from a continuation of strong flashes of lightning, which were followed by violent claps of thunder! The awfulness of this night was beyond description . . . *Seventh day.*–On this day in the morning, a ship hove in sight, which gave me fresh hopes; but they were soon banished by her steering another course, when she soon disappeared. I found myself now more forlorn, more miserable, and more hopeless than ever . . . *Eighth day*–the rock was so hot by the heat of the sun, that it was almost insupportable. I stripped myself of my jacket and trowsers, and bathed myself in the puddles of salt water which lodged in parts of the rock, and which were thrown there by sprays of the sea.[9]

Exhaustion took over, and that night Jeffery was able to sleep. On the following day he spotted another vessel and waved his hat furiously to attract attention. The schooner *Adams* was sailing from Martinique to America, and Captain John Dennis was sufficiently curious about this moving figure and the number of birds flying about to change his course. The next morning with the aid of his telescope he was able to make out Jeffery, who described his subsequent rescue: 'They had supposed me to be some unfortunate mariner who had been wrecked, and was the only survivor to tell the fate of his unhappy shipmates ... when, with the assistance of the crew, I got on board, the captain, and every one else, got round me with the most tender concern, supposing me shipwrecked. I related that *my Captain* had put me on that rock, for taking about a couple of quarts of spruce beer, and told them of my sufferings there! They were struck, as it were, for some time speechless.'[10]

With contrary winds, it took another five weeks to reach their home port of Marblehead*, 18 miles to the north of Boston, but during that time Jeffery recovered some of his strength. He was rescued just in time, since many American merchant ships were now stuck in port because of the Embargo Act, banning trade with all foreign nations, which the US government had recently passed following the attack on the *Chesapeake* by the *Leopard*. In America Jeffery continued to be treated well, as he later recalled:

When we arrived at Marblehead, *Joseph Dickson*, the mate, kindly took me to his house, and kept me nearly three weeks, until I was able to work. He generously went round to the inhabitants of the town with a paper, for a subscription for me. They came forward to relieve me, some with clothes, and others with money. John Wayman, a butcher, wanting a servant, and I, from my sufferings, being still in a very weak state, gladly went to him for my victuals, and remained with him three weeks. Israel Martin, a blacksmith, of Beverley, wanting a hand, engaged me to work at his business, and I remained with him two months, at eight dollars per month, board and lodging. From thence I went to Hambleton, and worked for David Dodge, blacksmith, three months, at nine dollars per month, board, &c. &c. From thence I went to Hipsidge, and worked with Amos Jones, blacksmith, five months, at ten dollars per month. From thence I returned to Hambleton, and was with John Adams, a farmer, and I laboured for six months on the farm. I went

---

* Now a noted yachting centre, Marblehead played a major role in the War of Independence and claims to be the 'Birthplace of the American Navy', from the time that privateers from this port were used to attack British supply ships.

thence to Whinham, and worked for Ziell Dodge, blacksmith, twelve months, at ten dollars per month.[11]

At this time Jeffery was unaware of the political storm that the story of his abandonment was causing in Britain. Sir Francis Burdett, a radical parliamentary reformer, would not let the matter rest. He was one of the two Members of Parliament for Westminster, the other being Captain Thomas Cochrane, who was on half-pay from the navy after being denied a role in the Walcheren expedition. On 15 February 1810 Burdett stood up in the House of Commons 'to call the attention of the House to a very interesting subject which he thought demanded their most serious consideration . . . that a sea-captain, in the British service, had been lately brought to trial by a court-martial, for a most unhuman act of wanton and deliberate barbarity towards a British seaman on board his own ship'.[12] Burdett was furious that Lake had been merely dismissed from the navy and asked whether the government 'meant to take any further steps upon a subject so disgraceful to the service, so materially interesting to the life and security of every seaman in his Majesty's fleet; a circumstance which, if so slightly passed over, might have the most serious effects in the naval service . . . for if such wanton tyrannical occurrences were once suffered to obtain with impunity, there would be an end of all order and good government in our fleets'.[13] In turn Samuel Whitbread, Member of Parliament for Bedford and another ardent reformer, expressed his outrage, saying that 'a case of more horrible cruelty could hardly be conceived. He had heard that sailors often find the approach of night dreadful, when their ship is sailing alone through the unknown seas: but what must have been the feeling of this unfortunate man, when, *on the approach of night*, he was left without provisions, or without clothes, alone on a *desolate* island?'[14]

On 6 April, three days after a major House of Commons debate on Jeffery, Burdett was found guilty of breach of privilege because of the language he had used in a letter to his Westminster electors, condemning the exclusion of reporters from the debates over the failed Walcheren expedition. It was voted to imprison him in the Tower of London, and crowds of supporters gathered around the Tower and in Piccadilly, where he lived. Violence broke out among the crowd in Piccadilly: 'The carriages of several Noblemen and Gentlemen . . . who, ignorant of the assemblage, drove that way, were assailed, and the windows of some of them were broken . . . About eight in the evening appearances became very alarming, nor was it long till the populace proceeded to various acts of outrage.'[15] They pelted the houses of many notable people with mud from the unpaved streets and broke their windows, as well as insisting 'that the inhabitants of Piccadilly and St. James-street should illuminate. Some refused and had their windows broken . . . The great majority, however, including the Club-houses, did illuminate; and these two streets were almost a blaze of light at 2 o'clock.'[16]

Governments were fearful of popular uprisings like this, and it was reported with great concern that 'the crowd at this time amounted to some thousands, extending through Piccadilly, beyond Berkeley-street, on the one side, and as far as Charles-street on the other. They employed themselves in compelling all persons who passed to do homage to them. The presence of the military did not prevent them from exacting this tribute. Such as refused to pull off their hats immediately were pelted with mud and dirt.'[17] Although the cavalry charged, resulting in many injuries, and the Riot Act was read, the disturbances continued, but Burdett was finally seized from his house on 9 April and taken to the Tower, only being released at the end of the parliamentary session in June.

In late April, after seeing a newspaper report about Jeffery, George Hassell, a merchant seaman, made a lengthy statement before the mayor of Liverpool, declaring that Jeffery was alive and well in America. A year earlier, while at the port of Beverly, to the north of Boston, 'he saw a person of the name of Jeffery, who, he understood, was by trade a blacksmith, with whom he had some conversation'.[18] Hassell added that 'Jeffery was well known in the neighbourhood of Marblehead and Beverley . . . and was generally called by the name of the "Governor of Sombrero," it being so notoriously known there that he had been put on shore by the order of the Captain of an English sloop of war.'[19]

The British consul at Boston arranged for Jeffery to set down his entire story, from his impressment at Falmouth to his rescue from Sombrero, and Jeffery signed this declaration with a cross, as was done by those who were illiterate. This report appeared in newspapers in Britain some weeks later, but his mother in Polperro was far from convinced, since she knew that her son could write and would have signed his name. To her this was further proof that he was dead. William Cobbett, the radical journalist who had published Burdett's letter about Walcheren that led to his time in the Tower, wrote a damning piece about the events surrounding Jeffery and urged that he should be brought home, declaring: 'There can be no reason for not doing it. The means are always at hand; and, there can be only one objection, which, indeed, may naturally occur: namely, that the poor fellow may be resolved never again to set his foot in England, or upon any land, or in any place or situation, where he may be exposed to the possibility of being again pressed on board an English ship of war.'[20] Cobbett was himself writing from Newgate Prison, where he had just started a two-year sentence for daring to criticise flogging within the army.

In America it was arranged for Jeffery to go to Halifax in Nova Scotia, and from here he was taken to England. On arriving at Portsmouth he was met by Samuel Whitbread, who wrote to Jeffery's mother: 'As you may not have heard the good tidings before this reaches you, I have the pleasure to inform you, that your son arrived at Spithead, in the *Thistle* schooner, yesterday. I have been on board her, and have seen him in good health and spirits; he says he has almost forgotten how to write, that he sent to you [a letter] by a friend of his from America some months ago—that he got his master to write the letter—that he made the deposition which you have seen, and put his mark to it.'[21] With the American ban on trade with Britain, it was a matter of chance whether letters reached their destination. In 1809, under the new president, James Madison, the extremely unpopular Embargo Act was replaced by one that permitted trade with all countries except France and Britain, and the following year this was replaced by a trade ban on Britain alone when France promised to repeal its own decrees against America.

Jeffery was ordered to the Admiralty in London and was given his discharge from the navy and all arrears of pay. He admitted that 'he had signed his *mark*, because it is the usual practice of seamen to do so, it being the least trouble'.[22] A representative from the Lake family next persuaded him to sign a paper not to prosecute Captain Lake, in return for which he was given £600. He then travelled to Polperro, in the company of a clerk appointed by the Lake family, in order to ensure his safe arrival with such a large sum of money. 'My mother,' Jeffery related, 'had been informed of my arrival only about half an hour before she saw me; and to describe this meeting is more than I can do. Suffice it to say, that when I saw my dear *parent*—we rushed into each other's arms, and I wept aloud . . . Neighbours and friends now flocked in, shaking me by the hand, and, with tears of joy, congratulated me on my deliverance.'[23] The following day his mother received one of two letters that Jeffery had written to her long ago from America – the other one never reached her.

Apart from the cloud over the incident with Jeffery on Sombrero, by early 1810 the situation in the West Indies was looking good for Britain. Naval supremacy there had been secured, and this also had a beneficial effect on trade with the East, because ships sailing to India and the East Indies from Britain would, at some point, be blown westwards. This was simply because they were dependent on prevailing winds for their speed. Whether they were bound for the West Indies or the East Indies, ships from Britain usually set a southerly course at least as far as the Cape Verde islands, off the west coast of Africa. Up to this point prevailing winds were from the west, but further south ships ran into the area of variable and unreliable winds around the equator. They tried to cross this region as quickly as possible, since they could become becalmed for days or even weeks and run dangerously short of supplies. South of this region, known as 'the doldrums', ships picked up the south-east trade winds, which blew them west towards the Caribbean and South America – a problem for ships sailing to India and the East.

The trade winds or 'trades' are steady, reliable winds that occur north and south of the equator from about the 30th parallel, and are caused by the rapidly rising hot air above the equator sucking in air from north and south. The rotation of the earth gives this air a direction, producing steady westerly winds north of the equator and easterly winds to the south. The name 'trade winds' derived from the fact that sailing merchant ships relied on them for a rapid voyage, and Basil Hall, an experienced naval officer of that time, pointed out that they were impossible to ignore: 'These vast currents of air, which sweep round and round the globe in huge strips of more than twelve hundred miles in width, are in a manner forced, more or less, on everyone's notice, from contributing essentially to that boundless interchange of the productions of distant regions by which modern times are so agreeably distinguished from the old.'[24] Outside the trades, winds were more variable, although immediately north and south of the trades the winds could generally be relied on to be westerly. Even routes relying on these westerlies could be locally disrupted by tides and currents, and seamen knew very well that the quickest route between two places was seldom the shortest – only for very short journeys were shipping routes a straight line.

For ships bound for the East and caught in the south-east trades, it was necessary to edge south while being blown westwards, in order to pick up westerly winds again. Since time was the important factor, rather than distance, it did not matter how far west the ships travelled – once into the westerly winds, it was usually straightforward sailing back across the

Atlantic and round the tip of South Africa before heading north again towards India. Some ships paused for a few days at a port in the West Indies or South America for fresh water or supplies, but even if they did not, this westerly leg of their journey had previously put them in danger from privateers operating from French colonies in the West Indies. With these bases now denied to them, the threat from the privateers gradually diminished.

Passing through the doldrums and the south-east trades was only the start of the problems for ships heading east. The pattern of prevailing winds in the Indian Ocean is seasonal, blowing from the south-west between April and September and from the north-east between October and March, so that ships from Britain aimed to arrive there in early summer and sailed for home in the autumn. Although the winds in the northern hemisphere did not impose such rigid restrictions, to make best use of prevailing winds ships tended to set sail from Britain for North America in the latter half of the summer, while those headed for the Caribbean and South America departed in midwinter. This seasonal rhythm of the sailing of merchant vessels to and from Britain made them predictable, and therefore extremely vulnerable to enemy warships and privateers.

With journey times between Britain and India averaging six months, and sailing times dictated by seasonal wind patterns, it was all but impossible to carry out instructions from Britain that might be many months out of date when they arrived in India. Consequently East India Company employees in India enjoyed a great deal of autonomy, while the Company itself struggled to control them by letters from London. This led to many dubious transactions and outright corruption and fraud, but even with legitimate trading there were widespread opportunities for profit, and many East India Company officials were extremely wealthy by the time they returned home. By 1810 the East India Company had become an agent of government, no longer relying on trade but on the collection of taxes. Large swathes of what is now divided into India and Pakistan were ruled by the Company through conquest or indirectly through alliances with hundreds of small states ruled by Indian princes. The Company relied on its substantial army of mainly native troops in India, but further east, as far as China, they had made few territorial gains and here they depended on their own navy and the Royal Navy to keep open the sea lanes for trade. For now, the Company had a monopoly on trade with India and China, and tea was of immense importance.

In his expedition to Egypt in 1798 Napoleon had already made one serious attempt to threaten Britain's hold on India, and there was always the possibility that he would try again. French officers and agents helped those Indian states actively opposed to the spread of British rule, and the Dutch, allies of France, still had colonies in the East Indies that provided bases for French ships and potentially for an attack on India itself. To counter this a fleet of British ships was kept in East Indian waters with instructions to blockade the Dutch settlements in the islands. This was an extremely difficult task with so few vessels, and in 1809 the commander in charge of this blockade, Rear-Admiral William O'Brien Drury, decided to shorten the odds, as he later explained to the Admiralty:

In consequence of His Majesty's Order in Council, and their Lordship's directions to put the Island of Java and the Moluccas [islands] under the most rigid state of blockade, I endeavoured to effect it with the few ships that could be spared from India; but finding it impossible to cover such an extent of coast, so as to answer the purpose of annoying or distressing the enemy to any extent, I judged it would best be done, by seizing upon the principal settlement in the Eastern Islands, securing their shipping and valuable crops of the Moluccas, and thereby fulfilling the intention of the blockade in a great degree, and at the least risk to the commercial and political interests of India.[25]

Just as East India Company personnel had great freedom to act on their own initiative, so did the commanders of the British Navy in eastern waters, and by the time Drury's dispatch, with his explanation of why he had attacked a particular island, arrived at the Admiralty, the Dutch had lost almost all their bases in the Moluccan Islands.

Drury had come out to the East Indies at the beginning of 1808 to serve under Edward Pellew. By then Pellew was again sole commander, no longer sharing the territory with Troubridge, who had instead been ordered to the Cape of Good Hope. In January 1807 Troubridge had left Madras, still in the forty-six-year-old warship *Blenheim* in which he had sailed from England with Mary Sherwood's convoy. He took with him the frigate *Java* and the sloop *Harriet*. At the beginning of March, off Madagascar, the *Blenheim* and *Java* were lost with all hands in a terrible hurricane.

When Pellew went home in early 1809, Drury took over as commander-in-chief. In the autumn of 1809 he sent Captain Edward Tucker with the frigates *Dover* and *Cornwallis*, the sloop *Samarang* and two companies of troops from the native regiments of India to attack the Dutch on the island of Amboyna (now Ambon). Tucker's force anchored off Amboyna on 9 December and began the attack on the 16th, using the ships to shield and hide a landing party of troops and marines in boats until the last possible moment. Pretending to sail away from the island, he allowed his ships to drift within reach of the chosen landing place, then turned and engaged the Dutch forts and gun batteries while the landing party stormed ashore. As these drove the Dutch and the native troops from their fortifications, a further force of seamen and marines with two small field guns was landed. An officer belonging to this second party sent an anonymous report to the *Calcutta Gazette*:

The party I belonged to had to perform a most fatiguing march, and a worse one I never made, with a view of gaining the height over the second battery. We succeeded in these points beyond our most sanguine expectation. The Dutch officers have since told us, we completely surprised them, they never could bring themselves to believe that so small a force would ever make even an attempt. On our appearing on the heights, they deserted the battery, and much about the same time the two batteries near the sea. We had now command of Fort Victoria [in range of the battery's guns], and amused ourselves next morning firing at Mynheer, his shells only reaching in return to the face of the hill, much to our comfort.[26]

By the end of that day much of the island was in British hands, and the Dutch stronghold of Victoria Castle was invited to surrender, which was done on the 19th. The island formally passed into British hands in mid-February 1810, but in the meantime Tucker mopped up Dutch outposts and strongholds on nearby islands, as well as capturing Dutch shipping in the area. It had all been deceptively easy, and certainly the Dutch authorities thought so: the Dutch commander was subsequently tried for treachery on Java and shot.

Amboyna was the headquarters of the Dutch in the Moluccas, and by May most of their settlements in the islands were in British hands, with the exception of Banda Neira, Ternate and a few outposts. Tucker's forces were now badly stretched and potentially vulnerable to a counterattack, so Rear-Admiral Drury instructed Captain Christopher Cole to sail with reinforcements from Madras. Captain Cole, from Marazion in Cornwall, had spent most of his naval career in the West Indies. He had more seniority than Tucker, and according to Cole's unpublished narrative of the expedition, he himself approached Drury and persuaded him to allow an attack on Banda Neira, or any other Dutch stronghold on the way to Amboyna. However it came about, Cole was given a very free hand to act, and he wanted to achieve something on his own account during the voyage. His ship, the frigate *Caroline*, was accompanied by another frigate, the *Piedmontaise*, the brig *Barracouta* and the transport brig *Mandarin*. The reinforcements that they carried were a hundred officers and men of the Madras European Regiment, while the *Mandarin* carried supplies and specie.

The ships sailed from Madras on 10 May, and soon Cole told Captain Charles Foote of the *Piedmontaise* and Captain Richard Kenah of the *Barracouta* about his intentions. Cole was determined to capture one of the spice islands because, as he said, 'it did not appear to me that any of the smaller possessions of the enemy would give us that credit which is so naturally looked forward to, from the successful issue of a service of this nature'.[27] After ten days' sailing they reached the island of Penang, in the Strait of Malacca between Sumatra and Malaya. Here the ships took on twenty artillery men, two field guns and twenty scaling ladders, but although Cole was able to question various people who had lived on Banda Neira, he was disappointed in not being able to obtain a map or plan of the island. He moved on from Penang on 10 June, sailing south-east down the Strait of Malacca, and five days later, off Singapore, he met Captain Richard Spencer in the sloop *Samarang*. Spencer had been with Tucker at Amboyna, and Cole was told by him that a record of the Dutch garrison of Banda Neira 'had been found at the capture of Amboyna and it stated the force at Banda to amount to more than seven hundred regular troops. Captn. Spencer seemed surprized at my determination to attempt the reduction of Banda before we were reinforced, and gave me all the information he had obtained by his active exertions under Captain Tucker.'[28]

Undaunted by Spencer's scepticism, Cole continued south-east, but on the 25th he was forced to halt off the coast of Borneo while repairs were made to the mainmast of the *Piedmontaise*, which had been struck by lightning. Because of the information from Spencer, Cole had decided to break off from the usual route and thread his way through unfamiliar waters to try to gain an element of surprise. He recorded that 'being anxious to get forward, and fearful that Daendels the Dutch Captain-General of Java and the Moluccas might by unusual exertions succeed in getting supplies and reinforcements thrown into Banda, before my arrival in that quarter, I was induced to try the passage between Borneo and Malwalli to enable us to get the quicker into the Sooloo Sea'.[29] It was reasonable to expect that once he heard about the capture of Amboyna, General Daendels, the Governor based on Java, would take steps to reinforce the remaining Dutch possessions, but the route that Cole was proposing to take was dangerous, because he was literally sailing into the unknown.

The first Europeans to explore the East Indies were the Portuguese and the Dutch, followed by the Spanish and the French. As part of the attempts to preserve their own footholds in the region, the sailors of these nations tended to keep any maps and charts to themselves, and the British, as relative newcomers, found it extremely difficult to obtain reliable information. To Cole, the route he proposed to follow, up the west and north coasts of Borneo and into the Sulu Sea, was a voyage through uncharted waters. It was to be more nerve-racking than he expected:

The passage proved the most dangerous I had ever navigated. The coral reefs were innumerable, and most of them but just covered with water, and not easily seen until the sun had risen considerably above the horizon. Our pilot had overrated his knowledge of this part of the navigation, but by an unceasing good look out, and strict attention, in the course of forty eight hours we had nearly cleared the shoals called by Dalrymple 'Felicia Proper' and the pilot had reported the ship past all danger, when we discovered a ship which had been recently wrecked on a coral reef just below the water's edge and directly ahead of us. The wreck was surrounded by piratical proas*, which fled at our approach. I went in my boat to examine the shoal and the wreck, and we found the deck of the latter streaming with blood that had been recently shed, and locks of human hair in many places, which proved that there had been a severe contest about the plunder. The *Piedmontaise* which had been ordered to proceed on, with the *Mandarin* in tow, whilst I examined the wreck, now made the signal for shoals in every direction between the NE, and SE; and the approach of night and the discovery of those shoals immediately in our track, obliged me to return to the ship, without pursuing the proas.[30]

As darkness fell, the *Barracouta* continued sailing, followed by the *Caroline*, but not without difficulty as Cole recorded:

---

* 'Proa' is a general Malayan word for 'ship' that was used by Europeans for a pirate vessel. Usually they were powered by a large triangular sail and carried an outrigger for stability.

In joining the *Piedmontaise*, the *Barracouta* was several times nearly on the rocks, but Captain Kenah's activity and perseverance carried her safe through every difficulty, and was of infinite service to the *Caroline* in her progress. At 6 in the evening we saw the small islands off the S.W. end of Cagayan Sooloo [now Cagayan de Tawi-Tawi]; and as the only directions published for the Sooloo Sea, mention the probability of a ship's being to the Easterrd [easternward] of the shoals on the NE coast of Borneo when these islands are in sight, I decided on running on, instead of anchoring and remaining quiet until the morning. The ships were put under easy sail, and the *Barracouta* leading was directed to steer a course for the night; and the other ships followed in her track. The night which was dark, rainy, and squally, was passed by all the ships in sounding, as quick as the lead could be sent to the bottom, and in momentary expectation of the signal for danger; but the small island of Manbahenawen [Mambahenauhan] close to us in the morning, gave some respite to our anxieties, for it assured us that our greatest difficulties were passed.[31]

The next problem was one of supplies, and so on 5 July, as Cole related, the ships

anchored at Sooloo [Sulu], where we obtained supplies of water, fresh meat, and vegetables in abundance, and many fair promises of friendship and amity from the Sultan. I thought it right to tell him my principal business in that quarter was to protect the merchants, and to punish all piratical proceedings, for the inhabitants of the smaller islands in this immense archipelago are addicted to the most cruel piratical warfare, and His Majesty of Sooloo is in some measure implicated in their proceedings. To give our force a more imposing appearance the *Barracouta* was converted [from a brig] into a ship, and as the alteration was made between daylight and breakfast, it occasioned no small surprise amongst the ignorant natives, and many inquiries from the Sultan whose fears induced him to give me a salute of thirteen guns, when I paid my visit of ceremony.[32]

What the crew of the *Barracouta* had done was to change the appearance of the ship overnight, since a brig had only two masts and a distinctly different pattern of sails from a ship. It seemed to the Sultan that one vessel had left, to be replaced by another, leaving him in doubt as to how large a force Cole had at his command.

After four days Cole set sail again, heading east into the Pacific, and was in sight of New Guinea by the 21st. He then turned southwards towards the island of Seram, which is due north of Amboyna and within easy distance of Banda Neira, but contrary winds and currents slowed his progress. The time was spent in preparing for the assault on Banda Neira, as he explained:

During our tedious passage the seamen had been constantly exercised in the use of the musket, pike, and pistol, and the scaling ladders were placed against the masts, and the men were practised in ascending them quickly with their arms [weapons] in their hands. Every arrangement had been made that seemed necessary to ensure success. Our men were in the highest health and spirits, and not a death had happened since our departure from Madras. The general orders for the attack had not only been delivered to the leaders of divisions, but they were read repeatedly to the men by the respective officers, and the greatest confidence and cheerfulness prevailed. The necessity of silence and steadiness, in the event of our making a night attack, was strongly enforced, and the most prompt and severe punishment held out against plunder and straggling.[33]

On 7 August the ships reached the island of Seram, after something of an epic voyage without adequate charts, through dangerous waters studded with islands. By taking this circuitous northern route, rather than heading south past Java, Cole had stayed clear of the usual sea lanes and avoided all the Dutch outposts so that no early warning would be sent to the garrison of Banda Neira. At Seram Cole picked up 'two Malay guides who professed to know the roads and situations of the batteries on Banda-Neira'[34] and continued on his way. The next day the ships made a stealthy approach towards their target and began preparations for the assault:

The weather on the 8th was very fine, with a haze round the horizon that favoured our near approach; and the ships were kept under easy sail [minimum area of sails spread for their required speed], to prevent as much as possible their being discovered before dark, as it was my intention to push the ships in suddenly against the batteries a little before daylight on the following morning. This day was occupied in making our final preparations; and at 2 o'clock all the boats were hoisted out, and the ammunition and provisions put into them. At 5 the ships were brought to, and at ½ past the small island of Rosengen became just visible through the haze . . . Great Banda appeared at the distance of ten or eleven leagues. My final orders were now given to

Captains Foote and Kenah, and after having told the men whom I had selected from the *Caroline*'s ship's crew to accompany me, how much I expected from them, the ships bore up for the lee point of Great Banda.[35]

They now suffered the first setback to their risky plan:

At 9 two shot were fired at us from the island of Rosengen, which was unexpected, for I never had received the smallest intimation of an out-post being there, and the night had become beautifully fine, with clear moonlight. My intention therefore of pushing the ships in against the batteries so as [to] produce any thing like a surprise, was frustrated, for the guns from Rosengen I concluded would alarm the islands, and my mind became naturally very anxious as to the result of any attack that might be made in open day against the enemy, whose force and means were so very superior to the strength of the little squadron under my orders.[36]

Around ten o'clock the moon set, and about three hundred officers and men clambered into the boats in the dark. As the boats headed for the shore, to be followed by the ships, the weather became squally, and although the rising storm gave them cover, it also made navigation difficult, as Cole explained:

My great object in venturing on this attempt was to get the place with the least possible loss. The badness of the weather and darkness of the night, which had increased to a very great degree, made it impossible for the boats to keep together in the open sea, and before their departure from the ships, they were directed to rendezvous, within and under the lee of the point of Great Banda. After a pull of two hours in a light gig towing two scaling ladders which the heavy boats had left behind them, I reached the point; and we found ourselves in smooth water, which gave us some relief, for the boat had been nearly stove to pieces several times, in our progress to the shore. The night was now so dark, that we could not see half the boat's length from us; and after pulling about in every direction two hours more, my anxiety may be conceived upon finding that Kenah in his gig was the only one of the party near me. We could not hail loudly for fear of being discovered, for our boats were nearly touching the bushes, and we had reason to believe that a battery must be close at hand. About three in the morning the ships appeared pushing past the point of rendezvous. They could not be seen until they were within an hundred yards of us; and I immediately went alongside the

*Piedmontaise*, told Captain Foote of our mortifications, and expressed my apprehensions that the night was too far advanced for us to meet the boats in time, when he answered that he was certain he had passed some of them, at a short distance from us. We pulled immediately in the direction pointed out, and in a few minutes I communicated with the boats he had seen, and explained to the officers and men, that we had not a moment to lose.[37]

The problems the boats had encountered in finding the rendezvous had seriously delayed the schedule of the attack, but soon they were in sight of the island. Fires were visible on the north point, and Cole interpreted this as a camp of troops who had been moved there to strengthen a known weak spot in the island's defences. He hoped that these troops had been taken from the main town and fort which he was proposing to attack, and with the storm now upon them, Cole ordered the boats to pull quickly for the shore. He described the scene from the boats:

A dark cloud at this moment rested itself on the mountains of Great Banda, and the rain falling heavy and thick gave the water in the harbour the appearance of one sheet of fire, undisturbed by the splashing of the oars, or the track of the boats. I could not help remarking to Lieutt. Pratt my Aid de Camp, and who accompanied me in my small boat, that although we were all wet and cold, the cloud was a cloak best suited to our necessities, and that it seemed a shield sent to us by Providence. We both agreed that the cloud would be a more effectual cover to our landing than any force we could have looked to, to help us, and that we should never see a black cloud again without thinking of this moment, and making it our 'obeisance'. About half past four the boats grounded on a coral reef at some little distance from the shore, and we thought we distinguished a battery to the left of us. Had the enemy discovered us at this moment, our party must have been cut to pieces even before they had reached the shore; but not the least confusion ensued and the boats were silently and coolly extricated from this trying situation, and at last struck the shore of Banda Neira . . .The cloud had accompanied us, and bursting, threw out a thousand forked lightnings, with quick peals of heavy thunder, and a deluge of rain.[38]

Once on shore they found that the Malay guides were useless, and Cole commented that 'the Malays are naturally very superstitious, and the circumstances of the weather had impressed them with the idea that evil spirits were working against us, and they had once or twice intimated that we ought to put back, and afterwards observed, that none but Englishmen or Devils would go forward'.[39] The weather had prevented them knowing where they had landed, but they soon found that they had rowed in right under the guns of a shore battery and so made hasty preparations for attack. Divided into two parties, the men took the battery with only moments to spare because 'the enemy had seen the ships a few minutes before, and an adjutant had just arrived with orders to open fire upon them. The muskets of the guard had been placed under a shed out of the rain, and the adjutant, and officer, and fifty men were surprised standing at the guns with matches lighted. They were instantly locked into the guard-room, and a party of twelve seamen left in charge.'[40]

Having landed without any effective opposition, they set off for the main stronghold, known as Castle Belgica, below which was a town. They soon found a local man to guide them and made their way towards the castle as rapidly as possible, as Cole recorded:

We had succeeded in seizing on a native as a guide, and as several of the Madras Europn. Regt. were Dutchmen or Germans, and many of our men spoke the Malay language, we had no difficulty in explaining to the native that he must instantly guide us by the shortest way to the Castle of Belgica. With a Pistol at each ear, to put him to death if he failed, and the promise of a handsome reward if he succeeded, he was led on to show us the shortest route, and our movement round the town was as rapid as possible, for the sound of the bugle told us the burghers were alarmed, and the militia assembling. A death-like silence was preserved whilst we passed the houses in the town, and the slaves who had just risen to their daily labour were heard laughing and conversing: and four native soldiers passed us, who taking us for a division of their own men faced about, and saluted.[41]

Cole's force had been split into three, the advance party, the centre and the reserve, and it took them about twenty minutes to thread their way up through the town to the castle above. As they came over the brow of the hill dawn was just breaking, and the castle was visible about a hundred yards away. They attacked immediately:

The scaling ladders were placed before the sentries challenged, and our guide was now suffered to make his escape. The outer work was escaladed in an instant, and a soldier was killed at the alarm bell, with the rope in his hand. The enemy opened a fire of musketry from the upper work, and three guns were fired, but in the confusion, they were fired from the opposite side of the angle which was escaladed. The musketry was smartly returned by the Reserve and part of the Centre who were placed among some bushes and underwood near the brink of the ditch, and who were directed to fire at the embrasures. The fire from our party was so well directed, that the attempts of the enemy to point guns at us were frustrated, except one gun pointed at the spot where some of us were standing, loaded with langridge, which had a match put to it twice, and at last burned [the] priming [without going off]. It would have occasioned great loss to us had it been fired; and I mention these circumstances, trifling in themselves, to point out more strongly our extreme good fortune.[42]

The castle, which was proving stronger than expected, was described by Cole as:

on a hill which has on three sides a gradual ascent, and the fourth side is abrupt and covered with bushes and shrubs, and had we known the exact nature of the position, this side would have been chosen for our operations. The work is of solid masonry, and is a regular pentagon. The outer wall is sixteen feet high, and had formerly a dry ditch round it, but from having been neglected the ditch is nearly filled up. There are six heavy guns on each angle . . . making in all thirty guns on the outer work. The inner walls are twenty four feet high and five guns in embrasures on each face, and the angles crowned by round towers thirty two feet from the ground. This work has twenty five guns, principally, twelve and nine pounders, on it, and the whole is bomb-proof. I believe no work could be better calculated to resist an escalade, and the enemy's numbers in Belgica exceeded our own.[43]

This was the kind of detailed information that had been desperately needed before the attack but had been impossible to obtain. Having climbed over the outer wall they found the ladders too short for the inner wall, and the gateways appeared too strong. Since this was their last hope of success, they ran for the gateways and their good luck continued, as Cole reported:

At the instant before our two parties reached the gateways, the Coll. [colonel] Commander with two officers and his orderlies, had, by running hard up the hill from his house which was at the bottom of it, arrived at the gates, and ordered them to be opened for his admittance. A desperate rush was made through the gateways, the guard was overpowered in an instant, and the Colonel and a few others fell after a short resistance. Numbers of the enemy precipitated themselves over the outer work, and we gained the interior of the inner work without further opposition, but even now a few hand grenadoes would have driven us out, for we could not find the staircases in the bomb-proofs, and there were numbers of grenadoes found ready fused in all directions afterwards on the walls, but the enemy were panic-struck, and allowed us to plant the ladders, and to scale the walls from the inside unmolested. Three hearty cheers were given, and I received the swords of four officers under the flag-staff on the upper walls.[44]

By attacking during the darkest part of the night and during the blinding violence of a tropical storm, Cole and his party of about 180 men had taken the main stronghold of Banda Neira in the face of overwhelming odds. Now, with the storm having just passed and the sun rising, Cole took a moment to reflect on the view of the island spread out below him:

The clouds were fast dispersing, and with day-light appeared the beams of the rising sun, which dispelled the vapours in the valleys, and discovered to us the whole of our situation. Some minutes were taken up in wonder, and admiration of the sublime scenery around us. The high hills, separated by deep ravines, were richly wooded to the very summits by a variety of the finest forest trees, which in some places appeared to take root in the ponderous masses of brown rock that broke through the surface of rich and varied foliage. Foo nong Appee, a volcanic mountain, vomited forth columns of smoke in quick succession, and the Signal Hill, high above us, and within the range of shells, fired guns of alarm. The nutmeg parks of Great Banda, and Banda-Neira were full in view, and afforded a beautiful contrast of cultivated scenery, to the grander features of nature which had first caught our attention; and Fort Nassau, several sea batteries, the town, and public buildings, lay at our feet. Neither of the ships were to be seen, and it was evident that the violence of the weather had driven them from the mouth of the harbour, and had also separated many of the boats to such a distance from the island that we could not reckon on their co-operation for many hours to come.[45]

Cole soon recovered from his reverie, for he realised it was essential to maintain the momentum of the attack before the Dutch had time to regroup and realise just how small the British force was that opposed them. He sent Captain Kenah to Fort Nassau to demand an immediate surrender from the Governor, carrying a sailor's shirt as an improvised flag of truce because they had brought no white flag with them. The lack of proper flags threatened to jeopardise the British success, for the English flag that had been hoisted over Castle Belgica was small, and the troops in Fort Nassau and the shore batteries did not seem to have noticed it. The *Caroline* frigate was now approaching the harbour and was within range of the Dutch guns. From the castle, Cole observed the ship:

She came in most majestically, and her gradual approach, inch by inch I may say, round a bluff point, was beautiful. Although she was hulled by the enemy's fire, she did not return a shot. The truce flag had been hoisted also, under the British Colours at Belgica, but it was instantly hauled down, and a shot fired, which fell into the centre of the nearest battery, and the enemy in the distant batteries turned round with dismay at this unexpected warning; nor had they, I believe, until this moment a thorough idea of their situation. Kenah had returned with the verbal submission of the Governor, but as the Dutch Colours were still flying in Nassau, and there was a great degree of hesitation in the Governor's conduct, I ordered Captain Nixon with the reserve and a few seamen to take charge of Belgica, and the remainder of the party to be ready with the scaling ladders at an instant, to follow me to the storm of Nassau; but observing great confusion in the batteries, and fearing that much blood might be shed if our anger was then let loose, I dispatched Kenah again to the Governor, to say that I should storm Fort Nassau in five minutes, if the Colours were not immediately hauled down, and that as the batteries had fired at the ship when the truce flag was flying, I could not answer for the consequences of our indignation. The colours were immediately struck, and just in time to prevent the broadside of the *Caroline*, which had now anchored, from sweeping the town.[46]

With the harbour under British control, Cole now felt secure since they could be reinforced from the ships. He considered their good luck: 'I looked round and saw my fine fellows about me, with scarcely a hurt that they would call a wound, and the fatigues and labours of the night crowned by complete success. A general feeling prevailed of the many wonderful circumstances that had occurred during the night to manifest the hand of Providence in our favour.'[47] In the following days the Dutch outposts also gave up, and Cole took the formal surrender of Banda Neira. He noted the ironic contrast between the two groups at this ceremony: 'The Dutchmen were in full dress, "Gold buttons, Small Swords, Cockd

Hats", &c. &c. but their countenances betrayed the sorrow and uneasiness of their minds. To give an idea of our appearance I will describe my own; an old round hat, a round jacket with epaulettes discoloured by bilge-water on it, a silk handkerchief round my waist with pistols stuck in it, and a dragoon sword with a brass scabbard by my side, completed my equip-ment, and finished a portrait more like Blackbeard the pirate, than a captain of a man of war.'[48]

The naval historian William James, writing a few years afterwards, was exultant in his praise of an enterprise that was more a speculative adven-ture of exploration than a well-calculated naval operation: 'Viewed in every light, the taking of the Banda isles was an achievement of no common order. Where are we to find, even in the annals of the British navy, more skill and perseverance than was employed in overcoming the difficulties of the navigation to the scene of conquest? Or where a greater share of address and valour, than was displayed by Captain Cole and his 180 brave associates, more than three fourths of them seamen and marines, in the crowning act of their bold exploit?'[49]

For his courage, skill and sheer good luck, Captain Cole was awarded a gold medal by the Admiralty and was knighted. The capture of Banda Neira and its associated islands brought Britain one step closer to domi-nation of the East Indies. The French islands of Mauritius (Île de France) off the east coast of Africa were captured at the end of 1810. These had provided bases from which warships and privateers could prey on home-ward-bound convoys from the East, so this threat had been removed. Captain Tucker followed up his success at Amboyna by an attack on Ternate, the last Moluccan island in Dutch hands. After a fierce fight the island was taken in August 1810. Now only Java remained in Dutch hands.

——— • ◆ • ———

# SEVENTEEN

# TRIUMPH AND TRAGEDY

If I Had an edication
I'd sing your praise more large
But I'm only a common foremast Jack
On board of le *Volage*

> A verse described by Byron, a passenger in the frigate *Volage*, as 'a
> mouthful of Saltwater poetry, by a Tar on the late Lissa Victory'[1]

Despite setbacks in the East, Napoleon was still considering reviving his conquest eastwards. He needed control of the Adriatic, since otherwise the British could land an army there and cut off his lines of communication and retreat. He also needed the Adriatic in order to dominate the Mediterranean again. The island of Corfu was already in French hands, and he controlled the ships and shipyards of Venice, as well as the port of Ancona to the south, so that by late 1810 his naval force in the Adriatic was superior in fire-power to the small squadron of British ships stationed there – the frigates *Amphion*, *Active* and *Cerberus* and the sloop *Acorn*. Napoleon decided that the British must be swept from the Adriatic, and he appointed one of his best naval commanders, Captain Bernard Dubourdieu, to take a French squadron to reinforce that of the Venetians and drive the British back into the Mediterranean.

After an exciting early life Dubourdieu had a reputation for professionalism and daring. He was one of very few French officers who had fought and taken a British frigate – the *Proserpine* in 1809. Although only thirty-seven, already he had been awarded the Cross of the Legion of Honour for his successes in the Mediterranean. He would soon be facing the British commander Captain William Hoste, who at the age of thirty also had a successful career behind him. As a protégé of Nelson, Hoste had been a young lieutenant at the Battle of the Nile, but narrowly missed Trafalgar. He had also served under Sir Sidney Smith and later Collingwood, who gave him command of the Adriatic.

In the autumn of 1810 Hoste learned that Dubourdieu had arrived in the Adriatic and was based at the Italian port of Ancona, and from that time there was a series of cat-and-mouse maneouvres and skirmishes between the two squadrons. The British ships were based at the island of Lissa (now Vis) off modern Croatia. This coast, like that of Italy opposite, was also under French control: Lissa was a precarious British foothold in the region. Donat Henchy O'Brien, who as a midshipman had escaped from Bitche in September 1808 and was picked up two months later by Hoste's frigate, the *Amphion*, was now a lieutenant on board that ship. O'Brien described how they went looking for Dubourdieu's squadron:

[On] reconnoitring Ancona on 17th October, we found that all our birds had escaped. Instantly every stitch of canvass that could be of use was spread, and our course was for Corfu . . . We fell in with a Sicilian privateer, that informed us she had just been chased by the enemy, who were steering for Corfu . . . In fact, the treacherous Sicilian had deceived us, and on the very day on which this ally had given us the false information, the French commodore having learned from a fisherman that the English squadron was on a cruise, entered Port St. George, landed troops, committed great havoc and devastation, destroyed our prizes, took away three neutral ships that we had detained, and steered for Ancona.[2]

Port St George was the anchorage at Lissa, and while Hoste was elsewhere Dubourdieu led this daring raid on 22 October – the day after the fifth anniversary of Trafalgar. In the absence of effective opposition, the French spent six hours recapturing the prize ships anchored there and driving the British shore parties into the hills. By the time Hoste returned, the French had retreated to the safety of their base at Ancona. Like Hoste, O'Brien was stung by the French success: 'This was a bitter drug of disappointment, and none felt it more severely than our gallant captain. I dined with him that day, and saw the big drop trickle down his manly cheek.'[3]

The raid was hailed as a great victory in French-controlled Europe, and the *Moniteur* newspaper enhanced it by twisting the facts to state that 'the

English squadron, though superior to the French in force and numbers, had most sedulously avoided measuring strength with it'.[4] Hoste realised that the version of events reported in the *Moniteur* would reach Britain before his dispatches, and on top of this humiliation he found out that Collingwood, who had died on 7 March 1810, was being succeeded as commander-in-chief of the Mediterranean by Admiral Sir Charles Cotton. Collingwood had been ill for some time. He had been almost continuously at sea since he sailed from Britain in 1804, and had not seen his wife and family since then. After Trafalgar he had inherited the Mediterranean command from Nelson, carrying it out efficiently and conscientiously, despite his failing health. Without his dedication and expertise in maintaining the blockades, the French ships in Mediterranean ports may well have managed to regroup and pose a significant threat once again.

In Collingwood, Hoste had lost one more link with Nelson, and even before Dubourdieu's raid, he was weary of the war: 'If ever I should (and why should I not?) get quietly home, and this war is past, I think the measure of my happiness will be to remain an easy, plodding, country farmer, with all my friends around me. I am almost tired of this unsociable life, but I have no right to complain, and must rough it through.'[5] Hoste suspected that Cotton might order him back to England, but he was retained because his experience in the Adriatic was valued. Captain George Eyre in the battleship *Magnificent* became his superior, but Hoste still had a great deal of freedom of operation, and his three frigates and a sloop were boosted by the addition of the frigate *Volage*.

After his raid Dubourdieu waited for further reinforcements before attempting a decisive assault on Lissa and the British. Hoste and his squadron continued to harass shipping, but on 12 March 1811 Hoste's ships began to leave Lissa, intending to sail to Dubourdieu's base at Ancona the next day and perhaps tempt the French into battle. As dawn broke on the 13th, the British were confronted by a forest of masts from ten warships accompanied by a gunboat. On board the *Amphion* O'Brien could see that 'they were not much more than a mile off Port St. George. The force of our long-sought enemy, whom we immediately recognised, was ascertained to be six ships, a brig, a schooner, xebec, and two gun-boats; certainly a very superior number – the disparity, to all appearance, overwhelming: but, strange to say, there was not a soul in the *Amphion*, from the chief down, who did not anticipate a complete victory: and I have been informed since, that the same feeling prevailed throughout the other ships.'[6]

Of the six ships O'Brien mentioned, five were frigates and one a schooner, with only one gunboat, not two, but it was still the largest enemy fleet that had been seen in the Adriatic. Dubourdieu had put together a force of French and Venetian frigates to deal with Hoste's squadron, and his smaller ships carried some five hundred troops to destroy the British base on Lissa itself. Hoste's squadron was outnumbered in both ships and cannons, and Dubourdieu had been training his crews intensively over the previous months. Despite this they still could not hope to match the skill and expertise of the British sailors, who were so confident of victory against the odds.

The British ships formed a line of battle, but the French were intending to break this line in two places, in an echo of Nelson at Trafalgar, to create a confused mêlée. Dubourdieu, with his crews outnumbering the British, wanted to create conditions in which Hoste's ships could be boarded. O'Brien watched as the French and Venetian ships approached:

Dubourdieu . . . was bearing down in two divisions to attack us. He, leading the starboard, or weather-one, in the *Favorita* [*Favorite*], a large frigate, followed by the *Flora* [*Flore*], *Bellona*, and *Mercure* brig; that of the lee was led by the *Danaë*, followed by the *Corona*, *Caroline* [*Carolina*], and small craft. Our ships were in a very compact line-ahead, the *Amphion*, *Active*, *Cerberus*, and *Volage*, having every sail set, that we might close as soon as possible. When nearly within gunshot, Captain Hoste telegraphed 'Remember Nelson!' which was answered by three loud cheers from the crews of our squadron, who manned the rigging on the occasion.[7]

The coming battle was to be a struggle for control of the Adriatic, but on top of that it was a matter of pride for Hoste, who felt he had been denied the opportunity of retaliation after the humiliation of Dubourdieu's raid on Port St George five months earlier. Now he had his chance, and as his commodore's pendant was unfurled from the *Amphion*'s mainmast, O'Brien said that he 'cried out most emphatically "There goes the pride of my heart!"'[8] The *Amphion* then tried a ranging shot, which just fell short of the bow of the leading ship, and within a few minutes a furious battle began. The seamanship of the British made it impossible for any enemy vessel to pass between them, and the ferocious gunfire they maintained prevented Dubourdieu breaking the line. Instead he attempted to swing alongside and board the *Amphion*, as O'Brien recorded:

A most tremendous fire was opened, and became general on both sides: ours was so well directed, and our ships so close in line, that the French commodore, who evinced great gallantry, was completely foiled in the attempt to board us on the starboard quarter, and which sealed his destruction, for at the moment that his jib-boom had nearly plombed our taffrail, his bowsprit and forecastle being crowded with boarders, himself in full uniform amongst the foremost, displaying great intrepidity, and animating his men, a brass five-and-a-half inch howitzer, which had been previously loaded with between seven and eight hundred musket balls, and well pointed, was discharged right at them. The carnage occasioned by this, together with an incessant fire of small arms from the marines and seamen, as well as round, grape and canister, from every great gun that could be brought to bear, was truly dreadful. Numbers of the poor wretches were swept away, and amongst the fallen was distinctly observed their gallant leader.[9]

By now the British ships were dangerously close to the shore and the signal was made for them to wear together, to reverse the order of sailing and head away from the coast. As the French attempted the same manoeuvre, the battered *Favorite* failed to make the turn and ran aground – Dubourdieu had been killed, and his ship was out of the battle. The French *Flore* managed to pass behind the stern of the *Amphion*, firing a broadside down the length of the ship. O'Brien, who was in charge of the main-deck guns, saw what was about to happen and ordered the gun crews to lie down, 'as by standing they were uselessly exposed, it being impossible to bring a gun to bear on the enemy at the moment. With the young gentlemen [midshipmen] or officers I left it optional to act as they pleased, and they remained erect with me, and I lament to say suffered in consequence of their gallantry, for Messrs. Barnard and Farewell, two promising young men, were immediately knocked down and taken to the cockpit, badly, though not mortally wounded.'[10]

The *Flore* and the *Bellona* successfully trapped the *Amphion* between them, and a fierce fight began. The *Danaë* also attacked the *Volage*, but soon realised the disadvantage of being too close because the British ship was armed with 32-pounder carronades. The *Danaë* regained the advantage by pulling away to a point out of range of the carronades, but still close enough for cannons to be effective. On board the *Volage* the gunpowder charges were increased in an attempt to improve the range of the carronades, but as a result these guns broke loose from their tackles, some overturned and some split open. This left the *Volage* almost defenceless, until the *Active* came to the rescue, and 'the *Danaë* made all sail to escape to Lessina, as did the *Carolina*, and the small craft scampered off in various directions'.[11]

The *Carolina* and *Corona* had been in battle with the *Cerberus*, and the *Corona* continued the fighting until the British ship *Active* intervened. The *Corona* then retreated, pursued by the *Active*, and this Venetian ship put up a desperate fight before being forced to surrender. Meanwhile the *Amphion*, still caught between the two enemy ships, concentrated on defeating the larger of the two, as O'Brien explained: 'We suffered much in the *Amphion* from the well-directed fire of the two ships, *Flora* and *Bellona*, so judiciously placed on our quarters, but the former being the most formidable, demanded our chief attention, and being to leeward, we were enabled by bearing up to close and pass ahead so as nearly to touch her, when we poured our starboard broadside into her larboard bow, and the consequence was, she soon ceased firing and struck her colours.'[12] The *Amphion* then tackled the *Bellona*, which also eventually surrendered, but in the meantime the *Flore* took the opportunity to escape, meeting up with the *Danaë* and reaching a safe anchorage on the island of Lessina. The battle was over, leaving the British with the *Bellona* and *Corona* as prizes. The *Favorite*, which had run aground, was set on fire by the crew and later blew up.

The battle had been hard fought. Some of the British ships, particularly the *Amphion* and *Volage*, were badly damaged, and Hoste himself was wounded by a musket-ball in his arm, and his face and hands were burnt. The casualties on board the enemy ships were far worse, however, and O'Brien was shocked by the scene in the *Bellona*:

It would be difficult to describe the horrors which now presented themselves; – the carnage was dreadful – the dead and dying lying about in every direction: the agonies of the latter were most lamentable and piercing. The surgeon, a herculean man, with an apron and his shirt-sleeves tucked up, attended by his assistants and others, bore a conspicuous part in the tragedy, being busily employed in examining wounds, ascertaining the bodies from whom the vital spark had actually fled, and superintending their interment, or rather launching out of the ports! Strange to say, every man stationed at one of the guns had been killed, and as it was supposed by the same shots [the guns being double-shotted], which passed through both sides of the ship into the sea. At another gun, the skull of one poor creature was actually lodged in the beam above where he stood, the shot having taken an oblique direction: in short, the scene was heart-rending and sickening.[13]

Initially the British squadron with its prizes returned to Lissa for repairs, and in the following days the crew of the *Favorite* was rounded up and taken prisoner. Hoste then led his ships and their prizes to Malta, where, as he wrote to his mother, they had a heroes' welcome: 'If I was to tell you our reception at this place yesterday, you would laugh at me, and call me a *vain*, foolish man. Indeed it is enough to make any man so, and I may in truth say yesterday was the proudest day of my life. The whole of the garrison manned the lines, and cheered us from the time of our entry into the port to that of our anchoring.'[14] In a later letter to her he said 'we have had balls and fêtes given to us by all classes here, and it is impossible to convey to you the sensation our success has given rise to'.[15]

As expected, Hoste soon received orders to bring his two most damaged ships and the prizes back to Britain for proper repairs, and, as was often the case with returning ships, they carried a few passengers from Malta. Among these was the poet Lord Byron, who, although not yet at the peak of his fame, was nevertheless a celebrity. He wrote to his friend John Cam Hobhouse from the *Volage*: 'We left Malta on the 2nd, with three other frigates, inclusive of the Lissa prizes, and we are on our way, they to glory, and I to what God pleases.'[16] The *Amphion*'s crew was paid off at Deptford on 12 August, and although Hoste was given congratulations and rewards, these were not in proportion to the strategic importance of his success. The battle at Lissa had destroyed any hopes of the French for securing a south European route to the East in the foreseeable future, as well as giving a further blow to the morale of the French Navy. Dubourdieu had been one of the best French commanders, and many experienced seamen had also been lost.

Like France, Britain still needed a constant supply of men to replace those who were discharged or died, but since so many had originally been pressed into service and had spent many years at sea, desertion was a major problem too. Whenever they had a reasonable chance of success many sailors took the opportunity to run away. The *Chesapeake–Leopard* affair of 1807 that had been sparked off by a dispute over deserters had not halted the major sources of aggravation between America and Britain – in the ruthless quest for recruits, Americans continued to be pressed into the Royal Navy, and American ships were still being searched for so-called deserters. In early 1811 the twelve-year-old Samuel Leech in the newly launched frigate *Macedonian* recorded one incident when they were about to leave the port of Lisbon: 'Being in want of men, we resorted to the press-gang which was made up of our most loyal men, armed to the teeth; by their aid we obtained our full numbers. Among them were a few Americans; they were taken without respect to their protections, which were often taken from them and destroyed. Some were released through the influence of the American consul; others, less fortunate, were carried to sea, to their no small chagrin.'[17] He added: 'To prevent the recovery of these men by their consul, the press-gang usually went ashore on the night previous to our going to sea; so that before they were missed they were beyond his protection. Sometimes they were claimed on our return to port.'[18]

The French-American traveller Louis Simond believed that 'the danger to which a real American sailor is exposed, of being forcibly taken away by the first English man of war met at sea, is certainly in the highest degree revolting, and will lead to interminable wars as soon as there is more equality of strength between the two nations'.[19] His prediction was gradually coming true, because two months after the battle of Lissa, a serious clash occurred between the *President* and *Little Belt* only a few miles from where the *Chesapeake–Leopard* encounter had taken place. Several seamen had recently been taken from American ships in that area, and in one incident the British frigate *Guerriere* had seized an alleged deserter from the merchant brig *Spitfire* just 18 miles off New York. As a result, Captain John Rodgers of the heavy frigate *President* was immediately given orders to set sail and cruise off the coast. One officer on board the *President* wrote to the *New York Herald*:

We learn that we are in pursuit of the British frigate who had impressed a passenger from a coaster. Yesterday, while beating down the bay, we spoke a brig coming up, who informed us that she saw the British frigate the day before off the very place where we now are; but she is not now in sight. We have made the most complete preparations for battle. Every one wishes it. She is exactly our force, but we have the *Argus* [sloop] with us, which none of us are pleased with, as we wish a fair trial of courage and skill. Should we see her, I have not the least doubt of an engagement. The commodore [Rodgers] will demand the person impressed; the demand will doubtless be refused, and the battle will instantly commence . . . The commodore has called in the boatswain, gunner, and carpenter, informed them of all circumstances, and asked if they were ready for action. Ready was the reply of each.[20]

In the evening of 16 May 1811 a warship was spotted off Cape Henry that was believed to be the *Guerriere*, but the vessel refused to show identification. A shot was fired, though it was never established who fired first, as subsequent reports from both sides were contradictory in every detail. Broadsides were exchanged, possibly lasting forty-five minutes, and the vessels then drifted apart. The *Chesapeake* and *Leopard* had been evenly matched, but at daylight the British vessel on this occasion was discovered not to be the frigate *Guerriere* but the much inferior sloop *Little Belt* (also called *Lille Belt*, its original Danish name before being captured at Copenhagen in 1807). The *Little Belt*, under Captain Arthur Batt Bingham, had earlier sailed from Bermuda with orders to meet up with the *Guerriere*. Ironically he had specific instructions 'to be particularly careful not to give any just cause of offence to the government or subjects of the United States of America'.[21]

The British had eleven dead and twenty-one wounded, some severely, while the Americans had only one wounded. In his report to the Admiralty, Bingham was of the opinion that the *President* had set out for a fight, even though Britain and America were not at war. 'By the manner in which he [Rodgers] apologized,' Bingham commented, 'it appeared to me evident, that had he fallen in with a British frigate he would certainly have brought her to action; and what further confirms me in that opinion is, that his guns were not only loaded with round and grape shot, but with every scrap of iron that could possibly be collected.'[22] The *Naval Chronicle* said that 'we have seen several private letters, all of which flatly contradict the assertion, that Captain Bingham fired first; and add, that the *President* fired the first single shot, and also the first broadside'.[23] The *President* was virtually unscathed, but the *Little Belt* limped into Halifax a near wreck, as Bingham described: 'His Majesty's sloop is much damaged in her masts, sails, rigging and hull, and as there are many shots still remaining in her side, and upper works all shot away, starboard pump also, I have judged it proper to proceed to Halifax.'[24]

Both governments did their best to downplay what had occurred. Opinion in America was mixed, but in many quarters it was believed that the earlier attack on the *Chesapeake* had been avenged. When the news reached London a month later, the British press was outraged, and one newspaper haughtily declared: 'Upon this extraordinary affair, we will only observe, that it betrays the hostile spirit of the American Commander. He had no right to question an English ship of war carrying English colours. He therefore was the aggressor, and upon his head lies the blood that has been shed . . . We give him joy of his triumph. The *President*, the great Leviathan of the American navy, overpowered a little English brig of 18 guns!!!'[25] Where the clash between the *Chesapeake* and the *Leopard* could be dismissed as an isolated incident, that between the *President* and the *Little Belt* was a warning of what was to come.

In the East, Dutch-held Java remained the single obstacle to British domination of trade, but on 4 August a massive naval force carrying nearly twelve thousand troops attacked the island. It took more than a month to overrun Java, during which time the captured Dutch ships and gunboats swelled the British fleet to over one hundred vessels, and sailors were called upon to build boat bridges across rivers, construct siegeworks and handle the artillery. When disease broke out among the troops, they were reinforced by marines from the ships, and in the latter stages of the campaign parties of seamen and marines were sent out to deal with the minor outposts. The Dutch finally surrendered their colony of Java on 18 September – the naval war in the East was effectively over, giving Britain rather than France the solid foundations of an empire that Napoleon had long dreamed of and lusted after.

In Britain itself the year 1811 was one of change brought about by Parliament finally deciding to declare George III insane. His illness and erratic behaviour had been causing concern for some time, and in early February the Prince of Wales was made Regent, initially with limited powers for twelve months. This was the start of what would be known as the Regency period, and was celebrated by a sumptuous banquet and fête on 19 June at Carlton House, the London residence of the Prince of Wales. It was a lavish meal with about two thousand guests, including the exiled French royal family. Such largesse did nothing for the general population, many of whom were suffering the effects of wartime shortages and the widening gap between rich and poor that was a side-effect of the early industrial revolution. Jobs and incomes were being squeezed, but the cheap food, clothing and other necessities that the British Empire would eventually supply had not started to flow into the country.

The winter of 1810–11 was severe, and the River Thames froze over so hard that men could walk on the ice from Battersea Bridge as far as Hungerford Stairs. In the countryside many people were starving and desperate, and inevitably violence broke out. In January 1811 Major-General Dyott, formerly at Walcheren and now military commander at Lichfield, wrote in his diary: 'A great deal of frost and cold weather in

January; shooting most days with tolerable success. I went to Beaudesert [Beaudesert House in Staffordshire] for a day's shooting with Lord Paget*, and never saw so much game in so short a time. We were not out more than three hours, and killed twenty-five pheasants, seven hares, and four rabbits.'[26] Such game animals were private property, however, and protected by severe laws – the punishment for poaching could be transportation. Home-grown wheat was also protected by duties that were introduced in 1804 to keep the price of imported wheat uncompetitive, but for most of the war food was so expensive that such laws were not needed. The high incomes of landowners and farmers were protected, but when prices rose, the poor starved. Many agricultural labourers, tenant farmers and their families were taking jobs in the industries, often at pitiful wages, and they had no hope of improving their lot. Although a few radicals spoke out in Parliament the landowners swayed the government, and corrupt elections and lack of a universal franchise for men, let alone women, ensured the status quo.

Under such conditions bad weather led to bad harvests, high prices, food shortages and then civil disturbance. Often the focus of resentment was the new labour-saving machines that put people out of jobs, and in 1811 Luddite attacks against factories began in the Midlands. In November Dyott wrote in his diary:

On the 7th I was ordered to Nottingham by a letter from the Commander-in-chief's secretary in consequence of the alarming riots that existed in that town and neighbourhood. The stocking manufacturers had committed great outrages by breaking the stocking-frames of such of their employers as would not increase the price of wages. I remained at Nottingham until the 14th, having distributed the 15th Dragoons and Berkshire Militia in the several villages where disturbances had happened to keep the peace and proceeded to Loughborough to attend a meeting of magistrates of the county of Leicester, there having been some symptoms of discontent in that country, but the appearance of a military force prevented any repetition of outrage, and I returned to Lichfield on the 15th.[27]

In fact there was uproar in the counties of Nottinghamshire, Derbyshire and Leicestershire that took seven regiments of troops to quell. This was

---

* Henry William Paget, who was later to lose his leg to a cannonball that narrowly missed Wellington at Waterloo.

only the beginning, as the attacks spread to textile areas in northern England. In all, the year the Prince Regent came to power was not a good one for the ordinary people of Britain, and it was to end in tragedy for the military.

The Baltic was essential for trade, but at the end of 1810 Sweden had declared war, leaving Britain no allies. With the Napoleonic decrees banning trade with Britain, all Baltic ports were closed to the British, but Vice-Admiral Sir James Saumarez, commander-in-chief of the Baltic fleet, had maintained friendly relations with Sweden. Using a system of foreign flags and false papers for merchant ships, trade between Britain and the Baltic countries was kept open. British warships escorted the merchant convoys, but with no base in the Baltic, they all had to leave before the onset of winter. On 1 November 1811 Rear-Admiral Robert Carthew Reynolds set out from the anchorage at Hanö, off the southeast tip of Sweden, in his 98-gun flagship the *St George*. Along with other warships, he was leading a convoy of over 120 merchant ships and had instructions not to leave any later because of the dangers from ice and worsening weather. Almost immediately the convoy ran into contrary winds, forcing the ships to turn back and severely delaying them. They were dogged by bad weather, and during the night of the 15th while at anchor off Nysted, a storm hit the convoy, and ships were dismasted and dragged their anchors. A large merchant vessel was blown across and cut one of the anchor cables holding the *St George*, which was driven into the shoals. In a desperate attempt to save the ship, all the masts were cut down with axes, but despite this the ship struck the bottom several times, the rudder was torn away, and the vessel ran aground. In this condition the *St George* managed to survive until the wind dropped, early the next morning, and temporary masts and a makeshift rudder were fitted, but it took another two days to refloat the battleship.

The merchantmen were in an equally distressed condition, several having been wrecked on the enemy coast and some having sunk. Thirty were badly damaged and limped back to a safe harbour near Hanö for repairs. The rest, seventy-six in all, were escorted to the Wingo anchorage off Gothenburg, where they arrived on 1 December. At Wingo the convoy met up with other British warships, including the *Victory* with Saumarez on board. He proposed that the *St George* should remain there while the other ships sailed with the convoy, but Reynolds insisted that his ship was capable of making the voyage, and in the end Saumarez allowed him his wish. The convoy was again delayed by contrary winds, not setting out for England until the 17th. A squadron consisting of the warships *Victory*, *Vigo*, *Dreadnought* and *Orion* as well as the brigs *Mercury* and *Snipe* led the way. Then came the *St George*, towed by the *Cressy*, and accompanied by the *Defence* and the brig *Bellete*, after which came the *Hero* and the brig *Grasshopper* leading the convoy of merchant ships. By the morning of Christmas Eve, the squadron led by the *Victory* had safely crossed the North Sea. Early on, the convoy of merchantmen returned to Wingo because of adverse winds and only set sail again on 21 December.

Because the *St George* seemed to be sailing well, the tow was cast off, but this squadron also decided to turn back to Wingo, and likewise headed for home again on the 21st. In the following days these ships managed to round the northern tip of Jutland but the weather, which had never been good, began to worsen again, and the *Bellete* was separated from the other three ships. Unknown to them, the merchant convoy led by the *Hero* had already passed them and was further south. Part of that convoy split off towards Hull and Scotland, while the *Hero* and *Grasshopper* continued to escort the rest of the convoy. News of the ships from the Baltic did not reach Britain until nearly two weeks later, when *The Times* reported:

We have with . . . regret to mention, that the fears entertained for the safety of the *Hero*, of 74 guns, Captain NEWMAN, are unfortunately realized. It is stated, that in a most dreadful gale, she struck on the Haak Sand, near the Texel, on which the *Minotaur* was lost last winter, and foundered. Every soul on board of her, it is added, perished. The *Grasshopper* sloop of war is also lost. She struck on the Haak, but got over it, and was subsequently wrecked. Captain FANSHAW, the Commander and the Officers and crew, were, it is stated, saved from the wreck, but are made prisoners of war in Holland.[28]

Because the ships were wrecked on the enemy coast of Holland, it was some days before a full picture of the incident emerged, in an account from one of the crew of the *Grasshopper*, showing that they were much further east than the pilots reckoned:

At half-past three [on 24 December] the hands were turned up, the ship being in broken water: we found we were on a sandbank, the pilot imagining it to be Smith's Knoll [towards the Suffolk coast]. The captain instantly ordered the brig to be steered S.S.E thinking to get out to sea, but she continued striking so hard [on the bottom] for a length of time, that we had almost given her up for lost, when suddenly and very fortunately, we fell into three fathoms water, upon which the captain caused an anchor to be let go, when we perceived the *Hero* again (as we then thought) also at an anchor, though she fired several guns and burnt blue lights: but alas! when the day broke we had the mortification of witnessing a most horrible scene, – the *Hero* was totally dismasted and on her larboard beam ends, with her head to the N.E. about a mile from us upon the Haeck's [Haake] Sand, as we then found we were inside of it, off the Texel Island.[29]

The *Hero* was already breaking up, and the damaged *Grasshopper* was trapped between a sandbank and the Dutch coast. There was no alternative but to surrender to the Dutch and ask for help:

The ship's company [of the *Hero*] were all crowded together on the poop and forecastle. As soon as daylight had well appeared, she hoisted a flag of truce and fired a gun, which we repeated, and very shortly after saw a lugger, two brigs, and several small vessels, plying out of the Texel to our assistance, but owing to the flood tide having made, and the wind blowing a perfect gale at N.N.W. the lugger was only able to come within two or three miles of us by two o'clock in the afternoon. In the meantime we hoisted out our boats, and made an attempt to get near the *Hero*, but the surf was so high, that it was all ineffectual, and we were under the cruel necessity of seeing so many of our brave countrymen perishing, without being able to render them any assistance.[30]

The crew of the *Grasshopper* was eventually taken off by the Dutch, with the loss of only one man. The *Hero* sank and there were no survivors.

These were not the only vessels of that convoy to be wrecked, for the *Grasshopper* seaman reported: 'I observed, likewise, about five miles to the northward of us, a vessel on shore, with her foremast standing, and another some distance from her, both of which I took to be the transports that were under our convoy. The [Dutch] commanding officer here has since informed us, that the telegraph has reported that eight or ten vessels were wrecked upon the coast to the northward . . . a transport, called the *Archimedes*, beat over the Haecks as well as ourselves, with the loss of her rudder, but has since been wrecked, though the crew are saved, and now prisoners of war, as well as we.'[31]

It took longer for news of the *Defence* and *St George* to reach Britain, but in early February 1812 newspapers began to pick up stories from the Danish press, and on the 10th the *Hampshire Courier* carried an account:

The Journals of Jutland are full of details, in part contradictory, relative to the shipwrecks of the *St. George* and *Defence*. It is natural that these dreadful scenes, having only for witnesses the sailors and fishermen, inhabitants of the coasts, should be related in different ways. It is known that the *St. George* carried 98 guns, 552 sailors and 200 marines. The crew of the *Defence* was 500 men in the whole; ten men from the *St. George*, and six from the *Defence*, are all that were saved: 1283 individuals perished in the waves. The *Defence*, which was very old, struck the ground first; she made signals with blue lights, that she was left without resource, and in a moment afterwards she went to pieces; what remained of her however, continued still visible, lying bottom upwards, and had at a distance the appearance of a church. Capt. ATKINS got alive to land, with six sailors, but expired a few moments after.[32]

This was on Christmas Eve, the same day that the *Hero* and *Grasshopper* were wrecked, but the warships *Defence* and *St George* were wrecked much further north, on the west coast of Jutland. The makeshift rudder of the *St George* no longer functioned, and the vessel drifted towards the coast. The captain of the *Cressy* decided to save his own ship, but the captain of the *Defence* remained with the *St George*, and both ships were driven ashore. Eyewitnesses did not agree as to whether the *St George* or the *Defence* ran aground first:

The *St. George* let go her anchors, but the violence of the wind drove her on shore, and the furious waves rolled over her without being able to break her, as she was of a very strong construction. This circumstance served only to prolong the sufferings of the unhappy crew. During the whole of the 25th, from four to five hundred men were seen clinging to the lofty deck of the vessel. It was impossible to come to their assistance, on account of the storm and unexampled agitation of the sea. On a sudden these men disappeared, and it was thought they had been carried away by a wave; but according to the account of one of the ten sailors, Admiral REYNOLDS, conceiving all succour impossible, had thrown himself in despair into the sea, and been followed by the greater part of the crew. Those who remained endeavoured to tie one another to pieces of wood, masts, and yards; and at length threw themselves into the sea, and attempted to gain the shore . . .

but with exception of ten they were all drowned, or crushed to death by the beating fragments of the wreck. The Secretary of Admiral REYNOLDS got to land, but expired immediately from fatigue and cold. There was found on him the portrait of his wife, with her address in London, and a note requesting those who might find his body to inform her of his unhappy fate. A child, eight years old, got on shore safe, fastened to a large piece of timber. His father and mother were on board the *Defence*: they followed him with their eyes, and when they saw him reach the land alive, they threw themselves into the waves, and died together![33]

In the following days a great many bodies were washed up on the coast and were buried in the sand dunes where they were found, an area known ever since as 'dead men's dunes'. The number of casualties from the Baltic convoy could not be calculated precisely, but over two thousand men and an unknown number of women and children were lost in the wrecks of the three warships, while the total death toll from warships, transport ships and merchantmen has been estimated at over five thousand. It was the worst single disaster to befall the British Navy during the entire Napoleonic Wars.

# EIGHTEEN

——·◆·——

# THE GREAT MISTAKE

Be it enacted, by the Senate and House of Representatives of the United States of America, in Congress assembled, that War be, and the same is declared to exist, between the United Kingdom of Great Britain and Ireland, and the dependencies thereof, and the United States of America and their territories . . . June 18, 1812 – (Approved.)

James Madison[1]

The year 1812, which had begun so badly for the navy, was not destined to greatly improve. All attention was on Europe, where at last Wellington's forces were gaining ground in Spain. After the victory at Ciudad Rodrigo in January, the British public was following the progress of the army through the Iberian peninsula, and for the first time since long before Trafalgar the army was beginning to eclipse the navy in popularity. In part the navy was a victim of its own success, having established a secure blockade of the Continent, adequate protection for trade and the annexation of the remnants of France's overseas empire. The problem was that many of these successes had been low-key and often far from home, with no great dramatic victories to capture the public imagination. The army now seemed to promise such drama, close at hand, with the possibility of British soldiers invading French soil in the foreseeable future, whereas the navy, which had cut off Napoleon's every attempt to spread his influence beyond mainland Europe, was taken for granted.

Wellington admitted privately that 'if anyone wishes to know the history of this war, I will tell them that it is our maritime superiority [that] gives me the power of maintaining my army while the enemy are unable to do so',[2] but it was the triumph and tragedy of victory in battle that grabbed the headlines. As ever, Sir Sidney Smith managed to summarise the situation: 'The *navy* has surely not the less merit for having worked itself out of employment by destroying all opposition on the coasts of the four quarters of the globe, & being the constant support of the army in all its operations, without which support it could not have accomplished any one of the objects for which its distinguished officers are so deservedly rewarded.'[3]

Through the spring of 1812 the ships of the navy carried on their routine duties of blockade, convoy protection and securing the supply lines for the soldiers in Spain, but a turning point was reached in June. War between France and Russia had seemed likely for some time and on the 24th Napoleon led his armies in an invasion of Russia. Almost a month later news arrived that America had declared war on Britain. The main point of dispute had been the British Orders-in-Council that restricted American trade, such as by requiring foreign vessels trading with an enemy country to call at a British port first and pay duties on their cargo. Ironically, these measures were repealed two days before America declared war, but *The Times* commented cynically: 'We have only to add our opinion . . . that as the Orders in Council have given occasion to the war, their revocation must or ought to suspend it; that as the hostilities of America have been built upon a foundation which is now withdrawn, the hostilities must fall to the ground likewise. There will even then be much to dispute about, which, after a proper regimen of misunderstanding, perverseness, and delay, may lead a second time to the same result.'[4] The only inaccuracy in this analysis was the supposition that news of the repeal would at least check, if not stop, the war, for the news was actually ignored in America, showing that the Orders-in-Council were the excuse, not the reason, for the hostilities.

The United States of America in 1812 was a large territory with a tiny population. There was no pressure on land, and indeed in some areas where the native Indians had been displaced, the settlers were too few in number to defend the land they had occupied. Despite this, some Americans felt it was their destiny, perhaps a God-given right, to own the whole continent, including a massive area to the west and Florida to the south, which were still in the hands of Britain's ally Spain, and the largely unknown Oregon territory in the north-west, which was mainly frequented by fur trappers and traders from both Canada and America.

Since the United States had only declared independence from Britain thirty-six years earlier, many Americans were also sensitive about anything that could possibly be construed as an infringement of their rights.

With the impressment of British sailors who had become American citizens and with interference in its trade, the United States felt increasingly provoked by Britain, and many politicians in Washington were urging that war was the only course, not just to win the battle of 'Free trade and sailor's rights' but also to push Britain out of Canada. Territorial expansion was now the primary military objective of those politicians dubbed the War Hawks, in order to obtain more land for settlement, to prevent Canada becoming a competitor in trade (by using the Great Lakes and St Lawrence River as a main shipping route) and to allow America to annex Florida. There was, too, a desire to curb the influence that Britain had over the Indian tribes, who were being pushed further and further west as America settled more land, while some politicians were seeking to gain financially. A presidential election was also looming in late 1812, and James Madison was fearful of not obtaining the nomination of his Democratic-Republican Party*.

The European nations, particularly France and Britain, viewed the emerging nation on the other side of the Atlantic as young and correspondingly naive, and as regards some of the Democratic-Republican politicians this was a fair assessment. Various arguments put forward in favour of the war were ludicrous, such as the idea that commerce with France was more important than trade with Britain, and yet before trade embargoes were imposed, exports to Britain and its colonies were ten times as great as those to France. The Federalists, who opposed the war and supported better relations with Britain rather than France, pointed this out during the debate, but were ignored. Although America was totally unprepared for a war there was in the country a confident anticipation of a victory, which relied on the expectation that Napoleon would soon defeat Britain. In reality the war was to last three years and achieve almost nothing.

Napoleon later claimed that his diplomacy manoeuvred America into declaring war on Britain. He had certainly done his best to deceive the

* Originally called the Republican Party, this became the Democratic-Republican Party and later the Democratic Party. Not to be confused with the modern Republican Party founded in 1854.

Americans, but in truth the Americans were faced with a stark choice. Both Britain and France were imposing stringent restrictions on American trade, so it was a question of declaring war on one and becoming allied to the other. An objective view suggested that since Britain now controlled the oceans and France was powerless to do so, America could ally itself to Britain without fear of reprisal. That would leave no excuse to invade Canada or Florida, and to some Americans – certainly many of those in government – an alliance with the 'republic' of France was more palatable than closer ties with their old colonial masters. Favouring ideals and opportunities for gaining territory over practicalities, America made the wrong choice and declared war on Britain.

At first the American Navy comprised only fourteen serviceable vessels, of which three were superior frigates – Captain Rodgers's *President*, Captain Hull's *Constitution* and Captain Decatur's *United States*. Five frigates were laid up, and of these the *Constellation* and *Chesapeake* were rapidly repaired. There were also 165 gunboats, though fewer than half were in commission. The navy had no battleships, but relied heavily on privateers, the privately owned armed vessels that were licensed to capture enemy ships. Both sides also had a small but growing force on the Great Lakes and on Lake Champlain. Even though the American Navy had only the eastern seaboard of North America to defend, this force was totally inadequate. Britain's Royal Navy was far superior, with around one hundred battleships and six hundred smaller vessels, but with the war continuing in Europe the navy was stretched to the limit, so that there was always a reluctance to provide the army or navy in North America with sufficient resources. If Britain had been able and willing to deploy all the resources currently engaged against Napoleon, America would rapidly have become a colony once more, with the Mississippi as its western border.

The initial aim of America was to invade Canada, and it was anticipated that this would be done very quickly and successfully, particularly as the population of British North America was so small, and the few troops were mostly concentrated around Quebec and Montreal in order to keep open the St Lawrence River. Simultaneous invasions at various points were planned, but they were uncoordinated and marked by indecision and delay. The American Army, under Brigadier-General William Hull, crossed into Canada on 12 July 1812, but five days later the British managed to capture the strategic American fort on Mackinac Island, in the north of Lake Huron.

Fearful of an Indian uprising on the frontier, by early August Hull pulled back his troops to Detroit and ordered the garrison at Fort Dearborn (now Chicago), on the south side of Lake Michigan, to withdraw. Major-General Isaac Brock, commander of the British troops, reached the Detroit River and demanded Hull's capitulation on the grounds that otherwise he would be unable to prevent a massacre by the Indians. Three days later Hull surrendered over two thousand men, a brig on Lake Erie, the Michigan territory between Lakes Huron and Michigan (including Detroit) and a great deal of weapons and supplies. This was a terrible blow to the Americans at the start of the war, and the fortunes of the Americans and Canadians would fluctuate throughout the following months without lasting gains on either side.

At sea the first action took place just five days after war was declared when a squadron left New York and spotted the British frigate *Belvidera*, which escaped into Halifax in Nova Scotia, and around the same time the privateer *Dash* captured the Royal Navy schooner *Whiting*, whose crew was unaware that war had been declared and were delivering diplomatic dispatches. On 17 July a British squadron captured the USS *Nautilus*, but the smaller sloop HMS *Alert* was captured by the frigate USS *Essex* on 13 August off the Grand Banks of Newfoundland. In Britain none of this was startling news, partly because America was so far away and information took so long to cross the Atlantic. People were still intent on the progress of Wellington in Spain and Napoleon in Russia – if the war with America was discussed at all, it was with the attitude that America was a naughty child throwing a tantrum:

We have often had occasion to lament the mistaken policy of our transatlantic brethren. It might have been supposed that a nation emanating from us, using the same language, actuated by the same spirit of liberty, would have shrunk with abhorrence from any kind of assimilation with the tyrant in France; that she would have joined us heart and hand in a contest for religion, order, morality, property, civilization, and every thing that has been held valuable by the wisest men. But no, – We see her taking advantage of our distresses to effect our ruin; we see her destroying her own commerce, because we shall have no share of it.[5]

By October news of the growing conflict was beginning to compete for attention in the newspapers, with *The Times* noting that 'the expedition of the Americans . . . has terminated not in the possession of

Canada by General Hull, but in the possession of General Hull and his army'.[6] But just three days later it had to report the first real setback in the conflict:

The disaster . . . is one of that nature with which England is but little familiar: it is the capture of one of her frigates, by the frigate of an enemy, and that enemy the Americans . . . The loss of a single frigate by us, when we consider how all the other navies of the world have been dealt by [with], is, it is true, but a small one: when viewed as a portion of the British navy, it is almost nothing; yet under all the circumstances of the two countries to which the vessels who fought belonged, we know not any calamity of twenty times its amount, that might have been attended with more serious consequences to the [country that was] worsted.[7]

This account cut right to the heart of the matter: the loss of a ship was of little importance, but the capture of a British ship by an American ship of the same size was unthinkable and likely to seriously undermine confidence in the British Navy. The frigate that had been lost was the *Guerriere*, which had encountered the American frigate *Constitution*. At the end of July the latter had narrowly missed being captured by a British squadron while on a voyage to New York. The fact that the commander of the *Constitution*, Isaac Hull (nephew of the now disgraced Brigadier-General William Hull), had displayed great skill and seamanship in escaping should have been a warning that the new enemy was of a different calibre from those the British Navy had fought in recent years, but it would take time for this information to be appreciated. Forced into the shelter of Boston harbour, Hull left again as soon as possible, rightly fearing that the widening British blockade might trap him there, and by mid-August he was cruising off the Canadian coast. On the 19th he spotted the *Guerriere*, the ship that had earlier caused so much friction over impressment of American seamen.

Neither ship was new, but the French-built *Guerriere* was of a lighter construction, and perhaps crucially the *Constitution* seems to have been better maintained and in better condition. The *Guerriere* was actually sailing to Halifax for a refit when the American frigate appeared. What surprised the British, however, was the high level of seamanship and gunnery of their opponents. Initially Captain James Dacres of the *Guerriere* tried to outmanoeuvre the American ship and wasted his opening broadsides, which fell short. Eventually he realised the enemy was too skilled to allow him an advantage, and decided on a straightforward gunnery duel, as Isaac Hull noted in his official report:

She [the *Guerriere*] continued wearing and manoeuvring for about three quarters of an hour, to get a raking position, but finding she could not, she bore up . . . I immediately made sail to bring the ship up with her, and five minutes before six P.M. being alongside within half-pistol shot, we commenced a heavy fire from all our guns, double shotted with round and grape, and so well directed were they, and so warmly kept up, that in 15 minutes his mizen-mast went by the board, and his main-yard in the slings, and the hull, rigging, and sails, very much torn to pieces. The fire was kept up with equal warmth for 15 minutes longer, when his mainmast and foremast went, taking with them every spar, except the bowsprit.[8]

Apart from differences in construction, the ships were not very evenly matched, with the *Guerriere* carrying mainly 18-pounder guns against the *Constitution*'s 24-pounders. Seeing a cannonball bounce off the side of the latter ship, an American sailor exclaimed that it must have sides made of iron, after which the ship bore the nickname 'Old Ironsides'. Even so, the *Guerriere* did damage some rigging of the *Constitution*, which pulled away from the helpless *Guerriere* for repairs. Captain Dacres had considered boarding as a last resort, but since the larger American vessel carried a much bigger crew, he thought better of it. His ship was too badly damaged for rapid repairs and an attempt at escape, so after consulting with his officers, he decided to surrender. The Americans were not sure whether the British had surrendered, though, and sent a lieutenant in a boat to enquire, who said, 'Commodore Hull's compliments, and wishes to know if you have struck your flag?'[9] After surveying his ship, now without a mast from which to fly a flag, Dacres replied, 'Well, I don't know; our mizzen-mast is gone, our main-mast is gone, and upon the whole, you may say we *have* struck our flag.'[10]

The casualties of the *Guerriere*, fifteen dead and sixty-three wounded, showed just how severely the vessel had been mauled during the half-hour that the ships had come within close range and traded broadsides. By contrast there were only seven men killed and seven wounded in the *Constitution*, whose crew was jubilant at their success, and an American officer wryly recorded that Hull, a portly man, had been so energetic during the fighting that he had 'split his tight breeches from waistband to knee'.[11] By the next day the *Guerriere* was in danger of sinking. All the men were taken off and the vessel was set on fire, eventually blowing up. While the British tried to recover from the shock that for the first time in many years a British ship, when not outnumbered, had been defeated in a fair fight, the Americans celebrated the victory in much the same way as the British after Nelson's success at the Battle of the Nile. Hull was rewarded with a ceremonial sword, pieces of plate and the freedom of the city of New York; medals were struck; songs and poems were composed; and Congress voted fifty thousand dollars to be distributed between the officers and crew of the *Constitution*. Beyond the immediate psychological impact on both sides of the Atlantic, the lesson provided by the incident – a lesson that the British Navy was reluctant to acknowledge – was that although the American Navy was tiny, its ships were manned by competent, determined and increasingly confident officers and crews.

With poor communications and the vast distances involved, it would take time for news of the capture of the *Guerriere* to reach all the ships of the British Navy. Before that, on 25 October, the American frigate *United States* under Captain Stephen Decatur in the mid-Atlantic sighted the British frigate *Macedonian* under Captain John Carden. As the ships approached each other, there was speculation among the crew of the *Macedonian*, which the fourteen-year-old powder monkey Samuel Leech recalled:

Our men were all in good spirits; though they did not scruple to express the wish that the coming foe was a Frenchman rather than a Yankee. We had been told, by the Americans on board, that frigates in the American service carried more and heavier metal than ours. This, together with our consciousness of superiority over the French at sea, led us to a preference for a French antagonist. The Americans among our number felt quite disconcerted, at the necessity which compelled them to fight against their own countrymen. One of them, named John Card, as brave a seaman as ever trod a plank, ventured to present himself to the captain, as a prisoner, frankly declaring his objections to fight. That officer, very ungenerously, ordered him to his quarters, threatening to shoot him if he made the request again. Poor fellow! He obeyed the unjust command, and was killed by a shot from his own countrymen.[12]

The *Macedonian* was cleared for action, and as it was Leech's first battle he noted every detail:

A lieutenant then passed through the ship, directing the marines and boarders, who were furnished with pikes, cutlasses and pistols, how to proceed if it should be necessary to board the enemy. He was followed by the captain [Carden], who exhorted the men to fidelity and courage, urging upon their consideration the well-known motto of the brave Nelson, 'England expects every man to do his duty' . . . My station was at the fifth gun on the main deck. It was my duty to supply my gun with powder, a boy being appointed to each gun in the ship on the side we engaged, for this purpose. A woollen screen was placed before the entrance to the magazine, with a hole in it, through which the cartridges were passed to the boys; we received them there, and covering them with our jackets, hurried to our respective guns. These precautions are observed to prevent the powder taking fire before it reaches the gun.[13]

From where he was stationed Leech could see nothing of the enemy ship and had to rely on his ears to work out what was going on: 'I heard a firing from some other quarter, which I at first supposed to be a discharge from our quarter deck guns; though it proved to be the roar of the enemy's cannon. A strange noise, such as I had never heard before, next arrested my attention; it sounded like the tearing of sails, just over our heads. This I soon ascertained to be the wind of the enemy's shot.'[14] It was not long before the two ships were trading broadsides, and the noise became almost unbearable:

The roaring of cannon could now be heard from all parts of our trembling ship, and, mingling as it did with that of our foes, it made a most hideous noise. By-and-by I heard the shot strike the sides of our ship; the whole scene grew indescribably confused and horrible; it was like some awfully tremendous thunder-storm, whose deafening roar is attended by incessant streaks of lightning, carrying death in every flash, and strewing the ground with the victims of its wrath: only, in our case, the scene was rendered more horrible than that, by the presence of torrents of blood which dyed our decks.[15]

What Leech did not see from his station at the guns was that, try as he might, Captain Carden could not manoeuvre his ship to make his broadsides effective. The American ship was so skilfully handled that whichever way the British ship turned, the *United States* was always off the bow, from where successive broadsides shot the *Macedonian* to pieces. All Leech could see, from his position, was the mounting devastation:

I was busily supplying my gun with powder, when I saw blood suddenly fly from the arm of a man stationed at our gun. I saw nothing strike him; the effect alone was visible; in an instant, the third lieutenant tied his handkerchief round the wounded arm, and sent the groaning wretch below to the surgeon. The cries of the wounded now rang through all parts of the ship. These were carried to the cockpit below as fast as they fell, while those more fortunate men, who were killed outright, were immediately thrown overboard. As I was stationed but a short distance from the main hatchway, I could catch a glance at all who were carried below. A glance was all I could indulge in, for the boys belonging to the guns next to mine were wounded in the early part of the action, and I had to spring with all my might to keep three or four guns supplied with cartridges . . . Two of the boys stationed on the quarter deck were killed. They were both Portuguese. A man, who saw one of them killed, afterwards told me that his powder caught fire and burnt the flesh almost off his face. In this pitiable situation, the agonized boy lifted up both hands, as if imploring relief, when a passing shot instantly cut him in two.[16]

Minute after minute the fighting continued, and all Leech could see were increasing casualties and the ship being destroyed:

The battle went on. Our men kept cheering with all their might. I cheered with them, though I confess I scarcely knew for what. Certainly there was nothing very inspiriting in the aspect of things where I was stationed. So terrible had been the work of destruction round us, it was termed the slaughter-house. Not only had we had several boys and men killed or wounded, but several of the guns were disabled. The one I belonged to had a piece of the muzzle knocked out; and when the ship rolled, it struck a beam of the upper deck with such force as to become jammed and fixed in that position . . . The schoolmaster received a death wound. The brave boatswain, who came from the sick bay to the din of battle, was fastening a stopper on a back-stay which had been shot away, when his head was smashed to pieces by a cannon-ball; another man, going to complete the unfinished task, was also struck down . . . Even a poor goat, kept by the officers for her milk, did not escape the general carnage; her hind legs were shot off, and poor Nan was thrown overboard.[17]

After over an hour of close-range conflict, the firing abruptly stopped, and Leech learned that the *United States* had pulled away to carry out repairs. The *Macedonian* was an unmanageable wreck, and by the time the

American ship returned, Captain Carden decided to surrender. Leech now had time to reflect on his own reactions:

I have often been asked what were my feelings during this fight. I felt pretty much as I suppose every one does at such a time. That men are without thought when they stand amid the dying and the dead, is too absurd an idea to be entertained a moment. We all appeared cheerful, but I know that many a serious thought ran through my mind: still, what could we do but keep up a semblance, at least, of animation? To run from our quarters would have been certain death from the hands of our own officers; to give way to gloom, or to show fear, would do no good, and might brand us with the name of cowards, and ensure certain defeat. Our only true philosophy, therefore, was to make the best of our situation, by fighting bravely and cheerfully.[18]

Now that the fighting had ceased and the ship had surrendered, the initiative passed to the Americans. Leech went below to help the wounded:

Pursuing my way to the ward-room, I necessarily passed through the steerage, which was strewed with the wounded: it was a sad spectacle, made more appalling by the moans and cries which rent the air. Some were groaning, others were swearing most bitterly, a few were praying, while those last arrived were begging most piteously to have their wounds dressed next. The surgeon and his mate were smeared with blood from head to foot: they looked more like butchers than doctors . . . I now set to work to render all the aid in my power to the sufferers. Our carpenter, named Reed, had his leg cut off. I helped to carry him to the after ward-room; but he soon breathed out his life there, and then I assisted in throwing his mangled remains overboard. We got out the cots as fast as possible; for most of them were stretched out on the gory deck. One poor fellow who lay with a broken thigh, begged me to give him water. I gave him some. He looked unutterable gratitude, drank, and died. It was with exceeding difficulty I moved through the steerage, it was so covered with mangled men, and so slippery with streams of blood. There was a poor boy there crying as if his heart would break. He had been servant to the bold boatswain, whose head was dashed to pieces. Poor boy! he felt that he had lost a friend.[19]

As he moved around the wounded and helped throw the dead overboard, Leech also noted the different reactions of the seamen after the fighting had ceased:

Some who had lost their messmates appeared to care nothing about it, while others were grieving with all the tenderness of women. Of these, was the survivor of two seamen, who had formerly been soldiers in the same regiment; he bemoaned the loss of his comrade with expressions of profoundest grief. There were, also, two boatswain's mates, named Adams and Brown, who had been messmates for several years in the same ship. Brown was killed, or so wounded that he died soon after the battle. It was really a touching spectacle to see the rough, hardy features of the brave old sailor streaming with tears, as he picked out the dead body of his friend from among the wounded, and gently carried it to the ship's side, saying to the inanimate form he bore, 'Oh Bill, we have sailed together in a number of ships, we have been in many gales and some battles, but this is the worse day I have seen! We must now part!' Here he dropped the body into the deep, and then, a fresh torrent of tears streaming over his weather-beaten face, he added, 'I can do no more for you. Farewell! God be with you!'[20]

The Americans took charge of the ship, moving most of the crew over to the *United States*, but Leech was left to look after the wounded. Soon he was helping clear the debris:

We took hold and cleansed the ship, using hot vinegar to take out the scent of the blood that had dyed the white of our planks with crimson. We also took hold and aided in fitting our disabled frigate for her voyage. This being accomplished, both ships sailed in company towards the American coast. I soon felt myself perfectly at home with the American seamen; so much so, that I chose to mess with them. My shipmates also participated in similar feelings in both ships. All idea that we had been trying to shoot out each other's brains so shortly before, seemed forgotten. We eat together, drank together, joked, sung, laughed, told yarns; in short, a perfect union of ideas, feelings, and purpose seemed to exist among all hands.[21]

Relations were also civilised among the officers, although Carden was saddened by having to surrender his ship, and Leech recorded that 'when Captain Carden offered his sword to the commodore [Decatur], remarking, as he did so, "I am an undone man. I am the first British naval officer that has struck his flag to an American;" the noble commodore either refused to receive the sword, or immediately returned it, smiling as he said, "You are mistaken, sir; your *Guerriere* has been taken by us, and the flag of a frigate was struck before yours." This somewhat revived the spirits of the old captain; but no doubt, he still felt his soul stung with shame and mortification at the loss of his ship.'[22]

The run of disasters for the British Navy was not to end before the year was out. On 29 December the British frigate *Java* met the *Constitution* off the coast of Brazil. The *Java* was carrying passengers, including the newly appointed governor-general of Bombay and his staff and over one hundred officers and men bound for the East Indies. It was to be a worse slaughter than the capture of the *Macedonian*. After over two hours of bitter battle the *Java* was completely dismasted, the captain, Henry Lambert, was mortally wounded and the ship was an unmanageable wreck. The first lieutenant, Henry Chads, took control and was helped with advice from senior naval officers among the passengers, but nothing was able to stop the ship being gradually knocked to pieces. Chads himself was wounded, and the eventual casualty figures reflected the unequal destruction: forty-eight killed and one hundred and two wounded in the *Java*, and just twelve killed and twenty-two wounded on board the *Constitution*. While held prisoner, an anonymous lieutenant from the *Java* wrote home to a friend: 'It is particularly to be remarked, that in no action [in] this war has so great a slaughter happened to that particular class of officers, the midshipmen, as occurred in this, there being no less than five killed, and four wounded.'[23]

Once again British seamanship had been matched by the Americans whose gunnery proved superior, and once again the strength of the American ships was thought to be the cause, as the *Java* lieutenant related:

From the manner in which this action was fought, and the unequalled injury the *Java* sustained beyond the *Constitution*, it appears evident that the American had advantages which do not belong to our frigates. It must strike every impartial observer, in noticing how rapidly the *Java*'s masts were carried away, one after the other; but it remains no longer a mystery, when it is known the *Constitution*'s masts are equal to our seventy-four's – and it was noticed by the officers of the *Java*, after the action, that the *Java*'s shot had passed through two of them; but so little did the Americans regard it, that when at St. Salvador, after the action, they did not attempt to fish [temporarily repair] the masts for security, before going to sea.[24]

The *Java* had been reduced to an unmanageable hulk, and being too far from an American port to make it worthwhile attempting to take the

wreck home as a prize, the passengers and crew were taken (
*Java* was blown up.

Through the first half of 1813 the Americans won further
actions between smaller ships, to the continued consternation of the
British. On 24 February the brig-sloop *Peacock* under Captain William
Peake was lost off Guyana's Demerara River to the American ship-sloop
*Hornet* under Captain James Lawrence. The action lasted only twenty-five
minutes, and among the nine dead was Captain Peake, with another
twenty-eight wounded. The senior lieutenant surrendered, but with 6
feet of water in the hold, the ship could not be saved, as Lawrence
described: 'Such shot-holes as could be got at were then plugged; guns
thrown overboard, and every possible exertion used to keep her afloat
until the prisoners could be removed, by pumping and bailing, but without effect, as she unfortunately sunk in 5½ fathoms of water, carrying
down 13 of her crew, and 3 of my brave fellows.'[25]

The *Hornet* headed straight home, reaching Martha's Vineyard three
weeks later. In early March Lawrence was promoted to the frigate
*Chesapeake*, which was fitting out in Boston. At New York the captured
officers expressed their gratitude to Captain Lawrence for their kind
treatment in a public letter: 'So much was done to alleviate the uncomfortable and distressing situation in which we were placed when received
on board the ship you command, that we can not better express our feelings than by saying we ceased to consider ourselves prisoners; and every
thing that friendship could dictate was adopted by you and the officers of
the *Hornet* to remedy the inconvenience we otherwise should have experienced from the unavoidable loss of the whole of our property and
clothes by the sudden sinking of the *Peacock*.'[26]

The British defeat was blamed on the failure to exercise the crews in
the use of guns, a recurring complaint at this time. Even where the crews
were exercised regularly, quite often this was done without actually firing
the guns, so as not to waste gunpowder and shot. Only the year before, Sir
Howard Douglas of the army was working in a combined operation in
Spain with Sir Home Popham's squadron and was 'scandalised at the bad
gunnery, which made him tremble for the laurels of the navy'.[27] In fact,
the *Peacock* 'had long been the admiration of her numerous visitors, for the
tasteful arrangement of her deck; and had obtained, in consequence, the
name of the *yacht*. The breechings of the carronades were lined with
white canvass; the shot-lockers shifted from their usual places; and nothing could exceed, in brilliancy, the polish upon the traversing-bars and

elevating screws'[28] – too much time had been spent on unnecessary polishing, at the expense of training.

While better training and practice would help in battles between individual ships, a more effective solution to the threat from the American Navy was blockade. Just a week before the *Peacock* sank, Captain Philip Bowes Broke* of the *Shannon* frigate had written: 'We yesterday spoke [to] a licenced *American*, who told us Sir John Warren was severely blockading *Chesapeake*, and had nearly cut off *Constellation*. This is the beginning of naval war to the *Americans*, and many a commercial town will feel the distress: I hope it may bring them to their senses. All their frigates are in harbour, but little *Essex*.'[29]

The blockade had started from a low level in 1812, but by February 1813 more British ships were available and the blockade covered the Atlantic coast from the Delaware to the Chesapeake. The coast of New England was spared the blockade at this stage, for the region's merchants were still happy to supply grain for Wellington's troops in the Peninsula, which was carried in licensed American merchantmen under the protection of the British Navy. It was also hoped that such a selective blockade would increase the dissension between the north-eastern states, which had opposed the war, and the rest of America. Already some American frigates were so securely trapped in port that they would take no further part in the war, and other American frigates were forced to wait weeks or months before they had a chance of slipping away. Towards the end of March the blockade was extended further south and as far north as New York, and gradually the stranglehold was completed. In 1814 even New England would be included, completing the blockade of the entire Atlantic coast of the American states.

As the war dragged on, many Americans were becoming increasingly disillusioned, particularly as the blockade of the ports began to bite, and it was not long before they were forced to clutch at every available means to keep some ships at sea, as one British newspaper reported:

The Americans, in order to do greater injury to our navy, have brought in a bill, ordering the use of torpedos and sub-marine engines to destroy British ships of war in American ports; and offering as a reward for such destruction, one half of the value of the vessel so destroyed. Our government possesses the means of retaliation for this designed mischief. The British ships of war had

---

* Pronounced 'Brook'.

taken on board at Bermuda, bombs, howitzers, rockets, &c, to bombard some American ports. We shall be glad to see the war carried on in earnest, and to find British vengeance effectually chastise American presumption and aggression.[30]

The Americans did their best to blow up the blockading warships, as William Stanhope Lovell, commander of the frigate *Brune*, recorded when a schooner laden with provisions was captured on 25 June 1813:

Small vessels, called coasters, were laden in this manner:—the upper part of the hold consisted of an assortment of all kinds, and the under filled with casks of gunpowder; they were then placed directly in the way of our ships at anchor off their harbours, their crews taking a boat and making their escape on shore when they observed ours near them in chase. A vessel of this kind was taken by the boat of the *Ramillies* (74), off New London, commanded by that most intelligent and excellent officer, Sir Thomas Hardy, who, suspecting from the manner she was thrown in his way that all was not right, had her anchored two good cables' length from his ship, and kept her there two or three hours before he would allow any person to go on board, thinking that by that time any mechanism invented for so diabolical a purpose would explode. After the above period poor Lieut. Geddes, whom I knew well, volunteered to go with the barge's crew to examine the cargo very carefully; Sir Thomas Hardy still felt doubtful, but was at length induced by the repeated solicitations of Geddes to allow him to go, but with particular injunctions to be careful. It is supposed that in hoisting up a cask of flour or biscuits they pulled the line that was made fast from it to the barrel of powder, the explosion immediately took place, when a lieutenant, midshipman, and barge's crew, sixteen in number, some of the best men in the ship, were blown to atoms.[31]

Lovell added that 'this fatal and melancholy catastrophe probably saved many of our gallant countrymen, as well as some of our men-of-war, by acting as a warning, and putting us on our guard against this *most dastardly* method of carrying on the war'.[32]

The British public were becoming as disillusioned as the Americans, because after nearly a year of war, the Americans had still not been beaten in a single-ship action and people were wondering what had become of the once universally victorious British Navy. At Boston, where the *Chesapeake* continued to be fitted out, the harbour was blockaded by the frigate *Shannon*. Captain Broke had been with the *Shannon* nearly seven years, and he was unusually diligent about instilling discipline and constantly training his men in gunnery, using floating targets such as empty beef casks. He had a passion for gunnery, introducing many innovations and adaptations for the *Shannon*'s guns.

By contrast, while many of the new crew of the *Chesapeake* were experienced naval seamen, very few of them were used to working together. There were some raw recruits, a handful were mutinous because of unpaid prize money and some of the officers were incapacitated through sickness. It was a crew, but not a team. Nevertheless, on Tuesday 1 June, Captain James Lawrence wrote to the Secretary of the Navy: 'I have been detained for want of men. I am now getting under weigh . . . An English frigate is now in sight from my deck. I have sent a pilot boat out to reconnoitre, and should she be alone I am in hopes to give a good account of her before night. My crew appear to be in fine spirits, and, I trust, will do their duty.'[33]

Lieutenant Provo Wallis of the *Shannon* later recalled that 'for some days previous to the 1st *June* . . . the weather in *Boston Bay* had been very thick and foggy, so much so that we had to guess our position. The morning of the above-named day, however, was ushered in by a brilliant sunrise, and the land near *Boston* sighted; but we were not without fear lest the *Chesapeake* had effected her escape during the thick weather . . . Having, however, stood in to reconnoitre, we were gratified by a sight of her at anchor in *Nantasket Roads*, a sure proof that she was ready for sea.'[34]

Broke immediately decided to send a challenge to Captain Lawrence: 'As the *Chesapeake* appears now ready for sea, I request you will do me the favour to meet the *Shannon* with her, ship to ship, to try the fortune of our respective flags.'[35] He included details of the manning and guns of his ship and added that 'my proposals are highly advantageous to you, as you cannot proceed to sea singly in the *Chesapeake*, without imminent risk of being crushed by the superior force of the numerous British squadrons which are now abroad . . . Choose your terms – but let us meet.'[36] The letter never reached Lawrence, as he had already decided to risk an encounter, leaving Boston at midday. There was an expectation of imminent success, and crowds of people gathered to watch. It was reported that 'so confident were the Americans of victory, that a number of pleasure-boats came out with the *Chesapeake* from Boston, to see the *Shannon* compelled to strike; and a grand dinner was actually preparing on shore for the *Chesapeake*'s officers, against their return with the prize!'[37] The encounter was being treated more like a baseball game than a battle.

Next, Broke reported, 'I took a position between Cape Ann and Cape Cod, and then hove to for him to join us – the enemy came down in a very handsome manner, having three American ensigns flying.'[38] Broke addressed his men: '*Shannons!* The *Americans* have, owing to the disparity in force, captured several of our frigates; but to-day, I trust, they will find out the stuff *British* sailors are made of when upon an equality. I feel sure you will all do your duty. In a word – remember, you have some hundreds of your brother sailors' blood to avenge!'[39] One seaman then asked: '"Mayn't we have three ensigns, sir, like she has?" "No," said Broke, "we've always been an unassuming ship."'[40] Unusually he also prohibited cheering, insisting on silence as they headed into battle. The *Chesapeake* was more ostentatious, as all the guns had stirring names, engraved on copper plates, including 'Yankee Protection', 'Liberty for Ever', 'America' and 'Washington', and while they approached the *Shannon*, Lawrence tried to encourage his men further with the words '*Peacock* her, my lads! *Peacock* her!',[41] referring to the destruction of that ship by the *Hornet*.

About 20 miles from Boston, at half past five, the *Chesapeake* met the *Shannon*. Two or three broadsides were exchanged, but right from the first broadside the training of the men of the *Shannon* proved devastating. Lieutenant Augustus Ludlow, acting first lieutenant of the *Chesapeake*, remarked that 'of one hundred and fifty men quartered on the upper deck, I did not see fifty on their feet after the first fire',[42] while the marksmen high up in the rigging of the *Shannon* told Midshipman Richard King 'that the hammocks, splinters, and wrecks of all kinds driven across the deck formed a complete cloud'.[43] The two ships became so entangled that the *Chesapeake* could no longer fire at the *Shannon*, and Lawrence gave orders for boarding, but in vain. He himself was then hit by a musket-ball and was carried below. His last words before he left the deck were 'tell the men to fire faster and not give up the ship. Fight her till she sinks!',[44] which became a future rallying cry for the American Navy of 'Don't give up the ship!'

Lieutenant Wallis related that Broke quickly assessed the situation and decided to board: '*Broke*, who saw the confusion on board of her, ran forward, calling out, "Follow me who can" and jumped on board, supported by all [about fifty seamen and marines] who were within hearing. A minute had hardly elapsed before the ships had separated, and a general cry was then raised, "Cease firing," and by the time I had got upon the quarterdeck from the aftermost part of our maindeck the ships had got so far asunder that it was *impossible* to throw any more men on board of her; but it was unnecessary, as they hailed, "We have possession."'[45] The Americans had given up the ship.

The gallantry of Broke's men was noteworthy, but the number of casualties was high, not least from 'friendly fire' that Broke bitterly regretted: 'My brave First Lieutenant, Mr. Watt, was slain in the moment of victory, in the act of hoisting the British colours; his death is a severe loss to the service.'[46] While they were hauling down the American colours and replacing them with the British flag, Lieutenant George Watt and some of the men surrounding him had been fired on by the *Shannon*, which mistook them for Americans, even though a cease-fire had been called. Broke himself was lucky to survive. 'Having received a severe sabre wound at the first onset,' he remarked, 'whilst charging a party of the enemy who had rallied on their forecastle, I was only capable of giving command till assured our conquest was complete, and then directing Second Lieutenant Wallis to take charge of the *Shannon*, and secure the prisoners.'[47] Wallis explained that 'my first care was to get the prisoners secured, which was an easy matter, as the *Chesapeake* had (upon deck) some hundreds of handcuffs in readiness for us'.[48] The Americans had been so sure of victory they were planning a triumphant return to Boston with the *Shannon*'s crew in handcuffs. At least sixty-one men were killed and eighty-five injured from the *Chesapeake*, and thirty-four killed and fifty-two injured from the *Shannon*. The battle gained the dubious record of being the fastest slaughter in naval history up to then, as it was all over in eleven minutes.

The *Chesapeake* with a prize crew and prisoners on board left Boston and headed for Nova Scotia, accompanied by the *Shannon*. Halifax was reached on 5 June, but thick fog meant they had to wait outside the harbour until the 6th, a Sunday. Some fifty years later the author and judge Thomas Chandler Haliburton recalled the events:

I was attending divine service in *St. Paul's Church* at that time, when a person was seen to enter hurriedly, whisper something to a friend in the garrison pew, and as hastily withdraw. The effect was electrical, for, whatever the news was, it flew from pew to pew, and one by one the congregation left the church. My own impression was that there was a fire in the immediate vicinity of *St. Paul's*; and the movement soon became so general that I, too, left the

John Wesley Wright

John Nicol, seaman, at
the age of sixty-seven

Captain Thomas Cochrane

Captain Charles Lydiard

Sir Samuel Hood

Donat Henchy O'Brien

J. Pelham del.

J. Brown sc.

Captain Sir William Hoste

Sir Home Riggs Popham

Edward Codrington

Stephen Decatur of the US Navy

James Lawrence of the US Navy

William Henry Allen of the US Navy

building to inquire into the cause of the commotion. I was informed by a person in the crowd than 'an *English* man-of-war was coming up the harbour with an *American* frigate as her prize.' By that time the ships were in full view, near *George's Island*, and slowly moving through the water. Every housetop and every wharf was crowded with groups of excited people, and, as the ships successively passed, they were greeted with vociferous cheers. *Halifax* was never in such a state of excitement before or since.[49]

Haliburton and a friend found a boat and rowed out to the *Shannon*, but were denied admission. Instead they were allowed to board the *Chesapeake*, but because the vessel had only a small prize crew, the carnage of battle had not yet been removed:

Externally she looked . . . as if just returned from a short cruise; but internally the scene was one never to be forgotten by a landsman . . . The coils and folds of ropes were steeped in gore as if in a slaughter-house. She was a fir-built ship, and her splinters had wounded nearly as many men as the *Shannon*'s shot. Pieces of skin, with pendant hair, were adhering to the sides of the ship; and in one place I noticed portions of fingers protruding, as if thrust through the outer wall of the frigate; while several of the sailors, to whom liquor had evidently been handed through the portholes by visitors in boats, were lying asleep on the bloody floor as if they had fallen in action and had expired where they lay. Altogether, it was a scene of devastation as difficult to forget as to describe. It is one of the most painful reminiscences of my youth, for I was but seventeen years of age.[50]

Once Captain Broke was taken off the *Shannon*, the surgeon of the naval hospital examined him: 'I was requested . . . to visit Captain *Broke*, confined to bed at the commissioner's house in the dockyard, and found him in a very weak state, with an extensive sabre wound on the side of the head, the brain exposed to view for three inches or more; he was unable to converse, save in monosyllables.'[51] Miraculously, he survived and returned to England in October. He would never serve at sea again, and although he lived to the age of sixty-four, he never fully regained his health.

Captain Lawrence survived for four days, but died of his wounds on 5 June just before they reached Halifax. He was thirty-one. His body was wrapped in the *Chesapeake*'s flag and laid on the quarterdeck, before being buried with military honours at Halifax on the 8th:

Six of the oldest navy captains carried the pall, which was one of the colours of the *Chesapeake*. This, they said, was considered a particular mark of respect by naval men, as it was a token that he had defended his colours bravely, and that at this time they should not be separated from him. The procession was very long, and everything was conducted in the most solemn and respectful manner; and the wounded officers of both nations, who followed in the procession, made the scene very affecting . . . There was not the least mark of exultation . . . even among the commonest people.[52]

Lieutenant Ludlow, acting first lieutenant of the *Chesapeake*, made reasonable progress, but died a few days after being transferred to the naval hospital. He was only twenty-one, and he was buried close to Lawrence. His last words were 'Don't give up the ship.'[53]

Once news reached America of the death of these two officers, Captain George Crowninshield from Salem in Massachusetts called for their bodies to be brought back to America. He was given permission to sail with a flag of truce to Halifax, and on 13 August he returned to America with the two bodies on board. At Salem a further funeral service took place, attended by thousands of people who came into the town. The coffins were then transported to New York, where some fifty thousand people watched the procession and a third funeral service took place, this time in Trinity Church. They were buried together in the churchyard and in 1847 their remains were removed closer to Broadway and a new, imposing mausoleum was erected in the Trinity Church graveyard, where it can still be seen.

The news had been slow to spread through America, but Richard Rush, comptroller of the treasury, later wrote: 'I remember . . . the first rumour of it. I remember the startling sensation. I remember, at first, the universal incredulity. I remember how the post offices were thronged for successive days with anxious thousands; how collections of citizens rode out for miles on the highway, accosting the mail to catch something by anticipation. At last, when the certainty was known, I remember the public gloom; funeral orations, badges of mourning, bespoke it. "Don't give up the ship!" the dying words of Lawrence . . . were on every tongue.'[54]

In Britain Broke was treated in much the same way as the Americans had treated Hull and Decatur. There was widespread public celebration, with guns fired, illuminations, bonfires and numerous speeches. Broke was knighted and showered with other honours and gifts, and in

Parliament John Croker, Secretary of the Admiralty, said that 'the action, which he [Broke] fought with the *Chesapeake*, was in every respect unexampled. It was not – and he knew it was a bold assertion which he made, – to be surpassed by any engagement which graced the naval annals of Great Britain.'[55]

The *Chesapeake* was brought to England and served in the Royal Navy until 1819, when the vessel was sold for dismantling, as described by a vicar of Fareham, near Portsmouth, who heard the story from Joshua Holmes himself:

She was sold by Government to Mr. Holmes for £500, who found he had made a capital investment on this occasion, and cleared £1000 profit. He broke up the vessel, took several tons of copper from her, and disposed of the timbers, which were quite new and sound, of beautiful pitch pine, for building purposes. Much of the wood was employed in building houses in Portsmouth; but a large portion was sold, in 1820, to Mr. John Prior, a miller, of Wickham, for nearly £200. Mr. Prior pulled down his own mill, and constructed a new one with this timber, which he found admirably adapted to this purpose.[56]

The watermill in Wickham became known as Chesapeake Mill and operated until 1970. Extensive historical and archaeological research has recently taken place into what is one of the finest surviving buildings constructed from old ships' timbers.

The war with America was literally brought home to Britain's shores with the arrival of privateers and warships that were beginning to be a serious threat to trade. In August 1813 the American brig-sloop *Argus* under the command of Captain William Henry Allen, from Rhode Island, was preying on shipping around the coast of Britain, having recently transported the minister for France and his aides from New York to the French port of Lorient. After a stint in the English Channel the *Argus* had sailed round Land's End and into St George's Channel (between Ireland and Wales), capturing and burning merchant ships, and 'by celerity of movement, audacity of action, and destructive energy, spread consternation throughout commercial England'.[57] The prizes were burned, because they were too far from a friendly port, and likewise captured prisoners were only briefly detained before being returned to shore.

One West Country newspaper reported that 'a correspondent at Ilfracombe informs us, that an American privateer [actually a naval vessel] called the *Argus*, was cruising last week near Lundy Island [in the Bristol Channel]. She is a long, low brig, with yellow sides and black head, and mounts 22 24-pounders. She took last Wednesday [10 August] a homeward-bound West India ship, a brig from Ireland with cattle, a sloop from St. Ives to Liverpool with clay, and a schooner. The crews of these vessels she put aboard a light brig, which has arrived at the Mumbles. – She has also taken a pilot-skiff, which she makes use of as a decoy.'[58] On the 13th the *Argus* captured and burned a merchant vessel laden with wine from Portugal, but exhausted crew members rescued some of the cargo and that evening became drunk. Early the following morning the flames from the burning vessel revealed their position near Milford Haven. The British brig-sloop *Pelican* under Captain John Fordyce Maples had only just left Cork with orders to search for the *Argus*. 'At 4 this morning,' Maples reported, 'I saw a vessel on fire, and a brig standing from her, which I soon made out to be a cruizer; made all sail in chase, and at half-past 5 came alongside of her . . . when, after giving her three cheers, our action commenced, which was kept up with great spirit on both sides 43 minutes, when we lay alongside, and were in the act of boarding, when she struck her colours.'[59]

In fact, the crew of the *Argus* cheered and fired first, followed by cheering and a broadside from the *Pelican*. The fighting could be heard in Milford Haven, where 'the inhabitants of this neighbourhood were this morning alarmed by a tremendous firing which appeared to be at some distance from the harbour'.[60] William Young, master's mate, was killed instantly as he led the boarding party. Another seaman, John Kitery, also lost his life, and five others from the *Pelican* were wounded. The *Pelican* returned to Cork, with some prisoners on board, while the *Argus*, manned by a prize crew, headed for Plymouth.

Ten men from the *Argus* were killed and another fourteen injured. Captain Allen was injured early on and had his left leg amputated by his own surgeon. When the ship reached Plymouth, Allen was examined by the highly respected surgeon of Millbay Prison, Dr George MaGrath, who realised he was in a dangerous state and advised that he should be moved to his hospital. Despite the best efforts to save him, Allen died four days after the battle. 'In person,' the *Naval Chronicle* lamented, 'he was about six feet high, a model of symmetry and manly comeliness, and in his manner and conversation a highly finished and accomplished gentleman.'[61] The funeral with military honours took place on the 21st, attended by a substantial procession, including many inhabitants of

Plymouth. Allen was buried in St Andrew's churchyard, next to eighteen-year-old Midshipman Richard Delphy, who had lost both legs in the action and had been buried the previous evening. Much of the churchyard has since been cleared, but the gravestone commemorating these two Americans has been restored and can be seen on a wall to the south of the church.

# NINETEEN

———•◆•———

# UP THE CHESAPEAKE

> Upon all occasions throughout this unhappy war,—between two nations speaking the same language, and descended in great measure from one common stock of ancestors,—it was certainly creditable to the Americans that they exhibited much kindness to British prisoners whom the fortune of war placed in their power.[1]

By the end of 1813 Napoleon was completely on the defensive as the forces allied against him began to close in. Wellington had fought his way up through the Iberian peninsula, compelling Napoleon to restore King Ferdinand VII to the throne of Spain, and had then invaded France from the south. In October Napoleon was defeated by a mainly Austrian and Russian army at Leipzig and was forced to retreat, and in November a Dutch uprising expelled the French from Holland. By January 1814 France was on the verge of collapse in the face of the invading forces, and Joachim Murat, who had been installed as King of Naples by Napoleon, changed sides in a bid to save his own throne. By the beginning of March the allies were so confident of success that they signed a treaty agreeing not to make a separate peace with Napoleon: they would defeat him first and decide the internal boundaries of Europe afterwards.

At the end of March the allies realised that in his haste to drive eastwards against them Napoleon had left the route to Paris undefended, and in a bold move of the kind Napoleon himself favoured, they pushed on towards the capital. By the 29th they were on the outskirts, and the authorities surrendered the city, fearing the consequences of a siege by which the Russians might take revenge for the fate of Moscow eighteen months before. When he found out Napoleon raced back towards Paris, but was too late to prevent the triumphant entry of the allies on the last day of March. Stunned by the news, he retreated to Fontainebleau and then the diplomatic wrangling began. Although he could no longer win, Napoleon still had sufficient military forces to cause a great upheaval before he was finally defeated. The allies decided it was better to negotiate, and they were led by the Russian Tsar Alexander.

At this stage Napoleon took some convincing that even his loyal forces were worn out by continuous campaigning and wanted peace. Many others who had held power under him were anxiously manoeuvring to save their careers, leaving the emperor to his fate. Over the following weeks diplomats shuttled between Paris and Fontainebleau as the future of France was decided. The Bourbon monarchy was to be restored, although after twenty-five years of exile there was little support for the members of the royal family in France, especially as they wanted to return to the conditions that prevailed before the Revolution. Napoleon was to go into exile, and owing to the generosity of the Tsar the island of Elba, between Italy and Corsica, was chosen, rather than somewhere more distant.

Even before Napoleon was cornered and forced to abdicate, there was an assumption that peace was near. In France the British parole prisoners were moved out of Verdun, initially to Blois and then on to Guéret, and among them was Lieutenant Frederick Hoffman, who had been there since 1812 after his ship ran aground on the French coast. After a wretched march during particularly severe winter weather, Hoffman had the good fortune to find lodgings at Guéret with the Countess de Barton. At this time Napoleon's regime still had a tight rein on the press and Hoffman had no inkling that the allied armies were closing in on the emperor. Within days news came that the allies were in Paris and Napoleon had abdicated. Unexpectedly soon, Hoffman was on his way to the city:

I will not describe our tiresome and wretched journey of nine days. At length we reached Fontainebleau, where we remained two days to rest ourselves as well as the horses. In passing through its forest, which is very fine, we were almost poisoned by the stench occasioned by dead men and horses. We saw the palace, and the ink on the table where Bonaparte had signed his abdication was so fresh that it came off by rubbing it a little with the finger. Two days after, we entered Paris, which we found in possession of the allied armies, and it was with the greatest difficulty that we procured lodgings even in the Faubourg St. Antoine. . . . During the three days we remained in Paris, I visited the Louvre and its stolen goods [looted from territories absorbed into the French empire]. It was a brilliant treat; never was any palace so decorated with such gems of art, nor, I hope, under the same circumstances, ever will be again. On the day Louis le Désiré [King Louis XVIII] entered, I paid a napoleon for half a window in the Rue St. Denis to view the procession.[2]

Louis XVIII made his triumphal entry into Paris on 3 May. Napoleon had left Fontainebleau on 20 April and travelled to Fréjus, where, nearly fifteen years before, he had arrived back from Egypt at the start of his climb to power. At Fréjus a British frigate, the *Undaunted*, was made available to take him to his new kingdom of Elba. Captain Thomas Ussher of the *Undaunted* recorded their first meeting: 'Soon after my arrival Count Bertrand, his Grand Marshal, informed me that it was the Emperor's wish to see me (he is still acknowledged Emperor, and Sovereign of Elba). When I was presented he said that he was once a great enemy to England, but now he was as sincere a friend. He said we were a great and generous nation. He asked me about the wind, weather, distance to Elba, and other nautical questions; he then bowed and retired. He was very dignified – still the Emperor.'[3]

Napoleon was pleasant and flattering because he felt safe only with a British escort, as he feared that some of the other allies were plotting his assassination. He spent his last night at Fréjus in the Chapeau Rouge, the inn where he had stayed on his return from Egypt, but possibly not for sentimental reasons since Ussher described it as 'a small Auberge, or hotel and, I believe, the only one in Fréjus'.[4] The next day Napoleon boarded the boat that would take him out to the *Undaunted*, as Ussher related: 'I informed him [Napoleon] that the boat was ready, and we walked together to where she was. He was handed into the boat by a nephew of Sir Sidney Smith's, who is my fourth lieutenant – rather odd coincidence. Lieutenant [George Sidney] Smith had been confined in prison for seven or eight years. I introduced him. The Emperor seemed to feel his conscience prick him: he only said, "Nephew to Sir Sidney Smith; I met him in Egypt".'[5]

The voyage to Elba was uneventful, and Napoleon insisted on a grand entrance when he arrived there. Ussher described how 'the yards were manned, and as soon as the barge [carrying Napoleon] shoved off a royal salute was fired, and the same by each of the French corvettes [in the harbour]. On the beach he was received by the mayor, municipality, and the authorities, civil and military. The keys were presented on a plate, and the people seemed to receive him with great welcome, and shouts of "Vive l'Empereur!".[6] It was a better reception than might have been expected, as Colonel Neil Campbell, the British Commissioner on Elba, commented: 'For several weeks the inhabitants had been in a state of revolt ... The spirit of the inhabitants is very inimical to the late Government of France, and personally to Napoleon, so that he will cer-tainly require the French troops [already stationed there] for his protection until his Guards arrive from France. He has also so strongly urged Captain Ussher and myself to land the marines, that we could not refuse.'[7]

In the days and months after the *Undaunted* sailed from Elba, Napoleon was left very much to his own devices. Officially he was regarded as an autonomous ruler of Elba who could not leave his island, rather than a prisoner to be watched and guarded. However, many of the allies, including Britain, were not entirely happy with the decision to send him there rather than somewhere more remote, so they stationed secret agents on Elba itself and in neighbouring ports. When Napoleon had been cornered by the allies, his wife and son were in Paris and were forced to flee before they became trapped in the city. Marie-Louise was Napoleon's second wife, having married her in the spring of 1810 after divorcing Josephine. The divorce was a political move as part of a delib-erate attempt by Napoleon to found a dynasty, since Marie-Louise was daughter of the Emperor of Austria. On 29 May, while Napoleon was still exploring his new Elba home, Josephine died at Malmaison. On the day of her funeral *The Times* recorded her death in just thirteen lines, referring to her as 'the mother of Prince Eugene',[8] who was not a son of Napoleon but of her previous husband. Three days afterwards, in a report from a correspondent at Paris dated 31 May, the comment was made in passing that 'the death of Josephine is universally regretted, and it is even said that it will occasion something more than a mere Court mourning at Elba'.[9] No one was sent to inform Napoleon, who read about Josephine's death in a newspaper some time later and was so overcome with grief that he shut himself in his room for two days.

By now many of the British prisoners in France were on their way home and 'prisoners from various depôts marched through Gueret for Bordeaux to embark there, all in great distress, for the French Government gave no clothing nor even arrears of pay due'.[10] The sudden removal of the prisoners hit the local population hard, for the majority of prisoners could not or would not pay the bills they had accumulated – a substantial sum at Verdun alone. In 1839 one newspaper stated that 'a deputation from the inhabitants of Verdun in France has just arrived in London to claim the payment of 3,500,000 francs (140,000 *l.*), the amount of private debts contracted by English prisoners detained in that city during the war'.[11] Some former prisoners made their way to the Channel coast of France to try to get home, and among these was Lieutenant Richard Langton, who had been at Verdun:

We quitted Boulogne at 10 a.m., and walking at a moderate pace, reached Calais ... in the afternoon. During the morning the atmosphere was too dense to permit a view of the cliffs of Dover; it however cleared about three o'clock. When first seen by several of the sailors of our party, three hearty cheers followed. These poor fellows invariably stopped at cottages where a bush hanging out on a poll [pole] over the door, denotes liquids [alcohol] may be purchased. These frequent stoppages gave rise to many ludicrous incidents during the day. As we approached Calais the sailors came to a decision to kiss every woman and shake hands with the men whom they might perchance meet. Several market women, mounted on asses, coming from thence were thus complimented, not, however, without a struggle. The 'Sailor's grasp' was by no means relished by two waggoners, if their exclamations and swearing were to be taken as proof. ... The Frenchmen were excessively enraged at the conduct of the sailors, bestowing on them epithets which it was well the latter did not comprehend, as, in such event, there would have been still further ground for their complaining. To those unacquainted with the character of a British sailor, the freaks alluded to may appear to have emanated from a feeling of revenge ... Quite the contrary; all they wanted, and to use their common expression, was a lark.[12]

Among the French people themselves there was rejoicing and relief at the peace. The Royalists celebrated the return of the king, and even many supporters of Napoleon were glad of an end to the years of fighting, conscription and, they hoped, the hardships of a besieged economy. In Britain the joy was unqualified, and up and down the country all manner of festivities were set in motion. At Lichfield Major-General Dyott wrote in his diary: 'A subscription made in Lichfield, and upwards of £700 collected for the purpose of giving a treat to all the lower class of people to commemorate the peace. Dinners were provided at the inns for near three thousand people, who were regaled with roast beef, plum pudding, and ale. I made a present of an ox, which was roasted whole and distributed.'[13] In London the Prince Regent ordered his own celebrations, which took longer to organise, as the *Liverpool Mercury* reported:

The preparations making to celebrate the Peace, at Carlton House, engross the attention of all the parties concerned. The Board of Works have received orders to erect an immense body of frame-work, eighty feet in height, in front of the Palace, occupying nearly the whole of the Court-yard. In addition to transparencies, there will be devices in variegated lamps of a most extraordinary description. Colonel Congreve has it in contemplation to exhibit his rockets in the Green Park, on the first night of the illumination. To give full effect to the scene, a bridge will be erected on the canal, and from thence the rockets are to ascend. To gratify John Bull, there will be such an effulgence produced as to set the elements on fire; no less than 10,000 rockets will ascend at one time. This is only intended as the first volley – there will be three of them.[14]

Near Little Dunham in Norfolk an obelisk was erected as a monument to the peace and carries the inscription 'In Commemoration of Peace John Drosier Esq. Erected this Obilisk Anno Domini MDCCCXIV'. Drosier is thought to have been a distant relation of Nelson, who is also commemorated by another inscription on the monument. The obelisk still survives and is a rarity: other monuments to the peace were planned but in many cases war broke out again before they were built or finished, so that most were eventually dedicated to the peace of 1815 rather than of 1814.

Not everyone in Britain was exultant about the peace. Many of the French prisoners-of-war were supporters of Napoleon and were unhappy at the prospect of being repatriated to a country ruled by a Bourbon king. Nevertheless, they were sent back to France, and by the end of August the *Morning Chronicle* could report: 'Of all the prisoners at Norman Cross, only one man remains; and he, in consequence of illness preventing his removal. The change produced by withdrawing the demand for the necessaries to supply ten thousand mouths is felt in the country round the depôt.'[15] Other Frenchmen were happy to return, but did not always have a pleasant homecoming, as Rifleman John Harris related:

Many of the French prisoners had volunteered into the English service, and were formed into four companies, called the Independent Companies. These were smart-looking fellows, and wore a green uniform ... on Napoleon's being sent to Elba, these men were all liberated and sent home to their own country, with four pounds given to each man; and gloriously drunk they all were at Portsmouth the night they embarked ... we were all sorry to hear (whether true or false I cannot say) that on their return, their uniforms betraying their having served us, they were grossly maltreated by their fellow countrymen.[16]

While the rest of Europe was at peace, Britain's war with America continued, but it seemed very far away and had little obvious effect on the population as a whole. Indeed, on 18 April the artist Joseph Farington recorded in his diary: 'James Boswell* said that when Francis Jeffrey, the Editor of the *Edinburgh Review*, was lately in America, he was in company with *Mr. Maddison* the *President* who was desirous to know from Jeffrey what the People of England thought of the War with America. Jeffrey declined answering till pressed to it. He then said, "Half the People of England do not know there is war with America, and those who did have forgotten it."'[17] Peace in Europe was what really mattered to the population on both sides of the Channel.

With the cessation of war in Europe, Britain was able to send many more troops and ships to America. In early April 1814, while Napoleon was still at Fontainebleau, Midshipman John Courtney Bluett sailed from England for Bermuda in the *Tonnant*, which was accompanying a convoy of troopships. When they heard the news of peace Bluett thought that 'the war with America must shortly terminate & I shall then return to England (I hope) to lead a domestic life. Give up the sea (for I despair of getting made Lieut) & endeavour to earn a livelihood without quitting my Native Country.'[18] As well as yearning after promotion to lieutenant, he was desperate to earn more money, since he was in financial difficulties: 'I have no money! Nor any means of getting any – and in this one single want, are summed up all the evils that can attack a man in this world.'[19]

The seaman James Durand was also about to leave for the West Indies. Durand was an American, from Milford near New Haven in Connecticut, and in 1809 had been taken off a Swedish vessel and forced to serve in the Royal Navy. When war broke out with America he and around thirty others on board his warship tried to give themselves up as

---

* Barrister and literary scholar, son of the more famous James Boswell.

prisoners-of-war, but to no avail – their pleas were ignored. In his case, he was a musician and his captain wanted him in the ship's band. At Bordeaux on board the new frigate *Pactolus*, Durand explained that 'we found it a rendezvous for all the shipping and all of our fleet. General Napoleon was a prisoner [at Fréjus], on his way to Elba . . . While we lay there, the aged and wounded troops were sent back to England and the other English soldiers came on board us too. They said that, since they had whipped Napoleon, they would have no trouble in subduing the U. States.'[20]

The *Pactolus* sailed from Bordeaux as part of a squadron under Rear-Admiral Pulteney Malcolm in the *Royal Oak* with Major-General Robert Ross on board. Captain Harry Smith of the 95th Regiment also embarked on board the *Royal Oak*, but somewhat nervously:

We soldiers had heard such accounts of the etiquette required in a man-of-war, the rigidity with which it was exacted, etc., that I was half afraid of doing wrong in anything I said or did. When I reached the quarters, the officer of the watch asked my name, and then, in the most gentlemanlike and unaffected manner, the lieutenant of the watch . . . showed me aft into the Admiral's cabin. Here I saw wine, water, spirits, etc., and at the end of the table sat the finest-looking specimen of an English sailor I ever saw. This was Admiral Malcolm, and near him sat Captain Dick, an exceedingly stout man, a regular representation of John Bull. They both rose immediately, and welcomed me on board in such an honest and hospitable manner, that I soon discovered the etiquette consisted in nothing but a marked endeavour to make us all happy . . . The fact is that Army and Navy had recently changed places. When I joined the Army, it was just at a time when our Navy, after a series of brilliant victories, had destroyed at Trafalgar the navy of the world. Nine years had elapsed, and the glories of the Army were so fully appreciated by our gallant brothers of the sea service, we were now by them regarded as the heroes whom I well recollect I thought them to be in 1805.[21]

Still feeling a little awkward, Smith entered the cabin:

The Admiral says, 'Come, sit down and have a glass of grog.' I was so absorbed in the thought that this large floating ship was to bear me away from all I held so dear, that I sat down, and seized a bottle (gin, I believe), filled a tumbler half full, and then added some water. 'Well done!' says the Admiral. 'I have been at sea, man and boy, these forty years, but d—— me, if

I ever saw a stiffer glass of grog than that in my life.' . . . I shall never forget the kindness I received on board the *Royal Oak*, and subsequently on board the *Menelaus* . . . and from every ship and every sailor with whom I became associated. Our Navy are noble fellows, and the discipline and the respect on board for rank are a bright example to the more familiar habits of our Army.[22]

Bermuda was the rendezvous for the troop transports and warships. There Sir Alexander Cochrane, who had taken over from John Borlase Warren as commander-in-chief of the North American station in the spring, was waiting in his flagship – the newly arrived *Tonnant*. Malcolm was his third-in-command and Rear-Admiral George Cockburn his second-in-command. In mid-July Edward Codrington joined them at Bermuda as Captain of the Fleet, initially on board the *Tonnant*. Writing home to his wife Jane, Codrington said: 'I like my chief (Sir Alexander Cochrane) very much, and I hope I shall make him as contented with me, by pursuing my inclination to meet all his wishes, and to make myself of material use to him.'[23] A few days later he added: 'My heart is very much in this war . . . I much like General Ross; and his troops, Malcolm says, are glorious fellows for the Yankees.'[24] Unlike Codrington's time at Walcheren, this expedition against America would benefit from close co-operation between the navy and army, many of whom were veterans of the Peninsular War.

Major-General Ross had overall command of the operation, and at the beginning of August the *Tonnant*, *Euryalus* and *Hebrus* left Bermuda so that the chief officers could reconnoitre their planned target, leaving the troops to follow on, although some were directed to Quebec to strengthen forces in Canada. Codrington wryly noted: 'We are now on our way to the Chesapeake (mind you don't tell the Yankees!).'[25] By mid-August they were sailing into Chesapeake Bay, but after his recent service in Spain, Codrington was not impressed: 'The wind does not favour our advance upon this unpicturesque river. Low, flat sandy banks, covered with pines, is all we see, and we cannot approach either shore on account of shoals. Never was there a greater contrast than betwixt this part of the American coast and Cataluña: not a thing is there here to attract the eye . . . the Chesapeake is like a new world.'[26]

They initially anchored off Point Lookout, between the Potomac and Patuxent rivers, and Captain Charles Napier of the *Euryalus* reported that they 'soon after joined Sir George Cockburn, who had been actively employed, feeling his way with a battalion of marines, and had kept the coast in a constant state of alarm'.[27] While they were waiting for the troops from Bermuda, help was given to Cockburn with his raiding parties along the Potomac River. Cockburn especially impressed Midshipman Robert Barrett of the *Hebrus*:

The excitement of the passing scene was imposing in the extreme to a youth of fifteen, like myself; and it is almost impossible to depict my boyish feelings and transport when, at the close of this spirit-stirring affair, I gazed, for the first time in my life, on the features of that undaunted seaman, Rear-Admiral George Cockburn, with his sun-burnt visage, and his rusty gold-laced hat – an officer who never spared himself, either night or day, but shared on every occasion, the same toil, danger, and privation of the foremast man under his command. These are the men who win a gallant sailor's heart! A glittering reward was set upon his head by the Americans.[28]

Barrett had only joined the navy in December, three years after his father drowned in the shipwreck of the *Minotaur*, of which he was captain. He now took part in some of Cockburn's raids and felt that 'this system of desultory warfare in various instances led to the petty plunder of poultry, sheep, and pigs. It was contrary to the strict orders which were issued, that nothing should be taken without payment; but what power on earth could possibly restrain the hungry stomachs of midshipmen and their numerous boats' crews, who were frequently from under the eyes of their commanding officers, and spread over an extended space of twenty miles upon the rivers of the Chesapeake?'[29]

On board one of the transport ships that were now arriving in the Chesapeake was a Scottish soldier, George Robert Gleig. In 1812 he had given up his university studies and plans for ordination to enter the 85th Regiment as an ensign, and was promoted to lieutenant a few months later. After serving in Spain his regiment had been ordered to America, and he had just enjoyed several days exploring Bermuda. Because of the heat, he was finding it unbearable cooped up on board:

The heat, indeed, became more and more oppressive every day, and the irksomeness of renewed confinement was more sensibly [sensitively] experienced from the long holiday which we had enjoyed on shore . . . on the 14th [August] . . . a signal was made by the admiral, that land was in sight. As yet, however, there was no appearance of it from the deck of our transport, nor, for a full half hour, could our anxious gaze be rewarded by the slightest trace of what it sought; but, at the end of that time, the low sandy point of Cape Charles began to show itself, and we rejoiced in the prospect of a speedy release from the ennui of a sea-faring life.[30]

Gleig detailed the sights around him:

The coast of America, at least in this quarter, is universally low and uninteresting; insomuch that for some time before the land itself can be discerned, forests of pines appear to rise, as it were, out of the water. It is also dangerous, from the numerous shoals and sand-banks which run out, in many places, to a considerable extent into the sea . . . This noble bay is far too wide, and the land on each side, too flat to permit any but an indistinct glimpse of the shore, from the deck of a vessel which keeps well towards the middle. We could distinguish nothing, therefore, on either hand, except the tops of trees, with, occasionally, a windmill, or a light-house; but the view of our own fleet was, in truth, so magnificent, as to prevent any murmuring on that account. Immediately on entering, we were joined by Admiral Cockburn with three line of battle ships, several frigates, and a few sloops of war and gun brigs . . . besides an equal, if not greater number of victuallers and transports . . . On board these ships was embarked a powerful reinforcement for the army, consisting of a battalion of seven hundred marines, an hundred negroes lately armed and disciplined, and a division of marine artillery . . . The sight was therefore altogether as grand and imposing as any I ever beheld; because one could not help remembering that this powerful fleet was sailing in an enemy's bay, and was filled with troops for the invasion of that enemy's country.[31]

The first target was a flotilla of American gunboats commanded by Captain Joshua Barney, which had been sent to the Chesapeake to try to stop British raids, but instead had taken refuge in the Patuxent River. The British now prepared to find and destroy them. As a diversion, Cochrane ordered the frigates *Seahorse* and *Euryalus* to lead mortar and rocket vessels up the Potomac to the port of Alexandria. Captain Charles Napier of the *Euryalus* and Captain James Alexander Gordon of the *Seahorse* had previously served in the Mediterranean, and Gordon had played a prominent part at Lissa, losing a leg soon after, but by the end of 1812 he was back in service with Cochrane in the Chesapeake. These Scottish captains set out on 17 August, with Gordon as the senior commander of the squadron. 'The river Potomac is navigable for frigates as high up as

Washington,' Napier remarked, 'but the navigation is extremely intricate . . . The best channel is on the Virginian shore, but the charts gave us
mostly very bad directions, and no pilots could be procured . . . The
American frigates themselves never attempted it with their guns in, and
were several weeks in the passage from the naval yard at Washington to
the mouth of the Potomac.'[32]

While Gordon's and Napier's squadron was carefully working its way
up the Potomac, the other vessels sailed up the Patuxent. Everybody
found the scenery beautiful, and Lieutenant Gleig observed that

the banks were covered with fields of Indian corn, and meadows of the most
luxuriant pasture; while the neat wooden houses of the settlers, all of them
painted white, and surrounded with orchards and gardens, presented a striking contrast to the boundless forests which formed a back ground to the
scene . . . there was the most complete line drawn between the regions
devoted to cultivation, and those still in a state of nature . . . Here, nature is
seen in her grandest attire; civilized man in his most pitiful state. The rivers
and forests are sublime beyond description.[33]

Even Codrington admitted that 'the sailing up the Patuxent is very
pretty',[34] though he noted the absence of any military opposition: 'I think
it may also be considered a comparatively extraordinary circumstance that
we have not found an enemy to assail us in the course of about sixty
miles that we have explored, although the cliffs which occasionally arise
on either bank offer facilities apparently irresistible to a people so disposed
to hatred and so especially hostile to the navy of England.'[35] When the
battleships found it too difficult to advance any further the fleet anchored,
and the next day the army was landed at the village of Benedict, some 10
miles away, which was 'one of the most sequestered and lovely hamlets in
existence', according to Barrett, and '. . . selected for the landing-place,
because a road proceeded from thence to Nottingham and Washington'.[36]
Lieutenant Gleig recalled how they reached Benedict:

As soon as the dawn began to appear, on the morning of the 19th, there was
a general stir throughout the fleet. A gun-brig had already taken her station
within an hundred and fifty yards of a village called St. Benedict's . . . Her
broad-side was turned towards the shore, and her guns, loaded with grape and
round shot, were pointed at the beach, to cover the landing of the boats . . .
The rest of the ships were several miles lower down the stream, some of

them being aground at the distance of four leagues from this point; but the boats were quickly hoisted out from every one of them, and the river was covered in a trice, with a well-armed and warlike flotilla. The disembarkation was conducted with the greatest regularity and dispatch. Though the stream ran strong against them, and some of them were obliged to row fourteen or fifteen miles backwards and forwards, so strenuously did the sailors exert themselves, that by three o'clock in the afternoon the whole army was landed, and occupied a strong position two miles above the village.[37]

The following day, 20 August, the army marched to Nottingham, with the Americans fleeing before them, as Gleig explained: 'We found this place (a town or large village, capable of containing from a thousand to fifteen hundred inhabitants) completely deserted. Not an individual was to be seen in the streets, or remained in the houses; while the appearance of the furniture, &c., in some places the very bread left in the ovens, showed that it had been evacuated in great haste, and immediately before our arrival. The town itself stands upon the banks of the Patuxent, and consists of four short streets, two running parallel with the river, and two others crossing them at right angles.'[38]

Boats from the warships were also rowed upstream in pursuit of the gunboats, because, as Codrington told his wife, 'Commodore Barney and his Baltimore flotilla are, it seems, gone up this river as high as possible, *out of harm's way*; and our troops will yet have a long march, and Cockburn a long run, to get at them.'[39] Two frigates began to inch upstream to Benedict as well – the *Severn* and the *Hebrus* with Midshipman Barrett on board, who many years later described the sight: 'A numerous flotilla of boats, well armed, and formed in three divisions, under the command of Rear-Admiral Cockburn, ascended the river in quest of Commodore Barney's seventeen gun-boats . . . Never, in the course of my life, have I since witnessed a more imposing spectacle than the numerous tenders, launches, barges, and cutters of the fleet presented, with their colours gaily streaming, whilst the sun glistened on their various fancy sails and the uniforms of the Royal Marines.'[40]

Midshipman Bluett was in one of the boats:

On the 22nd they [the army and boats' crews] communicated with each other at Nottingham village, which place Barney had left but a few hours before them, and had gone higher up to Pig Point. The assistance of the army not being thought necessary, they proceeded on their route to Washington and the boats pushed on to attack the enemy's flotilla but Barney finding the English resolute & not thinking himself a match for us, decamped with his men to Washington, leaving behind him a few men to blow up the flotilla – which they did the very instant our boats made their appearance round the point behind which they lay and so effectually did they execute their duty, that only one gun boat fell into our hands.[41]

The gunboat, Bluett thought, had been left as a booby-trap: 'For several boats finding that she was not on fire pulled on board and took possession of her – and one man going below found a train leading from the magazine, the cabin deck strewed all over with gunpowder and a lighted candle stuck in the center of it; fortunately they succeeded in putting it out, without any accident; thus was a flotilla of 20 sail destroyed without our losing a single man.'[42] In fact, the gunboat was probably not a booby-trap, but had failed to blow up with the others, when Captain Barney and his crews had fled their vessels and joined forces with the American army. Codrington was sorry that the gunboats had not been captured: 'It would have been more suitable to our future object to have got possession of these vessels, but it is at all events satisfactory to have forced him [Barney] to such a measure, by driving him up to the extremity of such a river, so distant from the Chesapeake into which it empties, and without any previous knowledge of the soundings. Pilots there are none to be had.'[43]

Because Cockburn's boats had no further targets, he hurried to join the British army, along with the marines and some of the seamen. The army was already marching from Nottingham through thick forests and tobacco plantations towards Upper Marlborough. On the 27th Codrington wrote that 'we got a note from Cockburn to say that our little army met the Yankees, at least double their force, at a place called Bladensburg, posted upon a hill, secured by works, and with ten guns'.[44] This was the Battle of Bladensburg. It was also known as the Bladensburg Races from the speed at which the Americans ran away, fortunately for the ill-prepared British, whose main army had not caught up with the advance guard. Midshipman Bluett described what happened:

The advance guard . . . consisted of 1500 men, part of which were seamen carrying pound rockets. Our brave fellows crossed the bridge in profound silence, without firing a single shot, and as they crossed opened to the right and left: proceeding firmly & steadily on, to form their little line, in front of the enemy, altho' exposed to a most galling cross fire of grape & bag shot from the artillery, & (till we opened fire) a well directed and continued fire from right to left of the American line. As soon as ever the little party was formed, they opened a brisk fire, and the rockets from the wings broke their line & disconcerted them considerably; but their artillery being out of musket shot was doing much damage which Ross perceiving, detached a party from each wing to storm the heights. This difficult service they performed instan-taneously & successfully – crawling on their hands & knees; and charging them in the very muzzles of their guns turned against them, struck such a panic into the Yankies that they fled precipitately, very wisely dropping their arms, and making the best possible use of their legs, accompanied in their flight by as many of their own grape shot as we could conveniently send after them from the pieces we had taken.[45]

Years later Midshipman Barrett, who regretted being ordered to remain with the boats at Benedict, wrote down what his messmate told him:

It was a glorious, but heart-rending scene, as the advance of the British army moved, in double quick time, up the hill, in face of a destructive fire . . . whilst ever and anon the exhilarating voices of the officers could be distinctly heard, cheering on the assault,— 'Hurrah! gallant 85th! push forward for the honour of Old England!' and nobly did all present do their duty in this short and decisive battle. This has ever been a sore subject with our Transatlantic brethren; so conscious were they of the cowardice and ill-conduct of the troops and militia then assembled for the defence of their capital, that, in my youthful days, one of the greatest insults which could be offered to an American, was to ask, in a bantering tone, with a grave face, if the gentleman had ever been present at Bladensburg races.[46]

The British then marched towards Washington, much to the horror of the Americans, who were totally unprepared and never believed that the city would be a target. The citizens, including President Madison, began to flee. Gleig remarked that Washington was 'completely in its infancy, few of the streets being finished, and many containing not more than three or four houses at wide intervals from each other. But from its situ-ation, it derives every possible advantage, and if it continue to be the capital of the United States for another century, it will become, I doubt not, one of the most flourishing cities in the world.'[47]

It was dark when they reached the city, and Gleig reported that they entered with a flag of truce, only to be fired upon by snipers, which enraged everyone, 'and having first put to the sword all who were found in the house from which the shots were fired, and reduced it to ashes, they proceeded, without a moment's delay, to burn and destroy every thing in the most distant degree connected with Government'.[48] James Scott was with Vice-Admiral Cockburn as his aide-de-camp and acting first lieutenant when he entered Washington, and by then the British had already set fire to parts of the city and the Americans destroyed others, as he described:

The position of the Capitol was elevated; the fiery beacon must have shed a sadly brilliant light upon the American habitations for miles around. The flames floated away in masses, which alighted upon the houses to leeward, set them in a blaze likewise. The Americans had been no less active in the work of destruction: they set fire to the Navy-yard; the *Essex* [actually the *Columbia*], a large frigate of sixty guns, measuring sixteen hundred tons, ready for launching; the *Argus*, a sloop of war of six hundred tons, all ready for sea. The wooden bridge across the Potomac, on the Virginia side, over which the greater part of the enemy's troops had retreated, was likewise destroyed; in fact, they anticipated our wishes, and by some of their acts saved us time, and an infinity of trouble. After the destruction of the Capitol, a party was ordered to take possession of the fort at Greenleaf Point.[49]

From Capitol Hill, Scott accompanied Cockburn's party into the city centre along Pennsylvania Avenue towards the house of the President, which had begun to be built by George Washington. Although occupied, it was still incomplete – later rebuilt from the ruins, it would become officially known as the White House:

The Admiral and General Ross then descended the Capitol hill, with about one hundred and fifty men, and entered the heart of the city, by the Pennsylvanian avenue. This was a fine and spacious causeway with a road on each side, for equestrians, outside of which were two broad pathways for the accommodation of the more humble pedestrian; the whole was beautifully planted with a row of trees separating them from each other. The President's palace, a handsome stone building, so lately the head-quarters of the enemy, stood at the extremity of the avenue, and was evacuated by the guard of soldiers, with their two field-pieces, only a few minutes before we made ourselves masters of the place.[50]

In the midst of the hardships of war, Scott came across an unexpected sight inside the White House: 'We found the cloth laid for the expected victorious generals, and all the appliances and means to form a feast worthy the resolute champions of republican freedom. A large store of super-excellent Madeira and other costly wines stood cooling in ice in one corner of the spacious dining-room . . . Fagged nearly to death, dusty, feverish, and thirsty, in my extremity I absolutely blessed them for their erring providence. Never was nectar more grateful to the palates of the gods, than the crystal goblet of Madeira and water I quaffed at Mr. Madison's expense.'[51]

Not only did he share in the presidential feast that had been confidently prepared for the expected American victors, but Scott also took a shirt belonging to Madison: 'The beautiful apartments were hastily visited; passing through the President's dressing-room, (which from its disordered state, opened drawers, and half-filled portmanteaus, must have been abandoned in the midst of packing up,) the snowy clean linen tempted me to take the liberty of making a very fair exchange; I accordingly doffed my inner garment, and thrust my unworthy person into a shirt belonging to no less a personage than the chief magistrate of the United States: the operation equalled in luxury and benefit the draught in the banqueting-room.'[52]

A portrait of the First Lady, Dolley Madison, who had packed up and saved many of the contents of the White House, was still in place and noticed by Scott: 'On the walls hung a small portrait of the President's lady . . . The Treasury was next visited, but the specie had been safely conveyed away. The building was fired before the discovery of a strong iron door, that resisted all the efforts made to break it open. It was presumed to be the stronghold and deposit of all the valuables. The window was forced in, and the first officer who descended into the apartment, gave information that it contained several weighty boxes.'[53]

There was much criticism of the burning of Washington, and Gleig blamed Cockburn: 'To destroy the flotilla [Barney's gunboats] was the sole object of the disembarkation; and but for the instigations of Admiral Cockburn, who accompanied the army, the capital of America would probably have escaped its visitation. It was he, who, on the retreat of that flotilla from Nottingham, urged the necessity of a pursuit, which was not agreed to without some wavering; and it was he also who suggested the attack upon Washington, and finally prevailed on General Ross to venture so far from the shipping.'[54] In his official dispatch Ross actually gave

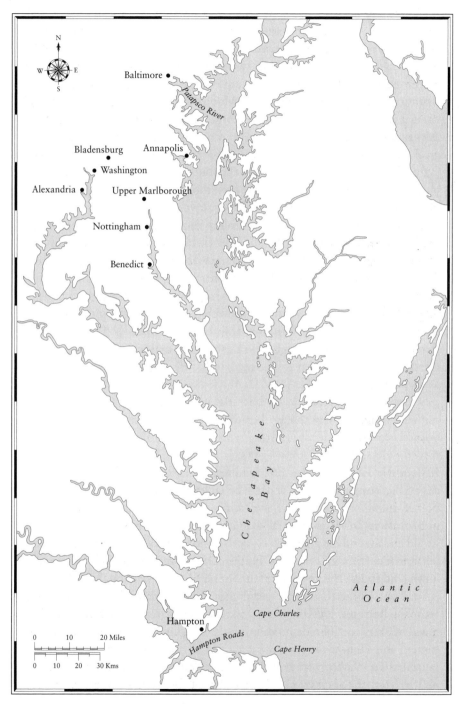

*Map of Chesapeake Bay*

thanks 'to Rear Admiral Cockburn, who suggested the attack upon Washington'.[55] It was often said that the burning of Washington was in retaliation for the burning the year before of York (now Toronto), the capital of Upper Canada, but when writing to his wife before the attack, Codrington said that they had been ordered to retaliate for the latest American excesses: 'By letting his [Madison's] generals in Canada burn villages again . . . he has led Sir George [Prevost] on one side, and Sir Alexander Cochrane on the other, to direct the severest retaliation in all parts till he remunerates the Canadians for their losses.'[56]

Lieutenant Gleig understood the need to destroy shipping and weapons, but lamented that 'it did not stop here; a noble library, several printing-offices, and all the national archives were likewise committed to the flames, which, though no doubt the property of Government, might better have been spared'.[57] Captain Harry Smith was also critical of the arson attacks: 'Admiral Cockburn would have burnt the whole [of the city], but Ross would only consent to the burning of the public buildings. I had no objection to burn arsenals, dockyards, frigates building, stores, barracks, etc., but . . . we were horrified at the order to burn the elegant Houses of Parliament and the President's house. In the latter . . . I shall never forget the destructive majesty of the flames as the torches were applied to beds, curtains, etc. Our sailors were artists at the work.'[58]

They left the White House burning, and Scott related that the office of the anti-British newspaper the *National Intelligencer* was next pointed out to Cockburn:

Its fate was decreed, and a few minutes would have seen it a prey to the devouring element – when a party of ladies, inhabitants of the adjoining houses, came forward to meet the Admiral (whom they only knew as a superior officer) to entreat that he would spare the building, as its destruction would endanger their property. The order was immediately countermanded; but a lieutenant and a party of blue jackets volunteered to pull the house down, and in less than two hours it was razed to the ground. The reams of paper, files of gazettes foreign and domestic, and all the inflammable materials, had been previously conveyed some distance in the rear, and a bonfire made of them . . . The demolition was effected by removing the window-frames, and then passing a stout rope round that part of the walls which separated the windows from each other; 'a long pull, and strong pull, and a pull altogether,' dragged them forward, and the whole superincumbent weight came tumbling down, and presented a mass of ruins in the time I have described.[59]

The women, very grateful that their homes had been saved from destruction, were bewitched by the charm of Cockburn, as Scott described:

The success of the fair petitioners emboldened others to advance, and in a few minutes the Admiral was surrounded by a host of lovely women . . . The kind affable manner in which he calmed their fears, his lively conversation and gentlemanly demeanour, soon won upon their better feelings, and insensibly chased away from their minds foes, captured city, defeat, and disgrace. The singular reunion of the victors and the families of the vanquished, took place in the Pennsylvania avenue, close to the scene, and while the destruction of the Intelligencer office was going on. It was only dissolved by one of the ladies inviting the Admiral to enter her dwelling and partake of the refreshments prepared for him; he accepted the welcome offer, and, courteously wishing the fair strangers good night, begged that they would retire to their pillows in confidence and peace.[60]

As Cockburn had been long reviled in the American press as a terrifying figure, Scott was obviously much amused by what occurred next:

I was about to follow my chief, but my steps were arrested by a gently urged request that I would favour them with the name of the delightful officer who had just quitted them. 'Why, that is the vile monster Cock—burn,' was my reply. A half-uttered shriek of terror escaped from the lips of some of them, as the dreaded name tingled on their ears. The announcement was electrifying. My plighted word had at last convinced them of the stounding fact that they had absolutely stood in the presence of, and amicably conversed with, that most venomous of all 'British sarpents,' and for whose head a reward of one thousand dollars had been publicly offered. Such was the state of American prejudice at that period.[61]

As Cockburn is pronounced 'Coburn' in Britain, Scott added a note that 'the Americans always pronounced the name as two long distinct syllables'.[62]

Almost like divine intervention, Scott recorded that Washington was struck by severe weather the following day:

About noon [on the 25th] one of the severest squalls, or more properly speaking tornadoes, which I ever witnessed, passed over Washington; trees were uprooted, plantations destroyed, and houses blown down, the conflict of winds setting at nought the industry and power of man. The tiles flew about in showers over our heads; it was found impossible to stem the whirlwind; and all those who were exposed to its fury were obliged to lie flat on the ground, as the sole means of resisting the effects of the tremendous blast. An officer on horseback turning the corner of a street encountered the hurricane, and both man and horse were dashed to the pavement in an instant. It was of brief duration, or the devastation to Washington would have proved of far greater magnitude than the mischief committed by the English.[63]

By this time Napier and Gordon had forced their way up the Potomac and captured Fort Washington and its supporting batteries. They reached Alexandria on the 28th, and the town surrendered. The Americans had earlier scuttled shipping, but the British ordered the vessels to be salvaged as prizes. At the beginning of September they began to sail back down the Potomac with their twenty-one prizes complete with cargoes, despite fierce firing from batteries that had been hastily erected to intercept their return journey. Napier recorded that 'this expedition lasted twenty-three days. The hammocks were only down twice—each ship was ashore [grounded] at least twenty times; but nothing could exceed the patience and good conduct of the ships' companies; and though every encouragement was held out by the inhabitants of Alexandria to induce the men to desert, there were only four or five out of the whole squadron who remained behind. The total loss was seven killed, thirty-five wounded.'[64]

Codrington thought their exploits were outstanding, as he told his wife: 'They overcame difficulties which would have dismayed many men in either of the two professions; and they have brought out twenty-one prizes, many of which they *weighed*, *caulked*, and *masted*, as well as *loaded*; and then forced their way through the most difficult shoal navigation, in spite of batteries erected to stop them, and a vast number of troops firing down on their decks in the narrow parts. The frigates were even obliged to take their guns out on account of getting aground, and put them in again. In short, it is nothing less brilliant than the capture of Washington.'[65]

The troops in Washington left the city after three days. Many American prisoners were given parole, including Captain Barney, while the care of the wounded British prisoners was entrusted to the Americans.

A rumour was deliberately spread that the next targets were Annapolis and Baltimore, and so the Americans hurried to reinforce those places, enabling the British troops to return safely to the boats, which they did at night, although they kept fires burning to deceive the Americans into thinking they were still encamped nearby. As they passed the site of the Battle of Bladensburg, the moon rose, and Gleig was horrified by the scene: 'The dead were still unburied, and lay about in every direction, completely naked. They had been stripped even of their shirts, and having been exposed in this state to the violent rain in the morning, they appeared to be bleached to a most unnatural degree of whiteness. The heat and rain together, had likewise affected them in a different manner; and the smell which arose upon the night air, was horrible.'[66]

They reached Benedict without serious incident, where the boats were waiting. 'We found the shore covered with sailors from the different ships of war,' commented Gleig, 'who welcomed our arrival with loud cheers; and having contrived to bring up a larger flotilla than had been employed in the disembarkation, they removed us within a few hours, and without the occurrence of any accident, to our respective vessels.'[67] Once embarked, Major-General Ross appointed Harry Smith to take dispatches back to England, but before leaving Smith asked Ross if he was going to attack Baltimore. He himself felt it would be a bad decision, as the men were suffering from dysentery and because Baltimore had been reinforced. Ross was emphatic – they would not attack Baltimore.

'The *Iphigenia* frigate, Captain King,' Smith noted, 'was to take me home, and Captain Wainwright of the *Tonnant* was to be the bearer of the naval dispatches . . . The day we were to sail in the *Iphigenia* . . . kind-hearted General Ross, whom I loved as a brother, accompanied me to the gangway. His most sensible and amiable wife was at Bath. I promised to go there the moment I had delivered my dispatches.'[68] Having been in the Peninsular War and then sent straight to the war in America, Smith had not been in England for seven years and was desperate to be reunited with his Spanish wife, if she was still alive. The journey back to England was rapid: 'The *Iphigenia* had a most extraordinary passage from the Chesapeake to our anchorage at Spithead. We were only twenty-one days. The kindness I received from Captain King I shall never forget.'[69]

At Portsmouth he and Wainwright travelled together by coach from the George Inn. 'I do not know what he considered himself,' Smith admitted, 'but I was of opinion that, as the bearer of dispatches to Government, I was one of the greatest men in England . . . Oh! the delight of that journey. I made the boys drive a furiously good pace. D—— me, if I had rather be beating off a leeshore in a gale, tide against me!'[70] After so many years of war Smith could not believe what he was seeing: 'The very hedgerows, the houses, the farms, the cattle, the healthy population; no naked slaves, no burned villages, no starving, wretched inhabitants, no trace of damnable and accursed war!'[71] The news they had brought caused great excitement, and Joseph Farington jotted in his diary for 27 September: 'The Park & Tower guns were fired today in consequence of the arrival of Dispatches from America with an account of victory over the Americans & the capture of the town of Washington.'[72] After Smith had delivered the dispatches and was reunited with his wife, they both set off for Bath, where 'we found poor Mrs. Ross in the highest of spirits at the achievement of our arms under her husband. Poor thing! at that very moment of her excessive happiness he was in a soldier's bloody grave.'[73]

# TWENTY

———•◆•———

## STAR-SPANGLED BANNER

O! say can you see by the dawn's early light,
What so proudly we hailed at the twilight's last gleaming,
Whose broad stripes and bright stars through the perilous fight,
O'er the ramparts we watch'd, were so gallantly streaming?
And the Rockets' red glare, the Bombs bursting in air,
Gave proof through the night that our Flag was still there;
O! say does that star-spangled Banner yet wave,
O'er the Land of the free, and the home of the brave?

First verse of 'The Star-Spangled Banner'

In the evening of 12 September 1814 Codrington wrote to his wife: 'The work of destruction is now about to begin, and there will probably be many broken heads to-night. The army with as many seamen and marines as could possibly be spared, were landed this morning, and are now on their march to the town of Baltimore, distant about fifteen miles by land, and twelve by water.'[1] The original plan, he told her, had been to sail immediately to Halifax in Canada, but Major-General Ross and Rear-Admiral Cockburn had persuaded Rear-Admiral Cochrane that they should first capture Baltimore, to the north-east of Washington on the Patapsco River. Codrington, though, had warned Ross that they did not have sufficient information about Baltimore: 'I was surprised that so sensible a man as General Ross should be led away by the opposite opinions,'[2] he remarked sadly.

Many of those around him thought that Ross was a weak leader, and Codrington agreed: 'I pointed out to him all the difficulties I saw in this attack, into which he was persuaded by Cockburn and a Mr. Evans*, who acts as quarter-master general in this army.'[3] Cochrane, in his report to the Admiralty, blamed the moon for the change of plan: 'The approaching equinoctial new moon rendering it unsafe to proceed immediately out of the Chesapeake with the combined expedition, to act upon the plans which had been concerted previous to the departure of the *Iphigenia*, Major-General Ross and myself resolved to occupy the intermediate time to advantage, by making a demonstration upon the city of Baltimore.'[4]

After finally leaving the Patuxent and Potomac, Midshipman Barrett of the frigate *Hebrus* related that

the fleet . . . once more reached the Chesapeake, and with a fine breeze, steered under all sail in the direction of Baltimore. As we ascended the bay, alarm guns were fired in all directions; thus testifying the terror which the inhabitants of the surrounding country felt at the approach of the British arms. Whilst thus standing to our place of destination, we had received the greater portion of the 44th Regiment—one part of whom were seated on our booms amidships, and the rest towing in our boats astern. As we passed the picturesque town of Annapolis (which is situate on the left side of the bay from the sea), we could plainly perceive the inhabitants flying in all directions. This was a mournful picture of the times, and should never be forgotten by America when some ruthless politician or party would again wish to plunge their country into war.[5]

By dusk on the 11th they anchored close to North Point, and Gleig commented: 'It was determined to land here, rather than to ascend the river, because the Patapsco, though broad, is far from deep. It is, in fact, too shallow to admit a line of battle ship.'[6] Midshipman Barrett later wrote that 'the approach by land to Baltimore from this position is through a woody peninsula, that varies in width from a few hundred yards to two or three miles; and the length of which may be estimated to be four or five leagues. One side of this narrow neck of land is washed by the Back River, whilst the other forms the shore of the Patapsco, and leads directly to the harbour of Baltimore.'[7] That night the men slept fully dressed, to be ready at a moment's notice, and Gleig was struck by the experience:

There was something in this state of preparation at once solemn and exciting . . . We lay at this time within two miles of the shore . . . Around us were

* Lieutenant Evans, Deputy Assistant Quarter-Master General.

moored numerous ships, which, breaking the tide as it flowed gently onwards, produced a ceaseless murmur like the gushing of a mountain stream. The voices of the sentinels, too, as they relieved one another on the decks; and the occasional splash of oars, as a solitary boat rowed backwards and forwards to the admiral's ship for orders, sounded peculiarly musical in the perfect stillness of a calm night. Though I am far from giving the preference, in all respects, to a sailor's life, it must, nevertheless, be confessed that it has in it many moments of exquisite delight; and the present seemed to me to be of the number.[8]

The troops under Major-General Ross, accompanied by Cockburn and several seamen, were landed very early the next morning, and the smaller ships then moved further up the river. Although Codrington thought that the attack should be postponed, he believed their enthusiasm would nevertheless ensure success: 'The bomb-vessels, brigs, and frigates are all pushing up the river with an eagerness which must annoy the enemy, I presume, as much as it delights me. Three frigates are aground abreast of us, hauling themselves over the banks into deep water by main strength, each trying to surpass the other.'[9] They spent all day getting within range of Baltimore, as Midshipman Barrett explained:

Thus parting from our gallant comrades, we proceeded, without delay, under all sail, in company with the frigates, sloops, and bombs, &c., to take up a position where we might be enabled to attack the sea defences of Baltimore. Leaving the line-of-battle ships, which, on account of their size, could not proceed any further than North Point, our frigates sailed through the mud for miles . . . Our boats were ahead sounding: I was in our launch, with the stream and kedge anchors, and cables coiled in her ready to heave the ship off if necessary; and willing to do all in my power, we measured off a line of spun-yarn, marked with three, four, and five fathoms, attached it to a marline-spike, and commenced the sailors favourite chant as well as the rest— 'And a—half—three! By the mark—three!' Notwithstanding all these precautions, we frequently grounded on the numerous shoals which abound in this channel; when I was constantly at work with laying out our stream and kedge anchors, to warp us off from the difficulty we encountered, until I was literally covered with mud from head to foot in the process. As there were only two or three pilots distributed through the fleet, and their knowledge of the navigation being confined to vessels of a smaller draught, most of our ships were guided in the passage solely by the lead. As we proceeded up the river, doubtless the Americans were struck with panic and amazement, for although they built frigates at this port, yet they always sailed down the river, flying light, as far as Annapolis, where, I was informed, they completed for sea, by taking in their guns, provisions, and water.[10]

Meanwhile the armed forces on land began to march towards Baltimore. Ross was in the advance guard, but about halfway to the city, in dense woods, he was shot by a rifleman concealed in a tree, and to the shock of everyone he died as he was carried back to the boats. William Stanhope Lovell was waiting in one of the boats at North Point and watched as Ross 'was brought down, wrapped in a union jack, attended by his aide-de-camp; I placed the body in my boat, and sent it on board'.[11] Ross was later taken to Halifax, where he was buried. The British detested the way American riflemen acted as snipers, and Midshipman Bluett commented on one incident that occurred the next day:

It was the custom of the Yankeys to conceal them[selves] in trees, and being excellent marksmen, they picked off a good many of our stragglers. Two seamen of the *Tonnant*, Denis Sulivan & Ino Robinson, the day after Genl. R. was killed, straggled away in search of spirits, and passing under a large tree, Robinson received a rifle ball through his hat, which being fired above him, absolutely grazed the skin off his ear, shoulder, finger & great toe; and Denis looking up found the Yankey perched in the tree; who seeing they had pistols, and his own piece discharged, begged them to shew mercy. Devil burn me if I do, says Denis, it was just such a spalpein [rascal] as you, killed our Genl – besides you've had your shot, it's our time now. I'll bet you a pint of grog Jack, I bring him down the first shot. Adone says the other, if you miss I'll try; they both missed, and then agreed that as they had their turn, it would not be fair play to kill the fellow; they therefore made him come down, and drawing their cutlasses placed him between them, and marched him arm & arm into the camp.[12]

After Ross was killed the army pushed on towards Baltimore, but within 5 miles of the city they came up against a formidable American force that was blocking a narrow neck of land. Lieutenant Scott commented on the actions of Cockburn while they prepared themselves for battle: 'Previously to the commencement of the attack, the Rear-admiral [Cockburn], who was well known to the enemy from his white horse and gold-laced hat, rode along the line from left to right, at a foot pace. The instant he was perceived, the fire of the enemy's guns seemed to follow him the whole length of the line; the shot might be seen grazing before, behind, under, and passing over his horse. I several times heard the troops, as he approached in front of them, jokingly exclaim, "look out, my lads, here is the Admiral coming, you'll have it directly".'[13]

Bluett detailed the attack: 'The command devolving on Col [Arthur] Brooke, he marched on to the attack, & the Americans laying their pieces over the paling, took deliberate aim at our men, advancing in the open field without firing a shot; as soon however as we were within pistol distance, we saluted them with a general discharge of small arms and artillery, and chargeing under cover of the smoke, came suddenly upon them, and routed them with great slaughter, so that finding it impossible to stand against us, they threw down their arms and ran like hares.'[14] Scott reckoned that 'it was a second edition of the "Bladensburg Races"'.[15]

Early the next day the troops began to move forward once more, in heavy rain, while the navy commenced a bombardment of Fort McHenry, situated to the south of the city and the key to its defences. 'At day break the next morning,' Cochrane reported, 'the bombs having taken their stations within shell range, supported by the *Surprize*, with the other frigates and sloops, opened their fire upon the fort that protected the entrance of the harbour, and I had now an opportunity of observing the strength and the preparations of the enemy.'[16] The bombardment lasted all day and into the night, and was recorded by Midshipman Barrett:

Early on the morning of the 13th, our squadron of five frigates, having three Admirals' flags hoisted, anchored in a line of battle, about one mile and three-quarters distant from the heavy batteries which defended the entrance of the port, or Baltimore harbour. Three bombs and a rocket ship also took up their position at a similar distance, and immediately commenced a heavy fire of shells and rockets upon the forts – several of which, we could perceive, fell far within the harbour. Such was the terror caused by the approach of the British Navy . . . that a complete chain of vessels were sunk across the entrance of the port; which presented a cheering and animating spectacle at this period to our jolly tars – for the harbour was pretty full of merchant-vessels, together with their beautiful new frigate, the *Java*, supported by a numerous flotilla of gun-vessels.[17]

According to Barrett, they were all confident of soon being able to fly the British flag over Baltimore's fort and were impatient for the order to move in closer:

About two o'clock in the afternoon, I was in the launch with our First Lieutenant, for the purpose of reconnoitring the harbour; when we had proceeded about three hundred yards ahead of our frigate, the fortifications opened a steady and deliberate fire, with their long, heavy guns, at the bomb-vessels, who, perceiving the enemy's shot passed over them, shifted their position about half a mile further out; and at this distance – two miles and a quarter, at least – we could perceive both the shells and rockets alight within the range of the harbour. During this cannonade, there was a large, flat gun-boat close to our launch, directed hither for a similar purpose, when a black man, who was standing up in the centre, was cut clean in half by one of the enemy's shot. This was a sufficient warning for us to shift our berth, and proceed on board our frigate.[18]

The British firing continued into the night, as he described:

All this night the bombardment continued with unabated vigour; the hissing rockets and the fiery shells glittered in the air, threatening destruction as they fell: whilst to add solemnity to this scene of devastation, the rain fell in torrents – the thunder broke in mighty peals after each successive flash of lightning, that for a moment illuminated the surrounding darkness. This was the period, fast approaching midnight, selected for the boats of the squadron to make a diversion in favour of our army, by feigning an attack on the fortifications which probably might flank their position. Musket flashes and continuous cheers along the flotilla added excitement and interest to a scene already imposing.[19]

The troops by now had come within a mile and a half of Baltimore, and Colonel Brooke thought that it was feasible to attack, but at this late stage Cochrane decided that the navy could not offer support because 'the entrance by sea, within which the Town is retired nearly three miles, was entirely obstructed by a barrier of vessels sunk at the mouth of the harbour, defended inside by gun-boats, flanked on the right by a strong and regular fortification, and on the left by a battery of several heavy guns'.[20] He sent a note to Brooke pessimistically concluding that 'a naval co-operation against the town was found impracticable',[21] and so Brooke agreed that the attack on Baltimore's fortifications should not proceed.

The decision to give up was a terrible blow after all their hard work, as Barrett clearly felt:

The boats returned on board, and, as the morning dawned, the storm had passed away, and the heavens once more assumed the aspect of serenity and peace – whilst the twinkling stars shone bright and clear, and the tranquillity of the night was broken only by the firing of the bombs, as they still continued with unremitting assiduity to hurl their destructive missiles on the foe. It is almost needless to add, that our men continued at their quarters during the whole of this night, and that the ships were all clear and ready for action, but their services were not required . . . Thus, after bombarding the forts and harbour of Baltimore [from smaller ships] for twenty-four hours, the squadron of frigates weighed, without firing a shot, upon the forenoon of the 14th, and were immediately followed by the bombs and sloops-of-war. In truth, it was a galling spectacle for British seamen to behold. And, as the last vessel spread her canvas to the wind, the Americans hoisted a most superb and splendid ensign on their battery, and fired at the same time a gun of defiance.[22]

Francis Scott Key became famous for having observed the bombardment. He was a lawyer who worked in Georgetown, a small settlement adjacent to Washington. At the time of the attack on the capital he was a volunteer in the light artillery, and he found out that his friend Dr William Beane had been taken prisoner by the British. Beane was a physician at Upper Marlborough and had himself been involved in capturing marauding British stragglers from the army. Because it was feared that Beane might be hanged, President Madison gave his approval for Key to go to Baltimore on board a vessel (the *Minden*) that was used as a flag of truce. He was accompanied by John Skinner, the American agent for prisoner exchanges, and the pair had caught up with the British fleet at the mouth of the Potomac, preparing for the expedition against Baltimore.

Because of the kindness shown to the wounded British prisoners, it was agreed that Beane could be released, but for the time being they all had to stay on board a frigate in case they leaked news of the plan of attack. Once the fleet neared Baltimore they were allowed to return to the *Minden*, with a guard of marines, from where they witnessed the bombardment. The previous year two new flags had been commissioned for Fort McHenry, including one that measured 30 by 40 feet with fifteen stars and eight red and seven white stripes (the official United States flag authorised in the Flag Act of 1794). As the three Americans watched they had no idea whether or not the town had surrendered, but in the morning the smaller flag was still flying over the fort, and as the British left, it was replaced by the huge one that so impressed Barrett. It survives today in the Smithsonian National Museum of American History in Washington.

During the assault Key began to jot down a poem, which he finished when back at Baltimore. The red glare of the rockets and the bombs bursting in the air of the first verse refer to the bombardment. Copies were printed and circulated under the title 'Defence of Fort M'Henry', and it was also printed in the *Baltimore Patriot* newspaper on 20 September, with an editorial comment that the song 'is destined long to outlast the occasion and outlive the impulse which produced it'.[23] It was sung to the tune of 'To Anacreon in Heaven', a British drinking song, and was adopted as the national anthem of the United States in 1931.

The British army retreated to North Point, where they were taken on board the various ships on 15 September. Both Cochrane and Brooke tried to put a positive emphasis on the expedition, and in his official dispatch Cochrane informed the Admiralty that 'the result of this demonstration has been the defeat of the army of the enemy, the destruction, by themselves, of a quantity of shipping, the burning of an extensive rope-walk, and other public erections, the causing of them to remove their property from the city, and above all, the collecting and harassing of his armed inhabitants from the surrounding country; producing a total stagnation of their commerce, and heaping upon them considerable expences'.[24]

Most of the seamen thought the retreat was a dreadful mistake, including Barrett: 'As a youngster of fifteen, in common with older heads than my own, I confess, I thought that, with the display of ordinary judgement, perseverance, and decision, upon the occasion, the batteries which defended the entrance of the port might have been graced with the colours of Old England; and the numerous merchant-vessels and shipping within the harbour have been our lawful prizes.'[25] It was wrong, he added, to think that the frigates could not get close to the fortifications: 'The truth is, I believe, pretty well known that our frigates could have approached within a cable's length of these batteries, if required, allowing the wind was fair; but how they were to retreat, in case of a reverse, with a foul wind, in shoal water, is quite another thing.'[26] Everyone had missed out on glory and prize money, and as they made towards Chesapeake Bay the mood was gloomy: 'It was with the batteries bidding us defiance – the weather scowling with a thick drizzling rain upon our proceedings – whilst our hearts and spirits were depressed in the extreme – that we retired down the Patapsco River, with far different sensations from those we experienced on entering it.'[27] The focus of attacks now shifted more than 1000 miles to the south-west.

New Orleans was one of the oldest and richest cities in America. It had been established by the French in 1718, and the city came under Spanish control after the end of the Seven Years' War in 1763. Much of the French architecture of the city was wiped out in disastrous fires in 1788 and 1794, but the rebuilt city continued to prosper, gaining its wealth from its position as a port at the mouth of the Mississippi, handling trade to and from great distances into the continent via river boats. After the slave uprising in 1791 on the French colony of Saint Domingue (later Haiti), the wealth and population of the city were boosted by an influx of refugee plantation owners and their slaves. Over the next few years the city rapidly changed hands, being ceded to France by Spain as part of Louisiana, which was then sold to the Americans by Napoleon. None of these changes seemed to check the rising prosperity of New Orleans, which could afford to be at the forefront of technological development: the first steamboat had arrived there in 1812. The city was now one of the great trading centres of the world, and an obvious target for the British.

An attack on New Orleans from the sea had been long in the planning, because the hot and steamy summer climate and the autumn hurricane season were not ideal times to launch an amphibious assault, and so it was necessary to wait for winter. The coastal territory to the east of New Orleans was the subject of dispute between America and Spain, so that although Pensacola was still in Spanish hands and could be used as a base by the British, Fort Bowyer, further west along the coast, had been captured and strengthened by the Americans, who knew that an attack would eventually be made on New Orleans itself. Fort Bowyer was situated at Mobile Point, protecting the approach to Mobile, which held the only other major American military force in the area besides New Orleans. A preliminary attack on this fort in September 1814 proved a terrible failure. The British ships were defeated by the shallow waters around Mobile Point and by the short range of their guns, which were largely carronades. The attack was beaten off with the loss of the frigate *Hermes*, one of only two British vessels to manoeuvre their guns within range of the fort. The *Hermes* ran aground and had to be abandoned and set on fire. It was not a good start to the campaign.

Apart from a few American gunboats, the British Navy had total

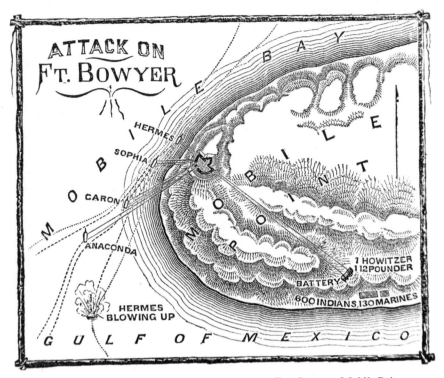

*Map of the failed attack in September 1814 on Fort Bowyer, Mobile Point*

control of the waters around New Orleans, but the failure to capture Fort Bowyer undermined the confidence of potential allies. The British had opened negotiations with the local Creek Indians and were relying on their support along with the Spanish and Portuguese. A third force was also approached by both sides – the pirates and smugglers based in the Bay of Barataria. Their ships had brought many of the refugees from Saint Domingue to New Orleans, and by 1814 they were well established, while their wealth afforded rich bribes that made them immune from the rule of law in their constant struggle with the governor of the city. They were led by two brothers, Jean and Pierre Lafitte, but in July 1814 the governor had scored a success by arresting Pierre and managing to hold him on charges of piracy.

Two months later the British had approached Jean Lafitte in an attempt to gain his assistance in the forthcoming attack, presenting a mixture of threats and promises. Lafitte was more concerned about what actions the New Orleans authorities were taking against him, since he knew that the shallow waters around his stronghold kept him out of effective reach of the British. He informed the governor about the British approach and offered his services to the Americans in return for Pierre's release and a free pardon. The authorities decided against this, but Pierre escaped from prison and Jean moved most of his stores, ammunition and men to the safety of a new base at Isle Derniere, about 40 miles to the west. When his old base was raided, however, twenty-six ships were seized, along with a few of his men and his eldest brother, Dominique You.

In late November the British forces began to assemble in Jamaica and embark on board the ships that were commanded by Cochrane. In all, there were around 7500 troops, including two black regiments from Jamaica, under the overall command of Major-General John Keane. At the same time the American Major-General Andrew Jackson, who was in charge of the defence of a vast area of the south, including the Louisiana and Mississippi territories, moved from Mobile, where he had been responsible for the strengthening of Fort Bowyer, to New Orleans itself.

Cochrane had already given up the idea of capturing Mobile first and attacking New Orleans from that direction, and on 10 December the fleet anchored among the small islands to the east of New Orleans. A nearby large lagoon, called Lake Borgne, was separated from the open sea by a bar too shallow for large warships to pass over. It was defended by seven American gunboats that had between them twenty-three guns. The British ships now started to transfer about a thousand marines and seamen into forty-five gunboats, each armed with a carronade. Once the Americans realised that this was not a landing party but a force intended to capture their own boats, they started to retreat and the engagement became something of a marathon rowing race. The British boats rowed through the afternoon and night of the 12th, against the wind and tide, but were eventually forced to stop to allow the men to eat and rest. By dawn the American boats, Codrington related, 'had increased their distance to eight or ten miles. On the 13th, at nine in the forenoon, the [British] boats had again, by great labour, reached nearly within shot of them, but were again obliged to anchor in order to feed and rest the people. At 10.30 they again weighed, and Captain Robert's division drove one schooner on shore. The Fort of Port Louis fired on the boats, but took fright and burned not only the schooner but the depôt of naval stores there. At eight in the evening the boats were again obliged to anchor, owing to sheer fatigue.'[28]

They finally caught up with the American boats the next morning, and having anchored just out of range to rest, began the attack at half past ten.

A fierce battle raged for two hours, but eventually the British won by sheer weight of numbers, having finally cornered the Americans. They paid dearly for the victory, however, with seventeen men killed and seventy-seven wounded against ten Americans killed and thirty-five wounded. Although the operation, which Codrington described as 'a most brilliant affair',[29] was successful and had given the British control of Lake Borgne, the American gunboats had delayed the British advance for several days. Perhaps its most important consequence was that it robbed Jackson of most of his ability to keep the British under observation – for the next few days he had no accurate knowledge of their movements.

The British began to set up an intermediate base on Pea Island, just off the mainland, inside Lake Borgne. This was a dismal operation, as most of the stores and troops had to be ferried in rowing boats, and the island itself offered nothing in the way of shelter or comfort for the troops, as Lieutenant Gleig lamented:

It is scarcely possible to imagine any place more completely wretched. It was a swamp, containing a small space of firm ground at one end, and almost wholly unadorned with trees of any sort or description. There were indeed, a few stinted firs upon the very edge of the water, but these were so diminutive in size, as hardly to deserve an higher classification than among the meanest of shrubs. The interior was the resort of wild ducks and other water fowl, and the pools and creeks with which it was intercepted abounded in dormant alligators. Upon this miserable desert, the army was assembled, without tents or huts, or any covering to shelter them from the inclemency of the weather . . . After having been exposed all day to a cold and pelting rain, we [had] landed upon a barren island, incapable of furnishing even fuel enough to supply our fires. To add to our miseries, as night closed, the rain generally ceased, and severe frosts set in, which, congealing our wet clothes upon our bodies, left little animal warmth to keep the limbs in a state of activity, and the consequence was, that many of the wretched negroes, to whom frost and cold were altogether new, fell fast asleep, and perished before morning.[30]

Midshipman Bluett also highlighted the terrible fate of the West Indian troops:

The weather was severe in the extreme; heavy rains in the day were succeeded by bitter frosts at night, insomuch that the poor unfortunate blacks that we had brought from the West Indies, unaccustomed to the sensation of cold, became wholly incapable of exerting themselves; and therefore were utterly useless and indeed an encumbrance; for they were obliged to have every thing done for them; and notwithstanding every care was taken of them, several died of the cold, so that this part of our force was entirely lost to us; or worse than lost for they stood in the way; and eat provisions that could ill be spared for we were all on two thirds allowance.[31]

It took days to land all the troops and stores, and the burden fell on the seamen, as Gleig described: 'On the part of the navy, again, all these hardships were experienced in a four-fold degree. Night and day were boats pulling from the fleet to the island, and from the island to the fleet, for it was the 21st before all the troops were got on shore, and as there was little time to enquire into men's turns of labour, many seamen were four or five days continually at the oar. Thus, they had not only to bear up against variety of temperature, but against hunger, fatigue, and want of sleep in addition; three as fearful burdens as can be laid upon the human frame.'[32]

Despite these extreme hardships, Gleig recorded that morale was remarkably high:

From the General, down to the youngest drum-boy, a confident anticipation of success seemed to pervade all ranks, and in the hope of an ample reward in store for them, the toils and grievances of the moment were forgotten. Nor was this anticipation the mere offspring of an over-weening confidence in themselves. Several Americans had already deserted, who entertained us with accounts of the alarm experienced at New Orleans. They assured us that there were not at present 5,000 soldiers in the State; that the principal inhabitants had long ago left the place; that such as remained were ready to join us as soon as we should appear among them, and that, therefore, we might lay our account with a speedy and bloodless conquest.[33]

Doubtless there was a tendency for the deserters to tell their captors what they wanted to hear, but when the British had first arrived the defences of New Orleans were in a poor state and Major-General Jackson was frantically trying to strengthen them. The longer the British were delayed, the more the chances of success slipped away from them. Jackson was daily hoping that reinforcements from Tennessee, Kentucky and nearby Baton Rouge would arrive in New Orleans. On 16 December Jackson declared martial law in the city, and soon after that Jean Lafitte offered his services to Jackson, and they were accepted. Lafitte and his men were particularly valuable as artillery men, and also they brought with them stores of arms and ammunition. Lafitte himself was useful to Jackson because of his detailed knowledge of the terrain.

After the loss of his gunboat flotilla on Lake Borgne, Jackson still had three gunboats, a schooner and a merchant ship that could be converted to a sloop, but he was desperately short of seamen. The local authorities had opposed impressment, but his declaration of martial law overrode their objections, and press-gangs trawled the streets for recruits. By the 17th nearly all the reinforcements had arrived, and more militia forces, including a battalion of Free Men of Color, had been raised locally. Of the latter Theodore Roosevelt, historian as well as politician, would later comment that they 'had gathered to defend the land which kept the men of their race in slavery; who were to shed their blood for the Flag that symbolized to their kind not freedom but bondage; who were to die bravely as freemen, only that their brethren might live on ignobly as slaves'.[34] In just a few days, though, the influx of extra men had dramatically improved the chances of a successful defence of the city.

While Jackson was organising his newly arrived troops, two British officers were reconnoitring the Bayou Bienvenu, a waterway leading from Lake Borgne to within a few miles of the city, where the army could be deployed for an attack. Having found that this route was viable, Cochrane and Keane decided to advance, but it was a hazardous plan as Pea Island was 60 miles from the mouth of the bayou and many of the boats would have to be rowed across Lake Borgne. The advance party spent twenty-six hours in open boats before they set foot on land, having crossed the lake and rowed up the Bayou Bienvenu as far as possible. By the evening of the 22nd about sixteen hundred troops were camped within 8 miles of New Orleans, but after the arduous journey they were exhausted and lacked both artillery and naval support. Worse still, a major of the American militia called Gabriel Villeré, whose small force had been overwhelmed and captured, managed to escape and raise the alarm. Already the element of surprise was lost.

Jackson reacted immediately and decided to attack the British camp as soon as possible. Gleig related that after sunset on the 23rd a vessel approached that they hoped was bringing reinforcements:

About half-past seven o'clock, the attention of several individuals was drawn to a large vessel, which seemed to be stealing up the river till she came

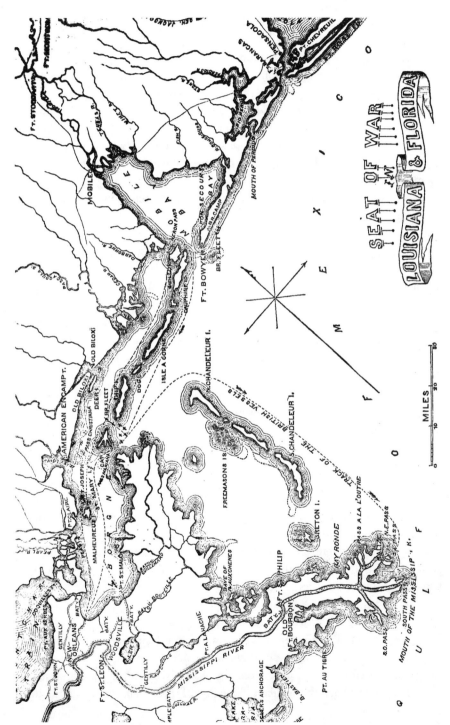

*Map of the New Orleans–Mobile area*

opposite to our camp, when her anchor was dropped, and her sails leisurely furled. At first we were doubtful whether she might be one of our own cruisers which had passed the port unobserved, and had arrived to render her assistance in our future operations. To satisfy this doubt, she was repeatedly hailed, but returned no answer, when an alarm spreading through the bivouac, all thought of sleep was laid aside. Several musket shots were now fired at her with the design of exacting a reply, of which no notice was taken, till at length having fastened all her sails, and swung her broadside towards us, we could distinctly hear some one cry out in a commanding voice, 'Give them this for the honour of America.' The words were instantly followed by the flashes of her guns, and a deadly shower of grape swept down numbers in the camp.[35]

The British now felt their lack of artillery, as Gleig complained:

Against this dreadful fire we had nothing whatever to oppose. The artillery which we had landed was too light to bring into competition with an adversary so powerful, and as she had anchored within a short distance of the opposite bank, no musketry could reach her with any precision or effect. A few rockets were discharged, which made a beautiful appearance in the air, but the rocket is an uncertain weapon, and these deviated too far from their object to produce even terror among those against whom they were directed. Under these circumstances, as nothing could be done offensively, our sole object was to shelter the men as much as possible from this iron hail. With this view, they were commanded to leave the fires and to hasten under the dyke.[36]

The ship was the schooner *Carolina*, whose broadside of seven guns was manned by expert gunners supplied by Lafitte, but as well as sending this downstream from the city, Jackson had deployed a force of some two thousand men backed up by field guns, so that the camp was soon under attack from land as well as the river. The first warning came from the sentries firing at the advancing Americans, and Gleig described the bloody combat that followed:

The heavens were illuminated on all sides by a semi-circular blaze of musketry. It was now clear that we were surrounded, and that by a very superior force and, therefore, no alternative remaining, but, either to surrender at discretion, or to beat back the assailants. The first of these plans was never for an instant thought of, and the second was immediately put into action. Rushing from under the bank, the 85th and 95th flew to support the piquets, while the 4th, stealing to the rear of the encampment, formed close column, and remained as a reserve. But to describe this action is altogether out of the question, for it was such a battle as the annals of modern warfare can hardly match. All order, all discipline were lost. Each officer, as he was able to collect twenty or thirty men round him, advanced into the middle of the enemy, when it was fought hand to hand, bayonet to bayonet, and sword to sword.[37]

Gradually the Americans were pushed back, and by daylight the attack had been repulsed. Gleig went to look for Captain Charles Grey, who had gone missing during the fighting: 'Having searched for some time in vain, I at length discovered my friend lying behind a bundle of reeds, where, during the action, we had separated, and shot through the temples by a rifle bullet so remarkably small, as scarcely to leave any trace of its progress . . . when I beheld him pale and bloody, I found all my resolution evaporate. I threw myself on the ground beside him, and wept like a child.'[38]

It was now the morning of Christmas Eve, and at six o'clock in the afternoon the British and American negotiators in Ghent signed a peace treaty after many months of wrangling. It would be some time before they found out, but the armies facing each other at New Orleans were technically no longer at war even though the treaty required ratification in America. Just a few hours later, on Christmas morning, Major-General Sir Edward Pakenham, fresh from the successful campaigns in Spain, arrived to take command of the British troops. Because there was a feeling that Major-General Keane might not be equal to the task, Pakenham had been sent out to replace Major-General Ross. According to Gleig, Pakenham 'now arrived in time to see his troops brought into a situation from which all his abilities could scarcely expect to extricate them. Nor were the troops themselves ignorant of the unfavourable circumstances in which they stood. Hoping every thing therefore, from a change, they greeted their new leader with a hearty cheer.'[39]

For Gleig, it was not enough to dispel the gloom of the meal he was having with some of his fellow officers: 'At so melancholy a Christmas dinner I do not recollect at any time to have been present. We dined in a barn; of plates, knives and forks there was a dismal scarcity, nor could our fare boast of much either in intrinsic good quality, or in the way of cooking. These, however, were mere matters of merriment: it was the want of many well known and beloved faces that gave us pain; nor were any other subjects discussed, besides the amiable qualities of those who no longer formed part of our mess, and never would again form part of it.'[40] The barn in which they sat was just out of range of the *Carolina*, which was continuing to bombard the camp, although occasionally spent cannonballs would bounce off the outside of the barn wall.

With most of his force pinned down by the bombardment, Pakenham's first act was to neutralise this threat, but to do so artillery had to be assembled. Under cover of darkness on the 26th, a battery was constructed on top of the levee*, and a dozen cannons of different sizes were installed there while shot was heated in furnaces. At dawn the next day the battery began to fire red-hot shot at the *Carolina*, which soon caught fire and within an hour blew up. On Christmas Eve the *Carolina* had been joined by a converted sloop, the *Louisiana*, and a couple of gunboats, but these fled after the loss of the larger ship. The way was now clear for the British to advance, although during the delay caused by the bombardment they had nearly been cut off by floods, when careless sentries failed to spot a party of Americans cutting the levee between them and the city. However, the breach was seen in time and soon plugged.

Although essential to allow the army to move forward, bombarding the *Carolina* had used about a third of the available ammunition, leaving the artillery dangerously short for the coming conflict. Because of the intense cold, very few of the remaining black troops were fit enough to join the advance, though a few helped manoeuvre the guns. Codrington, who had just shifted his quarters from a fisherman's hut to 'a double tent (one within the other), as being deemed warmer than the hovel',[41] was so cold that he told his wife he was 'clothed in two pair of trowsers and two coats, three waistcoats, and so forth'.[42] On the 28th Pakenham led a strong armed reconnaissance to probe the American defences, advancing in two columns supported by field guns and rockets. As they approached the American lines they came under flanking fire from the *Louisiana* and bombardment from the front, which Gleig recalled:

That the Americans are excellent shots, as well with artillery as with rifles, we have had frequent cause to acknowledge, but, perhaps, on no occasion did they assert their claim to the title of good artillery-men more effectually than on the present. Scarce a bullet passed over, or fell short of its mark, but

---

* The large flood-protection banks alongside the river were called levees.

all striking full into the midst of our ranks, occasioned terrible havoc. The shrieks of the wounded, therefore, the crash of firelocks, and the fall of such as were killed, caused at first some little confusion, and what added to the panic, was, that from the houses beside which we stood, bright flames suddenly burst out. The Americans expecting this attack, had filled them with combustibles for the purpose, and directing one or two guns against them, loaded with red-hot shot, in an instant set them on fire . . . The infantry, however, was not long suffered to remain thus exposed, but, being ordered to quit the path, and to form line in the fields, the artillery was brought up, and opposed to that of the enemy.[43]

If he was not exaggerating, Gleig seems to have been in the worst of the action, because the official report afterwards claimed there were fewer than sixty British casualties, but his comments about the accuracy of the

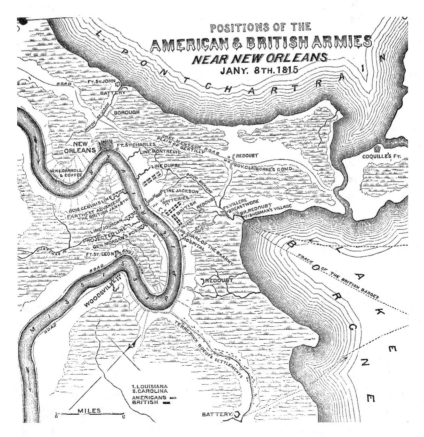

*Map of the New Orleans area*

American fire rings true. Much of their artillery was manned by Lafitte's men, at least equal in skill to British naval gunners, and most of the American troops were using rifles and were accustomed to singling out their victims. British troops, armed largely with muskets, still used the tactic of firing together at a target of massed troops – a target that the Americans, behind their defences, seldom presented. As the British held their ground and took cover, Pakenham assessed the strength of the American defences. More field guns were brought up, but by then several guns already deployed had been disabled, their wheels and gun carriages smashed. These were hauled back to the rear for repair by parties of seamen, while the army retreated out of range to wait until heavy guns were brought up from the ships of the fleet.

This was easier said than done, because the cannons had to be rowed all the way across Lake Borgne and up the bayou in small boats, and since the loads were so heavy and the boats so low in the water, sails could not be used for fear of capsizing. The Americans had not considered it even possible to bring anything but light field guns over this route, but in three days ten 18-pounder cannons and four 24-pounder carronades were ferried across and manhandled to the battlefield over land little better than a swamp. By New Year's Day 1815 everything was ready and the attack began, as Codrington described in a letter home:

On the 1st we had our batteries, by severe labour, ready in situations from which the artillery people were, as a matter of course, to destroy and silence the opposing batteries, and give opportunity for a well-arranged storm. But instead of so doing, not a gun of the enemy appeared to suffer, and our firing too high was not made out until we had expended too much of our *hardly-* collected ammunition to push the matter further. Such a failure in this boasted arm was not to be expected, and I think it a blot in the artillery escutcheon. We have by this allowed the enemy to increase our difficulties and gain spirits, and the harassing job of withdrawing the guns half buried in mud, occasioned by the pouring rain of that night, wore down the whole army as well as the poor Johnnies who had the heaviest part of that severe duty to perform.[44]

Once again the British were forced to withdraw, and Pakenham was said to be 'much mortified at being obliged to retire the army from a second demonstration and disposition to attack',[45] but Codrington was too harsh in putting all the blame on the artillerymen. Even before it started raining, the ground was sodden and unstable, and 'if you dug eight inches, water followed: hence to erect batteries with earth was impracticable'.[46] Sandbags were used to try to stabilise the ground, but there were just not enough, and it proved impossible to maintain an accurate fire. Jackson had solved this problem by requisitioning bales of cotton to form a firm base for his gun batteries, which did not become bogged down, and he had used every minute of the time to strengthen his defences while the British were bringing up cannons from their ships. Despite Codrington's poor opinion, the British artillerymen had actually scored at least as many direct hits as the Americans: it was lack of ammunition that was the main problem.

If Pakenham had brought up all his forces and pressed home the attack during his reconnaissance on 28 December, the Americans may have failed to hold their weak defences, but three days later the situation had changed. After a second withdrawal it was not just Pakenham who was dispirited, as Gleig recorded: 'Of the fatigue undergone during these operations by the whole army, from the General down to the meanest sentinel, it would be difficult to form an adequate conception. For two whole nights and days, not a man had closed an eye, except such as were cool enough to sleep amidst showers of cannon-ball, and during the day scarcely a moment had been allowed, in which we were able so much as to break our fast. We retired, therefore, not only baffled and disappointed, but in some degree disheartened and discontented.'[47] This was a drastic change from the 'confident anticipation of success' Gleig had experienced barely two weeks earlier. Jackson's delaying tactics had paid off, for now time was on the side of the Americans, who grew stronger and more confident as the British forces became increasingly despondent.

More British reinforcements were expected: a brigade commanded by Major-General John Lambert was coming from the West Indies, after stopping there for water and provisions. Pakenham decided to wait for Lambert's men before trying another assault, but he also decided on another plan of attack. He proposed crossing the river to capture the American gun batteries, and for this task he turned to the navy, as Codrington explained: 'A particular feature in the plan of attack was *our* cutting a canal into the Mississippi, into which river we were to take our boats in order to convey a force to the right bank, which, assisted by some of them as gun-boats, might surprise the enemy's batteries on that side by which our front was enfiladed, and turn them upon their line instead.'[48]

By 8 January the canal was dug and Lambert had arrived with reinforcements, but over two thousand men from Kentucky had arrived at
New Orleans, and although they were poorly armed and so ragged that
they had to be given clothes by the inhabitants of the city, the British
advantage was once again lost. On the morning of the 8th the attack
began with the naval operation to cross the river, but even Codrington
was unclear whether or not this was merely a diversion: 'I do not know
how far this measure was relied on by the General [Pakenham]. But as he
ordered and made his assault *at* daylight [dawn], I imagine he did not
place much dependence on it. By exertion which is beyond belief, we
dragged in fifty boats during the night, and Colonel Thornton, with his
remaining 85th (of about 300), and some seamen and marines amounting
to nearly as many more, were on shore by daylight. The whole operation
succeeded beautifully, and the guns in the enemy's batteries were
unspiked.'[49]

The Battle of New Orleans had begun, and the sailors led the attack on
the American gun battery on the other side of the river, as Gleig
described:

The bugle sounded, and our troops advanced. The sailors raising a shout,
rushed forward, but were met by so heavy a discharge of grape and cannister,
that for an instant they paused. Recovering themselves, however, they again
pushed on, and the 85th dashing forward to their aid, they received a heavy
fire of musketry, and endeavoured to charge. A smart firing was now for a few
minutes kept up on both sides, but our people had no time to waste in distant
fighting, and accordingly hurried on to storm the works, upon which, a panic
seized the Americans, they lost their order, and fled.[50]

Sixteen guns were captured, and despite some last-minute strengthening of the defences on that side of the river by Jackson, the batteries were
abandoned before the guns were properly spiked. From Codrington's
point of view, it was a complete success, but it came too late to be effective. Pakenham seems to have intended the gun batteries to have been
captured before his assault began, but he had not been informed that this
operation was running late because of the sheer effort needed to drag the
boats against the current along the new canal and into the river. Despite
the fact that these batteries could create havoc on one wing of the British
advance, Pakenham still began the attack at dawn, rather than wait until
the guns were captured.

The delay in capturing the guns on the opposite bank was not the only problem. Gleig observed the reaction of Pakenham when he surveyed his troops:

Instead of perceiving every thing in readiness for the assault, he saw his troops in battle array, indeed, but not a ladder or fascine upon the field. The 44th, which was appointed to carry them, had either misunderstood or neglected their orders, and now headed the column of attack, without any means being provided for crossing the enemy's ditch or scaling his rampart. The indignation of poor Pakenham on this occasion may be imagined, but cannot be described. Galloping towards Colonel Mullens, who led the 44th, he commanded him instantly to return with his regiment for the ladders, but the opportunity of planting them was lost, and though they were brought up, it was only to be scattered over the field by the frightened bearers. For our troops were by this time visible to the enemy. A dreadful fire was accordingly opened upon them, and they were mowed down by hundreds, while they stood waiting for orders. Seeing that all his well-laid plans were frustrated, Pakenham gave the word to advance, and the other regiments, leaving the 44th with the ladders and fascines behind them, rushed on to the assault.[51]

Sergeant John Spencer Cooper noted the terrible outcome: 'At the word "Forward!" the two lines approached the ditch under a murderous discharge of musketry; but crossing the ditch and scaling the parapet were found impossible without ladders. These had been prepared, but the regiment that should have carried them left them behind, and thereby caused, in a few minutes, a dreadful loss of men and officers.'[52] The attacking troops were faced with a hopeless task, and crucially Pakenham was killed, as Codrington told his wife:

It certainly required the best of the very Wellington stuff to stand up through such a fire as the enemy opened upon their near approach. The head of the assaulting column, however, shook, and in the endeavour to rally it and profit by the loss thus far sustained by a little further advance into the enemy's line, the gallant Pakenham received his mortal wound. General Gibbs, whose division was destined to assault, shared the same fate at about the same moment, each within fifty paces of the enemy's line, and General Keane received two musket-ball wounds and a severe contusion. Besides these, you will see a heartrending [casualty] list of the most gallant soldiers in our army.

Lambart [Lambert], our only remaining General, had but to retreat in the best manner he could, leaving the ground in front of the enemy's lines covered with killed and wounded. There never was a more complete failure.[53]

It was not long before Lambert, left as commanding officer, ordered a full retreat. Afterwards Captain Harry Smith of the 95th Regiment was sent to arrange a truce, which he recorded:

Late in the afternoon I was sent to the enemy with a flag of truce, and a letter to General Jackson, with a request to be allowed to bury the dead and bring in the wounded lying between our respective positions. The Americans were not accustomed to the civility of war, like our old *associates* the French, and I was a long time before I could induce them to receive me. They fired on me with cannon and musketry, which excited my choler somewhat, for a round shot tore away the ground under my right foot, which it would have been a bore indeed to have lost under such circumstances. However, they did receive me at last, and the reply from General Jackson was a very courteous one.[54]

That the American gunners came so close to hitting with a cannonball a single man advancing on foot is testimony to their great accuracy, which was responsible for the majority of the British casualties. After a truce had been agreed about three hundred wounded men were left in the care of the Americans and were treated well, but British losses in killed and wounded were terrible. Smith was with the burial party and commented that 'there were some awful wounds from cannon shot, and I dug an immense hole, and threw nearly two hundred bodies into it. To the credit of the Americans not an article of clothing had been taken from our dead except the shoes. Every body was straightened, and the great toes tied together with a piece of string. A more appalling spectacle cannot well be conceived than this common grave, the bodies hurled in as fast as we could bring them.'[55] On another part of the field, Gleig observed, 'within a small compass of a few hundred yards, were gathered together nearly a thousand bodies, all of them arrayed in British uniforms. Not a single American was among them; all were English, and they were thrown by dozens into shallow holes.'[56]

Many others were badly wounded, and Midshipman Bluett was one of those responsible for transporting them back to the warships. He was horrified by their suffering:

I have just heard from the wounded I am employed in carrying down to the fleet, the account of our *defeat*; within ten minutes from the commencement of the attack, the first and last gun was fired. And two thousand brave fellows were stretched on the field. I have now 350 of the wounded soldiers on board. I shall be three days going down, and the poor fellows wounds cannot be dressed for want of a surgeon. Having given up my cabin to the wounded & my decks being covered with them, I had last night no place to lie down; but placing a ladder against the mainmast, seated myself on one of the steps, and with my arms through another dozed away a bitter cold night, raining all the while, but what was my situation compared to that of the poor soldiers, whose miseries were increased by the torture of the wounds.[57]

The whole campaign against New Orleans proved to be a disaster made even more tragic by the fact that, unknown to them, the opposing sides were no longer at war. Gradually the British slipped away in a carefully planned retreat, and Jackson made no serious attempt to pursue them. By the end of January they were once again on board the ships of the fleet and Lambert was considering the next move – an attack on Fort Bowyer at Mobile Point, which the navy had unsuccessfully bombarded at the start of the campaign. This time troops were landed with artillery and siegeworks were dug to avoid any risk of unnecessary casualties. By 11 February everything was in position and once again it was Captain Smith who was sent in under a flag of truce. He found that 'the Major was as civil as a vulgar fellow can be. I gave him my version of his position, and cheered him on the ability he had displayed. He said, "Well, now, I calculate you are not far out in your reckoning. What do you advise me to do? You, I suppose, are one of Wellington's men, and understand the rules in these cases." "This," I said, "belongs to the rule that the weakest goes to the wall, and if you do not surrender at discretion in one hour, we, being the stronger, will blow up the fort and burn your wooden walls about your ears".'[58] After some discussion it was agreed that the fort would formally surrender on the following day, and at midday the Americans marched out and laid down their arms. Later that afternoon about a thousand troops arrived by ship to reinforce the garrison, but once they saw that the fort had surrendered, they returned to Mobile. Two days later news of the peace treaty arrived and hostilities ceased.

# TWENTY-ONE

## SWANSONG

How far is St Helena from the field of Waterloo?
A near way – a clear way – the ship will take you soon.
A pleasant place for gentlemen with little left to do.
(Morning never tries you till the afternoon)

From 'A St Helena Lullaby' by Rudyard Kipling

The war with America lasted through the early years of the Regency in Britain. This was a time of distinctive styles and fashions, and while British armies were fighting on American soil the architect John Nash was redesigning London – the construction of Regent Street and Regent's Park had begun in 1811. It was also the world of Jane Austen, whose work the Prince Regent enthusiastically admired. Her first published novel, *Sense and Sensibility*, appeared in 1811, followed by *Pride and Prejudice* in 1813, *Mansfield Park* in 1814 and *Emma* in 1815. She died on 18 July 1817 and the rest of her writing was published posthumously. With two brothers in the navy, Jane Austen was very well informed about the war with America. Charles Austen served for over six years in North American waters, ending as Flag Captain to Admiral John Borlase Warren, and in 1812 Francis was taken off blockade duty in Europe and his battleship was deployed against American privateers. Despite this, the war is barely mentioned in her books, because to the British it was never more than a sideshow, always upstaged by the situation in Europe.

Nevertheless, when news of the peace arrived it was a good excuse for a celebration in times that continued to be austere, and in Newcastle on 28 December 1814 'the news of peace with America was received with great joy. The Mayor immediately caused a salvo of 21 guns to be fired from the old castle, and the bells struck up a merry peal. A number of commercial travellers at Grieveson's, the Crown and Thistle inn, to demonstrate their joy on the occasion, were at the expence of illuminating the whole of the front of the inn, "G.R." and "United States" being displayed in variegated lamps, and sat down, at five o'clock, to an elegant dinner.'[1]

Throughout the winter Captain Charles Napier in the *Euryalus* was cruising off the North American coast, and from January 1815 he blockaded the frigate USS *Constellation* in Norfolk, Virginia. On 28 January, in emulation of Broke, Napier issued a challenge in writing to Captain Charles Gordon of the *Constellation*: 'I cannot help expressing my wish to meet the *Constellation*, and request you will inform me your terms and place of meeting, which I shall accept of, if in my power. Our force is twenty-six 18-pounders, twelve 32-pounders carronades, and 29-pounder. Complement, 294 men and boys. I trust, sir, you will believe that I have no personal hostility to you, and I have no other wish than to perform a grateful service to my country.'[2] Captain Gordon accepted the challenge, and Napier remarked: 'I have challenged the American frigate *Constellation*, and she has accepted of it. We shall meet in a few days. God grant us victory! I willingly will sacrifice my life to ensure it.'[3] The duel did not take place, as news of the peace arrived in time to stop it.

John Bluett, recently appointed as lieutenant, was in Cuba when the news reached him: 'Peace with America is considered as already ratified. I wish they could have continued the war a little longer, merely to give me an opportunity of recovering by prize money my losses in the *Hornet*'[4] – the *Hornet* had been shipwrecked, and Bluett had lost all his possessions. After hoping for war to continue he immediately felt remorse for what he had written: 'When I come to look at the above wish, it surprises me that I could commit so selfish an idea to paper.'[5]

The frigate *Pactolus* with the impressed American seaman James Durand had been in Bermuda after a stint blockading New London, Connecticut. The ship returned to the blockade of New London with dispatches on 25 February 1815, to be greeted by news of the peace – the Treaty of Ghent had been signed in America three days earlier, on George Washington's birthday: 'On our arrival there all the ships were dressed in their colors. A grand salute was fired by the ships and complemented by the forts in return. Our officers went on shore by invitation of the American officers, to attend a ball, the most superb that had been exhibited since the Revolution. Both parties were in full military uniform and attended by their guards. They convened at the hotel, with bells ringing and everything illuminated.'[6] After so much hostility, friendship was resumed surprisingly quickly.

In Britain the American prisoners-of-war had been following the negotiations at Ghent with intense interest, not least because peace in Europe had made the lives of these prisoners worse rather than better. After the French prisoners were repatriated in 1814, it had been decided to concentrate most of the Americans in the hated prison on Dartmoor. A seaman from Massachusetts, Henry Torey*, was twenty-one when he was captured off Martha's Vineyard in May 1813. He was first imprisoned at Melville Island, Halifax, but was subsequently sent to England, where he was held in a prison hulk at Chatham. In late 1814 he was moved to Dartmoor and was very dispirited on his arrival:

This is the latter part of the month of November; and the weather has been generally rainy, dark, dismal and foggy. Sometimes we could hardly see the sentinels on the walls. Sorrow and sadness within, gloom, fog, or drizzly rain without. If the commissioners at Ghent do not soon make peace, nor establish an exchange, we shall be lost to our country and to hope. The newspapers now and then enliven us with the prospect of peace . . . Whenever we see in the newspapers an article captioned 'News from Ghent,' we devour it with our eyes, but instead of substance, generally find it empty wind. We are wearied out. I speak for myself, and I hear the same expression from others. Winter is commencing, to add to our miseries. Poor clothing, miserable lodging, poor and inadequate food, long, dismal nights, darkness, foul air, bad smells, the groans of the sick and distressed, the execrations and curses of the half distracted prisoner, the unfeeling conduct of our keepers and commander— all, all, all conspire to fill up the cup of our sorrow.[7]

In mid-December, astounding news reached these Americans. Benjamin Palmer from Stonington, Connecticut, had originally been captured from the privateer *Rolla* and spent some time imprisoned in a hulk at Melville Island before being transferred to Dartmoor in October. He wrote in his journal: 'PEACE! PEACE! Huzza for Peace. This morning news was brought in that the preliminaries of Peace were signd on the 3d

---

* His memoirs are by Benjamin Waterhouse, but from various records Ira Dye (1987, p.316) has convincingly shown he was not the prisoner, who was more likely to be Torey, but his story was recorded by Waterhouse.

Inst . . . When this report was circulated through the Prison, it seemd as if the prisoners would jump out of their skins – all Buzz all talk & all Jaw.'[8] The next day the reports were of 'War! War! Rumors of War—The papers of today wear quite a different aspect.'[9]

At the end of the year, though, peace was confirmed, as Torey recounted:

On the 28th of this month, December, 1815 [actually 1814], the news arrived here that a treaty of peace was signed the 24th instant at Ghent. After a momentary stupor, acclamations of joy burst forth from every mouth. It flew like wild fire through the prison; and 'peace! peace! peace!' echoed throughout these dreary regions. To know that we were soon to return home, produced a sensation of joy beyond the powers of expression. Some screamed, holloaed, danced, sung, and capered, like so many Frenchmen. Others stood in amaze, with their hands in their pockets, as if doubtful of its truth . . . Some unforgiving spirits hail the joyful event as bringing them nearer the period of revenge, which they long to exercise on some of their tyrannical keepers.[10]

Nathaniel Pierce from Newburyport in Massachusetts had been captured only the month before and was taken to Dartmoor just as news of the peace arrived, 'which makes great rejoicing amongst the Prisoners, and on every Prison the American flag is displayed with the Motto Free Trade & sailors rights, which was never allow'd in this place before'.[11] Benjamin Palmer was also ecstatic: 'PEACE, PEACE, I cannot write any more at present',[12] and on the 30th he joyfully noted that 'we hoisted our saucy flags, on them are displayed Free trade and Sailors Rights in large capital letters—It humbles the British pride to see this Motto on our flag . . . This forenoon some English officers came up to see the prisoners & the band of No 4 played up Yankee doodle dandy. O it galls them.'[13] Although the treaty required ratification in America, as far as the prisoners were concerned the war was at an end. 'We calculate,' Torey commented, 'that the ratification of the treaty by the president of the United States, will arrive in England by the 1st of April [1815], at which period there will not be an American left in this place.'[14] Their high spirits were soon dampened when nothing was done to release them.

While the peace with America looked secure, from the outset many had been doubtful about the peace in Europe lasting while Napoleon remained on Elba, close to the continent he had dominated for so long.

Among these was Sir Sidney Smith, who was back in England in the summer of 1814. He had given up his command in South American waters in 1809, returning home that summer to a hero's welcome from the public, formal thanks from the merchants trading with South America and a variety of honours. For nearly three years Smith was on leave, basking in the limelight in Britain, being promoted to vice-admiral in July 1810 and in October marrying Caroline, the widow of the diplomat Sir George Rumbold. In July 1812 he had been given the post of second-in-command in the Mediterranean, under Sir Edward Pellew. On his way from Fontainebleau to Elba Napoleon, already gathering any useful intelligence, had enquired who was in command of the Mediterranean, and Colonel Campbell, the commissioner on Elba, recorded: 'I replied that I did not know, but that I believed Sir Sidney Smith was one of the admirals. He seemed to be moved by this, but quickly laughed it off.'[15] It is likely that what moved Napoleon was the thought that the prophecy that Smith had written while imprisoned in the Temple had come true – that fortune's wheel would turn and Smith would one day be as powerful as Napoleon was then, while the latter would himself be imprisoned.

Smith was in the Mediterranean for just under a year, but because of the boredom of blockade duty and deteriorating health he had relinquished his command. Back in London in July 1814 he had an unexpected visit from his old friend Hyde de Neuville, one of the French Royalists involved in his escape from the Temple in 1798. De Neuville had just become a diplomat in the service of the newly restored French monarchy and was collecting information on how the British viewed the situation in France. He noted how Smith was brutally blunt with him: '"But, do you not see a black speck, to which no one is paying any attention, on the other side of the Channel?" A map of Europe was beside him, and he went on: "Measure the distance between the Isle of Elba and the southern part of the coast of France. Is it anything to the man who has passed over the countries of Europe with such giant strides? Could he not within a few hours find himself again among his battalions?"'[16]

De Neuville was immediately struck by the danger of Napoleon returning. Smith then continued: 'Do you not know, the Emperor, at Fontainebleau, had already studied on the map the position of Elba . . . Your countrymen deceive themselves greatly, if they imagine that the prestige surrounding Napoleon's name has been destroyed by the recent reverses of France . . . If they will listen to you at Paris, advise them to watch the coasts.'[17] In fact, when Napoleon was first told he was being

sent to Elba, he was reported as saying: 'Elba? Who knows anything of
Elba? Seek out some officer who is acquainted with Elba. Look out what
books or charts can inform us about Elba.'[18]

Smith was already planning a new project: a campaign against the
white and black slave trade in the Mediterranean countries. This was to
evolve into a society called the Knights Liberators of the Slaves in Africa,
with Smith as its president, but in order to form this society he needed to
canvass potential members, and the ideal venue for doing so was at hand.
The allies against Napoleon had set up a congress in Vienna to decide the
boundaries of Europe, the fate of colonies annexed during the war, and
what, if anything, to do about Napoleon. Smith told de Neuville that
measures to combat the pirates who captured white slaves could also keep
a check on Napoleon: 'The question of the liberty of the seas, and the
means of putting down the piracy of the Barbary States, will be brought
forward at the Congress at Vienna. This shameful brigandage is not only
revolting to humanity, but fetters trade. The blockade of the African
coasts, and the undertaking on the part of the nations interested, to furnish a maritime force capable of re-establishing security, would enable
them, at the same time, to keep a watch over the Emperor's proceedings.'[19]

The Congress was formally opened on 1 November 1814, with most
heads of state attending, although the British Prince Regent was absent.
Initially he was represented by Lord Castlereagh and later by the Duke of
Wellington. The Congress attracted royalty, diplomats and statesmen,
and the atmosphere was one of a perpetual party with all kinds of amusements provided at enormous expense by the host, Emperor Franz of
Austria. This constant round of dinners, dances and entertainments was
soon joined by Smith, who also brought his new wife and three step-
daughters in his distinctive coach with his coat-of-arms painted on the
door panels.

While Smith and others lobbied for particular causes and the diplomats divided up Europe at a leisurely pace, Napoleon was apparently
getting to grips with his new kingdom, under the gaze of an array of
agents from various nations who were set to report on his behaviour. The
consensus was that if Napoleon decided to escape he would land in Italy
and perhaps try to join up with Murat, once one of Napoleon's generals
and now King of Naples. On Elba Napoleon set in motion plans for
improving the defences of the island, its infrastructure and industries,
and made an appearance of being totally absorbed in these projects. His

mail was opened and read, and visitors to the island were discreetly scrutinised, but he still managed secret communications with his supporters and used every means in his power to accumulate intelligence about events in Europe.

On the journey to Elba Napoleon had already commented to Captain Ussher that the Bourbon monarchy would be driven out again within six months and he felt that matters would be made worse by the allies' determination to reduce the power of France to stop the possibility of another war. This would, he believed, wound the pride of every Frenchman and have the opposite effect: 'France had no longer any fleets or colonies; a peace would not restore ships or San Domingo. Poland no longer existed, nor Venice; these went to aggrandise Russia and Austria. Spain, which is the natural enemy of Great Britain, more so than of France, was incapable of doing anything as an ally. If to these sacrifices were added that of a disadvantageous treaty of commerce with Great Britain, the people of France would not remain tranquil under it, not even six months after the foreign powers have quitted Paris.'[20]

The men who watched him suspected that Napoleon was merely biding his time before he made a bid to regain the power and position he had lost, but there was virtually no evidence, and in any case attention was focused on Vienna. By now it was apparent to Campbell, who monitored Napoleon for the British government, that Napoleon was spending beyond his means, not least because the allies had failed to pay the allowance they had promised him. Campbell was concerned that this might tempt Napoleon to sail for Italy, as he outlined in a dispatch to Lord Castlereagh: 'If pecuniary difficulties press upon him much longer, so as to prevent his vanity from being satisfied by the ridiculous establishment of a court which he has hitherto supported in Elba, and if his doubts are not removed, I think he is capable of crossing over to Piombino with his troops, or of any other eccentricity. But if his residence in Elba and his income are secured to him, I think he will pass the rest of his life there in tranquillity.'[21] This was a mistake, since already Napoleon was making preparations in readiness for any opportune moment to leave Elba and seize power again.

By Christmas it was not only Napoleon who was feeling pressed for cash: the Emperor of Austria had spent so much on the Congress he had a cash-flow problem and could not pay his troops, and there was no end in sight. The allies mistrusted one another and seemed no nearer an agreement than when they started. Only the British favoured the new

Bourbon monarchy in France because all the other major powers had at one time been allied to Napoleon. The former emperor was himself seen by each of the allies as a valuable asset, who at the very least would be a formidable commander of their armies if it came to a war. The British were also suspected of a covert plan to hold Napoleon in reserve as a threat to ensure their own requirements were met at Vienna. There was a feeling that a crisis was approaching and that war between the allies could well be the result.

To most people in Britain the peace seemed secure, and they were once again drawn to travelling to France and beyond. Among them was Emma Hamilton, now almost a destitute alcoholic, fleeing from her creditors. She took Horatia, her daughter by Nelson, with her to Calais, but her health rapidly declined. She was nursed by the fourteen-year-old Horatia until she died on 15 January 1815 and was buried six days later in the graveyard of the church of St Pierre. In London *The Times* merely noted 'DEATH OF LADY HAMILTON. – A letter from Calais, published in the Paris papers, says, that Lady HAMILTON died in that town the 16th instant.'[22] Of the London papers, only the *Morning Post* produced anything like an obituary, which was actually a lengthy character assassination that was picked up and embellished by the provincial papers: 'The origin of this lady was very humble, having been in her younger years a domestic . . . and she had experienced all those vicissitudes in early life which too generally attend those females whose beauty has betrayed them into vice, and which unhappily proves their chief means of subsistence. Few women, who have attracted the notice of the world at large, have led a life of more *freedom* . . . The *friendship* between Lady Hamilton and our great Naval Hero, Nelson, is too well-known to need any record in this place.'[23]

Despite a life less promiscuous and more useful than many of the aristocracy and most of the royal family, Emma was never to be forgiven for the sin of being born into the working class. After Nelson's death she had been gradually abandoned and ignored, and now the journalists could openly sneer at her. Horatia was taken back to England by the British Consul at Calais and put in the care of Nelson's sister, Kate Matcham, and her husband George. Later she lodged with his sister Susanna Bolton and her family, staying with them until she married the curate Philip Ward in 1822.

Perhaps fortunately for her memory, Emma's death was instantly eclipsed in the London papers by news from Vienna. Once the diplomats there heard about the signing of the peace treaty between Britain and America at Ghent, they soon overcame the final obstacles to agreement between the allies – it would be peace not war in Europe. Now useless as threats against opponents if the peace talks failed, Napoleon on Elba and Murat in Naples were liabilities not assets. France wanted to rid Europe of these final reminders of the exile of the Bourbon monarchy and began to receive at least tacit support from some of the other allies.

There was now peace in Europe and peace between Britain and America, but still the American prisoners were no nearer release. At Dartmoor in January 1815 there was an outbreak of smallpox, and towards the end of the month heavy falls of snow and bitterly cold temperatures added to the wretched state of the prisoners. Many deaths occurred not only from smallpox, but also pneumonia and typhus. John Seapatch from Massachusetts had been captured from a privateer off Halifax in November and was brought to Dartmoor on 27 December, but died on 7 February – at the age of twelve, he was the youngest prisoner to die there. A few days later Nathaniel Pierce noted gloomily in his journal: '11th This day Commences with disagreeable weather, and what we may call Dartmoor weather, for never was there a place I believe so disagreeable &c. unhealthy as this, great numbers die daily with the small Pox and other disorders, they average about five of a day, but we are in hopes shortly to be landed on that Blessed Eden the American shore.'[24]

In this desperate state the prisoners were very grateful towards Dr George MaGrath for all the care he gave them. He had served as surgeon on board the *Victory* until a few months before Trafalgar, and Nelson had regarded him highly. When writing to Emma Hamilton, Nelson had said of MaGrath that he 'is by far the most able medical man I have ever seen, and equally so as a Surgeon'.[25] Until recently he had been the surgeon at nearby Millbay Prison at Plymouth. While still waiting for their release, the prisoners drafted a letter to their President, James Madison, in which they praised the doctor:

It is impossible for us to speak of this gentleman in terms that will do justice to his superior professional science, brilliant talents, the exemplary virtues of his heart, the urbanity and easy accessibility of his manners, his unremitting assiduities and unwearied exertions, in combatting a succession of diseases of the most exasperated and malignant character, which prevailed among the prisoners . . . Dr. MaGrath's time and attention were fully occupied in the hospital, and in vaccinating the prisoners . . . This truly great man's exertions in the cause of suffering humanity, have been rarely equalled, but never excelled.[26]

Henry Torey agreed that their prison was

blessed with a good man for a physician, named M'Garth, an Irishman, a tall lean gentleman with one eye, but of a warm and good heart. We never shall cease to admire his disposition, nor forget his humanity . . . We owe much to the humanity of Dr. M'Garth, a very worthy man . . . Was M'Garth commander of this dépôt, there would be no difficulty with the prisoners. They would obey him through affection and respect; because he considered us rational beings, with minds cultivated like his own and susceptible of gratitude, and habituated to do and receive acts of kindness; whereas the great Capt. Shortland considers us all as a base set of men, degraded below the rank of Englishmen.[27]

Captain Thomas George Shortland had been in charge of Dartmoor Prison since December 1813. His naval career was distinguished, including action at the Dardanelles in 1807 and the Walcheren expedition in 1809, but he had started out with convicts in 1787 when he served on board the *Alexander*, the largest of the convict transport ships that sailed with the First Fleet to Australia's Botany Bay. To Torey, Shortland was 'the most detestable of men, and they [the prisoners] bestow on him the vilest and most abusive epithets'.[28] He did have some sympathy for the man, and had heard that Shortland once declared that 'I had rather have the charge of five thousand Frenchmen, than FIVE HUNDRED of these sons of liberty; and yet . . . I love the dogs better than I do the damn'd frog-eaters.'[29]

By the end of February everyone was very dispirited. 'Time hangs heavy on the weary and restless prisoner,' Torey wrote in his journal. 'His hopes of liberation, and his anxiety, increase daily and hourly. *The Favorite! The Favorite* [the sloop carrying the treaty to and from America], is in every one's mouth; and every one fixes the day of her arrival . . . Our anxiety increases every day. We inquire of every one the news. We wait with impatience for the newspapers, and when we receive them are disappointed; not finding in them what we wish.'[30] In their boredom they resorted to anything to pass the time, frequently gambling. Palmer related how he won one bet: 'One of my Messmates has met with quite a Misfortune having kept a louse (in the collar of his shirt) for 2 or 3 days past to run a race with one of mine—this being the day they were to run for a pot of Porter. He [took] off Shirt, but behold the Louse was gone. He was accordingly obliged to pay the bet.'[31]

One publication did lift their spirits, though, as Torey related:

Now and then we get a sight of Cobbett's *Political Register*, and when we do, we devour it, and destroy it, before it comes to the knowledge of our Cerberus.* This writer [the radical William Cobbett] has a manner *sui generis*, purely his own; but it is somewhat surprising how he becomes so well informed of the actual state of things, and of the feelings and opinions of both parties in our country. His acuteness, his wit, his logic and his surliness, form, altogether, a curious portraiture of an English politician. We now and then get sight of American papers, but they are almost all of them Federal papers, and contain matter more hostile to our government than the English papers. The most detestable paper printed in London is called *The Times*.[32]

While the Americans waited for release, on Elba Napoleon continued to make his preparations for escape. He had at his disposal the brig *Inconstant*, a xebec called the *Étoile,* as well as several smaller vessels, and his agents managed to secure two small merchant ships and were trying to obtain more. In all, seven ships were finally accumulated, but not all were armed and even their combined fire-power was no match for the British frigate *Partridge* that cruised around Elba and whose captain, John Adye, liaised with Campbell. On top of this, two French frigates were stationed to the north of Elba in positions that made it almost impossible for a flotilla even as small as Napoleon's to slip past unnoticed. Napoleon's prime concern seems to have been the *Partridge*, and when this ship sailed on a regular trip to Leghorn it was the chance that he had counted on. After embarkation on the afternoon of 26 February, his flotilla had to be rowed and towed by boats out from Elba because of the lack of wind, but the next day a light breeze allowed them to crawl away north of the island.

At Leghorn Campbell, who had been in Florence to hand over dispatches, watched anxiously as the wind failed and the *Partridge* was becalmed outside the harbour. On his return to Leghorn he had read the recent intelligence reports and was sure Napoleon was about to escape, so he was desperate to return to Elba. Once on board he wasted no time in persuading Adye they must sail at once, but the wind was so light that the ship inched along. The *Partridge* recorded spotting three ships on the

---

* The three-headed dog who guarded Hades, and a reference to Captain Shortland.

horizon, but did not stop to investigate and clawed its way on towards Elba.

To avoid contact with the British, Napoleon's ships altered course, heading straight for one of the French frigates. It is not clear how Napoleon circumvented this obstacle, but it is almost certain that one or both French frigates passively let him pass or actively helped him on his way. By the morning of the 28th the *Partridge* was in sight of Elba when the wind failed again. Campbell was rowed ashore and immediately saw that Napoleon and many of his troops were gone. He stopped long enough to find out that the destination was France, not Italy as expected, and the *Partridge* set off in pursuit. It was too late, as Napoleon was now too far ahead, and he began landing his small force at Golfe Juan, just west of Antibes. Campbell and Adye received news of the landing from a British ship on 7 March and learned that 'Napoleon had disembarked at midday on March 1, in Juan Bay between Antibes and Fréjus. In a few hours after, he had marched off towards Grenoble without opposition.'[33]

Napoleon's intelligence-gathering had proved better than that of all the allies, for he had a good idea of the strength of the support he could expect and he had proclamations prepared to rouse up the people in his favour. As Campbell followed his progress via intelligence reports, he correctly predicted that 'the test of Napoleon's success will be made at Grenoble, and that he will endeavour to bring it to that issue as soon as possible, before the accumulation of force [against him] renders his passage of the Isère more difficult'.[34] At the town of La Mure, a few miles south of Grenoble, Napoleon's advance guard found that troops were blocking the road ahead and beyond them was the strong garrison of Grenoble itself. On 7 March the two forces came face to face and for some time it was a stand-off, neither side willing to make a move. Napoleon studied the situation and sent emissaries to test the resolution of the opposing force and try to win them over. As Napoleon suspected, their commanders had not received clear orders and they were not sure what to do, particularly as they were aware that many of their troops were old supporters of Napoleon.

When he judged the time was right Napoleon sent an officer forward to shout out that the emperor was about to advance at the head of his men and that if they opened fire he would be the first to fall. It was a calculated risk, but Napoleon had plenty of time to judge the moment when the opposing troops were ready to defect. He led his troops forward with their muskets on their left arms and bayonets sheathed as a sign of peace, and 'throwing open his greatcoat to show himself more conspicuously, and calling out, "Kill your Emperor if you wish it!" the whole [body of soldiers blocking the road] immediately joined [him]'.[35] The bluff worked, and afterwards it was found that many of the troops blocking the road had not even loaded their guns because no such order had been given. With superb skill Napoleon had played on the drama of the moment, and as he approached Grenoble with the recently recruited soldiers leading the way to call out to their comrades in the garrison, they walked in through one gate while the few remaining royalists fled from another.

Grenoble was the turning point for Napoleon: after that his journey to Paris was more of a triumphal progress with old soldiers flocking to his eagle standards. He was well aware, however, that the spell he was casting over the people was extremely fragile. It would only need opposition from a strong force determined to stop him, and the bloodshed resulting from Frenchmen fighting Frenchmen would shatter the dream. On 20 March, his son's birthday, Napoleon entered the city from which Louis XVIII had fled the night before. From this day Napoleon would have barely four months before he was forced into exile again, because he made one fatal mistake. After receiving news that the Congress of Vienna had reached agreement, he assumed that this huge, expensive meeting would soon break up and the heads of state would be dispersed before they knew that he had left Elba. He counted on the distrust and jealousy between the members of the coalition to provide the opportunity for him to approach them individually with his old and successful tactics of dividing and conquering. The Congress had not broken up quickly, however, as those attending seemed reluctant to leave what had become a four-month-long party at the Emperor of Austria's expense. When news of Napoleon's escape reached Vienna in the early hours of 7 March, meetings were immediately convened and messages sent to halt the withdrawal of the allied armies. In the days that followed Napoleon was outlawed and the allies were reunited against him.

In the middle of March the American prisoners at Dartmoor heard the news that Napoleon had landed in France after his escape from Elba, and in order to annoy the British they cheered loudly in his support, even though they despised the French. 'There is but little love between us,' Henry Torey noted; '—yet we pretend great respect and affection for that nation and their chief, principally to torment overbearing surly John Bull.'[36] Also in mid-March, the ratified Treaty of Ghent was at last returned to Britain, and rumours began to filter through to Dartmoor, as

Nathaniel Pierce described: 'These 24 hours bring in thick & hazy weather and the American flag is hoisted on all the Prisons & have been ever since we receiv'd this glorious news. The Band also has been playing all over the yards and Prisons, now and then stopping and Cheering, & every man seems hardly able to Contain himself for joy; last night this Prison was illuminated & great joy prevails among us.'[37]

Torey also recounted the immense happiness: 'This long expected event threw us all into such a rapturous roar of joy, that we made old Dartmoor shake under us, with our shouts; and to testify our satisfaction we illuminated this *dépôt* of misery. Even Shortland affected joy, and was seen more than once, like Milton's Devil, *to grin horribly a ghastly smile.*'[38] He added that 'as there can now be no longer a doubt of our being soon set at liberty, our attention is directed to the agent for prisoners for fixing the time and arranging the means. Mr. Beasley had written that as soon as the Treaty was ratified he would make every exertion for our speedy departure. He must be aware of our extreme impatience to leave this dreary spot, whose brown and grassless surface renders it a place more proper for convicts than an assemblage of patriots.'[39]

The American agent, Reuben Beasley, was much hated by the prisoners, and Torey reckoned that 'his conduct is here condemned by *six thousand* of his countrymen'.[40] Unfortunately, America and Britain failed to reach any agreement about who should pay to charter ships to send home prisoners from their respective countries, and Beasley was in any case unable to find sufficient ships to charter. He further inflamed the prisoners by telling them that their daily allowance was to be cut now that the war was at an end. There was still no release for the six thousand increasingly frustrated and angry men, even though they were now technically free. Torey remarked that 'during the time that passed between the news of peace, and that of its ratification, an uneasy and mob-like disposition more than once betrayed itself . . . It may seem strange to some, but I am confident that there is no class of people among us more strongly attached to the American soil, than our seamen, who are floating about in the world and seldom tread on the ground.'[41]

Some of the prisoners vented their anger against Beasley by conducting a mock trial using an effigy of the man, as Torey explained: 'He was indicted for many crimes towards them and towards the character of the United States. The jury declared him guilty of each and every charge, and he was sentenced by an unanimous decree of his judges, to be hanged by the neck until he was dead, and after that to be burnt. They proceeded with him to the place of execution, which was from the roof of prison No. 7, where a pole was rigged out, to which was attached a halter.'[42] The effigy was then hung, cut down and burnt. After this incident it was believed that Captain Shortland became increasingly nervous, and some prisoners chalked on the prison walls 'BE YOU ALSO READY!'.[43]

At the end of March news of the British defeat at New Orleans reached the prisoners. 'Instead of shouting and rejoicing,' Torey said, 'as in ordinary victories, we seemed mute with astonishment . . . The more particulars we hear of this extraordinary victory the more we are astonished. We cannot be too grateful to heaven for allowing us, a people of yesterday, to wind up the war with the great and terrible nation, the mistress of the ocean, in a manner and style that will inspire respect from the present and future race of men.'[44] Everybody was despairing of ever getting away from Dartmoor, and on 1 April Pierce wrote: 'No news has come to us yet about our release from this dark hole of Despotism. It is now upwards of a month since the Peace was ratified by the President of the U. S. America. It is tedious indeed to lie in prison when our Countrymen are ploughing the Ocean and reaping the benefits thereof; no news except a report that we are to lie here until the arrival of Cartels from America.'[45]

On 4 April, Shortland was on business in Plymouth. That day the prisoners were angry because their bread allowance was unavailable, replaced with hard biscuit, which the contractor was apparently trying to shift before all the prisoners were released. A messenger was sent to Shortland to warn him about the mood of the prisoners, but everything was peaceful on his return the next day. Thursday 6 April also began in a fairly cheerful way, as Pierce recounted:

This day commences with light airs from the Eastward & Cloudy weather, first part of this day the Prisoners diverting themselves Gambling, playing Ball &c. At about 4 Oclock P. M. a sham fight was acted between the yard & Grass plot by about 300 men and it made fine sport indeed, throwing turfs of Grass at each other; the British envying our happiness order'd them out the grass plot which they complied with without the least resistance but before this a number of mischievous men have been making a Breach through the wall into the Barrack yard which they completed about the time their sport was ended in the Grass Plot.[46]

Benjamin Palmer believed that the hole in the wall (dividing part of the prison from the army barracks) had been made two days earlier and that the prisoners who were throwing turf were somewhat drunk. When the soldiers ordered the men to stop, they discovered the hole. By then it was early evening, when most prisoners were indoors. Captain Shortland was informed of the hole and immediately alarm bells were rung to alert the troops. Many more prisoners started to congregate to find out what was happening, and the lock on the gate leading to the marketplace was broken. The prisoners were ordered back, but refused, so the soldiers advanced with fixed bayonets. Hundreds of Americans now tried to retreat, but their numbers were too great. Somebody then shouted 'Fire!', though it was never certain if the order came from Shortland, from an army officer or even from one of the prisoners. Palmer, who thought that Shortland was drunk, wrote in his diary that he would remember this affair to the day he died:

The Soldiers gave an alarm that we were all coming out. The drum beat to quarters, and the Prisoners run towards the gate, where meeting the Soldiers, they were fired upon – and on running into the Prisons for safety were seen falling in all directions. The Soldiers followed on and fired Volley after Volley into the Doors & Windows without Mercy. Several who could not get [indoors] in time enough (owing to the crowd) were most inhumanly Butcher'd. Five Soldiers discharged their Muskets upon one man after he was Shot. Some that lay wounded on the ground were Jumped upon – and Bayonets plunged in them . . . One of our crew [John Washington of the *Rolla*] was Killed but my Messmates all Escaped – unhurt, being mostly in the House at this time. I was out but having no hand in the Sport [throwing turf], did not intend to Share in the danger, and wisely made my retreat in to the prison as soon as they commenced firing.[47]

Seven prisoners were killed outright, seven required amputation and over fifty others were injured less severely. Three men died later, the youngest being Thomas Jackson, a seaman from New York, aged fourteen, who was shot in the stomach. Nathaniel Pierce also thought that Shortland was drunk and was responsible for the massacre. The day afterwards he related that 'at about 9 Capt. Shortland & the Colonel came down to apologize for his firing upon us saying it was not his fault for he did not order them to fire. Which I knew is a positive lie for I heard him myself order them to fire upon them.'[48] Dr MaGrath, he noted, was horrified: 'After the surviving prisoners were all in, the Doctor sent for the wounded which was all sent into hospital, where Capt. Shortland appear'd to see them & in a most cruel manner threaten'd to run a man through who had lost an arm. But the Doctor prevented him & order'd him out & at last put him out after receiving several blows from the Capt. The Doctor a very humane man, it is said Cry'd like a child to see the slaughter & Blood shed that was made.'[49]

An inquest was held, with a verdict brought in of justifiable homicide, and a detailed inquiry followed. The eyewitness reports conflicted, and exactly what had happened was never ascertained, but each side blamed the other. This massacre prompted the Admiralty to arrange for transport ships to take the men back to America and settle the finances later. The first batch of prisoners, over two hundred in number, were released from the prison at the end of the month and marched to Plymouth, poorly clothed and ill-shod. One of those was Henry Torey, who said that 'at every step we took from the hateful prison, our enlarged souls expanded our lately cramped bodies. At length we attained a rising ground; and O, how our hearts did swell within us at the sight of the OCEAN! . . . This ground, said I, belongs to the British; but that *ocean*, and this air, and that sun, are as much ours as theirs.'[50]

They were forced to remain at Plymouth for a fortnight, and in that time Torey's attitude towards the British altered, as he found that most people there were well disposed to Americans: 'We were kindly noticed by several good people, who seemed to be rather partial to us Americans than otherwise. While there, I heard but very little uttered against America, or Americans. We were spoken to, and treated infinitely better than at Halifax [in Canada]. By the time of our embarkation . . . we felt considerable attachment to the people about us.'[51]

Pierce was not lucky enough to be released early, but towards the end of May he was optimistically 'employ'd knitting a pair of shoes, to walk down to Plymouth in, when it comes to my turn, but, the Lord knows when that will be'.[52] By early July most American prisoners were on their way home. They left behind at least 270 Americans and 1200 French who had died during their imprisonment, buried in the graveyard outside the prison. Memorials to both the French and Americans now mark their final resting place. Pierce was one of the last to leave, and witnessed the arrival of many French soldiers captured at Waterloo. On 2 July he wrote his last journal entry: 'There are now (2PM) 2000 Frenchmen entering the gates mostly soldiers. End pleasant & ends this journal for want of paper, tomorrow I leave this cursed Depot.'[53]

*

The road to Waterloo began when Napoleon's attempts to arrive at peaceful terms with the allies fell flat. This time the allies felt they could finally rid themselves of Napoleon and were determined to do so – if captured, he would be banished for ever. As their armies began to close in, Napoleon was faced with the choice of attempting pre-emptive strikes on individual allies or to remain on the defensive. Always predisposed to act boldly, he made the first move. A combined British and Prussian army was advancing on France from the north and although this force was one and a half times the size of his own, Napoleon counted on the uneasy alliance and less than unified command of his enemy to provide an advantage. He also knew that a defeat of the British was likely to make the current government fall, weaken the alliance against him and provide further opportunities he might be able to exploit. On the evening of 11 June he set out from Paris to lead his army into Belgium and head off the British and Prussians.

The Congress of Vienna had been finally brought to a close two days before, and Sir Sidney Smith and his family started the long overland journey to England. On 17 June they reached Brussels and learned that Napoleon and Wellington were about to confront each other just south of the city. Smith could not resist going to see what would obviously be a momentous battle, if not the decisive one, with the dictator he had fought and intrigued against for so many years. Leaving his family in Brussels he immediately headed for Waterloo. He seems only to have had an inscribed ceremonial sword with him and had to borrow a more serviceable one. He recorded how he arrived at the heart of the battle at the moment of Wellington's triumph:

Meeting Sir G. Berkeley returning from the field wounded, and thinking his sword a better one to meet my old antagonist *on horseback*, I borrowed it. Things went ill and looked worse at that time in the afternoon of the 18th June, 1815. I stemmed the torrent of the disabled and the *givers-in* the best way I could, was now and then jammed among broken waggons by a *drove* of disarmed Napoleonist janissaries, and finally reached the Duke of Wellington's person and rode in with him from St Jean to Waterloo. Thus, though I was not allowed to have any of the fun . . . I had the heartfelt gratification of being the first Englishman, that was not in the battle, who shook hands with him before he got off his horse, and of drinking his health at his table.[54]

After the battle Smith organised wagons to bring in the wounded from the battlefield to the dressing stations and to the hospital in Brussels.

As a fluent French speaker, he was asked by Wellington to arrange for the surrender of Arras and Amiens and to inspect the route that was to be taken by Louis XVIII on his return to Paris, to ensure it was safe and peaceful. Captain Harry Ross-Lewin of the 32nd Regiment, who had been in the disastrous Walcheren expedition, was returning from Waterloo when he came across Smith at the small town of Bavay:

When passing through the principal street of Bavay, my attention was arrested by the uncommon appearance of the arms blazoned on the panels of a coach, which was drawn up at the door of a British general's billet. 'Pray, sir,' said I to a little man who wore a travelling cap and was standing near, 'can you tell me whose carriage this is?' 'It belongs to your humble servant,' he replied, 'Sir Sidney Smith.' We entered into conversation. He had discovered Napoleon's cipher, and with it all that monarch's plans, from the papers found in the imperial carriage at Genappe. He also informed me that we would meet with no opposition before we reached Montmartre. Sir Sidney Smith carried his forage with him, and had a haystack raised between the hind wheels of his carriage. Some wags intended to put a coal of fire in this cumbrous appendage to the vehicle as he was going to start, but were by some means prevented from carrying this mischievous design into execution.[55]

Napoleon's carriage ended up on display at Madame Tussaud's in London, where it was destroyed in a fire in 1925.

Napoleon fled to Paris after the battle, arriving there on 21 June, and tried to rally what troops he had left, but his friends and commanders either abandoned him or turned against him, and he was forced to abdicate two days later. Smith's prophecy that Napoleon would eventually find himself imprisoned in the Temple after Smith had achieved power and glory had come true in spirit – but not in detail, because the tower that was Smith's prison had been demolished. Napoleon fled to Rochefort in the coastal area known as Basque Roads, where Thomas Cochrane's fireships had cause so much havoc among the French fleet in 1809. His last hope was for a French frigate to take him to asylum in America, but as so many times before, his plans were upset by the British Navy. The blockade of the area was too tight for French ships to evade, and with a hue and cry of French Royalists hot on his heels, Napoleon finally ran out of options. On 15 July he surrendered to the captain of a British ship.

# TWENTY-TWO

———·◆·———

# THE TURN OF FORTUNE'S WHEEL

You have already the hatred of all nations, in consequence of your maritime laws, and your pretensions to be mistress of the seas, which you say belongs to you by right. Then why not take advantage of it?

Napoleon, speaking to the physician Barry O'Meara on St Helena[1]

The victory at Waterloo in 1815 was celebrated in many ways, and on the morning of 24 July the schoolboy John Smart of Brixham in Devon was enjoying a holiday:

In common with most English schoolboys of that Waterloo year, we had an extra week's holiday at midsummer, and this was fortunate for me, as it tided me over my birthday on 24 July. It was a bright summer's morning when I sallied out after breakfast, with two half-crowns in my pocket, to meet Charlie Puddicombe and his younger brother Dick. Charlie was the biggest boy in our school; Dick was almost the smallest, and I and they were great chums. We met . . . on the quay, and at once began to discuss how we should spend the day and my money. Suddenly we spied two ships coming round Berry Head and into the bay – the first a large man-of-war, and the other a three-masted sloop.[2]

This was not an unusual occurrence, because the bay was a convenient anchorage for navy ships, particularly those on blockade duty in the Channel, but normally the boys would be confined in school, and John Smart recalled 'how thankful we were that no school bell would drag us away, but that we might stay to see all the fun!'.[3] Dick was sent running to fetch Michelmore Hawkins, the baker, while John and Charlie got a boat ready, for ships in the bay meant more sales for the local tradesmen, and the chance of some excitement, if not some extra pocket money, for the local schoolchildren. While they waited a boat from one of the ships landed two officers, one of whom immediately hired the 'old yellow postchaise'[4] and started out for London. Once he was on his way the other officer ordered the boat to take him back to the ship. Both officers had been unusually brisk, avoiding conversation, and giving out no news at all – it was the first indication of something out of the ordinary.

The boat was just pulling away when the baker arrived on the quay: '"Bean't he in a hurry, then?" said old Michelmore, who, in his floury coat and white hat, had just arrived with his apprentice boy from the shop. "Come, boys, let's be off to the ship".'[5] With Charlie and Dick on one oar, the apprentice boy on the other, John Smart was a passenger in the bow while the baker steered. 'He had a large sack with him containing new loaves,' Smart remembered, 'which he was taking as a speculation and as a suggestion for further orders.'[6] As they got nearer they could see other local boats:

[They] had stopped short of the ship, and were together, while in one of them a man was standing up, who, as we drew nearer, appeared to be in altercation with some one on board. Michelmore steered up to this boat and asked what was the matter. 'They won't let us come alongside, and they say as how they don't want no shore boats at all.' 'But they'll want some shore bread, I reckon,' said Michelmore, letting our boat drift onwards with the tide towards the ship. It was a grand-looking line-of-battle ship, with 74 guns, and with stern galleries and square cabin windows. The tide took us right under the stern, and there was a sentry with his musket in the poop, and an officer by him leaning over the rail, who said in a loud voice, 'Come, sheer off; no boats are allowed here.' 'But,' said Michelmore, as he made a grab at a lower-deck port-sill with his boat-hook, 'I've brought you some bread.' 'If we want bread,' replied the officer, 'we'll come ashore and fetch it, and if you don't let go I'll sink you.'[7]

By now the boat was right under the stern of the ship, and Smart was horrified 'to see the sentry drop his musket and seize a large cannon-ball, which he held exactly over my head. "Let go, you old fool, or by the Lord

I'll sink you!" said the sentry, and to my great relief Michelmore let go, and we were soon out of harm's way.'[8] To back up the sentries on deck, the ship lowered boats full of men armed with cutlasses to row round the ship and keep the shore boats at a distance, and Smart remembered the baker 'being most indignant. "Man and boy," said he, "have I sailed in these here waters, and never have I been so treated."'[9] As the other boats gave up and rowed back to the quay, the boys 'persuaded Michelmore to stay a little longer',[10] and Smart watched what was happening:

The patrolling boats were content in keeping us outside of their circuit . . . at a proper distance. One might well suppose that an English crew, so close to their own shores, would be as eager for communication as we were, and although no word came to us from the ship, we could see the men round the guns peering at us through the portholes. As we rounded the bows of the ship the tide caught us with great force, and . . . we were taken a little nearer than we would willingly have ventured. As the current swept us along, I noticed at one of the lower-deck ports a man nodding violently to us, but standing back a little, as if frightened at being seen. His eye caught mine for an instant as he put his fingers to his lips with a warning gesture.[11]

The boys and the baker did another circuit of the ship in their boat, and 'this time the man was still standing back, and even less visible than before; but his hand was just visible on the port-sill, and as we passed he let something drop from his fingers into the water'.[12] Smart later recalled that

we dared not approach, but we kept it in view as it drifted along. I had my hand dragging as if carelessly in the water, and when we were a good hundred yards clear of the ship, Michelmore steered so as to bring the object into my hand. It proved to be a small black bottle; but as the evident intention of the officers had been to prevent all communication, I was frightened to look at my prize, and could only clutch it in my hand with a fear that some one on board must have seen me. However, our curiosity was too great to brook delay, and we steered towards the shore, so that Michelmore's broad body was between me and the ship in case anyone was spying at us through a glass. It was a foreign-looking bottle, and as I drew the cork, its oiliness and perfume suggested that it had been used for some liqueur . . . In the bottle was a small piece of paper rolled up, and on the paper was written, 'We have got Bonaparte on board'.[13]

The secret was out, and it spread like a firestorm. As Smart put it, 'in five minutes after we reached shore, there was not a soul in Brixham, except babies, ignorant of the news'.[14]

The ships in the bay were the battleship *Bellerophon*, with Napoleon on board, and the frigate *Myrmidon*, which carried some of his entourage. When Napoleon had surrendered to the navy at Basque Roads, he had been forced to throw himself on the mercy of Frederick Maitland, captain of the *Bellerophon*. The British blockade of the French coast was so tight that in reality Napoleon had little other option, and Maitland was instructed not to promise anything to Napoleon, so delicate negotiations went on for several days. With the approach of the Royalists, Napoleon and his entourage boarded the *Bellerophon* on 15 July, still faintly hoping to be exiled in Britain or America. The British Navy having been the first to defeat Napoleon off the coast of Egypt, it was only fitting that it should take charge of the Emperor after his final defeat – especially since the *Bellerophon* had been in the thick of the fighting at the battles of the Nile and Trafalgar.

The journey from Basque Roads to Brixham in Torbay had taken nine days, and Napoleon held discussions with Captain Maitland and his officers on a wide range of subjects. Well aware of the historic occasion, many of the seamen noted down these conversations, especially anything odd. Midshipman George Home recalled that 'the Emperor seemed to entertain an idea that the Americans were bigger men than us, for whenever he saw any very stout man he asked if he was an American'.[15] Lieutenant John Bowerman of the *Bellerophon* was one of those who kept a journal, and his entry for Monday 24 July began: 'Early this morning we were close in with the land running into Torbay. Between five and six a.m. Buonaparte made his appearance on deck, and continued there until we anchored. He appeared delighted with the prospect, and his approach to England. Looking through his glass he frequently exclaimed in French "What a beautiful country!".'[16] Napoleon still talked of hoping to live the life of a country gentleman in exile among his former enemies in Britain, although many of his entourage were less optimistic, but when the first boat ashore returned the mood changed, as Bowerman recorded: 'The conjectures contained in the several newspapers which now reached us of the probability of his being sent to St. Helena cast a sudden gloom over the whole party . . . Buonaparte . . . solemnly declared that he never would go there.'[17]

The first boat ashore had carried a lieutenant to take dispatches to London. He held his tongue at Brixham, but when he changed horses at

Exeter he spread the news. By the evening carts and coaches crammed with sightseers from the city were flooding into Brixham, and the next day the *Bellerophon* was surrounded by all manner of craft from the local ports of Torquay, Paignton, Dartmouth and even further away that had been hired by people trying to catch a glimpse of the man who had dominated Europe for over a decade. John Smart, who had received the message in the bottle the day before, was amazed at the sight:

There never was before or since such an assembly of craft in Torbay . . . Torquay was little else but a fisherman's village in those days, and was only beginning to be known by health-seeking visitors as a salubrious hamlet in Torre parish, but the population, such as it was, seemed to have turned out altogether and crossed the bay. From Exmouth, Teignmouth, Plymouth, the boats and yachts continued to arrive all day . . . Gentlemen and ladies came on horseback and in carriages; other people in carts and waggons; and to judge by the number of people, all the world inland was flocking to see Bonaparte. The Brixham boatmen had a busy time of it, and must have taken more money in two days than in an ordinary month. It seemed a gala day as the boats thronged round the *Bellerophon*.[18]

Everyone was eager to find out all they could about Napoleon, and officers who came ashore from the ships were treated like celebrities, as recalled by Midshipman Home:

I was taken prisoner by some twenty young ladies, marched off to a fine house in the little town [Brixham], regaled with tea and clouted cream [Devon clotted cream], and bored with five thousand questions about Napoleon, the ridiculousness of which I have often laughed at since: What was he like? Was he really a man? Were his hands and clothes all over blood when he came aboard? Was it true that he had killed three horses in riding from Waterloo to the *Bellerophon*? Were we not all frightened of him? Was his voice like thunder? Could I possibly get them a sight of the monster, just that they might be able to say they had seen him? etc. etc.[19]

Midshipman Home did what he could to redress the balance and

assured those inquisitive nymphs that the reports they had heard were all nonsense; that the Emperor was not only a man, but a very handsome man, too; young withal; had no more blood upon his hands or clothes than was now upon their pure white dresses; that if by chance they got a look of him at the gangway they would fall in love with him directly; that, so far from his hands being red with blood, they were as small, white, and soft as their own charming fingers; and his voice, instead of resembling thunder, was as sweet and musical as their own. This account of the Emperor's beauty perfectly astonished the recluses of Torbay. Some misbelieved altogether, while the curiosity of others was excited beyond all bounds.[20]

It may have been an idealised picture that Home painted of Napoleon, but it was closer to the truth than that held by many of the British – after years of propaganda in the press, it was not just 'the recluses of Torbay' who believed him to be a monster who might literally not be human. The local newspapers carried accounts from people in the boats around the *Bellerophon* describing his physical appearance and behaviour, while anyone from the ship itself was pressed for details. *Woolmer's Exeter and Plymouth Gazette* carried the story:

By some passengers who came in the *Bellerophon* it appears that Bonaparte was quite at his ease on board that ship; took possession of the Captain's cabin, *sans ceremonie*, invited the officers of the ship to his table, talked with great freedom on the present state of things, said it was impossible for the Bourbons to govern France, and that Napoleon II would very soon be recalled to the throne . . . He acknowledged that England alone had ruined all his grand plans, and that but for her he had now been Emperor of the East as well as of the West. He walked on the poop and quarterdeck, conversed with the seamen, and affected great gaiety and unconcern. In short, such is the talent of this 'Child and Champion of Jacobinism', that before they arrived in Torbay he was considered by all on board as a *devilish good fellow*.[21]

Once the news spread, the national newspapers were quick to take up the story, and at first Napoleon's appearance was of greatest interest. In a time when the only forms of representing Napoleon were by drawing or painting, which in Britain were frequently distortions or outright carica-tures, people wanted to know if Napoleon was the devil incarnate as he was sometimes portrayed. *The Times* accordingly published a report from a correspondent in Dartmouth:

I was alongside his Majesty's ship *Bellerophon* last evening, and I saw Buonaparte very distinctly. Buonaparte walks the deck till six o'clock, at which time he retires to dine. He shows himself frequently to the spectators round the ship, and on retiring he pulls off his hat. He appears often looking at the people with his eye glass, and his picture which appeared in London about two months since, is an exact likeness of him. He wore a dark green coat, with red collar, buttoned close; cocked hat, two epaulets, light nankeen coloured breeches, and silk stockings the same colour. Every person on the quarter deck, both French and English, remain with their hats off when he is on deck. This I did not like to see, it hurt the feelings of all to see so much humility paid him . . . He reads the English newspapers, but appears afterwards very serious, no doubt not liking their contents. He, I am told, dreads the idea of going to St. Helena, and is very much afraid of being sent to that island.[22]

At this point the final decision on whether Napoleon should be exiled to St Helena or elsewhere had not been taken, and the newspapers were full of speculation. They also carried letters voicing strong opinions on the subject, and one that may well have been read by Napoleon was published by *The Times* on 26 July:

What is to be done with him? Is he after all his crimes to be suffered to go unpunished; or in what way is he to be brought to justice? . . . What punishment can be just, if the condemning him to death be cruel? He has, for a long succession of years, deluged Europe in blood, to gratify his own mad vanity, his insatiable and furious ambition. It is calculated, that every *minute* he has reigned, has cost the life of a human being. He has desolated the earth in its fairest portions. He has not only darkened the palace and the crowded mart with terror and dismay, but he has carried unutterable distress into cottage, and the mountain solitude.[23]

Napoleon had carried on unlimited warfare with the aim of making Europe a French Empire, and while people were relieved and sometimes surprised to find he was a man, rather than a supernatural monster, many held him responsible for their personal loss and would never forgive him. To the British, just as Nelson would always be a hero, Napoleon would always be an ogre.

As soon as the Admiralty heard that Napoleon was on board the *Bellerophon*, they decided that the ship must be moved to Plymouth for extra security against any rescue attempt, and John Smart watched the ships depart: 'The officer who had gone to London, must have travelled quickly, for on Wednesday morning, as soon after sunrise as the tele-graph could work, instructions had been sent to Plymouth, and these had been forwarded to Brixham. The ships weighed anchor at once and sailed for Plymouth, no secret being made of their destination. Boney having gone, the world no longer found anything of interest at Brixham. The visitors left us, and I went back to school. But at Plymouth the *Bellerophon* was still a greater attraction than it had been with us.'[24]

Although the anchorage at Plymouth was more secure, it was also more accessible for the sightseers, and it became increasingly difficult to keep them at bay. For Napoleon, these few days in Torbay and Plymouth, appearing on deck for the people of the nation he had tried so hard to conquer, were his swansong. On 31 July a letter arrived with the official decision of the British government – exile to St Helena. Arrangements were made to transfer Napoleon to the *Northumberland*, and on 4 August the *Bellerophon* set sail from Plymouth along the south coast of Devon. The *Northumberland* met the *Bellerophon* off Start Point on 6 August, Napoleon was transferred and the next day he was sailing from Europe into exile for the last time.

Napoleon was not to escape from St Helena, as he had from Elba, and after a long illness he died on 5 May 1821. There has been controversy ever since as to whether he was assassinated by being poisoned over a long period of time, or whether, as the official report claimed, he died of stomach cancer. Despite investigations over the years that have supported the official view, it is unlikely that the mystery will ever be resolved conclusively.

Sir Sidney Smith, the man who had dogged Napoleon's rise and fall, lived on into old age. After Waterloo he settled with his family in Paris, in part because the British government owed him a great deal of expenses, and until these were received he was in danger of being imprisoned for debt in Britain. It was a complaint all too familiar to senior naval officers and diplomats. At the end of 1815 he was invested with the insignia of a Knight Commander of the Order of the Bath by the Duke of Wellington at a celebration dinner at the Élysée Palace in Paris.

Smith continued to lobby for help for Christian slaves in North Africa, and eventually the British government sent out a fleet of warships to deal with the main slavers' base at Algiers. This was not commanded by Smith, as he had hoped, but by Sir Edward Pellew, who relied more on a show of force than Smith's more delicate style of diplomacy. In August 1816, after the Algerian shore batteries opened fire on Pellew's ships, they replied with such devastating broadsides that the town's sea defences were wrecked. The ruler of Algiers released over one thousand slaves and promised not to enslave any more Christians. After this Pellew, who had already been made the first Viscount Exmouth, became the commander-in-chief at Plymouth – a post that he held from 1817 to 1821. He then effectively retired, although occasionally making his voice heard in Parliament, and lived in Devon until his death in January 1833.

Smith eventually received the money the government owed him, but by that time he was ensconced in the Parisian social scene and was happy to remain there. His wife Caroline died in 1826 and was buried near the grave of Captain Wright in the Père Lachaise cemetery. Smith lived on in Paris and was awarded the Grand Cross of the Order of the Bath in 1838 by the young Queen Victoria. Two years later he died, at the age of seventy-six, and after a magnificent funeral he was buried beside his wife.

In the years that followed Waterloo, Smith was one of very few people who worried that Napoleon might return from St Helena. Most were happy to forget the French dictator and enjoy peacetime life, but even if Smith was no longer at the heart of the British intelligence network, he was a shrewd judge of politics. More than one plot was put forward to rescue Napoleon from exile, and Thomas Cochrane himself entertained an idea of persuading him to leave St Helena for South America. Cochrane had not served in the British Navy since his destruction of the French ships at Basque Roads and Gambier's court martial. In 1813 he was falsely implicated in and then wrongly convicted of a stock exchange fraud carried out by one of his uncles and was imprisoned. If it had not been for this fraud case, Cochrane would have played a part in the war against America, as he was about to sail there as flag captain for his uncle, Alexander Cochrane, when he was arrested. After his release he returned to his seat in Parliament but continued to be outraged at the corruption both in government and at the Admiralty, and was tired of the English prejudice against Scots like himself, so he did not hesitate when offered a post in Chile.

In 1818 he was hired by the Chilean government to command its fleet during its war of independence from Spain. He had already organised the building of the first sea-going steam warship for the Chileans, but this was not yet complete, so in August he took passage with his wife on a sailing ship for Chile, planning to stop at St Helena and persuade Napoleon to become Emperor of South America. On the way news arrived that the Spanish were grouping for an attack and he was needed in Chile immediately, so the diversion to St Helena was cancelled. In August 1812, despite efforts from his relatives to marry him off to a rich heiress, Cochrane had secretly married a sixteen-year-old orphan from Essex called Katherine Barnes. The marriage was later questioned and they were married twice more in 1818 and 1825.

Cochrane's success in Chile and then Peru, where he was accompanied by Katherine and their growing family, led other countries fighting for independence to seek his services, and after a brief time with the Brazilian navy he joined the Greek navy in 1827. Here he found he could do very little and returned to Britain the following year, having become the most famous admiral of the post-war years – the only British admiral since Nelson to achieve a global reputation. With a change of monarch and of government, Cochrane was rehabilitated into the navy and in subsequent years managed to clear his name and have his honours and position restored. He died in London in October 1860 at the age of eighty-five.

Cochrane was not the only one to be caught up in one of the plots to rescue Napoleon: in 1820 Tom Johnson the smuggler was hired to use a submarine to ferry him from St Helena to a ship waiting out to sea. The plot was discovered, and as Johnson took the submarine down the Thames so that another ship could tow it to St Helena, the vessel was captured by the British authorities and later destroyed. Johnson died in 1839 at the age of sixty-seven.

It was only a minority of senior officers who, like Cochrane, continued an active naval career as mercenaries. A few were kept on by the navy in peacetime posts, but the majority retired and occupied themselves with other pursuits. This was really only an option for those of the rank of captain and above, because half-pay for lieutenants and midshipmen was too meagre to live on. Lieutenant Hoffman, who had been a prisoner in France when Napoleon was exiled to Elba, wrote of his wartime naval service:

The days of my youth have floated by like a dream, and after having been forty-five years in the Navy my remuneration is a hundred and eighty pounds a year, without any prospect of its being increased. If the generality of parents would take my advice they never would send one of their boys into the service without sufficient interest [influence with senior naval officers] and some fortune. If they do, their child, if he behaves well, may die in his old age, possibly as a lieutenant, with scarcely an income to support himself; and if he should under these circumstances have the misfortune to have married and have children, God, I hope, will help him, for I very much fear no one else will![25]

In 1840 the Admiralty offered a special retirement rank of captain to the fifty most senior half-pay commanders under the rank of post-captain, and Hoffman was lucky enough to be one of them, so just nine years before he died he received his pay rise. Many other officers were not so fortunate. Even so, they were always better off than the seamen, who seldom had any income or pension to fall back on. For years they had been treated like children, told what to do at every hour of the day, and when allowed on shore for a short time they spent their money freely without any thought for the future. When peace finally came many ships were paid off and the newspapers made fun of the resulting antics of the sailors as they frittered away years of back-pay in a few days.

When the money ran out the sailors found circumstances had changed. The navy no longer wanted them, and there were far too few vacant places in merchant ships. Those who had a trade went back to it, but on land the majority were unskilled labourers, in competition with soldiers who were also redundant at the end of the fighting, at a time when many labourers were being laid off because their jobs could now be done by machines. Some of these men sailed for distant parts of the empire to seek a new life, but many were reduced to begging and crime. The situation was very similar in France, except that here sailors were vastly outnumbered by soldiers from Napoleon's disbanded armies. Some sailors had been prudent with their pay, and a few had grown relatively rich from prize money and were able to lead a comfortable life. Robert Jeffery, who had been given £600 for agreeing not to prosecute Captain Lake for stranding him on a desert island, should have been among these. In 1818 he married a woman from a village near to his home of Polperro, but two years later he died of consumption.

After such a long conflict most people were content to look to the future, but a few revisited places they had known during the war, and one such was Donat Henchy O'Brien. In May 1827, nearly two decades after escaping from the French prison at Bitche, he set out for the Continent with his wife, young son and nurse in order to relive some of his memories. One of his first stops was the site of the Battle of Waterloo:

At eleven o'clock we arrived at the inn of the village of Waterloo. This immense forest is said to cover sixteen thousand acres, one sixtieth of which is annually cleared to supply Brussels with fuel. I will not attempt to describe the varied and strong emotions that possessed and overwhelmed me on my traversing this mighty battlefield. I traced the positions of the two great hosts; marked the spots where the most deadly charges had been given; and where the cannon had done the most murderous work. Amidst my sorrows for suffering and sacrificed humanity, I confess that my heart glowed at the idea that it was here that the prowess, bravery, and genius of England had conquered the conqueror of the world; had annihilated revolutions; re-established monarchies; restored dynasties; and placed Europe once more on the basis of social order and international rights.[26]

He then moved on to visit 'the grave of a gallant Hibernian, Colonel Fitzgerald (whom I had known as a détenu at Verdun), surrounded by several others who had on that occasion immortalised the British charac-ter, and covered themselves with glory; and in honour of whom memorials have been erected, with which the walls of the little church of the village are lined . . . We were told that Miss Fitzgerald continued periodically to visit the shrine of her lamented brother, and that her piercing and piteous cries made it a most afflicting scene to witness.'[27]

The next stage of O'Brien's journey was part of the way along which the captured seamen were marched to their prisons, and he also tried to trace their escape routes. At Bitche they went to the best inn in the village, and just as they were preparing to visit the dreaded prison O'Brien saw that the landlady

suddenly fixed her eyes on me with astonishment. At first, her brows were knitted, then her eyes were dilated, with all the expression of wonder; and at last she burst forth with an ejaculation, '*Mon Dieu! je me souviens bien de vos traits, Monsieur; vous étiez un des aspirants de la marine royale anglaise*,' [My God! I recognise you, Sir. You were one of the midshipmen of the English Royal Navy] and after many other '*mon Dieus*,' she came to the catastrophe of my having been a prisoner in Bitche, and of my having made an escape which nobody could account for, except on something like the ground of miracle.[28]

O'Brien took his wife round the prison, conducting her 'to the exact point of the ramparts, from which my unfortunate companion

[Lieutenant] Essel, in attempting to escape, had been dashed to pieces. Grief for the loss of a friend thus sacrificed in youth, and under such unhappy circumstances, strongly oppressed me.'[29] Every detail was shown to his wife:

And the sensation of a female's mind may be conceived, when I pointed out the three lofty ramparts that I had scaled, and the point over which the rope was thrown, and by which I and my companions had descended to such an awful depth. Amidst serious matters the ludicrous often intervenes. Their brigadier [who was acting as guide] did not understand a word of English, and consequently, he knew not upon what we were talking; but our emphasis and earnestness aroused him, and he began to tell us a legend of a marvellous escape, effected by four English prisoners-of-war, who had scaled the three ramparts and got down to the glacis; and he added, that two of them were aspirants [midshipmen] of the British navy. And he concluded by shrugging his shoulders, and saying, that the English naval officers had the faculty of climbing and creeping 'comme des chats [like cats];' when I could not help laughing, but did *not* tell him that I was the very man who led the way on that occasion.[30]

In early July the travellers arrived at Verdun, but to O'Brien's disappointment his old gaoler was away, particularly as he remembered one incident: 'One day I asked this fellow, whether he imagined that there was any probability of the English prisoners being liberated from Verdun. He sarcastically answered, "*Oh! qu'oui, certainement* [Oh, for sure, certainly];" and he fixed our date of liberation when our ships of the line could sail over land, and batter down the tower and citadel. I should have liked to enjoy my revenge, by reminding him of his sarcasm, and of our having defeated his grand army, captured his Emperor, and destroyed his system and his power.'[31]

At the hotel O'Brien had to show his passport to the police: 'They were civil, and asked me if it was true that I had once been a prisoner-of-war, and had escaped by scaling the walls of Verdun and Bitche. I replied in the affirmative, and they expressed their astonishment, and retired.'[32] Before exploring the town he received a visit from an old friend, Dr John Graham, who had been surgeon of the shipwrecked *Hussar*. After the war ended he had remained in France, having married a Frenchwoman during his imprisonment. The subsequent tour of the town was tinged with disappointment: 'I had expected to find in the old burying-ground of the

English prisoners, tombs and epitaphs to many of my departed friends, but the site had been covered with stately edifices, and the bones of my countrymen had been removed, many years back, to a cemetery, aux faubourgs [in the suburbs] not far from Belle Ville. The mind is hurt at the desecration of the hallowed ground in which we have deposited the remains of those we loved and esteemed.'[33]

Eighteen years later, in the summer of 1845, Edward Boys went back to the Continent, because, he related, it was recommended that he should go to the spa waters near Liège in Belgium for the benefit of the health of his children and to help his own rheumatism: 'On arriving at Ostend, in a steamer, with about two-hundred passengers, we found the hotels so crowded, that it was necessary to proceed to Bruges, and there we took up our quarters at the Hotel de Commerce. Early in the morning, I enquired if anyone in the hotel knew of a Madame Derikre, who had formerly kept a public-house on the road to Blankenberg, called the "Raie-de-Chat," and if she were still living; when I was told she had been dead about four years.'[34]

He wandered around Bruges, to see if he could recognise any of the streets and hiding places from the time when he and his companions were waiting to get back to England after having escaped from prison in Valenciennes. The next day he hired a carriage to Blankenberge on the coast:

As we advanced into the country, the scenery became somewhat exciting, for I fancied I could recollect the very ploughed field where Hunter and I were chased by the gendarmes, when we were . . . reconnoitring, and had to plunge through a ditch, to escape into the wood. We soon reached the 'Cat,' under very different circumstances and feelings. As we entered the premises, almost everything became fresh in my memory; nothing seemed altered, except a new room at the side of the house . . . On enquiring after the former hostess, Madame Derikre, her successor told me she thought she had been living at Ostend about two years since; but a young man said he thought she had been dead about four years. We examined every part of the premises, and the very loft where I was so long concealed.[35]

He and his wife then walked to the beach and mounted the steps to the battery, from where 'nothing seemed altered in the village, or in the surrounding country'.[36] Returning to the hotel, they made copious enquiries, but could find no trace of the Derikre or Moitier family, until 'an old man, in the stable department of the hotel, stated that he knew them, and that the wife had been dead about four years'.[37] Boys refused to give up the search and went by train to Ostend, because the present landlady of the Cat thought she once lived there:

The following morning, on my arrival, [I] engaged an intelligent commissioner, named Pierre, to assist me. Having communicated to him the object of my return, we first visited the vegetable market, then some of the public offices, but could learn nothing encouraging, for Madame Derikre had latterly been too poor and too insignificant to be known by the authorities by that name, as she was generally called by her maiden name, Madame Robert, which I did not then know . . . We were again told that Madame Derikre had been dead four years. The Commissioner now began to be weary of the search . . . but as the name was not common, I saw no reason as yet for abandoning all hope, and, therefore, determined to proceed and endeavour to find out where this woman was buried four years' since . . . when halting, in earnest and somewhat audible conversation, on the bridge, a little decrepid old man, selling apples under a shed, rose and said, 'Pardon me, gentlemen, but it occurs to me, it is not Madame Derikre you seek, but the old "frau," called the "Aenglishe Reeker."'[38]

The old man knew that Madame Derikre had been receiving charitable assistance some months ago, and through this information Pierre found out the street where she lived, though he was convinced she was dead and that it was pointless discovering where she was buried. Boys insisted on continuing the search:

We rapped at door after door, but could find no one in that street who knew the name. At length a person told us there was an old blind woman, bed ridden, living on the upper floor of No. 20. An inmate of this house volunteered to ask if two strangers would be admitted, and immediately ran up stairs, but, suspecting some deception, or that preparation might be made for our reception, which it was desirable to avoid, I quickly followed her up into a back room, when to my horror I saw in a corner, sitting erect on a stump bedstead and palliasse, a withered remnant of human wretchedness, quite blind, and partially covered with a dirty tattered garment, and a substitute for a blanket. Painfully disappointed as I felt at the sight of this distressed object, and evident as it appeared that we had again failed, I approached the bed, intending to give something as a compensation for my intrusion, and retire.[39]

Something made Boys stay and ask a few questions, which led to a conversation about the late wars with England. He then asked her if she had heard of prisoners-of-war:

Encouraged by the ease and readiness of her replies, I then touched upon her age and occupation at that time. To all of which she surprised me with answers of remarkable clearness and accuracy, telling me she had assisted many young officers to escape, when she kept a public-house in the country. At length Pierre, who followed me up stairs, became very impatient, and asked if I was not now satisfied that this woman was the 'veritable Aenglishe Reeker?' Wait, was the reply (for seeing her miserable state, I could not entirely divest myself of doubt, and was anxious to elicit the truth), I have one more question to put, and then said to her, – 'Tell me, what were the names of the first four English, you say, you assisted to escape?' When, without the slightest hesitation, she quickly replied,—

'EDWARD BOYS,
ROBERT HUNTER,
FREDERICK WHITEHURST,
WILLIAM MANSELL.'[40]

Boys was completely astonished by her reply:

I hesitated for a moment, and then asked, if she had since seen this Edward Boys? She replied, 'Not since his escape; but when I was in England, I was sent to the Admiralty, and there told he was employed in the West Indies.' This again surprised me, at the same time that it dissipated all doubt as to her identity. After a moment's reflection, and knowing she was blind, I told her to give me her hand. She did so. I then added, – 'You have now the hand of Edward Boys!' She paused—trembled—slowly raised her head, and rolled her full black eyes round the ceiling, as if bewildered, and struggling for sight to recognise the man whose hand she now held in firm grasp. I could no longer endure the painful sight of such wretchedness in one, to whom I felt that, in early life, I was indebted to safety from the enemy, and for my subsequent good fortune.[41]

Leaving the room, Boys promised to return within an hour, and gave orders for Madame Derikre to be washed, dressed and given her dinner. He went to a shop with the woman of the house and bought numerous articles of clothing for the old lady. On his return he found her clean and dressed, and sat with her for about four hours:

Before I left, I told her she must now endeavour to make herself happy, as she would never again be in want, so long as I could minister to her necessities. That I should leave funds with a gentleman, or a banker, in Ostend, sufficient to give her, weekly, a franc a day, which should be continued during her life . . . To avoid increasing her apparent uneasiness of mind, I said, I must now leave you; to-morrow, my wife and daughters, who are at Bruges, will come and see you, and will carry out my promise should you survive me; therefore, I repeat, make yourself happy.' I kissed her, and took leave.[42]

His wife and daughters were jubilant at his success, and the next day they all went to Ostend, as Boys related:

We . . . found my poor old protectress sitting in the front room, clean and cheerful, ready to receive us, but unable to walk. My wife, daughters, and female attendant, were successively named to her, when to each she presented her hand, and had something pleasing to say, which had the effect of making a favourable impression, and showing she could appreciate kindness. Madame Derikre, having had time to reflect upon her change of circumstances within a few hours, described her feelings as so excited with gratitude when she went to bed, that she could scarcely believe her own senses, and feared that what had occurred was all a dream. When she was asked if she stood in need of anything else, she replied, 'Nothing, my good friends;' but, before we left the house, upon enquiry of the hostess, Madame Van Hecke, it was found advisable to add, to her property, a few necessary articles of bedding and linen to which she had long been a stranger. These were ordered, and Madame Derikre, as her wants were few, called herself the happiest woman in Ostend.[43]

News of the discovery of Madame Derikre soon spread, and Boys commented that others gave him money for her assistance and that she began to receive several visitors:

She was occasionally visited by Pierre, the Commissioner, who gave friendly publicity of her discovery, and thus induced the English to see her; these generally gave her something, which was always transferred to Madame Van Hecke, who received all, and supplied all. By these contributions, Madame Derikre's position, in the family, became reversed; for she was no longer a clog, but a profit: no longer a beggar, dependent on their bounty, with a pittance of eight francs a month from the parish, but one to whom all now looked up, desirous to please and to court. Whenever our own friends had occasion to pass through Ostend, she was sure to be visited, and complimented by them, which also had the effect of elevating her in the eyes of the natives; and, in some measure, restoring her to her former position in society.[44]

Boys visited her from time to time and learned more of what happened to her after she had helped him and his friends escape. The last time he visited her was May 1849, and the following month, at the age of eighty-three, she died.

After the massive upheaval of war, all Europe was changing rapidly. Steam power was spreading, driving machines for industry and trains and ships for transport. The era of sailing warships was over, and sailors would have to learn new skills and officers new tactics to fight the wars of the future. The conflict that had developed out of the chaotic attempt to spread the revolution beyond the boundaries of France had led to years of fighting and misery for millions of people. Although centred on Europe, it was truly a global war and would carry the title of 'The Great War' until it was surpassed by the horrors of World War I.

Napoleon's ambitions, though, had the most far-reaching consequences. At the time he clawed his way to power it was still possible for other European kingdoms to rival Britain in gathering colonies, building trade links and amassing an empire. It was Napoleon's desire to emulate the conquests of Alexander the Great that prompted a reaction from Britain, and as each French move was countered, territory was annexed and shipping destroyed or captured. Almost by accident at first, Britain found its territorial possessions and wealth increasing while its domination of world trade grew stronger. By the time of Waterloo no other European country could hope to match Britain in trade or command of the seas. The war that had begun as a response to the spread of revolutionary ideals on land had evolved into a war for all the oceans. Ultimately the massive empire over which Queen Victoria reigned was the unwitting gift of the French dictator who tried, and failed, to become Emperor of the East. As Sir Sidney Smith wrote in his prophecy to Napoleon, 'Fortune's wheel makes strange revolutions.'[45]

# NOTES

PROLOGUE: WITH CANNON AND CUTLASS
1. Long (ed.) 1899, p.284.
2. Dundonald 1861, p.93.
3. Dundonald 1861, p.94.
4. Dundonald 1861, p.93.
5. Dundonald 1861, pp.94–5.
6. Dundonald 1861, p.95.
7. Dundonald 1861, p.95.
8. Dundonald 1861, p.95.
9. Dundonald 1861, p.110.
10. Dundonald 1861, p.110.
11. Dundonald 1861, p.110.
12. Dundonald 1861, p.110.
13. Dundonald 1861, pp.110–11.
14. Dundonald 1861, p.111.
15. Dundonald 1861, p.111.
16. Dundonald 1861, p.113.
17. Dundonald 1861, p.113.
18. Dundonald 1861, p.112.
19. Dundonald 1861, p.112.
20. Dundonald 1861, p.112.
21. Dundonald 1861, p.112.
22. Dundonald 1861, p.113.
23. Dundonald 1861, p.113.
24. Dundonald 1861, p.113.
25. Dundonald 1861, p.114.
26. Dundonald 1861, p.114.
27. Dundonald 1861, pp.114–15.

1: GATEWAY TO INDIA
1. Las Cases 1835, p.59.
2. Barrow 1848, vol. 1, p.216.
3. Barrow 1848, vol. 1, p.216.
4. Barrow 1848, vol. 1, p.217.
5. Barrow 1848, vol. 1, p.220.
6. Barrow 1848, vol. 1, p.220.
7. Barrow 1848, vol. 1, p.220.

8. Barrow 1848, vol. 1, p.222.
9. Hyde de Neuville 1914, vol. 1, p.80.
10. Paris newspaper advertisement in *The Times*, 18 May 1798.
11. *The Times*, 7 May 1798.
12. Bourrienne 1829, vol. 2, p.296.
13. Bourrienne 1829, vol. 2, p.54.
14. Bourrienne 1829, vol. 2, p.49.
15. Nicolas 1845, vol. 3, pp.15–16.
16. Nicolas 1845, vol. 3, p.16.
17. Bourrienne 1829, vol. 2, p.56.
18. Nicolas 1845, vol. 3, p.19.
19. Nicolas 1845, vol. 3, p.19.
20. Nicolas 1845, vol. 3, p.18.
21. Bourrienne 1829, vol. 2, pp.70–1.
22. Bourrienne 1829, vol. 2, pp.63–4.
23. Nicolas 1845, vol. 3, p.31.
24. Nicolas 1845, vol. 3, p.230.
25. *Henry V*, Act IV, scene III.
26. Nicolas 1846, vol. 7, p.60.
27. Nicolas 1845, vol. 3, p.40.
28. Bourrienne 1829, vol. 2, p.71.
29. Ross 1838, vol. 2, p.208.
30. Bourrienne 1829, vol. 2, pp.84–5.
31. Bourrienne 1829, vol. 2, pp.85–6.
32. Thurman 1902, p.27.
33. Original Letters 1798, pp.48–50.
34. Desvernois 1898, p.105.
35. Nicolas 1845, vol. 3, pp.44–5.
36. Nicolas 1845, vol. 3, pp.42–3.

2: BATTLE OF THE NILE
1. Original Letters 1798, p.42.
2. Ross 1838, vol. 1, pp.210–11.
3. Original Letters 1798, p.44.
4. Original Letters 1798, p.44.
5. Ross 1838, vol. 1, p.215 footnote.
6. Nicolas 1845, vol. 3, p.67.
7. Nicolas 1845, vol. 3, p.67.
8. Nicolas 1845, vol. 3, p.68.
9. Elliot 1863, p.9.
10. Elliot 1863, p.10.
11. Elliot 1863, pp.10–11.
12. Elliot 1863, pp.11–12.
13. Jackson (ed.) 1900, p.21.
14. Jackson (ed.) 1900, pp.21–2.
15. Elliot 1863, pp.17–18.
16. Jackson (ed.) 1900, p.22.
17. Ross 1838, vol. 1, p.217.

18. Ross 1838, vol. 1, p.217.
19. Elliot 1863, pp.12–13.
20. Jackson (ed.) 1900, p.73.
21. Jackson (ed.) 1900, p.43.
22. Nicolas 1845, vol. 3, p.55.
23. Nicolas 1845, vol. 3, p.55.
24. Nicolas 1845, vol. 3, p.55.
25. Nicolas 1845, vol. 3, p.55.
26. Du Petit Thouars 1937, p.551.
27. Ross 1838, vol. 1, p.221.
28. Nicolas 1845, vol. 3, p.56.
29. Nicolas 1845, vol. 3, p.56.
30. Nicol 1822, pp.185–6.
31. Nicol 1822, p.186.
32. Nicol 1822, pp.186–7.
33. Saumarez archive SA/6/155.
34. National Archives Adm 36/14817 (2nd entry).
35. National Archives Adm 36/14817 (2nd entry).
36. Wellcome Institute Library, Vol. 10 Western Ms. 3676.
37. Nicol 1822, p.187.
38. Nicol 1822, p.187.
39. Nicol 1822, p.187.
40. Original Letters 1798, p.233.
41. Original Letters 1798, p.233.
42. Elliot 1863, p.13.
43. Willyams 1802, pp.52–5.
44. Willyams 1802, pp.55.
45. Willyams 1802, p.55.
46. Nicol 1822, pp.187–8.
47. Nicol 1822, p.188.
48. Willyams 1802, p.59.
49. Bourrienne 1829, vol. 2, pp.132, 141.
50. Nicolas 1845, vol. 3, p.89.
51. Nicol 1822, p.189.

3: SIEGE OF ACRE
1. Bourrienne 1829, vol. 2, pp.55–6.
2. Elliot 1863, pp.14–15.
3. Knight 1861, pp.113–14.
4. Knight 1861, p.115.
5. Knight 1861, p.116 footnote.
6. Nicolas 1845, vol. 3, p.74.
7. Barrow 1848, vol. 1, p.235.
8. National Archives FO 78/20, 85–88.
9. Barrow 1848, vol. 1, pp.236–7.
10. Barrow 1848, vol. 1, p.239.
11. Barrow 1848, vol. 1, p.249.
12. Barrow 1848, vol. 1, p.250.

13. Nicolas 1845, vol. 3, pp.455–6.
14. Nicolas 1845, vol. 3, p.122.
15. Original Letters 1799, p.225.
16. Historical Manuscripts Commission 1905, p.43.
17. Howard 1839, vol. 1, p.163.
18. Bourrienne 1829, vol. 2, pp.230–1.
19. Parsons 1905, p.209.
20. *Correspondance de Napoléon Ier Publiée par ordre de l'Empereur Napoléon III*, vol. 5 1860 (Paris), p.373.
21. Barrow 1848, vol 1, p.271.
22. Howard 1839, vol. 1, p.199.
23. *Naval Chronicle* 10, 1803, p.186.
24. *Naval Chronicle* 10, 1803, p.187.
25. *Naval Chronicle* 10, 1803, p.187.
26. *Naval Chronicle* 10, 1803, p.187.
27. Howard 1839, vol. 1, p.200.
28. *Naval Chronicle* 10, 1803, p.187.
29. Howard 1839, vol. 1, p.201.
30. Howard 1839, vol. 1, p.201.
31. *Naval Chronicle* 10, 1803, p.187.
32. *Naval Chronicle* 10, 1803, p.188.
33. Knight 1861, p.139.
34. Bourrienne 1829, vol. 2, p.230.
35. Barrow 1848, vol. 1, p.275.
36. Howard 1839, vol. 1, p.157.
37. Barrow 1848, vol. 1, p.278.
38. Barrow 1848, vol. 1, p.279.
39. Barrow 1848, vol. 1, p.285.
40. Barrow 1848, vol. 1, p.285.
41. Bourrienne 1829, vol. 2, pp.295–6.
42. Barrow 1848, vol. 1, p.308.
43. Bourrienne 1829, vol. 2, pp.243–4.
44. Barrow 1848, vol. 1, pp.293–4.
45. Barrow 1848, vol. 1, p.311.
46. Barrow 1848, vol. 1, pp.311–12.
47. Nicolas 1845, vol. 3, p.455.

4: FROM NAPLES TO COPENHAGEN
1. Dundonald 1861, p.88.
2. Parsons 1905, p.6.
3. Knight 1861, p.140.
4. Bourrienne 1829, vol. 2, pp.250–1.
5. Bourrienne 1829, vol. 2, p.265.
6. Bourrienne 1829, vol. 2, p.266.
7. Bourrienne 1829, vol. 2, pp.266–7.
8. Bourrienne 1829, vol. 2, pp.304–5.
9. Original Letters 1800, p. 5.
10. Bourrienne 1829, vol. 4, p.177.

11. Bourrienne 1829, vol. 4, pp.74–5.
12. Bourrienne 1829, vol. 4, pp.78–9.
13. Barrow 1848, vol. 1, p.385.
14. Dundonald 1861, p.90.
15. James 1826, vol. 3, p.9.
16. James 1826, vol. 3, p.10.
17. James 1826, vol. 3, p.10.
18. Nicolas 1846, vol. 7, p.80.
19. Parsons 1905, pp.33–4.
20. Parsons 1905, p.50.
21. Parsons 1905, p.50.
22. Harris 1843, p.vii.
23. Elliot 1863, p.23.
24. Elliot 1863, p.23.
25. Parsons 1905, p.51.
26. Oman 1947, p.384.
27. Parsons 1905, p.51.
28. Knight 1861, p.158.
29. Nicolas 1845, vol. 4, p.267.
30. *The Times*, 10 November 1800.
31. *The Times*, 5 January 1801.
32. Bourrienne 1829, vol. 3, p.270.
33. Nicolas 1845, vol. 4, p.279.
34. Fremantle (ed.) 1940, p.31.
35. Elliot 1863, p.27.
36. Fremantle (ed.) 1940, p.37.
37. *Naval Chronicle* 5, 1801, p.338.
38. Finlayson 1952, p.128.

## 5: WAR AND PEACE

1 Pettigrew 1849, p.444.
2. Millard 1895, p.85.
3. Millard 1895, p.85.
4. Millard 1895, p.86.
5. Nicolas 1845, vol. 4, pp.307–8.
6. Millard 1895, pp.86–7.
7. Millard 1895, p.87.
8. Millard 1895, p.87.
9. Millard 1895, p.87.
10. Millard 1895, pp.86–7.
11. Nicolas 1845, vol. 4, p.308.
12. Millard 1895, p.88.
13. Millard 1895, p.89.
14. Millard 1895, p.89.
15. Millard 1895, p.91.
16. Nicolas 1845, vol. 4, pp.308–9.
17. Nicolas 1845, vol. 4, p.312.
18. Finlayson 1952, p.131.

19. Nicolas 1845, vol. 4, p.310.
20. Nicolas 1845, vol. 4, pp.315–16.
21. Zealand 1804, pp.27–8.
22. Jackson (ed.) 1900, p.108.
23. Jackson (ed.) 1900, p.108.
24. Thursfield (ed.) 1951, p.110.
25. Dundonald 1861, pp.125–6.
26. Dundonald 1861, p.126.
27. Dundonald 1861, p.126.
28. Dundonald 1861, pp.126–7.
29. Dundonald 1861, p.127.
30. Dundonald 1861, p.129.
31. Dundonald 1861, p.130.
32. Ross 1838, vol. 1, p.345.
33. Dundonald 1861, pp.133–4.
34. Dundonald 1861, p.134.
35. Dundonald 1861, p.146.
36. Dundonald 1861, p.147.
37. Dundonald 1861, p.147.
38. Parsons 1905, p.215.
39. Parsons 1905, p.216.
40. Parsons 1905, p.217.
41. Parsons 1905, p.221.
42. Parsons 1905, pp.224–5.
43. *The Times*, 11 November 1801.
44. Ashton 1906, p.39.
45. Nicol 1822, pp.196–7.
46. Nicol 1822, p.197.
47. Nicol 1822, pp.198–9.
48. Sykes 1906, pp.101–11.
49. Sykes 1906, p.23.
50. Sykes 1906, p.109.
51. Sykes 1906, p.74.
52. Sykes 1906, pp.182, 184.
53. Burney 1846, p.285.
54. Bourrienne 1829, vol. 4, pp.301–2.

6: HOT PRESS
1. Nicolas 1846, vol. 6, p.100.
2. *Naval Chronicle* 9 1803, p.225.
3. *Naval Chronicle* 9 1803, p.243.
4. *Naval Chronicle* 9 1803, p.247.
5. Lewis (ed.) 1956, p.9
6. Lewis (ed.) 1956, p.9.
7. Lewis (ed.) 1956, p.9.
8. Sydney 1898, p.125.
9. Impressment 1835, p.11.
10. Robinson 1836, pp.2–3.

11. *The Times*, 9 May 1803.
12. Crawford 1851, p.102.
13. Crawford 1851, pp.102–3.
14. Crawford 1851, p.103.
15. Crawford 1851, p.104
16. Crawford 1851, pp.105–6.
17. Crawford 1851, p.107.
18. Crawford 1851, p.108.
19. Thomas Hardy 1897, *The Well-Beloved.*
20. *The Times*, 13 April 1803.
21. Marshall 1824, p.315.
22. *The Times*, 13 April 1803.
23. *The Times*, 19 April 1803.
24. *The Times*, 13 April 1803.
25. Headstone in St George's churchyard, Portland.
26. Headstone in, St George's churchyard, Portland.
27. Marshall 1824, p.316 footnote.
28. Marshall 1824, p.316.
29. Burrows (ed.) 1927, pp.26–8.
30. Nicol 1822, p.200.
31. Nicol 1822, p.202.
32. National Archives ADM 1/2141.
33. National Archives ADM 1/2141.
34. An 1887 recollection of Dolly Peel, South Shields Library.
35. An 1887 recollection of Dolly Peel, South Shields Library.
36. Hay (ed.) 1953, p.34.
37. Hay (ed.) 1953, p.36.
38. *The Times*, 13 April 1803.
39. Forester (ed.) 1954, p.43.
40. Forester (ed.) 1954, p.43.
41. Burney 1846, p.328.
42. Burney 1846, p.328.
43. Oman 1943, p.149.
44. Oman 1943, p.149.
45. Lewis (ed.) 1956, pp.16–17.
46. Lewis (ed.) 1956, p.38.
47. Nicol 1822, pp.201–2.
48. Nicol 1822, p.204.
49. Leyland (ed.) 1899, p.28.
50. Forester (ed.) 1954, pp.36, 38.
51. Forester (ed.) 1954, p.82.
52. Parkinson 1934, p.299.
53. Parkinson 1934, p.299.
54. Parkinson 1934, p.299.
55. Forester (ed.) 1954, p.86. Wetherell says January, but it was February.
56. O'Brien 1839a, p.6.
57. Forester (ed.) 1954, pp.92–3. Wetherell mistakenly believed they were wrecked on the Glenan Isles.

58. Forester (ed.) 1954, p.93.
59. Forester (ed.) 1954, pp.87–8.
60. Forester (ed.) 1954, p.96.
61. Forester (ed.) 1954, p.98.
62. Forester (ed.) 1954, p.100.
63. Forester (ed.) 1954, pp.100–1.
64. O'Brien 1839, vol. 1, p.11 footnote.
65. Forester (ed.) 1954, pp.104–5.
66. O'Brien 1839, vol. 1, p.15.
67. O'Brien 1839, vol. 1, p.18.
68. Forester (ed.) 1954, p.108.
69. Verdun 1810, vol. 1, p.125.
70. Choyce 1891, p.163.

7: INVASION FLEET
1. Robert Burns, 'Does Haughty Gaul'.
2. Rowbotham 1956, p.398.
3. Boswall 1833, p.211; John Donaldson later added 'Boswall' to his surname.
4. Boswall 1833, p.211.
5. Boswall 1833, p.212.
6. Boswall 1833, p.213.
7. Rowbotham 1956, p.401.
8. Boswall 1833, p.211.
9. Burrows (ed.) 1927, pp.37–8.
10. Crawford 1851, p.111.
11. Wheeler and Broadley 1908, p.213.
12. *Gentleman's Magazine* 73, 1803, p.730.
13. Crawford 1851, p.113.
14. Crawford 1851, pp.119–21.
15. Crawford 1851, pp.124–5.
16. *Naval Chronicle* 7, 1802, p.270.
17. Crawford 1851, pp.125–6.
18. Crawford 1851, p.126.
19. Crawford 1851, p.127.
20. Crawford 1851, pp.127–8.
21. Crawford 1851, p.130.
22. Crawford 1851, p.130.
23. Crawford 1851, pp.131–2.
24. Crawford 1851, p.135.
25. Crawford 1851, pp.135–6.
26. Lloyd (ed.) 1955, pp.31–2.
27. Lloyd (ed.) 1955, pp.31–2.
28. Lloyd (ed.) 1955, p.59
29. Lloyd (ed.) 1955, p.63.
30. *Naval Chronicle* 35, 1816, p.445.
31. *Naval Chronicle* 12 1804, p.16.
32. Brenton 1838, pp.143–4.
33. *Naval Chronicle* 36, 1816, p.3.

34. *Naval Chronicle* 36, 1816, p.14.
35. Lewis (ed.) 1956, p.49.
36. Lewis (ed.) 1956, p.49.
37. Lewis (ed.) 1956, p.49.
38. Barrow 1848, vol. 2, pp.136–7.
39. Crawford 1851, p.145.
40. Crawford 1851, pp.145–6.
41. Crawford 1851, p.146.
42. Crawford 1851, p.147.
43. Crawford 1851, p.148.
44. Crawford 1851, pp.149–50.
45. Lovell 1879, pp.37–8.


8: TURNING POINT
 1. Nicolas 1846, vol. 7, p.146.
 2. Burrows (ed.) 1927, pp.40–1.
 3. Burrows (ed.) 1927, pp.41–2.
 4. Burrows (ed.) 1927, pp.42–3.
 5. Burrows (ed.) 1927, p.45.
 6. *Correspondance de Napoléon $I^{er}$ publiée par ordre de l'empereur Napoléon III*, vol. 10, 1862, p.451 (Paris).
 7. *Naval Chronicle* 15, 1806, p.125.
 8. *Naval Chronicle* 15, 1806, p.125.
 9. *Naval Chronicle* 15, 1806, p.126.
10. *Naval Chronicle* 15, 1806, p.126.
11. *Naval Chronicle* 15, 1806, pp.130–1.
12. *Naval Chronicle* 15, 1806, p.131.
13. *Naval Chronicle* 15, 1806, p.131.
14. *Naval Chronicle* 15, 1806, p.126.
15. *Naval Chronicle* 15, 1806, p.126.
16. *Naval Chronicle* 15, 1806, p.134.
17. *Naval Chronicle* 15, 1806, p.127.
18. Desbrière 1907, p.114.
19. *Naval Chronicle* 13, 1805, p.358.
20. Dundonald 1861, p.176.
21. *The Times*, 11 September 1805.
22. Simond 1817, vol. 1, pp.97–8.
23. *Annual Register*, 1805 (1807), p.426.
24. Crawford 1851, pp.182–3.
25. Crawford 1851, p.183.
26. Crawford 1851, pp.188–9.
27. Crawford 1851, p.189.
28. *Jackson's Oxford Journal*, 16 November 1805.
29. Nicol 1822, pp.205–6.
30. Lewis (ed.) 1956, pp.50–1.
31. Lewis (ed.) 1956, p.51.
32. Lewis (ed.) 1956, pp.51–2.
33. *Naval Chronicle* 34, 1815, p.449.

34. Lewis (ed.) 1956, p.49.
35. *The Times*, 6 November 1805.
36. *Naval Chronicle* 36, 1816, pp.111–12.
37. Warden 1816, p.139.
38. O'Meara 1822, vol. 2, pp.182–3.
39. *Naval Chronicle* 36, 1815, p.121.
40. O'Meara 1822, vol. 2, p.24.
41. Alger 1904, p.75.
42. Rose 1923, pp.548–9.

9: IN EVERY SEA

1. Darton (ed.) 1910, p.245.
2. *Annual Register* for 1806 (1808), p.229.
3. O'Meara 1822, vol. 1, p.478.
4. Collingwood 1829, p.219.
5. National Archives, ADM 1/5126 no.53.
6. *Woolmer's Exeter and Plymouth Gazette*, 4 May 1809.
7. Pillet 1818, p.218.
8. Robinson 1836, pp.56–7.
9. Robinson 1836, pp.58.
10. Robinson 1836, pp.58–60.
11. Robinson 1836, pp.60–1.
12. Hawker 1821, pp.3–5.
13. Pinckard 1806, pp.36–8.
14. Pinckard 1806, pp.38–9.
15. Thursfield (ed.) 1951, pp.131–2.
16. Thursfield (ed.) 1951, p.132.
17. Richardson 1908, pp.225–6.
18. Knutsford 1900, p.258 footnote.
19. Hoffman 1901, pp.261–2.
20. Hoffman 1901, p.262.
21. Darton (ed.) 1910, pp.228, 231.
22. Darton (ed.) 1910, p.239.
23. Parkinson 1934, p.339.
24. Darton (ed.) 1910, p.239.
25. Darton (ed.) 1910, pp.240–1.
26. Garneray 1853, p.77.
27. Anon 1828, p.32; the soldier has been identified as probably Thomas Howell (p.iii of Hibbert (ed.) 1996, which omits this campaign).
28. Fernyhough 1829, pp.73–4.
29. Fernyhough 1829, pp.74–5.
30. Fernyhough 1829, pp.75–6.
31. Parkinson (ed.) 1949, p.40.
32. Parkinson (ed.) 1949, p.41.
33. Parkinson (ed.) 1949, p.41.
34. Fernyhough 1829, pp.79–80.
35. *The Times*, 5 May 1806.
36. Garneray 1853, p.77.

37. *Naval Chronicle* 15, 1806, pp.407–8.
38. *Naval Chronicle* 15, 1806, p.408.
39. *Naval Chronicle* 15, 1806, pp.413–14.
40. Fernyhough 1829, pp.89–90.
41. Parkinson (ed.) 1949, p.43.
42. Parkinson (ed.) 1949, p.43.
43. Parkinson (ed.) 1949, p.51.
44. Parkinson (ed.) 1949, p.54.
45. *Naval Chronicle* 17, 1807, p.242.
46. *Calcutta Gazette*, 19 November 1807 (in Sandeman 1868, pp.183–4).

10: CONFLICT AND COMMERCE
1. Greig (ed.) 1924, vol. 4, pp.184–5.
2. *Naval Chronicle* 26, 1811, pp.367–8.
3. Crawford 1851, p.288.
4. Crawford 1851, p.289.
5. Crawford 1851, p.290.
6. *Naval Chronicle* 17, 1807, p.320.
7. *Naval Chronicle* 17, 1807, p.320.
8. Crawford 1851, p.293.
9. Petrides and Downs (eds.) 2000, p.102.
10. Petrides and Downs (eds.) 2000, p.102.
11. Petrides and Downs (eds.) 2000, pp.102–5.
12. Howard 1839, vol. 2, pp.15–16.
13. Howard 1839, vol. 2, p.16.
14. Petrides and Downs (eds.) 2000, p.105.
15. Petrides and Downs (eds.) 2000, p.105.
16. Barrow 1848, vol. 2, p.230.
17. Crawford 1851, p.314.
18. Zimmerman 1925, p.26.
19. Lovell 1879, p.186.
20. Lovell 1879, p.186.
21. Lovell 1879, p.187.
22. Simond 1817, vol. 1, p.334.
23. Zimmerman 1925, p.136.
24. Lossing 1868, p.157.
25. Brooks (ed.) 1926, p.104.
26. James 1826, vol. 4, p. 483.
27. Collingwood 1829, p.316.
28. Collingwood 1829, p.317.
29. *The Times*, 22 August 1807.
30. *The Times*, 22 August 1807.
31. Chambers 1928, pp.383–4.
32. Chambers 1928, p.393.
33. Chambers 1928, p.393.
34. Chambers 1928, pp.393–5.
35. Chambers 1928, p.400.
36. Chambers 1928, p.401.

37. Chambers 1928, p.401.
38. Ross-Lewin 1904, p.74.
39. Chambers 1928, p.405.
40. Chambers 1928, p.411.
41. Chambers 1928, p.412.
42. Sturgis (ed.) 1899, p.12.
43. Chambers 1928, p.417.
44. Sturgis (ed.) 1899, p.12.
45. Ross-Lewin 1904, pp.80–1.
46. Petrides and Downs (eds.) 2000, pp.115–16.
47. Dundonald 1861, p.235.
48. Dundonald 1861, p.236.
49. Greig (ed.) 1924, vol. 4, p.231.
50. *The Times*, 13 February 1810.
51. *The Times*, 13 February 1810.
52. *The Times*, 25 October 1810.
53. National Archives ADM 37/1719.

11: THE SEA WOLF
1. Dundonald 1861, p.321.
2. *Naval Chronicle* 19, 1808, p.184.
3. *Naval Chronicle* 19, 1808, pp.184–5.
4. Howard 1839, vol. 2, pp.111–12.
5. *Naval Chronicle* 19, 1808, p.453.
6. *The Times*, 5 January 1808.
7. *Naval Chronicle* 19, 1808, p.57.
8. Reprinted in *Royal Cornwall Gazette, Falmouth Packet and Plymouth Journal*, 23 January 1808.
9. *Naval Chronicle* 19, 1808, p.425.
10. Dundonald 1861, p.242.
11. Dundonald 1861, pp.242–3.
12. Marryat 1872, p.45.
13. Dundonald 1861, pp.243–4.
14. Dundonald 1861, p.253.
15. Dundonald 1861, pp.253–4.
16. Dundonald 1861, p.257.
17. Dundonald 1861, p.257.
18. Dundonald 1861, p.258.
19. Dundonald 1861, p.260.
20. Dundonald 1861, p.260.
21. Dundonald 1861, pp.260–1.
22. Dundonald 1861, pp.263–4.
23. Dundonald 1861, p.264.
24. Dundonald 1861, p.264.
25. Dundonald 1861, pp.269–70.
26. Dundonald 1861, pp.273–4.
27. Dundonald 1861, p.279.
28. Raikes (ed.) 1846, pp.337–8.

29. Dundonald 1861, p.280.
30. Raikes (ed.) 1846, p.337.
31. Raikes (ed.) 1846, p.339.
32. Cockayne 1916, p.530.
33. Dundonald 1861, pp.321–2.
34. Dundonald 1861, pp.298–9.
35. Dundonald 1861, p.299.
36. Dundonald 1861, pp.302–3.
37. Dundonald 1861, pp.303–4.
38. Dundonald 1861, p.305.
39. Dundonald 1861, pp.305–6.
40. Dundonald 1861, p.309.
41. Dundonald 1861, p.310.
42. Dundonald 1861, pp.311–12.
43. Dundonald 1861, p.315.
44. Dundonald 1861, p.316.
45. Dundonald 1861, p.270.
46. *Bulletin from the London Gazette*, 7 January 1809.
47. Dundonald 1861, p.336.

12: BY LAND AND SEA
1. O'Brien 1839, vol. 2, p.7.
2. Boys 1864, p.45.
3. Boys 1864, p.47.
4. Boys 1864, p.18.
5. O'Brien 1839, vol. 1, p.99.
6. O'Brien 1839, vol. 1, p.108.
7. O'Brien 1839, vol. 1, p.240.
8. O'Brien 1839, vol. 1, p.240.
9. O'Brien 1839, vol. 1, pp.240–1.
10. Abell 1914, p.36.
11. O'Brien 1839, vol. 1, p.402.
12. O'Brien 1839, vol. 2, p.5.
13. O'Brien 1839, vol. 2, p.6.
14. O'Brien 1839, vol. 2, pp.47–8.
15. O'Brien 1839, vol. 2, p.48.
16. O'Brien 1839, vol. 2, p.49.
17. O'Brien 1839, vol. 2, pp.54–5 footnote.
18. O'Brien 1839, vol. 2, p.55.
19. O'Brien 1839, vol 2, pp.63–4.
20. Brett-James (ed.) 1981, p.131.
21. O'Brien 1839, vol. 2, p.146.
22. Brett-James (ed.) 1981, p.155.
23. O'Brien 1839, vol. 2, p.159.
24. Brett-James (ed.) 1981, p.162.
25. O'Brien 1839, vol. 2, p.163.
26. O'Brien 1839, vol. 2, pp.164–5.
27. O'Brien 1839, vol. 2, pp.168–9.

28. O'Brien 1839, vol. 2, pp.169–70.
29. Brett-James (ed.) 1981, p.168.
30. O'Brien 1839, vol. 2, pp.170–1.
31. Boys 1864, p.124.
32. Boys 1864, p.85.
33. Boys 1864, pp.86–7.
34. Boys 1864, p.94.
35. Boys 1864, pp.96–7.
36. Boys 1864, pp.97–8.
37. Boys 1864, p.100.
38. Boys 1864, pp.114–15.
39. Boys 1864, pp.121–2.
40. Boys 1864, p.144.
41. Boys 1864, p.151.
42. Boys 1864, pp.157–8.
43. Boys 1864, pp.161–2.
44. Boys 1864, p.163.
45. Boys 1864, p.166.
46. Boys 1864, p.169.
47. Boys 1864, p.170.
48. Boys 1864, p.184.
49. Boys 1864, p.188.
50. Boys 1864, p.239.
51. Boys 1864, p.264.
52. Boys 1864, pp.266–7.
53. Boys 1864, pp.268–70.
54. Boys 1864, pp.273–4.
55. Boys 1864, p.275.
56. Boys 1864, p.275.
57. Boys 1864, pp.276–7.
58. Boys 1864, p.277.
59. Anon 1828, pp.57–9.
60. Anon 1827, pp.63–4.
61. Curling (ed.) 1928, pp.126–7.
62. Curling (ed.) 1848, pp.186–7.
63. Curling (ed.) 1848, pp.193–4.
64. Curling (ed.) 1848, pp.230–2.
65. Curling (ed.) 1848, pp.232–4.
66. *The Times*, 23 January 1809.
67. Sturgis (ed.) 1899, pp.110–11.
68. Hall 1846, p.106.
69. Hall 1846, p.106.
70. *The Times*, 26 January 1809.
71. Anon 1828, pp.66–7.
72. Anon 1828, pp.67–8.
73. Hall 1846, p.111.
74. Anon 1828, pp.68–9.
75. Anon 1827, pp.73–5.

76. Curling (ed.) 1848, pp.234–5.
77. Anon 1828, pp.69–70.
78. *The Times*, 28 January 1809.
79. Sturgis (ed.) 1899, pp.124–5.
80. Anon 1827, p.83.

13: THE GRAND EXPEDITION
1. Marryat 1872, p.67.
2. Thomas Hood, *Ode to Admiral Lord Gambier, G.C.B.*
3. Dundonald 1861, p.341.
4. Dundonald 1861, p.338.
5. Dundonald 1861, p.342.
6. Dundonald 1861, p.356.
7. *Naval Chronicle* 21, 1809, p.428.
8. Richardson 1908, p.243.
9. Richardson 1908, pp.243–4.
10. Richardson 1908, p.244.
11. Choyce 1891, p.189.
12. Robinson 1836, pp.79–80.
13. Richardson 1908, p.246.
14. *The Times*, 27 April 1809.
15. Dundonald 1861, pp.377–8.
16. Choyce 1891, pp.191–2.
17. Richardson 1908, p.247.
18. Richardson 1908, p.249.
19. Robinson 1836, p.82.
20. Choyce 1891, p.192.
21. Richardson 1908, p.249.
22. *The Times*, 27 April 1809.
23. O'Meara 1822, vol. 2, pp.291–2.
24. Lewis (ed.) 1956, p.123.
25. Lewis (ed.) 1956, p.124.
26. Lewis (ed.) 1956, p.125.
27. Lewis (ed.) 1956, p.126.
28. Lewis (ed.) 1956, p.128.
29. *The Times*, 18 July 1809.
30. *Naval Chronicle* 23, 1810, p.118.
31. *Annual Register* 1809, p.223.
32. Gardyne 1929, p.172.
33. Maxwell (ed.) 1904, p.95.
34. Vane (ed.) 1851, p.274.
35. Taylor (ed.) 1853, p.129.
36. Taylor (ed.) 1853, p.129.
37. *Annual Register* 1809, p.223.
38. Liddell Hart (ed.) 1951, p.25.
39. Richardson 1908, p.258.
40. Richardson 1908, p.258.
41. Curling (ed.) 1848, pp.254–5.

42. Liddell Hart (ed.) 1951, pp.23–4.
43. *The Times*, 18 July 1809.
44. Liddell Hart (ed.) 1951, pp.24–5.
45. Anon 1810, p.308.
46. Liddell Hart (ed.) 1951, p.25.
47. Richardson 1908, p.261.
48. Anon 1827, p.86.
49. Sturgis (ed.) 1899, p.128.
50. Brenton 1838, pp.335–8.
51. Vane (ed.) 1851, p.298.
52. *Woolmer's Exeter and Plymouth Gazette*, 17 August 1809.
53. Liddell Hart (ed.) 1951, pp.27–8.
54. Richardson 1908, p.263.
55. Richardson 1908, p.263.
56. *Naval Chronicle* 22, 1809, p.207.
57. Richardson 1908, p.264.
58. Richardson 1908, p.267.
59. *Naval Chronicle* 22, 1809, p.208.
60. Yarrow 1975, p.185.
61. *Naval Chronicle* 22, 1809, pp.208–9.
62. *Naval Chronicle* 23, 1810, p.211.
63. Richardson 1908, p.273.

14: DISASTER

1. Richardson 1908, p.262.
2. Curling (ed.) 1848, pp.256–8.
3. *Naval Chronicle* 22, 1809, p.210.
4. *Naval Chronicle* 22, 1809, p.209.
5. Lewis (ed.) 1956, p.134.
6. Lewis (ed.) 1956, p.135.
7. Lewis (ed.) 1956, p.136.
8. Liddell Hart (ed.) 1951, p.33.
9. Fernyhough 1829, p.140.
10. *Naval Chronicle* 22, 1809, p.156.
11. Lewis (ed.) 1956, p.136.
12. James 1826, vol. 5, pp.204–5.
13. *Naval Chronicle* 22, 1809, p.155.
14. Robinson 1836, p.89.
15. Richardson 1908, p.269.
16. Anon 1828, pp.71–2.
17. Ross-Lewin 1904, p.128.
18. Robinson 1836, pp.89–90.
19. Petrides and Downs (eds.) 2000, pp.140–1.
20. Bourchier 1873, pp.141–2.
21. Bourchier 1873, p.147.
22. Bourchier 1873, p.147.
23. Liddell Hart (ed.) 1951, p.35.
24. Thursfield (ed.) 1951, p.370.

25. Richardson 1908, p.269.
26. Richardson 1908, p.273.
27. O'Meara 1822, vol. 1, p.256.
28. Richardson 1908, pp.269–70.
29. Robinson 1836, pp.90–1.
30. Lewis (ed.) 1956, p.138.
31. Anon 1828, p.73.
32. Pringle 1752, p.71.
33. Bourchier 1873, pp.152–3.
34. Vane (ed.) 1851, p.338.
35. Rocca 1816, p.92.
36. Yarrow 1975, p.188.
37. Rocca 1816, pp.95–6.
38. Rocca 1816, p.109.
39. Yarrow 1975, p.186.
40. Bourchier 1873, pp.143–4.
41. Yarrow 1975, p.188.
42. *Naval Chronicle* 22, 1809, p.283.
43. Petrides and Downs (eds.) 2000, p.147.
44. Liddell Hart (ed.) 1951, p.37.
45. Bourchier 1873, p.154.
46. Bourchier 1873, p.154.
47. Curling (ed.) 1848, p.132.
48. Curling (ed.) 1848, p.134.
49. Jeffery (ed.) 1907, pp.287–8.
50. Sturgis (ed.) 1899, p.131.
51. Bourchier 1873, p.156.
52. *Woolmer's Exeter and Plymouth Gazette*, 28 September 1809.
53. Jeffery (ed.) 1907, p.288.
54. Bourchier 1873, p.157.
55. McGrigor 1861, p.232.
56. McGrigor 1861, p.232.
57. Bourchier 1873, pp.158–9.
58. McGrigor 1861, pp.233–4.
59. McGrigor 1861, pp.234–5.
60. Bourchier 1873, p.161.
61. McGrigor 1861, p.236.
62. McGrigor 1861, pp.237–8.
63. Bourchier 1873, p.160.
64. *Cobbett's Parliamentary Debates* XV, 1810, appendix p.lvii.
65. McGrigor 1861, p.241.
66. *Cobbett's Parliamentary Debates* XV, 1810, appendix p.lviii.
67. *Cobbett's Parliamentary Debates* XV, 1810, appendix p.lviii.
68. Liddell Hart (ed.) 1951, p.39.
69. Richardson 1908, p.278.
70. Bourchier 1873, p.166.
71. Robinson 1836, p.94.
72. Richardson 1908, p.280.

73. *Annual Register* 1809, pp.225–6.
74. Sturgis (ed.) 1899, p.132.
75. O'Meara 1822, vol. 1, p.256.
76. Simond 1817, vol. 1, pp.84–5.
77. Simond 1817, vol. 1, p.157.

15: PRISONERS AND PRIVATEERS
 1. O'Meara 1822, vol. 1, pp.323–4.
 2. Abell 1914, p.41.
 3. Garneray 1853, p.82.
 4. Pillet 1818, p.228.
 5. Pillet 1818, p.230.
 6. Pillet 1818, p.229.
 7. Bonnefoux 1900, p.222.
 8. Bonnefoux 1900, p.222.
 9. *Naval Chronicle* 19, 1808, pp.285–6.
10. *The Times*, 26 November 1808.
11. *The Times*, 16 December 1807.
12. Abell 1914, p.75.
13. Fremantle (ed.) 1937, p.194.
14. Abell 1914, p.142.
15. Abell 1914, p.142.
16. *Alfred and Westminster Evening Gazette*, 26 April 1810.
17. *The Times*, 2 January 1810.
18. Abell 1914, pp.367–8.
19. Rattenbury 1837, p.50.
20. Rattenbury 1837, pp.50–1.
21. *The Times*, 13 August 1812.
22. Des Touches 1905, pp.426.
23. Des Touches 1905, pp.425–6.
24. *Western Antiquary* 1, 1882, p.107.
25. *Western Antiquary* 1, 1882, p.107.
26. *Western Antiquary* 1, 1882, pp.95–6.
27. Fraser 1906, p.393.
28. Fraser 1906, pp.391–2.
29. Bowers 1833, pp.218–20.
30. Bowers 1833, pp.221–2.
31. Bowers 1833, pp.222–3.
32. Bowers 1833, p.223.
33. Moody (ed.) 1959, p.240.
34. Brooks (ed.) 1926, p.54.
35. Moody (ed.) 1959, p.241.
36. Moody (ed.) 1959, p.241.
37. Bowers 1833, p.224.
38. Brooks (ed.) 1926, p.55.
39. Brooks (ed.) 1926, p.55.
40. *The British Neptune or Naval, Military, and Commercial Intelligencer*, 19 March 1810.
41. *The British Press*, 15 February 1811.

16: THE HAND OF PROVIDENCE

1. Evelyn 1674, p.15.
2. *The Times*, 8 March 1810.
3. *The Times*, 8 March 1810.
4. *The Times*, 13 February 1810.
5. *The Times*, 13 February 1810.
6. Greig (ed.) 1924, vol. 6, p.115.
7. Greig (ed.) 1924, vol. 6, p.116.
8. Jeffery 1811, pp.8–9.
9. Jeffery 1811, pp.9–10.
10. Jeffery 1811, p.12.
11. Jeffery 1811, pp.13–14.
12. *Cobbett's Parliamentary Debates* 15, 1810, cols. 424–5.
13. *Cobbett's Parliamentary Debates* 15, 1810, col. 425.
14. Jeffery 1811, p.24. Whitbread was the only son of the founder of a substantial brewery of porter in London.
15. *The Times*, 9 April 1810.
16. *The Times*, 9 April 1810.
17. *The Times*, 9 April 1810.
18. *The Times*, 1 May 1810.
19. *The Times*, 1 May 1810.
20. *Cobbett's Political Register* 18, 1810, col. 194.
21. Jeffery 1811, pp.27–8.
22. Jeffery 1811, p.19 footnote.
23. Jeffery 1811, p.15.
24. Hall 1846, p.26.
25. *Bulletin in the London Gazette*, 25 September 1810.
26. *Calcutta Gazette*, 6 March 1810, in Sandeman 1868, pp.237–8.
27–48. Captain Christopher Cole's report, Royal Naval Museum Manuscript: 1977/265.
49. James 1826, vol. 5, pp.471–2.


17: TRIUMPH AND TRAGEDY

1. Murray (ed.) 1922, p.39.
2. O'Brien 1839, vol. 2, pp.197–9.
3. O'Brien 1839, vol. 2, p.199.
4. O'Brien 1839, vol. 2, p.201.
5. Hoste 1887, p.159.
6. O'Brien 1839, vol. 2, p.204.
7. O'Brien 1839, vol. 2, pp.204–5.
8. O'Brien 1839, vol. 2, p.206.
9. O'Brien 1839, vol. 2, pp.206–7.
10. O'Brien 1839, vol. 2, p.210.
11. O'Brien 1839, vol. 2, p.212.
12. O'Brien 1839, vol. 2, p.212.
13. O'Brien 1839, vol. 2, pp.219–20.
14. Hoste 1887, pp.199–200.
15. Hoste 1887, p.201.
16. Murray (ed.) 1922, p.35.

17.  Leech 1844, p.28.
18.  Leech 1844, pp.28–9.
19.  Simond 1817, vol. 2, p.403.
20.  *New York Herald*, 3 June 1811, in Lossing 1868, p.186.
21.  *Bulletin from the London Gazette* for 1811, p.296.
22.  *Bulletin from the London Gazette* for 1811, p.293.
23.  *Naval Chronicle* 25, 1811, p.503.
24.  *Bulletin from the London Gazette* for 1811, p.293.
25.  *The British Press*, 20 June 1811.
26.  Jeffery (ed.) 1907, p.295.
27.  Jeffery (ed.) 1907, p.298.
28.  *The Times*, 4 January 1812.
29.  *The Times*, 30 January 1812.
30.  *The Times*, 30 January 1812.
31.  *The Times*, 30 January 1812.
32.  *Hampshire Courier, or, Portsmouth, Portsea, Gosport, and Chichester Advertiser*, 10 February 1812.
33.  *Hampshire Courier, or, Portsmouth, Portsea, Gosport, and Chichester Advertiser*, 10 February 1812.

18: THE GREAT MISTAKE

 1.  *Naval Chronicle* 28, 1812, pp.137–8.
 2.  Hamilton (ed.) 1898, p.409.
 3.  British Library Liverpool Papers Add. Mss 38258, f. 150.
 4.  *The Times*, 21 July 1812.
 5.  *Hampshire Courier, or, Portsmouth, Portsea, Gosport, and Chichester Advertiser*, 3 August 1812.
 6.  *The Times*, 7 October 1812.
 7.  *The Times*, 7 October 1812.
 8.  *Naval Chronicle* 28, 1812, pp.307–8.
 9.  Lossing 1868, p.444.
10.  Lossing 1868, p.444.
11.  Lossing 1868, p.443.
12.  Leech 1844, p.44.
13.  Leech 1844, p.44.
14.  Leech 1844, pp.44–5.
15.  Leech 1844, p.45.
16.  Leech 1844, p.45.
17.  Leech 1844, pp.45–6.
18.  Leech 1844, p.46.
19.  Leech 1844, pp.48–9.
20.  Leech 1844, pp.49–50.
21.  Leech 1844, p.50.
22.  Leech 1844, p.50.
23.  *Naval Chronicle* 29, 1813, p.452.
24.  *Naval Chronicle* 29, 1813, pp.452–3.
25.  *The Times*, 18 May 1813.
26.  Lossing 1868, p.699.
27.  Fullom 1863, p.167.

28. James 1817, p.202.
29. Brighton 1866, pp.366–7.
30. *Hampshire Courier, Or, Portsmouth, Portsea, Gosport, Winchester, Southampton, Isle of Wight, and Sussex Advertiser*, 29 March 1813.
31. Lovell 1879, p.170.
32. Lovell 1879, p.170.
33. Lossing 1868, p.701.
34. Brighton 1866, pp.193–4.
35. *The Times*, 30 October 1813.
36. *The Times*, 30 October 1813.
37. *Naval Chronicle* 30, 1813, p.69.
38. *Bulletin from the London Gazette*, 10 July 1813, p.380.
39. Brighton 1866, p.200.
40. Brighton 1866, p.167.
41. Brighton 1866, p.165.
42. Lossing 1868, p.705.
43. Lossing 1868, p.705.
44. Lossing 1868, p.706.
45. Brighton 1866, p.195.
46. *Bulletin from the London Gazette*, 10 July 1813, p.381.
47. *Bulletin from the London Gazette*, 10 July 1813, p.382.
48. Brighton 1866, p.196.
49. Brighton 1866, p.226.
50. Brighton 1866, pp.231–2.
51. Brighton 1866, p.196.
52. Brighton 1866, p.213.
53. Brighton 1866, p.223.
54. Brighton 1866, pp.257–8.
55. *Parliamentary Debates* 26, 1813, col. 1160.
56. Brighton 1866, p.444 (he wrongly says Farnham, not Fareham).
57. Lossing 1868, p.715.
58. *Flindell's Western Luminary*, 17 August 1813.
59. James 1817, appendix 42.
60. *The Times*, 18 August 1813.
61. *Naval Chronicle* 30, 1813, p.181.

19: UP THE CHESAPEAKE
1. Barrett 1841, p.460.
2. Hoffman 1901, p.329.
3. Anon 1955, p.10.
4. Anon 1895, p.25.
5. Anon 1955, pp.11–12.
6. Anon 1955, p.12.
7. Maclachlan 1869, pp.214–15.
8. *The Times*, 3 June 1814.
9. *The Times*, 6 June 1814.
10. Fraser 1914, p.307.
11. *The Times*, 18 October 1839.

12. Langton 1836, pp.236–7.
13. Jeffery (ed.) 1907, p.310.
14. *Liverpool Mercury; or, Commercial, Literary, and Political Herald*, 27 May 1814.
15. *Morning Chronicle*, 24 August 1814.
16. Curling (ed.) 1928, pp.190–1.
17. Greig (ed.) 1924, vol. 7, p.239.
18. Journal of Midshipman Bluett, Royal Naval Museum Manuscript: 1995/48.
19. Journal of Midshipman Bluett, Royal Naval Museum Manuscript: 1995/48.
20. Brooks (ed.) 1926, p.74.
21. Smith (ed.) 1910, pp.191–2.
22. Smith (ed.) 1910, pp.192–3.
23. Bourchier 1873, p.311.
24. Bourchier 1873, p.312.
25. Bourchier 1873, p.313.
26. Bourchier 1873, p.314.
27. Napier 1862, p.73.
28. Barrett 1841, p.457.
29. Barrett 1841, p.457.
30. Gleig 1826, pp.83–4.
31. Gleig 1826, pp.82–3.
32. Napier 1862, p.76.
33. Gleig 1826, pp.86–8.
34. Bourchier 1873, p.314.
35. Bourchier 1873, p.315.
36. Barrett 1841, pp.455–67.
37. Gleig 1826, pp.89–90.
38. Gleig 1826, pp.103–4.
39. Bourchier 1873, p.314.
40. Barrett 1841, p.458.
41. Royal Naval Museum Manuscript: 1995/48.
42. Royal Naval Museum Manuscript: 1995/48.
43. Bourchier 1873, p.315.
44. Bourchier 1873, p.315.
45. Royal Naval Museum Manuscript: 1995/48.
46. Barrett 1841, pp.459–60.
47. Gleig 1826, pp.132–3.
48. Gleig 1826, pp.125–6.
49. Scott 1834, pp.302–3.
50. Scott 1834, p.303.
51. Scott 1834, pp.303–4.
52. Scott 1834, p.304.
53. Scott 1834, pp.304–5.
54. Gleig 1826, p.148.
55. *Bulletin from the London Gazette Extraordinary*, 27 September 1814.
56. Bourchier 1873, p.313.
57. Gleig 1826, p.127.
58. Smith (ed.) 1910, p.200.
59. Scott 1834, pp.306–7.

60. Scott 1834, pp.306–7.
61. Scott 1834, p.308.
62. Scott 1834, p.308.
63. Scott 1834, pp.323–14.
64. Napier 1862, p.86.
65. Bourchier 1873, p.319.
66. Gleig 1826, p.141.
67. Gleig 1826, pp.145–6.
68. Smith (ed.) 1910, pp.206–7.
69. Smith (ed.) 1910, p.208.
70. Smith (ed.) 1910, pp.209–10.
71. Smith (ed.) 1910, p.210.
72. Greig (ed.) 1924, vol. 7, p.279.
73. Smith (ed.) 1910, p.217.

20: STAR-SPANGLED BANNER
1. Bourchier 1873, p.319.
2. Bourchier 1873, p.320.
3. Bourchier 1873, p.320.
4. *Bulletin from the London Gazette Extraordinary*, 17 October 1814.
5. Barrett 1841, pp.461–2.
6. Gleig 1826, pp.165–6.
7. Barrett 1841, p.462.
8. Gleig 1826, pp.167–9.
9. Bourchier 1873, pp.319–20.
10. Barrett 1841, p.462.
11. Lovell 1879, p.163.
12. Journal of Midshipman Bluett, Royal Naval Museum Manuscript: 1995/48.
13. Scott 1834, p.337.
14. Journal of Midshipman Bluett, Royal Naval Museum Manuscript: 1995/48.
15. Scott 1834, p.340.
16. *Bulletin from the London Gazette Extraordinary*, 17 October 1814.
17. Barrett 1841, pp.462–3.
18. Barrett 1841, p.463.
19. Barrett 1841, p.463.
20. *Bulletin from the London Gazette Extraordinary*, 17 October 1814.
21. *Bulletin from the London Gazette Extraordinary*, 17 October 1814.
22. Barrett 1841, pp.413–14.
23. *Baltimore Patriot*, 20 September 1814, in Sonneck 1914, p.65.
24. *Bulletin from the London Gazette Extraordinary*, 17 October 1814.
25. Barrett 1841, p.464.
26. Barrett 1841, p.465.
27. Barrett 1841, p.465.
28. Bourchier 1873, p.330.
29. Bourchier 1873, p.331.
30. Gleig 1826, pp.260–1.
31. Journal of Midshipman Bluett, Royal Naval Museum Manuscript: 1995/48.
32. Gleig 1826, p.262.

33.  Gleig 1826, pp.262–3.
34.  Roosevelt 1902, p.462.
35.  Gleig 1826, p.284.
36.  Gleig 1826, pp.284–5.
37.  Gleig 1826, pp.286–7.
38.  Gleig 1826, pp.294–5.
39.  Gleig 1826, p.301.
40.  Gleig 1826, pp.301–2.
41.  Bourchier 1873, p.333.
42.  Bourchier 1873, pp.333–4.
43.  Gleig 1826, pp.309–10.
44.  Bourchier 1873, p.334.
45.  Smith (ed.) 1910, pp.229–30.
46.  Smith (ed.) 1910, p.231.
47.  Gleig 1826, pp.317–18.
48.  Bourchier 1873, p.335.
49.  Bourchier 1873, p.335.
50.  Gleig 1826, pp.328–9.
51.  Gleig 1826, pp.324–5.
52.  Cooper 1869, p.130.
53.  Bourchier 1873, pp.335–6.
54.  Smith (ed.) 1910, p.240.
55.  Smith (ed.) 1910, p.241.
56.  Gleig 1826, p.332.
57.  Journal of Midshipman Bluett, Royal Naval Museum Manuscript: 1995/48.
58.  Smith (ed.) 1910, p.249.


21: SWANSONG
 1.  *Morning Chronicle*, 3 January 1815.
 2.  Napier 1862, pp.91–2.
 3.  Napier 1862, p.93.
 4.  Journal of Midshipman Bluett, Royal Naval Museum Manuscript: 1995/48.
 5.  Journal of Midshipman Bluett, Royal Naval Museum Manuscript: 1995/48.
 6.  Brooks (ed.) 1926, p.79.
 7.  Waterhouse 1911, p.184.
 8.  Palmer 1914, p.118.
 9.  Palmer 1914, p.119.
10.  Waterhouse 1911, p.186.
11.  Pierce 1937, p.26.
12.  Palmer 1914, p.125.
13.  Palmer 1914, pp.126–7.
14.  Waterhouse 1911, p.187.
15.  Maclachlan 1869, p.186.
16.  Hyde de Neuville 1914, vol. 2, pp.1–2.
17.  Hyde de Neuville 1914, vol. 2, p.2.
18.  Scott 1828, p.664.
19.  Hyde de Neuville 1914, vol. 2, pp.2–3.
20.  Anon. 1895, p.66.

21. Maclachlan 1869, p.319.
22. *The Times*, 26 January 1815.
23. *Trewman's Exeter Flying Post*, 2 February 1815.
24. Pierce 1937, pp.29–30.
25. Nicolas 1846, vol 6, p.36.
26. Andrews 1815, pp.245–6.
27. Waterhouse 1911, pp.176, 179.
28. Waterhouse 1911, p.177.
29. Waterhouse 1911, p.215.
30. Waterhouse 1911, p.205.
31. Palmer 1914, p.154.
32. Waterhouse 1911, p.206.
33. Maclachlan 1869, pp.388–9.
34. Maclachlan 1869, p.393.
35. Anon. 1895, p.117.
36. Waterhouse 1911, p.217.
37. Pierce 1937, p.36.
38. Waterhouse 1911, p.217.
39. Waterhouse 1911, p.217.
40. Waterhouse 1911, p.214.
41. Waterhouse 1911, pp.212–13.
42. Waterhouse 1911, p.214.
43. Waterhouse 1911, p.215.
44. Waterhouse 1911, p.216.
45. Pierce 1937, pp.38–9.
46. Pierce 1937, p.40.
47. Palmer 1914, pp.180–1.
48. Pierce 1937, p.41.
49. Pierce 1937, p.41.
50. Waterhouse 1911, p.264.
51. Waterhouse 1911, p.268.
52. Pierce 1937, p.52.
53. Pierce 1937, p.59.
54. Barrow 1848, vol. 2, pp.394-5.
55. Ross-Lewin 1904, p.291.

22: THE TURN OF FORTUNE'S WHEEL

1. O'Meara 1822, vol. 1, p.412.
2. Smart 1908a, p.321.
3. Smart 1908a, p.321.
4. Smart 1908a, p.322.
5. Smart 1908a, p.322.
6. Smart 1908a, p.322.
7. Smart 1908a, p.322.
8. Smart 1908a, p.322.
9. Smart 1908a, p.322.
10. Smart 1908b, p.382.
11. Smart 1908b, p.382.

12. Smart 1908b, p.382.
13. Smart 1908b, p.382.
14. Smart 1908b, p.382.
15. Shorter (ed.) 1908, p.300.
16. Shorter (ed.) 1908, p.311.
17. Shorter (ed.) 1908, p.312.
18. Smart 1908b, p.383.
19. Shorter (ed.) 1908, p.36.
20. Shorter (ed.) 1908, p.36.
21. *Woolmer's Exeter and Plymouth Gazette*, 29 July 1815.
22. *The Times*, 29 July 1815.
23. *The Times*, 26 July 1815.
24. Smart 1908b, p.384.
25. Hoffman 1901, p.334.
26. O'Brien 1839, vol. 2, pp.355–6.
27. O'Brien 1839, vol. 2, pp.358–9.
28. O'Brien 1839, vol. 2, p.395.
29. O'Brien 1839, vol. 2, pp.397–8.
30. O'Brien 1839, vol. 2, pp.398–9.
31. O'Brien 1839, vol. 2, p.410.
32. O'Brien 1839, vol. 2, p.411.
33. O'Brien 1839, vol. 2, p.412.
34. Boys 1864, p.298.
35. Boys 1864, p.299.
36. Boys 1864, p.301.
37. Boys 1864, p.302.
38. Boys 1864, pp.302–4.
39. Boys 1864, p.305.
40. Boys 1864, p.306.
41. Boys 1864, pp.306–7.
42. Boys 1864, pp.309–10.
43. Boys 1864, pp.313–14.
44. Boys 1864, p.315.
45. Howard 1839, vol. 2, p.309.

# SELECTED READING

Many books have been written about naval warfare in the Napoleonic period, and the majority concentrate on the later years of Nelson's life. Apart from a few books about the war with America from 1812 to 1815, there is little coverage of events after 1805. *The Command of the Ocean: A Naval History of Britain 1649–1815* by N. A. M. Rodger discusses the whole period in detail in a single scholarly volume, as does Peter Padfield's *Maritime Power and the Struggle for Freedom: Naval Campaigns that shaped the modern world 1788–1851*. *The Victory of Seapower: Winning the Napoleonic War 1806–1814* by Richard Woodman is also a well-illustrated introduction to the period, and his *Sea Warriors* describes the warfare of frigate captains from 1792 to 1815. *Wellington's Navy: Sea Power and the Peninsular War, 1807–1814* by Christopher D. Hall deals with the British Navy's involvement with the war in Spain and Portugal. For the period up to 1805, many of the major battles and minor incidents are covered in biographies of Nelson.

***Battles and Expeditions:*** Up-to-date coverage of the Battle of the Nile is given in *Nelson and the Nile: The Naval War against Bonaparte 1798* by Brian Lavery. Being a land battle won by a naval officer, the siege of Acre is covered by books about Napoleon's invasion of Egypt and campaign in Syria, such as *Bonaparte in Egypt* by J. Christopher Herold. For the Battle of Copenhagen in 1801, *The Great Gamble* by Dudley Pope remains the most comprehensive overview, while *The Battle of Copenhagen 1801: Nelson and the Danes* by Ole Feldbaek gives a Danish perspective.

The fight for Diamond Rock is detailed in *His Majesty's Sloop-of-War Diamond Rock* by Vivian Stuart and George T. Eggleston. Of the many books on the Battle of Trafalgar, the first choice has to be *Trafalgar: The Biography of a Battle* by Roy Adkins. Also recommended is *Trafalgar: the men, the battle, the storm* by Tim Clayton and Phil Craig. For those interested in facts and figures rather than a narrative, *The Trafalgar Companion* by Mark Adkin is an excellent reference book. *The Grand Expedition: The British Invasion of Holland in 1809* by Gordon C. Bond covers the Walcheren Expedition.

For the war of 1812 with America, *The British at the Gates: The New Orleans Campaign in the War of 1812* by Robin Reilly provides a readable discussion of the war as a whole, although mainly concerned with the Battle of New Orleans. *The War of 1812: A Forgotten Conflict* by Donald R. Hickey is a good, modern account of the conflict that also examines the American reasons for the war. *The Naval War of 1812* by Theodore Roosevelt is a classic account full of facts and figures, and *The Naval War of 1812* edited by Robert Gardiner is a well-illustrated introduction.

**Biographies:** Of the innumerable biographies of Nelson, mention must be made of *Nelson: Love & Fame* by Edgar Vincent, *The Pursuit of Victory: The Life and Achievement of Horatio Nelson* by Roger Knight and *Nelson: Britannia's God of War* by Andrew Lambert. For a rounded view, it is also necessary to read *Nelson's Women* by Tom Pocock, *Fields of Fire: A Life of Sir William Hamilton* by David Constantine and *Beloved Emma: The Life of Emma, Lady Hamilton* by Flora Fraser.

Other biographies of prominent figures of the period include *Cochrane: Britannia's Last Sea King* by Donald Thomas, *The Audacious Admiral Cochrane: The True Life of a Naval Legend* by Brian Vale, *Frigate Commander* by Tom Wareham (on Graham Moore), *The Real Hornblower: The Life and Times of Admiral Sir James Gordon, GCB* by Bryan Perrett, *The Man who burned the White House: Admiral Sir George Cockburn 1772–1853* by James Pack, *Admiral Collingwood: Nelson's Own Hero* by Max Adams, *A Thirst for Glory: The Life of Admiral Sir Sidney Smith* by Tom Pocock, *Beware of Heroes: Admiral Sir Sidney Smith's War against Napoleon* by Peter Shankland and *Remember Nelson: The Life of Captain Sir William Hoste* by Tom Pocock. *Marooned* by James Derriman tells the story of Robert Jeffery.

The life of Napoleon has also had many biographers, but *Napoleon Bonaparte* by Alan Schom and *Napoleon: A Biography* by Frank McLynn are particularly readable, as is *Napoleon and Josephine: An Improbable Marriage* by Evangeline Bruce.

***Ships:*** Several of the ships of this period have had books devoted to them, including *H.M.S. Victory* by Kenneth Fenwick, *Nelson's Favourite: HMS Agamemnon at War 1781–1809* by Anthony Deane, *Billy Ruffian: The Bellerophon and the Downfall of Napoleon, The Biography of a Ship of the Line, 1782–1836* by David Cordingly and *The First Bellerophon* by C. A. Pengelly. *The Construction and Fitting of the Sailing Man of War 1650–1850* by Peter Goodwin gives detailed and well-illustrated coverage of battleships, while *Navies of the Napoleonic Era* by Otto von Pivka gives facts and figures about all the ships and sailors of the period.

***How they lived:*** *Stephen Biesty's Cross-Sections: Man-of-War* by Stephen Biesty and Richard Platt is an excellent visual primer of life in the British Navy during the Napoleonic period, while *Life in Nelson's Navy* by Dudley Pope, *A Social History of the Navy 1793–1815* by Michael Lewis and *Sea Life in Nelson's Time* by John Masefield give vivid accounts of the frequent privations and infrequent pleasures of a sailor's life. *Heart of Oak: A Sailor's Life in Nelson's Navy* by James McGuane is an excellent photographic essay based on objects surviving from that period, and *Medicine Under Sail* by Zachary Friedenberg gives an overview of naval surgeons and the problems they faced. The pleasures and perils of food are covered in *Feeding Nelson's Navy: The True Story of Food at Sea in the Georgian Era* by Janet Macdonald. A handy and readable reference is *The Illustrated Companion to Nelson's Navy* by Nicholas Blake and Richard Lawrence. More academic but nevertheless accessible accounts are to be found in *Nelson's Navy: The Ships, Men and Organisation 1793–1815* by Brian Lavery and *The Wooden World: An Anatomy of the Georgian Navy* by N. A. M. Rodger.

Research into the experiences of women aboard navy ships has only been done systematically in recent years. Some information about such women can be found in *Female Tars: Women Aboard Ship in the Age of Sail* by Suzanne Stark, *Heroines & Harlots: Women at Sea in the Great Age of Sail* by David Cordingly and *She Captains: Heroines and Hellions of the Sea* by Joan Druett.

***Strategy, tactics, intelligence:*** There are many books that examine the naval strategy and tactics of the period, including *Nelson's War* by Peter Padfield, *Nelson against Napoleon: From the Nile to Copenhagen, 1798–1801* edited by Robert Gardiner, *The Campaign of Trafalgar 1803–1805* edited by Robert Gardiner and *Nelson's Battles: The Art of Victory in the Age of Sail* by

Nicholas Tracy. *Seamanship in the Age of Sail* by John Harland with Mark Myers is a well-illustrated account of its subject that provides an understanding of the possibilities and limitations of ship-to-ship warfare. *Secret Service: British Agents in France 1792–1815* by Elizabeth Sparrow is an excellent account of the espionage of the period, which is also covered by *Most Secret and Confidential: Intelligence in the Age of Nelson* by Steven Maffeo.

*Fiction:* Apart from non-fiction books about naval warfare during the Napoleonic period, there is a growing number of novels on the subject. The Jack Aubrey series by Patrick O'Brian, of which the first is *Master and Commander*, gives an accurate portrayal of naval warfare and conveys a flavour of how different late-eighteenth- and early-nineteenth-century society is from that of today. Also to be recommended is the Thomas Kydd series of novels by Julian Stockwin (the first one is simply called *Kydd*), which chronicles the lives and adventures of ordinary seamen rather than concentrating on the officers.

# BIBLIOGRAPHY

This is not a comprehensive list of all the books, articles and archives that we consulted during the preparation of this book, but includes the sources cited in the notes and those in the selected reading.

Abell, F. 1914 *Prisoners of War in Britain 1756 to 1815: A Record of their lives, their romance and their sufferings* (Oxford, London)

Adams, M. 2005 *Admiral Collingwood: Nelson's Own Hero* (London)

Adkin, M. 2005 *The Trafalgar Companion* (London)

Adkins, R. 2004 *Trafalgar: The Biography of a Battle* (London)

Alger, J. G. 1904 *Napoleon's British Visitors and Captives 1801–1815* (London)

Andrews, C. 1815 *The Prisoners' Memoirs, or, Dartmoor Prison; containing a complete and partial history of the entire captivity of the Americans in England* (New York)

Anon 1810 *A Collection of Papers relating to the Expedition to the Scheldt, presented to Parliament in 1810* (London)

Anon 1827 *Vicissitudes in the Life of a Scottish Soldier. Written by Himself* (London)

Anon 1828 'Journal of a Soldier of the Seventy-First Regiment, (Highland Light Infantry) from 1806 to 1815', in *Memorials of the Late War, vol. 1* (Edinburgh)

Anon 1895 *Napoleon's Last Voyages. Being the Diaries of Admiral Sir Thomas Ussher, R.N., K.C.B. (On Board the "Undaunted"), and John R. Glover, Secretary to Rear Admiral Cockburn (On Board the "Northumberland")* (London)

Anon 1955 *Napoleon Banished. The Journeys to Elba and St. Helena recorded in the Letters and Journal of two British naval officers: Captain Thomas Ussher and Lieutenant Nelson Mills* (London)

Ashton, J. 1906 *The Dawn of the XIXth Century in England: A Social Sketch of the Times* (London)

Barrett, R. J. 1841 'Naval Recollections of the Late American War, No. 1', *United Services Journal and Naval and Military Magazine*, pp.455–67

Barrow, J. 1848 *The Life and Correspondence of Admiral Sir William Sidney Smith G.C.B., volumes 1 and 2* (London)

Biesty, S. and Platt, R. 1993 *Stephen Biesty's Cross-Sections: Man of War* (London)

Blake, N. and Lawrence, R. 1999 *The Illustrated Companion to Nelson's Navy* (London)

Bond, G. C. 1979 *The Grand Expedition: The British Invasion of Holland in 1809* (Athens, Georgia)

Bonnefoux, P.- M.-J. de 1900 *Mémoires du Bon de Bonnefoux, capitaine de vaisseau 1782–1855* (Paris)

Boswall, J. D. 1833 'Narrative of the Capture of the Diamond Rock, effected by Sir Samuel Hood, in the Centaur', *United Service Journal and Naval and Military Magazine*, part II, pp.210–15.

Bourchier, J. 1873 *Memoir of the Life of Admiral Sir Edward Codrington, volume 1* (London)

Bourrienne, L. 1829 *Mémoires de M. Bourrienne, Ministre d'état sur Napoléon, vols. 2–4* (Paris)

Bowers, W. 1833 *Naval Adventures During Thirty-Five Years' Service by Lieut. W. Bowers, R.N., volume 1* (London)

Boys, E. 1864 (4th edn) *Narrative of a captivity, escape, and adventures in France and Flanders during the war* (London)

Brenton, E. P. 1838 *Life and Correspondence of John, Earl of St. Vincent, vol. II* (London)

Brett-James, A. (ed.) 1981 *Escape from the French: Captain Hewson's Narrative (1803–1809)* (Exeter)

Brighton, J. G. 1866 *Admiral Sir P.B.V. Broke, Bart., K.C.B., &c.: A Memoir* (London)

Brooks, G. S. (ed.) 1926 *James Durand: An Able Seaman of 1812* (New Haven)

Bruce, E. 1995 *Napoleon and Josephine: An Improbable Marriage* (London)

Burney, F. 1846 *Diary and Letters of Madame D'Arblay, Author of Evelina, Cecilia &c., Edited by her Niece, volume 6* (London)

Burrows, H. (ed.) 1927 *The Perilous Adventures and Vicissitudes of a Naval Officer 1801–1812: Being Part of the Memoirs of Admiral George Vernon Jackson (1787–1876)* (Edinburgh, London)

Chambers, C. 1928 'The Journal of Surgeon Charles Chambers of H.M. Fireship Prometheus', pp.367–466 in Perrin, W. G. (ed.) 1928 *Naval Miscellany III* (London)

Choyce, J. 1891 *The Log of a Jack Tar; or, the Life of James Choyce, Master Mariner* (London)

Clayton, T. and Craig, P. 2004 *Trafalgar: the men, the battle, the storm* (London)

Cockayne, G. E. 1916 *The Complete Peerage of England Scotland Ireland Great Britain and the United Kingdom, Volume IV* (London)

Collingwood, G. L. N. 1829 *A Selection from the Public and Private Correspondence of Vice-Admiral Lord Collingwood: Interspersed with Memoirs of his Life* (London)

Constantine, D. 2001 *Fields of Fire: A Life of Sir William Hamilton* (London)

Cooper, J. S. 1869 *Rough Notes of Seven Campaigns in Portugal, Spain, France, and America, during the years 1809–10–11–12–13–14–15* (London, Carlisle)

Cordingly, D. 2001 *Heroines & Harlots: Women at Sea in the Great Age of Sail* (London)

Cordingly, D. 2003 *Billy Ruffian. The Bellerophon and the Downfall of Napoleon. The Biography of a Ship of the Line, 1782–1836* (London)

Crawford, A. 1851 *Reminiscences of a Naval Officer during the late war with sketches and anecdotes of distinguished commanders, vol. 1* (London)

Curling, H. (ed.) 1828 *Recollections of Rifleman Harris* (London)

Curling, H. (ed.) 1848 *Recollections of Rifleman Harris (Old 95th.) with anecdotes of his officers and comrades* (London)

Darton, J. F. H. (ed.) 1910 *The Life and Times of Mrs. Sherwood (1775–1851): From the Diaries of Captain and Mrs. Sherwood* (London)

Deane, A. 1996 *Nelson's Favourite: HMS Agamemnon at War 1781–1809* (London)

Derriman, J. 1991 *Marooned: The Story of a Cornish Seaman* (Emsworth)

Desbrière, E. 1907 *La Campagne Maritime de 1805: Trafalgar* (Paris)

Des Touches, G. 1905 'Souvenirs d'un marin de la République', *Revue des Deux Mondes* 28, pp.177–201, 407–36

Desvernois, N. P. 1898 *Mémoires du Général Bon Desvernois* (Paris)

Druett, J. 2000 *She Captains: Heroines and Hellions of the Sea* (New York, London)

Dundonald, Thomas (tenth Earl of) 1861 *The Autobiography of a Seaman, Volume 1* (London)

Du Petit Thouars, B. 1937 *Aristide Aubert du Petit Thouars. Héros d'Aboukir 1760–1798. Lettres et documents inédits* (Paris)

Dye, I. 1987 'American Prisoners of War, 1812–1815', pp.293–320 in *Ships, Seafaring and Society: Essays in Maritime History* (ed. T. J. Runyan) (Detroit)

Elliot, G. 1863 (reprinted 1891) *Memoir of Admiral the Honble. Sir George Elliot written for his children* (London)

Evelyn, J. 1674 *Navigation and Commerce, Their Original and Progress. Containing A succinct Account of Traffick in General; its Benefits and Improvements: of Discoveries, Wars and Conflicts at Sea, from the Original of Navigation to this Day; with special Regard to the English Nation; Their severall Voyages and Expeditions, to the Beginning of our late Differences with HOLLAND; In which His Majesties Title to the DOMINION of the SEA is Asserted, against the Novel, and later Pretenders* (London)

Feldbaek, O. 2002 *The Battle of Copenhagen 1801: Nelson and the Danes* (Barnsley)

Fenwick, K. 1959 *H.M.S. Victory* (London)

Fernyhough, T. 1829 *Military Memoirs of Four Brothers engaged in the service of their country* (London)

Finlayson, J. 1952 'A Signal Midshipman at Copenhagen' *Blackwood's Magazine* 271, pp.121–37

Forester, C. S. (ed.) 1954 *The Adventures of John Wetherell* (London)

Fraser, E. 1906 *The Enemy at Trafalgar* (London)

Fraser, E. 1914 *Napoleon the Gaoler* (London)

Fraser, F. 1986 *Beloved Emma: The Life of Emma, Lady Hamilton* (London)

Fremantle, A. (ed.) 1937 *The Wynne Diaries, volume II, 1794–1798* (London)

Fremantle, A. (ed.) 1940 *The Wynne Diaries, volume III, 1798–1820* (London)

Friedenberg, Z. 2002 *Medicine Under Sail* (Annapolis)

Fullom, S. W. 1863 *The Life of Sir General Howard Douglas* (London )

Gardiner, R. (ed.) 1997 *Nelson against Napoleon: From the Nile to Copenhagen, 1798–1801* (London)

Gardiner, R. (ed.) 1997 *The Campaign of Trafalgar 1803–1805* (London)

Gardiner, R. (ed.) 1998 *The Naval War of 1812* (London)

Gardyne, C. G. 1929 *The Life of a Regiment: The History of the Gordon Highlanders from its formation in 1794 to 1816, volume 1* (London)

Garneray, L. 1853 *Voyages de Garneray, peintre de marine. Seconde partie, Aventures et combats; Les pontons anglais* (Paris)

Gleig, G. R. 1826 (2nd edn) *A Narrative of the Campaigns of the British Army at Washington and New Orleans under Generals Ross, Pakenham, and Lambert, in the years 1814 and 1815* (London)

Goodwin, P. 1987 *The Construction and Fitting of the Sailing Man of War 1650–1850* (London)

Greig, J. (ed.) 1924 *The Farington Diary by Joseph Farington, R.A., volumes 4, 6, 7* (London)

Hall, B. 1846 *Fragments of Voyages and Travels* (London)

Hall, C. D. 2004 *Wellington's Navy: Sea Power and the Peninsular War, 1807–1814* (London, Mechanicsburg)

Hamilton, R. V. (ed.) 1898 *Letters and Papers of Admiral of the Fleet Sir Thos. Byam Martin, volume 2* (London)

Harland, J. with Myers, M. 1985 (rev. edn) *Seamanship in the Age of Sail: An Account of the Shiphandling of the Sailing Man-of-War 1600–1860* (London)

Harris, W. S. 1843 *On the Nature of Thunderstorms and on the Means of Protecting Buildings and Shipping Against the Destructive Effects of Lightning* (London)

Hawker, E. 1821 *Statement Respecting the Prevalence of Certain Immoral Practices Prevailing in His Majesty's Navy* (London)

Hay, M. D. (ed.) 1953 *Landsman Hay: The Memoirs of Robert Hay 1789–1847* (London)

Herold, J. C. 1962 *Bonaparte in Egypt* (London)

Hibbert, C. (ed.) 1996 *A soldier of the seventy-first: The Journal of a soldier in the Peninsular War* (Moreton-in-Marsh)

Hickey, D. 1990 *The War of 1812. A Forgotten Conflict* (Urbana, Chicago)

Historical Manuscripts Commission 1905 *Report on the Manuscripts of J. B. Fortescue, Esq., preserved at Dropmore, volume 5* (London)

Hoffman, F. 1901 *A Sailor of King George. The Journals of Captain Frederick Hoffman, R.N. 1793–1814* (eds A. B. Bevan and H. B. W. Whitmore) (London)

Hoste, W. 1887 *Service Afloat Or The Naval Career of Sir William Hoste* (London)

Howard, E. G. G. 1839 *Memoirs of Admiral Sir Sidney Smith, K.C.B., &c., volumes 1 and 2* (London)

Hyde de Neuville, J. G. 1914 *Memoirs of Baron Hyde de Neuville: Outlaw, Exile, Ambassador, vols 1 and 2* (trans. Frances Jackson) (London, Edinburgh, Glasgow)

Impressment 1835 *Impressment of Seamen, and a few remarks on corporal punishment, taken from the private memoranda of a naval officer* (London)

Jackson, T. S. (ed.) 1900 *Logs of the Great Sea Fights, Volume 2* (London)

James, W. 1817 *A Full and Correct Account of the Naval Occurrences of the late war between Great Britain and the United States of America* (London)

James, W. 1826 *The Naval History of Great Britain During the French Revolutionary and Napoleonic Wars. Volume 3. 1800–1805* (London)

James, W. 1826 *The Naval History of Great Britain from the declaration of war by France, in February 1793, to the accession of George IV, in January 1820, volumes 4 and 5* (London)

Jeffery, R. 1811 *A narrative of the life, sufferings, and deliverance of Robert Jeffery, the seaman who was put on the desolate rock of Sombrero, December 13, 1807, and continued there eight days and a half, without any sort of provision* (London)

Jeffery, R. W. (ed.) 1907 *Dyott's Diary 1781–1845: A selection from the journal of William Dyott, sometime general in the British army and aide-de-camp to His Majesty King George III* (London)

Knight, C. 1861 *Autobiography of Miss Cornelia Knight Lady Companion to the Princess Charlotte of Wales. With Extracts from her Journals and Anecdote Books, volume 1* (London)

Knight, R. 2005 *The Pursuit of Victory: The Life and Achievement of Horatio Nelson* (London)

Knutsford, Viscountess 1900 *Life and Letters of Zachary Macaulay* (London)

Lambert, A. 2004 *Nelson: Britannia's God of War* (London)

Langton, R. 1836 *Narrative of a captivity in France, from 1809 to 1814, vol. 2* (London, Liverpool)

Las Cases, Comte de 1835 *The Life, Exile, and Conversations of the Emperor Napoleon, vol. III* (London)

Lavery, B. 1989 *Nelson's Navy: The Ships, Men and Organisation 1793–1815* (London)

Lavery, B. 1998 *Nelson and the Nile: The Naval War Against Bonaparte 1798* (London)

Leech, S. 1844 *Thirty Years From Home; or A Voice from the Main Deck. Being Six Years in A Man-of-War* (London)

Lewis, M. 1960 *A Social History of the Navy 1793–1815* (London)

Lewis, M. A. (ed.) 1956 *A narrative of my professional adventures (1790–1839) by Sir William Henry Dillon, K.C.H., Vice-Admiral of the Red, Volume II 1802–1839* (London)

Leyland, J. (ed.) 1899 *Dispatches and Letters relating to the Blockade of Brest 1803–1805, vol. 1* (London)

Liddell Hart, B. H. (ed.) 1951 *The Letters of Private Wheeler 1809–1828* (London)

Lloyd, C. (ed.) 1955 *The Keith Papers selected from the Papers of Admiral Viscount Keith, volume III, 1803–1815* (London)

Long, W. H. (ed.) 1899 *Naval Yarns. Letters and Anecdotes; comprising accounts of sea fights and wrecks, actions with pirates and privateers, &c. from 1616 to 1831* (London)

Lossing, B. J. 1868 *The Pictorial Field-Book of the War of 1812* (New York)

Lovell, W. S. 1879 *Personal Narrative of Events, from 1799 to 1815 with anecdotes* (London)

Macdonald, J. 2004 *The True Story of Food at Sea in the Georgian Era* (London, Mechanicsburg)

McGrigor, J. 1861 *The autobiography and services of Sir James McGrigor, Bart* (London)

McGuane, J. 2002 *Heart of Oak: A Sailor's Life in Nelson's Navy* (New York, London)

Maclachlan, A. N. C. 1869 *Napoleon at Fontainebleau and Elba: Being a Journal of Occurrences in 1814–1815 by the Late Major-General Sir Neil Campbell, C.B.* (London)

McLynn, F. 1997 *Napoleon. A Biography* (London)

Maffeo, S. 2000 *Most Secret and Confidential: Intelligence in the Age of Nelson* (London)

Marryat, F. 1872 *Life and Letters of Captain Marryat, vol. 1* (London)

Marshall, J. 1824 *Royal Naval Biography, vol. II part I* (London)

Masefield, J. 1905 *Sea Life in Nelson's Time* (London)

Maxwell, H. (ed.) 1904 (2nd edn) *The Creevey papers. A selection from the correspondence & diaries of the late Thomas Creevey, M.P.* (London)

Millard, W. S. 1895 'The Battle of Copenhagen (Being the Experiences of a Midshipman on Board H.M.S. "Monarch", as Told by Himself)', *Macmillan's Magazine* 72, pp.81–93

Moody, T. W. (ed.) 1959 'An Irish Countryman in the British Navy, 1809–1815: The Memoirs of Henry Walsh', *Irish Sword* 4, pp.228–45.

Murray, J. (ed.) 1922 *Lord Byron's Correspondence, volume 1* (London)

Napier, E. 1862 *The Life and Correspondence of Admiral Sir Charles Napier, K.C.B. from personal recollections, letters and official documents, volume 1* (London)

Nicol, J. 1822 *The Life and Adventures of John Nicol, Mariner* (Edinburgh, London)

Nicolas, N. H. 1845 *The Dispatches and Letters of Vice Admiral Lord Viscount Nelson, volumes 3 and 4* (London)

Nicolas, N. H. 1846 *The Dispatches and Letters of Vice Admiral Lord Viscount Nelson, volumes 6 and 7* (London)

O'Brian, P. 1970 *Master and Commander* (London)

O'Brien, D. H. 1839 *My Adventures during the late war: comprising a narrative of shipwreck, captivity, escapes from French prisons, etc. from 1804 to 1827, volumes 1 and 2* (London)

Oman, C. 1943 *Britain against Napoleon* (London)

Oman, C. 1947 *Nelson* (London)

O'Meara, B. E. 1822 *Napoleon in Exile; or, A Voice from St. Helena. The Opinions and Reflections of Napoleon on the Most Important Events of his Life and Government in his Own Words, volumes 1 and 2* (London)

Original Letters 1798 *Copies of Original Letters From the Army of General Bonaparte in Egypt Intercepted by the Fleet Under the Command of Admiral Lord Nelson, Part the First* (London)

Original Letters 1799 *Copies of Original Letters From the Army of General Bonaparte in Egypt Intercepted by the Fleet Under the Command of Admiral Lord Nelson, Part the Second* (London)

Original Letters 1800 *Copies of Original Letters From the French Army in Egypt. Part the Third, Consisting of Those Letters to the French Government, Intercepted by the British Fleet in the Mediterranean Which Have Been Published Here by Authority* (London)

Pack, J. 1987 *The man who burned the White House: Admiral Sir George Cockburn 1772–1853* (Emsworth)

Padfield, P. 1976 *Nelson's War* (London)

Padfield, P. 2003 *Maritime Power and the Struggle for Freedom: Naval campaigns that shaped the modern world 1788–1851* (London)

Palmer, B. F. 1914 *The Diary of Benjamin F. Palmer Privateersman, while a prisoner on board English war ships at sea, in the prison at Melville Island and at Dartmoor* (Hartford)

Parkinson, C. N. 1934 *Edward Pellew: Viscount Exmouth, Admiral of the Red* (London)

Parkinson, C. N. (ed.) 1949 *Samuel Walters Lieutenant, R.N. His memoirs, edited, with an introduction and notes* (Liverpool)

Parsons, G. S. 1905 *Nelsonian Reminiscences: Leaves from Memory's Log* (London)

Pengelly, C. A. 1966 *The First Bellerophon* (London)

Perrett, B. 1998 *The Real Hornblower: The Life and Times of Admiral Sir James Gordon, GCB* (London)

Petrides, A. and Downs, J. (eds.) 2000 *Sea Soldier: An Officer of Marines with Duncan, Nelson, Collingwood and Cockburn. The Letters and Journals of Major T. Marmaduke Wybourn RM, 1797–1813. Collected and transcribed by his sister, Emily Wybourn* (Tunbridge Wells)

Pettigrew, T. J. 1849 *Memoirs of the Life of Vice-Admiral Lord Viscount Nelson, K.B., vol. 1* (London)

Pierce, N. 1937 'Journal of Nathaniel Pierce of New Buryport, kept at Dartmoor Prison, 1814–1815', *Essex Institute of Historical Collections* 73, pp.25–59

Pillet, R.-M. 1818 *Views of England, During a Residence of Ten Years; Six of Them as a Prisoner of War* (Boston)

Pinckard, G. 1806 *Notes on the West Indies: Written During the Expedition Under the Command of the Late General Sir Ralph Abercromby, volume 1* (London)

Pivka, O. von 1980 *Navies of the Napoleonic Era* (Newton Abbot, New York)

Pocock, T. 1977 *Remember Nelson: The Life of Captain Sir William Hoste* (London)

Pocock, T. 1996 *A Thirst for Glory: The Life of Admiral Sir Sidney Smith* (London)

Pocock, T. 1999 *Nelson's Women* (London)

Pope, D. 1972 *The Great Gamble* (London)

Pope, D. 1981 *Life in Nelson's Navy* (London)

Pringle, J. 1752 *Observations on the Diseases of the Army in Camp and Garrison in Three Parts* (London)

Raikes, H. (ed.) 1846 *Memoir of the Life and Services of Vice-Admiral Sir Jahleel Brenton, Baronet, K.C.B.* (London)

Rattenbury, J. 1837 *Memoirs of a Smuggler, compiled from his diary and journal* (Sidmouth)

Reilly, R. 2002 (rev. edn) *The British at the Gates. The New Orleans Campaign in the War of 1812* (London)

Richardson, W. 1908 *A Mariner of England: An Account of the career of William Richardson from cabin boy in the merchant service to warrant officer in the Royal Navy [1780 to 1819] as told by himself* (London)

Robinson, W. 1836 *Nautical Economy; or, forecastle recollections of events during the last war dedicated to the brave tars of Old England by a sailor, politely called by the officers of the navy, Jack Nasty-Face* (London)

Rocca, A. J. M. de 1816 *Campagne de Walcheren et d'Anvers en 1809* (Brussels)

Rodger, N. A. M. 1986 *The Wooden World: An Anatomy of the Georgian Navy* (London)

Rodger, N. A. M. 2004 *The Command of the Ocean: A Naval History of Britain 1649–1815* (London)

Roosevelt, T. 1902 *The Naval War of 1812* (New York, London)

Rose, J. H. 1923 *Life of William Pitt* (London)

Ross, J. 1838 *Memoirs and Correspondence of Admiral Lord Saumarez. From Original Papers in Possession of the Family, volumes 1 and 2* (London)

Ross-Lewin, H. (ed. J. Wardell) 1904 *With "The Thirty-Second" In the Peninsular and other Campaigns* (Dublin, London)

Rowbotham, W. B. 1956 'The British Occupation of the Diamond Rock 1804–1805', *Journal of the Royal United Service Institution* 100, pp.397–411

Sandeman, H. D. 1868 *Selections from Calcutta Gazettes of the years 1806 to 1815 inclusive, Showing the Political and Social Condition of the English in India Upwards of Fifty Years Ago* (Calcutta)

Schom, A. 1997 *Napoleon Bonaparte* (New York)

Scott, J. 1834 *Recollections of naval life, volume 3* (London)

Shankland, P. 1975 *Beware of Heroes: Admiral Sir Sidney's War against Napoleon* (London)

Shorter, C. (ed.) 1908 *Napoleon and His Fellow Travellers* (London)

Simond, L. 1817 *Journal of a Tour and Residence in Great Britain During the Years 1810 and 1811, volumes 1 and 2* (Edinburgh, London)

Smart, J. 1908a 'Bonaparte on Board the Bellerophon, Torbay, 1815', *Notes and Queries* 10 series no. 226, pp.321–2

Smart, J. 1908b 'Bonaparte on Board the Bellerophon, Torbay, 1815', *Notes and Queries* 10 series no. 229, pp.382–4

Smith, G. C. M. (ed.) 1910 *The Autobiography of Sir Harry Smith 1787–1819* (London)

Sonneck, O. G. T. 1914 *The Star-Spangled Banner* (Washington)

Sparrow, E. 1999 *Secret Service: British Agents in France 1792–1815* (Woodbridge)

Sparrow, E. 2001 'What Nelson's blind eye didn't see', *BBC History Magazine* 2, pp.37–9

Stark, S. 1996 *Female Tars: Women Aboard Ship in the Age of Sail* (London)

Stewart, W. 1801 'Journal of the Baltic Expedition and Battle of Copenhagen', in *Cumloden Papers* 1871 (Edinburgh)

Stockwin, J. 2001 *Kydd* (London)

Stuart, V. and Eggleston, G. T. 1978 *His Majesty's Sloop-of-War Diamond Rock* (London)

Sturgis, J. (ed.) 1899 *A Boy in the Peninsular War: The Services, Adventures, and Experiences of Robert Blakeney, Subaltern in the 28th Regiment* (London)

Sydney, W. C. 1898 *The early days of the nineteenth century in England, 1800–20* (London)

Sykes, J. A. C. 1906 *France in Eighteen Hundred and Two* (London)

Taylor, T. (ed.) 1853 (2nd edn) *Life of Benjamin Robert Haydon, Historical Painter, from his autobiography and journals, volume 1* (London)

Thomas, D. S. 1978 *Cochrane: Britannia's last sea-king* (London)

Thurman, L. 1902 *Bonaparte en Egypte: Souvenirs publiés avec préface et appendices par le comte Fleury* (Paris)

Thursfield, H. G. (ed.) 1951 *Five Naval Journals 1789–1817* (London)

Tracy, N. 1996 *Nelson's Battles: The Art of Victory in the Age of Sail* (London)

Vale, B. 2004 *The Audacious Admiral Cochrane: The True Life of a Naval Legend* (London)

Vane, C. W. (ed.) 1851 *Correspondence, Despatches, and other papers, of Viscount Castlereagh, Second Marquess of Londonderry, volume VI* (London)

Verdun 1810 *A picture of Verdun, or the English detained in France, vols. 1 and 2* (London)

Vincent, E. 2003 *Nelson: Love & Fame* (New Haven, London)

Warden, W. 1816 *Letters Written on Board His Majesty's Ship the Northumberland and at Saint Helena* (London)

Wareham, T. 2004 *Frigate Commander* (Barnsley)

Waterhouse, B. 1911 'A journal of a young man of Massachusetts by Benjamin Waterhouse, M.D. (1754–1846)' in *Magazine of History with notes and queries* 18 (New York)

Wheeler, H. F. B. and Broadley, A. M. 1908 *Napoleon and the Invasion of England: The Story of the Great Terror* (London, New York)

Willyams, C. 1802 *A Voyage up the Mediterranean in his majesty's ship the Swiftsure, one of the squadron under the command of Rear-Admiral Sir Horatio Nelson, K. B. now viscount and baron Nelson of the Nile, and Duke of Bronte in Sicily with a description of the Battle of the Nile on the first of August 1798* (London)

Woodman, R. 1998 *The Victory of Seapower: Winning the Napoleonic War 1806–1814* (London)

Woodman, R. 2001 *The Sea Warriors: Fighting Captains and Frigate Warfare in the Age of Nelson* (London)

Yarrow, D. 1975 'A Journal of the Walcheren Expedition 1809', *Mariner's Mirror* 61, pp.183–9.

Zealand 1804 *A Tour in Zealand in the year 1802; with a historical sketch of the Battle of Copenhagen* (London)

Zimmerman, J. F. 1925 *Impressment of American Seamen* (New York)

# INDEX

Note: page references in *italics* refer to maps or charts